ARMAND HAMMER

ARMAND HAMMER

THE UNTOLD STORY

STEVE WEINBERG

EBURY PRESS

Published in Great Britain by Ebury Press,
an imprint of Century Hutchinson Ltd,
Brookmount House,
62-65 Chandos Place,
London WC2N 4NW

The author is grateful for the permission to include the following previously copy-righted material:

Excerpt from "Occidental's Giant China Mine Project Hits Snag as World Coal Price Plummets," by Amanda Bennett, August 10, 1983. Reprinted by permission of *The Wall Street Journal.* Copyright © 1983 by Dow Jones and Company.

Excerpt from "Hammer's Kremlin Connection," by Everett R. Holles, May 20, 1973. Copyright © 1973 by The New York Times Company. Reprinted by per-mission.

Excerpt from "Orkneys Depot for North Sea Oil Inaugurated by Hammer and Benn," by Peter T. Kilborn, January 12, 1977. Copyright © 1977 by The New York Times Company. Reprinted by permission.

Excerpt from "Man with the Golden Touch," by Spencer Klaw. Reprinted from *The Saturday Evening Post* © 1966 The Curtis Publishing Co.

Excerpt from "J. Carter Brown," by Larry Van Dyne. Copyright © 1988 by *The Washingtonian.*

British Library Cataloguing in Publication Data
Weinberg, Steve
   Armand Hammer: the untold story.
   1. United States. Entrepreneurship. Hammer, Armand,
   1898 -
   I. Title
   338'.04'0924

ISBN 0-85223-777-4

Printed and bound in Great Britain by
Butler and Tanner Limited, Frome and London

For Scherrie, Sonia, and Seth

Contents

Author's Note

WHY A BIOGRAPHY of Armand Hammer, after four of his own recountings of his life, including a best-selling autobiography as recently as 1987? The *Washington Post* provided the answer in its review of that book: "He has probably known more world leaders more intimately than anyone in history. Undoubtedly, he has been a force for good in the world. But we will have to wait for an unauthorized biography to learn how he operates."[1] Hammer's own accounts, like most autobiographies and authorized biographies, are neither objective nor complete. Even his ardent admirers acknowledge this — dozens told me that his true importance will be understood only when his life is chronicled by a biographer he cannot control.

I first heard of Hammer in the 1960s, as I began studying the langauge, politics, economy, and culture of the Soviet Union at the University of Missouri, where I was earning degrees in journalism. Hammer was almost seventy by then. It never occurred to me to become his biographer, however, until a conversation in 1984 with Barbara Matusow, an author in Washington, D.C. Matusow had done preliminary research for a Hammer biography. She had decided against tackling it but thought of me. With encouragement from our mutual agents, Elise and Arnold Goodman, and from my wife, Scherrie Goettsch, I began learning about Hammer in every moment that I could spare from running Investigative Reporters & Editors Incorporated, teaching journalism at the University of Missouri, and writing free-lance articles for magazines and newspapers. Later, I received vital, sustained help from Jennifer Josephy, my editor at Little, Brown; Deborah Jacobs, my copyeditor there; editorial assistant Kristen Hatch, also at Little, Brown; and free-lance editor John Stuart Cox.

I heard from many sources that Hammer would refuse to cooperate. That raised a legitimate question: Why proceed without his permission? The answer: Hammer is a significant public figure who has thrust himself into public view for nearly seventy years. By the 1980s, his name was a household word not only in the United States, but also in the Soviet Union, England, China, Libya, France, Israel, and other countries. Many people are fascinated by Hammer and affected by his actions. They deserve to know the fullest story possible.

Hammer never responded to my telephone calls and registered letters.[2] I went to great lengths to interview his associates, employees, and relatives. They included admirers as well as detractors; almost nobody was neutral about Hammer. In the end, I conducted more than seven hundred interviews, in person, by telephone, and by mail. I also unearthed hundreds of thousands of pages of documents.

Does lack of the subject's cooperation mean an incomplete or irresponsible biography? Incomplete, yes. His candor and access to his papers would have helped to paint an even richer word portrait. Irresponsible, no. Authorized biographers, such as Hammer's Bob Considine, often surrender their independence. Even unauthorized biographers who end up receiving cooperation sometimes agree to arrangements that compromise the truth.[3]

ARMAND
HAMMER

A Reckoning in Court

TO THE CASUAL observer, it appeared that Dr. Armand Hammer's amazing career had come to an end. In fact, it appeared he was about to die.

The date: March 4, 1976. The place: the Los Angeles courtroom of federal judge Lawrence Lydick. Attendants wheeled the seventy-seven-year-old tycoon into the courtroom from Cedars of Lebanon Hospital, where, according to his doctors, he had languished in unstable condition since January. Frail but still handsome, Hammer looked to be the remains of a truly charismatic man. Throughout the court appearance, he stayed hooked up to monitoring machines watched closely by medical specialists in an adjoining room.[1]

Hammer was present to plead to a charge of an illegal campaign contribution made four years earlier, during Watergate. Specifically, the federal government alleged that he had concealed $54,000 in donations to the reelection campaign of President Richard Nixon. Hammer seemed to believe he had done nothing wrong. But he pleaded guilty.[2]

Normally, he would have fought the charge all the way to the Supreme Court, fully expecting to prevail. Indeed, he had often used the courts to fight his tormentors, overwhelming them with millions of dollars' worth of legal talent. Such battles were second nature to him. Unlike many modern-day celebrities, Hammer was not famous simply for being famous. A man of action, he embodied both substance and significance. His decisions influenced the prices that Americans and citizens of many other nations paid for gasoline, coal, and chemicals used in household products. His practices helped determine the quality of the meat they ate, the purity of the air they breathed and the water they drank, the odds that they would benefit from a cure for cancer, the news they heard on the radio, the artworks they saw in museums — even the very survival of the planet, through his tireless efforts to reduce tensions between the superpowers.

Notwithstanding his deserved reputation for getting his way, he feared that continuing this court battle would kill him. By pleading guilty, Hammer knew, he could face a three-year prison term. He hoped, however, that the judge would spare him incarceration, a hope perhaps bolstered by the fact that Lydick formerly had been affiliated in law practice with Richard Nixon. Moreover, the judge had received more than one hundred letters on Hammer's behalf, from U.S. senators, billionaire industrialists, religious leaders, world-renowned entertainers, university presidents, and distinguished fellow jurists. Besides, what judge would send an influential, wealthy, famous, elderly, apparently dying man to prison?

The particulars of Hammer's offense began on March 30, 1972, during a lunch with Maurice Stans, Nixon's former secretary of commerce who was serving as finance chairman for the president's reelection campaign. The two men met in an expensive suite kept by Hammer at the Watergate apartment complex, in Washington, D.C. It was one of Hammer's favorite spots in the nation's capital, along with the elegant Madison Hotel, where he sometimes stayed because of the round-the-clock room service that catered to his taste for oyster stew, sweets, and grapefruit juice.

Stans had good reasons to believe that Hammer would make the lunch a fruitful one. Hammer was extremely wealthy and had been for more than fifty years, a self-proclaimed millionaire even before his graduation from Columbia University's medical college, in 1921. Some of the pharmaceuticals Hammer had sold to make his first millions had raised questions, to be sure, but Hammer had long since successfully swept them aside — as he had swept aside other questions about the whole range of businesses that he had dominated throughout his life. Each new venture had grown inexorably out of those preceding it, garnering him more money, influence, and publicity. Hammer's third wife, Frances Barrett, was wealthy in her own right and sometimes made campaign contributions in her own name to supplement those of her husband.

Stans had other reasons for optimism besides Hammer's wealth. Though more of a Democrat than a Nixon Republican, Hammer had courted U.S. presidents regardless of political party since Franklin Delano Roosevelt, doing all of them favors, sending them gifts, contributing money, trying to influence policy for his own good — which sometimes coincided with the national good and sometimes did not.[3] Hammer had grand dreams for the world, and for himself. Riches alone were not enough; he wanted influence, which he defined as getting things done his way by going to the top. (His version of the Golden Rule was enshrined on a plaque in the bedroom of his Los Angeles home: "He who hath the gold maketh the rule.") Probably no other private citizen had access to leaders of so many nations.

Stans also knew of Hammer's legendary philanthropy — ruthlessly doing good, said some detractors — and the legend was growing. The Armand Hammer Foundation, created in the late 1960s, was emerging as a major force in cancer research, just as it was in art. Hammer used his collections for political, diplomatic, and business purposes, as well as for philanthropic ones. His were among the world's best private collections and arguably were the last great ones built from scratch. Unlike most collectors, though, Hammer kept only a small fraction of his treasures at home. His art circled the globe year after year, bringing pleasure to millions of people, many of whom had never before been afforded an opportunity to view the Old Masters. Hammer thought nothing of spending millions of dollars for a single work of art to share with the world.

Many people knew all of these dimensions. But to Stans, Hammer was, first and foremost, the chief executive officer of Occidental Petroleum, the giant multinational oil company. Hammer had become involved in the oil business only after marrying Frances and moving from New York to Los Angeles in 1956, when he was fifty-seven. Occidental at that time employed just three persons and showed a net worth of almost zero. Hammer had viewed it solely as a tax shelter. But, with Hammer at the helm, Occidental had discovered oil and gas deposits in California. Within five years, the firm had burst into the ranks of the multinationals with a stupendous find against long odds in Libya. Probably no other twentieth-century businessman had taken a little company so far so fast, and so late in life.

Two years before his meeting with Stans, Hammer had altered the world's balance of power by breaking ranks with other Western oil companies and negotiating unilaterally the conditions for continued oil exploration with the revolutionary government of Muammar al-Qaddafi. The resulting agreement with Libya finished the old order and shifted power from the Seven Sisters to the long-exploited oil nations, which, through OPEC, began to show their muscle. Suddenly, consumers were paying higher prices for energy. For Hammer, the agreement was the foundation for the growth of his beloved company. Qaddafi allowed Occidental to continue producing profitably in Libya rather than nationalizing the company's primary source of crude oil.

Although Stans was accustomed to dealing with oil-company executives, Hammer was not quite the stereotype of Stans's experience. One headline writer aptly termed Hammer a "one-man flying multinational" because of his personal negotiations with desert sheikhs, Communist party leaders, and military dictators. Some of the biggest of these deals had failed to turn a profit for Occidental's stockholders, but Hammer pressed on: These arrangements allowed him to rub shoulders with heads of state, slaked his insatiable thirst for headlines, and more than anything else enhanced his aura of power.

As Hammer and Stans sat down to talk, Occidental was negotiating a multibillion-dollar fertilizer deal with the Soviet Union. Russia had special significance for Hammer. His parents had been born there. Hammer had gone there as a young man, in 1921, hoping to help the starving masses — and collect debts owed by the Bolshevik government to his family's pharmaceutical business. The duality of his mission foreshadowed the mix of altruism and self-interest that characterized Hammer's life for the next seven decades. He had planned to spend only a summer in the Soviet Union and return to New York City in time for a prestigious medical internship at Bellevue Hospital. Instead, because of a historic meeting with Lenin that dramatically improved his status, Hammer stayed a decade, making a fortune as the Communist party's favored capitalist. Known to every Soviet leader after Lenin, Hammer came to possess access to officials that was unmatched among foreigners in the Soviet Union. He secured landing rights for his private airplane and occupied a luxurious private apartment in a pleasant Moscow neighborhood — a gift from Leonid Brezhnev. But even with his connections, Hammer needed help from the Nixon administration to complete the fertilizer plan, the biggest deal ever with the Soviet Union. There was opposition throughout America to trading with a nation perceived as an enemy — especially when the arrangement called for shipping a scarce natural resource, a form of phosphate rock, overseas.

Hammer also had a China agenda for the Nixon administration. He dreamed of parlaying his reputation as a friend of Lenin's and of Communism into relations with the government that controlled the biggest market of all. It was going to be tricky; China and the Soviet Union were rivals. But Hammer was confident he could bring it off.

The Stans meeting had been arranged by Tim Babcock, hired by Hammer to open doors inside the Nixon administration. Babcock served in Occidental's Washington office, which Hammer had created to look after the corporation's interests and his own. A former Republican governor of Montana, Babcock was a favorite of Nixon's. Before the Stans meeting, Babcock had informed Hammer that a generous contribution could pay off in the future; Babcock had told Stans to expect a generous sum. But Hammer and Stans entered the meeting with different definitions of "generous." Hammer arrived with $50,000, and $4,000 of that was for tickets to a political dinner. According to Babcock, Stans suggested that $250,000 would be more appropriate. Stans has said he never mentioned the higher sum. In any case, they settled on a $100,000 contribution. Hammer promised to deliver the remaining $54,000 through Babcock within a week.

That deadline had special significance. A new campaign-finance law required candidates to reveal the names of donors who gave after April 7. Before the cutoff, donors legally could request anonymity. Hammer, who rarely did anything without fanfare, this time desired a low profile because of his normal identification as a Democrat and because of his wish to avoid future solicitations. Yet, when April 7 had come and gone, Hammer's contribution inexplicably had failed to reach Stans. The money did not begin arriving until five months later. By then, it was illegal to keep the names of donors anonymous. So, Hammer became involved in an elaborate cover-up to skirt the law.

When allegations of a cover-up reached federal prosecutors in the summer of 1973, common sense might have led them to dismiss such talk out of hand. Hammer was, after all, a multimillionaire with ready access to $54,000; why would he contribute the money five months late, when he could have contributed it so easily before the deadline? If Hammer had in fact waited until September to begin contributing in installments, why would he have told Nixon in a White House meeting on July 20, 1972, that he was a member of the One-Hundred-Thousand-Dollar Club (a conversation available to prosecutors because Nixon had recorded it on his secret taping system)? Hammer never would be so brazen as to lie to the president, would he? But the more lawyers on the Watergate Special Prosecution Force learned, the more they began to think they had a case against Hammer, no matter what common sense might indicate.

Any prosecutor delving into Hammer's past while considering whether to charge him would have been both impressed and suspicious. Yes,

Hammer was wealthy, and wealth generally confers its own kind of credibility. Yes, he was a generous philanthropist. Yes, he had access to the rulers of the Soviet Union, to other heads of state, from Japan to Peru, to presidents of the United States. But there was a criminal strain in his story as well. His father, Julius, a physician, had served time in Sing Sing for manslaughter after a patient died from an illegal abortion performed in his office. Julius had compounded the crime by orchestrating a cover-up after the death. The FBI possessed a fat file on Julius because of his lifelong involvement in Socialist and Communist movements thought to threaten the security of the United States.[4]

Then there was Armand's only child, Russian-born Julian. He had killed a man in 1955 during a drunken argument at his home. Julian's invocation of self-defense — bolstered by a skilled lawyer, whom Armand paid, and the intervention of a U.S. senator friendly with Armand — kept him out of prison. But afterward Julian was charged with other crimes, was sued by his victims, and ended up in a mental hospital.

As for Armand Hammer himself, government agencies had been concerned with him ever since the 1920s. Federal law enforcers sometimes refused to ignore his bending and breaking of the rules. The Internal Revenue Service, the Federal Trade Commission, and the New York State Liquor Authority all had taken him to task. As the Watergate campaign-contributions case was unfolding, the Securities and Exchange Commission was investigating him.

All of that was more than enough to make a federal prosecutor wonder about Hammer's character. How, a prosecutor might have mused, had Hammer survived and thrived, given his history? Long before Ronald Reagan became the Teflon president, Armand Hammer was the Teflon tycoon; it seemed as if nothing could stick to him. Like Reagan, he knew how to play the mass media like a violin. He perpetuated his image as an energetic, wealthy, well-connected altruist. Occasional media reports of Hammer's troubles were overwhelmed in the public consciousness by thousands of uncritical accounts. The handful of journalists who understood the need to dig deeper had difficulty. Because the record of Hammer's life was scattered around the globe, few writers had the determination, the time, and the money to piece it together. Those who tried sometimes received reprimands. A *New York Times* reporter wrote what Hammer perceived as a negative article in the Sunday newspaper. Hammer made some calls to the top. On Monday, there were conciliatory articles about him on page 1, by *Times* correspondents in Los Angeles and Moscow — with no indication to readers as to what had happened. A *Washington Post* reporter criticized Hammer's art collection, suggesting that some of the works were fakes. Within the week, the newspaper published a rebuttal article, under Hammer's own byline, that was longer than the original piece.

Normally cynical journalists became rapturous after an interview with "the doctor." The journalists knew they were being used. But they succumbed anyway to Hammer's personality. They knew he was vain, but they forgave him, rationalizing that a man of his accomplishments need not possess the humility of a saint. They excused many of his statements, saying that even if only half of what he said was true, he still had lived a far more significant life than ordinary mortals. A comment about Hammer by Stewart Toy, a senior writer for *Business Week,* is instructive:

> He is indeed an appealing man. An unabashed self-promoter, he is also gentle, witty, and somehow self-effacing at the same time. He radiates youthful enthusiasm for a long list of pet projects, from oil shale to world peace. He confides to enchanted visitors the latest gossip from Prince Charles or Deng Xiaoping. In my interviews with him for this magazine over the years, it has not always been easy to swallow his grand schemes for Occidental. But I have always come away charmed.[5]

All this, surely, would have piqued the interest of a prosecutor. Hammer's longevity was turning into a legend of immortality. Had he not known Lenin? His name was enshrined on the insides and outsides of buildings, on streets, art collections, scholarships, foundations, corporations. His name also was emblazoned where it was invisible to the naked eye — in the minds of thousands of people whose lives he had touched in unforgettable ways. Many of them said their lives had been enriched immeasurably by knowing Hammer. Many others said their lives had been devastated. In any case, he would live on after he died — or, as some wags had begun to say, *if* he died.

Hammer's high-cost, high-visibility quest for immortality was part of his desire for respect and respectability. He wanted to overcome the stigmas of being a first-generation American; of coming from an educated family nonetheless beset by financial fiascoes, including a stormy bankruptcy; of having a father who had spent time in prison; of being father to an only child who was in and out of police stations and mental institutions; of going through two failed marriages, the second of which had ended in a notorious divorce case; of obscuring his Jewish background as he made fortunes in anti-Semitic countries; of being labeled a Communist and a traitor because of his father's beliefs and because of his own dealings with the Soviet Union, China, and countries in their spheres of influence; of using sometimes unorthodox money-making tactics in the pharmaceutical, pencil, alcohol, cattle, meat-packing, and oil industries; and of experiencing repeated run-ins with government agencies.

The extent to which Hammer's quest for respectability had succeeded was shown by the disparate individuals who contributed blurbs for the dust jacket of his later, best-selling autobiography, *Hammer.* They included Jimmy Carter, Richard Nixon, Gerald Ford, George Bush, Edward Kennedy, Margaret Thatcher, Menachem Begin, Walter Cronkite, Barbara Walters, Dan Rather, Arthur Sulzberger, Jonas Salk, Isaac Stern, Mstislav Rostropovich, Irving Stone, Gregory Peck, Bob Hope, Norman Vincent Peale, Abigail Van Buren, and Ann Landers.

Still, for reasons obscure, Hammer had played fast and loose with federal laws governing campaign contributions after his lunchtime conversation with Stans. So the government's prosecutors pounced.

When Judge Lydick sentenced Hammer in late March 1976, the penalty was one year of probation and a fine of $3,000. The letters from the rich, the famous, and the powerful may have helped, as the dire medical reports may have helped. Looking terminally ill, Hammer was wheeled out of the courtroom, upset at this blot on his reputation but, in the main, relieved. A week later, he was back at work. Two months later, he was running the annual meeting of Occidental Petroleum Corporation in his usual velvet-fisted manner. Shortly thereafter he flew in his personal Occidental luxury airplane to Moscow, where he met with Soviet leader Leonid Brezhnev. Louis Nizer, Hammer's lawyer, called his client's recovery "a miracle."[6]

Twelve years later, in 1988, Armand Hammer celebrated his ninetieth birthday with gala parties on five continents.

PART I

AN UNUSUAL PATH TO MANHOOD

1

A Bankrupt Family

ARMAND HAMMER'S QUEST for respect and respectability might well have taken root in the garden of troubles tended by his paternal grandfather, Russian-born Jacob William Hammer. Armand's version is that his grandfather's inherited fortune in salt was stashed by the shore of the Caspian Sea. But a freak storm buried it beneath the waters, immediately impoverishing Jacob. From then on, it seemed that bad luck and his grandfather often were synonymous. Jacob's first wife was trampled to death during a synagogue fire in Odessa, leaving him a widower with two sons, William and Alfred. Jacob soon married Victoria Slepack, a widow with a daughter, Anniuta.

Victoria and Jacob would be the grandparents whom Armand Hammer knew well, whose influence he felt, and who lived nearby throughout Armand's childhood. Jacob spent time telling a young, impressionable Armand family lore, including stories about what life had been like in the old country. The Hammers were a close-knit clan; Jacob instilled some of that fierce family loyalty in his grandson. There would be much family shame for Armand to live with. But through it all, Armand, who became the titular head of the family while still in college, remembered the childhood lesson that blood is thicker than water.

Victoria Hammer's influence appears to have been the idealism that led her to challenge the established order — a quality Armand would possess in abundance. That idealism would account for the unusual kind of tycoon Hammer turned out to be: one who gave away much of his wealth for projects that he hoped might promote world peace.

In many accounts of his exploits, Armand is referred to by uninformed authors as Russian-born. His birthplace actually was New York

City, the destination of Jacob and Victoria Hammer when they left Russia. They might have been pulled to the east coast of the United States because of their certainty, shared by many immigrants, that the streets were paved with gold. But it is more likely they were pushed. Anti-Jewish pogroms beset the Odessa-Kherson area of Russia in the early 1870s. During a four-day stretch in May 1871, six persons were killed and twenty-one wounded, with hundreds of homes and businesses destroyed.[1]

There is evidence that Jacob and Victoria Hammer left their native land that same year with his two sons, placing her daughter with relatives in Russia. The evidence is inconclusive because of discrepancies among Hammer family members who claim to know the true story. Assuming the Hammers did leave in 1871, they departed a decade before the mass migration, when anti-Jewish elements began an especially widespread, vicious campaign.

Although Jacob and Victoria did journey to New York, they returned to Russia within a year or two. Julius Hammer, the only child from their union, apparently was born there on October 3, 1874, in Odessa. The return to the homeland turned out to be brief — Julius, it seems, was living in New York with his parents by 1875. The confusion over these dates stems from numerous, conflicting passport applications by Julius; his wife, Rose; Armand; Armand's brother, Victor; and Armand's half brother, Harry. Those applications show six different dates of birth for Julius, ranging from 1863 to 1875; and eight different dates of immigration, ranging from 1872 to 1891.[2]

When Armand later wrote about his family, the information had to be treated with caution. His 1932 memoir, published when his knowledge was the freshest, contains no hard information about that background. His 1975 authorized biography, his 1985 picture book, and his 1987 autobiography do contain some family information. None of it is documented, some is unverifiable, and some is demonstrably inaccurate. Certain details vary from book to book.

Despite confusion caused by contradictory family accounts, one verifiable item is that Jacob Hammer became a naturalized American on August 27, 1877.[3] But even after Jacob obtained his American citizenship, he and his family remained peripatetic, a word used to describe Armand decades later. The family used the access that their new passports provided to travel freely. They lived in France, where Jacob tried his luck at business, without success. They returned again to Russia but fared poorly there.

Finally, in 1890, Jacob and Victoria Hammer decided to settle in America. They chose the Branford–New Haven, Connecticut, area as their first home. Jacob found a job as an insurance agent. Julius, by then a husky teenager, took a job swinging a sledgehammer in a foundry, where he was exposed to management's exploitation of workers — and to competing political parties that hoped to enlist the exploited. The one impressing Julius the most was the Socialist Labor party with its twenty-five hundred members, about 90 percent of them foreign-born. Julius became a party stalwart.[4]

By 1892, the Hammers decided to give New York another try. It was to become the family's permanent base. Jacob continued his work as an insurance agent, joined the Republican party, and surrendered his Jewish heritage to Unitarianism — even as the family found itself living next door to a synagogue. (Jacob feared that being identified as a Jew might hurt business.) His son Julius, ready to fight injustice wherever he saw it, temporarily shelved his political activity in order to earn money for the family. He found a clerk's job at a drugstore in the Italian section of the Bowery, a marginal area of Lower Manhattan, and soon prospered. Hardworking Julius eventually bought out the owner, studied successfully to become a pharmacist, expanded into the manufacturing of pharmaceuticals, and employed his half brothers, William and Alfred, who became pharmacists, too.

The family grew after Julius met Rose Lipshitz. Rose had come to America about 1890 from Witebsk, Russia. When she entered the United States, she had used her mother's maiden name, Runyonson, on the immigration forms, which officials anglicized to Robinson.[5] She was probably fifteen at that time, although she subsequently changed her birth date so frequently that nobody was sure of her age. Hammer family documents show five dates of birth for Rose, ranging from 1865 to 1876.

When Rose arrived in New York, she moved in with an aunt, Racha Ettenberg. Within a year or two she married Max Ettenberg, a relative. Their son, Harry, was born in 1893. Apparently widowed soon after Harry's birth, Rose met Julius Hammer at a Socialist gathering; Rose, who loved a party, had gone not for the politics but for the fun. Generally, however, Rose had little time for fun: She was employed as a sewing machine operator in a garment factory and probably was the main money earner for her mother, Annie Lipshitz, her younger sister, Sadie, and her younger brothers, Willie and Eddie, all of whom had arrived in America after her. (Shimshon Lipshitz, Rose's father, stayed in Russia.) Together with her mother, she had also tried to boost the family income by running a restaurant in Brooklyn and by operating a summer resort outside of the city.[6]

Julius Hammer and Rose Lipshitz married in 1897. Their first home was at 406 Cherry Street on New York's Lower East Side, a small cold-water flat in a large Jewish enclave. That was their older son's home when he was born, on May 21, 1898. They called him Armand. For decades, Armand maintained that he was named after the hero in Alexandre Dumas's *La dame aux camélias,* a favorite work of Julius Hammer's, he said. Julius's Socialist comrades and anti-Communist Hammer haters insisted, however, that Julius named his first son for the arm-and-hammer symbol of the Socialist Labor party.[7] Eventually, the debate lost some of its force when, late in life, Armand conceded that the party symbol might have been a factor in the choice of his name.

Despite his anticapitalist political views, Julius, desirous of providing for his family's comfort, worked at being a successful capitalist. He owned eight drugstores. But they were not consistently profitable, partly because Julius's empathy for the downtrodden, growing out of his political philosophy, caused him to forgive debts. Hoping to find a more secure calling, Julius began medical studies at the College of Physicians and Surgeons, part of Columbia University, the same year Armand was born. Julius's decision fit into a trend among East European immigrant Jews. In 1890, only a few dozen were doctors or lawyers. By 1900, the number had grown to hundreds.[8]

The 1900 census showed the Hammers living at 72 Lewis Street, a few blocks from Armand's birthplace. Jacob, fifty-four, and Victoria, fifty-two, shared the home with Julius, Rose, Armand, and probably Harry, although the census taker failed to list Armand's half brother. Victor was born in 1901, completing the nuclear family. By then, the Hammers had moved out of Manhattan, across the Harlem River to 1470 Webster Avenue in the Bronx. In 1902 Julius graduated from medical college. Thereafter he began selling his drugstores, moved the family to a spacious house, which he bought for $13,000 at 1488 Washington Avenue in the Bronx, and opened a medical practice in a wing of the new home. It was a dramatic change of atmosphere: The family had traded crowded inner-city quarters for a large house in semirural tranquillity, all by moving no more than ten miles. The house became home for Rose Lipshitz's family, too. By 1906, its residents included Rose's mother, Rose's sister and two brothers, and a maid. Armand's grandmother and grandfather lived in the neighborhood.[9]

Yet Julius Hammer's finances were more precarious than most people realized. Without question, Armand grew up in a financially unstable household. As early as 1903, Julius was talking to Henry Kuntz — his friend, lawyer, and sometime business partner — about filing for bankruptcy. Julius began transferring his assets to his wife, his mother-in-law, and employees of his remaining drugstores. It looked like a scheme to shield assets from potential creditors. Finally, in 1906, Julius declared bankruptcy, listing assets of about $1,400 and liabilities of more than $16,000. His creditors believed he was lying about his assets. They charged him with "destruction or concealment of books and records with intent to conceal his financial condition . . . fraudulent concealment of his properties, consisting among others of the house and lot at 1488 Washington Avenue," and four other counts of wrongdoing.[10]

The court-appointed special master sided with the creditors, openly accusing Julius of deception. His report commented acidly on Julius's claim that he had sold the fixtures from one of his drugstores to his mother-in-law, Annie Lipshitz: "There's no evidence of consideration other than the bankrupt's unsupported testimony that he got cash money from Mrs. Lifschitz [sic], but he cannot remember what he did with the money. His bank books and checkbooks have been destroyed as rubbish and there is no means of tracing the money." The report questioned the failure of Julius's lawyers to call Mrs. Lipshitz as a witness and scoffed at the claim that they were unable to locate her: "She was a very important witness in regard to certain transactions concerning the sale of the pharmacies, and by the failure to produce her the inference is properly drawn that her testimony would not assist the bankrupt."[11]

The report expressed similar skepticism about other transactions. Julius said he had surrendered control of one pharmacy to his clerk and transferred control of a second to the husband of his mother-in-law's sister, who also happened to be the brother of Rose Hammer's first husband. "The proceeds of the Rivington Street sale [one of the pharmacies] are being paid monthly to the bankrupt for his use out of the profits of the business. . . . In omitting all reference thereto in his schedules, he has been guilty of a false oath," the report concluded, adding that Julius had destroyed his financial records in a calculated, fraudulent manner.[12]

The fierce loyalty and apparent lack of scruple among Hammer family members were demonstrated by their courtroom testimony. Rose Hammer's aunt Racha Ettenberg swore she had purchased one of the drugstores from a clerk who was an employee of Julius's. But, she added, the store had suffered a fire several months before the bankruptcy hearing. She had collected $800 from the Home Fire Insurance Company, she said. The agent on the policy? Jacob Hammer. Julius Hammer testified on four occasions during May and June 1906. Many of the questions involved transactions that had occurred no more than eighteen months earlier. He repeatedly responded, "I do not recall." When Rose Hammer testified in the proceeding, she answered the same way. An exasperated lawyer for a creditor told Rose, "Answer my question. Who told you to say 'I do not remember'?"[13]

The proceeding, stretching over years, almost certainly affected young Armand, even though it is likely that, at age seven, he had little idea of its seriousness. The bankruptcy might have helped create the siege mentality that Hammer family members evinced ever after. The relative painlessness with which Julius and Rose escaped from bankruptcy court, despite the untruthfulness of their testimony, almost surely impressed upon everybody that cover-ups and convenient memory lapses could be useful tactics. Later in life, Armand was known for his elephantine memory — until called to the witness stand as a defendant, when his recall sometimes seemed to leave him.

Notwithstanding the bankruptcy, the Hammers remained in their Bronx home, which provided Armand with a mostly pleasant physical environment as a youth. There was occasional strife in the neighborhood, however, as recalled by neighbor Irwin Hymes. One day, probably in 1907, four brothers named Maguire taunted Hymes, his brother Sidney, Armand, and Harry. Hymes said that Harry took on the eldest Maguire and "whupped him" behind the Hammer residence. That ended the taunting, Hymes said. Armand himself recalled a similar incident, in which Irish youths called the Hammers anti-Semitic names during a ride on the Third Avenue El. Armand reminisced about how the normally placid Harry drove them off with his boxing prowess.[14]

Whether such unpleasantness was a factor in the decision by Julius and Rose Hammer to send Armand to live away from home is uncertain. Ten-year-old Armand went to Meriden, Connecticut, and stayed there five years with the family of George Rose, a foundry laborer and Socialist colleague of Julius's. One explanation from Hammer family lore for this step is that Armand had fallen in with undesirable companions at Public School Number 4 in the Bronx. Another is that the family thought he needed fresh country air. Armand has said that his playing hooky from school to visit a New Jersey amusement park was the last straw for his parents. But all of those versions fail to explain why Harry, too, was sent away, to live with Rabbi Saul Wellington's family in Waterbury, Connecticut, or why two years later Victor went to live in Pleasantville, New York, with the family of prominent Socialist Daniel DeLeon. Perhaps Julius and Rose wanted the boys away from home because of the drawn-out bankruptcy proceedings. Perhaps the Hammers needed help getting back on their feet. Or perhaps Julius and Rose were simply overcommitted. There is evidence that the Hammers were never destitute: Julius and Rose traveled overseas, Julius invested in the Clay-Godsen Chemical Manufacturing Company, and he was generous to the Socialist Labor party as well.[15]

Whatever the reason for Armand's stay in Meriden, it seems not to have done any lasting harm to his psyche, unless a possible feeling of abandonment should be regarded as causing his lifelong quest for public adulation. When he returned to his parents' home in 1913, after completing two years at Meriden High School, he entered Morris High School in the Bronx. There he studied English, German, Latin, algebra, geometry, biology, physics, history, drawing, and elocution. He graduated in 1915 with good grades, some ability as a pianist (thanks partly to a first-rate private teacher), and impressive oratorical skills.[16]

A telling account of the atmosphere at Morris High School came from a classmate, Marie Syrkin, later a Brandeis University professor. She recalled that the student body was composed mostly of children of recently arrived immigrant families. The students tended to be neatly dressed and socially aware. With war consuming Europe, the majority of contestants in the class oratorical contest talked about peace. The winning orator spoke of World War I as the war to end war. It was Armand Hammer, whom nobody had the foresight to choose as most likely to succeed.[17] Armand's topic was an early indication of his passion for peace. After he earned his fortune, he spent much of it crusading for peace, often in the private chambers of heads of state. His critics accused him of using peace to call attention to himself. Self-aggrandizement was an element, but the evidence dating back to adolescence supports his sincerity.

By autumn 1915, Armand was ready to begin his undergraduate studies at Columbia University, Julius's alma mater. Armand wanted to be a family-practice doctor like his father. He would serve humanity while making a comfortable living. Rose Hammer already had singled him out as the most gifted of her three children. Armand's father, meanwhile, was immersed in doctoring and in radical politics, which would eventually get him into such trouble that Armand, while still a student, would assume the role of chief of the clan.

2

Radical Politics

IN AUGUST 1907, Julius Hammer, having emerged pretty much unscathed from his messy bankruptcy, took a break from his medical practice for a trip to Stuttgart, Germany, where an international Socialist conference was trying to decide policy questions. About nine hundred delegates attended. The *New York Times* editorialized that the twenty-one U.S. delegates, Julius among them, were traitors to their country. In the American delegation were Daniel DeLeon, Julius's ideological mentor, and Boris Reinstein, who had close ties to future leaders of the Soviet Union. Julius also met V. I. Lenin. Bertram Wolfe, who knew Julius well and who was a scholar of Lenin's works, wrote that Armand's father became "the most discreet and able of Lenin's men of confidence that I found in the Socialist party."[1]

Beginning that year, Julius served in numerous party posts. He also contributed money, even though his finances were sometimes precarious.* In partial compensation, he signed up a number of patients from

---

* In November 1913 Julius wrote to party headquarters asking for repayment of loans totaling $90 because his mortgage payment was in arrears. But the Socialist Labor party was having its own money troubles. A week after receiving Julius's letter, the national secretary sent him $15. Three weeks after that, the secretary asked "Comrade Hammer" if he would accept the remaining $75 "in literature and prepaid subscription cards. We could stand that very much better because it would be a gradual liquidation of the indebtedness." Throughout the next year, 1914, there was regular correspondence between Julius and party headquarters about their mutual needs for cash. When Julius received a plea for a loan of up to $500, he replied that he had no money on hand but would try to come up with something by month's end. In the meantime, he wondered, could the national secretary do him the favor of procuring a particular translation of Karl Marx's *Das Kapital*? (Socialist Labor party archives, State Historical Society of Wisconsin, Madison.)

among his Socialist connections. Indeed, the busy practice kept Julius away from party matters more than he liked. In December 1915, he wrote the national secretary an apology for his slowness in corresponding: "I often lack the minimum necessary time for sleep and food. It is now almost like a battle time, battling against the worst epidemic of la grippe and consequent pneumonia than ever any that I experienced."[2]

When he found time, Julius actively recruited Socialist Labor party members. Two contacts were his mother, Victoria, and his son Armand, both of whom signed membership applications in 1916.[3] Armand later said that he was never a Socialist or a Communist. His signature on that 1916 application casts doubt on his blanket denial. But, considering that he was an eighteen-year-old student, quite likely being pressured to sign by his father, the application mostly demonstrates Julius's zealousness.

The Bureau of Investigation (later known as the Federal Bureau of Investigation) had agents watching Julius Hammer. One surveillance report noted that in 1914 a suspected dangerous radical had visited the Hammer home, where he had "secured dynamite" to turn over to another suspected radical.[4] It seems out of character for Julius to have been dispensing dynamite, and many law-enforcement surveillance reports about him and Armand turned out to be inaccurate. But, true or untrue, law-enforcement authorities believed the dynamite story, and they acted on their perception of the Hammers as dangerous dissidents.

However independent Armand Hammer may have been of his father's politics, the youth undoubtedly was profoundly impressed by Julius's dedication to humanity through medicine. With Julius as an inspiration, Armand worked diligently to make it through the undergraduate program at Columbia University, which enabled him to enter medical college, just as Julius had done. While an undergraduate, Hammer sought companionship by joining Phi Sigma Delta, a small Jewish fraternity. Besides the fraternity, he joined the fencing team, and participated in wrestling, debating, the Sophomore Show, and the Varsity Show.[5]

His graduating class had 350 students, its ranks having been depleted by World War I. Two of his seventeen fraternity brothers left school to serve in the military, as did 45 percent of his overall class. The Columbia yearbook for 1919 noted that "more and more of us are answering the nation's call as the academic year draws to a close. There is a gigantic task ahead of those who are able to remain at Columbia and to carry on the work of their classmates." Armand's service appar-

ently consisted of working with the Mount Sinai chapter of the Red
Cross in New York. As a young man in a hurry, he preferred service
close to home, which allowed him to receive his bachelor's degree on
schedule so he could begin medical college.[6]

All in all, life had been good to the Hammers during Armand's
undergraduate years. After the fallout from the bankruptcy cleared,
Julius had built a thriving medical practice, with many Jewish immigrants from Russia among his patients. He acquired interests in several
pharmaceutical companies as well. Thus the Hammers could afford
two servants in the house. The family spent summers on the beach at
Belmar, New Jersey, staying in an upper-crust hotel, and enjoyed an
occasional retreat at Edgemere, New York, by the Atlantic Ocean. In
1917, an expansive Armand wrote to a young female cousin that if she
helped her mother take care of a baby, he would give her a long ride
when he bought his new car.[7]

Shortly thereafter, while still a student, Armand moved into a place
of his own at 183 West Fourth Street, Greenwich Village. Strikingly
handsome, with penetrating, soulful eyes, he considered the charming
former carriage house an ideal domicile for an unmarried ladies' man.
A high-ceilinged living room, complete with skylight, and a balcony
leading to the bedroom gave the place a romantic atmosphere. He bought
a grand piano and played it for his guests. A new car was parked
outside. He entertained often; alcohol was easy to obtain, even during
Prohibition, because the Hammer family business handled bonded liquor, which could be sold for medical reasons if prescribed by a doctor.[8]

The idyll didn't last long. As Armand progressed through medical
college, Julius became embroiled in the most serious troubles of his
adult life — first because of his political activity, then because of his medical practice. In 1918, he was expelled from the Socialist Labor party, a
victim of intramural doctrinal squabbling. Undaunted, he jumped parties. By early 1919, he was involved in establishing the Left Wing Section of the Socialist party of the United States. It was an early Communist beachhead in America, a revolutionary Leninist organization.
Julius immediately gained a position of power. Bertram Wolfe provided a description of Julius during this period, noting that when he
presided at acrimonious meetings, he appeared to be fair to all factions,
despite his identification with only one. Wolfe termed Julius "a robust,
stocky, swarthy man, always faultlessly dressed in a dark blue or black
suit. He wore, as the badge of the medical doctor at that time, a dignified black Vandyke." While Lenin found many Communist leaders
outside the Soviet Union disappointing, Wolfe said, he "had nothing
but good to say of Julius Hammer."[9]

To those espousing less radical politics, Julius's activities appeared to threaten the security of the United States. Federal law-enforcement agencies watched him closely, intensifying their surveillance in 1919 when the fledgling Bolshevik government of the Soviet Union authorized Ludwig Martens to open an unofficial diplomatic mission in New York. The United States refused to recognize the Bolshevik regime until 1933, which meant that the Soviet Union had no embassy in Washington, but the Russian Soviet Bureau, headed by Martens, was a functional alternative for a time. Though Martens proved to be an inept ambassador, he had able people around him, including Julius Hammer, who contributed to the operating budget, accepted a titled position, and cut back on his medical practice to devote time to the cause.[10]

Julius's reasons for working so closely with Martens were several. Certainly, the Soviet Bureau was a potential pipeline into Russia for the Hammer pharmaceutical firm. As Martens was organizing the bureau, Julius and Armand were gaining control of the Allied Drug and Chemical Corporation. That company had been created in 1917 by the Hammers, who amalgamated pharmaceutical firms in which Julius and other physicians had built up interests over the years. The Hammers agreed in April 1919 to pay a partner for his stock. One way they hoped to recoup the buyout money was by selling medical supplies, such as chloroform and ether, to the war-torn Bolshevik government through Martens. The Bolsheviks were having trouble obtaining such needed supplies because of an Allied blockade, which the United States was condoning.[11]

Julius was motivated by altruism as well. Trade with the Soviet Union was perceived as financially risky and unpatriotic by most businesspeople. It is likely that the Hammers profited little from whatever medicines they got into Russia; the Soviet government was having trouble paying bills in 1919, and Julius had little inclination to press the matter. His loyalty to the cause overrode his business instincts. Armand has said the amount Allied Drug grossed in its dealings with the Soviets was $150,000 at most, and about half of that came from sales of oil-well machinery, not medicine.

Julius, meanwhile, was working hard for the Socialist cause. He carried the titles of manager, chemico-pharmaceutical division of the commercial department, and acting director of the financial department. While other employees of the Russian Soviet Bureau earned up to $100 a week, Julius waived his salary. He made contact with the Ford Motor Company about selling much-desired American cars and tractors in the Soviet Union. He blanketed the country with letters intended to stimulate Soviet-American trade. For example, he sent a request to Stevens and Company of Providence asking to negotiate a contract for eyeglass frames and mountings. The goods would be sent to the Soviet Union, "conditioned on the procuring of export licenses for their shipment." As happened at many companies receiving such letters, suspicious executives queried the State Department for advice; the reply came back that export licenses to the Soviet Union "are not now being granted." [12] Almost all of Julius's efforts were frustrated. Although some American businesses wanted to trade with the Russians, the policy of the U.S. government acted as a powerful disincentive.

When Julius and Martens wrote to the National City Bank, claiming all the money deposited there by the pre-Bolshevik Russian government, bank officials asked the State Department what to do. One enraged bureaucrat responded that the Hammer-Martens letter "constitutes an affront to this government and renders [Martens] persona non grata. I recommend that Martens . . . be deported forthwith as an undesirable alien." The State Department never did recognize Martens's credentials. American authorities harassed the Russian Soviet Bureau, even seizing its paperwork in a raid. Martens received subpoenas to appear in front of various government tribunals. Then, in March 1920, deportation proceedings began. The case was handled by J. Edgar Hoover, a young lawyer just beginning a lifetime of government service. Thanks to Hoover's work, Martens was forced to leave the United States. Upset but undaunted, he traveled to Moscow to take up residence, along with Boris Reinstein and other Socialist friends of Julius's. [13] (Hoover first heard of the Hammers through the Martens case; he never forgot the Hammer name during his five decades at the FBI, trying to sully Armand Hammer's reputation in successive administrations.)

The United States did not deport Julius, but his world was caving in nonetheless. In their detailed surveillance reports, federal agents accused Julius of activities meant to foment revolution. The reports had a nasty, anti-Semitic tone. To complicate matters, the Hammer pharmaceutical business was mired in a dispute with its bought-out partner.

The biggest problem of all developed on July 5, 1919, when Marie Oganesoff entered Julius's medical office, in a wing of the Hammer family home. Mrs. Oganesoff, thirty-three, was married to a former czarist diplomat who had remained in the United States after the Bolshevik Revolution. She had given birth to a son, then thirteen, before accumulating a medical history of miscarriages, abortions, and general poor health. Mrs. Oganesoff, who conversed with Julius in Russian, arrived in a car driven by her chauffeur, accompanied by her son and her maid. The maid entered the office with her while the chauffeur and son stayed outside.

With no nurse present, Julius performed the abortion that Mrs. Oganesoff said she so desperately needed to preserve her physical and mental health. She left his office shortly after entering. A day later, she was gravely ill. Six days after the abortion, she died. The Bronx County district attorney heard about the suspicious-sounding death — either from another doctor or from Mrs. Oganesoff's distraught husband. A grand jury took testimony from the husband, the maid, the chauffeur, a police detective, and three doctors who possessed knowledge about the case. In August 1919, the grand jury indicted Julius Hammer for first-degree manslaughter. He was arrested, then released on $5,000 bail to await trial.[14] Armand, understandably devastated, took charge of the family. He was barely twenty-one years old.

3

Convict Father, Millionaire Son

WITH THE ARREST of his father, Armand Hammer began to demonstrate the intelligence, guile, and tenacity as a businessman that would make him world-renowned. His assumption of his father's mantle was an astonishing performance, one that few could have accomplished at his age — twenty-one — especially while earning a medical degree at the same time.

Even before Julius's indictment, Armand was shouldering more responsibility than the average person his age. With half brother Harry in military service, brother Victor still sheltered, grandparents Jacob and Victoria in their declining years, Rose occupied trying to keep the family's morale from sinking, and Julius consumed by medicine and radical politics, the family needed a leader. Armand had begun to play a role in the family pharmaceutical business while still an undergraduate. Now he took over. He was a smooth talker, handsome, aggressive, possessed of a good head for numbers, and given to true enjoyment in turning a profit.

Before Armand took up the reins of Allied Drug and Chemical Corporation, an unwelcome distraction had arisen, in April 1919. Former partner Charles Fingerhood sued Julius for allegedly telling others that Fingerhood had robbed the corporate treasury. Rather, Fingerhood charged, Julius had exaggerated the company's financial problems, suggesting it was on the verge of bankruptcy, in an attempt to panic Fingerhood into selling his stock. Fingerhood said that, acting on this false information, he had transferred his stock to Julius for about $1,500. In a later account Armand put the amount at $20,000, at variance with the court papers. Fingerhood said that once he came to believe the stock's value was many times higher than $1,500 he tried to buy it back for the original sales price, but Julius refused.[1] Fingerhood's story rang false in many particulars, especially considering that he was an accountant while Julius was a mediocre businessman. But believing Armand's retrospective version is difficult, too; it fails to square with extant court records.

Also puzzling is Armand's account of his relationship with Max Steuer, a famous lawyer he retained in the Fingerhood case.[2] Armand has said that Steuer agreed to write a letter to Fingerhood for a flat fee of $1,000. The letter had the desired effect; Fingerhood dropped his suit, according to Armand's version. Then Steuer tried to charge $10,000 for his service, supposedly backing down when confronted by Armand. Yet the court records show that Fingerhood *did* sue (although they do not indicate the outcome of the suit); no letter from Steuer or anybody else appears to have dissuaded him. Furthermore, Steuer's name was signed to numerous documents in the case, not just to one. It is possible but unlikely that Armand's version referred to an unknown, separate dispute with Fingerhood. It is also possible that Armand exaggerated the incident to demonstrate his prowess when pitted against a legal legend.

But the Fingerhood case did not prevent Armand from throwing himself into running Allied Drug; throughout his life he would always welcome a challenge. Before his involvement, the company had been a modest operation, employing about two dozen people to manufacture, package, and distribute medicines to doctors. It undercut competitors by using plain packaging. Allied Drug was getting along with a limited number of products, including Velògen, a "toilet article for skin, and surgical lubricant"; and ADACCO Salt, "a saline laxative," manufactured at its main plant, on upper Third Avenue in New York City.[3] Armand decided to revamp the business. Using hindsight, some Hammerologists have commented that Armand was a lucky kid, nothing more. In fact, when Armand Hammer was long past being a kid, detractors still were calling him lucky. The truth is that while there are many lucky tycoons, there are few lazy, lucky tycoons. Without question, Armand earned his early success by combining hard work and what some observers have considered opportunism. The formula exploited by Hammer might not have appealed to other businessmen, but it served him.

His success started with the company's experiencing rising sales on its tincture of ginger, which was 85 percent alcohol, although it never had been a major item in the Allied Drug line. Armand, puzzled, decided to visit one of the customers placing large orders of the tinc-

ture, a druggist in Richmond. Apparently incredulous at Armand's na-
iveté, the druggist took him into a back room, where he poured the
tincture into a glass of iced ginger ale. The result was an instant, powerful highball. This occurred at the beginning of nationwide Prohibition. In December 1917, Congress had approved a constitutional
amendment to ban alcohol consumption. By January 1919, the needed
three fourths of all state legislatures had ratified the amendment, which
took effect a year later. Congress approved the Volstead Act in October
1919, establishing the enforcement mechanism for Prohibition. Under
the circumstances, drinkers were not picky — they would consume what
was legal, and live with the taste.

Armand realized that his company could make a fortune by increasing its stock of tincture of ginger. He arranged a $1 million line of
credit with banks. Then he learned as much as possible about ginger-
exporting countries from the U.S. Department of Commerce. His next
move was to hire agents to buy ginger production in India, Nigeria,
and Fiji. Armand has said he cornered the world ginger market, forcing larger companies to buy their supplies from Allied Drug. The firm's
work force grew to fifteen hundred employees. The fledgling medical
student was taking $30,000 a day to the bank. He ended up with more
than $1 million of income for 1919.

If Hammer truly cornered the ginger market, he did it quietly.
Newspapers, magazines, and trade publications appear to have ignored
the amazing feat. But then, there would have been good reasons for
Hammer to keep a low profile. Buyers of ginger from Allied Drug
might have been upset to learn that its mastermind was a student backed
by a father with a poor credit history who was active in radical politics
and under indictment for manslaughter. Also, the morality of selling
tincture of ginger per se was questionable. At the 1918 meeting of the
Flavoring Extract Manufacturers' Association of the United States, the
talk was about federal Internal Revenue Department efforts to prevent
nonbeverage alcohol from being diverted to beverage purposes. A Tennessee tincture of ginger manufacturer told delegates he had stopped
selling the product, despite its profitability, because customers were
abusing it. The association's lawyer reported that the state of Oregon
had banned the product's manufacture and sale. At the association's
1919 convention, the group's president told of "unscrupulous" manufacturers' shipping large amounts of ginger into dry states. He warned
the membership: "If you continue to countenance such transactions upon
the theory . . . that you might just as well sell it as the other fellow,"
everybody might be put out of business by the federal government.[4]

By 1921, the House of Representatives was hearing disturbing testimony about the ghastly abuses of what was being called Jamaica ginger, or "jake." The president of the Flavoring Extract Manufacturers' Association testified in defense of Allied Drug and other member companies. But as scientists began to get a handle on the effects, there was no denying the dangers. Outbreaks of Jamaica ginger poisoning occurred in Wichita, Kansas; Oklahoma City; and Cincinnati. Thousands of drinkers suffered paralysis of the arms and legs. Some deaths were attributed to complications from imbibing jake. Although tincture of ginger was supposed to be available by medical prescription only, a bootleg version was being sold by pharmacists in two-ounce bottles.[5]

Maybe Armand Hammer did wrestle at the time with the propriety of selling tincture of ginger. But it appears doubtful. In his 1987 autobiography, he dismissed the matter by saying that he never considered himself a bootlegger, no matter what others believed. As long as it was legal, Armand determined that it was an appropriate way to make money. In other words, if it was legal, why worry? When the sale of tincture of ginger became illegal, Allied Drug got out of that line, using its profits to buy commonplace surplus government drugs and chemicals.

Allied Drug's profits would help to pay for the expensive defense of Julius Hammer against the manslaughter charge. It was difficult at first for Armand to take command of the defense effort — he was traumatized. Not even wealth at an early age could cushion a son completely from the shock of his father's facing prison as a convicted felon. In later years, when Armand was able to discuss his feelings publicly, he likened his reaction to that of Charles Dickens when his father was imprisoned. Armand speculated that Dickens's nightmare contributed to his genius as a novelist. He left unsaid whether Julius's trial acted as a spur to his own success.

When Armand began building a defense team, he contacted Henry Kuntz, who had advised Julius fifteen years earlier, during his bankruptcy troubles. In the interval, Kuntz had served time in prison for illegally instructing a client on how to disguise assets — in a bankruptcy case. After Kuntz was released, Julius had given him a job at Allied Drug. Asking Kuntz to set up the defense turned out to be a mistake, which stemmed from Armand's sometimes puzzling inability to judge a person's character accurately. One of the two lawyers chosen by the disbarred Kuntz to defend Julius was the man who had prosecuted Kuntz. Kuntz's other choice possessed no trial experience, reportedly showing up at the courthouse in a chauffeured Rolls-Royce and wearing a frock coat and monocle — creating an impression almost guaranteed to alienate the jurors. Armand has suggested that Kuntz retained the former prosecutor with the hope of winning support for a pardon. The other lawyer may have been a longtime Kuntz crony.[6]

When Armand realized Kuntz's legal team was making a shambles of Julius's defense, he hired another lawyer to conduct a salvage operation. It was too late. Testimony began on June 21, 1920, at the Bronx County Courthouse before Judge Louis Gibbs and a jury of twelve men. Albert Cohn (the father of Roy Cohn) and his fellow prosecutor had an easy time. Although Armand blamed incompetent defense lawyers and dishonest witnesses, there was a factor he refused to accept: Julius Hammer's case was weak. A thorough reading of the evidence almost surely would lead most people to conclude he was guilty. He may have been a skilled, caring doctor, but he botched the care of Mrs. Oganesoff, and she paid with her life. Then he lied about the cause of death in an attempt to escape responsibility. A prosecution brief set out the damning evidence succinctly. The brief quoted medical experts who criticized Julius for performing the curettage in his office instead of in a hospital, operating without removing the patient's clothing, failing to have a nurse present, and neglecting to prescribe bed rest.[7]

The tensest moment in the trial came on the second day, when a juror told the judge that an unidentified man had offered him $1,000 if he would vote for Julius Hammer's acquittal. Despite the attempted bribe, the juror promised the judge, he would be able to continue to serve in an unbiased manner. The judge accepted the assurance but then polled all the jurors after newspapers published articles about the alleged bribe attempt. It appeared that a mistrial would result. Julius's lawyers inexplicably failed to push for one, however, and the judge let the case proceed.[8]

The defense called seven doctors, all of whom testified to Julius's good character and his medical skills. But none could explain away the death. On June 26 the jury returned a verdict of guilty.

Armand began to engineer an appeal. He hired new lawyers, including a well-known trial attorney, a law school professor, and a former judge. Opinion was deeply divided about Julius's conviction. One doctor, an official at Bronx Hospital, told reporters that some of his colleagues were refusing to perform legal therapeutic abortions because of the conviction. The official said that women who needed abortions to save their lives would die as a result of the "stupid verdict." The *Journal of the American Medical Association* noted the doctor's outrage but two weeks later backtracked, reporting that the Bronx County Medical Society actually supported the abortion law as written and was doing nothing as an organization on Julius Hammer's behalf.[9]

Meanwhile, several hundred doctors signed a petition asking the judge to go easy on Julius and calling for the penal law to be amended before similar cases arose. There are indications that Armand organized this petition drive. It backfired. The district attorney announced an investigation into whether names had been forged. The judge denounced the petition effort from the bench. He called it objectionable propaganda, adding that doctors who obeyed the law on abortions had nothing to fear. On July 19, 1920, after hearing unconvincing arguments from Julius's lawyers, the judge sentenced the defendant to a minimum of three and a half years and a maximum of fifteen years in prison. The prosecution had pushed hard for prison time; Assistant District Attorney Cohn told the judge that Hammer had allowed his patient "to die like a dog," then tried to cover up the cause of death by attributing it to influenza.[10]

In later years, Armand cited an influenza epidemic as one of many factors that could have killed Mrs. Oganesoff, especially considering her overall bad health. He offered as other explanations political intrigue at Tammany Hall, where the city bosses disliked Julius's Socialist activities; incompetent defense lawyers; spiteful detectives from the district attorney's office who resented having been turned away from the Hammer house when they first went there to question Julius; and the bile of the dead woman's husband, who might have blamed himself for continually impregnating his frail wife but who — a former czarist diplomat thrown out when the Bolsheviks took power — transferred the blame to Julius, a Communist scapegoat. Armand's were pat, appealing scenarios from a son trying to live with having a felon for a father.

All this hypothesizing could not prevent Julius Hammer's entering Sing Sing Prison, in Ossining, New York, on September 18, 1920. The *New York Times* assigned a reporter to cover the event. The reporter noted that Julius "was fitted out in a suit of convict gray and assigned to the idle company, until he can be sent to the yard company to heave coal and do other rough work temporarily. More suitable employment will be found for him later." Three days after Julius walked through the prison gates, a *Times* editorialist commented that the doctor's incarceration was a strong refutation of the oft-heard refrain that there is a special law for the rich and another law for the poor. "The verdict stood," the editorial said, "and the criminal is behind bars, certainly for three and one-half years and perhaps for the better part of fifteen. The evidence against Dr. Hammer was clear, his condemnation fully deserved, and his punishment errs, if at all, on the side of lenience, not severity."[11]

Such attention must have been terribly painful to Armand, and there was no letup. On December 7, 1920, the *Times* reported the arrest of William Cope, a public relations man, for his refusal to answer grand jury questions about his role in the Hammer case. Two of those questions were "Who paid you one hundred dollars a day in the Hammer case?" and "Who employed you as a publicity man in the Hammer case?" Cope was found guilty of contempt by the court, fined, and sentenced.[12]

Julius's ignominy was back in the news again in January 1921, when the first appeal on his behalf failed in state court. The five-judge panel voted unanimously against him. Justice Samuel Greenbaum said in his opinion that the appeal turned on one question: "Was the patient when she came to the doctor's office . . . in such a physical condition that he honestly believed that in order to save her life it was necessary to procure her miscarriage?" The appellate judges suggested that even if the abortion had been justified, Julius was negligent and untruthful afterward. (Armand later wrote that there had been a 3-to-2 split decision by the original appeals judges, but there is no mention of such a decision in the court record.) A second appeal also failed. That opinion, 4 to 2 against Julius, was handed down December 16, 1921.[13]

For many years, Armand had trouble dealing publicly with the reality of Julius's conviction. His memoir *The Quest of the Romanoff Treasure,* published in 1932, contained not a single reference to his father in its 241 pages. A profile of Armand in the *New Yorker* of December 23, 1933, said only that in 1920 Julius Hammer's "far-flung activities were interrupted by a protracted absence." With Julius in prison, the Hammers sold their beloved Bronx home to Benjamin Diamond, Julius's medical partner. They took refuge at the Hotel Ansonia in Manhattan.[14] Armand ached but knew what he had to do — complete medical school and run the pharmaceutical business to support his family. He would get on with his life.

4

Young Doctor

A RMAND HAMMER was anything but a typical medical student. Because of the family business and his father's imprisonment, he missed a lot of his lectures yet managed to graduate with his class due to his intelligence, stamina, and wealth. One solution to his attendance problem was paying classmates to take thorough notes in his absence, then studying the notes during the wee hours. It would have been simpler to scrap his studies and devote full attention to the family business. But Hammer hated to stop short of achieving his dreams.

At least two times, Hammer did come close to leaving medical school — but not because he wanted to. In one case, he had delivered a breech baby while on call during his final year of studies. When he received a summons to the dean's office the next day, he thought he would hear praise for a successful delivery under adverse conditions. Instead, the dean threatened him with expulsion: Why had he failed to call for help? Thinking quickly, Hammer turned the argument around, putting the assembled faculty members on the defensive. Would they have wanted him to leave the mother in distress while he telephoned for help? Help that might have failed to arrive in time? The dean allowed Hammer to remain in school. This anecdote might be at least partly untrue, for Hammer's version names Samuel Lambert as the dean at the time, yet records at the College of Physicians and Surgeons show Lambert had left the deanship two years earlier.[1]

Another narrow escape came after a pharmacology examination. Hammer had missed the class lectures, so he prepared for the examination by reading the assigned textbooks. Unfortunately for him, the test questions were based on the professor's lectures, not on the textbooks. Hammer had no idea of the correct answers. He walked out of the examination, despondent. The next day, he visited the professor, relating the situation that had led to his failure. The professor gave Hammer a second chance. Hammer rose to it and earned an A in the course.

Despite such close calls, Hammer made a good enough impression to win election to Alpha Omega Alpha, a medical student honorary society with membership based on grades and leadership, and to graduate on schedule. His class photograph shows him with 104 classmates — five of them women, the first female graduates from the medical college. His friends in the class, such as Maxwell Rosenzweig, Milton Thomashefsky, and Daniel Mishell, almost surely knew the details of Hammer's unorthodox student career. But not everybody did. Surviving classmates said in interviews that they had known little about Hammer then, partly because they almost never saw him.[2] Hammer had an interest in remaining fairly inconspicuous during medical college, not only because of the unusual way he made it through, but also because of the embarrassment he must have felt at his father's plight. It was to be the last extended period of Armand Hammer's life during which he would purposely stay out of the public eye.

As he approached graduation, Hammer started angling for a prestigious internship at Bellevue Hospital, in New York. He was determined to leave the family business and set up a medical practice. Hammer used guile in his quest for the bacteriology and immunology internship, scheduled to begin in January 1922. He researched the interests of the doctor who controlled the selection, learning that the man was an avid collector of etchings. After cramming knowledge about etchings into his head, Hammer stopped the eminent doctor during hospital rounds to praise his place in the pantheon of collectors. Mistakenly believing himself in the presence of a fellow collector, the doctor invited Hammer to his home. Hammer subsequently received the internship. Relating the story in his autobiography nearly seven decades later, Hammer betrayed no hint of shame at his tactics.

One advantage of working at Bellevue Hospital was that it would keep Hammer in New York, near his father. Julius was doing as well in prison as could be expected. Armand has said that he never heard his father express bitterness about being in prison. Rather, Julius used it as an opportunity to help less fortunate inmates, who elected him secretary of the Mutual Welfare League of Sing Sing. After Julius's final appeal failed, there were rumors of a governor's pardon, which the district attorney announced he would fight. Meanwhile, the state of New York formally revoked Julius's license to practice medicine.[3]

While Julius Hammer tried to make the best of serving hard time, Armand was about to start a new, dramatic, and entirely unexpected life, one that would determine not only his future, but also the future of the entire Hammer family. Armand had become captivated by newspaper accounts of the famine in Soviet Russia. With seven months between his medical college graduation and his Bellevue internship, he decided to use his medical skills to help the victims of starvation and typhus. He could also visit the spots where his parents were born and reared, meet relatives still living in Russia, and maybe collect some of the $150,000 owed to Allied Drug by the Bolshevik government. He was determined to leave business management for good as soon as he could, placing Allied Drug and Chemical Corporation under the apparently sound direction of Harry Hammer and experienced chemist Alfred Van Horn.

Such plans took shape in his mind even before his medical college graduation, in June 1921. Hammer requested a passport from the U.S. government on April 16, 1921. The strikingly handsome young man in the passport photograph described himself as twenty-two, five feet seven inches, and as having gray eyes and brown hair, and residing at the Hotel Ansonia, Seventy-third and Broadway, New York. Hammer said he wanted to travel for about four months for "commercial and pleasure" purposes. He would visit England, France, Norway, Sweden, and Holland. Nowhere did he mention the Soviet Union.[4]

In 1921, an American wanting to travel to the Soviet Union faced a formidable challenge, in part because the American government discouraged such travel, but also because the Soviet government was selective about issuing visas. Nevertheless, before his departure, he arranged to ship a field hospital and a well-stocked ambulance by freighter to Riga, Latvia, whence the equipment and supplies would continue by train to Moscow. He had purchased the field hospital from government surplus stocks. The ambulance was brand-new. His cost for both reportedly exceeded $115,000.

Unknown to Hammer, key figures in the U.S. government were aware of his destination. On June 11, 1921, William Cope, the same Cope alleged to have coordinated a publicity campaign on Julius's behalf during his manslaughter trial a year earlier and who had refused to answer grand jury questions about his role, wrote to J. Edgar Hoover at the Justice Department, in Washington:

Dr. Armand Hammer, an intern at Bellevue Hospital . . . is going to sail for Europe . . . in July. . . . He is going overseas, I am advised, to carry some messages for [Ludwig] Martens, the deported Soviet ambas-

sador, and I am told that he will bring back some important papers for
those interested in the Soviet movement in this country. . . . Right now
. . . Hammer has a stock interest in the Allied Drug and Chemical
company . . . Martens has a half-interest in these factories, although I
believe the ownership is rather well concealed.[5]

On June 14, 1921, Hoover wrote to the State Department, asking
whether Hammer had applied for a passport and whether he mentioned Russia as a destination. The State Department replied that a
passport had been issued but that the application made no reference to
the Soviet Union. Hoover decided to let Hammer sail anyway. Perhaps
federal agents wanted to see what he would carry on his travels. Perhaps State Department officials believed they had no grounds to halt
his departure, because in 1921 it was legal (although inconvenient and
imprudent) for an American to travel abroad without a passport. On
July 12, the U.S. Embassy in London cabled Washington, confirming
that Hammer had sailed on July 5 from New York aboard the S.S.
Aquitania: "We propose to have him thoroughly searched on arrival,
and all documents he is carrying sent to this office for scrutiny. As he
is an American citizen, I thought we had better let you know."[6]

In describing his dramatic journey from New York to Moscow,
Hammer has emphasized different reasons at different times for its
purpose. Exactly what he told his questioners when he was detained in
Southampton, England, is unavailable in currently open files. But in
some of his earliest published remarks, Hammer said he was carrying
a letter of introduction from his father to Lenin, by then the preemi-
nent figure in the Bolshevik government. Hammer expressed surprise
at his detention. Trying to figure out what had triggered it, he concluded — being unaware of Cope's letter — that Scotland Yard had in-
tercepted his own cable to the Soviet representative in Berlin. Hammer's cable mentioned that he was sailing for Europe carrying a film
given to him by Charles Recht, the New York lawyer for Ludwig
Martens and other political radicals. Recht wanted Hammer to deliver
the film to Martens in Moscow; the footage showed Martens being
deported from the United States. It never occurred to Hammer that
anybody would consider the film politically sensitive. He had not learned
yet that just about anything involving the Soviet Union aroused suspicions within the United States and Allied governments.

At the end of his two-day detention, Hammer reportedly received
apologies, first from the Scotland Yard policeman who had questioned
him, then again at the Yard's London headquarters. His possessions

were returned to him, except for the film, which British authorities sent to the U.S. Embassy, along with a letter (translated from the Russian) that had accompanied it. The letter, written at the Cinematographic Association of the American Society for Technical Aid to Russia, was a proposal to Martens to arrange for movie projectors to be sent from America. After viewing the confiscated film, J. Edgar Hoover judged it to be undramatic. "I can see, however, how the film could be put to good propaganda uses either in this country or in Russia," he said. The Justice Department began tracing Hammer's mail and examining his bank accounts.[7] Meanwhile, Hammer — oblivious to the depth of his government's suspicions — reached Berlin, where he expected to pick up a visa into Russia from the Soviet consulate. His determination to continue on to the Soviet Union had remained strong, despite the upsetting delay.

In Germany, Hammer received an unpleasant surprise. The visa was not ready, a supercilious Soviet bureaucrat told him. Hammer cabled Moscow, asking for expeditious handling of his visa request. He made it known that he had shipped the field hospital and ambulance as a donation to the Bolshevik government. The reply that his visa would be forthcoming came not from a minor functionary, but rather from Maxim Litvinov, who later became the Soviet ambassador to the United States. The quick response from somebody as important as Litvinov probably is explained by Armand's invocation of the names Charles Recht, Ludwig Martens, and Julius Hammer. Why else would the Soviet government have granted a hard-to-get visa to a youthful small-business man about to begin a career as a doctor in America? F. A. MacKenzie, a foreign correspondent for the *Chicago Daily News,* had applied for a visa at about the same time as Armand Hammer. It took MacKenzie three months to obtain his, even though the Bolshevik government wanted more publicity in the Western world.[8]

With permission granted to enter Russia, Hammer traveled to Riga — then independent of the Soviet Union — to meet Boris Mishell, the uncle of Hammer's medical school friend Daniel Mishell. Armand had recently hired Boris as the European representative for Allied Drug and Chemical Corporation, and he was vital to the change about to occur in Armand's life. Russian-born, Mishell had immigrated to the United States at age seventeen. He ended up running a yarn business in New York City. But he longed to travel, so he sought opportunities overseas. He was fluent in Russian, a language Armand had yet to learn. Mishell, seventeen years older than Armand, became a second father to the young man, whose real father was incarcerated thousands of miles away. While they were together in Riga, Mishell taught Armand quickly, explaining, among other things, how much to pay customs officials when they held baggage hostage in expectation of a bribe.[9]

After saying good-bye to Mishell, Hammer journeyed by train from Riga to Moscow, where a representative of the Soviet Foreign Office met him and showed him to his hotel. The hotel was filthy. Armand was left on his own in a huge, devastated city where he was ignorant of the language and where many residents were near starvation. Unable to adjust at first, he stayed inside, learning Russian at the self-imposed pace of one hundred words a day. Later, after consuming the canned sardines he had brought with him in his luggage, he ventured outside, to a club serving bootleg food, where he could eat decently as long as he could pay the price. This routine was broken only by a visit to Nikolai Semashko, the Soviet public health minister, who thanked Hammer for his offer of medical help but did nothing to take advantage of his skills. Uncharacteristically discouraged, Hammer began thinking about returning to the United States.

Before he could make his arrangements, however, he received an invitation from Soviet officials to join a train excursion, led by Ludwig Martens, to the Ural Mountains, where the travelers were to inspect the parlous state of local industry. Hammer accepted with alacrity — anything would be better than life in the ravaged capital — and after three unexplained postponements in as many days, the party set out.

PART II

AMERICAN CAPITALIST IN COMMUNIST RUSSIA

5

Meeting Lenin

ALTHOUGH ARMAND HAMMER was more worldly than most
twenty-three-year-olds, none of his experiences had prepared him
for the sight of mass starvation he encountered along the route of
the four-day train ride from Moscow or for the wealth of precious
stones and minerals he encountered at his destination. Hammer has
recorded his impressions of that journey in four separate books, the first
published in 1932. An independent account of the trip, published
in 1922 — a decade earlier than Hammer's earliest recollection
— came from A. A. Heller, another foreigner on the train to the
Urals.[1]

In his 1932 memoir, Hammer identified Heller as simply an American writer sympathetic to the Bolsheviks. That thumbnail description
omitted a lot. Hammer and Heller knew each other from New York;
Heller was an incorporator of Allied Drug and Chemical Corporation.
He was also a Russian-American businessman believed to be subsidizing a Soviet publishing operation in the United States with profits from
his own industrial company in New Jersey. In his account, Heller said
he was in the Soviet Union to represent Russian-American workers
thinking of returning to their homeland because of dissatisfaction with
America and to help the Bolshevik cause. Parts of Heller's book have
a propagandistic bent, but the scenes that include Hammer appear to
be straightforward and accurate.

One of Heller's entries, for September 18, 1921, reads:

A party consisting of Dr. Hammer, Grisha, and myself started out this
morning from Ekaterinburg on an automobile trip to the Kasli factory,

which is celebrated all over Russia for its art castings. Our machine was an old Stevens car without a top, with a seat which barely held three. The chauffeur and his assistant were in front. . . . The distance to the factory was about one hundred and thirty versts [one verst is equal to two thirds of a mile] and the chauffeur assured us we could make it in three or four hours. . . . About twenty versts out, something went wrong with the motor. The chauffeur refused to go further and suggested sending his assistant on foot to the nearest village, six versts away, to call up Ekaterinburg for another car. Before doing this we decided to look into the cause of the trouble. This was soon discovered by our enterprising doctor [Hammer], who thereupon took the wheel, to the great disgust of the chauffeur, and started off at a good pace. He did not mind the bumps or turns of the road or the peasant carts loaded with grain and hay which kept getting in our path, and we should have gone on splendidly if one of the tires had not burst while we were passing through a village.[2]

The journey resumed after the tire repair, but more engine trouble forced the group to stop at midnight to sleep in the open car as a cold rain fell. Hammer improvised a toaster from a tin can, and the travelers had warmed bread for breakfast. After setting out again, in daylight, the car ran out of benzene fuel and left the party stranded. Hammer, Heller, and the rest of the group finally reached Kasli that night, entering on a peasant's hay cart. Hammer's refusal to be discouraged by adverse conditions in a strange land was obvious from Heller's account. The week after the fiasco with the car, the group reached the town of Alapayevsk. Another American on that leg of the journey was Lucy Branham, described by Hammer as "a plucky little social worker and former suffragist." Again, his brief characterization failed to reveal significant information. It is quite likely that Hammer and Branham were acquainted before this meeting on Soviet soil. Branham's passion was diplomatic recognition of Russia by the United States. She brought greetings to Soviet laborers from American union leaders.[3]

On the party's agenda in the Urals was a visit to a group of asbestos mines. A narrow-gauge railroad ran part of the way; they accomplished the rest of the journey by automobile on a muddy wooden roadway. The mining operation was fairly modern, having been built about twenty years earlier. But the idle site had been neglected. Heller noted that the deterioration was slight; he guessed a modest investment would make the mines operational again. As Hammer later recalled, it was at the mines that he had an idea. What the Russians needed most was food;

in the United States there was plenty of grain. Why not have his family business ship grain to the Soviet Union? In exchange, Hammer could profit by exporting from Russia the commodities that he saw everywhere, unused and unappreciated — furs, lumber, and semiprecious stones. Hammer suggested the idea to Martens, who took it up in person with the proper authorities in the Urals and by telegraph with Bolshevik leaders in Moscow. Making a profit never even entered his mind, Hammer has said; somehow, though, the contract ended up including a 5 percent commission for the Hammers on each end of the deal.

Hammer's offer became known during a speech by Martens to a group of mostly unemployed miners near Alapayevsk, assembled to hear what the beleaguered Bolsheviks planned to do about renewing production. Martens "told of the agreement which the Ural Industrial Board had concluded with Dr. Hammer for the delivery of one million poods [one pood equals thirty-six pounds] of flour, and he assured his audience that the workers in the Urals would have part of the food necessary to get some of the factories going," according to Heller's account. Hammer was greeted as a hero at every train station on the remainder of the trip. The news had spread that the young American doctor would supply grain to the masses.[4]

Martens's own version, written decades later, suggests a different progression of events. He noted that

> the wheat question was the central question of the economy of the time. The enormous attention . . . which V.I. Lenin devoted to that question is therefore understandable. Before me lies a note sent to V.I. Lenin of November 17, 1921, in which I informed him about the fact that the first steamship of wheat was leaving New York in accordance with the agreement with American concessionaires . . . the first who received an industrial concession from us. I succeeded in interesting an American firm in a concession for the Alapaievsk deposits of asbestos. Among the conditions of the concession was the obligation of the firm to deliver to the Urals in a very short time one million poods of wheat.[5]

If Martens's version is truthful, it was his idea to bring American grain to the Soviet masses rather than Hammer's spontaneous humanitarian impulse.

Whoever originated the idea, Lenin liked it. He cabled Martens in the Urals to confirm the report. When Martens cabled back that it was accurate, Lenin asked to see Hammer in Moscow. Hammer was present with Martens at the telegraph office during the exchange of cables.

It was the first time he was recognized by a head of state, and it made an indelible mark on him. For the remainder of his life, Hammer would negotiate by starting at the top.

Lenin and Hammer met the day after the Urals group returned to Moscow. Hammer devoted ten pages to the meeting in his 1932 memoir. Subsequent versions sometimes add or alter details. For example, Hammer said in his later writings that Boris Reinstein accompanied him to the meeting inside the Kremlin; his 1932 version never mentions Reinstein's name. A Socialist Labor party colleague of Julius Hammer's, Reinstein had returned to the Soviet Union after many years in the United States. His task in the Bolshevik regime was to cement relations with American radicals. Reinstein was part of Lenin's inner circle and thus an immense help.[6]

Hammer found Lenin shorter than he expected — Hammer, only five feet seven, had an advantage of four inches. But Lenin's shortness soon faded from Hammer's mind. Lenin's full concentration, piercing stare, and dedication to the betterment of Soviet society engendered trust in Hammer. Lenin wondered: Would Hammer operate the asbestos mines in the Urals as the first American concessionaire in the Soviet Union? Hammer apparently had enough presence of mind to mention the primitive mining technology, the inefficient Soviet bureaucracy, and potential labor problems. Lenin said those concerns would be handled with dispatch; meanwhile, Hammer should prepare a provisional contract. Upon leaving the meeting, Hammer evidently entertained no doubt about accepting the opportunity. He wrote to his professor at Columbia University, asking to postpone his internship at Bellevue Hospital.[7]

Lenin paid personal attention to the negotiations. He wanted the contract to spell out the grain and asbestos agreements as formal concessions, partly for public relations purposes: "What we want to show and have in print . . . is that the Americans have gone in for concessions. This is important politically." In a letter eight days later, Lenin said that

> special attention must be given to our thorough, actual fulfillment of the terms. . . . We must make a special effort to nurse the concessionaires. This is of exceptional economic and political importance. . . . A point to be specially cleared up [is] whether this should be made public. There is much indication that it is of great importance for us to have this concession and the contract publicized as widely as possible.[8]

Why did Lenin maintain such intense interest in a relatively minor deal? It appears that three factors were at work. One was Julius Hammer's prominence in American Socialist politics — heightened by what Lenin thought was his martyrdom in prison. Lenin's perceptions were set out in a letter in which he said he had heard details about the grain deal from Boris Reinstein. According to Lenin, Reinstein reported that

> the American millionaire [Julius] Hammer, who is Russian-born [and] is in prison on a charge of illegally procuring an abortion — actually, it is said, in revenge for his Communism — is prepared to give the Urals workers one million poods of grain on very easy terms (five percent) and to take Urals valuables on commission for sale in America. This Hammer's son and partner, a doctor, is in Russia and has brought Semashko $60,000 worth of surgical instruments as a gift. The son has visited the Urals with Martens and has decided to help rehabilitate the Urals industries.[9]

A second explanation for Lenin's interest was Armand's entrée through Reinstein and Martens. They pushed the Hammer family's case because culmination of the bargaining in an actual contract would redound to their credit. A third factor was Lenin's desire to build business relations with the United States as a step toward diplomatic relations. The Soviet government, still unstable, was fearful of England and France and hoped America would halt any hostile plans by its allies. Simon Liberman, then chief of the Soviet timber industry, wrote that Lenin's concessions "were the bait which would help him to overcome the political hostility of foreign capitalists toward Soviet Russia. . . . He would create, in one foreign country after another, influential groups of capitalists vitally interested in preserving peaceful relations with Moscow."[10]

As Armand conducted negotiations in Moscow, news of Lenin's offer reached the American public. The first report, in the *New York Times,* carried this headline: "LOOK INTO SOVIET ASBESTOS GRANTS / FEDERAL AGENTS INVESTIGATING CHEMICAL COMPANY HEADED BY DR. HAMMER, CONVICT / MOSCOW TELLS OF DEAL / WILLIAM HAMLIN CHILDS SAYS ALLIED CHEMICAL AND DYE CORPORATION USES NO ASBESTOS." The newspaper's report served nobody well. The Hammer family faced unwanted publicity once again concerning Julius's imprisonment. William Hamlin Childs was forced to admit ignorance about the affairs of his own company in the *New York Times,* for thousands of people to see. Readers of the *Times* would have understood Childs's bewilderment, however, had they known the newspaper was guilty of confusing the Hammers' Allied Drug and Chemical Corporation with Childs's larger, unrelated firm, named Allied Chemical and Dye Corporation.[11]

Federal agents began investigating the new development. A New York agent from the Bureau of Investigation sent a memorandum to headquarters that included information from a listening post in London, where sources cited a "jubilant announcement" by Soviet officials concerning the asbestos concession. The Soviets said "a deposit of $50,000 in gold in the state bank is the only formality that remains to make the contract valid."[12] Hammer later told the banking story differently, saying that the state bank's president suggested he should have the honor of being the first depositor. Hammer, needing rubles anyway for day-to-day transactions, agreed to deposit $5,000, receiving passbook number one in return.

Despite the confusion in the United States, the contract negotiations in Moscow were going smoothly, thanks to Boris Mishell, who had joined Hammer there. Hammer knew he needed somebody more worldly than he, somebody fluent in Russian. Mishell told Hammer to grab the opportunity; why not ask for special treatment, knowing that Lenin was anxious to complete negotiations? Mishell and Hammer composed an addendum of special terms. Their bid worked. The contract signed by the Soviet authorities contained the five points from the addendum: The Hammer concession would be granted offices and warehouses, and militiamen to protect the sites; employees with American citizenship could travel freely within the Soviet Union and leave the country at will; radio and telegraph stations would be at the concession's disposal; the Bolsheviks would assist in transporting freight and employees; and the government would appoint a committee to moderate disputes. Hammer obtained office space on favorable terms in a building that had housed the workshop of Karl Fabergé, the jeweler whose creations for the last two czars of Russia were becoming legendary for their quality.[13]

The Soviet press began to trumpet the Hammer concession. In Moscow, Hammer became a figure of importance. His living situation improved dramatically after his meeting with Lenin. The Soviet authorities moved him to a mansion popularly called the sugar king's palace, in memory of the wealthy capitalist who had built it in czarist times with money from a sugar beet fortune. The Bolsheviks had transformed it from a single-family home to a guesthouse. Being placed there as a lodger by the Bolsheviks conferred the unmistakeable status of distinguished guest. Clare Sheridan, an English artist and writer, was another foreign guest who lived there. She described it as standing

> behind iron railings and sentried gates. . . . The old family servant remained . . . who tried to look after his master's bric-a-brac and waited on the strange new government guests at table. The interior decoration

. . . was modern German Gothic, the furniture imitation Louis Sixteenth, upholstered with real petit point. There were innumerable bronzes
and Sèvres china ornaments and figures. There were gaps on the walls
where the best pictures, Corots chiefly, had been removed to museums.
Lions by Rosa Bonheur, late Victorian family portraits and others had
been left. . . . The general effect, although vulgar, was sumptuous and
comfortable.[14]

Boris Mishell lived in the sugar king's palace as well; he brought his
wife, two sons, and one daughter to Moscow as soon as was possible.
Armand had the Mishells as his extended family while his own family
worked on arrangements to join him. But with Julius Hammer imprisoned, the timing was necessarily uncertain.

Although Armand appreciated the luxuries, he had little time to
enjoy the sugar king's palace. He had a shaky asbestos-mining operation to oversee a long way from Moscow — and he knew almost nothing about asbestos mining. In addition, he needed to find wheat to ship
from the United States to the Soviet Union, locate the ships to carry it,
select goods to send back to America, and make arrangements to sell
those goods once they arrived. Harry Hammer and other Allied Drug
employees provided vital assistance at their end; Mishell carried much
of the burden in Moscow. Federal agents believed Julius was master-
minding the deals from his cell in Sing Sing, since they were unable to
accept that young Armand could be calling the shots.

All these tasks had to be performed by Armand in an atmosphere
of hostility fostered by the United States, combined with uncertainty
on the part of Russians about how to treat capitalists in a fledgling
Communist society. Shifting attitudes within the Soviet government
during the 1920s toward private enterprise frustrated foreign capitalists
as well as indigenous entrepreneurs trying to make their way under
the New Economic Policy. They became known disparagingly as NEP-
men. Yet another obstacle was the difficulty of transporting goods between the United States and the Soviet Union. The U.S. Shipping Board
asked the State Department about the advisability of American vessels'
carrying cargoes to Russian ports. The State Department replied it would
be ill advised to allow American ships in the ports; the risks of ship
hands being imprisoned or the vessels being seized were too great.[15]

Hammer took the risks, though; he was determined to deliver the
first shipment of wheat on time, no later than December 25, 1921. On
its arrival, the Soviet Union was to have goods ready for loading to the
United States. Those might include "artistic valuables, furs, leathers,

bristles, hair, sausages, caviar, crafts goods, cigarets." The ship containing the first cargo of Hammer's grain arrived at either Revel, Estonia, or Riga (depending on which of several accounts is correct) and sailed back to the United States loaded with furs, hides, lace, rubber, and caviar.[16]

Armand returned to America shortly thereafter for a brief stay, partly to supervise the sale of the Soviet goods. Lenin took advantage of the occasion to send a bon voyage letter that contained greetings for Julius and other Socialist leaders confined at Sing Sing. Armand may also have traveled home because Allied Drug was changing its identity — perhaps to make it harder for government agents to track, perhaps to better reflect its new emphasis. Allied Drug became the Ural American Mining and Trading Company in December 1921. In January 1922, the name changed again, to the Allied American Corporation.[17]

When Armand returned to Moscow in the spring of 1922, he had a lot on his mind, including the operation of a distant asbestos mine; his continuing attempts to have his father's conviction overturned, or at least his release from Sing Sing effected; his desire to persuade his kid brother, Victor, a twenty-year-old college student in the United States, to come to Moscow to help in the concession; and his uncertainty about whether to reject, once and for all, the prestigious Bellevue Hospital internship that he had worked so hard to obtain just a year earlier. Yet even the eternally optimistic Armand could not possibly have foreseen that all of these concerns were about to be subsumed in the amazing expansion of his Soviet operations.

Baron of the Brown House

DURING ARMAND HAMMER'S RETURN TRIP to Moscow in the spring of 1922 he stopped in London. While browsing in a shop run by Leonard Partridge, a well-known antiques dealer, Hammer noticed a monkey, cast in bronze, looking at the skull of a human. The monkey's perch was Charles Darwin's *Origin of Species*. Hammer bought the sculpture. After reaching Moscow, he arranged a meeting with Lenin through Boris Reinstein. Hammer presented the sculpture to Lenin, who was immediately taken with it. Lenin's delight made an impression on Hammer.[1] He realized world leaders could be moved, maybe even swayed, by unexpected kindnesses. From then on, Hammer paid calls at the top with carefully chosen gifts in hand.

Lenin interpreted the sculpture to mean that humanity would be annihilated if nations failed to achieve peace. Should that occur, a monkey might well pick up a human skull and wonder about its origin. The bronze monkey later sat on a desk in Lenin's study, which was kept just the way he left it on his last day of work, in 1923. Visitors would call it the most striking of all Lenin's gifts from foreigners. Tour guides at the Moscow museum where the office was replicated would point out the monkey, telling of Lenin's prescient reaction to it more than twenty years before nuclear weapons became reality and praising Hammer for his decades-long role in Soviet-American relations.[2]

Despite Hammer's pleasure at Lenin's reaction, something more immediate than the theoretical destruction of humankind was on the young entrepreneur's mind during the early months of 1922: asbestos mining and import-export arrangements. Lenin stayed on top of the concession, too. He worried that Hammer might be upset by low-quality goods provided for export to the United States, directing that "our obligations under this concession are performed with absolute strictness and accuracy, and in general we must pay greater attention to the whole business." When Hammer and Boris Mishell complained about an intransigent Soviet bureaucrat, Lenin handled the problem himself and obtained an apology from the Soviet official in charge. Lenin informed Joseph Stalin, who would emerge as his successor, that the Hammer concession "is a small path leading to the American business world, and it should be used in every possible way."[3]

The logistics of the grain shipments became moot earlier than expected. Mishell noted in private correspondence that after two of the planned four shipments, Soviet authorities asked the Allied American Corporation to cancel the remaining boatloads.[4] Russian crops were doing well, and U.S. wheat prices were rising to unacceptable levels. But the Soviets had been impressed with Hammer's abilities during the truncated arrangement. As a result, Allied American received the Bolshevik government's blessing to be the exclusive representative of American companies trading with the Soviet Union.

The key to the arrangement was the Ford Motor Company or, more specifically, Henry Ford, the embodiment of American capitalism. The evidence about how the Hammers and Ford first met is inconclusive. One apparent link was Alexander Gomberg, called Uncle Sasha by Armand. Gomberg's wife, Anniuta, was the daughter of Victoria Hammer, Armand's paternal grandmother. Gomberg maintained residences in Paris and Odessa and had operated a Ford Motor Company dealership near Odessa before World War I. Armand realized quickly that the Soviet Union needed a great number of tractors to mechanize its agricultural production. So he asked Gomberg whether Henry Ford might want to enter the postrevolutionary Soviet market in a big way. Gomberg replied that Ford was not only anti-Communist, but also anti-Semitic. Nonetheless, Gomberg offered to help set up a meeting.

Hammer has said he traveled to Detroit, where he met with Ford over lunch and continued talking into the afternoon. Ford agreed to allow Russian employees of Allied American to visit Detroit for training and gave Hammer permission to take automobiles and tractors to Moscow for display. Within hours, Hammer has said, he persuaded Ford to make Allied American his sole agent in the Soviet Union. Hammer's quick success was remarkable — if it happened that way. Some researchers do not believe Hammer's account, pointing out that archivists at the Ford Motor Company have failed to locate proof of a face-to-face meeting between Hammer and Henry Ford. Other researchers accept Hammer's version or at least acknowledge he played a significant role in Russia for Ford. Still others never mention Hammer; their evidence about Ford sales in Russia suggests Hammer either was unaware of what the automotive company already was doing in Russia before 1922 or embellished his own importance. Available documents are inconclusive about a face-to-face meeting but indicate an important link between Allied American and Ford Motor Company's Russian operations.[5] Whatever the details, it is impressive that Hammer captured the Ford sales market in the Soviet Union, a market other companies would have fought to monopolize.

An interview published by a Soviet magazine in 1922 quoted Hammer as saying of his Ford representation: "In the course of the year, we have delivered tractors, trucks, and light automobiles and at the present time together with the Ministry of Foreign Trade we are working out a plan to disseminate tractors on a mass scale." A State Department official noted that Allied American "recently completed a contract with the Soviets on behalf of Ford Motor Company for the delivery . . . of sixty Ford cars. It is said that the cost . . . will be $630 each, and that they will be sold for about $1,600 each." Hammer traveled throughout Russia receiving orders. When about fifty Fordson tractors arrived at Novorossiysk, Hammer and his employees picked them up and drove them to Rostov, more than 150 miles away, in a tractorcade. Russian onlookers had no idea what to make of the noisy procession. There were rumors of an invasion by Western tanks. As the correct information spread down the line, Hammer was greeted warmly by Anastas Mikoyan, then a local Communist party secretary, among others.[6]

By spring 1923, Hammer and Mishell had built an import-export empire in the Soviet Union, using Ford Motor Company as the foundation. Allied American was representing up to three dozen companies doing business with the Soviet government. An advertisement on page 1 of the Moscow telephone directory told of offices there, in New York City, and in Berlin, Petrograd, Riga, and Rostov, and mentioned the firm's concession for asbestos mining and its contract with Ford.[7] Hammer spoke of his company in messianic terms. He billed himself as much more than a profit-oriented capitalist: He was helping a struggling nation achieve self-sufficiency, aiding the American government's balance of trade, and making a contribution to international understanding.

The U.S. government failed to share Hammer's viewpoint about the nobility of his enterprise. A State Department memorandum noted that one of his clients, the Moline Plow Company, was selling a mower in the Soviet Union for $93, with one third of the price going to Allied American as a commission. The memorandum writer fumed about Allied American's principals being Armand Hammer, the son of "a well-known radical," and Boris Mishell, "a naturalized American of Russian-Jewish origin." A *New York Times* article about the Hammer operations led a State Department official to comment that Allied American was "controlled by the Russian Foreign Trade Monopoly Bureau, which in turn is manipulated by the Soviet government. The statement . . . that this corporation is American-owned and American-directed is false."[8]

One part of the family's import-export business was obtaining Russian furs, then shipping them to the United States. Armand compared the fur-gathering operation with that of the Hudson Bay Company during pioneer times on the North American continent. The Hammers' outposts dotted Siberia and the Urals. Trappers obtained provisions from the Hammers as winter rolled in and headed for the wilderness. In the spring, they returned with pelts and collected payment. Allied American entered into a partnership with Sutta and Fuchs, a prominent fur business that sold Russian imports through a New York auction house. The agreement was mutually beneficial — Sutta and Fuchs had been denied its own trading permit, so turned to the Hammers.[9]

On July 14, 1923, the Hammers and the Soviets formalized the exclusive import-export arrangement, signing a contract in Moscow. Allied American promised to import goods worth a minimum of $1.2 million a year into Russia and to export goods valued at the same amount. With the chief export being furs — including pelts from sables, minks, beavers, and squirrels — the Hammers established a subsidiary, the Allied American Fur Sales Agency Incorporated. Other items exported by the Hammers included caviar, lumber, and sheep intestines used in sausages. The imports to the Soviet Union were varied, including, besides Ford automobiles and tractors, asbestos-mining machinery. The Hammers took a 10 percent commission off the top; the Soviets received 50 percent of the remainder. Reports indicated the Hammers were handling at least $6 million a year. Walter Duranty, the *New York Times* correspondent in Moscow, called the Hammer-Soviet contract precedent-setting because of the independence the Russians gave the Hammers.[10]

Pravda played down the Hammers' autonomy, noting that the Soviet government had representation on the Allied American board of directors. Further details about the arrangement were revealed inadvertently years later, after the Internal Revenue Service brought a case against Allied American for taxes allegedly owed from 1923. The agency claimed that the Hammers owed an additional $1,390 because of a nondeductible payment to the Soviets. Allied American responded that the payment was properly deductible as an ordinary and necessary business expense. The U.S. Tax Court sided with the Hammers. But documents filed with the court seem to indicate greater Soviet influence on Allied American operations than was generally admitted by Armand, giving credence, to some observers, to the State Department view of Soviet manipulation.[11] Armand Hammer's detractors have used documents from the case in their decades-long quest to portray him as a Communist tool, an enemy of America.

If the Bolshevik government truly treasured Hammer as a tool, it certainly could have provided him with easier ways to earn money. The asbestos concession in the Ural Mountains, which covered several hundred acres, turned out to be troublesome. Before World War I, Russia had produced more asbestos than any other nation except Canada. During the disarray of the Bolshevik Revolution, production stopped.[12] As Hammer tried to revive it, a continuing problem was the distance between Moscow and the mine site. Hammer has told of a visit to the mines by him and his brother Victor. The train service over the last leg of the journey, about one hundred miles, was so unreliable that they traveled instead by sleigh, through snow-covered forests.

Poor transportation also meant difficulty in getting promised food to the miners. Part of the grain that Armand Hammer shipped from the United States was supposed to be routed to the Urals. Hammer learned that the first shipment of twenty-five grain-filled railroad cars had been halted by a station commander who wanted a bribe. Allied American complained to higher authorities, who executed the corrupt functionary. Hammer related the incident so matter-of-factly that his detractors have used it as evidence of his hard-heartedness, of his concern for profit before human life despite his decades of humanitarian pronouncements. Hammer's supporters replied that all he did was report a business problem; he had no control over how the Bolshevik hierarchy dealt with it.

Despite these troubles, mining began more or less on schedule. The Soviets and Hammer marked the opening by staging a ceremony filled with speeches about Soviet-American goodwill. Hammer spread the excitement to the United States, returning to New York for a meeting behind closed doors at the Commodore Hotel. Businessmen in attendance hoped to emulate Hammer by tapping the Soviet market but worried about receiving financing from commercial banks in the face of continuing American nonrecognition of the Bolshevik regime.[13]

Back in Moscow, Hammer talked to a correspondent for the Soviet publication *Ekonomicheskaya Zhizn* (*Economic Life*), whose report quoted him:

> We received only one covered working shaft for the output of asbestos, which was in a highly neglected condition. Also, in it slag had been dumped in large piles in many places. . . . In addition, the entrances and tracks for taking away the mined ore were not completed. The grading factory with its equipment and devices, except for the building itself, was received in such a condition that all its appurtenances and devices needed more or less significant repair. The real estate also demanded significant repairs, somehow — the barracks, the living quarters, and all of the auxiliary buildings.

Hammer told how railroad tracks were laid, electric lights introduced in town, the meeting hall repaired, and worker dwellings built. He said the inherited problems would prevent Allied American from achieving its production goals for the first year. But area workers should be grateful, Hammer implied — summer employment in 1922 reached 1,100 workers; for 1923, employment was expected to be 2,200. Every worker received heated and lighted living quarters; the town also possessed a new school with two teachers for the fifty students, a meeting hall, and a hospital. In view of such amenities, Hammer wondered why rumors of a strike at the mines persisted. Walter Duranty, who had become friendly with Hammer, chronicled the concession's progress for the *New York Times*. Duranty reported that a sample shipment of asbestos from the Ural mines had reached New York. Like the Soviet newspaper, he quoted Hammer at length on the obstacles overcome.[14]

Soon, *Ekonomicheskaya Zhizn* announced that asbestos sales might pick up because of a new organization "for marketing roofing materials, which has had widespread dissemination abroad in view of its fire resistance and acid resistance. . . . If one recalls how very widespread fires are in the Russian countryside, then the use of these shingles for roofs must take on special interest."[15] The asbestos concession showed a profit in 1925 due to the increased Russian demand for the natural resource as a fireproofing material, as well as for insulation in pipes, boilers, and refrigeration units. Unfortunately for the profitability of the mines, exporting the asbestos was financially unsound because the world market was soft as a consequence of Canadian overproduction.

Despite Hammer's expressions of benevolence, the operation of the concession by a foreign capitalist caused resentment that not even Lenin's blessing could erase. *Pravda* published an ill-tempered article that said:

> During these twenty-three months he [Hammer] has invested about 300,000 gold rubles, one-third of which have been expended for the reestablishment of the mines. . . . The mines have turned out . . . asbestos for which there is no use in this country. . . . In Russia, says Mr. Hammer, there are many sad things that are even worse than the thirty-five percent of third-class asbestos. One is the press. The papers generally have overlooked everything good done by the American company, but always put out something that is bad. For instance, one of the papers wrote once that the workmen of the American concession are being eaten up by bugs. Another time it wrote that on the American concession there is only one cubic sazhen of living area for every four people. Or again that a strike has broken out at the mines which in fact never took place.[16]

When the American consul in Riga sent the *Pravda* attack to the State Department, he noted that "the tone of the report of the interview is throughout very sarcastic. Perhaps, one may infer, the concession is not going as well as public statements made by Mr. Hammer and previously published in the Soviet press would lead one to believe." Six weeks later, however, *Pravda* published a correction based on "supplementary material . . . furnished to the editor." It turned out the interview had been with Armand's brother Victor. The printed apology noted that the mine was operated by the family of Julius Hammer, a longtime American Socialist; that Allied American was not "rapacious," thus distinguishing it from other concessionaires; and that it had spent large sums to improve the mine.[17]

Any pain associated with the asbestos mining was alleviated somewhat for Armand by the reuniting of his family — in Moscow. It happened in stages. First, Harry Hammer applied for his passport on June 8, 1922. Then Victor applied, eleven days later.[18] Victor had studied at Colgate University, then at Princeton. His mother, Rose, disliked his wild friends and their incessant partying. Victor was planning to pursue an acting career, but his mother's disapproval combined with Armand's desire to have him in Russia proved persuasive. Armand used psychology wisely, telling his brother that he could study at the Moscow Art Theater. Before Victor left New York, Armand arranged for him to learn shorthand and typing. Victor complied, making him a valuable assistant to his overextended brother.

The truly unexpected event was the early release of Julius Hammer from Sing Sing. He had been sentenced to a minimum of three and a half years, which would have meant freedom no sooner than March 1924. But on January 23, 1923, the New York State Board of Parole approved his release. Julius left prison on April 5. Even before then, he had been lobbying for permission to leave the country. On March 11 and again on March 23, 1923, Julius wrote L. S. Reingold, his parole officer at the Jewish Board of Guardians. Julius asked that he be allowed to leave for Moscow as soon as possible and to stay as long as necessary. He claimed that Armand had suffered a breakdown due to the strain of operating the family businesses.[19]

Julius presented affidavits from Boris Mishell and Victor testifying to Armand's poor health. It was no wonder that Armand had succumbed to the pressure, Julius wrote. Until recently, he had been "a student all his life. He calls me now to relieve him of this continuous drain upon his health, and in view of his illness and of the fact of my being a physician and a devoted father, I am most anxious to go to his side." Julius, expressing no remorse about his crime, added that he had been wrongly convicted: "It was only a question whether my judgment was correct in considering the operation absolutely necessary to preserve the life of the patient."[20]

Reingold granted permission for Julius to leave the country on March 30, 1923. On April 3, Julius wrote an official at the U.S. Commerce Department, appealing to the commercial instincts of the federal official as he recounted Allied American's history:

> Before its incorporation, I shipped to Russia oil well machinery purchased in this country, which I sold to a department of the Russian government, which conducts a foreign trade monopoly and therefore was the only party with whom business in Russia could be done. I was duly paid for this merchandise. For some years before the war, my brother-in-law Mr. Alexander Gomberg was an agent for the Ford Motor Company. As a result of this situation, the Allied American Corporation was organized to continue developing business along these lines.

Julius noted that a report detailing Allied American's "brisk and lucrative business with Russia" was on file at the Commerce Department. He mentioned his Socialist Labor party background but added that he never had advocated violence or anarchy; his desire to leave for Moscow quickly had nothing to do with his political views. Business and his son's health were his only concerns, he swore. Julius received his passport on April 12, 1923, to the consternation of State Department and Bureau of Investigation agents, who considered him dangerous. By late April, he and Rose Hammer had arrived in Riga, where Boris Mishell, accompanied by the supposedly gravely ill Armand, traveled from Moscow to greet them.[21]

Julius's involvement in the import-export business, which Armand later tended to dismiss as subordinate to his own efforts, focused initially on the Ford connection. On June 1, 1923, Julius wrote to Henry Ford about establishing a manufacturing plant in the Soviet Union, preferably at Rostov-on-Don. Soviet officials in that region had received three hundred tractors with accessories, plus a considerable supply of touring cars. Julius told Ford that the Soviets "are firmly convinced of the superiority of the automobiles and tractors of your manufacture for Russian conditions and needs," but for economic reasons "the production of these models by you on Russian territory, employing Russian materials and labor, would be highly welcomed. . . . The general outlook makes the success of such an enterprise definitely assured. The need for large numbers of tractors is most urgent; many tens of thousands would be required to take the place of the perished draught animals."[22]

Two days later, Julius wrote another Ford Motor Company executive, using Allied American letterhead stationery adorned with a drawing of a Fordson tractor. Julius said that "I found Russia to exceed all my expectations. Reconstruction is going ahead at a more rapid rate than in any other countries in which I visited in Europe. . . . Living is more interesting here, with arts maintaining their excellent standards. The coming crop promises to be a bumper one. The effect of this will be to accelerate the restoration of Russian industry and commerce." Julius later reported that he had filled $400,000 in orders for the Ford Motor Company during 1923.[23]

The Hammers were able to travel freely in the Soviet Union thanks to extraordinary internal passports. Armand's passport letter, issued with the approval of Lenin, said:

> The bearer, Dr. Armand Hammer, is the secretary of the Allied American Corporation, the first stock company to receive from us a franchise, namely the one for the asbestos mines in the Ural Mountains. This firm has also a contract for supplying to Russia a party [sic] of grain in exchange for Russian goods, and it has also the exclusive agency for our automobiles, trucks, and tractors of the Ford Company of America, as

well as the agricultural implements of the Moline Plow Company. I
urgently request all representatives of the Foreign Trade Department /
Vneshtorg or the railroad administration and all other representatives
of Soviet government in Russia and abroad to render to the representatives of this corporation all due attention and all possible assistance by
removing unnecessary formalities, et cetera.[24]

The Hammers found opportunities for a social life as well as a business life in Moscow. There was a special reason to rejoice in November
1924, when New York governor Alfred Smith granted a pardon to
Julius. By then, the Hammers had a suitable place for celebrating. It
was known as the Brown House, probably the most opulent private
residence occupied by Westerners in all of Moscow. Built by a textile
merchant in czarist days, it had been leased by Armand from the Soviet
government. Previously the mansion had served as headquarters for
the American Relief Administration, an organization that in the first
few years of the decade had saved thousands, maybe millions, of Soviet citizens from starvation. The house contained about thirty rooms.
It was conveniently close to shopping, the Moscow Art Theater, and
the circus. A food shop for diplomats and correspondents was around
the corner. Hotels and the telegraph building were within walking
distance.[25]

Journalist Eugene Lyons, who later lived in the mansion, left a detailed description:

> The house was excessively ornate within and without, its doors rein-
> forced with elaborate grillwork, its stone facade tortured with sculptured
> decoration, and a broad inner stairway of gleaming marble spiraling
> majestically to the upper story. The place was filled with rococo statuary
> and paintings, and reindeer heads looked down in astonishment from
> the vestibule walls. The generous proportions of all the rooms, especially
> the immensely high-ceilinged ballroom, represented heady freedom. . . .
> A former cloakroom off the vestibule was large enough to serve as my
> office. . . . The vast kitchen, with its oven as broad as a field, was
> upstairs.[26]

"Visiting Americans carried back tall tales of the splendors and com-
forts in which we luxuriated," Armand later recalled. The home became an unofficial American embassy in the absence of diplomatic relations. Guests included H. G. Wells, Gene Tunney, Mary Pickford,
Douglas Fairbanks, John Dewey, Will Rogers, and Walter Duranty.
Lucita Williams and her husband, Albert Rhys, an internationally known

journalist, were grateful recipients of Hammer hospitality; they lived in the Brown House off and on during the 1920s. Lucita Williams recalled in a memoir the amazing variety of guests, many of them involved in the Bolshevik government or American radical politics. Her memoir focused on Rose Hammer, whom Mrs. Williams called a fun-loving, caring hostess.[27]

One early set of important visitors was a delegation from the U.S. Congress. Senators William King of Utah and Edwin Ladd of North Dakota, and Representative James Frear of Wisconsin — accompanied by well-known journalist Isaac Don Levine — arrived during August 1923. It was a daring trip, especially because of widespread opposition in the United States to recognition of the Bolshevik regime. Senator King had been an opponent of trade with the Soviets, but the trip converted him. He became a friend of Armand Hammer's, later performing political favors for him.[28]

The Hammers took advantage of their special status, looking for financial opportunities wherever they could. They profited from black market money transactions. Victor served as Armand's dealer, exchanging new American currency at favorable rates for rubles, which the Hammers needed to pay short-term bills in their businesses. Armand and Victor began buying works of art — secular and religious — and all manner of czarist bric-a-brac at bargain prices. Some of it they stored; some of it graced the mansion. Armand learned about Arabian horses after receiving one as a gift from General Semen Budenny, a military commander who was the father of the Red Cavalry.[29] Collecting both art and Arabian horses became prestigious, lucrative pastimes of Armand's later in his life.

One sad note associated with the Hammer family reunion in Moscow was the wedge that Julius's arrival drove between Boris Mishell and Armand. For nearly three years, the Mishells had been Armand's second family. Joseph Mishell, Boris's oldest son, remembered his own arrival in Moscow to join Boris: "My father and Armand met me at the Moscow train station. I had received my ticket for the journey from Harry Hammer in New York City. When I got off the train, I had not bathed in four days. Armand and my father took me to a Russian bath. A three-hundred-pound Russian man started pounding on my back. I asked Armand, . . . on a nearby table, how to tell the man to go easier. Armand told me a word, but it turned out that it meant 'harder.' Armand laughed. I ended up working at Allied American Corporation as an office boy decoding cables. Boris spent a lot of time at the asbestos mines in the Urals." The Mishell boys and their sister

Louise took Russian lessons at home. The same teacher then worked with Armand. Robert Mishell, Boris's youngest son, recalled that before Julius and Rose Hammer arrived, "Armand was practically a member of our household in the Soviet Union . . . Armand was almost like a son to dad, and Julius Hammer resented that relationship. . . . He put a chill on it."[30]

The split was inevitable. Julius told Boris to leave the country, and the Mishell family moved to Chicago, where Boris opened a factory for the National Yarn Corporation. The *Chicago Daily News* published a glowing profile of him, which noted that F. A. MacKenzie, the newspaper's Moscow correspondent, had shared the sugar king's palace with Mishell and Armand during 1921. The article gave all the credit to Mishell for the breakthrough in Soviet-American trade — Boris's small revenge, perhaps.[31]

Caught up in the drama of his Moscow life, Armand dropped his plans for a medical career. One of his college mentors, the celebrated researcher and writer Dr. Hans Zinsser, visited the Soviet Union in 1923 on behalf of the League of Nations and reportedly sought to persuade his former student to resume his career in medicine. But Hammer turned aside Zinsser's entreaties. He did become licensed as a doctor in New York and renewed the license regularly.[32] But it was symbolic only. Moscow was his new home.

7

Pencil King

AFTER THE MISHELLS' DEPARTURE, the reunited Hammer family was more fiercely cohesive than ever. Working together, its five members were a formidable combination of brains, daring, persistence, and the right connections. However, all was not well. The U.S. government cast a long shadow. Some federal agencies were softening their opposition to trade with the Soviet Union, but official policy still discouraged entrepreneurs. Moreover, agents from the State Department and the Bureau of Investigation continued their surveillance of the Hammers. Another ominous sign was Lenin's death, in January 1924. Armand was a mourner at the funeral. Thereafter Stalin began to consolidate power — despite Lenin's warning about him to Bolshevik leaders. It became increasingly clear that Stalin did not share Lenin's views about providing industrial concessions to Western capitalists.[1]

What appeared to be most threatening of all to the Hammers' continued stay in Moscow was the disintegration of the import-export concession, precipitated by the Soviet government's creation of the Amtorg Trading Corporation. Amtorg began operations in 1924; its purpose was to give the government control over what it hoped would become a booming foreign trade. One immediate adverse effect was less business from the Ford Motor Company. The Hammers' import-export turnover dropped — from about $6 million in 1924 to about $1.5 million in 1925, an amount below the minimum required by the contract. The U.S. consul in Riga wrote that during 1925 "Soviet government and cooperative organizations practically dominated the foreign trade, and companies with participation of private interests played a negligible role."[2] On March 3, 1926, *Ekonomicheskaya Zhizn* announced the expiration of the Hammer import-export concession.

Most foreigners would have given up. But that never seriously occurred to Armand. As he would do so often, he turned what seemed to be a problem into an opportunity. His instincts and intellect told him there had to be other possibilities besides asbestos and automobiles in Russia.

Before he could concentrate on his next Russian venture, however, he had to deal with a bizarre denouement to his involvement with a bank in the Baltic state of Estonia, which was temporarily free of Soviet domination but tied to its giant neighbor. The Hammer family's ownership of an Estonian bank was shrouded in mystery then and still is today. Armand has said he bought the bank to handle trade matters in the Soviet Union; using Russian banks carried a stigma in the West, and transactions through American banks had proved too complicated. So the Hammers availed themselves of a bank of their own to expand their business in the face of competition from Amtorg.

American government officials viewed the purchase as sinister, their normal reaction to any transaction involving the Hammers. A State Department report summarized the Hammers' Estonian banking connection:

> Early in 1924, Dr. Hammer, representing the Allied American Corporation, obtained control of the Harju Bank at Reval, Estonia, the purchase price for which was said to have been $250,000 American currency, of which $35,000 to $50,000 was paid down at the time of the purchase. This acquisition aroused some press comments at the time. Ostensibly the bank was to finance the export of butter from Russia. There was some suspicion, however, that the Moscow authorities might have advanced part or all of the funds to purchase the bank to obtain a means of transferring funds abroad surreptitiously if desired. Plausibility is given the theory that the Allied American Corporation could not have financed the undertaking itself, in view of its failure to have made any considerable money up to that time from its Russian concessions, and the probability that a large part of its funds were tied up in the asbestos concession which was then being developed and from which little income had been received.[3]

The American consul in Riga reported the Estonian government's unhappiness about foreigners' buying the nation's fourth-largest bank, but the transaction appeared to be legal. The consul noted that the

Soviet legation in Revel had transferred its account to the Harju Bank as a sign of support for the Hammers, then added:

> As regards the business of the Harju Bank under the new owners, all informed people in Reval believe that there is something far deeper than the ostensible butter shipments which the bank proposes to finance. The Allied American Corporation will be able to get its money out of Russia through the Harju Bank and also will be able to make profitable financial transactions for the Soviet authorities.

State Department officials transmitted the information to J. Edgar Hoover, about to ascend to the directorship of the reorganized Bureau of Investigation. Hoover apparently did nothing, but his distrust of the Hammers increased.[4]

Whatever the purpose of the family's ownership of the Harju Bank, there was little time for the Hammers to accomplish it. By mid-1925, the bank was out of business. It had been less sound than the Hammers believed, apparently the result of adverse banking conditions in Estonia combined with alleged embezzlement by the prior owners. Armand had placed Alexander Gomberg, his uncle who helped negotiate the Ford Motor Company contract, in charge of the bank. Gomberg may have failed to detect unsound loans made by bank officers, aggravating an already bad situation.[5] The Hammers left the banking business and returned their focus to Moscow and replacing the income from their import-export concession.

Armand heard from an English shipbuilding corporation wanting a partner in Russia. He discussed the opportunity with Leonid Krassin, a top Soviet trade official. Krassin discouraged such a plan, saying the Russians wanted to build their own ships. Instead, Krassin urged Hammer to acquire his own concession. Hammer was mulling that over when the epiphany happened — during a search in Moscow shops for a lead pencil, of all things. The best price Hammer could find was the American equivalent of 26 cents; in the United States, 3 cents was common. Why did the Soviets charge so much? Hammer wondered. He began to research the market and learned that the Russians were importing pencils from Germany. Before World War I, a German group had operated a small pencil factory in Moscow, but it was defunct. Hammer discovered that although the Soviet government wanted to resume production, its plan was still on the drawing board. So, armed with an idea for reviving the industry, he visited the vice president of the Soviet central concession committee, who was both enthusiastic and skeptical. What did Hammer know about manufacturing pencils?

Nothing, Hammer replied with his typical confidence, but he would learn. He promised his company would deposit $50,000 in the State Bank as a guarantee of good faith. Production would begin within twelve months; moreover, the factory would turn out $1 million worth of pencils during its first year of operation. The Soviet government was impressed enough to sign a contract.[6]

Americans learned of Hammer's newest venture through an aside in a *New York Times* article published in October 1925 that touted his other Russian ventures. The main topic was the import-export concession, which reportedly had shared with the Soviets a $600,000 profit during the previous fiscal year and was shipping large amounts of leather and cotton to the United States. The aside stated that the Soviets had signed a contract allowing Allied American "to take over and re-equip on highly favorable conditions two large pencil factories in Moscow."[7]

Before doing anything else, Hammer traveled to Nuremberg, Germany, to learn everything he could from employees of the Faber pencil factory. At first, employees feared being fired if caught talking to an upstart who planned to compete against established German manufacturers, maybe even steal their talent. But Hammer finally found a source of information: George Baier, a disaffected engineer at Faber. Baier had lived in Russia before World War I while helping to build a pencil factory there and had married a Russian woman. As a result, when he returned to Germany, he was treated like a traitor by the pencil companies for daring to promote competition in another land. By 1925, he was ready to return to Russia, so he jumped at Hammer's offer of a good salary and bonus plan based on production. Baier then helped Hammer hire other workers willing to move to Moscow.[8] Hammer obtained Russian visas for them and ordered machinery for the factory. He followed a similar plan in Birmingham, England, where he learned the technology of steel-pen manufacturing.

Construction of the Moscow factory required about a thousand laborers, who also built cottages for the foreign workers. The cottages were clustered near newly laid-out gardens, clubhouse, school, restaurant, and hospital. The Soviet government required some of the improvements; others were insisted upon by the workers themselves before they would agree to leave their homelands. By May 1, 1926, the factory had begun operation.

During its first year, the Hammer concession grossed about $2.5 million from its manufacture of pencils and pens. The retail price in Russia of a pencil dropped to the equivalent of 5 cents. A grateful Soviet

government thereupon cut off pencil imports, giving Hammer a near-
monopoly. Even the American balance of trade benefited as American
firms supplied cedarwood to the Moscow factory. (Eventually, the
Hammers obtained wood within the Soviet Union.)

Victor Hammer became centrally involved in the day-to-day operation, keeping a diary of how to improve the manufacturing process. He
worked on the production lines and used his own experience to gauge
the appropriate piecework rate. The Hammers believed Russian laborers worked harder when compensated on a piecework basis rather than
with an hourly wage. Armand apparently realized that such capitalist
thinking might cause trouble down the road, but in the short run his
goal was the greatest production possible.[9]

Soviet publications, still eager to promote foreign investment on Soviet terms, used the Hammer pencil concession as an example of how
American capitalists could profit in a Communist state. The *Economic
Review of the Soviet Union,* published by Amtorg, reported that for 1926
the Hammer pencil concession grossed slightly more than 7 million
rubles, at a time when one ruble equaled 52 cents in American money;
in 1927, that gross rose to nearly 8.5 million rubles. The annual profit
approached 1 million rubles, even after a hefty payment to the Soviet
government. In addition to pencils, the Hammer factory was turning
out sharpeners, steel pens, and rulers. Because the efficient factory was
producing more than the Soviet market could absorb, the Hammers
exported pencils to England, Persia, and China.[10]

Alexandre Barmine, a Soviet official, was assigned to explore ways
of capturing some of the Hammer concession's business for the state.
Barmine served as a director of the Soviet International Book Company, whose main purpose was to import certain items for use in Soviet
schools. When the company decided to expand into the manufacture of
school supplies in competition with the Hammers, it was in for a nasty
surprise. Barmine recalled that

> foreign concessionaires, who had been given contracts to manufacture
> certain of these articles inside Russia, were growing rich under our eyes.
> The largest of these companies was run by an American, Dr. Hammer.
> The state . . . undertook to make cheap pencils, but the quality was so
> bad that they could not compete with Dr. Hammer's more expensive
> goods. The concessionaires, who had obtained permission to export their
> profits . . . must have laughed at our inefficiency.[11]

A neutral observer, British journalist Ellis Ashmead-Bartlett, told of a pencil factory in Moscow run by a foreigner with considerable success because the demand for pencils amounts to a famine, where wages are nearly one hundred percent higher than those paid in the two government-run pencil factories. Yet owing to efficient private management, the profits are far higher. Places on the benches are eagerly sought after by men and women who formerly occupied distinguished social and administrative positions. Professors, authors, generals, former captains of industry, ex-government officials, and ladies of noble birth sit side by side — at the cutting machines and lead-filling machines, at the trimming and painting plants, and in the packing rooms — with humble industrial workers. Their only ambition is to sink their individuality, and to destroy all records of their past in order that they may keep their jobs. Nevertheless, the government agents and spies are constantly tracing their lineage and former careers and insisting on their being turned into the streets to make room for the genuine proletariat.[12]

With the Hammer pencil concession occupying a privileged position in the Bolshevik economy, U.S. government surveillance reports became more shrill. As a result, when the Hammers tried to renew their American passports from Moscow, State Department officials questioned them closely. Julius sought a renewal in August 1925 for his first trip to America since his release from prison. The State Department considered a denial until Senator William King, who had visited Armand at the Brown House two years earlier, apparently intervened on Julius's behalf. In 1927, when Julius applied for another renewal, the State Department required him to complete its "Affidavit to Explain Protracted Foreign Residence and to Overcome Presumption of Non-Citizenship."[13] The American consul in Berlin thereafter found discrepancies between what Julius stated in the affidavit and what he had said during an interview. Julius, worried that the decision would go against him, mobilized American companies that retained him as their Soviet representative to intervene. The American Rule Manufacturing Company said Julius was its valued representative in Moscow, Berlin, and Paris. The Amalgamated Leather Companies was less forthcoming with its praise but asked the State Department to allow Julius's reentry — he allegedly owed $27,000 on account, and the company wanted to collect the debt in person.

Soon, trouble for the Hammers was emanating not only from the American government but also from the regime of Joseph Stalin. In 1928, Soviet accountants spent five months going through the pencil concession's finances, apparently because of concern about the amount of money being exported by the Hammers. The Hammers had obtained the right to export their profits at the rate of 1.95 rubles to the dollar after approval of the concession's financial records by the Soviets. But the Soviets hated to see that money going abroad.

Pravda entered the debate by publishing an article based on discussions with workers at twenty-four concessions, including the Hammer pencil factory. *Pravda's* sources said a director of the pencil concession, who was unnamed in print, took pretty female employees for rides in his car and sometimes took them to his home. Armand also received criticism for allegedly pitting skilled craftsmen against unskilled laborers and for refusing to allow workers to attend a Moscow Soviet plenum on the writer Maxim Gorky, even though the workers' contract mandated time off with pay. The *Pravda* sources charged that Hammer kept anxiety high by spreading layoff rumors. When a layoff did occur, he blamed the union's factory committee, thus sowing distrust. Employees said that working conditions were poor and that Soviet labor inspectors allowed the conditions to continue, leaving the impression that Hammer had bribed them. The article cited forty-two accidents at the Hammer factory during the first half of 1928, compared with twenty-eight at a comparable state-run pencil factory during the full year of 1927.[14]

A month later, *Pravda* published a related article criticizing five concessions, including the Hammers' factory. "The feverish race for profits" was deemed responsible for an unsanitary courtyard and poor ventilation at the pencil factory, where, *Pravda* also claimed,

> the pens taken from the electric tempering oven are sorted by hand in heavy metal sieves. Ten-pound drums in which . . . the pens are polished are lifted to a height of one or two meters by the worker alone. The workers who finish the pencils carry boxes with pencils to and fro. Each such box weighs thirty-five kilograms. According to the existing statutes for women in production, it is allowed to lift not more than twelve kilograms.

Because there was no lunchroom, workers at the Hammer factory ate next to their machines. The locker area reportedly was full of rats and bedbugs.[15]

Hammer, who thought of himself as a benevolent employer, found himself portrayed as a capitalist monster. But instead of publicly rebutting the criticisms, Hammer — perhaps threatened with the loss of his factory — told a Soviet publication aimed at Americans that running a concession in Russia was no problem:

Abroad I have often been asked whether the successful functioning of concessions is possible in the Union of Soviet Socialist Republics. The best answer to this question is supplied by the facts themselves, namely, the successful and profitable operation for a number of years of many sound concession enterprises. Rumors are being circulated in foreign circles to the effect that concessions in Russia are bound to fail because of the prevailing conditions, that the labor question offers insurmountable difficulties, et cetera. . . . As one of the pioneers in the concession field in the Soviet Union . . . I have had an opportunity to closely observe the causes which have led to the liquidation of some of the concession enterprises. My opinion is that the main reasons for failure of these concessions were either the shortage of capital, or the inability on the part of the concessionaire to recruit a satisfactory staff of employees among the native Russians. . . . Foreign capitalists, including Americans, are seeking new fields for investments. Russia, with its enormous natural resources and a population of 150 million requiring manufactures of all kinds, offers a market of incomparable possibilities.[16]

Hammer's statement led outsiders to believe all was well. The leader of an American delegation to Moscow wrote home about Hammer's factory turning a net profit of 100 percent annually and also mentioned smooth labor relations and happy, productive workers. A visiting Russian-American businessman described the pencil factory as "employing some eight hundred workers, mostly women, and all on a piecework basis, with an air of intense application that belies the claim that individual initiative has been destroyed."[17]

But all was not well; Hammer had fallen from favor under Stalin. Probably nothing he might have done would have been good enough. The *Chicago Daily News* correspondent in Moscow filed a story headlined "SOVIET STORMS OVER BONUS FOR PENCILMAKERS / EDITORS ACCUSE AMERICAN EMPLOYER IN MOSCOW OF BRIBING WORKERS." The article cited an attack in *Pravda* against the Hammers for sharing with fifty-five employees $4,000 in bonus money, bonuses the Soviets labeled capitalistic rubbish. By the end of 1929, the Bolsheviks had decided to purchase the Hammer concession. Again, the *New York Times* stood up for the Hammers: "It is admitted that the Hammer interests made big profits, but they built up the big and profitable business at their own risk. The Hammer interests were the first Americans to do business in Russia, and — profits or no profits — they have not been treated overgenerously."[18]

In his 1932 memoir, Armand exhibited no bitterness about the takeover of the pencil concession, instead defending the Russian state. He noted that the concession had grown to the point where it needed outside financing, but obtaining capital in Western nations for a Russian venture was difficult. The most sensible solution was to work out a sale to the Bolsheviks, he said.

As the Hammer family's reputation rose and fell, Moscow during the second half of the 1920s continued to be their playground. Victor Hammer was the first to fall deeply in love with a Soviet woman. In 1925, he married Vavara Sumski, a twenty-two-year-old native of Moscow.[19] Their only child was born there two years later. They named him Armand, tangible evidence of Victor's reverence for his older brother. Victor, Vavara, and little Armasha lived at the Brown House, where the marriage foundered early. Vavara's mother caught her committing adultery and reported her unfaithfulness to Victor. By 1929, Victor and Vavara had divorced. When Victor decided to return to New York, he asked permission to take his young son, who had an American passport. Vavara apparently agreed, reluctantly, but the Soviet authorities said no. Victor, crestfallen, left the Soviet Union unsure whether he would see his son again.

Armand had an eye for Russian women, too. His good looks and his Model T Ford — one of the few private automobiles in the Soviet Union — helped attract female companions. Until 1925, he played the field. When he finally did fall in love, his romance was the stuff of soap operas. He met Olga von Root during 1925 in the resort town of Yalta, where she was appearing in concert under the stage name Olga Vadina. A stunning beauty with a beguiling gypsy repertoire, she was one of the best-known entertainers in Russia. Armand, vacationing in Yalta, was smitten when he saw her onstage. Mutual acquaintances introduced the two after the show.

Olga had received an upper-class, conservative upbringing. Her father was a czarist general descended from Germans who had come to Russia centuries earlier to serve in the military. During her childhood, Olga had studied voice in Petrograd. Armand has said that when the Bolsheviks attempted to take over the government, Olga's father remained loyal to the czar and commanded a White Russian army unit during the civil war. Olga reportedly sang in cabarets to support her mother, sister, and brother in Kiev. Olga finally persuaded her father to side with the Bolsheviks, perhaps saving the family from execution. He became an instructor at a military academy, while she became famous as a singer.

Olga had fair skin, light blue eyes, blond hair, and a disarming smile. Within a week of first meeting, the impetuous new lovers were on a train to Moscow, where Olga filed for a divorce from her stage-manager husband. After two years of courtship, Olga and Armand married, on March 14, 1927. He was twenty-eight, she was twenty-two.

Lucita Williams, who with her journalist husband, Albert Rhys, lived in the Brown House intermittently as the Hammers' guests, wrote that

> when Armand brought home his beautiful bride [to the Brown House], the vivacious gypsy singer Olga, Mother Rose accepted her as though she were her very own daughter. That was all very well, but Armand always had ideas of his own. He wanted his bride to have her own abode. In no time he had set up a small jewel of a house behind a high fence, a place that we greatly enjoyed visiting as we would a museum, only this was warm with Hammer hospitality. And Olga would sing for us enchantingly. I basked in the atmosphere of all the treasures Armand had picked up here and there to satisfy his aesthetic tastes.

Olga gave birth to their son, Julian Armand Hammer, on May 7, 1929, in Moscow.[20]

According to American journalist Eugene Lyons, the Hammers, "in a great house[,] . . . dispensed hospitality with a baronial hand." Negley Farson, Moscow correspondent for the *Chicago Daily News,* wrote in 1929 about a party at the Brown House for a visiting delegation of eighty-six American businessmen, many of whom had brought along their wives and children. At two-thirty in the morning, Farson said, a jazz band was still "banging out hot black-bottoms." The poet e. e. cummings used the mansion as a setting in his cryptic book *Eimi*; Julius Hammer appeared as the character Chinesey.[21]

The gaiety at the Brown House ended as the Hammers began negotiating with the Soviet government about the disposition of the pencil concession. Armand was part of a four-person committee formed to iron out the details. Two members represented Allied American Corporation; the other two represented the Bolsheviks. In some ways, the negotiations were typical of other terminations. As one scholar observed: "A standard propaganda ritual was practiced before expropriation of each concession. The ritual consisted of increasingly stronger criticism of errors or supposed errors committed by the concessionaire. Nothing appears to have been too remote or insignificant to escape attention."[22]

The Soviet newspaper *Izvestia* tried to put the onus on Hammer:

In consequence of the financial difficulties experienced over the course of an extended time by the Hammer concession, the concessionaire posed before the main concession committee the question of a pre-term buyout of his enterprise by the government and a cessation of activity of the concession agreement. Despite the large dimensions of the credit given the concessionaire in the State Bank, the absolute inadequacy of his own means and the difficulty of obtaining foreign credits have threatened the enterprise with financial disaster. The government did not remain unsympathetic to the proposal of the concessionaire — although it had the right to refuse the buyout — and took the path of an amicable agreement.[23]

Without question, the Hammer pencil concession had had a positive impact on the Soviet Union, producing the tools of literacy for a developing nation. Millions of Soviet citizens, including Nikita Khrushchev, Leonid Brezhnev, and Konstantin Chernenko, learned to write using Hammer pencils. Some Russians treated their Hammer pencils as collector's items because of their quality.[24] The pencil concession made Armand Hammer a household name in the Soviet Union, increased his fortune, and proved to him that with daring, anything is possible in business. His special status would be demonstrated by the Bolshevik government's settlement over the pencil factory; probably no other concessionaire received such generous compensation. In fact, the settlement launched Hammer on his next career.

PART III

REACHING FOR RESPECT

8

Selling Art Like Shoes

WHEN ARMAND HAMMER entered the Soviet Union in 1921, he knew nothing about asbestos mining, but he operated asbestos mines. He knew nothing about importing grain, about exporting furs or caviar. Yet within two years, he was handling millions of dollars' worth of goods for his family business and three dozen other companies. He knew nothing about manufacturing writing instruments, but he became a household name in pencils.

Hammer also knew nothing about buying and selling art when he arrived in the Soviet Union. But by the time he left Moscow in 1930, he possessed a major collection of art objects and owned a gallery in New York. During the 1930s, in fact, he gained two of the things he wanted most — money and publicity — by selling czarist art ranging from masterpieces to bric-a-brac. In the process, he turned the American art establishment upside down.

From the beginning of the Hammers' sustained art-buying spree, Victor, who had taken art courses in college, played a major role. Between them, Victor and Armand have provided numerous accounts of how they began to collect Russian art. The accounts differ mainly in emphasis; the basic elements are fairly consistent. A synthesis might read like this: After the Bolshevik Revolution, many frightened, wealthy Russians abandoned their homes, leaving precious items behind. Walking through Moscow, any foreign guest could buy them at bargain prices. The Hammers, never inclined to pass up a bargain, had reason to buy after moving into the Brown House: The mansion's thirty-odd rooms needed table service for entertaining, rugs for the floors, and paintings for the walls. So Armand put Victor in charge.[1]

Victor found religious icons everywhere and snapped them up. Because previous owners had treated them like religious objects rather than precious works of art, the icons had been casually repainted as needed when they passed from father to son. Victor developed a method to strip away the centuries of overpainting to reveal the magnificent original underneath. He also dealt in fine china. At restaurants, he and Armand might enter for a meal and leave as the new owners of china from czarist palaces. The managers were pleased to get rid of the china, which dishwashers complained broke too easily. In the basements of czarist residences, the Hammers discovered brocade religious garments about to be burned to melt down the gold in the fabric. They bought them by the armload.

Armand and Victor faced some competition for art during their decade in Moscow. The other chief buyers were the ambassadors from France and Germany. Because of their diplomatic privileges, they were able to send possessions back home with little trouble. The Hammers, however, had a great deal of red tape to cut. They had to register their purchases with the Moscow museum administration, whose inspectors visited the Brown House periodically to make sure nothing had been removed illegally. The Hammers were uncertain whether the Soviet government would allow the treasures to be exported, but they were such an attractive investment that Armand decided to bank on somehow finding a way. Besides, he had learned something about himself during this period of acquisition: He enjoyed art for art's sake. It stirred his emotions and intellect much as music had done when he was a youngster studying piano.

When Armand decided to leave the Soviet Union after the government terminated his pencil concession, he negotiated permission to export the art after payment of a tax that ranged from 15 percent to 35 percent, depending on the item involved. The Soviet government's decision to allow the art out of the country provoked criticism from pre-revolutionary Russian nobles who had once owned the items, but their complaints were futile. Nikolai Tolstoy, the grandnephew of Leo Tolstoy, summed up the anti-export sentiment:

> At the time of the revolution, there occurred massive expropriation of the wealth of the imperial family, the aristocracy, and other rich. Many art treasures were acquired by the new Bolshevik ruling class, but most were retained by them collectively as property of the state. Almost at once a number of rich and unscrupulous foreign entrepreneurs descended on Petrograd and Moscow like kites on a rotting carcass. Very

soon they came to profitable arrangements with the Soviet authorities, whereby they exported shipments of art treasures at prices which in the West were knockdown, but in Soviet Russia provided valuable foreign currency at a time when the economy was suffering from ever worse difficulties.

Tolstoy singled out the Hammers, whom he called "a singularly unpleasant clan: Themselves of Russian origin, they discovered at an early date the profitable conjunction of Socialism and secret art deals with the Soviets."[2]

Robert Williams, a historian specializing in the Soviet Union, knew nothing about Armand Hammer when he began a research project during the 1970s. In his book, *Russian Art and American Money*, Williams told of his revelation:

> The buying of Russian art in America was an extraordinary sales campaign by both the Imperial and Soviet governments. As my research progressed, it became increasingly apparent that Russian art was a valuable export commodity intended to earn credit — economic and political — in the United States, especially in the years prior to American recognition of the Soviet Union in 1933. A crucial figure in this campaign turned out to be Dr. Armand Hammer.

By the time Hammer received permission to remove his Russian art treasures to the United States, he had established an outlet by which to sell them: In 1928, what eventually became known as Hammer Galleries opened in New York City with Harry and Victor in charge. The business began in partnership with Emery and Steffy Sakho, established art dealers doing business as the Peasant Art Importing Company. Emery Sakho, while in Moscow in 1928, had met Hammer at the Brown House, where he saw some of his collection. So impressed was he that he offered a full partnership on the spot. Armand accepted. Soon thereafter, theatrical impresario Morris Gest joined the team — about the same time that Sakho was in danger of losing all his assets to the 1929 stock market crash.[3]

Gest was in Moscow to line up entertainers for the American stage when he met Hammer. Both flamboyant, they liked each other at once, so they pooled their resources to buy out Sakho. All of a sudden, the Hammers were transformed from amateur collectors investing in somebody else's business to professional gallery owners in a highly competitive field. Because Gest's theatrical productions made headlines regularly, he drew attention to the gallery. So did the name, L'Ermitage

Galleries, meant to recall czarist Russia. The display room was well situated, at 3 East Fifty-second Street, in Manhattan. There seemed to be ample reason for optimism.[4]

But Gest turned out to be a drain on the assets of the gallery, despite the glamour that he lent. He is another early example of Hammer's poor ability to judge character. Gest borrowed nearly $20,000 from the Hammers to buy stock when he was already overextended in the theatrical world. He filed for bankruptcy in 1930, leaving Harry Hammer with an unpaid claim of $10,000, L'Ermitage Galleries with a claim of $18,700, and Importers of Antique Art with a claim of slightly more than $21,000.[5]

Some of the difficulties during the early years of the Hammer gallery almost certainly were attributable to Armand's absence from day-to-day management. When he, Olga, Julian, and Julian's nursemaid left Moscow toward the end of 1930, they settled in Paris. There, Olga shifted easily between her bohemian companions and high society, where audiences appreciated her singing. She and Armand moved into a château in Garches, a Parisian suburb. Benefiting from his Russian decade, Hammer opened a private bank, dealing in promissory notes issued by the Soviet government. Foreign businesses selling to the Soviets were paid partly in cash, partly in notes. Hammer had conducted his own commerce in Moscow that way. He believed the Soviets would pay the full value of their notes; other businessmen were not so sure. They sold their notes to Hammer for far less than face value. Better thirty cents on the dollar than nothing, they calculated. When the Soviet government paid the notes in full, Hammer made a nice profit.[6]

H. R. Knickerbocker, a journalist who observed the phenomenon, wrote about private bankers, such as Hammer, who capitalized on reports of the Bolsheviks' demise. A sarcastic Knickerbocker said that with each rumor, "the Parisian money lenders . . . knot their ties more hurriedly in the morning, get down to business earlier, for that day there will be fat pickings." The brokers initially would reject offers from the panicked sellers, finally pretending to give in at discounts of 45 percent or higher,

> which is to say that for a note drawn by the Soviet Trade Delegation
> for $100,000 payable in full with six percent interest in one year to the
> French or American or other manufacturer who has sold . . . to the
> Soviet government, the black broker pays $55,000. He tucks the note
> away in his safety deposit box, and at the end of the year, if the Soviet

government has not resigned and fled to Sweden disguised in green spectacles, the patriotic emigré will collect.[7]

While Armand was thriving in Paris, and Harry and Victor were struggling in New York, pleading vainly for Armand's help, Julius and Rose were shuttling in and out of the Soviet Union on two main missions. One was negotiating the terms of the pencil-concession settlement; the Soviet government was in no rush to complete negotiations, possibly because it had little currency on hand to pay the Hammers. The second mission was to ship the family's art objects from the Brown House, the Moscow warehouses, and other European sites to Hammer Galleries.[8]

As always, the U.S. government was attempting to discern what the Hammers were up to. A December 1, 1931, State Department memorandum carried the heading "Dr. Julius Hammer and His Russian Enterprises." It showed continued mistrust of the Hammer family:

> There appears to be no recent direct evidence to substantiate the suspicion . . . that Dr. Hammer has acted as a Communist agent, and he seems to have been engaged principally in commercial activities. But the apparent importance and financial magnitude of such activities are somewhat surprising when it is considered that Dr. Hammer was previously a practicing physician in a small way, and that he served a prison term in New York for an illegal operation. Should any indication appear that Dr. Hammer has acted either as a Communist agent or as a commercial agent of the Soviet regime, information to that effect would be received with interest.

British intelligence officials, meanwhile, were telling American diplomats that Armand and Victor Hammer were Soviet agents "who both continue to carry out secret missions for the Soviet government and travel between the United States and Europe for that purpose." British intelligence also labeled Olga Vadina a spy in the service of the Bolsheviks.[9]

Ironically, the State Department, so wary of the Hammers, became involved in helping obtain the release of the star-crossed Julius from a German prison. The American embassy in Berlin heard on December 11, 1931, of Julius's arrest in Erfurt, Germany. The notification came in a telegram from Henry Hollis, a former U.S. senator from New Hampshire who was practicing law in Paris. One of his clients there was Armand Hammer, private banker. Hollis asked the American embassy to do all it could on Julius's behalf.[10]

The U.S. government sent a representative to Erfurt, where he learned that the Hammers allegedly owed German manufacturers about $100,000 in connection with materials ordered for the Russian pencil concession. One manufacturer had asked German authorities to detain Julius until he paid all monies owed. Armand has said the litigant held a grudge because the Hammer pencil concession had sued him for providing inferior materials. He also said the same German creditor had conspired with a pencil-concession accountant to defraud the Hammers. The German authorities — after studying the web of intrigue — agreed to release Julius if all parties worked out a settlement. Julius, meanwhile, was as equable about the German jail as he had been about Sing Sing; he never showed distress, instead making the best of what for most people would have been a nightmare. After his release, Julius resumed his travels in search of art for Hammer Galleries.[11]

For a while, Victor shuttled between New York and Russia, too, buying art and visiting his young son. But sometime during the 1930s, the Soviet government withdrew permission for him to enter the country. Perhaps the visa withdrawal meant that the Hammers had fallen from favor during the anti-Semitic, xenophobic regime of Stalin or that they were paying for their identification with Lenin. On the other hand, some inveterate Armand Hammer watchers, especially those on the political right, believe Hammer never fell from grace but that the Soviets simply gave him a lower profile to facilitate keeping him in their service.[12]

One thing is certain: Whatever Hammer family members did to get their art out of Russia, they had to work mightily to sell it in New York. In the first place, Russian émigrés, some of them anti-Semitic, were suing to halt sales of what they considered their rightful property. More serious, the Depression had caused a collapse in the price of art. So in 1931, belatedly heeding the pleas of his brothers, Armand left Paris — Olga, Julian, and the family nurse stayed behind — and himself assumed control of the gallery in New York. He moved back into the converted carriage house on West Fourth Street and got down to work.[13]

The gallery's account books validated Harry and Victor's alarms. But Armand, never doubting his ability to engineer a turnaround, followed the credo that there are no bad businesses, only bad businessmen. He decided the gallery would try something else — selling through downtown department stores. If the masses wouldn't flock into what they perceived as snooty, high-priced art galleries, then he would take the merchandise to the masses. He sought marketing advice from S. L. Hoffman, a dress manufacturer who had succeeded by emphasizing volume sales and who had been introduced to him by the lawyer representing them both.[14] Armand blanketed the country with letters to department store executives. Expecting an enthusiastic response, he told Victor to conduct an inventory and appraisal of the gallery's holdings. Victor prepared a price tag for each item, complete with its history. The tags were emblazoned with the crest of the czars, the two-headed eagle. Joseph Finder in his book *Red Carpet* termed such sales tactics "lowbrow huckstering," akin, perhaps, to selling art like shoes. Armand himself used the metaphor of a traveling circus to describe what he was doing.

At first, it appeared department store executives had no interest in a traveling circus. The country's major outlets either ignored Armand or turned him down. But finally, a positive reply came from Joseph Laurie at the St. Louis department store of Scruggs, Vandervoort and Barney. Hammer set out for Missouri. His plan, and Laurie's enthusiasm for it, were rewarded: Men and women from all walks of life fascinated with nobility mobbed the store when the sale opened on a winter day in 1932. With help from gee-whiz newspaper coverage, clever advertising, and word of mouth, the Hammers had a success on their hands. The news spread to department store executives in other cities.[15]

The Hammers next took their treasures to a store in Buffalo, where the local newspaper published an advertisement reading: "Hengerer's presents a $200,000 collection of royal Russian antiques and jeweled objects, an authentic close-up of Russia in these personal treasures of the late czar." Armand and Victor gave public lectures on the provenance of the works in auditoriums filled to capacity.[16]

When the Hudson galleries in Detroit booked Armand Hammer and his traveling treasures, the *Detroit News* publicized not only the art, but also Hammer's views on the Soviet Union. It was one of his first experiences as a pundit. The reporter quoted Hammer as saying that the Soviet wish for world economic liberation was a "messianic hope, a poet's dream. . . . The materialization of the Five-Year Plan may require fifteen, twenty, or perhaps fifty years. But it is a plan nevertheless, remarkably adapted to the Russian psychology, which demands some concrete objective."[17]

In San Francisco, the Hammers convinced the Emporium department store to give the exhibit floor space. A local newspaper article (more free publicity) valued the items on display at $500,000: "The exhibit includes old world antiques, brocades and fabrics, vestments, chasubles, imperial silverware, porcelain, Russian icons, glassware, crown jeweled objects of art in diamonds, emeralds, rubies, and sapphires."[18]

The assurance of long-running success arrived with an invitation from the prestigious Marshall Field and Company department store, in Chicago. Milking the forum for all it was worth, Armand hired a Russian prince to display the sales items there.[19] Another innovative part of the marketing plan was Hammer's first memoir, published when he was just thirty-four years old. The idea came from Ray Schaeffer of Marshall Field's. Hammer composed the book partly from memory, buttressed by a diary of his decade in the Soviet Union. His publisher chose the romantic title *The Quest of the Romanoff Treasure.*

With photographs of Russian jewelry and a ringing endorsement of Soviet-American trade, Hammer's book helped promote not only his art sales but also American recognition of the Soviet government. The *New York Times* reviewer opined that Hammer's dramatic tales must be accurate because that newspaper's Moscow correspondent, Walter Duranty, had said so in the foreword. The review noted that "Dr. Hammer seems to be one of those enviable people to whom things happen, one of those magnets of destiny that inevitably become centers of events."[20]

The publicity surrounding the czarist art sale was not quite an unalloyed boon, for it further enraged the czar's descendants. Marie Romanoff sued L'Ermitage Galleries in 1932, claiming it was selling her treasures. She described monogrammed white porcelain plates, a monogrammed white porcelain double-tiered candy dish, and a Russian icon in the shape of a cross. But her suit failed to stall the sales juggernaut.[21]

At the beginning of 1933, the Hammers scored their biggest coup to that point — a show at Lord & Taylor, in downtown Manhattan. A brochure promoted "the Hammer collection of Russian imperial art treasures from the Winter Palace, Tsarskoye Selo, and other royal palaces." The show attracted wealthy buyers enamored of the riches from czarist yesterdays. In fact, Hammer Galleries had begun doing business with some of the wealthiest buyers of all, including Marjorie Merriweather Post.[22]

Robert Williams, in *Russian Art and American Money,* accused the Hammers of dishonest promotion in their shows at Lord & Taylor and elsewhere: "What the Hammers called crown jeweled objects of art were actually the debris of Russian hotels, monasteries, shops, and palaces which the Hammers were getting from the Soviet government." Yet Armand made believers of the masses and the media. The *New Yorker* magazine reported that in less than a year, the Hammers had sold more than $500,000 worth of their czarist treasures at Lord & Taylor:

Only the other day, a Chicago woman paid $17,000 for a gold and lapis lazuli [Fabergé] Easter egg. One of the most valuable single items is a diamond and lapis Easter egg with a miniature of the czarevitch. Yours for $50,000. For $2.50, you can get Dr. Hammer's book, *The Quest of the Romanoff Treasure,* in which there is a photograph of the Easter egg.[23]

Meanwhile Hammer Galleries, which had moved to the street level of the Waldorf-Astoria Hotel, moved again, to a more prestigious location — 682 Fifth Avenue. John D. Rockefeller, Jr., owned the building, a fact that Armand's defenders mentioned later when anti-Communist activists threatened to blackball him because of his Soviet ties. In particular, Senator Styles Bridges commented that "if there were any doubt about the Hammers' reputation or loyalty to this country, Mr. Rockefeller's agents who made a careful investigation . . . would not have approved and signed the lease." The Hammers also opened a gallery branch in Palm Beach, Florida, with a staff that included Mikhail Gounduroff, a Russian prince. He had wandered into the Hammers' New York gallery one day, down and out. Armand, seizing an opportunity as always, hired Gounduroff for Palm Beach: Czarist art sold by a prince appealed to the class-conscious residents of that city.[24]

Armand established himself not only as a marketing genius, but also as an authority on Fabergé. He recognized the inherent value, as well as the snob appeal, of Fabergé's creations. Victor had acquired some of Fabergé's Easter eggs from the Bolshevik regime just before the Hammers left Moscow. At one time or another, the Hammer family possessed as many as fifteen Fabergé eggs. The queen of England, who owned ten, was their main competitor at the time.

As the Hammers mounted more shows, publicity mushroomed. *Time* magazine praised an exhibition of 194 Russian icons spanning seven centuries, "the largest collection . . . ever shown in the United States." *Time* termed Armand and Victor "two of the most startling characters" in the art world.[25] And that they were.

Beer by the Barrel

TAKING THE ART WORLD by storm was not enough for Armand Hammer in the 1930s. His desire for wealth, influence, and fame had been fed by his early successes. He saw new opportunities to achieve his goals, and he grasped for them. But even the most prescient observer would have been unlikely to guess in which direction Hammer would branch out.

The new venture was cooperage, colloquially known as barrel manufacturing. Several paths taken previously by Hammer converged in such a way that making barrels seemed in retrospect ordained by fate. One of those paths was Hammer's first attempt at influencing American politics. Former senator Henry Hollis, Hammer's attorney in Paris, was friendly with New York governor Franklin Roosevelt, who was about to run for the presidency as the Democratic candidate. Hollis suggested Hammer become involved in presidential politics, now that he was living in the United States. Hammer found he agreed with Roosevelt's program — especially diplomatic recognition of the Soviet Union. On July 28, 1932, Hammer sent a telegram to Roosevelt expressing support.[1]

More to the point, Hammer's study of Roosevelt's program made him aware that Roosevelt as president might push for the repeal of Prohibition. That realization set Hammer to thinking about the need for barrels. It took daring by Hammer to make any plans based on the possible end of Prohibition. The Eighteenth Amendment to the Constitution had taken effect in 1920; legislatures in forty-seven of the forty-eight states had ratified it, indicating widespread support.[2] No constitutional amendment approved by Congress and ratified overwhelmingly by the states had ever been repealed. For Hammer's plan to succeed, something unprecedented in American history would have to happen.

Hammer knew instinctively there would be a barrel shortage if legal mass production of alcohol ever resumed. During Prohibition, companies that produced wooden staves for beer barrels had folded. Quality staves needed to be air dried for up to two years; if Prohibition were to end soon, brewers could not afford to wait that long to slake the thirst of a nation. So Hammer went to work. He learned that seasoned white oak is nearly ideal for barrel manufacturing. He knew firsthand that the Soviet Union possessed it in abundance — during the 1920s, the Hammer import-export concession had shipped Soviet white oak barrel staves to Germany. Therefore, when Prohibition in fact ended, in 1933, Hammer was ready to use his connections in the Soviet trade ministry to buy white oak and have it transported to New York.

It proved to be a smart business move. The Soviets sold the white oak to Hammer at $105 for one thousand staves, below the world market price of $180. American timber companies were unprepared for the demand; as a result, the few old-line cooperage firms still operating were searching desperately in Germany, Poland, and Yugoslavia for white oak. With its unmatched supply of Soviet white oak contracted for, the A. Hammer Cooperage Corporation registered to do business in June 1933.[3] The next month, Hammer obtained a line of credit with the Trust Company of North America, run by principals from the New York City law firm of Schapiro, Wisan and Schapiro — the same firm that had represented the Hammer businesses for years. It seemed to be a cozy financing arrangement.

Obtaining orders for barrels was no problem at all. Since breweries were working overtime to produce alcoholic beverages, they needed every barrel they could find. One of Hammer's first customers was Anheuser-Busch of St. Louis. Hammer traveled there from New York in July 1933, returning home with a contract worth $95,000. The cooperage plant was using a separate family firm, A. Hammer and Company, as its sales agent. Hammer was producing barrels at a main plant in Brooklyn and at a contract shop in Marcus Hook, Pennsylvania. Within a short time, he opened another factory, in Milltown, New Jersey.

Advertisements showed a Hammer employee using a "Hammermeter" to test, in just ten seconds, whether a company barrel complied with government standards. The Hammermeter technique received praise from the Hamm Brewing Company of St. Paul, which quickly bought more than fifty thousand barrels from the Hammer factory. Other customers included breweries in Los Angeles, San Diego, Baltimore, and Belleville, Illinois. When some Massachusetts brewers needed to be sold on the virtues of traditional wooden barrels over those of newfangled steel models, Hammer visited them, carrying the message that steel barrels were too loose at the welds and rusted easily.[4]

Hammer, always pushing for publicity, got it, despite operating what journalists normally would have considered a business with little news potential. His showmanship, combined with his knowledge of how to manipulate reporters and editors, paid off in national attention. *Time* magazine, already aware of Hammer as a showman in the art world, reported: "Sensing the beer keg shortage, he had wangled out of Moscow last May a contract for the entire Russian output of the proper air-dried wood," adding that a Hammer barrel cost $9.25, "cheaper than they can be imported." Hammer wrote to *Time* that the article had brought him several mailbags of letters, not to mention calls. He said he had received offers of timber tracts in dozens of states: "Innumerable propositions have been made to me to participate in a great variety of businesses, ranging from breweries to perfumeries. I have had many offers to augment my collection of czarist treasures by acquiring jewels and works of art which once belonged to bygone crowned heads of Europe."[5]

The *New Yorker* noted that Hammer drove from Manhattan to the Brooklyn barrel factory in a Rolls-Royce. He "works so hard that he sometimes falls asleep in his clothes, too exhausted to go to bed. . . . He still has his Greenwich Village house, which he uses for entertaining. He likes to play the host in a bartender's coat, and sometimes spends the entire evening behind the bar, mixing drinks."[6]

Meanwhile, the U.S. government was still watching him. Some investigators assumed he had established ties with organized crime, apparently because of the barrel company's negotiations with Kings Brewery, believed to be run by racketeers. But if Hammer were consorting with organized crime figures, the government was unable to build a case strong enough to initiate prosecution. All the agents could do was gripe to each other. One later wrote J. Edgar Hoover at the FBI that the barrel business contained plenty of opportunities to violate the law and that the Hammers were "individuals of unsavory reputation."[7]

Hammer soon encountered a more troublesome enemy to his business than Hoover — the bank owned by his lawyers. In June 1934, the Trust Company of North America sued Hammer over a financing arrangement the bank had made with him a year earlier. Hammer, normally astute in business, had been taken when he signed the original loan papers, and, too late, he knew it. The notification came as Hammer needed cash, fast, to pay the Soviet government's Amtorg Trading Corporation for white oak about to arrive in port. It was only after the shipment left Russia that a bank officer told Hammer he must cough up a $50,000 bonus to receive the needed $100,000 line of credit.[8]

Hammer was stunned at the usurious rate, and he balked. He had known the principals in the bank for years. In fact, he trusted them so implicitly that he had given Jacob Schapiro power of attorney during his decade in the Soviet Union. The lending officer responded that Amtorg quite likely would sell the shipment elsewhere if Hammer failed to pay when it arrived. Hammer knew that could mean cancellation of his Amtorg contract, which in turn would spell financial ruin for the barrel business. He paid the bank its bonus under protest, commenting acidly to the lending officer that the only thing left out of the deal was the arsenic.

The bank kept upping the ante, with Hammer's company eventually paying finance charges of nearly $63,000 and interest of almost $10,000. A lawsuit by Schapiro's bank added insult to injury. The bank claimed Hammer was shifting the barrel factory's assets to Tennessee without the bank's knowledge and asked the court to liquidate Hammer's company as well as award damages of nearly $230,000. Hammer responded that he was producing barrel staves in Oneida, Tennessee, because he had lined up domestic supplies of wood. But he said there was no intent to break the loan agreement with the bank. The bank's case rested on the contention that Hammer was an amazingly accomplished businessman at age thirty-six who never would have been bamboozled into signing an unjust agreement. Eventually, the court ruled that Hammer indeed had violated his contract with the bank. But, the court added, the Trust Company of North America was barred from relief because of its "unconscionable, oppressive, unreasonable, and over-reaching" behavior.[9]

The lawsuit had hurt Hammer's barrel operations deeply for three years. That Hammer was able to gear up the business after the court fight was remarkable, especially considering the demands made on him by his art gallery — not to mention the turmoil in his personal life.

Hammer and Olga had been drifting apart almost from the time she arrived in the United States from Paris with their son, Julian, and Julian's Russian nursemaid in 1931 or 1932. Olga, who spoke English poorly, liked to spend her time with other émigrés, whom Armand found boring. He preferred looking to the future; why waste time reminiscing about the old days? Olga showed no interest in business, while Armand lived for business challenges. He frequently traveled on behalf of the art gallery and the cooperage factory. By most accounts, he was an uninvolved father, and he did not seem to be a model husband.

Living in America instead of Moscow or Paris accentuated the differences between Armand and Olga. They tried to work out their problems. They spent winters in Palm Beach after Hammer Galleries opened its branch there. Olga liked the high society, but unhappily for her the season did not last all year. She tried to resume her singing career, but it never took off. Olga and Armand bought an eight-room house on five acres in Highland Falls, a suburb of Monroe near West Point, New York, where she and Julian spent much of their time; Armand joined them when he chose to.[10]

With his marriage on the rocks, Armand found his attention wandering to other women. He has admitted he was searching for a new wife. From the audience, he fell in love with actress Helen Hayes when he saw her perform the role of Mary, Queen of Scots. He sent gifts to her from Hammer Galleries. A couple of years later, Hammer met her for a date after her performance as Queen Victoria. He preserved the memory in his diary for March 11, 1936 — an entry he reproduced in his 1987 autobiography. An elderly Helen Hayes said she was "flattered" when Hammer published the account of their only date.[11]

Another woman on Hammer's mind was the less well known but nonetheless entrancing Frances Barrett Tolman, who had entered his life as a result of the czarist treasures sale at Marshall Field's, in Chicago, where she had bought several items. They saw each other periodically after that and, Armand has said, talked of their love for each other. Frances's millionaire husband, Elmer, was nearly thirty years older than she and in poor health. Frances could not bring herself to seek a divorce. She and Armand limited themselves to clandestine correspondence. Armand also kept up with Frances from conversation with his brothers, Victor and Harry, who mixed socially with the Tolmans.

By the end of the 1930s, Armand and Olga had separated. Their divorce became official on November 29, 1943, in Las Vegas. Armand was absent from the proceeding. Olga retained custody of Julian, who reportedly was attending private school in Tucson, Arizona; Armand received custody for two weeks at Christmas, as well as during August. Reflecting on his relationship with Julian decades later, he seemed wistful but not remorseful. He told of a Saturday at the zoo with Julian, then about ten. It was fun, and Hammer swore there would be many more days like it. But there were not. "It could not be helped," he concluded.[12] It was one of the few matters in his life that he seemed to leave to fate. The obvious conclusion is that he cared too little to control fate in his relationship with his son.

As part of the divorce, Hammer agreed to pay for Julian's schooling and give Olga $75 a week. Olga obtained permission to sell the Highland Falls home and move to Southern California. Although she and Armand had little to do with each other after the divorce, Olga remained friendly with the rest of the Hammer family until her death, in 1967.[13]

At the divorce proceeding, the judge asked Olga what had caused the split. "We could not get along together, and he has another woman," Olga replied. That other woman was Angela Carey Zevely, whom Armand had met about five years earlier at a Greenwich Village party. She was glamorous, intelligent, acerbic, and possessed of a good head for business. Born in Pittsburgh, trained as a singer at the Boston Conservatory of Music, she had pursued a career in opera and network radio. She was forced to abandon it after an automobile accident impaired her hearing. Angela had married young, eventually obtaining a divorce on grounds of desertion. By the time she met Armand, she had begun buying farmland in Monmouth County, New Jersey. They started to look at acreage together, expanding their farm greatly in the next few years. Angela and Armand married in December 1943, three weeks after his divorce from Olga.[14] The ceremony took place at Victor's Park Avenue apartment, with family acquaintance Judge Bernard Botein presiding. Armand was forty-five, Angela forty. Armand has said he was ready to have children and settle down on the farm. It was not to be.

10

Selling Spirits, Too

ALTHOUGH ARMAND HAMMER'S PERSONAL LIFE was unhappy before he married Angela Zevely — and would become unhappier during that marriage — he separated it sufficiently well from his career to continue conquering worlds. To be sure, he suffered from personal troubles, but not as much as most people. Nobody, not a problem wife, not a problem son, would stand in the way of Hammer's latest business deal or his sought-after meeting with a head of state. Life was too short to think about the emotional needs of others.

Hammer had a wide circle of acquaintances and legions of admirers, including countless recipients of his philanthropy. But many people who knew him well disliked him, and even his admirers doubted whether he had any true friends. For Hammer, however, wealth and adulation seemed to substitute for friendship. In the 1930s, he had begun to achieve sporadic national attention. During the 1940s, he was in the spotlight more frequently. One of the ventures that put him there was the Hammer Galleries' decade-long dispersal of the art collection of William Randolph Hearst, beginning in 1941.

The venture entailed selling the fantastic artworks owned by the newspaper tycoon, who had decided to jettison about two thirds of his vast collection to avoid inheritance taxes and build badly needed cash reserves. For decades, Hearst had bought art indiscriminately. The collection carried an estimated value of $50 million; using 1989 prices, it probably was worth $1 billion. Yet initial sales attempts by Hearst met with little success. When items sold at all, they often brought just one tenth to one half of his original purchase price. In 1940, Hearst's administrators called on Hammer to put life into the sale, recalling his pioneering use of department stores to sell czarist treasures.[1]

Hearst harbored reservations about using such lowbrow tactics for what he considered treasures more significant than Russian knick-knacks. His trustees, however, convinced him to follow Hammer's example. An important advocate was Charles McCabe, a Hearst executive whom the Hammers had met in Chicago during their 1932 sale. McCabe was impressed not only by what he saw then and later, but also by what he heard from Karl Bickel, a United Press executive who had met Armand and Victor in the Soviet Union during the 1920s. In 1940, McCabe was the publisher of the Hearst-owned *New York Mirror*. His approach to Sovietophile Hammer on Hearst's behalf was especially ironic because of Hearst's loudly voiced suspicions about the Bolshevik regime.[2]

Hammer accepted the offer from the Hearst organization, on his terms — a 10 percent commission, plus freedom to set the prices on individual items — and began negotiating with the R. H. Macy and Company department store. Macy's, too, insisted on the right to establish a price for each item. Hammer responded that Macy's employees lacked the expertise; besides, Victor already was pricing the thousands of items in the Bronx warehouses used by Hearst. Armand and Victor accompanied Macy's employees to one of the warehouses. As Hammer feared, there was profound disagreement. In one instance, a Macy's employee put a price of $29.95 on a set of seventeenth-century vases that had cost Hearst $20,000. After negotiations with Macy's broke down, Hammer approached the Gimbel Brothers department store through Frederic Gimbel, a customer of Hammer Galleries. Hearst was furious when he found out, outraged that his treasures would be displayed in a store with a reputation for bargain-basement sales. Hammer placated him by persuading Gimbel's management to devote floor space at Saks Fifth Avenue to the sale. Gimbel's generally refrained from publicizing its connection to Saks, fearing it would offend upper-crust customers.[3]

The sale began at Gimbel's and Saks on January 20, 1941. Hammer scored a publicity coup when he convinced the press that they should treat it as a legitimate news story. As a result, he received the kind of attention that advertising dollars never could have bought. The advance article on page 1 of the *New York Times* noted that "art experts interested in the sale say it can only be compared in quantity to the exhibition of collections as large as those of the British Museum and the Paris Louvre combined."[4]

The collection required 150 volumes to catalog it. At his press conference, Hammer, clearly enjoying the limelight, described items with his usual flair, increased sales never far from his mind. The *Times* reporter present recounted how Hammer called attention to an "unimportant-looking little mug," which he termed as possibly the most significant piece of English silver in the entire United States. Hammer showed the reporter the will of Archdeacon Wright of Oxford, who once had owned the tankard. The archdeacon had valued it at only £5 sterling, a tiny amount in light of its rarity in the modern world. Hearst had paid about $30,000 for the piece; Hammer hoped it would bring much more than that at the department store.[5]

To heighten interest, Hammer employed another technique — founding a monthly arts magazine that subtly promoted the Hearst sale and the role of Hammer Galleries in it. He was delighted with his creation, pronouncing it "elegant." The first issue of *The Compleat Collector* appeared in November 1940, subtitled "A monthly discourse on the fine arts for the contemplative man's recreation." Inside, it called itself "a monthly message of goodwill from dealer to collector." The initial issue carried an article about the joys of owning art that immodestly said, "Currently, in special exhibits, the Hammer Galleries . . . whose great collection of treasures from the palaces of old Russia has long been known in this country, is now presenting these splendid and historical relics." The next issue emphasized the galleries' involvement in the upcoming Hearst sale. During the magazine's life, Hammer wrote many of the articles himself, sometimes capriciously using the name Braset Marteau, "arm and hammer" in French.[6]

One thing failed to go according to Hammer's grand plan. He was unable to attract one of the nation's most prominent persons to the sale, First Lady Eleanor Roosevelt. He asked Mrs. Roosevelt to open the sale officially on a date convenient to her, saying it was filled with significance because it would democratize art collecting. The profits from the preview would go to the Infantile Paralysis Fund, a cause of President Roosevelt's. Mrs. Roosevelt declined.[7]

But Hammer certainly suffered no disappointments when it came to personal publicity. The *New York Sun* published an upbeat profile of him under its standing headline "WHO'S NEWS TODAY." The *New York News* offered a breathless Sunday feature about Hammer and the sale, reporting that John D. Rockefeller himself "hankers, your scribe hears, for the Cellini cup — agate, ruby and gold-encrusted — at $25,000." Other interested buyers included actress Ginger Rogers, and Mrs. Wendell Willkie, the wife of the 1940 Republican presidential candidate. The feature told of how the smaller, more exclusive exhibition at Saks

Fifth Avenue contained a Van Dyck portrait of Queen Henrietta Maria selling for $375,000. The most expensive item for sale at Gimbel's was a Flemish tapestry priced by the Hammers at $199,894. Befitting a bargain-basement department store sale, the merchandise often carried such amounts on the price tags rather than the more expensive-sounding round numbers normally found at art galleries. An enterprising reporter interviewed Miss Monahan, one of Hammer's grade school teachers, who was attending the Gimbel's exhibition. "She remembered him as a good boy but not too smart," wrote the reporter, "which just goes to show you."[8]

A decade's accumulation of positive publicity about the czarist treasures and the Hearst sale helped bring new business to Hammer Galleries. Hammer sold items on consignment that had belonged to such well-known collectors as Clarence Mackay and Dorothy Payne Whitney and disposed of the furnishings from the *Corsair,* J. P. Morgan's yacht. One of the Hammers' most valued new customers was King Farouk, who ruled Egypt from 1936 to 1952. Farouk, a legendary sybarite, possessed a large appetite for expensive and often frivolous items. Hammer obtained permission to place the phrase "by appointment to His Majesty the King," along with a replica of Farouk's coat of arms, on the gallery stationery. The Hammers' role was to find Farouk the items he desired, whatever his whim might be. Their sales to Farouk brought in millions of dollars.

Armand's relationship with Gimbel's department store, which helped handle the Hearst sale, led to his next business success — even as the dollars kept rolling in from the Hearst collection. Again, Hammer quickly assumed a major role in an industry about which he knew little at the start. That industry was distilling. Frederic Gimbel was a key figure in this new venture. He and Hammer had become friends; in fact, Gimbel served as best man at Hammer and Angela Zevely's wedding. Armand and Frederic did well by each other: The Gimbels profited nicely from the Hearst sale, while the Hammers used the visibility of the Gimbel stores to generate business. The Gimbel brothers also cut the Hammers in on the Kende Galleries, an in-store art business that recorded millions of dollars of annual sales.

Hammer already was somewhat familiar with the distilling industry from selling barrels to brewers. However, the cooperage factories operated by Hammer were suffering declining sales; he had capitalized on his Russian supplies at the end of Prohibition, but less resourceful manufacturers eventually had caught up. So Gimbel's tip — to buy stock in the American Distilling Company, headquartered in Illinois — came

at a propitious time. American Distilling had fallen on hard times early
in World War II and therefore decided to dispose of 245,000 barrels of
bulk whiskey in its inventory. The plan was to give a barrel of bourbon
as a dividend for each share of stock outstanding.[9] Hammer bought
5,500 shares at $90 each just before leaving with Angela on their hon-
eymoon. Gimbel's department store was prohibited from buying the
stock itself, but the company could sell the alcohol if it was purchased
from an appropriate party. Hammer obtained a wholesaler's license
from New York State, enabling him to become that party. The bourbon from Illinois was then put up in fifths and marketed by Gimbel's
as the Cooperage brand. Before he knew it, Hammer had sold 2,500 of
his 5,500 barrels of bourbon through the department store.

Hammer, seeing money to be made on a continuing basis, decided to
forge ahead with his own distilling company rather than simply sell
the remaining 3,000 barrels to Gimbel's. It was a risky move; World
War II was hard on the liquor industry. Some distilleries produced
alcohol for use in smokeless gunpowder. Distilleries still manufacturing
whiskey were troubled by domestic grain shortages as the federal government shipped corn, wheat, and rye overseas.

Hammer possessed enough confidence to tackle such a challenge,
expert opinion be damned. He has said his confidence was bolstered by
a surprise visit during 1944 to Hammer Galleries by a chemical engineer whom Hammer has identified only as "Mr. Eisenberg." They had
met in Russia "seven or eight years before," according to an account in
Hammer's 1975 authorized biography, by Bob Considine. That would
have placed the meeting in about 1936. But Hammer has steadfastly
maintained that he never set foot in the Soviet Union between his
departure in 1930 and his dramatic return in 1961. In any case, Eisenberg supposedly divulged his methods of producing vodka in the Soviet
Union, where he had stretched straight whiskey by a factor of five
through the addition of 80 percent neutral spirits. Eisenberg said if
Hammer bought a distillery, it could use rotting Maine potatoes to
produce the spirits. Hammer immediately recognized a brilliant plan.
Whether Eisenberg benefited financially was left unsaid. To confuse
matters, Angela Zevely Hammer later testified that her own knowledge
of how to extract alcohol from potatoes was crucial to the genesis of
the business. Her testimony contained no mention of anyone named
Eisenberg.

Whoever was the progenitor of the potato plan, Hammer liked the
possibilities. He started looking for a plant to buy, settling on the Nahum Chapin Distilling Company, in Newmarket, New Hampshire. Like

other distilleries, it had been hurt by the federal government's grain cutbacks, so the owners decided to manufacture alcohol for war purposes. But the U.S. Reconstruction Finance Corporation had placed conditions on its conversion loan that Nahum Chapin management found unacceptable. In August 1943, the government had foreclosed on the Nahum Chapin mortgage, then advertised the property for sale. Since there were no bidders, the government had bought it. When Hammer decided to acquire the plant, he found friendly receptions in the offices of Senators Styles Bridges, from New Hampshire, and Owen Brewster, from Maine, both of whom figured that their state's economy would benefit. The senators arranged an appointment for Hammer with Donald Nelson, head of the U.S. War Production Board. Despite the board's mandate to give priority to defense material, Nelson granted Hammer approval to manufacture potato alcohol for human consumption.

The angry previous owners of Nahum Chapin later claimed Hammer had obtained the factory from them with help from government bureaucrats. They complained to Senator Bridges:

> The company understands that Mr. Hammer . . . with the help of the Reconstruction Finance Corporation, purchased and installed the boilers and equipment which the company had arranged to purchase but which the Reconstruction Finance Corporation had refused to finance; that he has operated the plant at full capacity in the manufacture of beverage alcohol; that his is the only concern in the United States which has been permitted to make and distribute beverage alcohol, while all other distillers had to make alcohol for industrial use only; that this discriminatory privilege was of enormous benefit to his associates.

The memorandum called Hammer's profits "unconscionable."[10]

Hammer hired Hans Maister from the American Distilling Company, the firm that unwittingly had launched Hammer in the business. An expert fermentologist, Maister had produced neutral spirits from potatoes in Europe before coming to America. Bridges introduced Hammer to leaders of the American Farm Bureau Federation, who in turn introduced Hammer to Maine potato growers. Hammer bought rotting potatoes for as little as ten cents a one-hundred-pound sack, sometimes after the spuds had been judged unfit for human consumption. As the Newmarket distillery started turning out its product, Gimbel's in New York City bought it, advertising it under the Gold Coin label.[11] It sold briskly.

Despite the successful start-up, there were anxious moments. The federal government kept changing the rules determining which commodities were eligible for use, when they were eligible, and the allowable price for the finished product. In August 1944, as the Newmarket distillery was humming along on rotten potatoes, the government unexpectedly told distillers that they could use grain again. Hammer feared he was ruined — he calculated that few consumers would buy potato alcohol when they could buy grain alcohol instead. But the government reversed course soon thereafter, saving Hammer's business. At another point, Hammer's distillery was forced to switch from dehydrated to whole potatoes. An inefficient conveyer used to bring whole potatoes to the cooker smashed the spuds, resulting in loss of starch, from which the alcohol was derived. Equipment for removing stones from large lots of potatoes worked poorly and thus damaged the machinery. Fermentation was complicated by contaminated shipments of yeast. As delays beset the plant, the already rotten potatoes in nearby railroad cars rotted further, making them unusable. An ironic problem for Hammer was the shortage of new barrels for storing whiskey. He had stopped producing enough for his own use, a mistake. So Hammer switched to the production of corn whiskey, the only type that legally could be stored in used barrels. It made sense in the short term, but he had to live with the worry that the value of corn whiskey would drop if new barrels became available.[12]

Meanwhile, journalists began to take notice of Hammer's maneuverings in a new field, emphasizing his successes. The *New York Times* reported on the latest venture of the man best known recently in Manhattan for the Hearst sale and on the angry reaction of old-time distillers to his intrusion into their field. The executive director for the Conference of Alcoholic Beverage Industries called the War Production Board's ruling a new "high in absurdity." The newspaper carried his outburst under the headline "PREDICTS DELUGE OF POTATO ALCOHOL / DISTILLERS' SPOKESMAN ATTACKS WAR PRODUCTION BOARD FOR ALLOWING SMALL PLANT TO MAKE BEVERAGE / SEES PUBLIC CHEATED / INSISTS GRAIN SPIRITS SHOULD BE DRUNK."[13]

A War Production Board study defended Hammer's special treatment, saying his distillery had been released from compliance with normal restrictions "because the difficulty of transporting its small output to consuming points made it impractical to incorporate the unit into the industrial alcohol program."[14] Unlike Hammer, other distillers were ill equipped to use rotting potatoes. Hammer, a novice, had possessed more foresight than the established distillers.

Hammer decided to go head-to-head with the industry giants. First he acquired United Distillers of America Limited for a reported $730,000 from a Canadian company. United Distillers already produced such well-known brands as Jesse Moore, a spirit blend; Paul Revere rye and bourbon bottled in bond; and Auld Grimsby Scotch-type. With its name and assets he transformed A. Hammer Cooperage Corporation into United Distillers of America. Hammer also purchased West Shore Wine and Liquor Company, which enabled him to sell its brands of Roamer whiskey and Buckingham scotch. The purchase helped him circumvent regulations from the Office of Price Administration that were hurting his company's profitability. Anxious to expand into other money-making lines, he paid an estimated $240,000 to acquire the Blue Grass Distillery, at Gethsemane, Kentucky.[15] Hammer did not want to be caught short again by a federal grain holiday; acquisition of grain distilleries would reduce his vulnerability.

By mid-1945, everybody in the distilling industry was becoming aware of this daring upstart. *Spirits,* an industry magazine, published a profile under the headline "Armand Hammer, M.D.: Independent Distiller Has Fantastic Saga." The author said that Horatio Alger himself never would have dreamed up such a character. In the summer of 1946, Hammer paid an estimated $3 million for the Dant Distilling Company plant, in Dant, Kentucky. The new company planned to blend its potato neutral spirits with Kentucky bourbon whiskey under the name of American Bar Blended Whiskey.[16]

By October 1946, *Spirits* felt compelled to publish a sequel to its first Armand Hammer story. The article said that "a powerful new personality is forging toward the top in the distiller set . . . the fellow who in a couple of years has acquired eight distilleries with a productive capacity of about forty million proof gallons of whiskey and neutral spirits annually, and bottling capacity of three million cases a year." The company moved its headquarters to the seventy-eighth floor of the Empire State Building; Hammer's decorating there made his office "among the swankiest in the industry," the magazine commented. Hammer, always looking for an angle, had obtained the office space after an airplane crashed into the building at that lofty height during bad weather; the previous tenants harbored understandable qualms about returning. The disaster was a propitious accident for United Distillers — Hammer had been looking in vain for a prime Manhattan location.

What made the United Distillers offices especially elegant was Hammer's purchase of centuries-old paneling that had adorned the Old Treaty House in Uxbridge, England. When the paneling left England in 1929 for America, British commentators had treated the sale to New York antiques dealer Louis Allen as a national disgrace. Seventeen years later the British campaign continued for return of the paneling to Uxbridge. Despite the uproar, Hammer was delighted with his acquisition. One of the paneled rooms became his personal office. The other served as the United Distillers tasting room. Hammer purchased part of a third room from an Italian Medici palace, for meetings of the corporate board.[17]

Hammer's strategy and flair captivated the industry. While other distillers cut back, Hammer "was buying plants on the general theory that the shortage might continue, and anyway there would always be a place for an independent. Sure enough, the shortage did continue, and Armand's company is now just about the largest privately owned distillery set-up in the nation," *Spirits* noted. The company was doing what came naturally in each geographic area, producing rye in Maryland and Pennsylvania; bourbon in Kentucky; and neutral spirits in Louisiana, New York, and New Hampshire. Hammer's vision received acclaim from U.S. Representative James Auchincloss of New Jersey, who told colleagues that United Distillers planned to use surplus grain in the manufacture of alcohol fuel. Hammer had visited Cuba to examine the process. More than two decades before fuel shortages struck the United States, Hammer was telling American distillers how they could use 200 million bushels of surplus grain annually to produce 500 million gallons of alcohol. That alcohol when mixed with gasoline made an excellent motor fuel, Hammer said. Auchincloss told his colleagues they should listen to this tycoon with the "brilliant mind."[18]

As the 1940s progressed, Hammer attempted to wield his new prominence to influence occupants of the White House, as well as members of Congress. Investigators scattered throughout the bureaucracy who knew his past were suspicious of his motives; FBI files on him grew fatter. One day in 1951 — after reviewing various reports on Armand Hammer, his brothers, and his parents — J. Edgar Hoover wrote in the margin: "A very bad group. I well remember the Hammers when I was presenting [the] case against Ludwig Martens." The navy intelligence office compiled a report captioned "The Hammer Galleries, Armand Hammer, et al." It summarized investigations by the military and others, including the Treasury Department and the New York State Liquor Authority. The report noted Hammer's "lengthy pro-Russian record." Congress published reports resurrecting the specter of Julius Hammer as a dangerous Communist.[19] The Internal Revenue Service moved against Armand's distilling company after receiving information from an informant on September 11, 1946. The agency alleged tax deficiencies of about $517,000. The case dragged on for thirteen years before Armand prevailed.

Despite such problems, Hammer's campaign to become an intimate at the White House continued unabated. His efforts had begun with the administration of Franklin Roosevelt, and his main advocate there was Senator William King, who first met Hammer as part of the 1923 congressional delegation to the Soviet Union. King regularly consulted Hammer for his views on foreign affairs. In the early part of World War II, at King's request, Hammer devised a plan for American financial aid to England and France in return for leases of military bases in the Western Hemisphere. Hammer knew of previous proposals, but he believed they had failed to take British objections into account. On September 21, 1940, Hammer wrote directly to President Roosevelt, telling of his concern about Britain's ability to continue its heroic struggle. Hammer hinted that he possessed inside knowledge of the British position on Lend-Lease and asked for a meeting with Roosevelt. The president's secretary sent a neutral reply.[20]

Hammer, not ready to give up, tried to get the attention of the Roosevelts in other ways. He sent Eleanor Roosevelt white-oak-and-northern-pine ice buckets bearing the trade name Icesavers from his cooperage factory. Mrs. Roosevelt's secretary sent a thank-you, in which she said the First Lady would use the gift at her Hyde Park residence. In October 1940, Hammer sent a telegram to the president, who was nearing the end of a reelection campaign. Hammer said he had tried to air a dramatization about the benefits of the New Deal, but a New York radio station had rejected the show. Hammer suggested that the president order an investigation by the Federal Communications Commission. The ploy worked; the station aired the program during the week of the election. It used cases from the Social Security Board, and the actors were people who actually had benefited from old-age pensions and unemployment insurance. Hammer and Mrs. Irving Berlin paid for the time. A New York newspaper columnist called the show "one of the most novel broadcasts of the campaign." Franklin Roosevelt's secretary sent a thank-you; Eleanor Roosevelt replied separately, commenting, "What a grand thing you did to help the president."[21]

On November 26, 1940, the *New York World-Telegram* published an approving editorial based on a Lend-Lease pamphlet printed by Hammer. Senator King urged the White House on November 27 to give Hammer time with the president. Hammer, who was already in a Washington hotel, lobbied independently. On November 28, he finally achieved his goal of a White House meeting with Roosevelt. It was

reported on seriously by the *New York Times,* whose article was based
on an interview with Hammer. But at a press briefing, Roosevelt treated
the meeting mockingly. Asked about his conference with Hammer on
naval bases, the president responded, "Never talked about it." When
the questioner said Hammer had given the impression of a substantive
discussion, Roosevelt replied:

> No, he gave me a long book here which I have not had a chance to look
> at yet. If you are really interested, you may look at it. It has 28,636,940
> news clippings . . . these news clippings are on a bill proposing settle-
> ment of world war debts. I thought it was political, but it is not, for it
> says "leasing of Pacific bases and granting credits to Great Britain," and
> then each paper that has favored it editorially with the circulation of the
> paper after it, and there are 28 million of these, and oh yes, favorable
> editorials for buying the earth, 5,557,580; unfavorable, 456,832. It is a
> very interesting compilation which I have not had time to scan. (laugh-
> ter)[22]

Perhaps Hammer never saw the transcript of the press briefing. If
he did, he chose to ignore it. In his 1987 autobiography, Hammer wrote
that President Roosevelt received the volume of clippings "with great
interest. The next day he even brought them with him to a White
House press conference." It was an uninformed, or disingenuous, interpretation. Hammer has said that after his meeting with the president,
Roosevelt adviser Harry Hopkins visited him several times at his art
gallery to discuss Lend-Lease. Eventually, Congress adopted a version
of his proposal, Hammer claimed. Yet there appears to be no mention
of Hammer's role in Hopkins's publicly available papers. Nor does
Hammer's name appear in any of dozens of books about Lend-Lease.
One possibility: President Roosevelt, Hopkins, and their compatriots
followed Hammer's advice but insisted he keep a low profile because
of his ties to the Soviet Union. Another possibility is that Hammer
exaggerated his role to build an image as a loyal American.

After the passage of Lend-Lease, Hammer channeled his energy into
other ways to serve his president and his nation. He believed the best
tactic to defeat the Germans was to bomb their industrial centers. To
spread his views, Hammer paid for a campaign called "Knock Out
Germany Now — by Air!" In addition, he tried to help the federal
government plan for a return to a peacetime economy by making a
presentation to the National Resources and Planning Board, chaired by
Frederic Delano, the president's uncle.[23]

After Roosevelt's death, in April 1945, Hammer did what he could

to get the attention of President Harry Truman. He sent a telegram to
the White House pledging support to the new chief of state. Later, he
wrote Truman on United Distillers stationery with a promise to distribute one million pounds of wheat flour through the United Nations
Relief and Rehabilitation Administration, which was trying to combat
famine overseas. Hammer said he would obtain the flour from his company's federal allotment to its Baltimore plant. Hammer wrote the
president that he had helped the American relief effort during the Russian famine twenty-four years earlier. He vividly remembered the sight
of starving children crying for scraps of food. If other Americans had
seen such hunger, they would want to help as well, Hammer said.[24]

Hammer milked his gift of wheat flour for every possible ounce of
publicity. Journalist Drew Pearson discussed the Hammer letter to
Truman on his radio program. The *New York Times* published an article about the pledge. Hammer received additional coverage when he
presented the flour to Fiorello La Guardia, the former New York mayor
who headed the Relief and Rehabilitation Administration. Then Hammer met with former president Herbert Hoover to talk about the relief
effort. Before serving as president, Hoover had directed American aid
to the Soviet Union during the early 1920s — at the very time Hammer
was shipping wheat there by his own devices.[25]

On July 19, 1946, Truman agreed to meet Hammer, after receiving
a memorandum from his White House staff saying that "Dr. Hammer
owns one of the finest and most attractive antique stores in New York
City, [and] recently personally contributed fifty thousand tons of grain
to help feed Europe, and is very anxious to meet the president. . . .
Hammer has no favors to ask." At the White House meeting, Hammer
gave Truman a red calfskin portfolio from the desk of Russia's last
czar; Hammer had acquired it from the Soviet government in 1927.
Afterward, the *New York Times* reported that Hammer would tour
Europe to examine the famine-relief effort, then organize American
businessmen to combat it further.[26] Truman later named Hammer to
his Citizens' Food Committee.

Charles Luckman already had accepted Truman's appointment to
direct the committee. His goal was to conserve one hundred million
bushels of grain and ship them to Europe. A large portion of that
amount was to come involuntarily from distillers, whose leaders were
angry about a threatened sixty-day shutdown in the name of conser-
vation. Luckman worried about whether he truly possessed the authority to enforce the shutdown. Just before he was to ask the distillers for
a voice vote — one he feared he would lose — Hammer passed him a

note. You have the support of the president, the note said, and nobody in the room wants to be recorded as opposing Truman. Why not call the roll, forcing each man to go on record? Luckman took Hammer's suggestion; his proposal passed 14 to 7.[27]

While Hammer endeavored to become a force at the White House, he had — as usual — many other balls in the air. He was involved in redeeming Julius's reputation during his father's final years. He was trying to hold together his marriage to Angela. He was preoccupied with the sticky emigration case of his namesake nephew — Victor's son — who still lived in Moscow. Furthermore, Hammer had to worry about fending off attacks aimed at himself and members of his family, attacks that threatened to brand them as traitorous Communists in the accusatory atmosphere created by U.S. Senator Joseph McCarthy and others of his ilk. If such allegations stuck, they would harm Hammer's drive for respectability, as well as hurt his expanding business empire.

11

Domestic Difficulties

ALTHOUGH ARMAND HAMMER was preoccupied with mastering new business ventures, he devoted considerable attention to family matters. His involvement in the latter perhaps grew out of a feeling of duty, strongly reinforced by practicality: Hammer knew that unless he removed the stains on the family's record, they would forever hinder his drive for social acceptance and wealth.

One of his more determined efforts was orchestrating Julius Hammer's bid for reinstatement as a medical doctor. The state of New York had revoked Julius's license to practice medicine in 1922, after his conviction. But Julius never lost his desire to practice again. Nor did he and Armand accept the correctness of the guilty verdict. So in 1942 they sought his reinstatement. The timing seemed right, with many American doctors off at war.

Bernard Barron served as a character witness. A prominent Manhattan lawyer, he studied the court record of two decades earlier, then told the New York State Board of Medical Examiners that Julius's imprisonment had been unjust. Other testimonials came from former New York governor Alfred Smith and James Gerard, a onetime ambassador to Germany and law partner of one of Julius's attorneys. On July 7, 1943, Julius regained his license to practice medicine and commenced a limited practice at age sixty-nine.[1]

Julius and Rose celebrated their fiftieth wedding anniversary four years later. Family and friends gathered for a lavish party at the Barbizon Plaza Hotel, where Julius and Rose had taken an apartment overlooking Central Park. How the three sons signed the guest book typified the differences in their personalities. Harry, the eldest and most reserved, signed simply "Harry J. Hammer." Victor, the youngest and most outgoing, signed "Victor," then followed with a gushy note. Armand, the dominant brother, wrote: "Until the diamond wedding anniversary, *Dr.* Armand Hammer"[2] (emphasis added).

A year later, Julius, seventy-four and still an ardent Socialist, died after a heart attack. He was buried in Middletown, New Jersey, near the rural estate of Armand and Angela Hammer. Armand has said that his mind was a blank during the week of his father's death, but the memory of Julius lived; in his later years Armand spoke often of his father's legacy. In the 1970s, he donated $5 million to Columbia University to build a health sciences center named after Julius and himself. In comments at his eighty-eighth birthday party, he told hundreds of well-wishers: "From my father Julius I learned it is not what a man accumulates but what he gives away that counts in the final great reckoning."[3]

Hammer's absorption with family was not always so generous, especially when it conflicted with his quest for respectability. Another preoccupying concern was the plight of Victor's son, Armand, called Armasha to avoid confusion with his renowned uncle. Armasha lived with his mother, in Moscow, but by the time of Julius's death he had reached his majority. Victor wanted him to immigrate to the United States, and evidence suggests that Armasha wanted to do so. Victor had found happiness in 1941 when he married Ireene Seaton Wicker, a native of Quincy, Illinois. Ireene had been making a name as the creator, writer, and solo performer of a children's radio show when Victor met her during the czarist art sale in Chicago; she was attending to interview a Russian prince brought in by the Hammers for publicity. At that time, she was married to another show business professional, but she divorced him three years before marrying Victor, who had not remarried after breaking up with his Russian wife. Ireene had lost her son, a volunteer fighter pilot, in World War II, and her daughter was living overseas after marrying an American serviceman. Ireene wanted Armasha, Victor's only child, in New York with them. So did Victor, who made forceful appeals for help to White House aide Harry Hopkins, the personal secretary of former ambassador to Moscow Joseph Davies, and others — all in vain. The Soviet government repeatedly refused to let Armasha emigrate.[4]

The evidence indicates that Armand was not enthusiastic about helping Armasha. To be sure, at first he may simply not have had the power. But from 1961 onward, when he undoubtedly possessed influence in Moscow, he apparently never pushed for Armasha's release. His relationship with his nephew was sometimes cool, sometimes hostile, usually volatile. An unsuccessful father himself, he may not have understood why Victor was so anxious to bring Armasha to America — Armand and Victor had very different emotional makeups.*

Although Victor was devoted to his older brother, Armand sometimes treated him offhandedly, even callously. Armand treated Ireene shabbily as well, despite the national renown she had attained as radio's "Singing Lady." In the years to come, she played a big part in the family's affairs but received not a single mention in the authorized biography of Hammer, by Bob Considine, and only one, unpleasant footnote in Hammer's 1987 autobiography. Like others who earned Armand's disfavor, Ireene essentially became a nonperson.

She also, from an early date, evidently became an embarrassment. In the postwar anti-Communist hysteria, she was blacklisted and lost her job. She fought back, forcing a right-wing newsletter called *Counterattack* to retract false charges made against her, but the damage was done. Although her talent remained intact, her days as a star were over.[5]

Armand apparently did little to help her. There is evidence he protested to *The Sign* magazine concerning an article it had published about her and asked Francis Cardinal Spellman to intervene with the magazine on Ireene's behalf. But Armand opposed filing a libel suit, fearing that information about Julius's political activities — not to mention the Hammer family's period in Russia — might resurface, hurting business. He had his own reputation to protect.†

There was irony in the patriotic Ireene's being smeared as a Communist sympathizer while Armand — who had lived for a decade in Bolshevik Russia, who knew Lenin, who had made a fortune while building up Soviet industry — escaped public calumny. Hammer did not deserve to be accused unfairly either, of course, but he would seem to have been an easy target for Joseph McCarthy. Roy Cohn, Senator

* Victor finally received permission from the Soviet government in 1956 to visit Armasha, who had just become the father of a daughter. Ireene and Rose Hammer made the trip, too. It was an emotional reunion. (Victor Hammer papers and Associated Press report in the *New York Times,* July 23, 1956.)

† Six years after her blacklisting, Ireene wrote to her husband: "Surely I can get [a job] now . . . surely the ridiculous hogwash because I am married to a man whose Russian father is supposed to have been a Communist, because I entertained Spanish refugee children, because I criticized the Taft-Hartley Act, because I sang Russian gypsy songs, because I did not fight back in case it might reflect on the business as Armand warned me — well, surely, all this claptrap must be unimportant by this time." (Ireene to Victor, August 25, 1956, collection of Ireene Wicker Hammer and Victor J. Hammer.)

McCarthy's influential aide, knew about him; Cohn's father had prosecuted Julius in the abortion trial. A possible explanation for Hammer's
escaping unscathed was that he worked to do so, contributing money
and favors to politicians who were his supporters. His special guardian
was Senator Styles Bridges, Republican of New Hampshire, a fire-
breathing, hard-line anti-Communist. Senator Albert Gore, Democrat
of Tennessee, helped, too. Hammer was friends with both men, as well
as a business partner of Gore's.

Although Hammer's powerful allies helped maintain his public image, they were unable to keep him from all harm. Behind the scenes,
his ties to the Soviet Union haunted him in every administration, although mention of this drag on his quest for respect is conspicuously
absent from all of his books. The most telling controversy had its genesis in Hammer's desire to lease a former army ordnance works in
Morgantown, West Virginia, as a plant for United Distillers of America. The army had built the Morgantown works during World War II
to produce ammonia. The plant, closed after the war, later geared up
to produce anhydrous ammonia for fertilizer needed in postwar Germany and Japan. By 1950, the army was ready to put the plant in moth-
balls again, unless it could find a private enterprise to lease it. Three
private concerns were eager: Allied Chemical and Dye Corporation,
Mathieson Chemical Corporation, and Hammer's United Distillers.[6]

The Army Corps of Engineers decided Hammer's bid was the best
of the three, but the Defense Department rejected them all after determining that the plant should use natural gas instead of coke. The bidding was reopened. Only Hammer's company and Allied Chemical
participated. Once again, the army favored Hammer's bid. This time,
Senator Matthew Neely, a West Virginia Democrat, intervened. He
told the army he preferred to have Allied Chemical operate the plant
in his home state. Neely dragged the White House into the fray, charging that New York State Democratic chairman Paul Fitzpatrick was
employing unfair influence on President Truman to swing the lease to
Hammer. Fitzpatrick denied the charge, although he did ask U.S. Representative Emanuel Celler, a New York Democrat who chaired the
Judiciary Committee, to argue Hammer's case. Meanwhile, Hammer
implored the other West Virginia senator, Harley Kilgore, to help
counteract Neely's opposition, which Hammer said was based on false
information. With so much at stake, Hammer mobilized United Distillers bankers to testify about the financial stability of his company,
which was small compared with the competition.[7]

Notwithstanding Hammer's efforts, the army decided in favor of

Mathieson Chemical, which had not even entered the second-round bidding. Allied Chemical had been disqualified by the Justice Department and the Federal Trade Commission, which found adverse antitrust implications. As for Hammer's company, the army's public statement said that it was too small and inexperienced to produce ammonia on such a large scale.[8]

There was more to the decision than that, but Hammer was in the dark. Relying on the army's public rationale, he complained to Representative Carl Vinson, a Georgia Democrat who chaired the House Armed Services Committee. Vinson found Hammer's complaints valid but defended the award to Mathieson Chemical. Vinson stressed the need to have the Morgantown plant operating as soon as possible to reduce the nation's annual fertilizer shortfall. "United [Distillers] was jilted at the church door, but that does not make the engagement to Mathieson and the proposed lease a nullity," Vinson said. He told his colleagues that the "committee must not be used as a forum for driving shrewd bargains, for obtaining business advantages by delays and frustrations which amount to little more than a mild form of blackmail. We have been careful to avoid this in this case, while at the same time we have given all interested parties a full opportunity of presenting all the facts to us."[9]

With the assistance of Representative L. Gary Clemente, a New York Democrat, Hammer got a hearing before the House Armed Services Committee. He hired influential representation: former U.S. senator Scott Lucas of Illinois and Wendell Berge, previously assistant attorney general in charge of antitrust. Hammer was impressive as a witness, until he danced around his Soviet connections during an exchange with John Courtney, special counsel to the committee. Courtney, wanting to know more about Allied American Corporation's business during the 1920s, asked where the company had maintained offices. Hammer replied: "This country and abroad. Our main office was in New York. We had branches all over Europe — London, Paris, Berlin, and other countries."

Courtney: What other countries, Doctor?
Hammer: Well, we had an office in Moscow — at that time we had a concession agreement. We had an office in China. We had an office in Latvia. We had branches in various cities throughout the world.
Courtney: Did your business carry you to them?
Hammer: Oh, yes. I made three or four trips a year to Europe during that time.

Courtney: To visit these branch offices?
Hammer: That is right.[10]

Hammer's testimony contained no other reference to his astounding
ten years in the Soviet Union. He probably thought it was a sensible
omission, given the anti-Communist hysteria in the United States. When
army officials testified, they said nothing about Hammer's Soviet decade either, instead casting doubt on the financial statements of United
Distillers. Archibald Alexander, undersecretary of the army, told the
committee that "various asset items seem questionable."[11]

Hammer was fooling nobody about his past, which had played a role
in the army's award of the lease to Mathieson Chemical in the first
place. This was borne out on November 27, 1951, when Mark Galusha,
a staff member of the Senate Armed Services Committee, wrote secretly to Styles Bridges, suggesting the senator stop advocating Hammer's bid. Galusha said he had discussed the Morgantown case with
the army's general counsel, who revealed

> on a confidential basis that the Army . . . objected to the leasing of the
> plant to United Distillers because of Dr. Hammer's previous connections
> in Russia. His Federal Bureau of Investigation file indicates that he spent
> ten years in Russia . . . and that during this time he was awarded the
> pencil and asbestos monopoly. At the conclusion of the ten-year period
> he brought out of Russia large amounts of valuable assets. . . . The
> Army . . . states that his company should not be given contracts, nor
> should he hold any position of public trust within the Department of
> the Army.[12]

Hammer's opponents used the FBI to damage United Distillers' position as the debate raged over the Morgantown lease. The bureau's
New York office sent a teletype marked "urgent" to other offices;
someone with influence had asked for all damaging information on
Hammer from the bureau files. The teletype asked all offices to "ex-
pedite. . . . Bureau has requested this matter be given preferred attention." Responses arrived from Chicago, Newark, and Washington, D.C.
All said sensitive information had been located. Bridges wrote to his
files: "There is reason to believe that the gossip and unfounded rumors
about the Hammers being pro-Soviet or pro-Communist have been used
by competitors of United [Distillers] in a whispering campaign brought
to the attention of the House and Senate Armed Services Commit-
tees."[13]

Later, for public consumption, the anti-Communist Bridges minimized his efforts on Hammer's behalf. In an interview with *The Re-*

porter magazine, he said Hammer "felt he was the highest bidder, but they gave it to somebody else and I never paid much attention to it. . . . My interest in it was relatively slight." When the magazine later published an exposé of Bridges, it devoted significant space to the Morgantown controversy. The article stated that during the debate an assistant to army undersecretary Alexander received a call

> from a fairly prominent New Jersey politician. The caller emphasized that Hammer's company was incorporated in New Jersey and that it might be advantageous all around if Hammer were to receive the Morgantown contract. [The caller] then said it would be worth $100,000 to Alexander's campaign [for U.S. senator from New Jersey] if the Morgantown award went to Hammer. There was no indication that Hammer knew of this attempted bribe.

Bridges excoriated *The Reporter* on the Senate floor. Albert Gore also spoke out, protesting what he believed to be the magazine's unfair treatment of Hammer: "This private citizen has had aspersions cast upon his character and patriotism. I could see no reason for that except as a means of attacking the senior senator from New Hampshire."[14]

The army's distrust of Hammer perhaps explained an earlier rejection as well. In 1949, United Distillers had proposed selling its Saf-Tone antifreeze to the Defense Department. Ordnance officials responded that the antifreeze failed to meet military specifications. Hammer asked Bridges to intervene. Bridges wrote to the secretary of defense, who sent the controversy to the Munitions Board. Bridges obtained an appointment for Hammer with the Munitions Board chairman.[15] In the end, Hammer's efforts failed. Whether the military told Bridges at that time about its blacklist is uncertain.

The government's behind-the-scenes labeling of Hammer as untrustworthy showed up again when Hammer applied for a passport in 1952; the State Department turned him down on the grounds that he was a "suspected Communist." State Department documents cited Hammer's activities in the Soviet Union during the 1920s; his favorable passages about the Bolsheviks from *The Quest of the Romanoff Treasure;* his father's political affiliations; his 1937 membership in the Institute of Pacific Relations, a left-wing think tank; and his hiring of an alleged member of the Communist party as a United Distillers employee. The State Department quoted a "former acquaintance and business associate [who] does not consider subject [Hammer] subversive but states he is unscrupulous and 'would do business with the devil if there were a profit in it.' "[16]

All in all, the distilling business was beginning to be a problem for Hammer. It was filled with unsavory characters; associating with them could link a distiller to organized crime in the minds of law-enforcement agents, a link the already suspect Hammer could do without. Moreover, the New York State Liquor Authority had disciplined Hammer's wholesale and distilling companies for failing to file information about terminated employees; selling industrial alcohol without the appropriate licenses; wrongly storing liquor in the basement of the Empire State Building; and offering liquor at unauthorized prices. The agency suspended United Distillers' wholesale license for ten days and canceled the license of its subsidiary, West Shore Wine and Liquor Company.[17]

Hammer, often accused of using predatory tactics in his business dealings, felt he was being preyed upon by the Big Four distillers — Seagram, Schenley, National, and Hiram Walker. He complained during a House of Representatives hearing that the Big Four were trying to drive companies such as United Distillers out of the marketplace: "In the past year, our company has negotiated with many distributors who expressed their desire to do business with us and add our line, but finally they had to tell us that they could not obtain consent from their principal distributor, and therefore were in no position to jeopardize their main line." Hammer told the committee that from 1944 to 1947 he had been forced to give the Big Four part of United Distillers' government grain allocation in exchange for scarce barrels.[18]

In view of all this, Hammer decided to start unloading his distilleries. The New Hampshire plant was the first to go. To Hammer's displeasure, the sale occurred under the glare of negative publicity. Senator Bridges was taking heat for his assistance to Hammer in obtaining the distillery; the criticism was an offshoot of a dispute over the placement of an air force base. Bridges favored a site in the Portsmouth-Newington area. The state's other senator, Charles Tobey, sided with the opponents of placing the airfield there. John Hoyt, town clerk of Newington, dredged up the Hammer connection to use against Bridges in the battle over the base. Hoyt told reporters he planned to ask Bridges "to make full revelation of his and Senator [Owen] Brewster's association and friendship with Armand Hammer of United Distillers." Hoyt wanted to know why Bridges was such a frequent visitor at Hammer's New Jersey rural estate and why the senator spent so much time in Florida aboard Hammer's "palatial yacht." The people of New Hampshire were wondering about "the ten-million-dollar profit realized by Hammer's World War II distillery at Newmarket," Hoyt said. Georgia

Mason, a Bridges constituent who also opposed the air force base, wired the senator that a "great many people [are] becoming concerned about your association with Dr. Armand Hammer in [the] Newmarket distillery."[19]

Still, Hammer departed from the distilling business on an upbeat note, thanks to his marketing genius. He had been planning to announce that United Distillers would drop the price of its 100 proof bottled-in-bond J. W. Dant bourbon from $5.39 for a fifth to $4.95. The advertisements were in production when Armand received an excited telephone call from his half brother, Harry, who had asked for a bottle of Dant bourbon at a liquor store only to be told by the proprietor that the store did not carry it. Instead, the proprietor reached under the counter for a little-known bourbon. He told Harry it was reserved for his best customers. Its quality was excellent. The price: $4.49. Armand changed the advertisements at the last minute to match that amount.

So low a price for an established brand was a daring move, and it shook up the industry. Within months, Dant shot to number one on the sales charts, pushed by Hammer's strategy of stamping a crown onto the bottle. His brand was advertised as "the crown jewel of Kentucky bourbon." Hammer promoted it by sending an actual crown and jewels on a national tour. In some cities, he invited prominent local women to pose for photographs wearing the jewelry. To build further goodwill, Hammer donated proceeds from these appearances to charity. It was a variation on the czarist-treasures marketing strategy from two decades earlier. The media loved it. When Victor visited Dallas, a newspaper there published a photograph of him with a diamond necklace reportedly worth $250,000 alongside a bottle of Dant bourbon. Victor told the newspaper that the jewelry had belonged to the Austrian branch of the Hapsburg royal family. A San Antonio newspaper reported that Victor would have a police escort from the airport to a retail liquor convention because of the valuable jewelry accompanying him. The results were sensational. *Spirits* magazine called the rise in J. W. Dant sales "the success story of the year."[20]

Hammer nevertheless opted to sell off most of United Distillers' assets — while the company was perceived as a hot property. United Distillers dismantled its opulent headquarters in the Empire State Building; Hammer donated the historic Uxbridge treaty and reception rooms to Queen Elizabeth II in honor of her coronation. It was a magnanimous gesture, one that helped Hammer later when he aggressively began to cultivate the royal family. He and Lewis Rosenstiel, the chairman of Schenley Industries, negotiated for the bulk of United Distillers' business, sometimes talking from their respective yachts in Florida. The sales price was reportedly $6.5 million.[21]

At the time of the sale, the Internal Revenue Service was investigating Hammer. The government eventually sued United Distillers and West Shore Wine and Liquor for about $500,000 in back taxes, alleging that returns filed for 1945 and 1946 had been fraudulent. Hammer has credited Arthur Groman, his Los Angeles lawyer, with determining that the decision would turn as much on Hammer's credibility as on the law. To bolster that credibility, Hammer suggested lining up his acquaintances Eleanor Roosevelt, Beardsley Ruml, and David Wilentz as character witnesses. Ruml was chairman of the R. H. Macy department store company and of the Federal Reserve Bank of New York. Wilentz, as New Jersey attorney general, had prosecuted Bruno Hauptmann in the Lindbergh baby kidnapping case. According to Groman, Eleanor Roosevelt assured a Hammer victory by testifying to his excellent reputation and the high esteem in which President Roosevelt had held him. That version, as recounted by Hammer's authorized biographer, Bob Considine, must be treated cautiously, however. The book contains inaccuracies, including the year of the hearing. Moreover, there is no evidence in publicly available files of Mrs. Roosevelt's testimony. Certainly the judge's ruling was not a complete vindication, for he commented that accounting procedures used by Hammer's company could have been "a vehicle of fraud." But the government had at most proved gross negligence, not fraud, said the judge.[22]

The millions Hammer earned from the sale of his distilling empire in no way meant retirement. During the same period that he painstakingly built and then sold United Distillers, he was becoming dominant in another business: Aberdeen-Angus cattle breeding. Angela Zevely was responsible for stimulating Hammer's interest in the breed — by the time they met, she had learned about animal husbandry on her New Jersey farm forty-five miles south of New York City. Her land near Red Bank, New Jersey, was known as Nut Swamp. On her original twelve acres, Angela kept sheep, pigs, and chickens. Hammer's contribution was to take her unfocused interest in animals, add cattle, and expand the farm into a profitable enterprise.

Breeders in Scotland had developed Aberdeen-Angus cattle, and in the 1870s the breed found popularity in the United States. One attraction was the breed's high percentage of edible flesh to total carcass weight when compared with that of other breeds. Hammer discerned a logical connection between the cattle and distilling — one by-product of whiskey was mash, which made good cattle feed. Another attraction to Hammer was that working with cattle allowed him to use his medical training, albeit on an unexpected type of patient. Trying to keep the animals healthy, and curing the ones that inevitably took sick, were challenging. Hammer became fascinated with the genetics of breeding great cattle.[23] For many of his competitors, the cattle business was a tax shelter to be operated by hired hands. For Hammer, it became a passion.

At first, the Hammer farm was home to a few cattle treated as pets, until one day when Armand and Angela attended an Aberdeen-Angus auction. Armand bid impulsively for one of the cows. He ended up not only with the cow, but also with the manager of the herd from which it came. The manager was restless with his employer and liked the thought of building a quality herd, fast, for Hammer.

Angela formed the Shadow Isle Corporation, eventually transferring a 50 percent interest to Armand. The farm grew to more than 200 acres as nearby land came onto the market. On their property stood a fifteen-room homestead with a well-stocked wine cellar; three baths; a three-car garage; seven servants; a beachhouse; a boathouse with sailboats, motorboats, and rowboats; and two farm buildings. A second spread of 72 acres contained two dwellings and eleven farm buildings. Later, the cattle operation spilled over to a separate farm of 363 acres that Hammer purchased in Colts Neck, seven miles from Shadow Isle. The land contained three dwellings and fifteen farm buildings. Armand and Angela invited United Distillers and Hammer Galleries employees to parties on their vast lawn. When they entertained dignitaries from the realms of business, politics, or the arts, the menu might include champagne, caviar, Angus steak, and pheasant under glass.

Armand bought an airplane so he could jet around the country and conduct Aberdeen-Angus business quickly when time was short; it contained a bed, a bar, easy chairs, and cooking facilities. To accommodate the plane, he built a landing strip on their farm. He bought a second, eighty-foot yacht, too, and refurbished it. Thereafter he commuted by yacht from a marina near the farm to United Distillers headquarters, in Manhattan, docking at a nearby boat basin. When Hammer needed a car, he had a Cadillac at his disposal, with an M.D. license plate.[24]

Mary Kotick Feinstein, an employee of Gimbel's working with the Hearst art collection directly under the Hammers throughout the 1940s, watched as Armand juggled his businesses. While the Hearst sale was in progress at Gimbel's, Feinstein and Victor Hammer would write daily reports about each customer so that "even if Armand were absent, he knew what had happened. He was always hands-on, all business, but with a sense of humor. . . . He maintained an informal relationship with the salespeople and pumped them for details regarding the customers, though he had more formal relations with his secretaries and the other employees. He had high standards, would not stand for inefficiency. He was not mean, but he was demanding — and brilliant." Harry Hammer was there every day but did little of substance, Feinstein said. "I called him the dignity man. He looked right, dressed right. When Armand and Victor would disagree, Harry would settle it." Sometimes Armand's son would be at the New Jersey farm or hanging around Gimbel's, Feinstein said. "He was such a nice boy, and so handsome. . . . Too bad Armand's relationship with Julian was so difficult in the ensuing years." Feinstein said that Angela "was brilliant, beautiful, frustrated by her deafness. She began to drink heavily."[25]

For a time, Angela was a full partner in the cattle business, which, in September 1949, held its first annual auction. The top price paid for a bull was a hefty $4,000; the top price for a cow reached $6,000. Hammer persuaded New Jersey governor Alfred Driscoll to attend; the governor auctioned off some heifers, with Hammer donating the proceeds to charity. By then, Hammer was obsessed with owning the prize bull of the Aberdeen-Angus breed: Prince Eric of Sunbeam. The first time he attempted to buy Prince Eric, a Wisconsin breeder named L. L. O'Bryan outbid him, paying $35,300. While stewing about losing, Hammer received a call from Leo Mac Cropsey, a Crystal Lake, Illinois, veterinarian. Cropsey had heard rumors that Prince Eric was losing his potency and so might be on the market. Hammer called O'Bryan, received permission to perform tests, traveled to Wisconsin to conduct them, and satisfied himself that Prince Eric could be induced to perform at top levels once again. Hammer offered the owner $75,000. O'Bryan demanded $100,000. Hammer left in a huff but later agreed to the price, paying O'Bryan the highest amount ever reported in the trade. Prince Eric turned out to be worth the money.[26]

Prince Eric quickly occupied an honored spot on the stationery of Shadow Isle Farm, all by himself in the lower left-hand corner. In the upper right-hand corner were drawings of three other prize animals — Prince Barbarian of Sunbeam, Prince Sunbeam the 249th, and Prince Sunbeam the 328th. To care for them, in 1951 Cropsey joined Shadow Isle Farm as manager. That same year, Hammer claimed a new record sale at public auction when Shadow Isle received $57,000 for one of its bulls.

Through the sales, Hammer met breeders whose vocations were in fields of use to him: oil barons, members of Congress, and the like. He forged a relationship with Jay Walker, a wealthy Tulsa businessman. When Walker's daughter Martha lost her husband in an auto accident ten days before the birth of their daughter, Hammer insisted Martha use his Florida yacht to help her recover from the tragedy. She accepted the offer, cruising off Florida with the captain and cook at her service. It was a kindness she never forgot.[27]

With Prince Eric at Shadow Isle, Hammer was on top of the Aberdeen-Angus world. He bought cows for less than $1,000 each, impregnated them with Prince Eric's semen, and then sold them while still pregnant for $5,000. A cow accompanied by one of Prince Eric's calves and pregnant with another fetched $20,000. Hammer has said that in Prince Eric's three years at Shadow Isle, the bull brought in about $2 million.

Not every customer was a happy customer. Richard Allen, a Virginia breeder, said he bought bulls from Hammer hesitantly, because he had heard that Shadow Isle Farm pedigrees might be unreliable. Allen said that a deceased neighbor of his allegedly had paid top dollar for a prize bull from Hammer, only to find that its belly had been painted. Two breeders, one from Illinois and one from Indiana, sued Hammer for allegedly selling defective cattle. Neither lawsuit went to trial, but the Illinois plaintiff received a $12,000 settlement.[28]

Those two lawsuits were insignificant compared with what was to come in connection with Hammer's Shadow Isle venture. The first blow arrived on August 13, 1953, when Prince Eric died just short of his eleventh birthday. Meanwhile Armand and Angela had begun to disagree about the operation of Shadow Isle Farm — Angela's name had stopped appearing in advertisements as of August 1952. Furthermore, the disagreements between the two involved more than business. On July 8, 1953, Armand had moved out of the main house, claiming that Angela's "cruel and inhuman treatment" was destroying his physical and mental health. He moved to another house on the property. On August 13, the day of Prince Eric's death, Angela charged Armand with locking her out of their house in Manhattan. Amid this, Hammer's accounting firm warned him of unpleasant tax burdens from the sale of United Distillers — burdens that could be lightened by unloading his cattle. So Hammer announced a three-day dispersion sale at Shadow Isle beginning May 10, 1954.

Hammer advertised with characteristic flair, billing the dispersion as "the sale of the century." He told how the previous seven auctions at Shadow Isle had resulted in 634 head of cattle selling for more than

$2.7 million. At the dispersion sale, 500 cattle would be auctioned, a record. In the May 1954 issue of the *Aberdeen-Angus Journal,* Hammer placed a multipage advertisement filled with testimonials to himself and his herd from leading industry spokesmen. The 352-page sales catalog weighed three pounds. Angela, who said she had not been consulted, threatened to stop the sale with a court injunction. She and Armand reached agreement just days before it was scheduled to begin. Buyers arrived from thirty-seven states and two Canadian provinces. Every hotel in the vicinity was filled. American and overseas newspapers covered the event. When it was over, the gross topped $1 million for the first time in the industry's history.[29]

As the sale faded into memory, Armand and Angela Hammer focused their energies on ending their marriage. It was a protracted, ugly, exceedingly public spectacle. In October 1954, Angela sued Armand for an accounting of their money, some of which she believed had been diverted from the cattle business to buy art for Hammer Galleries. That same month, she sued for an official marital separation. Armand replied by suing for divorce. Angela wanted to fight it out in the New York State courts because she thought the laws there would afford her a better settlement. Armand, too, felt that the New York laws would favor his wife, so he filed for a New Jersey divorce. Angela charged that he "knew full well that he could not obtain a divorce in the state of New York against me for the only ground recognized . . . adultery. He hopes to use the New Jersey courts as his pawns to deprive me of my marital rights on a set of fictitious charges of cruel and inhuman treatment." Armand prevailed on the jurisdictional issue, but that was just the beginning.[30]

Armand's divorce petition said that almost from the beginning of the marriage, Angela had "imbibed alcoholic beverages in excessive amounts, resulting in protracted periods of intoxication, during which periods she abused plaintiff, using vile language towards him and calling him a dirty Jew. Defendant is of a different religious faith." Armand's filing quoted Angela as saying to his face that "it is too bad Hitler did not take care of all the Jews." Armand portrayed Angela as a woman consumed by jealousy: At one point, she reportedly accused Armand of sleeping with the wife of an employee, then told the employee of her claim. Understandably upset, the man and his wife threatened to sue Angela for defamation. Armand said he talked the couple out of suing but later fired the alleged cuckold because of the poisoned atmosphere resulting from Angela's accusations.[31]

Armand's allegations also covered the night of April 8, 1952, when after a cattle auction Angela's "abusive and drunken conduct" at a local hotel shocked the guests. She supposedly appropriated the checks from that sale; Armand said he stopped payment on them, then shamefacedly asked the customers to write new ones. Furthermore, Armand claimed, on July 7, 1953, he awakened to find Angela standing over him with a lit cigarette, threatening to burn his eyes out; the next day, she hit him in the face and knocked his glasses off. Armand said such verbal and physical abuse had caused him "nervousness, sleeplessness, and gastrointestinal dysfunction" requiring medical attention.[32]

Nor was Angela willing to be served with the divorce papers. A Monmouth County, New Jersey, deputy sheriff told the court that when he tried to serve the papers as she was leaving a dentist's office, she denied her identity, then threw the papers out of her Cadillac as she drove away. Angela, rejecting Armand's allegations, countered with some of her own. She said a recent hospital stay that Armand attributed to alcoholism was caused, instead, by Armand's cruelty. She charged that Armand threatened to "beat her brains out" while holding a metal pipe. She said once he actually had physically assaulted her. The incident purportedly occurred on their yacht — Armand blackened both of her eyes after she chided him "about his undue attention to one of the female guests at a social event." Supporting testimony came from Angela's sister, who swore she had witnessed the assault. The sister also gave short shrift to Armand's assertion that Angela had caused his illness: "The plaintiff is a man of boundless energy, possessed of an iron will and strong determination, and is not one whose mental and physical condition can be easily affected by other persons."[33]

The couple fought about property and money. Armand contended that Angela needed little financial support, saying that her share of the New Jersey land and buildings was worth at least $500,000 and that the jewelry he had given her steadily over fifteen years was insured for at least $50,000. Armand's personal secretary told the court that she often received Angela's bills at United Distillers and paid them with Armand's personal checks. Angela countered that Armand possessed "tremendous personal wealth" of at least $20 million, much of it hidden from her. Angela said Armand "has always boasted and vaunted of his successful schemes and financial manipulations, who lives by the philosophy that money can buy everything and everybody." She charged that he had organized nominal corporations or used friends and relatives as fronts to hide his assets.[34]

As the court battle dragged on, Angela told Red Bank–area merchants to bill Armand for her food and farm materials, but Armand's lawyer notified them that Angela was buying in excess of her allowance as set by the court: "Please be advised that you will at your risk furnish any supplies or other items to Mrs. Hammer." Angela requested that the court compel Armand to pay her legal fees, suggesting that the high cost of her lawyers was caused by the necessity of matching Armand's high-priced representation. Armand's legal retinue included Louis Nizer, one of the best-known trial attorneys in the United States. It was the beginning of an enduring legal, business, and social relationship between the two dynamic men.[35]

Viewing the divorce decades later, one cannot easily determine who was telling the truth about such normally private matters. Six persons who viewed the Hammer-Zevely marriage firsthand provided information for this book. One of them said Angela appeared to have a drinking problem early in the marriage; the other five said they had seen no evidence of a drinking problem. All six had trouble picturing Angela the way Armand portrayed her. There is no question that some of Angela's charges against Armand were false or exaggerated and that some of Armand's charges against Angela were equally false or exaggerated. For example, Armand said Angela cooked up a story that Julian had spied on them through their bedroom window, then reported the details of what he saw to Olga Vadina. Armand suggested that Angela meant to poison his relationship with his former wife and their only child. Indeed, a story about such an incident appeared in the *New York Daily News,* which said Julian "spied on their bedroom capers through binoculars and tattled to his mother, the first Mrs. Hammer." But *Daily News* files show the story was false — the report of the incident came from an entirely different divorce case and was mistakenly attributed to the Hammers. The newspaper published a correction after a complaint from *Angela's* lawyer.[36]

Whatever the truth, the dispute caught the fancy of the media; published reports spread the details of the quarrel across the country. The *New York Daily News* used a story accompanied by photographs of the couple under the headline "WIFE SUES TO NAIL TEN MILLIONS OF HAMMER $$; SAYS HE CHISELED." The reporter called the battle "one of the biggest husband-and-wife legal disputes ever recorded."[37] The court proceeding — combined with the intense pressures of business and the intractable problems of Julian — left Armand depressed. He began to suffer stretches of despondency. Considering his normally limitless energy and a can-do attitude that bordered on zealotry, such depression clearly signaled an unusually rough time for him. Hammer drew strength from a variety of sources: his late father's example; the poem *If,* by

Rudyard Kipling; the collected sayings of Roman emperor Marcus Aurelius; and Dale Carnegie's writings on self-improvement. By focusing his strong will on his troubles, Hammer snapped out of his depression and overcame his medical ailments, which included gallbladder, kidney, and prostate troubles.

The divorce settlement, approved in January 1956, hastened Armand's recovery. Angela received only $1,000 a month. Armand agreed to pay some of her outstanding bills (including property taxes and utilities), transfer two of their cars to her name, pay about $30,000 of her legal fees, make a lump-sum cash payment to her of $12,000, surrender his personal property in the residences in New Jersey, return Shadow Isle Corporation stock to her, and resign as an officer and director of the corporation. Angela and Armand divided the New Jersey acreage. Later, Armand sold seventy-eight acres from the settlement for more than $400,000. One disappointment was his failure to recover three handwritten letters from Lenin to him, as well as an inscribed photo. Hammer assumed that Angela had exacted revenge by hiding, destroying, or selling the financially and sentimentally valuable items. He searched the world for them, unsuccessfully.[38]

The decree brought far more joy than unhappiness, however. Within days of the judgment, Hammer had remarried and started a new life.

12

Going West

A RMAND HAMMER'S NEW LIFE in California, like so much
else that happened to him, grew seamlessly out of his past. This
time, however, an unpleasant shock interrupted the smooth flow of
events: a murder charge filed by the state of California against his only
child.

After Olga and Armand were divorced, in 1943, Julian Hammer
lived with his mother — first in Las Vegas, for a short time, then in
Southern California. Olga tried to be a supportive mother, but her
bohemian life-style consistently undermined her intent. Flora Chell, who
met Olga in 1942 and became her friend, said that by the time the pair
reached Los Angeles the adolescent Julian clearly was heading for trouble. Nor was Julian's absentee father much help. When Olga on one
occasion called the Hammer family in New York asking what to do,
Chell said, it was Harry, not Armand, who traveled to California to
take Julian in hand.[1]

Armand's way of handling Julian was to give him money to spend.
To be sure, he occasionally tried to establish a relationship with the
boy, taking him on a fishing trip to Canada, for instance, and flying
him and Angela along on a United Distillers business trip to the Dominican Republic. But the good times with Julian were few and far
between. Sometimes when Julian called on his father at the office for a
long-awaited outing, Armand would ignore him until it was too late
for the planned get-together.[2]

In 1948 Julian had enrolled at Marshall College, in Huntington, West
Virginia, but left in 1951 without a degree. Living in that locale had
separated him from his father. Moreover, after Julian left college and

entered the military, his service had kept him and Armand even farther apart. Nevertheless, it appeared that Julian might settle down when, in 1954, at the age of twenty-five, he married Texas-born Glenna Sue Ervin, a twenty-three-year-old divorcée with a young daughter. By the spring of 1955 they were expecting their first child.[3]

The murder charge stemmed from a reunion between Julian and Bruce Whitlock, his college roommate, on May 7, 1955. Whitlock, just released from military service, had moved into an apartment in the Los Angeles area not far from Julian's, and the two men were celebrating Julian's twenty-sixth birthday. The party began in the afternoon with beer drinking. Before dinner, the young men switched to martinis. Glenna Sue, five months pregnant, cooked and served the meal. The trio went to a Russian restaurant owned by a friend of Julian's after dinner. There the men drank some more and began arguing over a $200 gambling debt that Julian supposedly owed Whitlock. Julian said that he had no recollection of incurring the debt, but he and Whitlock agreed to flip a coin for double or nothing. Julian lost.[4]

The rest of the story follows Julian's account under oath. The group returned to the Hammer household, where Julian wrote out an IOU. Whitlock rejected it. Instead, he asked for Julian's car and clothes. The tension mounted. Whitlock knocked Julian to the floor, threatened to rape Glenna Sue, and then jostled her. The altercation shifted to the bedroom, where Whitlock barred Julian's path to the closed door. Frightened, partly because Whitlock had served time in prison for auto theft and partly because he had been a Golden Gloves boxing champion, Julian grabbed a pistol he kept in a drawer of the night table and warned Whitlock to stop advancing. When Whitlock kept coming, Julian fired twice, killing him. Julian then called the police.[5]

The judge presiding at Julian's arraignment for murder doubted some of Julian's account and so refused to dismiss the charges against him. Armand thereupon retained a law firm whose defense counsel, Arthur Groman, filed a compelling brief, asking that the murder charge be set aside on grounds of self-defense. Glenna Sue backed Julian's story, and with the only other witness to the homicide dead, the judge dismissed the charges.*

---

* Julian may have received assistance from his father's political connections. On July 2, 1955, Armand sent a telegram to Senator Styles Bridges telling him that the case against Julian had been dismissed and expressing a father's heartfelt gratitude. Hammer never forgot Bridges's kindness. Years after the senator's death, he donated money to the custodian of the Bridges papers in the hope that a favorable biography would result. Hammer told the custodian that Bridges's farsighted proposals had made the world a better place. Moreover, after Julian's release, a lifelong, close working relation-

Thus began the longest sustained period of happiness in Armand's life.

By the time of Julian's misadventure, Armand's secret love, Frances Tolman, was a widow. She and Elmer Tolman had bought a house in Los Angeles in 1946 from actress Gene Tierney and her fashion designer husband, Oleg Cassini. Tolman died there in 1954, leaving Frances the house, valuable land in Illinois, cash, and other assets. In 1955, Frances was well-off financially. She was also an intelligent, gentle, dignified, attractive woman. She had not forgotten Armand, nor had he forgotten her. Frances had read of his lurid divorce in a tabloid while sitting in a beauty parlor. Then she learned of Julian's troubles in the local newspapers. She sent a telegram to Armand in care of Hammer Galleries, where he happened to be when it arrived.[6]

Armand was thrilled. The next day, he flew from New York to Los Angeles, showing up unannounced at her home (the telegram contained an address but no telephone number) to propose marriage. The private wedding took place on January 25, 1956, six days after Armand's divorce from Angela.[7]

Armand and Frances decided to live in the five-bedroom, five-bath home with a swimming pool that she already owned at 10431 Wyton Drive, a pretty, upper-class Los Angeles neighborhood near a park. The conventional wisdom at that time was that Hammer had retired to sunny California — he was fifty-seven, she fifty-three. But such was not quite the case. When he married Frances, Armand was involved in numerous ventures that he was loath to give up. Nor did he want to become a full-time resident of California; he refused to surrender his beloved bachelor's carriage house in Greenwich Village and to sever his ties to his art gallery. Moreover, despite the dispersion sale of the Aberdeen-Angus herd, he had not left the cattle business either, instead forming a partnership with a fellow breeder, Senator Albert Gore.[8]

Nevertheless, he and Frances made Los Angeles their home and, in the spirit of affluent retirees, worked on assembling an important art collection (largely through the good offices of Hammer Galleries, now moved to 51 East Fifty-seventh Street) and bought and restored the late president Franklin Roosevelt's summer house on Campobello Island, in New Brunswick, Canada. Neither venture, however, was the newlyweds' alone.

---

ship arose between Hammer and Groman. Thereafter, Groman was Hammer's lead lawyer among an army of lawyers. (Bridges papers, New England College, Henniker, N.H.; and personal papers of James Kiepper. Hammer's letter is dated April 4, 1978; Kiepper sent it to the author July 15, 1988.)

Armand, Victor, and Harry had begun building an art collection together, partly for the love of the quest, partly for the prestige and publicity, before the marriage. Thereafter they acquired in a single transaction the entire collection of one Charles Russell, an artist from Montana who had died in 1926. In 1957 and 1958 they displayed the combined Russell-Hammer collections from San Francisco to New York as "the private collection of the Hammer brothers." The collection featured Dutch, Flemish, German, and Italian paintings from the fifteenth, sixteenth, and seventeenth centuries.[9]

Armand acquired some of the pictures in the collection on the advice of Anthony Reyre, a British art restorer. One of the prize acquisitions turned out to be controversial. It was *The Letter,* by Gabriel Metsu, a seventeenth-century Dutch painter. W. R. Valentiner, who had attributed the painting to Metsu, later reversed himself, saying the original was at a Baltimore gallery. Still convinced he owned the original, Hammer transported the picture to Baltimore, where the gallery director compared them side by side and acknowledged that Hammer had the original.

In 1958 the collection was shown at the Municipal Art Gallery in Los Angeles. Hammer announced his intention to donate it to a public institution, eventually bestowing it on the University of Southern California. John Walker, director emeritus of the National Gallery of Art, in Washington, D.C., commented that the collection constituted "an important group of Old Masters intended for study purposes . . . invaluable in a university museum." By the time of the donation, newspapers were calling the pictures the Armand Hammer Collection — the names of Victor and Harry had disappeared. A 1965 catalog contained a verbatim reprint from the 1957 catalog for the Russell-Hammer collections, with the exception that all plural references to "the Hammer brothers" had been altered to Armand's name alone. (After the donation to the university, Hammer began to assemble a new collection — a much more ambitious one, with nobody else's name attached.)[10]

Hammer's other "retirement" enterprise likewise had originated several years before his remarriage and likewise relied heavily on his brothers. In 1951 Hammer Galleries had previewed 1,450 items, mostly china and silver, from the private collection of Franklin and Eleanor Roosevelt and donated some of the proceeds to the National Foundation for Infantile Paralysis, a favorite Roosevelt charity. Partly as a result of that gesture, the next year they were afforded an opportunity to buy Campobello, on the island where FDR's parents had lived and where Franklin had courted Eleanor. Elliott, the second of the Roosevelts' four sons, had inherited Campobello from his father and needed money; he sold the huge, run-down thirty-four-room house to the Hammers for a reported $5,000.[11]

Owning, and restoring, Campobello gave Armand exactly what he had hoped: instant stature as a philanthropist apparently motivated by a desire to save a national treasure. The perception took hold even though Hammer had earlier said in a candid moment that he had thought of Campobello "mainly as an investment." Hammer wanted to be a statesman who counseled presidents; the newspaper reports of the Campobello purchase had conferred that status on him by noting that he had known Franklin Roosevelt "personally," even though there was only one recorded meeting between them.[12] Then and later Armand exploited Campobello for all the public relations it was worth.

However, it was Victor and Ireene who did the work of restoration. In Eleanor Roosevelt's papers, every piece of correspondence from the Hammers is written by Victor or Ireene, and nothing written by Eleanor is addressed to Armand. There was a genuine fondness between the Victor Hammers and Eleanor, a fondness from which Armand was excluded.[13]

Bette Barber, whom Harry Hammer had married after an extended bachelorhood, also became involved in the Campobello restoration. As had Armand and Victor before him, Harry fell in love with an intelligent, talented professional woman. Trained as a photographer and journalist, Bette produced a thirty-six-page pamphlet about Campobello, dedicating it to Rose Hammer and her three sons. It was filled with photographs meant to identify the Hammers with the estate in the public mind. A picture of Armand showed him playing the piano in the house while Victor and Ireene cuddled. Bette's Campobello photography exhibit opened in New York, with the proceeds going to the March of Dimes. Eleanor Roosevelt attended the opening.[14]

Campobello was a legitimate historic site, so it is reasonable to suppose that Hammer could have sold it for a large profit. In Considine's authorized biography, there is a passage about Hammer's "indignantly" rejecting a $500,000 offer for Campobello from a buyer wanting to commercialize the property. In his autobiography, Hammer slightly revised the story, saying he rejected the huge amount without thinking twice. Maybe the rejection occurred as Considine and Hammer told it. But that was not the whole story. Hammer entertained thoughts of selling Campobello, and the Roosevelts knew it. Franklin Junior said "there were [Roosevelt] family discussions about whether Armand Hammer would sell Campobello. It concerned us." During the summer of 1956, the Hammer brothers talked to a firm called Previews about disposing of Campobello.

Ireene Hammer and her daughter, Nancy, pleaded with Armand to reconsider. Ireene promised to cut back on entertainment and renovation expenses and cited the lucrative business the Campobello connection brought Hammer Galleries. In a prescient passage, she said the property's value was sure to increase: "Perhaps in ten years, maybe less, Franklin Delano Roosevelt can be more dispassionately and accurately judged for his greatness, and when he is, look what you have here! To sell now or even to put this place on the public market will bring us little money and lots of criticism, complete destruction of the fine publicity the family received for buying it, restoring it." Noting that Armand had not visited Campobello for two or three years, Ireene begged him to take a few days off from his busy schedule to see the changes for himself: "The mood is different. The aimlessness has disappeared. The tension is gone. It is something very special and much too precious to give up without serious and thoughtful consideration. . . . This is the only time I have been so bold as to interfere in order to ask, no, to fight for something. I think this is worth fighting for." If Armand were to continue to push for a sale, Ireene swore she would try to buy Campobello herself. Nine days later, Victor told Ireene that "the prospect of selling Campobello does not make me happy either, but it is one of those things that has to be faced." [15]

No sale occurred in 1956. But Armand refused to drop the idea. In 1959 he tried to sell Campobello for $60,000 through an advertisement in a Canadian newspaper. The next day, the *New York Times* reported the offer. Victor, reached by a *Times* reporter, said the Canadian newspaper had published the advertisement mistakenly. He added, perhaps defensively, that the Hammers had spent at least $60,000 improving the property. Notwithstanding the negative reaction to a possible sale, the Hammers continued to correspond with real estate brokers about Campobello.[16] But they never found the right buyer at the right price. In the end, Armand almost surely was pleased he had not sold to commercial developers, despite the profit he might have made. When Campobello did leave the Hammers' ownership, it was under circumstances that brought considerable goodwill, and international renown, to Armand.

During his "retirement" in Los Angeles, Hammer was involved in yet another venture, one in which he played a more hands-on role than at Campobello, where he was mainly the front man burnishing the family's image. The venture — as did so many others — harked back to his decade in the Soviet Union, where he had started with asbestos mining. This new enterprise involved mining, too, but the commodity was jade; it had grown out of Hammer's negotiations with Maxwell Perry, a Russian-born entrepreneur who had sold pencils in China during the late 1920s for Hammer. The two men had never lost touch, and in 1954 Perry had introduced Hammer to the jade business. Intrigued, Hammer helped Perry purchase a jade mine in Fremont County, Wyoming. Hammer and Perry established the headquarters of their new firm, Imperial Jade, at the Aberdeen-Angus farm in Colts Neck, New Jersey. Perry and his wife, Galina, lived there, enabling them to operate the jade business and care for the livestock as well. Among the investors were Frances, Victor, and Harry Hammer, and Hammer Galleries executives. Armand studied the jade business, even borrowing hard-to-find books from the Library of Congress through Senator Gore.[17]

When Hammer became part owner of Imperial Jade, its assets included 230 pounds of rough jade, $15,000 worth of finished or nearly finished merchandise, and $7,000 worth of equipment. The company advertised flower-design cabochons, rings, pins, and earrings "hand cut and carved in the Orient from our own jade." Looking for expertise, Hammer hired a seasoned sales manager, but within a year the manager resigned.[18] By late 1957, Hammer faced up to the need for his direct involvement. Thereafter he called on customers himself to pep up moribund sales.

But new complications arose because of a lawsuit filed by one of Imperial Jade's directors, Joseph Imhoff. Imhoff alleged fraud by Hammer in the handling of the company's assets. Hammer offered to settle for about $35,000. Imhoff refused. Fifteen years after he filed the lawsuit, the dispute ended, without Imhoff's prevailing.

In this case, Hammer's way of doing things had provoked legal action by somebody who should have been an ally. The evidence offered by Hammer's antagonists sometimes appeared to contain the ring of truth, but knowing something and proving it to the satisfaction of a judge or jury were different matters. In other cases, the charges against Hammer clearly were unfounded. When Hammer decided to fight, no legal expense was too large. As a result, Hammer usually won in court, but sometimes those victories were hollow given the huge costs, the loss of time, and the residual bitterness. The Imhoff lawsuit fell into that category.

The jade venture never took off, partly because Armand's attention was so divided. By 1957 he was devoting most of his time to new business interests in California. Hammer Galleries received only about one day a month of his time. Imperial Jade often received no more. However, Hammer never regretted buying the mine. Small potatoes though it was, he loved giving away jade key rings to friends and acquaintances. He sent one to President Dwight Eisenhower in 1958, along with a booklet on the beneficial qualities of jade. Hammer told the president that the Wyoming mine was the only commercial jade operation in the Western Hemisphere and that it produced jade as good as the Orient's.[19]

A more ambitious and time-consuming project for Hammer came with his purchase of the Mutual Broadcasting System, one of the world's largest commercial radio networks. Hammer's acquaintances initially expressed surprise at his involvement. Broadcasting was far afield from his other ventures and had no obvious organic link to his past. They finally realized that Hammer entertained visions of becoming another David Sarnoff or William Paley. Albert Gore wrote Hammer after learning of the Mutual Broadcasting purchase, "It should be a great challenge to one in retirement, particularly when the retired man has no other interests whatsoever other than oil and cattle, jade, art, real estate, stocks, bonds, a lovely wife, and a few other things."[20]

When rumors of a Mutual Broadcasting System sale began to circulate in the summer of 1957, Hammer's name never even came up. The leader of the buyers' syndicate appeared to be Paul Roberts, a Los Angeles radio station manager. The network, with about five hundred affiliates, was under the management of RKO Teleradio Pictures; in 1956, the network had reported a loss of about $400,000. Roberts signed an option to buy the network on July 25, 1957, agreeing to pay about $13,000 for the stock, plus $537,000 to reduce the network's indebtedness.[21]

Hammer's unexpected involvement in the purchasers' syndicate came at the urging of Frieda Hennock. Six years Hammer's junior, she had grown up in the same Bronx neighborhood and graduated from the same high school as he. Hennock had become a successful criminal lawyer while still in her twenties, at a time when few women practiced criminal law. She had received help from Hammer in 1948, when President Harry Truman appointed her as the first female member of the Federal Communications Commission. At that time Paul Fitzpatrick, New York State Democratic chairman, had asked Hammer to help win the seat for Hennock, so Hammer intervened through his acquaintance, Robert Taft, the Republican leader of the Senate. Hennock gained a reputation as a competent, strident, and independent commissioner during her six-year term. After leaving the FCC, she lined up Roger Stevens, a real estate broker turned theatrical producer, to finance the Mutual Broadcasting purchase. When Stevens pulled out unexpectedly, Hennock approached Hammer.[22]

Hammer knew the radio network was in weak shape, but he liked the price. Paul Roberts signed an agreement with Hammer and several partners whereby they promised to furnish almost all the money. (Armand and Frances sank some of their own money into the network — about $53,000 apiece.[23]) Roberts held on to some of the stock and assumed some of the debt, but Hammer received majority control of the board of directors. Ownership of Mutual Broadcasting was transferred to the Hammer-Roberts group on August 7, 1957, with Hammer as chairman and Roberts as president. With the stroke of a pen, Hammer was on a par with top executives of the major networks.

Thereafter Hammer and Frances started commuting between Los Angeles and New York. It was a wearing business, certainly the antithesis of a slow-paced retirement. Hammer, as usual, was incapable of taking a backseat to anybody. Despite his lack of technical knowledge about the radio business, he consolidated power at the network in his own hands. On February 27, 1958, the Hammer group called a board of directors meeting without Roberts's knowledge. The result was a reconstituted board, lacking any representatives of the Roberts group. Hammer quickly engineered the removal of Roberts, who allegedly was taking kickbacks from advertisers in return for discounted airtime. Hammer learned about the alleged scheme when an unhappy advertiser blew the whistle.

To get the goods on Roberts, Hammer and other Mutual directors secretly had searched his desk at night. They emptied drawers at Hammer's insistence. The documents they found were so incriminating, Hammer has said, that the next day he told Roberts to leave without protest or prepare to be prosecuted. For public consumption, Roberts said that he had tried to buy out Hammer because of different views about the network's programming but that Hammer prevailed. Privately, Roberts and his partners sued the Hammer group. Without hesitation, Hammer offered to purchase the stock options of the dissatisfied group, thereby averting a messy trial.[24]

Now firmly in control, Hammer visited the FCC to assure the commissioners that Mutual Broadcasting had no intention of folding. He bore gifts of jade for each commissioner, even though Jack Blume, Mutual's Washington lawyer, told him to drop the gift-giving plan.

"The propriety of how he would conduct himself was important," Blume said. "I told him that very clearly, but he did not listen." Blume knew it could be illegal for the commissioners to accept such a gift. Indeed, he said, some commissioners were offended, but Hammer barely noticed. Nothing discouraged him.[25]

Blair Walliser watched Hammer at this time, first as an executive with the Colgate shave cream account — one of Mutual's largest advertisers — then as a Mutual executive working for Hammer. "Of course, Armand is persuasive," Walliser said. "Everybody is charmed by him. I took a chance [in going to work for Hammer], even though the value of the network was zero."[26] Nobody was thriving under the arrangement that Hammer inherited, in which network affiliates owned the newscast on the hour and Mutual the newscast on the half hour. So Hammer decided that Mutual should provide more programming, including more news, sports, and features. The network signed journalist Walter Winchell and singer Kate Smith, both legends. It was another example of Hammer's penchant for drama. Before long, he was claiming he had achieved a quick turnaround, transforming Mutual into a money-making operation within months. Some industry observers were skeptical.

Then, just as suddenly as Hammer had gained control of the network, he surrendered it. The buyer, at a reported $2 million, was Hal Roach Studios, which was controlled by Alexander Guterma. *Television Digest,* putting the best face on the sale to Guterma, commented that it "gives shaky Mutual Broadcasting System a new lease on life — whether continuing as at present with news, commentary, and special events only . . . or revamped into a full-blown competitor of ABC, CBS, and NBC radio networks. . . ." Hammer, who negotiated the deal without the intervention of a broker, received a consulting contract and a position on the reconstituted board of directors. Walliser said Hammer and Guterma were two of the craftiest negotiators he had ever seen.[27]

How much Hammer knew about Guterma is uncertain. But he certainly could have chosen a sounder buyer. As *Broadcasting* magazine said after the fact, "Five months later, the Securities and Exchange Commission . . . announced that it was investigating Guterma's financial dealings. Later, a federal grand jury alleged that Guterma had pledged the use of Mutual Broadcasting System as a propaganda instrument for then Dominican Republic dictator Rafael Trujillo. Guterma was eventually sentenced to federal prison for stock fraud." The once-proud Mutual Broadcasting System entered bankruptcy court.[28]

Why had Hammer sold the network so precipitately, especially when he could have built it into a base for influencing public policy? Part of the answer was the hectic pace of the venture, especially the cross-country commuting. Walliser said Hammer's health was cracking under the strain; he had developed noticeable nervous tics. Although Hammer normally was stoic about his health, he has admitted it was poor during the 1950s. The pain from gallbladder disease, kidney stones, and prostate problems seemed unbearable at times. Another part of the answer was the lack of financial promise in the face of competition from other networks. Jack Blume said that "Armand Hammer was interested in making money. He did not care if he was doing the right thing or doing it the right way. He was always picking up the phone, always rushing to catch a plane, instead of listening. When he saw that he would not turn a fast buck with Mutual Broadcasting, he sold it."[29]

Whatever the truth of such speculation, the major reason for Hammer's willingness to sell Mutual seems clear — he had become deeply involved with another business that would be an obsession for the rest of his life. That business was oil.

PART IV

OIL TYCOON

13

Accidental Occidental

WHEN ARMAND HAMMER entered the oil business through the back door in 1956, he knew almost nothing about it and had no intention of becoming deeply involved. The company that drew his attention was Occidental Petroleum Corporation of Los Angeles, which since its founding in 1920 had done nothing to distinguish itself. Its little-known stock traded on second-tier West Coast exchanges. For 1955, Occidental Petroleum had reported assets of just $79,000. A new management had come on board, hoping to energize the company before it slid into oblivion. Shortly after that, Hammer — newly married and adjusting to Los Angeles — lent Occidental $50,000. Frances lent an equal amount. More and more, she was becoming Armand's partner in business as well as his partner in life, thanks to the money left her by her first husband.[1]

Armand and Frances never anticipated that they would make money through their investments in Occidental. On the contrary, they expected to lose it. In return for their loans, they received interests in two wells that Occidental planned to drill. But their expectation was that they would be dry holes, a tax loss to shield their personal wealth, which was in the highest tax bracket, from the federal government. Occidental as a tax shelter had been the idea of Sam Shapiro, a relative of Armand's who practiced accountancy in Los Angeles. Shapiro was a stockholder in an oil company owned by Dave Harris, who doubled as the new president of Occidental. If that first loan from the Hammers had resulted in the expected dry hole, it probably would have been the end of Armand Hammer, oilman. But the wells — one in Fresno County, California, another one near San Jose — came in.[2]

Before they knew it, Armand and Frances were hooked on the adventure of oil and gas exploration. Frances was so excited she had them buy a mobile home and then drive it to the newly drilled oil fields for overnight vigils. Frank Barton, a Los Angeles energy lawyer doing work for Harris, invited Hammer to lunch at the Los Angeles Petroleum Club to tap his financial resources further. But Armand showed no interest in becoming an owner of Occidental; Armand and Frances agreed only to another loan, this time for $112,500 each. Hammer acquaintance Louis Abrons, a Russian-born New York real estate developer, contributed about $225,000.[3]

Occidental used the money to acquire drilling rights in the Los Angeles suburb of Dominguez, land on which there already were producing wells. The owner of the rights was J. K. Wadley, a Texas wildcatter who needed a cash infusion. Wadley was torn about selling but shed his reluctance on meeting Hammer, whom he liked. (Wadley later called Hammer and H. L. Hunt the two keenest businessmen he ever knew.) The rights became Occidental's on October 16, 1956, for $1 million in cash and $750,000 in eighteen-month notes.[4] The day after Wadley, Hammer, and Hammer's lawyer Arthur Groman agreed on the transaction, Hammer drove to the area, buying a camera en route to take photographs of an honest-to-goodness producing field.

Shortly thereafter Occidental Petroleum and the Union Oil Company of California entered into a contract under which Occidental sold its crude oil from the Dominguez field to Union, which then distilled and marketed it. When Union Oil later requested termination of the contract, Hammer wrote to Styles Bridges, who reportedly had influence with Union chairman Reese Taylor. Hammer's letter betrayed his concern with image over substance, for he told Bridges that continuation of the contract was more a question of prestige than money.[5]

Prestige through association with larger oil companies assumed less importance in Hammer's mind as Occidental's good fortune accelerated. One of the Hammers' early investments — the Amber Lease, west of Bakersfield, California — turned out to be one of the most substantial. Together, Armand and Frances owned a 34 percent interest in the lease. That $100,000 investment grew to more than $5 million for Armand and $6 million for Frances by the time they decided to sell. It was all quite dizzying. During 1957, a resuscitated Occidental Petroleum drilled eight new wells and redrilled two others. Armand was involved deeply by then. In July he assumed the presidency, about the same time he started his management role at Mutual Broadcasting. Occidental sank more than $100,000 into the radio network, in addition to the personal investments of Armand and Frances. The two corporations were connected in Hammer's mind; he wanted Occidental to thrive through diversification.[6]

As usual, Hammer transformed whatever he touched, reshaping Occidental's board of directors in his image. Dave Harris stayed until early 1960 but possessed less and less authority in the company he had struggled to lift from near-worthlessness. Hammer added technical expertise in the person of Nico Van Wingen, a petroleum-engineering professor at the University of Southern California. He added political and business clout with Neil Jacoby, an acquaintance of Frances's who taught business administration at the University of California–Los Angeles and had served as an economic adviser to President Dwight Eisenhower. For marketing genius, he tapped Frederic Gimbel, his friend, who had retired to Los Angeles after helping run the family department store in New York.[7] Added legal skills came with Arthur Groman, who had defended Julian against the murder charge.

Maury Leibovitz played a vital role in the company's early growth, as Hammer's financial adviser. Hammer had met Leibovitz, an accountant, by chance in a restaurant; Leibovitz impressed Hammer with his insight into corporate finance. As a result, when Hammer was considering buying a company, he consulted Leibovitz. Meeting during normal business hours was complicated because Leibovitz had decided to switch careers, enrolling at the age of forty as a psychology student at USC. Hammer, used to working around the clock anyway, consulted with Leibovitz at unorthodox hours.[8]

After Leibovitz earned his doctorate, he joined the USC faculty as an assistant professor of clinical psychology but continued to answer Hammer's calls. Occidental employees viewed Leibovitz as a mysterious gray eminence. Some believed he provided valuable guidance; others considered him a rubber stamp for Hammer's ambitious expansion plans. Although Leibovitz never joined Occidental Petroleum in an official capacity, he did become an officer of Hammer's art gallery in later years. There he received credit for the fabulously successful marketing of contemporary artist LeRoy Neiman.[9]

In his early years at Occidental, Hammer needed help from Leibovitz: When he assumed the presidency, the full-time staff consisted of just three people. It was a tenuous existence. Hammer learned that Occidental was renting its office furniture. Its building lease was month to month because the landlord lacked confidence that Occidental would be around to pay off a long-term contract. The situation looked more stable after six months of Hammer's presidency. At the end of 1957,

Occidental reported assets of nearly $2 million and an annual profit of about $36,000. That was a far cry from the holdings and earnings of the major oil companies, but it represented a substantial improvement. Hammer was one of the largest shareholders at the time, although he never came close to owning 50 percent of the stock. His control, then and later, was based not on accumulation of stock, but rather on his forceful personality, keen mind, capacity for work, and incessant salesmanship. He persuaded acquaintances, and acquaintances of acquaintances, to buy Occidental Petroleum shares when those shares appeared to be nearly worthless.

Never before had Hammer been forced to think about satisfying stockholders or reporting earnings for the world to see, but he adapted beautifully to taking the helm of a public company. He employed management principles aimed at fast growth. One of these was to seek the advice of technical experts. He learned the identities of the best geologists, petroleum engineers, and drillers, then offered stock options to them as an inducement to join the company. Hammer believed employees with a chance to become rich by owning part of Occidental would perform more aggressively, which in turn would lead to faster growth.

Hammer bought Occidental cachet with Wall Street analysts by obtaining a listing on the American Stock Exchange. The company had completed its first significant acquisition — the drilling business of Eugene Reid, who at the time was briefly and uncharacteristically down on his luck. Dry well after dry well had set the experts wondering about him, and his company had lost money for three consecutive years. To some financial analysts, Hammer's willingness to give Reid 160,000 shares of Occidental stock for three drilling rigs and fifty-four seemingly marginal wells in Kern County, California, looked foolhardy. Hammer, however, believed instinctively that Reid would be a key player in a bright future for Occidental.[10]

Reid's son, Eugene Junior, better known as Bud, came with the acquisition. A geologist with valuable experience at other companies, he strengthened Occidental's nucleus of scientists. Bud had opposed selling the family business to Occidental Petroleum: "If I had had anything to say about the merger with Occidental, I would have said do not touch it with a ten-foot pole. I had been a Shell Oil engineer, and my calculations on Occidental were pessimistic. I thought Occidental's assets were overstated and Reid company's assets were understated. Dad [who died in 1971] went ahead because of Armand Hammer, because Dad saw something of his entrepreneurship, his ability to raise money from others." Bud received stock options at $4 a share (the price later reached $120). Eventually he persuaded fellow Stanford alumni Richard Vaughan and Robert Teitsworth to leave other employers for Occidental.[11] In the end, Bud, Vaughan, and Teitsworth helped turn the tide for Occidental.

One immediate benefit accruing to Occidental from the Reid purchase was that a Wall Street broker started promoting its stock. Louis Rezzonico, Jr., had known the Reids before the merger with Occidental and was impressed with their knowledge of the oil business. "They told me that Occidental might be a pig in a poke," Rezzonico said, "but I went ahead. I did not even know Armand Hammer at first. Dad and I came from the Wall Street scene — we tried to get a following for the stock." Rezzonico's father, a dentist, was a major stockholder in Pepsico, where he served on the board of directors. Louis Rezzonico, Sr., eventually accumulated so much Occidental stock that he joined the board, retaining his position until his death, in 1969. Through his connections, the elder Rezzonico interested prestigious Wall Street brokerages in Occidental.[12] The younger Rezzonico worked for several of those brokerages, all of which had the ability to lend respectability to Occidental and Hammer.

In the Reid acquisition, Hammer had used low-priced shares of Occidental stock as bait, which minimized the damage if the risky move went sour. It was a strategy that, with minor variations, worked again and again. In one case, Hammer wanted to acquire Parker Petroleum, a company headquartered in Oklahoma. Parker had filed for bankruptcy in 1958, the victim of a costly Texas gas-well blowout, mismanagement, or both, depending on who was testifying. Hammer, sensing a bargain and a nice fit with his company, began to acquire Parker shares for Occidental, compensating the sellers with Occidental stock. When he had acquired a substantial equity, he offered to operate Parker, pay its creditors, and remove it from bankruptcy.[13]

Under Hammer's plan, Occidental would pay $1 for each of 1.3 million shares of Parker stock, making Occidental a 51 percent owner. The bankruptcy judge thought the plan made sense, but the Securities and Exchange Commission judged it unfair to Parker shareholders. Stung by the agency's criticism and sobered by a pessimistic revised estimate of Parker's assets, Hammer decided he wanted out.[14]

But that was not the end of the affair. By then a new judge, Stephen Chandler, had assumed jurisdiction because the previous judge had died. Chandler ruled Occidental could not walk away from its obligations and ordered Hammer to proceed with the Parker reorganization. At the same time he disparaged Hammer from the bench, suggesting Hammer might be planning to "milk" Parker's profits. There were reports that Chandler in his chamber called Hammer a "son of a bitch" and labeled Occidental executives in general "shady characters, pirates, and vultures." Hammer asked a higher court to remove Chandler from the case on the grounds that the judge had demonstrated "personal bias." The appeals court took Chandler off the case, allowing Hammer to escape the Parker morass.[15]

Judge Chandler was not the only person who bridled at Hammer's methods. Some Occidental stockholders disliked the way he controlled the company during his first years there. The most publicized early challenge came from Milton Jaffe, who sued Hammer and his hand-picked directors for alleged fraud. Jaffe charged that Hammer "completely dominated" the board, whose members unfairly "reaped huge financial profits" because of Hammer's alleged manipulative genius. Occidental called the lawsuit "vicious and utterly without merit." Jaffe failed to prove his assertions conclusively.[16] The evidence left no doubt, however, about Hammer's acumen in profiting for himself as Occidental began to prosper.

Because of Hammer's early successes, many — probably the vast majority — of Occidental's early stockholders loved him. But there was always a vocal, litigious minority of unhappy stockholders who kept Occidental under siege in courtrooms across the nation. Later, after the company became the target of repeated legal actions by the SEC, that group grew in size. Through it all, Hammer's conduct was the main focus of concern. Few Fortune 500 corporations have come so totally under the sway of one person, especially one who owned such a tiny percentage of stock.

Hammer's solo performance was especially impressive because he was a novice in the energy business, while many of his subordinates had been in the industry for decades. It was, from the beginning, one of those mysteries of human chemistry. The other officers of Occidental were intelligent people, many of whom saw Hammer's flaws: his dominance of the corporate hierarchy, his desire to cut ever-bigger deals, his thirst for publicity that would propel him into the corporate and social elites. Some of the executives and directors most captivated by him admitted he lacked the qualities they would choose in a friend. Yet they voluntarily became planets in orbit around Hammer's blinding sun. Later, many of those planets left orbit involuntarily, fired to settle real or imagined scores. A few, belatedly aware they were becoming the kind of sycophants they so despised, left voluntarily.

Hammer exercised his will during his early years at Occidental to chart an unusual course for the company, a course that harked back to his entrepreneurial roots in the Soviet Union. There was speculation among Hammer watchers — especially those who were obsessively anti-Communist — about whether he had served as a Soviet agent in the West, complete with a control officer based in Moscow. Even many Hammer watchers with a world view more accepting of Soviet-American détente believed he must have agreed to some kind of formal quid pro quo with the Russian government to obtain his special status there.[17] But if Hammer in fact entered into such an agreement, its existence has been well concealed. American federal agencies that kept him under surveillance for seven decades either failed to find it or chose to keep it secret.

Rather, what Hammer appears to have had in his favor since 1960 was the trail he blazed as an American entrepreneur in the Soviet Union in the 1920s. That advantage without doubt made his case unique, that and his distinct point of view. He had three goals: to establish Occidental as a multinational corporation, promote peace through trade, and renew the kind of citizen diplomacy he had practiced with Lenin.

The time seemed ripe in 1960 for Hammer's renewal of contact with the Soviet Union. Soviet leader Nikita Khrushchev had visited the United States in 1959, a breakthrough in relations between the two countries. Moreover, Khrushchev knew about the Hammers. When Eleanor Roosevelt entertained the Soviet premier at Hyde Park in September 1959, a *New York Post* columnist reported that the "guest list . . . included Victor Hammer, the art dealer. . . . When Victor Hammer was introduced to the guest of honor and asked [him] if he remembered the Hammer pencil factory, Khrushchev said, 'Who does not remember it?' "[18] Thanks to Eleanor Roosevelt's intervention, the Soviet government allowed Armasha, then age thirty-three, to visit Victor in America in 1960.*

Like Khrushchev, President-elect John Kennedy knew about Hammer. The two had met on three occasions: once in the late 1950s during a twenty-minute chat after a committee hearing involving Senator Kennedy and Senator Gore, who introduced them; a second time dur-

---

* After he returned to Moscow, Armasha reportedly spoke harshly about his uncle Armand. Some of the Russians in Armasha's social circle believed that Victor wanted his son to defect and that Armasha had considered doing so. But they speculated that Armand Hammer was opposed because of the damage a defection could do to his plans for a renewal of lucrative links to the Soviet Union. (Correspondence between Victor and Armasha Hammer, Victor Hammer papers; and Finder, *Red Carpet.*)

ing a Kennedy fund-raising dinner in Los Angeles in 1960, when the senator, then a presidential candidate, stopped by Hammer's table for a brief word; and a third time, in December 1960, when Hammer's yacht *Shadow Isle* just happened to encounter Kennedy's yacht at Palm Beach. Hammer next saw Kennedy from a distance — at the inaugural on January 20, 1961, as Gore's guest. Later that same week, Gore and Kennedy spoke at a White House reception. Kennedy said something about the Soviets' employing slave labor to produce crabmeat for export. The U.S. government gave credence to the reports, he said, which the Soviets vigorously denied. Gore suggested to the president that he send Hammer to investigate firsthand.

While such high-level contacts were developing, Hammer used his Gore and Roosevelt connections to increase his chances of meeting top Soviet officials if and when he visited Moscow. Victor asked Eleanor Roosevelt to write introductions to the Soviet leadership for his brother. Armand sent along suggested wording, one paragraph of which read: "Dr. Hammer was a friend of my husband and myself and my sons and has visited us in the White House and we have visited him in his home. We hold him in high esteem." Mrs. Roosevelt revised the letter by pointedly removing the words "and myself" and changing the *we*'s to *they*'s.[19] She was willing to send a helpful letter, probably because of her fondness for Victor and Ireene, and because the Hammer family had helped her sons Elliott and James. But she could not bring herself to call Armand her friend.

Hammer asked Gore — who apparently harbored no reservations about Armand's character — to help beyond the initial suggestion to Kennedy. To make sure Gore understood his role in the young Soviet Union, Hammer sent the senator a copy of *The Quest of the Romanoff Treasure*. On Hammer's behalf, Gore wrote to Anastas Mikoyan, by then a high-ranking minister, the same man who had met Hammer in the early 1920s during the delivery of Fordson tractors to the Soviet provinces.[20]

The upper-echelon interventions worked. Armand and Frances Hammer departed for the Soviet Union in early February 1961, less than a month after Kennedy's inauguration. Yet, although Hammer indicated otherwise, there is evidence that Kennedy knew little or nothing about the trip until Hammer's return. All planning appears to have been done through Luther Hodges, Kennedy's secretary of commerce, who had demonstrated interest in the Soviet Union before joining the Kennedy cabinet, having visited Russia in 1959 as governor of North Carolina.[21]

The urgency Hammer attached to his journey probably sprang more from his own mind than from anything anyone in the Kennedy administration said. Hammer was impatient to make Occidental Petroleum an international force, to enter the realm of citizen diplomacy. He sensed the wisdom of returning to the Soviet Union in 1961 to play his Lenin card. As Soviet historian Nina Tumarkin observed:

In 1930, Stalin had laid Lenin to rest in the granite Lenin mausoleum as the emerging Stalin cult gradually eclipsed and ultimately eroded the formalized veneration of Lenin. Now, in 1961, the reverse process took place as the immortal Lenin arose to drive Stalin into the nether regions of the Kremlin Wall . . . Lenin's spirit was restored to its original exalted status and achieved new heights.[22]

On his way to the Soviet Union, Hammer stopped in Rome — one of several side trips suggested by Hodges — where he met U.S. foreign service officials. Despite his lack of experience in Italian affairs, Hammer showed no hesitation in pointing out problems bedeviling trade relations between the two countries. He saw that American corporations had failed to demonstrate the requisite ingenuity to break into the increasingly attractive Italian market. Grounded in pragmatism as he was, he did not issue a general indictment and leave it at that; he provided specifics. For example, the Italians preferred the technology of American refrigerators but refused to buy the huge ones produced for the American market. Why had U.S. manufacturers failed to discern that? he wondered. He was amazed to find only twenty-eight IBM computers in Italy — with just a dozen experienced operators to make them run. Why had the company failed to train more Italian-speaking technicians?[23] Such perceptiveness illustrated to his new friends in government how he had been able to dominate the marketplace in so many realms.

Hammer visited Libya, too; at the time it was a seemingly inconsequential stopover, but not from Armand's viewpoint. The large, underdeveloped kingdom was beginning to experience a land rush by Western oil companies; Hammer's count showed nineteen oil companies doing business there, with an equal number hoping to. Some of those companies had entered into agreements with individuals claiming to have influence with the king. Hammer, seeking to undercut them, wrote Hodges about the importance of the Libyan oil reserves, recommending American government assistance to develop closer commercial ties. Despite the problems of doing business in Libya, he was excited by the possibilities there for Occidental. Indeed, he could hardly wait to present his ideas to his board of directors.[24]

When Hammer arrived in Moscow on February 11, he did so with uncharacteristic discreetness. That was calculated. He had no idea how the Soviets would treat him after a thirty-year hiatus, and until he could be certain of a successful mission, he saw no reason to publicize his presence. Officials in the U.S. Embassy were skeptical that he would accomplish anything. He seemed to almost everyone to be an anachronism. But the embassy staff was in for a surprise. Hammer's association with Lenin turned out to be magic, especially when combined with an imprimatur of sorts from the Kennedy administration.[25]

Hammer's first meeting occurred on February 14, with V. M. Vinogradov, Soviet chief of trade for Western countries; M. N. Gribkov, chief of the American trade section; and William Morrell, Jr., the American embassy's liaison for economic affairs. Hammer explained his dual role as a private citizen and emissary for Hodges and Gore. Expressing doubt that Congress would ease trade restrictions, he suggested the Russians accomplish change through the White House and cabinet agencies.[26]

The next day, Hammer met with Anastas Mikoyan, first deputy premier. Hammer's Russian was rusty, but he used it to good effect during the session. The two men reminisced about their first meeting in the Russian provinces four decades earlier, then got down to business. Mikoyan expressed hope that the crabmeat ban would be lifted. He also articulated his views about settling Lend-Lease debts from World War II, most-favored-nation trade status, inadequacies of recent U.S. secretaries of commerce, Vice President Richard Nixon's hostile comments during a 1959 Moscow visit, American shortsightedness in failing to obtain Soviet orders for steel pipe, and direct commercial airplane service between the two nations.

Hammer responded that the Soviet government needed to improve overall relations with the United States before receiving credits and most-favored-nation status. He offered a specific suggestion: The Soviets could send their top paintings on a tour of America, with Eleanor Roosevelt chairing a committee to supervise the undertaking. Mikoyan liked the idea. Hammer then turned the conversation to cattle breeding, showing Mikoyan the 1954 dispersion-sale catalog and relating the virtues of American meat.[27]

After the meeting with Mikoyan, Hammer's business in Moscow appeared to be finished. His hoped-for meeting with Khrushchev did not appear to be panning out. So he and Frances turned their attention to a family reunion, having dinner with Vavara Hammer, Victor's first wife; Armasha; and Larissa, Armasha's wife. In a letter home describing the event, Frances said she and Armand were leaving for London the next day, then flying to New Delhi, where Hammer was scheduled to meet Prime Minister Jawaharlal Nehru.[28]

But Frances and Armand were in for a pleasant surprise. At Mikoyan's urging, Khrushchev decided to meet Hammer face-to-face. The session took place on February 17 in Khrushchev's Kremlin office. By Hammer's reckoning, it lasted two hours and five minutes. Also present was Anatoly Dobrynin, chief of the American division for the Soviet Ministry of Foreign Affairs and later ambassador to Washington.

Khrushchev and Hammer conducted their conversation in Russian. Khrushchev began by discussing the Aberdeen-Angus sale catalog that Hammer had given Mikoyan. He had enjoyed American meat on his visit to the United States, he said, and he conceded that it was better than Soviet beef. Hammer, ever the inspired supplicant, promised to ship a bull to Khrushchev to complement some Angus heifers already sent by President Eisenhower and Lewis Strauss, the former chairman of the U.S. Atomic Energy Commission and a fellow cattle breeder.[29]

Hammer then presented Khrushchev with a copy of *The Quest of the Romanoff Treasure*. The interpreter translated the final two pages into Russian. In those pages, written nearly thirty years earlier, Hammer had raised the question of whether "the Russian experiment of government ownership on a vast scale . . . will be successful." He had seen progress during the first decade of Bolshevik rule:

> Whatever may be said of a socialist system, the centralized control of the sources of supply and production has much to recommend it. Will some scheme of such centralized control be evolved to take the place of our present wasteful and planless system of overproduction? The present world-wide economic crisis would seem to indicate that we may yet have to borrow a page from Russia's Five-Year Plan.

Khrushchev remarked that the passage showed "considerable understanding and farsightedness." He gave Hammer an engraved gold automatic pencil to commemorate the factory Hammer had operated.[30]

When Hammer told Khrushchev he had been denied permission to visit the factory, Khrushchev told Dobrynin to see about arranging it.[31] Hammer then proceeded to the U.S. Embassy to report to the acting American ambassador in Moscow. During their discussion, a call came from the Kremlin that a Russian driver would pick up Armand and Frances for a trip to the pencil factory.

At the plant, Hammer was thrilled to discover that some of the old employees remembered him. One woman tearfully embraced him while recalling it was she who had taught Victor how to work the machinery. The celebration in the boardroom included caviar, champagne, and vodka. Khrushchev later used Hammer's factory visit to score propaganda points, telling his appreciative Russian audience: "When I received this American, he asked permission to visit the factory and look it over. He left satisfied and several of the old workers remembered Hammer and said 'See how our former boss is pleased.' "[32]

The next day Hammer, tired from the celebration, saw Khrushchev again, at a reception for Communist leaders of other nations. Khrushchev met Frances there and flirted with her. After the reception, Hammer canceled his trip to India (and also Japan and Thailand) so he could return to Washington with an immediate report for the Kennedy administration.[33]

On February 25, Hammer met with Senator Gore and Secretary Hodges in Washington. Hodges had prepared for the meeting by talking with Llewellyn Thompson, the American ambassador to the Soviet Union, trying to glean what he could about the Hammer-Khrushchev session. Hodges and Thompson were suspicious of Hammer. They could not figure out why Khrushchev had received him while refusing to see official government representatives. In a memorandum to Secretary of State Dean Rusk, Hodges commented that "we had a security check made on Dr. Hammer, which, as you probably know, was not too conclusive." With Hodges and Gore listening, Hammer reviewed his three major meetings in Moscow, adding an account of a recent two-month visit to the United States by his nephew, Armasha. Hodges wrote Rusk: "According to Dr. Hammer, the nephew has no desire to migrate from the Union of Soviet Socialist Republics. The nephew is satisfied with the Soviet Union, particularly so since the death of Stalin."[34]

Hammer's reports led to a reconsideration of the American ban on importation of Soviet crabmeat. Until reading Hammer's findings, American officials had failed to understand how upset the Soviets were. On February 26, 1961, Rusk wrote the president that he wanted to approve crabmeat imports:

> We believe that it is of great importance at this juncture to take some action which would further our objective of developing the channels of communications with the Soviets. Removal of the ban on the importation of Soviet crabmeat would be a tangible demonstration of our desire to improve United States–Soviet relations. It would remove a barrier to

. . . trade which Soviet leaders apparently regard as particularly discriminatory.[35]

By now burning to circulate the news of his coup in seeing Khrushchev, Hammer sent a written account to Eleanor Roosevelt through Victor.[36] She in turn sent a copy to Adlai Stevenson, the U.S. ambassador to the United Nations. Soon, the blackout surrounding Hammer's visit ended. On March 7, United Press International released a story that began with Hammer's suggestion to Khrushchev about paying off the Lend-Lease debt in exchange for increased trade. The *New York Times* followed the next day with an account of the meeting, supplied by Hammer.

The media attention and high-level Soviet contacts only whetted Hammer's appetite — he yearned to make a personal report to President Kennedy. Working through James Roosevelt, he prevailed. On September 15, 1961, he, Roosevelt, and the president chatted briefly. The meeting was not on the president's official schedule. There may have been no special reason for that, or it may have been an intentional omission by a president worried about Hammer's links to the Soviet Union, links responsible for Hammer's equivocal security check. Hammer has said Kennedy not only thanked him for improving Soviet-American relations but also expressed interest when told of Khrushchev's comment that Communism must attain a higher standard of living for its peoples to compete with capitalism.

Thereafter, for the next two years, until the president was assassinated, Hammer gave frequent advice to the administration. One initiative was meant to help the Allied powers gain permanent access to West Berlin. He formulated a detailed plan, then asked Gore to present it to the White House. He also offered to use his access to Khrushchev on the proposal's behalf.[37] The initiative circulated at high levels but apparently failed to influence ongoing negotiations. In fact, Hammer never succeeded in becoming a Kennedy administration insider.

Outside Washington, however, he gained widespread publicity and enough goodwill to last him a lifetime by donating Campobello to the U.S. and Canadian governments. Armand has explained the donation by saying that his mother's death, in 1960, and Eleanor Roosevelt's death, on November 7, 1962, set him to thinking seriously about Campobello's future because it was vacant so often. He said a donation had been in the recesses of his mind since August 10, 1962, when President Kennedy dedicated a new bridge between Lubec, Maine, and Campobello Island. In his dedication speech, Kennedy had noted that the bridge was a symbol of better U.S.-Canadian relations; a park at Campobello, Hammer opined, would strengthen the bonds even more.[38]

Hammer acted on May 10, 1963, after hearing a report of a meeting between Kennedy and Canadian prime minister Lester Pearson at which the president expressed a wish for an international park in memory of Franklin Roosevelt. Hammer has said he promptly called Senator Edmund Muskie of Maine, who allegedly supported the gift. Muskie, however, has said he remembers no such communication.[39] Hammer called James Roosevelt, who said he would inform Kennedy about the donation — as a Roosevelt son, as a friend of Hammer's, and as Hammer's representative in Congress.

Within hours, Hammer received a message from the White House that the president would call the next morning. Hammer was ecstatic. He set up recording equipment to capture the call in his home, complete with loudspeakers so family members and Occidental executives could hear the conversation. The president called at the appointed hour. Hammer asked if he had received a copy of the telegram concerning the donation. When Kennedy said no, Hammer put the president on hold while he went to search his bedroom for the text. To his horror, he could not find it. Frances, beside herself, scolded him for keeping the president waiting. Hammer picked up the telephone, apologized, then recited the text of the telegram as best he could from memory. Later, when comparing the recording of the conversation with the text of the telegram, Hammer found he had repeated it verbatim.[40]

After talking with Hammer, Kennedy announced news of the donation to the media. The acclaim was immediate. Most of the articles credited Armand alone; Harry and Bette, Victor and Ireene, received virtually no attention, even though they were more involved in the renovation of Campobello than Armand had been.[41] Hammer used the gift to heighten his visibility at the White House and in Congress, bombarding the president, senators, and representatives with examples of the outpouring of gratitude.

Hammer also offered Kennedy the use of his indoor pool during an upcoming visit by the president to Los Angeles. The invitation specified that the pool was glass-enclosed, with sliding doors connecting it to the garden. Hammer informed Kennedy that the pool was thirty-four feet long and twenty feet wide; the water was kept at 95 degrees Fahrenheit and the air at 80 degrees. Kennedy politely declined the invitation. Disappointed but unbowed, Hammer, through James Roosevelt, asked the president to autograph a picture. Kennedy complied, giving Hammer another inscribed memento for the growing collection displayed prominently in his office. Kennedy also appointed Hammer a trustee of the Eleanor Roosevelt Memorial Foundation, newly created to raise $25 million for causes that had been close to the First Lady's heart — UN programs, human rights, and cancer research.[42]

Meanwhile, negotiations between the United States and Canada over Campobello were under way. Such a donation, to two governments, was unprecedented. The negotiations had proceeded far enough by January 1964 that Lester Pearson and Lyndon Johnson, who had succeeded to the presidency after the assassination of Kennedy the previous November, met to sign the Roosevelt Campobello International Park agreement. Hammer, who attended the White House ceremony, curried favor afterward with Johnson's staff by sending thank-you notes and Campobello guidebooks to them.[43] (Although Hammer negotiated at the top, he understood the importance of cultivating underlings — in administration after administration, he sent gifts to midlevel White House and cabinet department employees. In the long run, he asked for big favors in return. But in the short run he requested only a photograph with an inscription.) To Mrs. Johnson, Hammer presented not only the Campobello guidebook, but also jade gifts.*

After passage of the enabling legislation, Mrs. Johnson spoke at Campobello on August 20, 1964, praising Hammer by name. Armand sent her his thanks for her generous words, enclosing $1,000 from himself and another $1,000 from Frances for Lyndon Johnson's election campaign. Mrs. Johnson responded by saying that "my words about you and your brothers spoken at Campobello were not adequate to express all that was in my heart. Everyone is so grateful to you for your gift in memory of our beloved President Roosevelt and his wife."[44]

Thereafter Hammer took advantage of the Campobello donation to build bridges to the Johnson White House, Congress, and the federal bureaucracy. For the first time he truly had the ear of a president. Throughout the rest of Johnson's term, Hammer used his access to promote himself and Occidental Petroleum. Partly as a result, in the 1960s Occidental started a metamorphosis that transformed it into one of the world's largest companies.

---

* Interestingly, Hammer remained a Kennedy family supporter while cultivating the Johnsons, despite Lyndon Johnson's hatred for Robert Kennedy. When Robert ran for the Democratic presidential nomination, in 1968, Hammer was one of his few wealthy business supporters. Even after Kennedy's assassination, on June 6, 1968, Hammer retained access to the Kennedy power and mystique because of an ongoing relationship with Senator Edward Kennedy. (Charles Spalding oral history, March 22, 1969, conducted by Larry Hackman, John Fitzgerald Kennedy Library, Boston.)

14

Shaking Up the Seven Sisters

THE CHAIRMAN of Occidental Petroleum possessed boundless optimism — about bringing hostile nations to the peace table, finding cures for dread diseases, and making profits in business ventures. During the 1960s, Armand Hammer needed every bit of that optimism. Few Wall Street analysts gave Occidental much chance of becoming a multinational company, let alone one that would rise to the top twenty of the Fortune 500. After all, Occidental's gross for 1960 was only $2.5 million, and the bottom line showed a net loss of $127,000.[1]

If Hammer truly had been interested in retirement with Frances, 1961 would have been a smart time to do it. He and she possessed more than enough money to live well, and Occidental had turned out to be a tax shelter for their income. Hammer had achieved his triumphant return to the Soviet Union; his meeting with Khrushchev would have allowed him to practice statesmanship as a citizen-diplomat in his retirement. He could continue to build his art collection and make a name for himself as a philanthropist in the war against cancer.

As it turned out, he achieved all those goals, and many more, but without retiring. Nor did it take long for his eternal optimism to be rewarded. A turning point for Occidental came in 1961, with the discovery of gas in the Lathrop field, about ninety miles southeast of San Francisco, in the vicinity of Stockton. The acquisition of the Eugene Reid drilling company in 1959 was the necessary condition for the discovery. Without the scientific knowledge and youthful enthusiasm of employees such as Bud Reid, Richard Vaughan, and Robert Teitsworth, Occidental might have ignored the well-concealed potential of the Lathrop field.

A hint of the big break appeared in the December 19, 1960, issue of *Oil and Gas Journal,* an industry publication. An article by Bud Reid, Vaughan, and Teitsworth carried the headline "Why Explore in California's Sacramento Valley?" The authors made a case that it was logical to look for natural gas in the as yet untapped valley, which extended 205 miles, from Redding to Modesto. Reid, Vaughan, and Teitsworth were back in print sixteen months later. This time the headline said "Sacramento Valley Booms Ahead."

What had occurred between those two articles was the playing out of a hunch. At least two multinational companies already had drilled in the Lathrop field. But Occidental's Teitsworth thought the giants had given up too easily. Occidental moved in equipment, planning to drill to 8,600 feet if necessary, approximately 3,000 feet deeper than anybody else. It was not a decision made lightly. Hammer had encountered difficulty raising enough money to proceed. He sold ten drilling investment units for $32,000 apiece; Frances bought one, and he bought half of a unit to help the cause. But banks had refused to lend Occidental additional money at what Hammer considered a fair rate, so he ordered drilling to proceed with no assurance of adequate financial reserves.

When Gene Reid reached 6,500 feet with nothing to show for it, Hammer began to feel queasy. Then the good news arrived: At 6,900 feet, Reid found what turned out to be the second-biggest gas field in California history, worth hundreds of millions of dollars.[2] Hammer wrote the stockholders that Occidental could receive net income of nearly $11 million a year for each of five years under a contract being negotiated with Pacific Gas and Electric Company.

Executives of the latter had been discouraging when first approached; the utility already was obligated to bring gas in from outside California, and Occidental's supplies threatened to upset that plan. Hammer thereupon approached the city of Los Angeles with an offer to sell the new gas at prices lower than the utility's lowest rate. Pacific Gas and Electric quickly changed its tune and signed long-term agreements to buy Occidental Petroleum's supply.

For the first time it looked as if Occidental could begin to pay dividends, and maybe expand its exploration program. Hammer told his wife her $32,000 unit was worth $1 million. Frances called Morrie Moss, an investor and later a company director, who said he planned to hang on to his units for a while; he thought they would be even more valuable than $1 million each. Frances followed Moss's advice, which turned out to be correct.

Hammer now allowed himself to dream of competing with the major oil companies, known popularly (and sometimes derisively) as the Seven Sisters: Exxon, Gulf, Mobil, Socal, Texaco, British Petroleum, and Royal Dutch Shell. No longer the proprietor of a money loser whose main function was to shelter outside income from taxes, Hammer acquired the Signet Oil and Gas Company, increasing Occidental's reserves through expansion as well as exploration. About this time a newspaper columnist called Occidental one of "the new Cinderella companies. It is finding oil and gas where the smart money in the business knew it could not exist." At the end of 1961, Occidental had 159 producing oil and gas wells. Revenue for that year had jumped to more than $4 million from less than $3 million the year before. The bottom line showed a $1 million profit.[3]

Financial analysts and business journalists marveled at the way Hammer raised money from Occidental directors, stockholders, and companies outside the oil and gas world. A *Business Week* reporter wrote of Hammer's success in obtaining $6 million — $4.5 million of it from Occidental stockholders' buying units costing a minimum of $15,000 each. The same reporter wrote wonderingly of a $15 million advance payment by Mutual Life Insurance Company of New York in exchange for future gas finds from the Lathrop field — an insurance-company investment that paid off for both sides.[4]

Occidental's California discoveries opened diversification possibilities for an entrepreneur as daring as Hammer, who decided the company should expand into the fertilizer business. He had overseas markets in mind, including the Soviet Union. Such an expansion would fit neatly into his conception of Occidental Petroleum as a natural-resources conglomerate; his experience with the Mutual Broadcasting System had taught him the dangers of trying to build a widely diversified company. In the ensuing expansion, Hammer mixed his rapaciousness for the big score with his keen sense of how to make deals that gave the impression of helping all the parties involved. There would be obstacles — he knew many Occidental directors, executives, and stockholders would be content to play safe, to remain a profitable, small independent oil and gas company sticking to its business in California. But Hammer wanted to be the biggest. His instincts told him that in order to do so, Occidental needed something to offer foreign leaders whose countries were bursting with natural-resource potential.

It seemed obvious to him that developing countries he had visited needed to achieve self-sufficiency in food production. Accordingly, those nations needed affordable fertilizer that could nourish crops on marginal land. Thus the deal: In return for fertilizer, they could offer natural resources that were doing little good sitting in the ground.

To traditional businesspeople, some of them Hammer's own, his plan sounded risky. But by then he had gained control. The chief opponent on his board of directors was Gene Reid, who wanted Occidental to stick with domestic oil and gas exploration. Hammer never fully convinced Reid of the wisdom of overseas ventures, but Reid never found the votes on Hammer's handpicked board to prevail. One secret of Hammer's control, despite his minority stock ownership, was the tangible wealth that the Lathrop field discovery bestowed on many of the directors. They might have joined the board originally as a favor to Hammer, but he had returned the favor by fattening their bank accounts through the appreciation of Occidental shares.[5]

A lesser-known weapon was the sheaf of undated resignation letters from directors that Hammer possessed. One of those directors was Hugh Ten Eyck, who joined the board after the company he worked for merged with Occidental. "It was a dominated board," Ten Eyck said. "You could speak freely, but you knew that [Hammer] always had that manila envelope with your undated resignation letter. . . . You signed that letter because he told you to. What were you going to do [when he asked]? Resign on the spot?"[6]

Robert Rose, Occidental's general counsel and a director, not only signed the undated resignation letter but said Hammer threatened to use it against him. The directors knew the practice was wrong — Hammer had received specific legal advice against it — but they failed to speak out publicly against him. Between 1962 and 1972 Hammer received undated resignation letters from ten directors. Nine of the executives were part of Occidental's management, which meant they depended on Hammer's goodwill for their salaries. During that same period, Hammer allowed fifteen other directors, ten from management and five outsiders, to serve without submitting such letters. Clearly, he trusted some directors to do his bidding more than he did others. When the Securities and Exchange Commission many years later learned about the practice, it reprimanded Hammer.[7] But by then the practice had served its purpose — Hammer's control of the board had been of such long duration that most Occidental employees and stockholders took it for granted.

Another way Hammer retained his iron grip was through his superb recall, aided by copious notes. He scribbled throughout meetings on folded paper that he divided into three vertical columns. Afterward, he gave the notes to his secretary, Dorothy Prellwitz, who cross-referenced them and placed them in a binder. Hammer worked around the clock seven days a week. He expected everybody to be available whenever he called. Stories of his telephone calls at three o'clock in the morning are legion. He thought nothing of interrupting wedding anniversaries, birthdays, and out-of-town vacations. When employees were unavailable, he could be unforgiving.[8]

Wielding his dominance, Hammer encountered little trouble in obtaining approval for the early acquisitions that he had targeted to transform Occidental into a multinational natural-resources conglomerate. A significant early purchase was International Ore and Fertilizer Company. It marketed agricultural chemicals in fifty-nine countries. Hammer had heard from the U.S. commercial counselor in Tripoli, Libya, that International Ore would be a good outlet to market ammonia produced by a proposed Occidental fertilizer plant in Libya — a proposal Hammer believed would help his company win an oil concession from the Libyan monarchy in upcoming competitive bidding.

Hammer eventually decided he wanted more than a marketing agreement, though; he wanted to buy International Ore. Seeking out Hugh Ten Eyck, then an Interore executive, Hammer entertained him on his yacht, offering him an attractive package to join Occidental if the sale went through. Ten Eyck soon thereafter met Hammer in Italy, where Henry Leir, the owner of International Ore and other natural-resource companies, was staying. Ten Eyck voted in favor of the merger: "I felt we had gone as far as we could go as a marketer." But the Hammer-Leir negotiations got off to a bad start. "Both men were afraid the other would take him in," Ten Eyck said. In the Montecatini hotel where the negotiations were in progress, Ten Eyck happened to see lawyer Joseph Alioto, soon to be elected mayor of San Francisco. Alioto, on vacation with his family, coincidentally represented Leir. Ten Eyck said the sale would benefit everyone if the two tycoons could agree; Alioto consented to enter the negotiations. "I had to shuttle between their rooms," Alioto said. "You could not put them together." With Alioto's assistance, Hammer and Leir found a middle ground in the wee hours of the morning.[9]

Hammer's version of the negotiations differs substantially from those of Ten Eyck, Alioto, and Leir. It also contains a telling anecdote: Before departing for Italy, Hammer said he had researched Leir's likes and dislikes. Hammer's conclusion — Leir was a snob. Accordingly, Armand and Frances flew to London, where they bought the most expensive white Rolls-Royce they could find. They shipped the car to Paris and motored from there to Italy, to the hotel where Leir awaited. According to Hammer, the car caused a sensation when it pulled up.

In fact, he said, King Olaf V of Norway, a guest at the swank hotel, rushed outside to admire it. In Hammer's account, found in his 1987 autobiography, Leir was so impressed that he was primed to reach quick agreement on a merger.

This account may have been a great story to tell friends, but the evidence is overwhelmingly against it. Ten Eyck and Alioto agreed that Hammer's original premise was faulty; Leir was no snob. "Mr. Leir thought it [the Rolls] was gauche," Alioto said. "He got around in a Bentley, believing it to be less conspicuous." Ten Eyck and Alioto also agreed that the negotiations went poorly at first, not smoothly, as Hammer said. Leir himself recalled, "I have known Armand Hammer personally since 1963 . . . I feel we are on good terms. But when I saw his last account of the Interore transaction, I resented it. It is simply not true."[10]

In any case, Hammer obtained the company, which proved to be a vital element in Occidental's rise. After closing the deal, he sent a telegram to the White House, telling President John Kennedy that James Roosevelt would be requesting a meeting in which he and Hammer could discuss how Occidental would feed the world's hungry masses, thus making Communism less attractive to them.[11]

An acquisition that fit with International Ore was the Best Fertilizer Companies, which operated plants in the western United States. Best needed gas from Occidental's California fields to produce ammonia, an ingredient in its products; Hammer wanted a fertilizer manufacturer in Occidental's stable to work with the International Ore marketing organization. Hammer began negotiations with Lowell Berry, the founder of Best Fertilizers. The two men met on May 21, 1963 — Hammer's sixty-fifth birthday. They reached agreement quickly, but both men were too strong-willed and proud to be partners. The next year, Hammer fired Berry, citing his conduct during labor problems at the industrial site in Lathrop, California, which produced ammonia dedicated to fertilizer manufacturing, as well as other hazardous chemical substances. The union members at the plant had struck on July 31, 1964, and Hammer had thereupon ordered Berry to attend a negotiating session with the union on August 26. Berry had refused. Hammer had stepped in, reportedly helped settle the strike, and then fired Berry for alleged disobedience and mismanagement. Motivated partly by his previously expressed anger at his $50,000 annual salary — $10,000 less than both Hammer's and Gene Reid's — Berry sued. After an eighteen-day trial, Hammer largely prevailed, although Berry salvaged some pension benefits.[12]

While the case was in court, Hammer struck at Berry, asking Sena-

tor Albert Gore to convince the Treasury Department that it should
investigate the Lowell Berry Foundation. Gore did mention the matter
to the Treasury Department but, queasy about the propriety of his
intervention, soft-pedaled it.[13]

In the end, Berry got revenge of sorts. The Lathrop plant, which
Hammer alleged had been poorly managed by Berry, caused big problems for Occidental. The SEC cited Occidental for its failure to disclose
the costs associated with environmental contamination by the plant.
The federal government and the state of California sued Occidental for
discharging hazardous wastes there. Workers claimed their handling of
toxic chemicals at the plant had caused them to lose their fertility.
Newspapers published articles with headlines that sullied the company's image. Internal memorandums told of how water from the plant's
waste pond trickled into a neighboring field, where a dog waded into
it, licked itself, and died. Still, despite the troubles, from a strictly commercial standpoint the Best acquisition made sense; the operation found
an important niche in a newly synergistic company. Occidental added
smaller fertilizer-related companies at a rapid pace after that.[14]

Yet another controversial acquisition during 1963 — part of Hammer's impatience to put Occidental into the fertilizer business — was
Jefferson Lake Sulphur Company, headquartered in New Orleans. The
company mined sulfur, used in fertilizer production. At the time of the
merger, Occidental listed assets of about $42 million. Adding Jefferson
Lake's assets of about $35 million thus nearly doubled Occidental's size.
The acquisition also gave Occidental a presence in Canada, where a
Jefferson Lake subsidiary produced natural gas and extracted sulfur
from hydrogen sulfide gas.[15]

Some Occidental executives were nervous about Jefferson Lake, which
reportedly had approached Hammer out of financial desperation. Sulfur prices were volatile, many of Jefferson Lake's key indicators looked
weak, and Hammer seemed to be pursuing size for size's sake. To give
Occidental more visibility, Hammer had been aching to secure a listing
on the New York Stock Exchange. The Jefferson Lake merger had
given Occidental enough assets for Hammer to submit a listing application. If his plan worked, it would be a devilishly fast progression —
from the Pacific Stock Exchange to the American Stock Exchange to
the Big Board in just seven years. Approval was by no means certain,
however. The SEC had raised questions about the close relationship
between Hammer and a brokerage firm called Gilligan, Will and Company that specialized in Occidental trading on the American Stock Exchange. But the federal government decided against charging Occiden-

tal with wrongdoing in the Gilligan, Will matter. The New York Stock Exchange eventually approved Hammer's application. Occidental stock began to trade there in March 1964. Victor, Harry, and an ecstatic Armand joined together on the exchange floor to celebrate the occasion. A few weeks later, Occidental reported 1963 revenue of nearly $35 million, with a profit of almost $7 million.[16]

Hammer concentrated on making Occidental self-sufficient in the fertilizer business as quickly as possible, which accounted for the large number of acquisitions in so short a time. As the company explained:

> Balanced fertilizers contain three basic nutrients — nitrogen, phosphorus, and potassium. Nitrogen is available in the form of ammonia or urea. Phosphorus is available in the form of phosphoric acid, a derivative of phosphate rock. Potassium is a derivative of potash. In addition, sulphur is an essential basic element used in the manufacture of commercial fertilizer and agricultural chemicals.[17]

Hammer decided to buy the potash from outside suppliers, given market conditions at that time. Everything else he elected to bring under the Occidental umbrella.

Acquiring ammonia and sulfur by purchasing existing companies was relatively simple. Breaking into the phosphorus market, which Hammer proposed to do next, was more complicated — a small number of companies dominated North American phosphate-rock reserves, which many experts believed to be available in significant minable quantities only in Hillsborough and Polk counties, Florida. In September 1963, Hammer hired George Brooks, an astute thirty-six-year-old mining engineer, to direct a phosphate exploration program. Brooks had worked for Armour Agricultural Chemical Corporation, one of the companies entrenched in Hillsborough and Polk counties. He told Hammer there were plentiful phosphate deposits in Hamilton County, Florida, farther north than the conventional wisdom allowed. Hammer gave him the go-ahead. At first, the two men got along well enough, but Brooks soon chafed under Hammer's suffocating oversight and business practices. Brooks had served his purpose by the time of his unhappy departure the next year.[18]

Meanwhile, A. A. Guffey, who had joined Occidental about the same time as Brooks after fourteen years in the phosphate industry and who stayed for the rest of his career, agreed with Brooks about the untapped areas. "We knew that Continental Can and Owens-Illinois owned reserves there. Dr. Hammer knew [General] Lucius Clay at Continental Can. We outbid Monsanto for the rights. Dr. Hammer was the more clever one." In fact, Hammer had obtained information about the price that the Monsanto Company — which dwarfed Occidental — planned to bid for the reserves. He then submitted a higher bid. The Continental Can board of directors was inclined to favor Monsanto anyway. But Hammer had a link to Clay through Wall Street titan Robert Lehman, a fellow art collector whose firm had accepted up-and-coming Occidental as a client.[19]

Pushed by Lehman and Hammer, Clay in turn rammed through Occidental's bid. Suddenly, Occidental had the rights to mine phosphate beneath 5,300 acres on the Suwannee River, a bit south of the Georgia border, in Hamilton County, Florida. Hammer could hardly wait to get going. When he appeared at the ground-breaking, a reporter present for the *Florida Times-Union* wrote that curiosity about the new plant "was only slightly greater than interest in the personal background of the company's president . . . [Hammer] is one of the most interesting persons to ever visit this county."[20]

Occidental began mining phosphate rock in August 1965. A year later, the company christened its phosphate chemical complex about one mile from the main mine. To cater the dedication party, Hammer hired the person who provided food for guests at the Texas ranch of President Lyndon Johnson. During the ceremony, he stressed the five hundred new jobs and the $30 million annual payroll that Occidental was bringing to the depressed local economy. Ever the globalist, he added that the output would help feed a world in which 50 percent of all inhabitants suffered from malnourishment.

Much of the rock from the mine site was used as raw material in the adjacent processing plant. The rest traveled to Jacksonville, Florida, where Occidental had access to a deep-water port from which to ship its resources all over the world. Some of the ships departed loaded with superphosphoric acid, produced at still other Occidental facilities in Florida. Superphosphoric acid, often known by its acronym, SPA, contained greater quantities of phosphate per pound than did traditional phosphoric acid. Dealing in SPA meant savings in freight costs — Occidental could transport the equivalent of three normal-sized shiploads in one freighter — and less expensive storage. SPA had other virtues, as advertised by Occidental. It was less corrosive, contained fewer impurities, resulted in minimal sludge settlement, and possessed a higher-than-average concentration of plant nutrients when used in liquid fertilizers.

Occidental, meanwhile, had developed SPA through the acquisition of patent rights from Nordac, a British company. In early 1964, Occidental had constructed an SPA pilot plant in Uxbridge, the same English town to which Hammer had returned the historic paneling that once graced his United Distillers office in the Empire State Building. Next, Occidental built an SPA plant in Lakeland, Florida. It in turn worked so well that the company erected a second SPA plant, adjacent to the chemical plant and mine site in Hamilton County.

As Armour and Company executives saw what was unfolding at Occidental, they were not amused. Armour sued, asking courts in Delaware, Florida, and California to forbid former employees hired away by Occidental from sharing trade secrets about SPA production. Later, Armour alleged that Occidental had infringed on a patent. Occidental countersued. Several Occidental executives involved in SPA production at that time said Hammer had lured people from Armour and other established companies specifically to gain expertise about SPA production.[21]

One such employee was Ernest Csendes, who testified that he had feared legal action by Armour if he jumped into SPA research immediately after joining Occidental and believed he had obtained Hammer's promise that such duties would be three to five years away. Soon thereafter, however, Hammer allegedly pressured him to help Occidental sell SPA technology in Morocco. Csendes said he told Hammer that "he was crazy," that he could "take his contract and eat it." An angry Hammer reportedly hung up on Csendes but later apologized; he needed Csendes's know-how too much at that time to drive him away.[22]

Whether Hammer had committed an actionable offense by hiring Armour employees was a question for the judge to decide. The importance of the case to each company was indicated by the length of the trial — forty-two days. After four years of posttrial legal maneuvering by both companies, the resolution favored Hammer. Some insiders saw it as one of the most important victories in Occidental Petroleum's early history, since a defeat would have altered Hammer's plans profoundly by making it close to impossible to succeed in the fertilizer business overseas. With the court battle over, he was free to begin serious negotiations on what would become the largest contract in history between an American corporation and the Soviets.

As Occidental's fertilizer operations expanded, the rest of the corporation was growing in all sorts of directions — some of them surprising. Occidental explored deals overseas that its stockholders barely knew existed. The negotiations must have appeared unplanned, even rash. All along, however, Hammer was keeping the larger picture in mind. The key elements in that picture were Libya and the Soviet Union. The big break in Libya came during 1966; the big break in the Soviet Union came in 1972. When they occurred, many stockholders and Wall Street analysts saw them as bolts from the blue. They were actually painstakingly won triumphs for Hammer, victories for his hands-on brand of management.

To achieve the first big opportunity, Hammer traveled several paths. The buildup of the domestic fertilizer business was one. A logical outgrowth was ventures in foreign nations that Hammer had marked for secondary roles in his drive toward Libya. Demonstrating serious interest in those nations would give Occidental visibility as a player in the multinational energy sweepstakes. Hammer hoped Libya's King Idris would notice tiny Occidental Petroleum amid the huge Seven Sisters. As a prelude to bidding for oil concessions in Libya, he concentrated on Saudi Arabia, where Occidental and King Faisal agreed to build a $33 million ammonia-urea plant, in Dammam. The kingdom would provide all the money. Hammer signed a twenty-year management contract. For its effort, Occidental would receive 10 percent of any profits and 5 percent of sales. The unused output would be purchased by Occidental for sale elsewhere.[23]

Occidental's Saudi Arabian contract demonstrated that Hammer was serious about operating in Arab nations. Thereafter he strengthened that impression by meeting with King Hassan II of Morocco about copper recovery and agrichemical manufacturing. He then shipped Aberdeen-Angus cattle to Hassan. When the king visited the United States, Hammer sponsored a dinner in his honor at the exclusive Lotos Club in New York.[24]

Hammer also kept tabs on negotiations to establish Occidental fertilizer ventures with Nicaragua, Venezuela, Singapore, and Turkey, in addition to Saudi Arabia, Morocco, and Tunisia. The dizzying overseas negotiations served many purposes in Occidental Petroleum's fledgling decade under Hammer: They allowed Hammer to practice his special brand of citizen diplomacy with heads of state, a practice — some would say an obsession — of his since his meeting with Lenin, in 1921; they gave Hammer the attention he craved; they provided Occidental with visibility in cash-poor, resource-rich nations; and they held out a promise to Wall Street analysts and Occidental stockholders of good times to come.

With the Lathrop field discovery, in 1961, the value of Occidental's stock had begun to climb. In 1962, its shares on the American Stock Exchange ranged from $10 to $22. In 1965, with its overseas activity in motion, the stock, by then trading on the Big Board, reached $34. But Hammer seemed to know his plans for abroad would take years to pay off. As a result, he concentrated on other internal and external measures in an attempt to achieve a healthy, growing bottom line in short order.

Uncharacteristically, he decided to launch Occidental in the real estate field. On the surface, real estate might have seemed like a logical venture for Hammer — it was, after all, a permanent resource that appreciated in value, especially in cities such as New York and Los Angeles, where Hammer had spent most of his life. Many other tycoons had built fortunes in real estate or had dealt in it profitably after becoming wealthy. But Hammer was different. His only significant personal investment in real estate at that time had more to do with sentimentality than with profit.

In 1962, he had finally acquired title to his beloved carriage house in Greenwich Village. The seller was the estate of Alfred Maclay, a banker, gardener, book collector, and president of the American Horse Shows Association; the property had been in the Maclay family since 1857. Hammer paid $58,500 to the estate and slept in his Manhattan home whenever he could. The owner of Pâtisserie Claude, next door to Hammer's house, said that "whenever he is in town, people ask me who lives there because they see two or three limousines in front. I do not tell them. He likes privacy. . . . He is a very nice man, though he does not say hello. His first words are 'How is business?'" Claude said Hammer, known for his sweet tooth, did him an unexpected kindness: "When I opened my shop it was very difficult. On July fourth I was here early, depressed. Armand Hammer came in at six A.M. and bought everything in my case. I closed up and went home for the holiday. I was very happy." Generally, though, Hammer traveled the few feet between his limousine and his house without mingling.[25]

At the same time Hammer bought the carriage house, he became an economic force in the neighborhood through an entity called the Hambrig Corporation, not part of Occidental. Hambrig bought adjacent Village properties from the same Maclay estate, for investment purposes. The other partner in Hambrig, shorthand for Hammer-Brignole, was Michael Brignole, proprietor of an Italian grocery on the same block as Hammer's house.[26] Brignole's father had operated the store when Hammer first moved to the neighborhood, while a college student, and Michael, thirteen years younger than Hammer, eventually became the boy Friday for Hammer himself and for 183 West Fourth Street.

Hammer repaid Brignole's loyalty by encouraging him to invest a reported $30,000 in the then-struggling Occidental Petroleum. Brignole held on to his Occidental stock as the price skyrocketed, even though he could have sold it a decade later and retired comfortably on the proceeds. In his will, Brignole wrote: "I request that my trust retain all shares of Occidental Petroleum as long as my friend Dr. Armand Hammer remains as an officer of the company." Brignole died of a heart attack in 1987 at age seventy-five. By then, he was living with his wife in retirement on Staten Island. But when Brignole's body was discovered at nearly midnight, it was not in his home. Rather, it was at Hammer's Manhattan house. Although elderly and financially comfortable, Brignole had not stopped doing chores for Hammer.[27]

Hammer and Brignole dissolved the Hambrig Corporation five years after forming it, selling the properties at a tidy profit. By then, Hammer had tried to make real estate pay off for Occidental, too. The company's first foray into land came with the acquisition of S. V. Hunsaker and Sons in mid-1964 for stock valued at about $5.6 million. Hunsaker had been building homes and apartments in California since 1938. By the end of 1965, Occidental also had acquired the Family Realty Corporation and the William Development Corporation from William Weinberg. The companies had been buying and selling undeveloped land in Southern California and Arizona since 1959. Hammer gave Weinberg Occidental stock valued at slightly more than $5.3 million. In March 1966, Occidental bought Monarch Investment Company for stock valued at about $2.6 million. In August 1966, Occidental used close to $4 million in stock to buy Deane Brothers.[28]

Each firm had real estate that Occidental added to its assets, then quickly sold for what appeared to be multimillion-dollar gains. In time Hammer consolidated all real estate operations under the Deane Brothers name. It stayed that way until 1969, when Hammer announced a merger of the home-building and real estate development subsidiaries into Occidental Petroleum Land and Development Corporation. The reorganization verged on desperation; things had gone poorly. New housing starts and home sales had begun a marked drop in Southern California soon after Occidental's entry into the business. At the end of 1966, while Hammer was working endless hours to make the company look profitable, the real estate subsidiaries were carrying 441 unsold new houses at a book value of more than $9 million. The book value of houses sold but then repossessed was more than $6 million.

The SEC began to examine the real estate transactions as part of a larger investigation of Occidental and Hammer. The agency had shown a worrisome interest several years earlier in Occidental's accounting for land spin-offs. After a 1966 meeting involving Occidental executives, their lawyers, and the federal agency's representatives, Hammer had issued an order that all major real estate transactions should be reviewed by independent auditors before closing. But the SEC staff expressed doubts that much had changed.

Some of the principals in the transactions who testified before the agency in closed sessions during 1970 and 1971 offered insights into how Hammer conducted business. Lawrence Weinberg, William Weinberg's brother and business associate, said the sale of the Family and William corporations had had its genesis with Maury Leibovitz, accountant for the Weinbergs as well as Hammer's influential adviser. Just one week after Occidental had acquired Family Realty and William Development, it sold a substantial portion of the unimproved land owned by those two companies — to Lawrence Weinberg. The quick sale allowed Occidental to record a gain of $2.9 million on its books. William Weinberg took his newly acquired Occidental stock to a bank, where he offered it as collateral for a $3 million loan. The bank approved the loan, on condition that Occidental either provide additional collateral, purchase the stock, or find an outside purchaser should Weinberg's shares turn out to be insufficient. Surprisingly, Occidental agreed.[29]

Later, William Weinberg granted a foreign investor an option to purchase his shares at $44 apiece. The foreign investor paid Weinberg $1 million just for the option to buy later. If the investor failed to exercise the option by a certain date, it would expire. As another condition of the bank loan, Occidental substituted its own bank note of more than $3 million for William Weinberg's note. Why Hammer agreed to such seemingly unfavorable arrangements became clear during Lawrence Weinberg's testimony: William Weinberg had begun looking for a buyer of his Occidental stock because its volatility worried him. Word of the possible unloading had reached Hammer, who told William Weinberg the rumors were depressing the market for Occidental shares. Hammer was constantly promoting the stock — to friends, business associates, doctors, and lawyers. Hoping to eliminate the problem quickly, Hammer said he would find a purchaser. He did — a mysterious European firm called the Hall Establishment, with offices in Switzerland and Liechtenstein. Hammer's contact there was John Tigrett, a Tennessee toy manufacturer turned European financial representative for J. Paul Getty, James Goldsmith, and other tycoons. It transpired that Tigrett had bought the $1 million option from William Weinberg. The latter thereupon had applied the sum to reducing the debt incurred when Lawrence Weinberg purchased the very land belonging to him just a week earlier.[30]

There were legal complications growing out of William Weinberg's selling his shares, however. So Washington lawyer Myer Feldman, representing Occidental on one side of the deal and the Hall Establishment on the other, asked the SEC for a letter signifying that it would take no action should the option be exercised. The agency duly issued the letter, and Hammer then arranged the purchase of the shares. Feldman was well connected, having worked in the Kennedy and Johnson White Houses. While Feldman was serving on Kennedy's staff, he and Hammer had corresponded.[31] They also knew each other through the Eleanor Roosevelt Memorial Foundation board of trustees, to which both had been named by the president.

In 1971 the SEC heard additional testimony about Occidental's suspicious real estate dealings from Lawrence Kagan, who had sold Monarch Investment Company to Occidental in 1966. Like the Weinberg transaction, the Monarch acquisition had yielded a quick paper profit for Occidental: Within a week, Occidental sold a substantial portion of Monarch's unimproved land for a reported gain of more than $2 million. Kagan said his link with Occidental Petroleum was Maury Leibovitz, who had initiated acquisition discussions after a chance meeting on a flight from Los Angeles to New York. At the hearing Kagan was asked about Hammer's role in the land transactions under investigation; for example, did he provide specific, formal instructions? "I would say anything that comes out of Dr. Hammer's mouth, that is, instructions, is formal as far as I am concerned," he replied. After the commission's inquiry, Occidental slowly eliminated its real estate division, turning over management of the properties to Shapell Industries, a successful builder and developer. When that occurred, in 1975, Occidental's real estate operation was millions of dollars in the red, while the rest of the company was thriving financially.[32]

Hammer's real estate acquisitions for Occidental served his purpose, however — to bulk up the bottom line, thus making the company more attractive to investors and giving it credibility with overseas governments whose rulers wondered if they should award contracts to such a relatively tiny firm in competition with seasoned multinationals. Those rulers were looking for alternatives to dealing with the Seven Sisters, whose perceived arrogance and exploitative terms were maddening.

Even before branching into real estate, Hammer combined his new foreign focus with an assault on the Kennedy White House; he believed in dealing at the top in every country, including his own. As he prepared to conquer markets in Libya and the Soviet Union, therefore, he began to knock at that door, using Senator Gore and the Campobello donation as entrées. Then, tragically, Kennedy was dead.

Hammer thereupon started all over again with Lyndon Johnson. Shortly after Johnson's succession, he sent a telegram to the White House, pledging support. Always one to drop a name when it would help, he said, "For many years I have heard our mutual friend John Mecom sing your praises. Now I know it was well deserved." (Mecom, a Texas oilman, and Hammer went back to 1951, when they had met on a transatlantic cruise and Hammer had started Mecom in the cattle business.) Thereafter President Johnson became increasingly aware of Hammer — through the Campobello ceremonies, through various aides whom Hammer cultivated, through mutual acquaintances such as Mecom. One pressure point was Representative James Roosevelt, who insisted the White House staff make an appointment for Hammer to see Johnson. The president's aides and Johnson himself were wary of Hammer's hucksterism and of the uncertain nature of his links to the Soviet Union. Myer Feldman said that "Lyndon did not want to see Hammer because he was extremely cautious of anyone even remotely suspicious."[33]

After the Campobello ceremony at the White House, Hammer, working through Roosevelt and Johnson aide Lawrence O'Brien, obtained a photograph with the inscription "To Dr. Armand Hammer, with high regards and best wishes, Lyndon B. Johnson." Hanging in Hammer's office, it gave visitors the impression of special status at the White House. With Hammer, impressions mattered a great deal. The next trick would be to change the impression into reality. Accordingly, on May 5, 1964, Roosevelt called a Johnson assistant, who wrote down this version of the congressman's plea: "I have a very good friend named Armand Hammer, president of Occidental Petroleum. He formerly owned Campobello and gave it to the government. Two or three years ago, President Kennedy sent him as a private citizen to Russia to negotiate the crabmeat controversy with Khrushchev. He has now been asked by Khrushchev to come back, and it has been approved by the Commerce Department. He is to leave at the end of May and would like very much to have a few minutes with the president before he goes, both to be sure it is all right to go and also for a few suggestions." On May 6, White House aide Jack Valenti turned down Roosevelt's request. Valenti wrote on July 20 to McGeorge Bundy, another White House aide, about a possible Hammer-Johnson meeting: "What should the president do about this? Congressman Roosevelt keeps calling. This man [Hammer] is obviously a big contributor to him. As I understand it, this man had some contact with Secretary [of Commerce Luther] Hodges. In my conversation with Secretary Hodges, he was not too high on Dr. Hammer having an appointment with the president."[34] Bundy replied: "Pass Hammer to one or another of us on staff. President should not have to see him."

Undaunted, Hammer worked to win over Lady Bird Johnson and daughters Lynda and Luci, knowing they could provide access to the president. In April 1965, Lynda wrote Hammer a thank-you for some earrings; Luci thanked him for a pin. The next month, Lady Bird wrote Hammer that she deeply regretted being unable to visit an exhibition by Russian artist Pavel Korin at Hammer Galleries.[35] She began to develop a fondness for Hammer. His strategy was working. Hammer also succeeded in building relationships with White House aides, especially W. Marvin Watson, who later became postmaster general in the cabinet. (Watson went to work for Occidental Petroleum at the close of the Johnson administration.)

On June 17, 1966, Myer Feldman called Watson at the White House about adding Hammer's name to the guest list for King Faisal's state dinner. Hammer and the king knew each other from Occidental's venture in Saudi Arabia. In fact, Hammer was planning to take the king to lunch during his visit. Hammer's executive assistant, Thomas Wachtell, already had written to those handling the state dinner, trying to lay the groundwork for an invitation. The king's brother, Ahmed Abdul Aziz, cabled President Johnson and endorsed Hammer's wish to be added to the guest list.[36] An overwhelmed Johnson gave his approval.

The dinner went well, but the next day Faisal made disparaging remarks about Israel that caused New York City mayor John Lindsay and New York governor Nelson Rockefeller to cancel receptions for the king.[37] Hammer appeared nonplussed, having denied or downplayed his Jewish heritage most of his life. Being considered Jewish might hurt business in anti-Semitic nations, exactly where Hammer was seeking Occidental's fortune. The uproar caused by Faisal's remarks gave Hammer no pause about operating in Saudi Arabia.

On the day of the state dinner, Hammer had stopped at the White House to visit Watson. Recounting the meeting for the president, Watson wrote: "Armand Hammer . . . was in today. He says he has twenty-five that he would like to do without. You will recall that Mike [Myer] Feldman brought him in." The "twenty-five" referred to a donation of

$25,000; Hammer had contributed to Johnson in the past. His name appeared on a December 1966 list of twenty-seven "principal support-ers" compiled by Johnson's finance chairman.[38] The supporters received a bust of the president as a Christmas remembrance.

As was his practice, Hammer presented Watson with a jade key ring. On the heels of that gift, he mailed Watson a *Saturday Evening Post* profile of himself.[39] He asked Watson to give the article to the president, underlining passages about how Occidental's development of fertilizer plants in underdeveloped countries would help feed a hungry world. Hammer had sent the *Saturday Evening Post* profile to the White House at least one time previously; social secretary Bess Abell acknowl-edged it in a letter dated April 15, 1966.*

On New Year's Day, 1967, Armand and Frances Hammer sent en-couragement to a president beset by protest over Vietnam, reminding Johnson of the wisdom attributed to another beleaguered president, Abraham Lincoln. They were words Hammer sometimes applied to himself: "If I were to read, much less answer, all the attacks made on me, this shop might as well be closed for any other business. I do the very best I know how, the very best I can, and I mean to keep doing so until the end. If the end brings me out alright, what is said against me will not amount to anything. If the end brings me out wrong, ten angels swearing I was right would make no difference."[40]

As Johnson became more comfortable with Hammer, favors started coming Hammer's way. The president invited the Hammers to a black-tie White House dinner for the Moroccan king, where they rubbed shoulders with three cabinet members, a Supreme Court justice, four senators, six representatives, three governors, and private-sector lumi-naries such as Conrad Hilton and Walter Cronkite.[41] Three months later, Myer Feldman called White House aide James Jones to complain that Hammer never had received a photograph of himself with John-son at the dinner. Jones took care of the matter.

The president reappointed Hammer to the board of the Eleanor Roosevelt Memorial Foundation and sent him a White House invita-tion to the swearing in of Alexander Trowbridge as secretary of com-

---

* Sending articles about himself to the White House was a pastime with Hammer. Often, the tactic got him the attention he craved. For instance, when Hammer mailed coverage of Occidental's plans to beautify its oil drilling sites to Lady Bird, Bess Abell praised him on behalf of the First Lady: "It is so encouraging to see the efforts of public-spirited businessmen to protect the beauty of our cities, and your portable tower to screen oil rigs is certainly ingenious!" Abell added her own postscript: "You are certainly a man of many interests!" (Abell to Hammer, April 15, 1966, Lyndon Baines Johnson Library, Austin, Tex.)

merce. Hammer reciprocated by sharing his insights into the battle against inflation, telling the president to raise taxes — advice that contradicted Johnson's top advisers and was abhorrent to most business executives. No matter, Hammer said; his advice was based on clearer vision than that possessed by others. Some months later, Armand and Frances received a coveted invitation to the Johnson ranch itself.[42]

Of Hammer's many attempts to win recognition at the Johnson White House, however, the most successful probably was his gift of two bronze sculptures by western artist Charles Russell. The stratagem started at a White House dinner to honor the shah of Iran. Senate Majority Leader Mike Mansfield of Montana took Hammer aside to say how nice it would be for the White House to have a Russell bronze to complement its Frederic Remington bronze; Mansfield knew Hammer had purchased the contents of Russell's house a decade earlier. Hammer decided to donate *Meat for Wild Men,* which depicted native Americans on horseback attacking a buffalo. It arrived at the White House in time for that same week's dinner honoring Mansfield's twenty-five years of congressional service. Mansfield was touched and grateful. On October 23, 1967, he inserted two items into the *Congressional Record.* The first was a column by *Washington Star* society reporter Betty Beale, telling the tale of the Hammer donation. The second was a flattering profile of Hammer from the previous day's *New York Times.* Mansfield called Hammer "one of the most successful businessmen in the nation."[43]

White House curator James Ketchum wrote Hammer that Lady Bird Johnson "exclaims with delight and great pride when she points out this unique bronze to her guests. Needless to say, her joy will be shared by the millions of Americans who come to the White House each year to see and benefit from its vast, historic collection, in which your Russell bronze holds now such an important place." Mrs. Johnson was indeed grateful. In her diary for August 22, 1967, the night of the White House dinner for the shah, she noted how Hammer "told me the marvelous news that he wanted to give the White House a Charles Russell bronze. He knew we had a Remington. I struggled with myself one moment and then said, 'You are testing my loyalty.' And he said, 'What do you mean?' And I said, 'You know, there will be a Lyndon Johnson Library within two or three years and the artists of the Southwest are among my husband's favorites. But it will be marvelous for the White House to have it.' But I got no further. He said, 'I will give one to the Lyndon Johnson Library, too.' What a great addition those would be!"[44] The second bronze chosen by Hammer was Remington's *Bronco Buster.* At the time, the two bronzes had an estimated value of $175,000.

All of Hammer's goodwill and largess paid off. On June 19, 1968, he received the White House Oval Office meeting for which he had been campaigning. Accompanied by W. Marvin Watson, he saw the president, and the next day he returned for an off-the-record lunch about plans for the Johnson Library in Austin, Texas. Those invited were a select group of twenty-five influential people, many of them extremely wealthy. The president also helped Hammer's image by appointing him to an advisory committee on trade policy.[45] It looked impressive on a résumé.

Privately, many on Johnson's staff and Johnson himself continued to waver about how to treat Hammer; high-level policymakers spent inordinate amounts of time considering whether the president should see him at all. The ambivalence within the administration was suggested by a round of memorandums beginning with a plea from Hammer to Watson about obtaining the president's imprimatur for a trip to the Soviet Union. Hammer said he would be willing to disguise the purpose of his trip if that would please Johnson. He attached a six-page letter and six exhibits meant to strengthen his case by demonstrating his influence. He then stressed the problems of Soviet agriculture, noting the dependency of the Russians on grain from the United States and Canada. Hammer wanted to convince the Soviets that with American help they could be agriculturally self-sufficient. In return, he suggested, the Soviets could be pressured to push North Vietnam to the peace table. He added that if he unofficially proposed the plan and it was rejected, the White House would lose no face.

Watson summarized Hammer's material for the president, with a request for a yes-or-no response. Johnson turned it over to his adviser W. W. Rostow, with this notation: "Be very, very cautious about this and do only what you and [Secretary of State Dean] Rusk can justify. It does not appeal to me much." Rostow wrote Watson about the proper course to take, but the memorandum has remained classified as secret. Rostow then sent a sanitized letter to Hammer, saying the White House would have no objection to his visiting the Soviet Union — as a private citizen.[46] With such a lukewarm response, Hammer postponed the trip.

15

Fame

B Y THE MID-1960s, Armand Hammer had arrived. Nothing he
had done previously had so caught the public imagination as his
being an oil tycoon. From John D. Rockefeller on, Americans had been
fascinated by oil barons, and Hammer was no exception.

One observer who saw a legend in the making was Lloyd Unsell,
president of the Independent Petroleum Association of America, where
his career spanned forty years. Unsell occasionally criticized Hammer,
when his maverick ways violated the welfare of the industry as a whole,
but he became an admirer after he compared Hammer with hundreds
of other oil-company executives: "I have followed Armand Hammer
with awe . . . I cannot think of any success story comparable to that
of Occidental. You cannot put it down to sheer luck. You have to credit
the adventuresome spirit of an unusual personality. . . . I remember
when I first heard that Hammer was getting involved with Occidental.
I thought, based on what I know of this man, I ought to hock my
house and buy Occidental stock. Looking back, I wish I had. . . . Most
of the international oil companies are run by men who came up through
the ranks, who worked thirty-five to forty years to get up from the
bottom — explorationists, geologists. Then you have Armand Hammer
at an age when most men are thinking of retirement, with no previous
oil experience, who on the strength of his instincts is a big success. . . .
I read *The Quest of the Romanoff Treasure,* and that gave me my first
impression of Armand Hammer. I was impressed by the unusual per-
suasion he used to get the pencil factory going in the Soviet Union. I
have wondered how Hollywood resisted making a movie out of that
book."[1]

Sustained attention from the media became the crucial element in Hammer's metamorphosis from occasional news maker to international celebrity, a household name. The *Los Angeles Times* published a profile in 1962 that read as if written by Hammer himself. The opening paragraph said Hammer "is a physician who never has treated humans. He has found too much fun and much more profit in diagnosing and treating businesses. . . . His latest patient is Occidental Petroleum Corporation." That same year the *New York Times* published a wholly uncritical feature by Hedrick Smith, later to become a best-selling author of a book about Russia. Smith observed that Hammer's business activities "have been so profitable that even Premier Khrushchev inquired last year about his secret for success." Trying to explain Hammer's achievements, Smith quoted a distilling-industry competitor about how Hammer would enter an industry "he does not know anything about. Before long, he knows more about it than people who have been in it all their lives. And then he surrounds himself with top management." Later that year the *New Yorker* published a profile in which it commented that nearly thirty years had passed since anyone from the magazine had lunched with Hammer; the interview had taken place in an expensive restaurant suggested by Hammer, who ate minute steak as he spun yarns of his meeting with Khrushchev.[2]

The profiles began to show a sameness; Hammer was getting his story down pat. Compared with the actual events, an Associated Press feature distributed on New Year's Day, 1966, seemed a mixture of fact, exaggeration, and fiction that became the staple of almost all Hammer portraits thereafter. Perhaps the only exception was the insightful piece by Spencer Klaw in a 1966 issue of the *Saturday Evening Post,* at that time one of the most popular magazines in the United States. Klaw captured Hammer's character in the opening paragraphs:

People who have only a casual acquaintance with the career and personality of Dr. Armand Hammer, a sixty-seven-year-old nonpracticing physician who has been making a considerable splash lately as a financial operator, sometimes take him for a confidence man. The assumption is a natural one. Hammer's ideas for making money often have the suspicious sweep and simplicity one associates with plans for harnessing the power of volcanoes, or for recovering the lost treasure of the Incas. . . . Hammer's reminiscences are no more plausible than his projects. He may recall, for example, how he became the proprietor, at the age of twenty-seven, of the only pencil factory in the Soviet Union; or how, when Prohibition was repealed, he forehandedly cornered most of the

world's supply of beer-barrel staves. Hammer also likes to embellish his
stories with recollections of such improbably assorted personages as Prince
Abdullah, brother of King Hassan II of Morocco; Nikita Khrushchev;
and the late Senator Robert A. Taft.

Hammer does not look like the kind of man who dines with Moroccan princes or builds factories in the Soviet Union. Short, smiling, and
comfortably upholstered, he goes about in an elderly camel's-hair coat
and a limp Borsalino hat, chuckles disarmingly at his own anecdotes,
and might well be mistaken for an old-fashioned country doctor. In a
way, this is reassuring; no confidence man in his right mind who wanted
to pass for an international financier would get himself up like Hammer. But even when one has hit on this comforting theory, a glance
from Hammer can quickly arouse one's suspicions all over again. Hammer's brows are divided by two very deep vertical furrows which give
his eyes at times a look of hypnotic intensity, like the eyes of a mad
scientist in an old horror film or the author of a book on *Conquering
Life Through Will Power*. As it happens, Hammer's stories are true.[3]

Although unique in most ways, Hammer was in one way a type.
Author Leo Braudy noted that "the urge for fame mingles one's acceptance of oneself with the desire for others . . . to recognize that one is
special." That observation is especially significant in the modern-day
media world, where, Braudy said,

> honor becomes less a matter of personal satisfaction and personal values
> than of an external recognition that makes that inner honor "real" . . .
> the spiritual glow conveyed by being recognized means finally not hav-
> ing to say who you are. Touched by the magic wand of this secular
> religion, the aspirant moves beyond the usual social context of achieve-
> ment to a place where there is no career, no progress, no advance, no
> change — only the purity of being celebrated for being oneself. . . . In
> a world of increasing anonymity and powerlessness, where every day on
> the news life goes on without you, your name in print or your picture
> in the papers promises at least a moment of respite from despair. For, if
> an image lasts beyond death, it implies that its possessor is more than
> human.[4]

Hammer, indeed, wanted respite from mortality. But he knew the
attention would dissipate if Occidental failed to continue its spectacular
growth, if he failed to continue demonstrating his business acumen
mixed with his citizen diplomacy. He need not have worried. The seed
planted in Libya was coming to fruition.

Libya had been on Hammer's mind since his visit there in 1961. Richard Vaughan, a key geologist during Occidental's early growth, said that he first mentioned Libya to "the doctor" in 1960 but that Hammer referred to it only rarely until 1964. "The Libyan operation was one that Dr. Hammer was personally involved with, and he obviously was playing it very close to his vest because neither I nor any of my associates in the geological division were aware that . . . studies were being made," Vaughan said.[5]

Hammer tried to convince his government it should do more to open Libya to independent American oil companies, Occidental included, of course. Hammer wrote an angry letter from Tripoli to the U.S. secretary of commerce about a government decision to drop out of an international trade fair scheduled for the Libyan capital. Noting that exhibiting would cost the government as little as $25,000, Hammer said Libya was a friendly nation that had become the sixth-largest petroleum producer only six years after the discovery of oil there. Libya wanted to expand its agricultural industry, but the United States had no Agency for International Development program to train the Libyans. The Iron Curtain and European countries, however, had established training programs. Skilled at perceiving other people's interests besides his own, Hammer argued that the United States needed Wheelus Air Force Base, in Libya, whose lease expired in six years, so why not give aid to Libya?[6]

Hammer was convinced Occidental would profit if it could gain a foothold in the kingdom. Thanks to his research, he knew Occidental had a better chance of competing in Libya than in other oil-producing nations. In most parts of the world, the Seven Sisters already controlled the market. But Libya had initiated a new way of awarding drilling concessions. King Idris gave specific exploration areas to separate bidders rather than awarding nationwide rights to one company. The monarchy divided the eighty-four available concessions among the conglomerate oil majors and the smaller independent firms — seventeen companies in all.

The majors disliked the system evolving in Libya and disliked Hammer for trying to exploit it. His efforts produced incredulity, even mirth — who was this upstart, anyway? — but also hostility. Despite the favorable omens Hammer saw, it was a bold move for his company to attempt to win a concession in Libya. A successful bid would be just the first step. Exploration would be tremendously expensive, with no promise of a return.

Hammer decided to face the challenge. His plan was innovative: offer the Libyans more than just money to take the oil out of their

ground. The acquisition of International Ore and Fertilizer was calculated to build up Occidental's agricultural-chemicals business so it would
have something tangible to offer to crop-poor Libya. Senator Albert
Gore wrote Hammer an introduction to the U.S. ambassador in Libya,
Allan Lightner, a career diplomat posted there in mid-1963. Lightner
recalled Hammer's visit: "He found me at home, just strolled into my
garden where I was with my family. He was with someone carrying
his briefcase for him, was on his way to Tobruk to see the king. He
told me he hoped to get the king interested in giving him a concession.
He was feeling around before making his attempt. He stayed for dinner, and we were fascinated by his stories. He has the gift of gab and
there is nothing he would rather talk about than himself. He gave
everyone at the dinner table jade key rings. We mentioned having taken
the queen to Kufra, a sacred oasis near the Sudanese border for her
ancestors and for the king's ancestors, too. She took photographs back
to show the king, and they were both thrilled over the queen's excursion. Hammer made note of it all, including Kufra's potential for un-
derground water."[7]

During Hammer's meeting with King Idris, he took the measure of
the monarch. His conclusion: The king was a traditional elderly Arab —
religious, living modestly, concerned about his subjects but influenced
by his less holy aides. James Akins, director of the State Department's
Office of Fuels and Energy, testified, "The Idris regime was certainly
one of the most corrupt in the area and probably one of the most
corrupt in the world. Concessions were given . . . on the basis of payments to members of the royal family. This was widely known
throughout Libya." Persons working for Western oil companies and
the U.S. government in Libya during the 1960s believed Hammer spread
money around but was not the only oil executive to do so. Although
Hammer's conduct might have been usual in kind, it probably was
unusual in degree: A perception was abroad that he contributed more
generously and strategically than anybody else. G. Henry Schuler, who
represented Grace Petroleum and later Nelson Bunker Hunt in Libya,
believed Hammer did something rash to become a player after missing
the first round: "Hammer was bringing up the rear on getting into
Libya. He had nothing going for him, and was desperate to get into
the bidding. There was no assurance he would get good acreage even
if he got into the bidding. His [initial] efforts were the laughingstock
of the Libyans and the other oil companies, and turned people off."[8]

Some of Hammer's dealing occurred on September 17, 1964, at Claridge's Hotel, in London. It was there that Herbert Allen, a New York
investment banker who represented Occidental, introduced Hammer to

Ferdinand Galic. Galic said that he was an Italian citizen with homes in St. Moritz and Paris, that he had graduated from a university in Prague, and that he had entered Libya during 1951 with an introduction from the king of Yugoslavia. The exotic Galic had met Herbert Allen through Charles Allen, Herbert's partner, at a bankers' dinner in Paris. Accompanying Galic to Claridge's was a man introduced to Hammer as General de Rovin. De Rovin had met Galic in Paris recently and bragged of his influence in Libya. Allen, Galic, and de Rovin thought Hammer might be interested in their services.[9]

On the same day as the Claridge's meeting, at a separate get-together set up by the director of Occidental's European office, Hammer talked with Taher Ogbi. Ogbi was a sometime minister in the Libyan government, a man believed to have access to the king's adviser Omar Shalhi. Hammer wanted such access: Months before the clandestine meetings in London, Occidental had submitted an informal bid for a Libyan oil concession. Hammer was shuttling Occidental employees in and out of the country to work on winning a concession. He had also hired James Lawler, a geologist headquartered in Rome, to prepare reports on seven tracts in Libya. Lawler had kept Hammer abreast of political developments as well as scientific findings, but Hammer worried that that was not enough. The purpose of the London meetings, therefore, was to determine how to strengthen Occidental's chances for success. On September 18, 1964, Hammer signed agreements with Galic, de Rovin, and Ogbi, who promised to use their connections in Libya on Occidental's behalf. On December 17, he and Herbert Allen signed an agreement covering cost sharing and profits of any oil discoveries resulting from Galic's influence in Libya.[10]

As it happened, Hammer, usually the crafty one, had been bamboozled. The clandestine contracts became more troubling the more he learned. De Rovin "turned out to be an international crook and swindler and bankrupt man," Hammer later testified.

> The whole thing looked like a big promotional swindle and everybody in it was engaged in a lot of hot air, so I decided then that we had to be careful to see that these people did no harm to us in Libya, and although I had made up my mind to terminate them immediately . . . I felt I was better off to wait until such time as we were sure that they could not harm us in Libya. So I waited until sometime later and then made my move and served notice on all of them.[11]

The showdown occurred in June 1965, again at Claridge's. Galic, de Rovin, and Ogbi were unhappy when Hammer told them he was terminating their agreement. Galic threatened to sue but signed a waiver after Occidental agreed to pay him $200,000. Allen and Company did sue — after the oil had begun to gush — asking for more than $100 million. During a bizarre twenty-one-day trial, testimony centered on three questions: Was there a valid joint-venture agreement between Allen and Occidental? If there was, did Occidental terminate it illegally? And, was it Galic who turned up the oil concessions in Libya for Occidental, as he and Allen claimed?[12]

Hammer feared if Occidental were to settle or, worse, lose in court, Wall Street would perceive him as untrustworthy. So he sent employees, lawyers, and investigators around the globe seeking evidence. Louis Nizer, representing Occidental, devoted most of a chapter to the Allen lawsuit in his autobiographical memoir *Reflections Without Mirrors*. Nizer said Hammer prepared for a case unlike any other client: "Hammer looks forward to taking the stand. As in his business deals, he prepares thoroughly. Hours mean nothing. I have been called 'slave driver' by many clients . . . but Hammer does not understand why we quit at three in the morning. He studies every fact, every date, and the principles of law involved."

Concerning the Allen case, Nizer commented that

> the author of the *Arabian Nights* could not have provided a more engrossing scenario. We were engaged in a fascinating struggle, filled with mystery, intrigue, forged documents, and miracles, such as the discovery of an ocean of water beneath the Libyan desert. Naturally, then, Hammer enjoyed the drama while hiding his anxiety, while I, as lawyer, shared the anxiety without appreciating the drama.

Nizer believed Occidental had an airtight defense. But, he worried, "was there ever a suit in which a surprise witness or document did not suddenly appear to upset all calculations? The Allens produced such a document. It detonated in our midst and almost drove us to surrender. Then we recovered our stance and fought on more determinedly than ever."

That document was a letter from Libyan oil minister Fuad Kabazi to Galic, dated before the awarding of any concessions to Occidental. The letter testified to the close relationship between Kabazi and Galic; it also testified to the importance of the Allen company's financial standing in the awarding of concessions. The letter was devastating — only it was phony. Analysis by Occidental's experts showed it had been concocted by Kabazi long after the date it carried in order to help Allen and Company win the case. Presumably Kabazi had been promised a cut of the proceeds in the event of an Allen victory. Thereafter Ham-

mer and Nizer convinced the judge that Occidental was being victim-
ized; the judge ruled in Occidental's favor on every point. He felt
compelled, however, to say he found Hammer's testimony to be of
questionable credibility on some points, an observation made by other
judges in other cases.[13] Such criticism of his integrity notwithstanding,
Hammer said the judge's ruling saved his good name, and it certainly
saved Occidental hundreds of millions of dollars.

With no help coming from Galic, de Rovin, Ogbi, or Allen and
Company, Hammer initiated another clandestine operation in his effort
to win a Libyan concession. It involved a different cast of characters:
Hans-Albert Kunz, Kemal Zeinal Zade, and Wendell Phillips. On October 6, 1965, Hammer signed an agreement under which all three men
would receive a share of Occidental's oil revenues should it find anything of value in the ground. Kunz and Zeinal Zade were little known
outside Libya, where they had operated for years. Phillips, on the other
hand, was a fabled explorer, archaeologist, author — and promoter. The
New York Times called him "the world's largest individual holder of
oil concessions," adding that he "was the first Westerner since Lawrence of Arabia to become a tribal sheik." Through his travels, Phillips
had become friendly with the sultan of Muscat and Oman, who reportedly had introduced him to King Idris of Libya. Hammer later
denigrated Phillips's influence, claiming all he did for Occidental was
bring Kunz and Zeinal Zade into the picture. Hammer's remarks came
during a lawsuit in which Phillips's heirs accused Occidental of cheat-
ing on Libyan royalty payments to the estate.[14]

David Orser, who went to Libya for Mobil Oil Corporation in 1960
and joined Occidental there in 1968, said that during the first half of
the 1960s Occidental "was just one of fifty gangs trying to get in the
door. I had heard of Phillips, Kunz, and Zeinal Zade long before I met
them. . . . The Libyans would sometimes seek out people like that to
bring in new business, to do favors. Mobil did not use people like them,
but Occidental was the new boy on the block and had to play differently." Hammer continued his relationships with Kunz and Zade into
the late 1980s. He and Kunz finally fell out over royalty payments from
the Libyan wells. Kunz had received at least $23 million over eighteen
years but said Occidental owed him far more than that.[15]

Whoever else deserved credit for Occidental's entry into Libya, there
was no question that Hammer earned a large share. Kabazi, Libya's
minister of petroleum affairs from 1961 to 1962 and again from 1964
to 1967, said that when he was approached by Taher Ogbi about Occidental's chances, he expressed doubt about the company's ability to

finance the venture. On the other hand, Occidental took the initiative in exploring the possibilities, something few other companies its size had done, Kabazi said. Hammer had Occidental's annual report translated into Arabic and delivered to Kabazi. Statements from Occidental's bankers at Chase Manhattan helped convince Kabazi that the company not only was serious, but also financially able. Hammer solicited an endorsement from Signal Oil and Gas Company, which promised to assist Occidental with refining and marketing any oil discovered on Libyan territory.

When Kabazi examined the 120 competing oil-company bids beginning in July 1965, Occidental's stood out. It was, Kabazi said, "very thick, and had, I think, a leather binding and everything, and with the nice Libyan color ribbon and so on. It was very fancy and colorful."[16] Hammer had devised a special sheepskin diploma on which to submit the bid; it was bound with red, green, and black ribbons, the colors of the Libyan flag — a transparent but effective appeal to the king's patriotism. The bid included proposals for an ammonia plant, production of fertilizer from the residue of Libyan gas, deployment in Libya of an Occidental process to preserve perishable foods during shipping, educational assistance for Libyan students, and a promise to spend 5 percent of Occidental's Libyan oil earnings for agricultural development of the Kufra oasis. The Kufra proposal was the most imaginative of all the inducements in Hammer's package and quite likely the most effective. Hammer understood from geological data that the oasis, in southeastern Libya, lay on top of a large aquifer. He also knew from Allan Lightner that it was a symbolic spot for the king, whose father was buried there.

Hammer's special attention to the proposal produced the desired result. On February 20, 1966, Occidental surprised its competitors by receiving two of the most sought-after concessions to drill in the Sirte Basin. Occidental agreed to pay a one-eighth royalty to the Libyan government on any discovery, plus a 50 percent tax on any profits. Occidental's negotiators and the Libyan government signed the final contract on March 29, 1966; Hammer, as usual, was upbeat, announcing that "the concessions are surrounded by multibillion-barrel oil fields, so we think the concessions will be producers."[17]

Hammer's optimism was one thing. Actually finding oil, then extracting and marketing it, would be another, and represented a difficult, expensive undertaking. Occidental spent $2 million on seismic tests, then $1 million on each of three consecutive dry holes. Within the company, executives privately were referring to Libya as "Hammer's folly." Eugene Reid's skepticism echoed through Hammer's mind as he worried about a revolt by his normally agreeable board of directors. But that never happened.

The first successful well came in during mid-November 1966, at the smaller of the two concessions, known as the Augila field. David Orser, for one, was not surprised when success arrived. Orser worked for Mobil Oil in Libya at that time and later commented that "we were keenly aware at Mobil that the Occidental people had got potentially valuable concessions. . . . Some oil companies that also won concessions during 1966 could not or did not carry through and develop the concessions. We were interested and impressed at how Occidental handled the former Mobil land; Occidental drilled one successful well right over a Mobil campsite. . . . Occidental used new technology well. They could see things that older technology did not allow you to see. Occidental was lucky enough and bright enough to bring all that into play." [18]

At Occidental's 1967 annual meeting, Hammer said the oil was plentiful and low in sulfur content. Clean oil during a time of rising environmental concern was especially welcome. A *Wall Street Journal* reporter attending said the audience was "giddy with the recent price appreciation of its stock. . . . Obviously in an ebullient mood, the usually affable Dr. Hammer had approximately one thousand persons in the Grand Trianon room of the Beverly Wilshire Hotel . . . laughing and applauding almost his every gesture." Occidental hired Ira Cobleigh, a Ph.D. in economics and a financial writer, to produce a pamphlet based on the annual meeting. Cobleigh said Hammer "received an ovation not unlike that of a Roman general back from a winning campaign, or the late Babe Ruth pointing prophetically to the left field wall." [19]

Beneath the surface giddiness, Hammer was painfully aware that he had to find a way to move the oil from the concessions to the coast and then find a way to sell it outside Libya. That meant spending a lot of money to build an infrastructure. Esso, an industry giant, offered to help after an overture from Hammer. Esso agreed to pay $100 million in exchange for half of Occidental's Libyan operation, sweetened by the opportunity for Occidental to use refining and marketing systems already in place. Hammer was torn. He hated to share the wealth, yet the offer was more than Occidental's net worth. Hammer felt obligated to present the offer to his board of directors. The board voted to accept, so Hammer entered into further arduous negotiations with Esso, apparently completing them successfully.

Then, with no warning, the directors of Esso's parent company, Standard Oil of New Jersey (which in turn was owned by Exxon, one of the Seven Sisters), rejected the proposed contract. Hammer suspected a setup, retaliation by the major companies that would leave Occidental stuck with millions of barrels of unmarketable oil. But he was unable to prove a conspiracy. Then, after he announced another major find in Libya, Standard of New Jersey called again, according to Hammer, this time sending one of its directors to California accompanied by seventeen lawyers. Hammer, bargaining from strength, asked for $200 million this time. The Standard Oil team agreed to the terms, and everybody celebrated. But, again, the full Standard Oil board said no. Something seemed amiss, and Occidental was back to square one. Certain that the Seven Sisters were conspiring against him, Hammer decided to consult the federal government.

On May 15, 1967, Hammer met with four high-ranking State Department officials, including Eugene Rostow, undersecretary of state for political affairs. Rostow had joined the Johnson administration after serving as the dean of the Yale University law school. There was plenty of law to discuss at the meeting, because Occidental was thinking of negotiating a Libyan partnership with Gulf Oil. Hammer wondered if the Export-Import Bank or some other government entity would make the deal more enticing for Gulf by offering political-risk insurance. Rostow said he would ask the Justice Department about the legality of various alternatives.[20]

Meanwhile, Hammer was focusing on whether it was feasible to go it alone. The big question was how, or even whether, Occidental could build a pipeline quickly and affordably. No existing pipeline in Libya would do. Hammer approached the one company that in his opinion could handle such a massive project: the Bechtel Corporation, a multinational construction and engineering company headquartered in San Francisco. Bechtel had begun working in Libya about a decade earlier, building pipelines for oil companies and foreign governments that were early concession holders.

Hammer was in the unusual and potentially unpleasant position of suppliant. He told Stephen Bechtel, Sr., about Occidental's need for a pipeline to traverse up to 150 miles of desert from its wells to the closest usable Mediterranean port, at Zueitina. Hammer also mentioned the need for a terminal at the port itself. But, he said, his company could not afford to pay cash. Furthermore, Occidental had no assurance of customers for the oil if it reached port. Convinced that Hammer would come up with the money, Bechtel authorized the work on credit.

Hammer attributed the grand gesture to the sometimes inexplicable but vital human factor in business.

The truth was more complicated. Bechtel executives reportedly were split about whether to take a risk on an Occidental pipeline. Some worried about Hammer's ability to pay and about the adverse effects if major oil companies canceled contracts out of resentment. But Stephen Bechtel saw a potential profit, so he sent skilled negotiator Raphael Dorman to talk with Hammer. The risk paid off in the long run. Hammer's business around the globe eventually meant many millions of dollars to Bechtel.

The Libyan government also had doubts about an Occidental-Bechtel partnership. The Libyans believed Bechtel was too prosperous and therefore wanted to award the pipeline contract to smaller companies of Libyan origin. Hammer compromised, agreeing to award subcontracts — for example, transport and catering — to companies designated by the Libyan government. He worked feverishly to help his chances with side deals, including an executive airplane for the Libyan minister of petroleum affairs.[21]

His push to complete the pipeline quickly meant grueling, even inhuman, conditions. The temperature in the Libyan desert reached 120 degrees Fahrenheit during the day. Hammer ordered the work to proceed around the clock, necessitating the stringing of lights on poles across the desert. Disgruntled Bechtel supervisor John McGuire became a whistle-blower. He recalled the details for Senate investigators, who wrote:

> The frenzy that encompassed Occidental's operations was disastrous to life, limb, and property. Sixteen-hour days and rampant drinking were givens. . . . The desert heat did get to the brain . . . and some grown men actually came up to McGuire and cried at his feet, begging him to let them leave the country. Occidental and Bechtel, incidentally, did not bother to tell their employees what was in store for them before they were sent to Libya. . . . McGuire said that there was absolutely no adherence to any kind of safety standards. In all of his many years of travel for different multinational corporations, McGuire said, he never saw anything that even approached the conditions he witnessed in Libya in 1968. . . . McGuire was never sure of the reason for the dynamic push, why Occidental was in such a hurry to get the crude out. . . . McGuire said that Occidental and Bechtel personnel were forever pouring on the heat, working the Arab laborers into the ground. For example, when the Arab laborers would get down on their knees and pray to Mecca six

times a day, McGuire said, "the Occidental-Bechtel people were crawl-
ing all over them."[22]

Bechtel executives vigorously denied the charges by McGuire, who, the
company noted, was a disgruntled former employee.

Whatever the truth about working conditions, the pipeline was completed ahead of the projected deadline. There was at least one reason
for Hammer to rush the construction: The closing of the war-torn Suez
Canal in June 1967 had made Occidental's Libyan oil, located as it was
west of the canal, more valuable because it could be transported with
relative speed to Europe and beyond. The cost of the accelerated construction turned out to be nearly $150 million, but Hammer was not
complaining. By being able to transport its oil in a timely fashion, Occidental Petroleum more than recouped the extra expense.

On November 3, 1967, the American ambassador in Tripoli wired
Washington that Hammer had been at the embassy to discuss dedicating the pipeline as early as mid-January 1968: "Hammer expects King
Idris to attend and in order to point up importance American investment in Libya desires extend invitation to select Congressional delegation. . . . Embassy believes pipeline opening might provide non-
political context for Congressional visit and suggests such assistance to
Dr. Hammer as circumstances will permit."[23]

Hammer approached not only the State Department about recognizing Occidental's achievement, but also the White House. Through
Johnson's aide Marvin Watson, Hammer requested that a presidential
message be read at the opening of the pipeline and terminal. W. W.
Rostow of the White House staff summarized his opposition in a memorandum of April 22, 1968, one day before the dedication:

> In the oil trade, a message would be interpreted as a favor to Occidental
> in contrast to numerous other American companies already operating in
> Libya. We have not done this for anyone else. . . . Our oil experts be-
> lieve such a gesture toward Libya would make life more difficult for us
> in Saudi Arabia and Iran, by calling attention to what we are doing for
> their main competitor. Particularly, when the shah of Iran visits the
> president in June, he may ask us to press American companies to in-
> crease their liftings from Iran to produce greater revenues. We want to
> minimize the problem for the president insofar as possible. We do not
> think Libyan-American relations need this gesture, although it is a big
> project done by American investors and we are proud of it. . . . A
> message would put the president in a position of blessing a $100 million
> overseas investment. Although in the long run this strengthens our bal-

ance of payments position, it is something of a drain at a time when the president is stressing restraint.[24]

Rostow's argument dissuaded Johnson from acceding to the request, but the lack of a presidential message could not have dimmed Hammer's satisfaction much. The brief desert ceremony, staged at a cost of approximately $1 million, indeed attracted the Libyan king, as well as Senator Gore and about eight hundred other people. Christopher Rand, an Arabist who had worked for Bechtel, in his book *Making Democracy Safe for Oil* imputed huge significance to what Hammer had done:

> This volume of oil entering international distribution channels just eight hundred miles off Europe, outside the control of the major oil companies, posed one of the first major challenges to a system which had held sway for thirty years. Since the Suez Canal was now closed . . . its [Occidental's] oil was more valuable in Europe. The newcomer promptly played its part in jolting the system to its foundations.

Hammer was pleased by the oil moving through the pipeline and by the arrangements he made during construction to refine and sell it. He had read in an industry publication that Signal Oil and Gas Company was thinking of selling its European refining and marketing operations, so he called Claude Geismar at Signal, suggesting the company could solve its crude-oil shortage by taking Occidental's output. Signal would receive a commission on its sales of Occidental's oil. Hammer threw in the bonus of paying for an option to buy Signal's European operations if everybody thought it would be advantageous. The Signal board of directors accepted the offer. As the oil started to flow through the pipeline during February 1968, Hammer exercised the option to buy. Occidental, in one stroke, had found a way to dispose of its entire Libyan production in-house without a large outlay for construction. Geismar agreed to manage the European operations for Occidental and join the board of directors.[25]

With the Libyan discoveries, it seemed Hammer was everywhere. *Oil and Gas Journal* published its first full-scale piece about him on August 14, 1967, a sign he had arrived in the oil business. A personality profile in the *New York Times* appeared under the headline "FROM BOURBON TO OIL WITH A MIDAS TOUCH." Reporter William Smith ended by asking, "Why is Dr. Hammer still working sixteen hours a day seven days a week when he has achieved both fame and fortune?" For the answer, Smith let Hammer have the last word: " 'Believe me, I would pay Occidental to let me work.' " On the Libyan discovery, Smith quoted an unnamed Wall Street analyst: "With one fell swoop, it placed Occidental in the class of the major petroleum giants." Paul Steiger, describing Hammer in the *West* magazine of the *Los Angeles Times,* said, "In all the world there have been few who can claim to have socked it away with quite so much verve or in so many different ways as this shrewd and daring little man."[26] Occidental's stock moved from a first-quarter 1967 high of $50 to more than $100 a share by November 1967. The board of directors voted in favor of a three-for-one stock split. Many days, Occidental was the most heavily traded issue on the New York Stock Exchange.

In the midst of this success, one of the few realistic profiles of Hammer appeared, in *Fortune* magazine. Author Stanley Brown wondered about Occidental's Libyan production peaking in a relatively short time:

> What happens then depends on Hammer's ability to solve several problems, including the concentration of earning power in Libya, the absence of an apparent successor to the energetic but aging doctor, and the pressure on world oil prices as new discoveries in areas such as the Persian Gulf, Nigeria, Alaska, and the North Sea bring enormous quantities of crude oil into the market.

Brown acknowledged the rise in Occidental to $100 a share but also noted the dampening effects of a New York Stock Exchange decision to raise the margin requirements on purchases, a ruling designed to reduce speculative buying and selling.[27]

More negative was a front-page article by Byron Calame in the November 27, 1967, *Wall Street Journal.* The article tied Occidental's gyrating stock price to questionable public relations tactics. Calame observed that at the end of September 1967 the stock was selling at $66, then soared to $122 on November 13 after frequent announcements about Libyan oil discoveries. A sell-off dropped it to $94, but a week later it was up to more than $103, apparently because Occidental announced a stock split and an increased dividend. A major part of the article concerned Occidental's reporting of nonrecurring items without separating them from operating profit.

Multiple announcements of the same blessed event came in for scrutiny, too. Calame told of an October 16, 1967, news release about a fourth oil discovery in Libya. Two weeks later, a separate news release referred to the same discovery without making it clear that there had been a previous announcement. Calame reported that Occidental used the controversial accounting practice of spreading out expenses from dry holes by writing them off only as the company sold oil from producing wells. The American Petroleum Institute told Calame that thirty-five of thirty-seven oil companies checked used a more conservative method. Calame noted, too, how Occidental "is known for its careful cultivation of good will within the financial community. . . . Near Los Angeles . . . recently, a half-dozen brokers were to be found on Dr. Hammer's seventy-two-foot yacht, sipping champagne and digging into a buffet lunch when they were not fishing."

Occasional skepticism aside, it seemed as if everything was going Hammer's way at home and overseas. Even when an acquisition attempt ultimately failed, Hammer had the ability to emerge as the perceived winner. In one such instance, the unsuccessful takeover of Kern County Land Company — a raid, as the target termed it — led to a profit that defrayed the huge cost of the Libyan pipeline and terminal. Lawsuits growing out of the bid reached the United States Supreme Court. It was one of many controversial transactions not mentioned by Hammer in his autobiography.

The brouhaha began when Hammer paid an uninvited call during mid-April 1967 on Dwight Cochran, Kern County Land's president. Cochran expressed indignation about what he considered to be a raid and refused to discuss the proposal. Three weeks later, on a Sunday morning, Cochran was playing golf when Hammer called his home. Mrs. Cochran took a message. Realizing its importance, she sent a messenger to the golf course. When Cochran returned Hammer's call, he learned Occidental would be announcing an offer to buy Kern stock at $20 a share over the last price on the New York Stock Exchange. After meeting Cochran the next day, Hammer expressed optimism. But Cochran said he was strongly opposed to the offer, telling reporters it "came as a complete surprise."[28]

Certainly Cochran was not surprised at the attractiveness of his company as a takeover target. Some of its western landholdings were devoted to farming and cattle; much of the land was ideal for oil and gas exploration. At Occidental's annual meeting two days after the offer, Hammer said Kern had been unsuccessful in its oil and gas exploration. "We believe we can help them," Hammer said. The original offer would have given Occidental about 11 percent of Kern's stock, but as the days passed, Hammer raised his sights until it appeared he might aim for majority control. Cochran was furious, using terms such as "power grab" and "opportunistic" to describe Hammer in communications urging resistance by Kern's stockholders. From Cochran's viewpoint, there was good reason to oppose a merger with Occidental. Kern's management was horrified at Hammer's promotional style: how he hyped Occidental to Wall Street analysts and potential stockholders, how he brazenly predicted future earnings and inserted quotations from positive media coverage in the company's annual report. Kern moved conservatively, generally refraining even from issuing news releases.[29]

Cochran searched for ways to stop Hammer. After Occidental had acquired about 20 percent of Kern's shares, Cochran proposed marriage to what he considered a more compatible partner — Tenneco, a diversified energy-based company. Now it was Hammer's turn to be furious. There was Occidental with a $75 million investment, and all it had to show for it was a minority position. Hammer threatened to halt the marriage to Tenneco, then went to court to force Kern to open its books for examination. After acrimonious negotiations, Hammer decided to allow the Tenneco merger. His price: Occidental would give Tenneco an option to acquire its Kern shares. In exchange for the option, Occidental would receive $10 a share — nearly $9 million up front.[30]

The Tenneco stockholders approved the arrangement at a special meeting. Kern shareholders approved the merger the next day. Occidental refrained from voting its shares, hoping to avoid what was looming as a serious legal problem. Section 16-B of the Securities Exchange Act prohibited profits by an insider during the first six months of its stock ownership. Occidental believed it could not fairly be called an insider. But to play safe, Hammer insisted on delaying the sale of Occidental's shares until December 1967, after six months had passed. Louis Nizer petitioned the Securities and Exchange Commission for an exemption from Section 16-B, but the agency denied it. Meanwhile, Kern and Tenneco, becoming impatient, were moving to consummate the merger. If they moved too quickly, Occidental would lose any legal protection it might have gained from a December closing date.[31]

Hammer and Nizer devised a strategy to delay the merger. They agreed to pay the costs of small Kern stockholders to file lawsuits in state and federal courts throughout the country, lawsuits whose purpose was to delay the merger, if not overturn it. Kern, seeing what it believed to be litigation based on "vexation and harassment," sued the small stockholders, hoping to expose the true nature of the delaying tactics. Cecil Munn, a litigator hired by Kern County Land, submitted a compelling, melodramatic brief addressed to the genesis of the controversy. Munn's conclusion was straightforward:

> A series of assaults to block or impede the reorganization of Kern County
> Land Company into the corporate family of Tenneco originated and are

controlled and fomented by Occidental Petroleum Corporation in its effort to obtain a $20 million quick profit at the expense of innocent shareholders. The mastermind behind their many-fronted attack is Mr. Louis Nizer of the New York bar, acting as counsel for Occidental.[32]

The federal judge accepted Munn's conclusion, noting that whoever was footing the bill for the tiny shareholders had deep pockets:

It is apparent that the obvious expenses of the litigation in some instances will exceed the entire value of the plaintiff shareholder's stock, and in all instances will be more than the difference between the claimed value and the figure he is getting under the reorganization plan. The plaintiffs in those cases have insisted that they did not expect to be held responsible for the expenses, and have claimed that they did not know who was putting up the money for such expenses.

Naming Occidental specifically, the judge said that

there is little doubt that somebody with a lot more at stake and a much stronger motive for delaying the closing than these named plaintiffs was furnishing an almost unlimited expense account to finance this weird a pattern of delaying actions. The timing, the coordination, the connection of the same lawyer with all the cases, and the ever-present, mysterious source of money to foot the heavy expenses were not just happenstance.[33]

Hammer's delaying tactics failed to keep Kern and Tenneco from merging before December 1967. In the short term, that was fine — Tenneco exercised its option to purchase Occidental's shares in Kern. Occidental received about $95 million in the transaction, of which about $20 million was profit, before expenses. But in the long run, the picture was less clear. Without the protection of the six-month hiatus, Occidental could be forced to disgorge its profits. Kern and Tenneco moved to achieve just that result and won the first round: A judge said Occidental had to pay back more than $23 million.[34]

Frantic, Hammer hired prestigious lawyer Whitney North Seymour to argue the case at the appeals courts, which ruled that Occidental was innocent of violating Section 16-B. The decision, arrived at on narrow legal grounds, had nothing to do with Occidental's outrageous behavior in seeking to stall the Kern-Tenneco merger. Hammer's opponents were outraged. They sought review by the United States Supreme Court and received it. On May 7, 1973, the Supreme Court ruled 6 to 3 — in Hammer's favor. But not even that decision put an end to the litigation arising from the takeover attempt. Occidental Petroleum's legal bills mounted, eating up a portion of the huge profit. [35]

Julian Rogers, who worked for an Occidental subsidiary and had owned Kern stock before the takeover attempt, sued for a finder's fee. Rogers presented evidence that it was his idea to acquire Kern. He testified that he had attended a meeting in Hammer's office during which Hammer had asked about how to implement the transaction. Rogers suggested hiring an investment banker, but Hammer reportedly replied, "Oh, no, they would want three hundred thousand dollars just to talk to them. That's out." Hammer authorized Rogers to explore alternate means. When Hammer responded to Rogers's claim in court, his vaunted memory deserted him. A jury decided that Occidental indeed owed Rogers for his idea and awarded him $850,000 in May 1975. When Occidental told Rogers it would press an appeal, he bitterly accepted a settlement that reportedly was about $100,000. In 1978, Occidental finally disposed of the last lawsuit attempting to strip away the $20 million profit from the Kern deal.[36]

Hammer made bids for other firms in a less contentious atmosphere. Probably the most significant for Occidental's future was that for the Permian Corporation. It was one of many companies that seemed to fit well into the big picture being painted by Hammer. The successful drilling in Libya drove up Occidental's stock, making it attractive to companies that Hammer wanted to acquire. Permian, based in Midland, Texas, was an oil-gathering, transporting, and reselling operation, a middleman with a high gross. The key figure was Walter Davis, Permian's founder and CEO, who met Hammer during 1963 through Terry Sanford, the governor of North Carolina, Davis's native state. Davis and Hammer were impressed with each other, despite their different styles and backgrounds. Davis, rough-hewn and salty, began to discuss a merger with Hammer on August 4, 1966. By October 27, the two men had reached agreement. Occidental used stock valued at more than $54 million to acquire Permian. Davis described Hammer as "the greatest financial and business genius of our time." Hammer said Davis was "being groomed for the presidency. We acquired Permian principally to get him. I see in him the kind of executive I have been looking for." Other executives at Occidental failed to understand Hammer's enthusiasm for Davis, whom they considered crude and lacking in people skills. Hammer never had reason to regret the acquisition of Permian itself — the company helped Occidental's growth immensely — but the honeymoon with Davis soured quickly. Davis was the first of many men to be hailed by Hammer as the heir apparent, only to be later forced out.[37]

After buying Permian, Hammer acquired the McWood Corporation, headquartered in Abilene, Texas, whose business was much the same as Permian's. Next he bought Garrett Research and Development Company, a purchase that led him into a near-obsession with the potential of synthetic fuels. Judging by the rise in Occidental's stock prices, investors and brokers approved of the transactions. Encouraged, Hammer went after bigger fish, starting with Signal Oil and Gas. He already had bought that company's European operations; now he wanted it all. The merger would have just about doubled Occidental's size overnight, in one of the largest oil-company transactions ever. The perception among some investors was that Hammer's offer surpassed Signal's true worth. He pressed on anyway. As rumors abounded that the Justice Department was looking into antitrust violations, the stock prices of both companies dropped, for whatever reasons. Signal's chairman, Samuel Mosher, publicly questioned the merger, while other Signal executives worked to negate Mosher's opposition. With everything in disarray, the two companies dropped plans for the merger in February 1968.[38]

The indefatigable Hammer did not miss a beat. If Signal was off-limits, well, there were lots of other targets out there. Hammer knew King Idris could not last forever and, although optimistic about Occidental's future in Libya, realized it made sense to diversify on a grand scale while the company prospered. One motive was to make Occidental so big it would be takeover-proof. Hammer liked being the shark; he had no desire to be swallowed by a larger fish. So during 1968, he engineered the acquisition of not just one but two huge corporations.

The first was Island Creek Coal Company, headquartered in Cleveland, the third-largest coal firm in America. The cost: $150 million of Occidental Petroleum stock. Next came the largest merger in U.S. business history up to that time — the acquisition of Hooker Chemical Company for $800 million. Occidental was now a company with more than $1 billion in annual revenue. The acquisitions vaulted it from number 102 to 48 in the Fortune 500.[39]

In the short run, the acquisition of Hooker caused unpleasant ripples amid the general rejoicing. The Federal Trade Commission charged that the acquisition illegally reduced competition in the manufacture of diammonium phosphate and blended fertilizers. Occidental signed a consent order, agreeing to divest some of its operations within three years to stimulate competition. To complicate matters, Representative Hale Boggs, a Democrat from Louisiana and one of the most influential members of Congress, complained to the SEC that Occidental had violated insider-trading rules when acquiring Hooker, a company from his home state. The agency found no evidence persuasive enough to prosecute Occidental.[40]

In the longer run, Hammer's acquisition of Hooker Chemical stained his and Occidental's names irrevocably. But as 1968 turned into 1969, it appeared nothing would dampen Occidental's performance as the hot stock of the late 1960s. Senator Gore sent Hammer money to cover the purchase of a thousand Hooker Chemical shares at $50 each. J. Paul Getty wrote Hammer from his English estate, commenting that Occidental's statements, sent by Hammer, were "an amazing story of what one man can do today. We all know there were titans in the past, but most of the present generation believe that conditions today do not permit a small independent to become a great major oil company. You have proved that it is still possible, and I congratulate you."[41]

There was plenty to gloat about. On November 16, 1968, Hammer told the New York Society of Security Analysts an anecdote, perhaps apocryphal, that had been related to him: A director of Ford Motor Company acquainted with Hammer met the chairman of a major oil company. The Ford director needled the oilman about Occidental's beating the Seven Sisters to the big stakes in Libya. The oilman decided to make a proposal to Occidental about purchasing its Libyan production. So he sent an emissary to Los Angeles. The emissary returned with the news that he could not conclude a deal because Hammer knew nothing about the oil business. Hammer laughed at the story. So did the security analysts. Hammer continued: "By now, I believe our competitors feel that perhaps there is more orthodoxy in our operations than appears on the surface. But in a world engulfed in rapid . . . changes, we remain committed to a policy of vigorous, imaginative seeking and seizing sound opportunities for growth . . . by cutting through red tape. In that sense, we plead guilty to not being as orthodox as some of our competitors." Asked about the political situation in Libya under the aging King Idris, Hammer replied, "I think Libya is one of the most stable countries outside the United States."[42]

Hammer had reason to be confident about Libya. Even the water exploration at Kufra had worked out surprisingly well from a public relations standpoint. At Occidental's annual meeting on May 21, 1969 — Hammer had mandated his birthday as the date for the stockholders' get-together — he told how Occidental was growing barley and alfalfa and was grazing livestock at the oasis. He predicted food self-sufficiency for Libya within a few years. He was so enthusiastic that he informed a congressional committee two months later that water "is now being used to transform the Libyan desert and economy, and may prove in the long run to be more valuable to Libya than the discovery of oil."[43]

King Idris told Hammer that "Allah sent you to Libya." The king reportedly asked if he could rename the royal birthplace Hammer. Armand said he diplomatically declined, asking if he could name one of Occidental's oil finds the Idris field. The flattered king consented. Dudley Miller, who directed Occidental's Libyan operations, gave Hammer credit for Kufra: "It was great public relations, but it was truly close to the doctor's heart. He likes agriculture, and had every intention of making North Africa the breadbasket of Europe."[44]

PART V

THE WIDE WORLD
OF OCCIDENTAL

16

Hot Spots

ALTHOUGH BY THE END OF THE 1960s Armand Hammer was riding high at Occidental Petroleum, he had failed to achieve what he considered adequate public attention and acclaim. The attention, if not the acclaim, was about to increase exponentially, however. For in September 1969, Hammer found himself thrust onto the world's center stage as the lead in a long-running drama.

The site of the theater was Libya. The play had begun away from the public eye three and a half years earlier, when Hammer won drilling concessions, and moved into the public eye on September 1, 1969, when a self-styled Libyan revolutionary council overthrew King Idris, the seventy-nine-year-old monarch who had reigned since 1951. Because Hammer had obtained Occidental's lucrative concessions by courting the king, he was distressed to see Idris unceremoniously dethroned while undergoing medical treatment in Turkey. The bloodless revolution took most foreigners by surprise. There had been political unrest two years before, but most of Idris's subjects saw no compelling reason to oust him. He was generally benevolent, lived modestly by the standards of other monarchs, and had increased the nation's wealth through his ability to handle the fiercely competing oil companies since the discovery of black gold, in 1957.[1]

"There was always talk of ferment in Libya during the late 1960s. There was talk of the king abdicating. But the question was, to whom?" said Michael Arra, a lawyer who went to Libya to represent Mobil Oil and ended up working for Hammer. "The Shalhi family was favored by the king, but not widely liked. You had to assume that whatever happened within the Libyan government, you would find a way to keep producing." Arra, moreover, had confidence in Hammer's ability to handle any situation: "Dr. Hammer has a great sense of geopolitical relations, almost like Henry Kissinger. . . . He looks at the long-term in front of him, as well as behind him. He has an ultimate belief in the value of natural resources. Their prices might fluctuate, but they will never be worthless. He would have been a good head of the World Bank or the Agency for International Development or some such. . . . He would use the personal touch with Libyan ministers, ask them about their children, help them get their children into American schools. . . . He was accessible to everybody."[2]

After the coup, foreign experts had difficulty determining who possessed influence in the government. The initial announcement of the cabinet contained no mention of Muammar al-Qaddafi. Although Hammer, too, was in the dark, he sounded sanguine. One of his first public statements appeared four days after the coup: "We have been in contact with our management in Libya, who have advised us that they are having good relations with the new Libyan authorities, who have assured the oil companies operating in Libya that they will honor all concession agreements." Hammer watchers discounted his optimism as self-serving, but in fact he had good grounds for his statement; the new government was placing little emphasis on renegotiations with the oil companies. Premier Mahmoud Maghreby said there would be "no spectacular changes in oil policy."[3]

Hammer, however, understood that if the government ever decided to squeeze the oil companies, Occidental perhaps would be the most vulnerable. There was a difference between Occidental and every other major producer in Libya: its much heavier dependence on that country's oil. Hammer also realized the importance of making peace with a government that had displaced the monarchy with which he had been identified. So he played what he perceived as his strong suit — himself. Certain of his ability to sway heads of state, he arranged to visit Libya, ignoring contrary advice from Occidental's staff there. To this end, he sent John Boles, a former university economics professor with Middle East contacts, as an advance man.

Boles called at the U.S. Embassy on October 6 to announce that Hammer would arrive on October 13. The embassy wired the State Department that "Boles asked if embassy considered visit good idea at this time. Economic counselor replied . . . it probably [would] be best . . . if Hammer deferred visit until January . . . especially since only purpose . . . was apparently establish contact with members new regime." The embassy staff explained the potential problems with an immediate visit by Hammer:

Contacts by embassy with members of new regime still difficult to establish [in] view of regime's preoccupation with governmental organization, its investigations into activities of old regime . . . and heavy workload on limited number of personalities chosen for governmental positions on basis [of] their political reliability and freedom from any taint of corruption, which increasingly stands out as major thrust against former leadership.[4]

Hammer, not always one to heed advice from his government, listened this time. He did not have the luxury of sitting idly. He had problems elsewhere.

One of those problems was far from the Libyan desert, in the tiny coastal town of Machiasport, Maine. What became known as the battle of Machiasport had its genesis in the mind of Jack Evans, a retired energy-company executive who directed the Independent Fuel Oil Marketers of America. Evans was looking for oil to import. The state of Maine was seeking an oil company to build a refinery that would provide jobs and supply New England with lower-cost fuel for its harsh winters. Residents had experienced a shortage of home heating oil during the winter of 1967–1968; they wanted to avoid a reprise. Evans approached numerous oil companies with his plan. The answer was always no. Their executives had no interest in crossing swords with the rest of the industry, which abhorred the thought of imports cutting into domestic sales.[5]

Evans's acquaintance John Buckley, editor of *Petroleum Intelligence Weekly,* suggested contacting Occidental about supplying Libyan oil for the proposed refinery. It burned clean at a time when environmentalists were gaining political clout. Furthermore, Buckley liked Occidental's spare corporate structure, which allowed for quick decision making, and also was impressed by how well Hammer treated his wife, Frances. On the negative side, Buckley noticed that Hammer "was not strong on corporate niceties and bureaucratic reviews; he had a tendency to take shortcuts compared to an Exxon or a Mobil." In May 1968, Evans circulated a memorandum about building a refinery to handle imported oil, with 25 percent ownership going to Occidental. A vital part of the plan was to obtain foreign-trade-zone status for Machiasport, allowing Occidental to bring its Libyan oil to the refinery duty-free.[6]

The procedure for establishing a zone already existed; Hammer was determined to take advantage of it. He testified that "foreign trade zones are designed to keep jobs that might otherwise go abroad in this country. Zones are designed to keep facilities, including oil refineries and petrochemical plants, from being built offshore. Further, zones offer an ideal vehicle to help this country solve one of its most pressing international problems — our balance of payment difficulties."[7] If Occidental received the foreign trade zone, as Hammer expected, the next steps would be obtaining import permits from the Interior Department, starting construction of the refinery, and selling oil by some time in 1969. When the Interior Department received Occidental's formal application for a refinery, an enraged industry learned Hammer was requesting a quota of 100,000 barrels a day and promising to supply heating oil to New England's independent marketers at 10 percent below prevailing prices.

Before the unveiling of the Machiasport plan, competitors had perceived Hammer as an upstart who knew little about the oil business. His imaginative — and possibly questionable — tactics in Libya had done nothing to endear him to managements failing to find oil there. Many of those competitors wanted to make Hammer squirm. Their distress at his attack on the industry's oil-import quota system was sincere. Hammer knew he was questioning an article of faith. As he told a congressional committee,

> I believe we need some system of import controls. But I also agree that the present system keeps new United States competitors, like Occidental, who discover large quantities of oil outside the United States, from getting fair access to the United States market. It also places certain regions, such as New England, at a distinct disadvantage. . . . Because foreign oil imports are strictly controlled, refiners naturally choose to build new capacity in the areas that are close to domestic supplies which they must use. This eliminates the necessity of moving the domestic crude over long supply routes in high-cost United States flag tankers. This economic factor, in turn, explains to a large extent why East Coast refining capacity has declined by almost 200,000 barrels daily, while in Texas and Louisiana refining capacity has risen by almost 1,250,000 barrels daily during the ten-year period in which the oil import program has been in existence.[8]

Appealing to the interests of others, Hammer threw in a national security argument: "It should be emphasized that the size of the Maine refinery, plus its domestic location, will give United States armed forces an added measure of supply security in the event of emergency. The plant's location in Maine will help achieve another strategic goal . . . the dispersal of the nation's refining capacity, now heavily concentrated along the United States side of the Gulf of Mexico." Hammer rejected charges of profiteering:

> Occidental is not asking for any exclusive or any privileged position. If any other oil company would make a proposal that has the same advantages to the nation and to the people of New England that Occidental proposed, I believe that their proposal would receive the same consideration. . . . If Atlantic Richfield can offer the same terms or better terms, we welcome competition. We did not initiate this. The state of Maine came to us when every other oil company refused to do anything to help the people of New England.[9]

The major producers were having none of Hammer's line. Continental Oil Company executives wrote Stewart Udall, secretary of the interior, and C. R. Smith, secretary of commerce, that Occidental's plan

> will have an extensive and detrimental impact upon the entire nation. If approved, the mandatory oil import program will be crippled or destroyed and the security of this nation will be seriously threatened; the real purpose and intent of the Foreign Trade Zone Act will be circumvented and distorted; Occidental Petroleum Corporation will receive enormous giveaway profits approximating one billion dollars, and the alleged benefits to New England will be largely illusory, and far outweighed by the cost to other parts of the nation and by the inequities and dislocations that will result throughout the petroleum industry.

The American Petroleum Institute asked President Lyndon Johnson to reject Hammer's proposal, even though Occidental was a member. *Oil and Gas Journal* reported on the organization's "unprecedented action in taking a stand on a specific import proposal."[10]

Lloyd Unsell, the spokesman for smaller oil companies, was one of Hammer's most effective opponents. His homework included obtaining Hammer's out-of-print memoir, *The Quest of the Romanoff Treasure,* to plumb the depths of its author's mind. Unsell commented:

> One cannot help but get the feeling that Hammer's exploits in Russia provided the strategy which Occidental is using to get its proposed trade zone refinery. . . . The . . . Romanoff treasure, as lucrative as it proved to be, would pale into insignificance should Hammer succeed in his quest of the Machiasport treasure. To begin with, many people have been no less than amazed that any company would take the position that it is entitled to a special deal outside of the rules such as Occidental seeks at Machiasport. Such special treatment is not incredible at all,

however, compared to the high privilege to which Hammer became accustomed in Russia.[11]

Employing sarcasm, Unsell said that Hammer's formula was to promise
benefits to as many people as possible. If Hammer were to be believed,
he said, Occidental's refinery would be the first with "more sex appeal
than Liz, more feeling for motherhood than Whistler, and more . . .
goodies for more people per dollar . . . than the Department of Health,
Education, and Welfare. . . . How the Republic progressed this far
without this deal is a real headscratcher." Unsell likened Hammer's
plan to a giveaway game, in which the advertising made it sound as if
everybody won although nobody paid. The world was not like that,
Unsell said: "Somebody has to put up the house stakes. Guess who?"[12]

Hammer, enjoying the combat, called a session in Occidental's New
York office. Peter Bradford, an aide to Maine governor Kenneth Curtis, described the meeting, which was attended by Curtis, Hammer's
lawyer Louis Nizer, his lobbyist Myer Feldman, and New England oil
marketers. The meeting was vintage Hammer. He kept everybody
waiting, a reminder of his importance:

> From the moment he arrived, a miniskirted secretary with a British
> accent interrupted the meeting at five-minute intervals to bring him
> phone messages, some of which he left the room to return. In his ab-
> sence, Nizer philosophized about the importance of cooperation and the
> evils of the major oil companies, while Feldman passed out political
> assignments. When the independents raised the question of their share
> of the refinery, they were told that such discussions were premature.[13]

The New Englanders worried about Hammer's desire for complete
control: "To Armand Hammer, friend of Lenin and of every Democratic president since Roosevelt, a thirty-eight-year-old governor and a
state of less than one million people were objects to be used, albeit
nicely, since the association was potentially a long one," Bradford wrote.
Andy Nixon, at the meeting as an aide to Governor Curtis, was taken
aback at Hammer's cruel treatment of underlings. "He could be
charming, but I would have to say he was a most inconsiderate person.
He seemed not to care about people; he used them up and discarded
them." Later, Nixon — who became an oil-company executive himself — answered a telephone call at 2:00 A.M. from Hammer, who wanted
to talk to a Washington lawyer in whose home Nixon was staying.
Nixon refused to help, telling Hammer the lawyer was asleep. "He got

very angry," Nixon said. "He couldn't believe anyone would say no to him."[14]

The Maine representatives expressed added concern about the participation of Fred Vahlsing, Jr., as a representative of Occidental. Hammer and Fred Vahlsing, Sr., had had a long association through their mutual interest in cattle breeding. Fred Senior was a respected figure credited with making Maine potatoes a household staple. His son, however, a businessman who was a supporter and friend of Senator Edmund Muskie's, was not perceived by everybody as respectable. A *New York Times* profile told of Fred Junior's notoriety in Maine: "The legendary Mr. Vahlsing is beginning to run into difficulties along a broad front that could affect the 1972 presidential race. Financial headaches at one company in Maine have been felt throughout the state. Charges of stream pollution by the company are being used in an attempt to embarrass a potential presidential candidate [Muskie]." Bradford described Vahlsing as "an ebullient man given to boasting of his extensive political contacts."[15]

With all his high-powered help, Hammer had no doubt he could make the refinery a reality. But building such a controversial refinery meant more than convincing Lyndon Johnson. Many agencies would have to approve. Bradford wrote that Hammer failed to realize how limited his influence would be when opposed by so many powerful forces: "He was able to arrange White House meetings, to get Cabinet officers on the telephone, to be named to presidential commissions, but these were trappings traditionally available to large contributors. . . . Misled by the doctor's apparent strength, Occidental permitted itself to be drawn into a war of attrition."[16]

The war became harder to win when Hammer got on the wrong side of Representative Hale Boggs. Boggs, of Louisiana, was predisposed to oppose Machiasport because of his many campaign contributors at major oil companies. Boggs called a news conference in which he alleged that Occidental had attempted to bribe him into favoring the refinery. Three days later, he used fifteen pages of the *Congressional Record* to discuss the alleged bribe. He said it had been offered during a visit to his office by executives of Occidental's new subsidiary, Hooker Chemical. The executives told him, he said, that they wanted to contribute to his reelection campaign. He asked if they expected him to drop his testimony against Occidental's refinery at an upcoming hearing in return. When the men said yes, Boggs claimed, he angrily walked out. "They immediately wrote me a letter . . . which is . . . an obvious attempt to justify what happened in my office and to avoid the viola-

tion of the statute," Boggs said. One paragraph of that letter, signed by
E. W. Mathias, said, "Lest there be any misunderstanding, Mr. [James]
Baldwin and I want it abundantly clear that there is no relationship
between the discussion regarding the campaign contribution, and the
Maine refinery." Boggs demanded that the FBI check into the matter.[17]

The dramatic charges by Boggs received attention in high places.
White House aide W. DeVier Pierson wrote President Johnson: "The
attached clippings show what a big deal the Maine foreign trade zone
project is. Hale Boggs held a wild press conference Friday in which he
accused Occidental of trying to buy him off to drop his opposition to
the project. It was carried in the Sunday *New York Times.*" Similarly,
Representative Wayne Aspinall of Colorado asked the president to delay Occidental's foreign-trade-zone application until completion of a
thorough investigation: "In a matter of such importance involving such
a large benefit to a single company, an immediate investigation of all
matters involved is essential. . . . If the charges all proved to be true,
and our government had already granted the special treatment which
has been requested, we might well have a very serious scandal on our
hands."[18]

Hammer was enraged, writing the president that Aspinall's letter
was part of an attack by competitors gouging New Englanders, who
needed fuel oil. Hammer said Boggs had invited the Hooker representatives to his office to entrap them. Expanding on the charges, he sent
the president sworn statements by Hooker representatives to the effect
that they had done nothing to bribe Boggs. He also included a Nizer
memorandum, which said that even if Boggs's statements were true,
no law had been broken.[19]

Attacking Boggs backfired on Hammer. This was one time when a
combative strategy made no sense. Johnson and Boggs were friends.
The miscalculation probably stemmed from Hammer's overweening
desire for legitimacy. He had come so far, only to see his name sullied
by the word of one politically motivated opponent who had congressional immunity. The Boggs episode hurt Occidental's chances to win
Johnson administration approval for Machiasport. But the main reason
Hammer failed to carry the day with Johnson was that he ran out of
time. Richard Nixon, a Republican, was by then the president-elect;
Johnson saw no reason to make a decision bound to anger important
Democratic contributors no matter which way he ruled. In December
1968, his lame-duck secretary of commerce announced that Nixon would
inherit the controversy.[20]

During the transition from Johnson to Nixon, Hammer kept the issue on the front burner by persuading Senator Thomas McIntyre of New Hampshire to call a sympathetic hearing, allowing Occidental to score points in the media. He continued to take his case to the public after Nixon settled in. He received an introduction from Senator Alan Cranston of California, who called him "an outstanding citizen" and a "man of genius." Hammer promised not only plentiful, clean, lower-cost oil, but also a $7 million donation to a marine resources foundation established by governors of the New England states. Hammer distributed a pamphlet called "Let Us Keep the Record Straight on Machiasport." The twenty-five-page propaganda piece had the look of authority, containing twenty-nine footnotes and a statistical table.[21]

As the debate about Machiasport continued, Hammer had to adapt to circumstances beyond his control, something he had learned to do well during his decade as a concessionaire in the Soviet Union. Part of his effectiveness was putting the best face on a bad situation. About the time of the Libyan coup, he had demonstrated his adaptability by unveiling a new feature of the Machiasport plan, denying that the shift had anything to do with the uncertainty in Tripoli:

> While we initially planned to import a large percentage of crude oil from Libya at Machiasport, our current plans are to use up to seventy percent Venezuelan oil. . . . It makes economic sense for us to sell Libyan oil to the rapidly growing and nearby European markets than to Maine, and to use largely Venezuelan supplies for Machiasport. Venezuela is as close to Maine as ports on the United States Gulf Coast.[22]

Hammer wanted to avoid a public admission of anxiety about Libya; that could have devastated Occidental's stock price. So he portrayed his new emphasis as being in the public's interest. But, in fact, using Venezuelan oil was entirely in Occidental's interest. As Peter Bradford noted, Hammer's plan

> sought to draw the Venezuelan government into the quota struggle on Occidental's side. Venezuelan oil interests had demonstrated considerable past leverage with the State Department, and Occidental was hoping that the leverage would influence Secretary of State William Rogers's conduct as a member of the Cabinet Task Force on Oil Import Controls. Second, Occidental had submitted bids for exploration concessions on Venezuela's Lake Maracaibo, and [Hammer's] offer of a large United States market share would make those bids more appealing to the Venezuelan government. Because Venezuela crude was exceptionally high in sulphur and difficult to desulphurize, the doubling of the Venezuelan

role made the refinery less compatible with the promise of low-sulphur
fuel for the East Coast. Furthermore, because Venezuela had no deep-
water ports, the supertanker savings dwindled.

Hammer's revisions of the original plan meant it was unlikely that he
would be able to deliver a 10 percent reduction in the cost of home
heating oil, something he conveniently omitted from his statement,
Bradford noted.[23]

Hammer lobbied Nixon about Machiasport, sending a letter through
John Ehrlichman, the president's influential assistant for domestic affairs. Hammer expressed concern that the Cabinet Task Force on Oil
Import Controls had heard mostly evidence from opponents of Machiasport.[24] The letter precipitated debate within the White House staff
about whether the president should respond, thereby injecting himself
into the controversy. The staff drafted a letter for Nixon on White
House stationery, but in the end the president delegated the reply to
his assistant Peter Flanigan, who had met with Hammer during the
transition. The controversy had acquired political overtones, which made
Nixon cautious about getting involved. Crosby Noyes, in his column
for the *Washington Star,* explained the awkwardness of the situation for
Maine senator Edmund Muskie, who favored Machiasport and planned
to run for president on the Democratic ticket. Muskie was a darling of
the conservationists, who opposed building a huge refinery on the beautiful Maine coast. On this issue, however, Muskie was on the side of an
oil company perceived as an enemy by the environmentalists. Fred
Vahlsing's identification with Occidental's plan was especially harmful
to Muskie. Hammer again wrote Nixon through Ehrlichman, suggesting that the Noyes piece had been planted by an Occidental competitor.

The president avoided a decision by ordering further studies. The
oil-state senators were delighted but lay low so Nixon might avoid
being charged with selling out to the Seven Sisters. Almost all members
of Congress from New England, on the other hand, were upset by the
delay. Hammer looked for alternate channels of influence. He met with
Robert Finch, who served Nixon on the White House staff and as
secretary of Health, Education, and Welfare. Finch talked to Flanigan
about helping Hammer. Flanigan in turn wrote George Lincoln, head
of the Office of Emergency Preparedness at the National Security Council:
"As you can imagine, he [Hammer] made a pitch for his Machiasport
refinery. . . . I am not particularly sympathetic to Hammer, but I do
think you might wish to review this proposal so that there will be an
administration position."[25] When Hammer finally admitted to himself

that the Machiasport plan was dead, he salvaged something by appearing to drop the plan voluntarily, thereby defusing some of the oil industry's resentment and winning gratitude from Nixon staffers by taking the president off the hook.

It is hard to say exactly why Hammer's clout failed. The most obvious answer is that even he was no match for the combined might of the large oil companies. Muskie said the increasing strength of the environmental movement, peaking as Hammer was pushing his plan, probably was the factor that hurt most. President Johnson's surprise lame-duck status was damaging, too. He wanted to return to Texas, where even a former president would be a pariah at the Petroleum Club if he gave in to Hammer. Not one to dwell on his rare defeats, Hammer virtually ignored Machiasport in his 1987 autobiography, devoting only four paragraphs to it. There was no mention of Boggs, Vahlsing, or Hammer's sometimes brilliant, sometimes misguided lobbying. His scant analysis placed the onus on the greed of the major oil companies.

While Hammer was preoccupied pushing for the Maine refinery and trying to decipher what was going on in Libya, trouble arose for him in a spot more remote than either Machiasport or Tripoli. That spot was the Persian Gulf sheikhdom of Umm al Qaiwan, a Trucial State, in southeast Arabia. What happened there during 1969 and 1970 — with Hammer in the middle, as always — had international repercussions, poisoning relations among four nations. For a time, it appeared war might result. Hammer's emotional references to Umm al Qaiwan seventeen years later, in his autobiography, demonstrate the depth of the agony it caused him.

At first, there was no sign of trouble. Hammer courted the sheikhdom on the recommendation of Texas oil tycoon John Mecom, who had been drilling offshore there until running out of money. Hammer had learned a lot about the oil business from Mecom, so he was inclined to follow his advice about Umm al Qaiwan. After contacting the kingdom's ruler, Hammer and the ruler's son — the crown prince — met at Claridge's Hotel, in London. The prince told Hammer what the price would be to assume Mecom's concession: $1 million for the first year, $217,000 for the sheikh's personal account, and $444,000 that would go to various other recipients. Later, the sheikh requested another $200,000, paid by Occidental to a Swiss attorney through a Liechtenstein investment partnership. The attorney transferred the money to an international businessman, who delivered the cash.[26]

The cloak-and-dagger nature of the transactions perhaps should have suggested that somebody was worried about the morality and possibly the legality of the payments. But Hammer apparently did not think twice about the arrangement. How could the payments be construed as bribes in a country with an absolute ruler? It was ludicrous to talk about bribing the sheikh to influence himself. Occidental simply was paying the costs of doing business, he rationalized. The concession would go to the highest bidder, and Hammer had no intention of being out-bid. Given the possible financial return on an oil strike, the price was right, Hammer thought. So Hammer and the crown prince signed a forty-year concession agreement.[27] The British Foreign Office, which maintained jurisdiction over the sheikhdom's international relations, approved it. Hammer announced the arrangement from London, term-ing the $1 million payment a "bonus." With the anxious situation in Libya, Umm al Qaiwan looked to be a promising alternative source of oil. Armand and Frances flew to the sheikhdom for a celebration. They sat on the floor of the ruler's huge tent, while servants brought course after course of exotic, sometimes unidentifiable delicacies, one of which turned out to be eye of sheep.

Hammer was so encouraged by his reception that he sent Occidental representatives to the neighboring sheikhdoms of Ajman and Sharjah to negotiate drilling rights in their territorial waters. Negotiations pro-ceeded smoothly in Ajman, but Sharjah's ruler, to Hammer's dismay, ended up signing an agreement with a small California company called Buttes Gas and Oil. It was a fateful loss for Occidental. In early 1970, Buttes unexpectedly announced that under its Sharjah concession it had the right to drill in precisely the offshore area claimed by Occidental under its Umm al Qaiwan agreement. Buttes based its claim on an extension of Sharjah's territorial waters from three miles offshore to twelve miles. According to Buttes, Sharjah's ruler had issued the decree in September 1969, two months before Occidental signed its agreement with Umm al Qaiwan. Hammer wondered why he had heard nothing about the decree at the time of its issuance. The answer from Buttes: Sharjah's ruler had put the decree in a coat pocket after signing it, then had forgotten to take it out.[28] Sharjah's legal experts, however, said the ruler had a solid argument based on a twenty-nine-mile doctrine estab-lished in the Continental Shelf Convention. Those legal experts found no basis for Umm al Qaiwan's thirty-seven-mile claim.

Outraged, Hammer pored over nautical maps with his experts. Con-vinced Sharjah had backdated the agreement in conspiracy with Buttes, Hammer decided Occidental would continue to drill. John Tigrett,

Hammer's overseas consultant, said Umm al Qaiwan would back Occidental all the way. But neither Hammer nor Tigrett had figured on the intervention of a much more powerful nation — Iran. The shah said his country owned the legal claim to the territorial waters. Iran had claimed the area for many years, but had paid little attention to it previously. The possibility of oil wealth suddenly stimulated the shah's interest. Hammer referred to him as perfidious. The British government, responsible for the external relations of the sheikhdoms, tried to cool off the situation by urging Sharjah to settle with Iran and ordering Occidental to halt its drilling. Hammer ignored the order, unwilling to abandon Occidental's large investment, especially when he believed he was in the right.

On June 1, 1970, Royal Navy crewmen boarded the Occidental drilling barge in the Persian Gulf. Overpowered, Occidental withdrew temporarily. Hammer filed lawsuits against the British government and Buttes. He also opened negotiations with the Iranian government, in effect conducting his own foreign policy. Eventually, he and Iranian negotiators concluded an agreement that would have allowed Occidental's drilling to continue, with the proceeds from any marketable oil being paid into a Swiss bank account — to be divided upon resolution of the dispute. The shah, however, kept Hammer hanging by doing nothing to carry out the agreement. Hammer was reluctant to resume exploration in the face of unresolved court proceedings and the threat of armed intervention.[29]

Anxious to motivate the shah on Occidental's behalf, Hammer looked for ways to ingratiate himself. The shah took advantage of the opening, arranging for Occidental to purchase up to 200,000 barrels a day of oil from the country's nationalized energy company. The deal was not quite what it appeared to be. Iran wanted to buy military aircraft manufactured in the United States but needed Western currency to do so. Hammer had agreed to be the conduit, pledging to pay Iran 30 percent of the oil's true price, then use the other 70 percent to purchase dozens of fighter planes for the shah's arsenal. But the shah never intended to sell the oil to Occidental. He outsmarted Hammer by showing Occidental's offer around to obtain better prices from the Seven Sisters, who were anxious to freeze Hammer out of Iran. The shah then used the handsome profits to buy the American aircraft anyway. Hammer has said the shah's chicanery cost Occidental hundreds of millions of dollars.[30]

Hammer was unable to prevail in the various courts where he brought suit over the Umm al Qaiwan quagmire, mainly because a variety of judges said they lacked jurisdiction. Successfully suing governments for misconduct in business turned out to be fruitless under then-current legal doctrine. Some of the antagonists contended that Hammer had received British Foreign Office permission to sign the Umm al Qaiwan agreement only because of connections, not on the merits of his case. It turned out that Hammer had befriended Sir John Foster, an English barrister and member of Parliament. Foster understood the complex situation well, having served as the British government's legal adviser to Umm al Qaiwan. Hammer's opponents suggested that Foster had taken the liberty of signing the official permissions in the minister's anteroom, quite possibly without prior communication between the Foreign Office and Umm al Qaiwan.[31]

Detractors suggested further that Hammer had paid Lord Roy Thomson of Fleet Street to visit Persian Gulf rulers on Occidental's behalf. As part of the bargain, Thomson, the British media magnate, might have ordered favorable coverage for Hammer in the pages of his newspapers. Hammer also contacted Douglas MacArthur II, U.S. ambassador to Iran, who, in light of Occidental's claim and its reputation at the embassy as a responsible American company, arranged for Hammer to meet with the shah to discuss the matter directly. Foster later became an Occidental director, and Thomson thrived financially as a business partner of Hammer's. After his retirement from the Foreign Service, in 1972, MacArthur eventually performed work for Occidental as a consultant and was offered a spot on the board of directors, which he declined because of doubts about whether he would be kept fully in the picture.[32]

Yet all of Hammer's connections failed to accomplish the vital objective — convincing Iran that it should take itself out of the dispute. If that had occurred, the British government almost surely would have allowed Hammer to continue his drilling. Because of the shah's unwillingness to compromise, Occidental never finished its explorations in the promising waters of the Persian Gulf. Feeling deceived, Hammer swallowed his pride and learned from the experience. When the shah tried to trick him several years later on another deal, Hammer was wary. Meanwhile, because of the shah, Hammer's sizable investment was lost, and huge legal fees made a bad situation even worse. The longest-running, most expensive lawsuit of all stemmed from Hammer's indiscreet combativeness. At a press conference in London — called mainly to discuss Occidental's operations in Libya and Europe — Hammer lashed out at Buttes Gas and Oil during the question-and-answer session. Buttes officials sued Hammer for slander. Hammer responded with a suit for libel, based on a circular sent to Buttes shareholders. The British courts were saddled with the case for more than a decade, causing a judge to comment sarcastically about the "interminable action. . . . No expense had been spared, no stone unturned. It looked like outdoing *Jarndyce* versus *Jarndyce* [a long-running case from Charles Dickens's *Bleak House*], except that the present litigants were not likely to run out of money."[33] Neither side ultimately prevailed in the welter of litigation.

Nevertheless, despite temporary setbacks, at the beginning of the 1970s Hammer had reason to be optimistic. Yes, Machiasport and Umm al Qaiwan had been costly defeats. But Hammer's reputation as an influential statesman and business wizard nonetheless remained intact. He publicized his many successes and hoped that few would notice the failures. In fact, few did. Observers figured anybody willing to take such chances in the first place would come up short once in a while. Occidental Petroleum was a thriving company, undertaking daring ventures in every part of the world. Fortunately for Hammer, some of those ventures would be spectacularly successful, because, in Libya, the time bomb was about to explode.

17

Hammer and Qaddafi

AFTER THE SEPTEMBER 1969 coup in Libya, Armand Hammer relied on his intelligence network to learn what the new government was thinking. Under King Idris, the oil companies had had a good deal as long as they kept paying royalties into the treasury and kept the right palms greased. Hammer had proved himself especially adept at operating in Libya. Unlike most chief executive officers, he learned Libyan customs and negotiated in person with the king's ministers. Because of his long experience with heads of state, he was comfortable doing so.

Yet, despite his negotiating ability, Hammer was apprehensive about Muammar al-Qaddafi and his ministers. In their minds, Hammer was identified with King Idris. One early action by the revolutionaries was to rename Occidental's Idris field. Hammer knew that Qaddafi realized how vulnerable Occidental Petroleum was because about 90 percent of its production came from Libya. Occidental was the third-largest producer in Libya, at about 600,000 barrels a day, but the Oasis consortium and Esso, numbers one and two, had various sources of oil. After these three, there was a huge drop-off; the number-four producer reported about half as many barrels a day as Occidental.[1]

Hammer's intelligence came in large part from his experienced staff on the scene. Probably the best connected of the Americans was George Williamson, who went to Libya in 1960 at age twenty-four to work for Nelson Bunker Hunt's oil company. Williamson knew just about everybody of importance in Libya by the time he joined Occidental's operation the month after the overthrow of King Idris. Hammer trusted Williamson, apparently looking upon him as the successful son that

Julian was not. While diplomats, Wall Street analysts, and stockholders feared nationalization by the revolutionary government, Williamson and his colleague Dudley Miller told Hammer to be confident. "When it came time to deal with the Qaddafi government, I did not think it would be that hard," Williamson said.[2]

That time did not arrive immediately. The new rulers of Libya needed to organize themselves. For several months, Qaddafi's degree of influence in the Revolutionary Command Council was unclear to many outsiders. Although he would become a household name as leader of a nation seemingly bent on world terrorism, in the early stages of the new government the twenty-seven-year-old military officer was unfamiliar. As Qaddafi solidified his position at the apex of the regime, he shuffled his ministers. Izz al-Din al-Mabruk received the position of petroleum minister in January, and suddenly the regime started to pay attention to the foreign oil companies. Five days after his appointment, Mabruk began negotiations with twenty-one companies. A week after that, Qaddafi addressed their representatives. The message was threatening — if the oil companies failed to negotiate sensibly, Libya would train technicians to operate the firms, then nationalize them. That ultimatum made Qaddafi more effective as a negotiator than King Idris ever had been. The king's ministers repeatedly had asked for more money from the oil companies but never seriously employed the threat of nationalization.

Before long, the Libyan government took the step that Hammer had feared; Mabruk singled out Occidental to begin separate talks, on February 6, 1970. Hammer had few cards to play, and none looked like a winner. With an introduction from press magnate Lord Roy Thomson, he visited Egyptian president Gamal Abdel Nasser, one of Qaddafi's mentors.[3] Hammer knew it was in Nasser's interest to act as a mediator because Libyan revenue from Occidental's operations was helping pay for Egyptian military hardware. Nasser did speak to Qaddafi on Hammer's behalf, apparently to no avail. In any case, several months later Nasser was dead.

Rumors flew that Libya would settle for nothing less than a price increase of 40 cents a barrel; most oil companies said a 10-cent increase was the maximum they could live with. They worried about what a large hike would signal to other governments all over the world that desired more oil revenue. As always, Hammer was the maverick thinker. He believed 40 cents a barrel was reasonable when viewed from the Libyan perspective. Unlike most oil-company chiefs, he put himself in the shoes of the negotiator on the other side. An American diplomat noted that Hammer thought "Libyan leaders were probably not Communists or Soviet pawns, but instead very intense nationalists. He believes there is a good possibility of dealing successfully with the Libyans . . . provided we approach them with patience and understanding of their sensitivities, aspirations, and determined nationalism."[4] Qaddafi had no sense of Hammer's unique thinking early on, however, nor did Hammer telegraph it. In those first months, he told his negotiators to keep the price increase minimal, if possible.

With both sides appearing to be intransigent, talks halted for weeks at a time as one party found a new position proposed by the other to be insulting. Losing patience, Qaddafi in June 1970 reduced Occidental's allowable production by 300,000 barrels a day. The official Libyan position stated that the reduction was meant to conserve oil that Occidental was depleting at an unacceptable rate. That probably was true, but it strained credulity to think of the reduction as totally unrelated to the price talks. In August, Occidental offered an increase of 20 cents a barrel; Qaddafi said no and reduced Occidental's maximum daily production by another 60,000 barrels.[5]

Occidental was feeling the pinch. Although Hammer had strained relations with other American oil companies, he decided it would be foolhardy to stand alone if he could obtain help. Maybe one of the Seven Sisters would supply Occidental with oil to replace the lost Libyan barrels. Such a guaranteed supply would allow Hammer to resist a steep price increase, which, if conceded, might later be forced on other American companies. On July 10, 1970, Hammer called on Kenneth Jamieson at Esso. Hammer was not coy. The cutbacks imposed by Qaddafi were making it difficult for Occidental to fulfill its contracts. But, according to Hammer's version, he said he would resist price increases if Esso would sell oil to Occidental at a small profit, maybe a 10 percent markup. Jamieson later recalled Hammer's requesting the oil at cost. Jamieson was cool, Hammer said, replying only that the company would consider the request. Despite the urgency, Hammer complained, Esso took two weeks to reply. The answer: Occidental would have to pay current market price. Jamieson said twenty years later that he told Hammer Esso was unable to sell Occidental oil at cost because of existing contracts. "I did offer to sell him oil at our lowest third-party price and thought I could get Shell to agree to the same arrangement. . . . I heard nothing from Hammer." In any case, as a result of the failure to agree, relations between the companies deteriorated so completely that their Libyan representatives reportedly stopped speaking to each other. Jamieson clearly resented Hammer's version of the Occidental-Esso negotiations, calling it "a batch of fiction." The sale of oil from Esso to Occidental would not have stopped the movement toward higher oil prices in the Middle East, Jamieson said.[6]

Hammer knew then that he was on his own. Occidental tripled its tanker-fleet capacity so as to be able to transport crude oil from non-Libyan supply points to European refineries in the event of nationalization. Through a Liberian subsidiary registered in Bermuda, Occidental owned three ships and chartered another forty-seven, leasing them at profitable rates. It seemed a prudent move at the time; Hammer was not the sort to let fate take its course. But later, that expanded tanker fleet would haunt Hammer by causing severe damage to Occidental's bottom line as charter rates dropped precipitately. George Williamson wrote that Occidental "came out quite well on the renegotiation of all of our crude-oil contracts after the last round with the Libyan government. What is very discouraging to all of us is to have the profits of our marketing and refining operations being more than wiped out by shipping losses." Hammer renegotiated rates to Occidental's advantage when he could, but some of the charter services were furious enough to sue. In one case, an English judge ruled that Hammer had participated in a fraud to obtain a new contract.[7]

By the end of August 1970, Williamson was telling Hammer that nationalization of Occidental's Libyan operations might be announced any day, to commemorate the revolutionary government's first anniversary. Without hesitating, Hammer called Fred Gross, the pilot of the Occidental jet that was in practice Hammer's personal aircraft. He asked Gross how long it would take to ready the jet for a trip to Libya. Several hours, Gross answered. Hammer replied that they would leave that day.*

There was good reason for worry. John Boles, Hammer's assistant who specialized in Middle Eastern economy and culture, said, "I was concerned about Dr. Hammer going to Libya after Qaddafi, because of his Jewish faith. I am not sure how he was perceived, as a Unitarian or what. We just did not say anything. I put together a scrapbook of Dr. Hammer pictured with various Arab leaders, and showed it around the Libyan embassy in Washington. That was where we had to get a visa for the doctor. I was hoping the Libyans would look at the scrapbook and say he must be all right if he knows all those people."[8]

Clearly, Hammer was not to be deterred. In the airplane en route to

---

* Although used to traveling around the globe on a day's notice, Frances Hammer opposed this unplanned journey. She was unable to talk her husband out of it, however. The stockholders would never forgive him if Occidental were nationalized and he did not go there, Armand told her. A frightened Frances stayed behind.

Tripoli, however, he took precautions. He decided that his presence should be known only to Occidental and Libyan negotiators at the scene. A low profile would protect his image as master negotiator in case of a failure. Hammer arranged to fly from Tripoli to Paris each night to guard against being held hostage and to have access to a secure telephone. The travel was arduous for a seventy-two-year-old man — it would have been arduous for a man half that age — since the plane arrived in Paris about 2:00 A.M. and departed again for Tripoli four hours later.

On touchdown in Tripoli, Williamson met Hammer at the airport, escorting him to the office of Abdul al-Salam Jalloud, Qaddafi's chief deputy prime minister. Hammer has said Jalloud had a revolver strapped to his waist, although other Occidental negotiators present remember no such thing. Jalloud had a stormy personality, but he greeted Hammer warmly; he was pleased that a chief executive had arrived to negotiate, not an underling.

Still, he was blunt. The negotiations should be simple, he said: Either Hammer should grant Libya a 40-cent increase on each barrel or Occidental would be nationalized. Hammer disliked the message but was impressed by Jalloud's negotiating savvy. Later he said wistfully to an aide that he wished he could hire Jalloud to work for Occidental.

Negotiations stretched out over five days. Hammer's low profile was so complete that the American embassy was unable to confirm rumors he was in Tripoli. When Boles received a query in Los Angeles about Hammer's whereabouts, he replied that Hammer was not in Libya. Later, he said he himself had been kept in the dark about Hammer's trip. An Occidental executive in Tripoli, however, finally informed the embassy of Hammer's visit. The executive could provide little other information, commenting that only Hammer and Williamson knew "how far Occidental is prepared to go."[9]

In the event, Libya got an increase of 30 cents a barrel, with another 2 cents each year for five years. Hammer also agreed to an increase in the tax on oil-company earnings from 50 percent to 58 percent, a significant departure from the status quo. In return, Libya promised to cancel Occidental's production cutbacks, subject to certain conditions meant to keep the fields from being depleted too quickly.

Hammer and Libyan oil minister Mabruk were ready to sign the secret agreement when, at the last minute, Hammer asked Mabruk to attach an authorization from the government stating that the minister possessed the proper authority. Mabruk replied that he had an authorization in his desk but could not show it to Hammer because it was a private government document. Hammer was suspicious. Without such an authorization in Hammer's hands, Qaddafi could later claim the agreement was meaningless. Hammer insisted Mabruk discuss the matter with Jalloud. Mabruk left the room, returning to say that Hammer could view the authorization but could not make a copy.

Hammer asked for time to think about the new development and pulled Williamson outside. Telling him that something was fishy, he resolved to leave Tripoli on the spot, without flight clearance from the Libyans. It was 2:30 in the morning. The pilot, Gross, said that taking off without clearance might cause the Libyans to fire on the plane. Hammer decided to take the risk. Minutes later the jet rose majestically and cleared Libyan airspace without incident. A few hours later, Hammer was safe at the Ritz Hotel in Paris.

Stunned, the Libyans finally relented. The next day Williamson received a copy of the authorization, and he signed the agreement on Hammer's behalf at 2:00 A.M. Because the Libyan negotiators abstained from alcohol, Williamson and Dudley Miller drank orange soda pop with them to celebrate. Williamson recalled commenting that "everybody who drives a tractor, truck or car will be affected by this."[10]

On September 4, 1970, Qaddafi announced the settlement to the world. For his part, Hammer did more than put the best face on a bad situation; he sounded downright heroic, telling a group of London bankers that "I came at the last minute and probably averted the Libyan government's intention of taking unilateral action against the [oil] industry." Using hindsight, hundreds of commentators have analyzed Hammer's decision to compromise with Qaddafi. Libyan expert Henry Schuler said Hammer made a dangerous decision "by admitting that past dealings were not fair. This convinced the Libyans that they had all the power in the world. Maybe Hammer was right that prices had been too low. . . . But the way he did what he did set in train the oil price rises in the 1970s. Hammer did the right thing for Occidental; he was able to pass through the increases to consumers. The question is, did he have a broader responsibility?"[11]

James Cook, in a *Forbes* cover story about Hammer, commented that the agreement

was the beginning of the end for the age of cheap energy. . . . Occidental's Libyan settlement may have been the most important single event since the end of World War II, and one that marked a turning point for the modern world. Hammer had saved his Libyan concession at a terrible price to the industrial world, but he did so at remarkably little cost to himself. Prices went up so rapidly thereafter that Occidental, and most other producers, were able to make more and more money on an increasingly smaller share of an immensely large pie.[12]

As predicted, the other oil companies operating in Libya capitulated to the pressure in the wake of Hammer's settlement. Other oil-rich nations then called for price and tax increases; under the auspices of the formerly toothless OPEC, they issued joint demands impossible to resist. Such pressure brought Western oil companies to the realization they should have reached months earlier — divided they would fall; united they might stand.[13]

In his autobiography, Hammer has suggested it was Sir David Barran, the chief executive of British Petroleum, who made the first approach to work in tandem. The date was December 11, 1970. Hammer reportedly took Barran's call from a hospital bed, where he was recovering from a kidney stone operation. Barran said he was afraid that the Libyans would demand further price increases of Occidental, then expressed his hope Hammer would resist. Hammer said he wanted to resist but could afford to do so only if the Seven Sisters supplied him with oil at cost to replace Libyan-ordered cutbacks. According to Hammer, Barran replied that he found such a request reasonable. Barran, however, provided an alternate account — one supported by Hammer himself in court testimony — that seems to contradict the autobiography. Barran said it was Hammer who called first, in early October. The two men followed with a meeting on October 9 in London. Afterward, Hammer assigned consultant John Tigrett to negotiate with Barran.[14]

Whatever the truth about who called whom first, the discussions led somewhere: On January 11, 1971, representatives of twenty-three oil companies met in New York. The federal government said it would set aside antitrust concerns for the special occasion. The meeting took place under a shadow stretching from Tripoli — Qaddafi was insisting that Occidental and Nelson Bunker Hunt return to the negotiating table to discuss further price increases. The Western companies, realizing the urgency this time, agreed to a Hammer-inspired safety-net arrangement. Any company suffering cutbacks or nationalization would receive oil from other companies in quantities based on previous Libyan production. The Justice Department gave qualified approval to the collusion. It was a painful agreement for the oilmen in the room, hating Hammer as they did. Gordon Brown, who observed the sessions for the State Department, said, "In a strange way, fear of Mr. Hammer was the driving force behind the actions of the United States government and the oil companies. We never knew what Mr. Hammer was thinking, and his representatives at the meetings were very discreet. We assumed that only Mr. Hammer knew for sure what was in his mind. That caused lots of befuddlement." [15]

The arrangement involving Occidental and its sister oil companies was a halfway measure at best. For years to come, Libya would have the upper hand. Hammer lived in uncertainty about just when Qaddafi would make new demands, but lower profits were better than the financial disaster of nationalization. Discussing Libya in public, Hammer tried to sound optimistic. At the end of 1971, he told Occidental's stockholders that "relations with the government of Libya are good, and we are operating in a spirit of mutual respect." Meanwhile, he used the time he had bought to reduce his company's dependence on Libyan revenue. It was a global quest that included exploration in Venezuela, Peru, Nigeria, the North Sea, Ghana, the Spanish Sahara, Sierra Leone, the Persian Gulf, Canada, Jamaica, Nicaragua, Honduras, and Trinidad and Tobago. [16]

The search for new sources of revenue took on fresh urgency in 1973, when the Libyans sought 51 percent ownership of the foreign-owned oil companies operating there. Hammer flew to Malta for a strategy session with George Williamson, David Orser, Dudley Miller, and John Tigrett, abruptly canceling a seventy-fifth birthday party in Los Angeles. The Libyans were pressuring Occidental to be the first to agree to control of its local operations by the government. In the past, Hammer might have resisted vigorously. By this time, however, it was clear the Libyans meant business. Forty-nine percent ownership sounded better than nothing, especially because the Libyans were willing to compensate Occidental with a payment of $136 million. Hammer decided to accept it. Ray Vicker of Dow Jones News Service wrote about the agreement before it was supposed to be public, thanks to a chance meeting in Moscow with Hammer at which Occidental's chief executive talked openly about Libya. A surprised Occidental public relations department in Los Angeles disavowed the story, but Vicker had it right, straight from the boss's mouth. [17]

As part of the new arrangement, a three-man administration committee came into being, composed of two members from the Libyan government and one from Occidental. The dark joke within the company was that the Occidental representative got to vote in case of a tie. James Patten, an Occidental lawyer posted to Libya, said the Libyans on the negotiating bodies "were sharp, knew the oil business, and were pleasant to work with." Patten expressed admiration as well for Hammer's ability to buck opposition within Occidental about staying in Libya. Executives in Occidental's stateside exploration division "always wanted to walk away from Libya in a snit. But Hammer had more sense than that," Patten said.[18]

Unlike other foreigners, Hammer tried to understand Qaddafi as something other than the devil incarnate. He commented that Qaddafi was "a combination of uncanny cleverness, idealism, perhaps fanaticism, and he certainly wants to raise the living standard of his people." Hammer apparently never met Qaddafi, but not for lack of trying. Occidental's David Orser said, "The doctor really wanted us to get him an appointment with Qaddafi. We always thought it was because he wanted another chapter for his next book."[19]

Under 51 percent Libyan ownership, the sky did not fall. Drilling and exploration returned to normal until late 1975, when an ugly altercation broke out over two related issues: the way the company was compensating the government, and the amount of oil Occidental was pumping. Hammer requested arbitration, warning Libya he would withhold $440 million until the dispute was resolved. The Libyan petroleum minister, upping the ante, said no Occidental employees or their dependents could leave the country until Hammer capitulated. That edict covered 520 people, of whom 230 were American citizens.

The U.S. government was worried that the conflict would escalate. Hammer wrote to President Gerald Ford, asking for White House support. One of Hammer's Washington executives, former Nixon and Ford aide Noel Koch, kept the National Security Council, State Department, and members of Congress advised. Assessing the situation, the London *Sunday Times* put its money on Occidental, noting that the Libyan government had "misjudged Hammer, or rather it forgot just how clever a capitalist is the man who built Occidental. . . . Only people who have not kept an eye on Dr. Hammer's past and present capitalist coups could be so naive as to imagine he could be easily caught out."[20] After several tense months, Hammer and the Libyans approved a settlement generally perceived to be a victory for Occidental.

Occidental held on in Libya until the administration of Ronald Reagan forced American companies to pull out their American employees during a political and military offensive against Qaddafi. Hammer reluctantly complied, reporting to the president that only non-Americans were operating the oil fields. Rumors kept cropping up that Occidental and other companies were allowing Americans to travel into Libya anyway. On January 10, 1985, Deputy Secretary of State Kenneth Dam

wrote Hammer, demanding that "if your company has American employees who reside in or travel to Libya, you forgo this practice by
asking those now in Libya to depart, and those planning to go not to
do so." As relations worsened, Reagan ordered an end to all trade with
Libya but allowed Occidental to operate through foreigners in the short
term if the company promised to sell soon "in a manner consistent with
the policy goals of the United States government." When *New York
Times* columnist Flora Lewis alleged that Hammer was trying to reverse Reagan's evacuation order, Hammer angrily denied it, pointing
out that Libyan operations constituted only 1 percent of Occidental's
business at that time. Still, even as Occidental searched for a buyer of
its Libyan concessions, Hammer never lost hope that he would regain
control of them one day.[21]

Without question, by giving in to Libyan demands during the August 1970 negotiations in Tripoli, Hammer changed the balance of power
in the world. But for him personally, what was widely perceived as a
cave-in to revolutionaries was worth it — he saved Occidental from
disaster. Despite the added bill every consumer paid as a result of
Hammer's agreement, and others that followed, his reputation not only
survived largely untarnished, but even thrived in the minds of the public. Nor did his months-long front-page celebrity during the Libyan
negotiations end when the situation there finally calmed. On the contrary, it took off like a red star, this time over the Soviet Union.

Détente Through Trade

A RMAND HAMMER apparently played no significant role in Soviet-American relations from 1930 until 1961, when he decided
the time was right to reestablish commercial ties with Russia and worked
hard to meet Nikita Khrushchev. Thereafter, as he had done with
American presidents, he devoted countless hours to cultivating Soviet
leaders: Leonid Brezhnev, Alexei Kosygin, Yuri Andropov, Konstantin
Chernenko, and Mikhail Gorbachev. His record of unofficial contacts
was unmatched by any other private citizen.

In these meetings, Hammer usually took the discussions beyond considerations of vanity or greed. His devotion to the cause of world peace
was constant. He pushed his agenda for peace when it would have been
easier to ignore the topic. As he put it,

> I am a man who can look back over a lifetime of involvement in world
> affairs . . . and can appreciate the fact that communications can lead to
> understanding — and understanding can lead to peaceful relations. I am
> practical enough to know there are still many obstacles in our path, but
> I think for the first time we are finding ways around them, and that
> one important means to détente is through trade. . . . As a nation we
> do not buy the Soviet ideology. Neither do they buy ours. But there is
> no reason why we cannot trade with each other instead of threatening
> each other with nuclear bombs.[1]

After the breakthrough in 1961, Hammer solidified his standing with
Khrushchev. He sent messages and gifts, then started lobbying for a
second meeting, using the Soviet embassy in Washington and the
American embassy in Moscow as his channels. When that meeting failed

to materialize quickly, he asked Senator Albert Gore to help. Gore, in a sensitive position as a member of the Senate Foreign Relations Committee during a time of strained superpower relations, decided against writing Khrushchev directly, but he did send letters to the U.S. and Soviet ambassadors.[2]

Hugh Ten Eyck, an Occidental executive who traveled to Moscow with Hammer in 1964, recalled having the clear impression that Hammer was on his way to regaining his special status there: "I always had thought that his stories about Lenin were exaggerated, until I went through Lenin's office with an Intourist guide. She pointed out the brass monkey on Lenin's desk. I said the man who gave that to Lenin is in the next tour group. She left our group like a shot to see this legendary man. . . . He was treated like a god over there."[3]

During the 1964 visit, Hammer met first with the chief of the Foreign Trade Department's American division. The meeting held out promise for Occidental's plans in the Soviet Union. His next move was unorthodox, a harbinger of how he would operate in the future. He sought a meeting not with a higher-level trade minister, as most negotiators would have done, but rather with the minister of culture, Yekaterina Furtseva. Art was a universal language that Hammer spoke fluently, so he mixed it with business, suggesting an exhibition of Grandma Moses paintings in Russia. Furtseva was enthusiastic. She counterproposed that the Soviets send works from Moscow to the United States. Good, Hammer replied, already one step ahead of her. How about a show featuring the sculptor A. A. Neizvestny, and how about opening it at Hammer Galleries in New York? Furtseva hesitated on settling the details. But her excitement caused her to say just what Hammer had hoped: How about a meeting with Khrushchev?[4] It was one of the first times he used his art collecting to open doors at the top. It would not be the last.

Hammer's second meeting with Khrushchev occurred during a reception for Walter Ulbricht, the leader of East Germany. Khrushchev took Hammer aside while Mrs. Khrushchev entertained Frances separately. The conversation covered lots of ground, including the possibility of a visit by President Lyndon Johnson to Moscow. Then Hammer turned the talk to business affairs: Occidental had become a fertilizer powerhouse. The Soviet leader had spoken often about improving the yields of his country's cropland. Maybe a deal could be beneficial to all parties. Khrushchev was interested, especially if Hammer could help soften the attitude of Congress toward trade with the Soviet Union. He then reiterated his admiration for the Aberdeen-Angus bull that Hammer had sent in 1961; it had been bred to more than five hundred Soviet cows, he said. Hammer replied that he would be delighted to help the Soviets produce better steaks. The conversation had gone well. Armand and Frances helped themselves to the elaborate spread of food, wine, and champagne, and left.[5]

Encouraged by Khrushchev's responses, Hammer pushed to close a deal. He started talking publicly about the preliminaries as if they were completed contracts. Such talk was calculated: Although negotiations with the Russians enraged Hammer's anti-Communist detractors, the reaction from stockholders usually was positive. After all, the Soviet Union was a vast market. If Hammer could tap it for Occidental, that would bode well for the corporate bottom line.[6]

About a month after meeting with Khrushchev, Hammer told a New York Society of Security Analysts meeting that a fertilizer deal with the Soviets was in the works. Part of his payback for sending the Soviets fertilizer, he said, would be the exploitation of natural gas in Kamchatka. When questioned by journalists for confirmation, the U.S. Commerce Department refused comment. That might have been for reasons of national security, or because federal officials knew nothing about the arrangement. Hammer frequently seemed to act first and inform the authorities later. He filled in the blanks with a September 1964 announcement from London, in which he disclosed that Occidental and British associates expected to sign a contract for up to ten Soviet fertilizer plants at $100 million each.[7]

The announcement prompted Soviet authorities to promote Hammer in the controlled press, where he had appeared so frequently four decades earlier. *Izvestia* published an eleven-hundred-word excerpt from *The Quest of the Romanoff Treasure,* commenting in an editor's note that

> Soviet people of the older and middle generations probably remember the name Hammer. [He] probably was the first businessman from the other side of the ocean to understand the advantages of developing trade relations with the young Soviet Russia. In Moscow there was a pencil factory named after Hammer . . . Hammer pencils were widely known. . . . The other day Armand Hammer was a guest of *Izvestia.* . . . He said that he was struck by the titanic progress the Soviet Union had made.

Theodore Shabad, Moscow correspondent for the *New York Times,* said Hammer was "being depicted as a man who may break the ice in trade relations."[8]

But the grand plan went awry. Escalating American intervention in Vietnam cooled relations with the Soviet Union. Then Khrushchev fell from favor, leaving Hammer without an enthusiastic advocate in the Kremlin.

Soon after Khrushchev's ouster, Hammer made his third trip to Moscow within the year, as one of ninety-two American business executives there to discuss trade. He co-chaired a lunch for Anastas Mikoyan and met with Andrei Gromyko and Alexei Kosygin. Those discussions indicated to Hammer that Khrushchev's survivors failed to share his fervor for the vital role of better fertilizer in Soviet agriculture. Hammer called Occidental's British associates to cancel the arrangement.

During that Moscow visit, however, Hammer fostered a connection that served him well when the atmosphere for trade and personal diplomacy again became propitious. He agreed to talk with Soviet journalist Mikhail Bruk, who wrote for the Novosti Press Agency. The resulting article, which appeared in *Soviet Life* magazine, kicked off a Hammer-Bruk relationship.[9] From then on, although Bruk maintained his identification as a Communist journalist, he spent increasing amounts of time in Hammer's service, with the blessing of the Kremlin. Americans in Moscow found Bruk mysterious, especially his ability to speak English with no trace of an accent. He was well connected, drove a Western automobile, and loved to talk. They assumed he worked not only for Novosti and Hammer, but also for Soviet intelligence.

Meanwhile, one project begun during the thaw with Khrushchev came to fruition. The paintings of Grandma Moses traveled to Moscow as planned. In return, the Soviets sent portraits by Pavel Korin to Hammer Galleries, even allowing Victor Hammer to become involved in selecting the works.[10] Although the exchange was not the stuff of front-page headlines, it was a signal that the Soviets would do things for Hammer that they would do for nobody else.

Given his preoccupation with Libya at this time, Hammer was unable to focus all his brainpower on the Soviet Union immediately after Khrushchev's downfall. But he kept his antennae up for openings into the land of his ancestors. The first opportunity came through Cyrus Eaton, a fabulously successful capitalist, fifteen years Hammer's senior, who had made his fortune in steel and railroads. Eaton had shown little interest in Soviet-American relations until he was past seventy, but when the subject caught his attention, it became his passion. He visited the Soviet Union first at age seventy-two, and the people he met there loved him. In the late 1960s, Hammer approached him and his son Cyrus Junior in their hometown of Cleveland to discuss buying their coal interests, which would have supplemented Occidental's entry into mining through the recently acquired Island Creek Coal Company. The elder Eaton assigned his son to discuss the matter. Hammer arrived at Cyrus Junior's home at dinnertime; the conversation unexpectedly continued long into the night.[11]

"He wanted to know what we were doing and planning to do in the Soviet Union," Cyrus Junior said. "He told me that he wanted to do business again with Russia, but that he had no current connections there. He saw great possibilities for Hooker Chemical in the Soviet Union, but its conservative management might oppose him. So he wanted to get in through us."[12]

Nothing came of the coal talks, but Hammer and the Eatons agreed to something else — Occidental's purchase of a 55 percent interest in an Eaton subsidiary doing business in Communist nations. Occidental also assumed some of the subsidiary's debt load. "After we became partners, I talked to Hammer one or two times a week, especially after my trips to Russia," the younger Eaton recalled. "His calls often came at two A.M., or at a restaurant when I did not even think I had told anyone that I would be there." During the conversations, Hammer heard ideas he liked. One was for the construction of an international trade center in Moscow, which then sorely lacked offices and display space for foreign businesspeople. Hammer was impressed with the Eatons' contacts, especially Dzherman Gvishiani, son-in-law of Soviet leader Alexei Kosygin.[13]

When Hammer and the elder Eaton finally met, Hammer regaled him with stories of the early years in the Soviet Union. Then Hammer requested Eaton's help in obtaining permission for the Occidental jet to land in Moscow; flying the plane into Moscow would be a status symbol. Eaton interceded with Gvishiani. Hammer was ecstatic when permission arrived, but the relationship with Eaton did not remain cordial for long. As usual, Hammer moved to take control and eventually fired Cyrus Junior. Smart but not cutthroat, the younger Eaton lacked adequate defenses, and it was Hammer who ended up benefiting from the entrée to the Soviets more than the Eatons, who had developed the contacts.

"Entrepreneurs have to be ruthless," Cyrus Junior said later. "I guess you could say that about my father. Usually with that success they have to step all over people." Unwilling to prolong the unpleasantness, he decided against suing for breach of contract after being dismissed by Hammer. He was dismayed but resigned to the situation. Like so many other people dismissed by Hammer, he still respected him: "I am not blaming him. He is very astute, an unusual person, a maverick."[14]

Ara Oztemel was another entrepreneur who felt used as Hammer pushed for preeminence in Soviet-American relations. Oztemel had been building trade ties to Russia for twenty years when Hammer called. The meeting that resulted angered Oztemel so much that Paula Smith, profiling him for *Dun's Review,* began her article with a mention of Oztemel's continued irritation over the matter three years later. Oztemel recalled how, in early 1972, he received a call from Hammer. The two men never had met. When they talked in Oztemel's office, according to Oztemel,

> Hammer replayed all the legends about himself, accompanied by photos of Lenin and the pencil factory. Then, as I know now, he spent the next three hours picking my brain. His approach was that he envied me, that if he were a young man he would be doing the things he heard I was doing. And, by the way, what was I doing? Perhaps we could do something together. But he was too old to reenter the Russian market after such a long absence. Would I tell him some of my transactions anyway? What, for instance, did I do with nickel? Well, it did not take him two months to announce that Occidental Petroleum was entering the market for Russian nickel, was going to do this and that, all in a way that very strangely resembled everything I told him about my own operations and plans.

Oztemel believed Hammer's announcement was the factor that killed other nickel transactions for a while. Hammer responded dismissively that Oztemel's contract was so minuscule as to be impractical for Occidental, so why copy it?[15]

Hammer believed his big breakthrough with the Russians was about to occur. He desperately wanted everything to click. One concern he mentioned to almost nobody was the potential problem of his nephew, Armand, Victor's son, who still lived in the Soviet capital. By then in his midforties, Armasha was perceived as a big spender and a playboy. Armand worried about Armasha's defecting to the United States, a possibility that had surfaced in discussions with Victor. With the passage of time, defection had come to seem less likely because Armasha would be leaving a family behind, but Armand still worried that his nephew's behavior could cause trouble. They began to see each other more often as Armand jetted to Moscow, but familiarity seemed to breed contempt rather than respect. Armasha complained that Uncle Armand refused to treat him as an adult, assigned Mikhail Bruk to spy on him, and ordered his mail opened. But despite his bitterness, Armasha realized he needed Armand more than Armand needed him, so he tried to be agreeable.[16]

While keeping an eye on Armasha, Armand was moving toward the deal of the century with the Soviet Union. The timing was propitious. George Kennan, the diplomat-scholar recognized as one of America's leading experts on the Soviet Union, noted that

> the Soviet government has always attached . . . great importance to the possibilities for the development of Soviet-American trade. The reasons for this are no doubt various. They include such practical considerations as a desire to tap America's rich resources of advanced technology, the need for heavy importations of American grain to make up domestic agricultural deficiencies, and so on. But there has always been a curious feeling on the part of Soviet leaders that a willingness to expand trade, or at least to make public gestures in that direction, is a symbol of a desire to strengthen political relations, particularly in the case of a capitalist country, and therefore has high political significance.[17]

The Soviets could not have wished for a better choice than Hammer. After all, Lenin had sanctioned him decades earlier. Many Soviet officials revered him because of that connection, all the more so after the appearance in 1970 of an *Izvestia* interview emphasizing his links with the great leader. The American ambassador in Moscow, Jacob Beam, summed it up for the State Department in a memorandum entitled "Armand Hammer joins Lenin adoration campaign." Beam said that

> in general, Hammer gives a picture of Lenin which coincides with the official Soviet image. Hammer concludes the interview with a statement that he plans to visit the Union of Soviet Socialist Republics in the near future. This visit, he says, reflects his desire to make a personal contribution to the development of Soviet–United States business relations. Such a contribution would be "the best way to honor the memory of the great Lenin." For the Soviet reader, the message must be that if the capitalists revere Lenin, the ordinary man in the street positively loves the great leader.[18]

Hammer's uncharacteristic low profile during his Soviet negotiations of the late 1960s and early 1970s probably stemmed from his knowledge that many powerful people in America opposed trading with a country perceived as the enemy. But while he deferred to such opposition, he brooked none inside Occidental, where he knew resistance would be minimal. He already had the board of directors under control — a dissenting vote by a director was virtually unknown — and in 1972 he consolidated his control by assuming the presidency in addition to the chairmanship.

Some assistance in putting together the big deal came from outside Occidental. Key figures included Sargent Shriver, a Kennedy in-law who had served as director of the Peace Corps and ambassador to France; influential Washington attorney Max Kampelman; international-trade lawyer Samuel Pisar; onetime American Communist David Karr, by then a deal maker *extraordinaire* based in Paris; and, on the Soviet side, Dzherman Gvishiani, Kosygin's son-in-law.[19] President Richard Nixon helped set the stage with his highly publicized May 1972 trip to Moscow, and the Soviets agreed to help end the Vietnam War. All the omens looked good.

They were. In July Hammer and the Soviets signed a preliminary protocol covering oil and gas resources, agricultural fertilizers and chemicals, metal treating and plating, solid waste disposal, and hotel construction. Hammer announced the plan to the world during a heavily attended news conference on July 18 in London.[20] The timing of the announcement served the Soviet Union well. Earlier that day, Egyptian president Anwar as-Sadat had announced the expulsion of twenty thousand Soviet advisers from his country, an embarrassment in the U.S.S.R.'s drive for world hegemony. The press conference helped divert attention from Russia's humiliation in Egypt.

Hammer downplayed the tentative nature of the agreement. The Soviets had asked him to omit dollar figures from the announcement; he did their bidding, on the surface. But Occidental executives had informed journalists ahead of time (off the record) that the transactions would be in the multibillion-dollar range. Asked at the press conference about a reported figure of $3 billion, Hammer responded disingenuously, "I wonder where they got that from." When the *Times* of London correspondent pressed the point, he replied, "I do not know whether the figure is ridiculous or not. I just said that I do not know where it came from." As one journalist noted perceptively, "Dr. Hammer is his own best public relations man, shattering one myth after another and making just the sort of comments that he knows will look good in print. . . . Once one gets down to talking about specific risky ventures, the promoter . . . aspects of Dr. Hammer's character shine forth strongly."[21]

The announcement from London caused the New York Stock Exchange to go crazy. Trading of Occidental shares came to a halt because of Wall Street's inability to process all the buy orders. When trading resumed late in the afternoon, more than a million shares changed hands, the day's largest volume. A few voices questioned the enthusiastic reaction. In the *New York Times,* for example, William Smith said Hammer's announcement contained few facts. Energy experts expressed puzzlement about how to interpret the surprising announcement. " 'Why the hell do the Russians need Armand Hammer?' was the tersest comment," according to Smith's story. The majority of the analysts interviewed by Smith talked about Occidental's lack of experience in areas where the Soviets required the most help: "The answer to the question why Dr. Hammer may simply be because the Russians know Dr. Hammer far better than any other businessman from the non-Communist bloc." [22]

Alan Abelson, writing in the financial weekly *Barron's,* was sarcastic, commenting that "Occidental's past seems filled with glowing promises that somehow are never quite realized. Dr. Hammer in his restless quest for corporate charisma has ventured far afield, from South America to Africa. Now, the Soviet Union. All that remains, really, is China. And, of course, the moon." [23] Associated Press reporters in Moscow received instructions to be wary of Hammer's announcements because of fears that he was using the wire service to boost Occidental's stock.

The Securities and Exchange Commission requested a copy of the July 18 news release and a transcript of the London press conference. Occidental's general counsel complied. The news release contained the notation "Approved by the Soviet Union." SEC attorney John Carleton reported: "There is no question that the combination of the Hammer news conference and the rumors attending this agreement led thousands of investors to believe that Occidental had completed a deal which would result in important and immediate financial gains for the company." [24]

Jewish groups attacked Hammer as a traitor for signing contracts with an anti-Semitic nation that refused to recognize basic human rights. It was bad enough that Hammer was making millions by dealing with Qaddafi and other anti-Semites in the Middle East, the Jewish groups said. Now he was currying favor with the Soviet Union, too. [25]

Hammer had expected that reaction. The skeptic who surprised him, though, was Peter Peterson, U.S. secretary of commerce and chairman of the U.S.-Soviet Commercial Commission. Visiting Moscow to negotiate most-favored-nation treatment, trade credits, and other commercial matters in the aftermath of President Nixon's visit, Peterson fielded questions about an Occidental-Soviet "multibillion-dollar deal" from journalists. One of his answers suggested that the Occidental deal might contain less than met the eye. The company's stock dropped. Ironically, what Peterson knew about the Occidental-Soviet negotiations had come from Hammer himself. Peterson had been in Morocco the previous day, about to travel to the Soviet Union, when he received an unexpected call. It was Hammer telephoning from his airplane, which was winging its way to North Africa, apparently from Moscow. Hammer wanted to meet with Peterson before he left Morocco to discuss the latest developments. "It was rather puzzling to us that such an understanding simply to negotiate would have warranted such a sudden and major unplanned trip," Peterson said. "By the time I got the message he was already in the air. Given that he had come so far, we felt simple courtesy required that we spend some time with him. So, James Lynn, undersecretary of commerce; Hal Sonnenfeldt, senior deputy to Henry Kissinger; and I did meet with him."[26]

Peterson was unimpressed by what he heard from Hammer. About his answer at the Moscow press conference, he said later, "It would have been wrong on two grounds for me to confirm that a huge deal had been made. One, of course, was that it was not true. I spoke the truth as I understood it, that it was simply an agreement to negotiate a possible deal. The second was that a big deal was against United States policy at that time." Peterson was under "strict instructions" from the president and Kissinger to refrain from prematurely announcing any major agreements; Nixon insisted on linkage between large transactions and progress on foreign policy matters, such as Vietnam and arms control. Knowing nothing about Hammer's London announcement, Peterson was unaware that his skepticism would cause a drop in Occidental's stock.[27]

Hammer was furious, and he said so to Nixon during a White House meeting on July 20, the day after Peterson's public remarks. The meeting was otherwise cordial. Nixon was pleased that Hammer had stressed to reporters the importance of the administration's breakthrough on East-West trade. It certainly did not hurt Hammer that he had been a major contributor to the president's reelection campaign — a member of the One-Hundred-Thousand-Dollar Club, as he reminded Nixon. Never one to pass up an opportunity, he also mentioned that his art collection was about to open in Ireland; he hoped Nixon's daughter Julie would attend. Ingratiating himself further, he agreed to give Occidental executive Marvin Watson time away from the company to help with the president's reelection campaign. Watson had served in the Lyndon Johnson cabinet, but Hammer apparently thought Watson would have no hesitation in joining a onetime fellow Texas Democrat, Governor John Connally, as a supporter of the Republican candidate. Watson said later that he did no work on Nixon's behalf.[28]

Hammer left wearing cuff links from the president, while Frances sported a special pin. White House press secretary Gerald Warren was noncommittal about the meeting, but a newspaper dispatch said, "When a reporter suggested that Nixon would not have met [Hammer] if the president was opposed to the deal, [Warren] agreed this was so." The president never reprimanded Peterson, although he apparently gave Hammer the impression a reprimand would be issued. A *Washington Post* editorialist expressed the same doubts as Peterson, writing that Hammer had proceeded without waiting for the signing of a bilateral trade agreement, which the secretary of commerce was trying to negotiate in the Soviet capital. "Whether the new Hammer announcement has removed some incentive from the Russians to compromise on issues bearing on the trade agreement, or whether the announcement has only whetted the Russians' appetite for further deals they can make only by concluding the trade agreement, remains to be seen," the editorial said.[29]

Several months later, Peterson signed a Soviet-American protocol covering trade matters. Hammer was pleased. His separate negotiations obviously had not undermined the talks between the two governments. Furthermore, the comprehensive general pact would help Occidental with its specific projects. Welcome praise arrived at Hammer's office from A. W. Clausen, president of the Bank of America in San Francisco:

> We have just read of Occidental Petroleum's exciting agreement with the Soviet Union. Congratulations! The possibilities of expanded trade with the Union of Soviet Socialist Republics are enormous. President Nixon's visit has done much to enhance these possibilities, and your recent visit and arrangement with the Soviet Union is in the early vanguard of establishing the probabilities.

Hammer sent the Clausen letter to White House aide H. R. Haldeman, commenting that it was much like other letters he had received. Hammer asked Haldeman to encourage Peterson to mention Occidental favorably. In addition, he asked Nixon's former secretary of commerce, Maurice Stans (somebody acutely aware of Hammer's fat-cat status), to intervene forcefully with Peterson.[30]

Hammer made sure Occidental's deal of the century stayed in the news as he filled in the blanks of the agreement to agree. He commuted between Los Angeles and Moscow as if it were a ride between the suburbs and downtown. The slightest new wrinkle in the negotiations spawned another press release. Hammer met Kosygin in September, announcing afterward that Occidental had permission to open a permanent Moscow office. The two men discussed construction of the international trade center — Cyrus Eaton's project until the breakup with Hammer. Kosygin was praised by Hammer, who told reporters the Soviet leader would have been a first-rate businessman in the capitalist world. Hammer also met with Nikolai Patolichev, the Soviet foreign trade minister, to close an $80 million contract under which the Soviets would supply nickel in exchange for metal-finishing equipment to be used in automobile and truck plants. It was the first specific contract to emerge from the previous July's signing. Then Hammer disclosed he had agreed on a "preliminary letter of intent" for the transfer of American phosphate to the Soviet Union in exchange for ammonia and urea.[31]

Much of this press agentry was attended by compliments for Hammer, although there were occasional naysayers, such as Robert Kaiser, Moscow correspondent of the *Washington Post,* who took note of Hammer's four visits to Moscow during 1972, during which he held a private meeting with Premier Kosygin, donated a valuable painting by Goya to Leningrad's Hermitage Museum, and, as usual, received a great deal of publicity. "His performance angered many competitors and, reportedly, some of the Russians he was dealing with," Kaiser noted. "Whether the billion-dollar deals he has discussed in the past are ever to materialize remains to be seen. . . . [Because of the Lenin connection] it is still conceivable that he can bring off big deals which others could not."[32]

Big deals, of course, implied important contacts, and Hammer pursued both. For example, in 1972, as he was trying to close the Soviet fertilizer deal, he decided it was vital to see party leader Leonid Brezhnev. He likened Brezhnev to the chairman of the board of a major corporation, and he believed that all significant decisions were made at such a level. Hammer had talked with Kosygin and Nixon, but in his mind Brezhnev's blessing was necessary. The Goya gift was a means to that end. However, Hammer sensed something even more dramatic was needed if he were to meet the aloof leader.

The means came to hand in the person of Otto Kallir, owner of Galerie St. Etienne in New York. According to Hammer's version, he received an unsolicited call from Kallir, who claimed to possess two letters written by Lenin. In exchange, Kallir wanted masterpiece paintings from Soviet museums. Hammer viewed the letters, one from 1919, the other from 1921. They seemed authentic; he sent copies to Moscow, where authorities agreed. According to his own account, he then convinced Kallir that the request for Soviet treasures was unreasonable. Why not accept instead art from Hammer's collection, sweetened by $128,000 in cash? Kallir said yes.[33]

Kallir's associate at Galerie St. Etienne, Hildegard Bachert, told a story substantially different from the Hammer version. Bachert said Hammer and Kallir had known each other at least a decade before the transaction. During that period, Kallir's ownership of the letters was known to Hammer, who periodically raised the possibility of buying them. In 1970, Kallir was ready to entertain an offer, but Hammer responded indifferently. Then, all of a sudden in 1972, Hammer wanted the letters right away. The two men negotiated a sale, and both emerged happy. Bachert expressed perplexity at Hammer's disparaging tone toward Kallir in the 1987 autobiography.[34]

Whatever the case, Hammer barely could contain himself. He wrote to Brezhnev that because of the letters' historical significance, he had spared no effort to buy them from Kallir. They were intended, Hammer said, to demonstrate his goodwill for the leaders and peoples of the Soviet Union and his appreciation of a friendship with the sacred Lenin. Gvishiani delivered the letters to the Kremlin. Brezhnev was away, so chief Soviet theoretician Mikhail Suslov received the package. The normally reserved, inaccessible Suslov was thrilled. Armand and Frances, staying in the Lenin suite at the National Hotel, received word that Suslov wanted a meeting. At the session, a flattered Hammer learned that Suslov had studied all of the 1920s correspondence written by Lenin about the young American. Suslov gave Hammer a resolution thanking him for the letters, then presented him with a portrait of Lenin. After Brezhnev returned, he wrote a thank-you note stressing the value of Hammer's gift.[35]

Hammer had his opening to Brezhnev. On February 15, 1973, he met for more than two hours with the Soviet leader. Détente through trade was the theme. As Hammer did with almost every head of state, he fawned over Brezhnev, commenting later that he "has great wisdom, great empathy for the people of the world, and very clearly has a great desire to lower the few remaining barriers of the cold war and introduce Russia and America into an era of peaceful coexistence through trade." Hammer and Brezhnev discussed President Nixon, whom Hammer considered a great leader. The tycoon reassured Brezhnev that Nixon was no longer the Communist-baiting, right-wing demagogue of the 1950s. Nixon had the support of American voters, Hammer said, in his quest for détente through trade. Concerning the allegations of the political scandal becoming known as Watergate, Hammer reported that they appeared to amount to no more than a minor irritant.[36]

At the end of the session, Brezhnev displayed his warmth and generosity, according to Hammer's account, by giving him the gold watch and chain from his vest as a spontaneous gift. Brezhnev promised direct access for Hammer should Occidental encounter difficulties with the fertilizer exchange, the international trade center, the nickel/machinery contract, or a plan to import Siberian gas to the west coast of the United States. In effect, Hammer had obtained an imprimatur from the top as significant as the one from Lenin fifty-two years earlier. *Pravda* gave the meeting front-page coverage.[37]

After the Hammer-Brezhnev encounter, the U.S. Embassy staff gathered information from its sources, notifying the State Department that Brezhnev was worried about the slow pace of negotiations with Occidental, especially concerning the fertilizer deal:

> Price has been a stumbling block here, but this may now have been solved by Hammer accepting rock bottom price which gives him practically no profit. Hammer group thinks there is new sense of urgency about getting phosphate fertilizers moving into Union of Soviet Socialist Republics against backdrop of grain shortfall last year, bad beginning this year, and maximum effort under way to guarantee adequate grain output.[38]

That Hammer conceded on price when he had the Soviets over a barrel demonstrated how much he wanted to close the deal. It seemed clear to insiders that the transaction was more for Hammer's ego than for Occidental's bottom line.

A big splash came two months after the Hammer-Brezhnev meeting, when Occidental and the Soviet Union signed additional agreements; at that juncture, the fertilizer deal was carrying an $8 billion price tag. Later, with negotiations on firmer ground, Hammer said it was a twenty-year, $20 billion transaction. Indications abounded that the Soviets placed great importance on the barter arrangement. One sign was Hammer's appearance on Soviet television; another was the presence at the signing of not only the foreign trade minister, but also the chemical industry minister. Edmund Stevens, the most experienced of all Moscow correspondents, wrote that the signing was a "personal triumph for the American, which will confound his critics and detractors for a long time to come." Stevens distinguished Hammer from

other American businesspeople who rushed into the Soviet Union unprepared and left disappointed.[39]

The Soviet media explained the agreement to the masses. An *Izvestia*
article about Soviet-American trade commented:

> One can judge the mutually advantageous nature and possible scale of
> such cooperation by the recently signed agreement with . . . Occidental
> Petroleum. . . . Soviet organizations will purchase in the United States
> of America, on long-term credit . . . equipment valued at several hundred
> million dollars for the production of large amounts of ammonia and
> urea. In addition, after the construction of this complex, the Union of
> Soviet Socialist Republics will purchase in the United States of America
> every year over a period of two decades up to one million tons of super-
> phosphoric fertilizers. The equipment and acid that are purchased will
> be paid for by Soviet deliveries of ammonia, urea, and potassium chlo-
> ride. . . . The sum total of deliveries of goods involved . . . is estimated
> at eight billion dollars. Both sides stand to gain. . . . Our agriculture
> will receive additional amounts of chemical fertilizers . . . which are
> still in short supply. The base of the Soviet chemical industry will be
> developed, and Soviet-American trade will receive an important stimu-
> lus. This operation is also to the advantage of the United States of America,
> since otherwise it would have to purchase the necessary nitrogenous and
> other fertilizers not in the Soviet Union but in other countries without
> corresponding exports of its own fertilizers.[40]

When Hammer and the Soviets signed another set of contracts, in
June 1974, the stated dollar amount of $20 billion, if accurate, meant
the deal accounted for half of Soviet-American trade. Hammer's detractors criticized all the agreements to agree, wondering if there ever
would be a final contract, but Hammer sloughed off the remarks. He
knew it was necessary to start with a protocol, follow with a letter of
intent, and move on to a global agreement that set the stage for the
principal terms of understanding. Those terms, in turn, would lead to
the implementing contracts. If other businesspeople chose to keep quiet
until the final signing, that was fine with Hammer. He preferred to
trumpet each stage.

Although critics carped, the size of the deal gave Hammer tremendous leverage. When the Soviets asked for an unprecedented written
commitment to the transaction from the U.S. government, the Nixon
administration complied. Frederick Dent, secretary of commerce, exchanged commitment letters with his Soviet counterpart. Hammer had
lobbied Nixon hard to obtain the letters. His key instrument of persua-

sion was a missive to the president, which began with effusive praise for Nixon's dedication to peace and prosperity. Without using the term "Watergate," Hammer told Nixon how arduously he was spreading the message to politicians and journalists that innuendo must not be confused with fact. With the flattery out of the way, Hammer informed Nixon of the request for the unprecedented letter to the Soviets. He made such a favor sound routine: It simply would state that the Soviet-Occidental agreement conformed to policies established by the trade pact of October 18, 1972.[41] Nixon came through. Once Hammer had obtained the letter, he invoked it whenever the fertilizer deal appeared to be in trouble as a result of a change in American foreign policy.

Despite administration support of the deal, the *New York Times* published a Sunday article by part-time West Coast correspondent Everett Holles questioning the validity of the contracts:

> One Occidental official, accustomed to being caught off guard by Dr. Hammer's bold exercise of his financial and executive control of the company, spoke cynically of the deal, not as an Occidental undertaking but as "Dr. Hammer's latest fling. All I know is what I read in the papers," he said. "I do not know where all the money is coming from, but perhaps that is an insignificant detail." . . . Wall Street specialists and Occidental's competitors, many of whom regard Dr. Hammer as prone to careless optimism in publicizing Occidental's ventures, have been less than enthusiastic over his latest Russian deal. "He has a long-standing and well-documented habit of counting his chickens before they are hatched," said a West Coast oil executive. . . . Others suggest that Dr. Hammer may have become involved, in this latest "historic agreement," in a Soviet propaganda ploy aimed at paving the way for the visit of L.I. Brezhnev, Soviet Communist Party chief, to Washington in June. This fact may account for Dr. Hammer's uncharacteristic reticence to talk about the deal, they add. To some observers, April's announcement appears to be a "replay" of even more elaborate plans announced by Dr. Hammer last July, which the Russians have now seized upon as a means of combating opposition in Congress toward the Nixon-Brezhnev détente and the granting to the Soviet Union of more liberal credits and most favored nation tariff status.[42]

For somebody as conscious of his image as Hammer, the article in the world's most influential newspaper was a terrible blow. Hammer reportedly called Holles, then followed with a call to *New York Times* publisher Arthur Ochs Sulzberger. Holles was dispatched to Hammer's home for an interview. The next day, Holles's byline was on the front page, above his article about another Hammer-Soviet project. This time, the story was more complimentary. Accompanying it was a piece by the newspaper's Moscow correspondent emphasizing the importance of the Occidental-Soviet negotiations. It was an amazing recovery by Hammer, fully indicating the influence he could wield.

Troublesome articles were damaging, but more worrisome in the long run were doubts voiced by government policymakers. Hammer generally appeared to deal first and tell the government later; as a government unto himself, he could operate that way. But when the Soviet Union was on the other end, things became more complicated. Because so many American policymakers considered the Soviet Union the enemy, every private agreement received careful scrutiny. The gigantic fertilizer contract caught the Defense Department's attention because of deep Soviet ports being built for storage and shipment of the anhydrous ammonia. Pentagon analysts were concerned that the ports could also accommodate Soviet nuclear submarines.

A more sustained, less theoretical challenge came from natural-resources experts within the federal government, who wondered about the advisability of Occidental's exporting so much of America's phosphate rock to the Soviets. When Hammer had introduced Occidental into the phosphate business a decade earlier, he spent millions to explore parts of Florida untouched by the industry giants. The gamble had paid off. Even in the new mining area, however, supplies were exhaustible. The question was when.

Hammer believed Occidental owned adequate supplies to meet the requirements of the Soviet contract, and other contracts as well, without endangering domestic supplies. William Stowasser, a U.S. Bureau of Mines phosphate specialist, disagreed. When nobody consulted Stowasser about the impact of Hammer's $20 billion deal on America's natural-resource picture, the concerned bureaucrat took the initiative. In an eleven-page analysis of Hammer's transaction, Stowasser said the phosphate exports "will accelerate the depletion of the remaining reserves of this mineral that is so necessary to agriculture." Stowasser said Hammer had no sound basis for his estimate of 144 million tons of recoverable phosphate from the company's northern Florida mines. His own best estimate, Stowasser said, was 50 million tons, enough to fill just ten years of Occidental's twenty-year contract with the Soviets. Stowasser said he was worried that Hammer would eventually have to mine the Osceola National Forest deposits to obtain the additional phosphate. There were reasons to worry about the Soviet imports, too, he said. Potash from the Soviet Union would compete with Canadian producers and might destroy the American potash industry. Imports of Soviet ammonia and urea "will further increase the dependence of the United States on foreign supplies."[43]

Stowasser's criticism was well documented but little noticed. More emotional, louder complaints came from members of Congress, led by two hard-line anti-Communists — Representative Richard Ichord, a Missouri Democrat, and Representative John Ashbrook, an Ohio Republican. Ichord, chairman of the Committee on Internal Security (previously known as the Committee on Un-American Activities), looked for ways to shoot down Hammer's fertilizer deal. Committee research director William Shaw, who had worked as J. Edgar Hoover's speech writer, said in an internal memorandum that

> careful consideration has been given to the means by which the chairman could best call attention to the adverse impact Hammer's deals with the Soviets could have on our national security. It would appear that the most effective approach would be for the chairman to deliver a speech on the floor of the House pointing out Hammer's long-standing Kremlin connections and explaining how Hammer's trade deals appear to be designed to give an advantage to the Soviet Union. At the same time, an appropriate press release could be made which should engender public interest throughout the nation. The public indignation hopefully will cause the executive branch to closely scrutinize Hammer's negotiations with the Soviets to insure that these deals are not being carried out so as to adversely affect United States interests.[44]

Ichord delivered the speech Shaw had suggested five weeks later:

> In view of the current energy crisis in the Soviet Union and in the United States, and Dr. Hammer's well-known pro-Soviet background, I cannot help but question the effect such trade agreements might have on our national security. Should we in effect deal through agents? And even if it is desirable to deal through agents, is Dr. Hammer the proper person to carry on such extensive trade negotiations? Are these trade agreements negotiated by Dr. Hammer of benefit to the United States, or are they designed to further Soviet ambitions of world conquest? Could the Soviets take advantage of these trade agreements to create future energy crises in the United States? . . . Any citizen who is aware of Dr. Hammer's close association and friendship over the years with Kremlin leaders can very well question whether he is acting entirely in the best interests of the United States in these trade matters.[45]

Publicly, Hammer dismissed such attacks by saying, "Of course, there are hard-liners on both sides who will attempt to interfere with [the agreement]. There are as many Russians who do not want to make capitalists rich as there are Americans who do not want to help Communists with United States technology." Hammer went on to explain the transaction in high-minded language:

> The tree is planted and the roots are deeper than we ever dared hope. Now it is up to us to bring it to flower. When it starts to grow, our world and the world of our grandchildren may indeed be a happier and better place. What a marvelous challenge that is for we [sic] ordinary businessmen who so seldom have the opportunity to share in the accomplishment of such a great dream — to bring peace to the peoples of the world.[46]

Privately, Hammer labored to defuse congressional opposition. He wrote to Peter Flanigan, President Nixon's assistant for international economic affairs, that he had talked to three senators about the transaction, at Flanigan's suggestion. Each of the three had promised to raise no public objection, Hammer said. Flanigan responded in a "Dear Armand" letter that the administration was discovering "when we talk to members of Congress and explain the project, they understand its validity from a United States viewpoint. We will continue to work on this matter in an effort to bring it to a satisfactory conclusion."[47]

Despite such reassurance, Hammer had reason to worry about the financing of the deal. The Bank of America and nine other banks had agreed to lend $180 million to the Soviets to build the Occidental-inspired fertilizer complex. That covered about half the projected cost. For the remainder, Hammer this time was at the mercy of a U.S. government entity, the Export-Import Bank. The bank's officials seemed inclined to go ahead with President Nixon's blessing, but there were countervailing pressures from Congress.

In one of the biggest power plays of his career, Hammer took charge of the effort to win congressional authorization for such a major commitment to a project in the Soviet Union. He began by summarizing his concerns in a letter to Walter Sauer, the chairman of the Export-Import Bank, reminding him that the bank's participation was written into the Occidental-Soviet contract, that the Nixon administration and Soviets had exchanged letters of support, and that Occidental, its subcontractors, and the Soviet Union had spent large sums based on the Export-Import Bank's preliminary commitment eight months earlier. Sauer replied promptly to the effect that the bank's staff understood the advantages of the deal to the United States, thanks in large part to Hammer's persistence. Hammer was encouraged.[48]

The next month, however, William Casey replaced Sauer as Export-Import Bank chairman. That meant starting over to educate another top official. To make matters worse, Casey had chaired the SEC earlier in the decade while the agency was bringing serious charges against Occidental and Hammer. Casey was greeted by a cautioning letter from Senator Adlai Stevenson, an Illinois Democrat who chaired the subcommittee with jurisdiction over the bank's policies. Stevenson observed that

> as recently as January of 1973, the bank had no involvement with the Soviet Union. Since then, however, almost a billion and a half dollars in loans and guarantees have been extended to Russia and Eastern Europe for such major facilities. . . . Pending with respect to the Soviet Union are applications for an additional quarter of a billion dollars or more in loans for such things as a four-hundred-million-dollar chemical complex. . . . With transactions of this magnitude and type involving nonmarket countries with which the United States has had no substantial economic relations for the past thirty years, it is reasonable to expect serious inquiry about the policies which the bank is pursuing, particularly since they involve countries whose military posture and political systems are still, to a large extent, inimical to the best interests and values of the United States.[49]

Stevenson scheduled a hearing. But before Hammer's appearance, the senators heard Richard Stone, Florida's secretary of state, who was making what turned out to be a successful bid for the U.S. Senate. Accompanying Stone was Richard Glick, a chemistry professor at Florida State University. Stone expressed concern that the phosphate rock from his state, after being converted into superphosphoric acid by Occidental, could be employed militarily by the Soviets. Stone mentioned other reservations, too: Converting phosphate rock into superphosphoric acid took huge amounts of domestic energy, did it not? Occidental would be contributing to domestic phosphate shortages, would it not? Ammonia could be produced more efficiently at home than imported from the Soviet Union, could it not?[50]

Hammer was ready with the answers. As was his practice, he began by taking the high road: "I am, at seventy-five, one who can look back on a lifetime of involvement in world affairs and who sees the possibility that we, as American businessmen, may play an important role in assisting our government in its efforts to achieve a lasting peace between the world's two greatest powers. In my opinion, one of the ways to bring this about is through internationally beneficial trade."[51]

The fertilizer deal's benefits reached far beyond stockholders of Occidental, Hammer said. It would mean help for developing nations "who face the specter of famine which many economists and agronomists tell us may not be far off." Hammer expressed puzzlement at objections that the involvement of the Export-Import Bank meant giving away money rightly belonging to American taxpayers: "This, of course, is pure nonsense. Credit is a basic tool in any large international business transaction. If everything had to be done on a cash and carry basis, the wheels of industry would grind to a halt." Converting Florida phosphate rock into superphosphoric acid was energy-efficient, not wasteful: "By this process, we can deliver in one ship as much phosphatic material as would otherwise require four ships — three for the phosphate rock and one for the sulphur." As for the imported Soviet ammonia and urea, those commodities allowed the United States to save its own natural gas, which otherwise would be employed in the manufacture of domestic ammonia and urea.[52]

Hammer was especially scornful of the argument that Occidental's superphosphoric acid would be used by the Soviets for military purposes: "It is possible to convert superphosphoric acid into phosphorus, but it requires a lengthy and expensive process. It would be the height of economic absurdity for the Soviets to do this, since they would be taking an expensive fertilizer component for which they were paying a high price, reducing it back to basics, then extracting basic chemicals which they already have in large supply." To spur Congress, Hammer was unsubtle. He reminded the senators of the Nixon administration commitment in writing. He talked of lost profits for dozens of American suppliers. He raised the possibility of the Soviets' giving their phosphate business to Morocco.[53]

Still, despite Hammer's virtuoso performance, the conventional wisdom remained that Congress would scuttle the Export-Import Bank credit to the Soviets.[54] It is easy to understand how his detractors could have underestimated his clout at the White House: Hammer's decade of living in the Soviet Union, combined with his father's political activities, had made him suspect at the White House ever since the 1920s. If any president entered office neutral about Hammer, the thick FBI file on him was quite likely to alter that neutrality. Until his death, in 1972, J. Edgar Hoover showed no hesitancy about pulling out the file. After Hoover was in his grave, his legacy died hard. As a result, Hammer had to expend extraordinary energy to influence leaders of his own country. Yet, despite the obstacles, he had made his presence felt during every administration. The difference now was Hammer's renewed access to Soviet leadership. In an age of superpower tension, complete with nuclear bombs, no president could afford to ignore a diplomatic back channel like Hammer, despite his questionable reputation.

During the Johnson administration, Hammer had honed two techniques that advanced his influence: hiring experienced political hands to staff a full-time Washington office and funneling campaign contributions to the White House and key members of Congress.

For the Washington office, Hammer chose mostly well-connected Democrats, although it never lacked well-connected Republicans. The staff came from the White House, executive-branch agencies, Congress, and the statehouses. The number of personnel hovered around twenty, a substantial addition to the Occidental payroll. Almost everybody who worked there operated on the assumption that they served Hammer first, and then Occidental. If the interests of the doctor and the corporation coincided, all the better. William McSweeny, a former Boston newspaperman and Democratic National Committee official, emerged as Hammer's top Washington aide. Hired at a salary of $55,000 to launch the office in 1969, he soon was earning many times that amount. McSweeny was a master at putting powerful Washingtonians in his debt. He was also a master at staying out of the limelight while getting exposure for his boss.[55]

Hammer's other influential Washington representatives included Tim Babcock, former Republican governor of Montana, who just missed being appointed President Nixon's secretary of the interior; Jack King, another former newspaperman from Boston who had achieved recognition in Washington as the voice of the National Aeronautics and Space Administration; Rear Admiral Tazewell Shepard, Jr., son-in-law of Senator John Sparkman and former naval aide to President Kennedy; John Kyl, former Republican congressman from Iowa appointed by Nixon to a top position at the Interior Department; Noel Koch, special assistant to Presidents Nixon and Ford; and former senator Albert Gore, originally hired to manage Occidental's coal subsidiary, Island Creek Coal. Additional access in Washington came through paid lobbyists; Hammer used at least a dozen different lawyer/lobbyists on Occidental's behalf. Even though he had put together an effective Washington staff, often Hammer was his own best advocate in the corridors of power. Senator John Tunney, a California Democrat, said Hammer's personal visits distinguished him from other tycoons: "He believed in direct contact, unlike so many other business executives who would send their vice presidents. He knew that when you are dealing with big political egos, one-on-one contact works best. One time he and his entourage came with me on the Capitol subway when the bells started ringing for a vote. . . . Hammer called me personally after my election but before my swearing in. I cannot think of anybody else of his prominence who called without wanting anything. I was impressed. . . . He is a genius, and I have heard absolutely ruthless with his own people, but able to ingratiate himself with just about anyone, and willing to take on long odds to succeed."[56]

As the Occidental Washington office geared up during Nixon's first term, there was nothing subtle about Hammer's approaches to the White House. He gave Nixon not only money, but also loyalty, praising the president on television and in print for being willing to talk constructively to the Soviets. So it should have been no surprise when Nixon wrote Casey at the Export-Import Bank that the Occidental deal was indeed in the national interest. That letter broke the impasse. Casey announced the granting of the $180 million credit, the biggest ever to the Soviet government.[57] Perhaps coincidentally, the announcement came the same day as Occidental's annual meeting, which, as usual, was being held on Hammer's birthday. It was quite a gift.

Members of Congress expressed outrage; the below-market 6 percent interest rate especially angered them. Representative E. G. Shuster of Pennsylvania wrote a typical letter to Casey:

> It is absolutely incredible to me that the United States has agreed to assist the Soviets in the construction of a plant which will produce such a strategic material as agricultural fertilizer and to provide the financial assistance at such a low interest rate as well. When our own industries and businessmen are forced to pay interest rates that are nearly double that which we have offered the Russians, the finalization of such a proposal, in my mind, is totally indefensible.[58]

Shuster and other dissenters received a form letter from Casey defending Hammer's project.

The debate over the Export-Import Bank credit was especially emotional because it was conducted in the supercharged atmosphere of another debate, about whether the United States should use trade sanctions to punish the Soviet Union for its human rights stances. Many Americans believed it was unconscionable to trade with the Soviets while Jews were being denied permission to emigrate. The centerpiece of the controversy was proposed legislation sponsored by Senator Henry Jackson, a Washington Democrat, which linked trade to human rights.[59]

Hammer and chief executives of many other multinational corporations wanting to make money in Russia opposed Jackson. Hammer argued that if the United States tried to dictate Soviet policy, the Soviet government might restrict emigration even further to show it would not be bullied. He observed as well that the Russians had changed their views for the better since Stalin. A laissez-faire attitude would more likely lead the Soviets to relax their emigration policies, he said, adding that only a couple of hundred thousand people were involved and that he had not seen anti-Semitism in the Soviet Union during his decades there. Besides, Brezhnev had sworn to Hammer face-to-face that anti-Semitism no longer existed in the Soviet Union, and he had believed him, he said.[60]

American Jewish leaders were aghast at Hammer's remarks. They wondered whether he would stop at nothing to help the Soviets — and himself.

19

Dollars and Rubles

WITH HIS STATUS as the number-one American in the Soviet Union assured by the mid-1970s, Armand Hammer spent the rest of his career capitalizing on it. In addition to shepherding the $20 billion fertilizer deal through the hazards of international politics, he mounted numerous other initiatives. They were a curious mélange of potential profit makers and quirky projects of personal aggrandizement. The theme was the bigger the better — for Occidental's bottom line, for world peace through commerce, and, last but definitely not least, for Hammer's reputation.

Next to the fertilizer deal, the most ambitious of Hammer's Soviet ventures was one that never had much of a chance. Either Hammer refused to admit that to himself or realized it but therefore viewed the project as an even greater challenge. His plan was to move natural gas from northern Siberia to the west coast of the United States. The deal burst into the news in 1973, when Hammer starred at a Moscow press conference. Also present were Howard Boyd, chairman of El Paso Natural Gas Company, and Nikolai Osipov, Soviet deputy foreign trade minister. If the plan could be brought to fruition, Occidental reportedly would buy twenty supertankers to transport the gas and the Soviet Union would build a two-thousand-mile pipeline from the gas fields to a coastal port. Hammer involved Japanese firms in financing the multibillion-dollar project. The implications were mind-boggling. As the Associated Press reported from Moscow, "The gas agreement is tightly linked with the Soviet Union's détente efforts, at easing tension with the West, and [at] obtaining goods and technology from the capitalist world to bolster a sagging domestic economy."[1]

The importance of the project to Hammer and the Soviets was obvious to Theodore Shabad, Moscow correspondent of the *New York Times,* who was judging by some new high-visibility tactics. In the past, Hammer had avoided American reporters after meeting with Soviet ministers, preferring to give a sanitized version to the Russian-language media instead. Shabad said the strategy had been harming Hammer's credibility, something that apparently finally dawned on the parties involved: "Soviet officials, always sensitive to the image they project in the West, may have found such press relations counterproductive, and may have encouraged Dr. Hammer to discuss his projects with newsmen."[2]

In the United States, the project needed approvals from the Export-Import Bank and the Federal Power Commission, among other agencies. Senator Frank Church, an Idaho Democrat who chaired the subcommittee scrutinizing the deal, understood the scope of Hammer's plan:

> We are here examining something that is quite different from the ordinary intercourse of normal trade relationships. The projects which we propose to examine require huge magnitudes of investments. They are a claim on scarce capital and human resources in the United States, or they involve advanced technology not generally available in the Communist bloc nations. By their very nature, they have a high visibility factor, and thus have a tendency to become symbolic of the state of relations between the United States and these countries. Moreover, in some instances these projects involve our European or Japanese allies, either as competitors or collaborators. Hence our ties with these countries can be drawn into the web of relationships as well. There is consequently a strong public interest in careful examination of precisely in what way do these large investment projects fit into the process of détente.

Church opposed Hammer's plan, saying the proposed U.S. government loan guarantees and credits would be underwriting a project that violated the country's attempt to become independent of foreign energy supplies. When Church learned that Hammer had donated $1,000 to his campaign committee, the senator returned the money.[3]

Undeterred, Hammer visited Japan, where he announced that the Tokyo Gas Company would join Occidental and El Paso in the Siberian project. Furthermore, Occidental agreed to become partners with the Japanese in a second giant Siberian project, as well as an oil pipeline in Peru. Prime Minister Kakuei Tanaka promised to discuss the

Siberian projects with President Richard Nixon during an upcoming visit to Washington. Keyes Beech of the *Chicago Daily News* watched Hammer parade about Tokyo and noted that he was "traveling more like a visiting chief of state than a businessman. . . . The tycoon already has seen everybody here who matters, including Tanaka."[4]

In the early going, the project suffered a setback with the death of Raphael Dorman, the executive at the Bechtel Corporation assigned to help Hammer realize the dream, just as Bechtel had helped in Libya the previous decade. Dorman's death resulted from a heart attack in Moscow while he was there with Hammer. In the end, though, the natural-gas project gradually fell of its own weight. It might have been a good idea for all nations involved, but it was too big and too complex for American officials, who lacked Hammer's vision. By 1980, the project had become so much a hostage to the vagaries of international politics that it was effectively dead. A Commerce Department memorandum commented, "Since its inception, this project has faced tremendous financial and political hurdles, and in the wake of the Soviet invasion of Afghanistan has been moved even further onto the back burner."[5]

Hammer was disappointed but undaunted. He had already shifted his attention to a separate Occidental-Soviet project, the international trade center and hotel for foreign businesspeople in Moscow. The preliminary drawings showed office space for four hundred companies, a six-hundred-room hotel, and living space for 625 families. The Soviet Union attached such importance to the project that Anatoly Dobrynin, its ambassador to the United States, had attended the contract signing in New York. Drawings for the proposed complex contained a pool so Hammer could take the early morning swim that was part of his routine in every other city.[6]

Once again, Hammer was planning a Soviet project with U.S. government assistance in mind; the commitment from the Export-Import Bank would be $36 million. As the plans took shape and inflation took hold, costs soared from $110 million to $180 million. Skeptics appeared, but Hammer proved them wrong this time. Nine years after the unveiling of the drawings, seven years after the laying of the cornerstone, Hammer gave his dedication speech. Among those present at the festivities were U.S. Ambassador Arthur Hartman, Senator Robert Dole, Secretary of Transportation Elizabeth Hanford Dole, and Soviet dignitaries by the score. Occidental and forty-seven other foreign corporations that previously had occupied inadequate office space became ensconced in the new twenty-story building.[7]

A travel guidebook said of "Armand Hammer's hotel" that it was "the closest thing to a Moscow Hyatt. . . . The hotel caters almost exclusively to the foreign business community and offers conferences and secretarial services, Russian-language courses, a health club, and the businessman's club with live entertainment. There are two restaurants, one self-service cafeteria, a Japanese restaurant, and three bars." Philip Taubman, a *New York Times* Moscow correspondent, presented a different perspective, calling Hammer House a "modern complex on the banks of the Moscow River that has . . . every amenity the Russians imagine a Westerner could want, including flocks of prostitutes roaming the bars after dark. . . . The only people not welcome at the hotel are Russians, and the only currency not readily accepted is the ruble." The trade center remained the place to be in 1989 for business executives in Moscow, and it provided the Soviet government with a great deal of much-needed hard currency. Reports abounded, however, that the government refused to spend any of the profits on maintenance. The complex's director, Fyodor Kryuchko, complained publicly of broken elevators, dirty ceilings, faulty air-conditioning, and unappetizing restaurants in what had been Hammer's pride.[8]

Hammer wanted foreign businesspeople to have a golf course to accompany the other Western amenities. The game was unavailable in the Soviet Union. Although not a golfer himself, Hammer liked the symbolism of the ultimate capitalist sport in a Communist nation. Hammer said the idea "came to me . . . as I was flying into Moscow. The countryside, a scant half-hour's ride outside Moscow, is beautifully suited to a country club. And I thought, why not?" Some people informed about the project, however, gave credit to Robert Dwyer, a Portland, Oregon, lumber tycoon and avid golfer. Dwyer knew Hammer and suggested that Occidental become involved in a plan to build a course. He told a newspaper reporter how Hammer liked the thought that "golf was a great equalizer among people as soon as they stepped up to the first tee. He had me write it up as a proposal. It took me four hours to condense it to one and one-half pages, and he presented it to Brezhnev." Hoping to impress the Soviets, Hammer retained internationally known golf-course designer Robert Trent Jones, Jr. Worried about delays, Jones discussed the project with Brent Scowcroft, President Ford's national security adviser, then followed with a plea for help in making Hammer's dream a reality:

This project is an outgrowth of an offer made to and accepted by . . . Brezhnev in connection with the Moscow World Trade Center. It certainly has gained widespread attention, helping to prove that golf is a six-hundred-year-old sport of Scottish origin rather than an ideological symbol. At the moment, although fully approved by authorities in Moscow, this project is simmering on the back burner for a variety of reasons, including preparation of the 1980 Olympics which are consuming the energies of the Moscow people. Should President Ford care to indicate any interest in the golf course project to the appropriate diplomatic people . . . [that] would, I am told, nudge the golf project onto the front burner now.[9]

Hammer exploited the news-making potential of the plan. When the media picked up the story again in 1978, it was as if the idea were brand-new. Normally serious *New York Times* columnist James Reston had fun with it, commenting that perhaps it would be named the Hammer and Sickle Country Club: "No doubt Hammer made his offer in the spirit of détente and the reduction of international tensions, but golf is an addiction like vodka and produces more physical and mental tensions than any other form of human activity with the possible exception of sex." Even when the golf course seemed to fall victim to superpower disagreements over the Soviet invasion of Afghanistan, Hammer — bolstered by Jones's determination — refused to surrender hope. At age ninety, Hammer pronounced the project revived at a Moscow press conference during the Reagan-Gorbachev summit of May 1988, and construction began.[10]

Another Hammer sports-related venture with the Soviets also caught the attention of the public. Hammer had never before ventured into the realm of the Olympics, but the 1980 Games were different because the site was Moscow. The Soviet regime, looking to obtain Western currency, decided to sell commemorative coins and medals. Jockeying was fierce for the distribution rights, estimated to be worth $150 million. In September 1977, Hammer emerged the winner as part of a consortium involving Occidental Petroleum. The arrangement seemed incongruous. Colleen Sullivan, author of an investments column, noted that "the Soviet Union is selling its own legal currency around the world with the help of Western corporations using modern marketing strategies." But, she added, "when the name Armand Hammer surfaces in connection with the project, the incongruity vanishes." The silver-coin series totaled twenty-eight pieces, supplemented by six gold coins and five platinum coins. The total price to an investor was $3,665. Hammer promised 3 percent of the face value sold in the United States to the nation's Olympic team; that contribution was expected to reach $5 million. On the surface, it looked like a great deal for everyone concerned.[11]

Armand's mother, Rose, in her native Russia with her father.

Armand as a schoolboy.

From left: Brothers Harry, Armand, and Victor vacationing
at the beach in Belmar, New Jersey.

Armand's father, Julius, serving time in Sing Sing
Prison after being convicted in 1920 of performing
an abortion that caused a patient's death.

Armand (*left*) and Harry in Berlin during the 1920s.

Armand on an outing in Russia during his residency there in the 1920s.

The Brown House, Moscow, where the Hammers lived in palatial
splendor during the 1920s. (U.S. American Relief Administration, Russian
Unit, Collection/Hoover Institution Archives)

Olga, Armand's White Russian wife, with their son, Julian; about 1931.

Armand's parents, Rose and Julius, in Russia with Victor's son, Armasha,
and Armasha's mother, Vavara; early 1930s.

Armand's beloved Greenwich Village home at 183 West Fourth Street.
(Anne Fullam)

The fiftieth wedding anniversary of Rose and Julius, 1947. From left are
Harry, Julian, Rose, Armand, Julius, and Margaret Seaton,
Victor's mother-in-law.

Armand and his second wife, Angela, accept $100,000 for a half interest in their prize bull, Prince Eric; 1952. (UPI/Bettmann Newsphotos)

The Hammer family in happier times. *From left:* unidentified guest; Nancy Hammer Shelby (Eilan) with son Michael; Rose; Victor; Harry; Angela; and Armand.

A Sandor Klein portrait of Armand holding a Corot landscape.
(Courtesy of Sandor Klein, portrait painter)

After three decades away from Russia, Armand returns to meet
Nikita Khrushchev, 1961. (Bettmann Newsphotos)

Armand, Armasha, and Victor in Russia.

Armand (*center*) at the fiftieth anniversary of Hammer Galleries, 1978,
with Albert Gore (*left*) and the Lowell Thomases.

Armand and his aide James Pugash peruse the treasures of a Parisian
art gallery early on a Sunday morning, as Frances, Armand's third
wife, dozes. (Anthony Howarth)

Armand displays the Leonardo da Vinci manuscript he just won at auction
by bidding more than $5 million; 1980. (UPI/Bettmann Newsphotos)

Mikhail Gorbachev and Armand Hammer converse at the December 1987
U.S.-Soviet summit in Washington. (Reuters/Bettmann Newsphotos)

The Los Angeles mausoleum for Armand
Hammer's family, in a celebrity cemetery.
(Victor Cook)

The Los Angeles home of Frances and Armand Hammer. (Victor Cook)

The arrangement was not trouble-free, however. There were the usual charges from fervent anti-Communists in Congress and elsewhere that Hammer was giving assistance to the enemy. Another problem: The Soviets reportedly squeezed Hammer, asking for a larger share of the consortium's revenue as the value of gold and silver rose in the world market. According to the same reports, when Hammer resisted, the Soviets held back coins, which caused the consortium to fall behind on filling its orders. Hammer was in a bind; he needed the Soviet government's goodwill on many other projects. He agreed to pay more to the Soviets. A *New York Post* account put it baldly, saying "Hammer caved in." As a result, Hammer's coin group reportedly raised its prices to consumers. Still another problem: Because of international diplomatic tensions, the United States withdrew from the Moscow Olympics, hurting coin sales. Hammer believed President Jimmy Carter had made the wrong decision in withdrawing: "I went to those games and . . . I was disappointed that our athletes were not there. I felt very badly about it and I can tell you frankly that I do not believe boycotts work." [12]

It turned out that Hammer's acquisition of the distribution rights had a dark underside, at least according to the claims of Leo Henzel, president of United Euram Corporation. In late 1979, Henzel sued Occidental Petroleum and the New York investment banking firm of Loeb Rhoades, which played a role in the consortium. The story as told by Henzel went like this: He had produced a television special called "The Russian Festival of Music and Dance," which he sold to NBC. Problems developed with the marketing; to placate Henzel, the Soviets in March 1977 let him bid on the contract to distribute the Olympic coins. Henzel put together a consortium of large businesses. Dudley Cates, a Loeb Rhoades vice president, traveled with Henzel to the Soviet Union. Cates's associates at Loeb Rhoades suggested bringing Hammer into the deal, apparently in part because some consortium members had pulled out, in part because of Hammer's legendary ability to negotiate with Soviet leaders. Occidental agreed to take 70 percent of the deal, Loeb Rhoades took 22.5 percent, and United Euram took the other 7.5 percent. [13]

On a trip to Moscow soon thereafter, Cates was in Occidental's office without Henzel present. Hammer was there, along with three deputies. According to Cates, Hammer suggested cutting United Euram out of the consortium. When Henzel arrived later that day, Hammer offered him $250,000 to withdraw. Henzel refused. Hammer responded that he was out anyway. Cates, upset and perplexed, recounted the incident to his boss, John Loeb. But Hammer was determined. The next month, he approached Cates again about jettisoning United Euram. When Cates warned Hammer about a possible lawsuit by Henzel, Hammer reportedly replied, "I will hire Louis Nizer and I will be glad to pay him five times as much to defend such a lawsuit as I would ever pay Henzel." After Hammer succeeded in dumping Henzel, Cates said, "There is a term for what Hammer has tried to do to Henzel, and it is simply that Henzel has been defrauded. I think it is reprehensible."[14] Hammer fought back with high-priced legal talent and introduced Henzel's criminal record into the case. Occidental said it never would have signed a contract with Henzel if his past had been known.

Henzel responded that his criminal record was the result of a mistake and, anyway, was irrelevant to the main issue of his having been cheated by Hammer. Henzel added that Hammer was not exactly clean, having pleaded guilty in the Watergate campaign-contributions case and having signed consent decrees with U.S. government agencies concerning Occidental's business practices. Henzel's partner, Peter Yamanov, testified that when Hammer had offered to buy out United Euram,

> it was my impression . . . Hammer thought of Henzel and [me] as discardable baggage now that the contract had been won. . . . Hammer's explanation that they had to make room in the deal for a Mr. David Karr and his associate/friend Gvishiani — who happened to be the Soviet premier's son-in-law — did not convince me that Hammer was being fair. . . . I still cannot get over the greed of that man Hammer.

Henzel asked the court to force Occidental to disclose all payments to Gvishiani. Occidental denied making any payments.[15]

Much of Henzel's pending case appears weak legally, but his allegations hurt Hammer at least temporarily by linking him more publicly than before to David Karr. The coming together of Hammer and Karr in the Olympic coin consortium was extraordinary, as was their entire relationship. Karr, who had changed his name from Katz, had written for the American Communist newspaper *Daily Worker,* researched for muckraking Washington columnist Drew Pearson, managed a public relations firm, and become chief executive at a diversified corporation called Fairbanks Whitney. Eventually, Karr moved to Paris, where he put together business deals, including many with the Soviet Union. Karr and Hammer met in about 1970. Karr reportedly told Hammer, "You're always talking about your old friend Lenin. Why not go to the Soviet Union and do some business?" Hammer was trying to do just that. Karr helped negotiate the huge fertilizer deal and re-negotiate Occidental's financially disastrous Libyan oil-tanker rates. Like Hammer, Karr cultivated world leaders. In a 1975 letter to President Gerald Ford, he offered advice on U.S.-Soviet relations, mentioning his forty-eight trips to Russia in the past three years. In his cover letter, Karr invited White House press secretary Ron Nessen for a vacation on his yacht. Karr also had ties to President Lyndon Johnson, Greek tycoon Aristotle Onassis, and numerous American senators.[16]

When the Soviet Union insisted Hammer and Karr join in the Olympic coins transaction, the two men did so but with great reluctance because of recent disagreements. Charles Simonelli, an American businessman approved by Hammer to market the Soviet coins, remembered a Karr anecdote about the Russians telling him and Hammer they were partners, putting them in a room, and ordering them to iron out the details. Karr turned to Hammer and said, "Okay, we're in the coop together. Now, who's the chicken and who's the fox?"[17]

Shortly before Karr's death, in 1979, he told *New York Times* reporter Jeff Gerth he had "secretly testified against Armand Hammer during an investigation by the Securities and Exchange Commission and alleged, among other things, that Mr. Hammer had made payoffs inside the Soviet Union." Karr died suddenly in Paris just after a trip to Moscow. There were rumors of poisoning whispered by Karr's widow. Gerth and Roy Rowan of *Fortune* magazine investigated, and each wrote a major article about Karr's complex life. The official pronouncement, however, was that he died of natural causes. Karr's son, Andrew, said that "there was a lot of tension in the last years between my father and Armand Hammer," but he rejected rumors of foul play involving Hammer or others.[18]

John Tunney, former senator from California, was in business with Karr after the falling-out with Hammer. "I prefer not to talk about what Karr said to me about Armand Hammer — that is not fair to a dead man. They definitely were not getting along, although Karr still respected him." The widespread publicity about the Hammer-Karr relationship at the time of Karr's death convinced anti-Communists all the more that Hammer was the devil incarnate; after all, Karr was perceived by some self-proclaimed patriotic groups, rightly or wrongly, as one of the most significant Communist agents in the West.[19]

Henzel's allegations about the roles of Karr and Hammer in the Olympic coins caper caused trouble for Hammer the next time around. The tempest over his participation in the marketing of 1984 Los Angeles Olympic coins made the Moscow allegations appear to be a tiny

squall. This time, Occidental was teamed with investment banker La-
zard Frères in an entity called the Coin Group. The drama began in
1980, when the Los Angeles Olympic Committee solicited bids for marketing commemorative coins. The Hammer group won partly because
of its experience with the Moscow coins, combined with its willingness
to put up a $50 million guarantee. Congress began considering legisla-
tion to mint the coins, but disagreements among legislators caused costly
delays that led Hammer's group to reduce its guarantee by $20 million.

Hammer's leading opponent was Representative Frank Annunzio,
an Illinois Democrat who chaired the subcommittee with jurisdiction
over the program. Annunzio was concerned about reports that the Coin
Group had melted down some of the Moscow collector's items, attempted to manipulate the market, and hidden excess profits in secret
bank accounts. Annunzio also was critical of the Hammer consortium's
slow delivery of Moscow coins to American consumers, citing fifty
complaints to postal authorities. Fernand St. Germain, a Rhode Island
congressman who chaired the full committee, was in Hammer's corner,
however.[20]

The disagreements came to a head during House hearings in April
and May 1982. Mary Brooks, former director of the U.S. Mint, charged
the Hammer consortium with being "probably the most high-powered
group ever unleashed upon the Congress. Their vision of the United
States Mint as a gigantic money machine . . . is the most ambitious
program in the history of the modern world. . . . The spectacle of the
greatest nation . . . with the strongest currency . . . allowing its money
to be consigned to a private group for sale and profit is outrageous."
Hammer replied that he was puzzled by such outrage. His group hoped
to make a profit, sure, but the Los Angeles Olympic Committee would
receive a minimum of $30 million even if Hammer had to eat red ink.
Attacking his role in the marketing of the Moscow coins was unfair,
he said, for several reasons:

> The payment made to the United States Olympic Committee from sales
> of the 1980 Moscow Olympic coins represented one of the largest sources
> of revenue for the committee. Although the United States Olympic ath-
> letes did not participate in the Moscow games due to President Carter's
> foreign policy decision, our organization paid from its own proceeds the
> sum of over $400,000 . . . although we had no obligation to do so. . . .
> I would also point out . . . that the Moscow Olympic coin program was
> a success despite the fact that sales were made during a time of unprec-
> edented increases in the values of gold and silver. One result is that we

found ourselves under contract to customers to sell coins at prices which were substantially less than the actual value of the coins. Nevertheless, all such contracts were fulfilled. I cite this not only to demonstrate the propriety with which we carried out the Moscow coin program, but also because it is the very kind of problem which creates risks and dangers which are best borne by the private sector.[21]

In an attempt to demonstrate his concern for the public interest, Hammer noted that he had torn up his first contract with the Los Angeles Olympic Committee to

permit rebidding, so that there could be no accusation of favoritism and so that everybody would have a fair chance to bid on this coin program, and I remember you thanked me for that. . . . The coin group entered into a new contract with the Olympic committee in which we agreed to reduce our guarantee from $50 million to $30 million because of the reduction in the number of coins. And then when nothing happened and there were further delays, my partners particularly felt frustrated and they asked me to join them in withdrawing from the program and cancel our contract, to which I reluctantly agreed. But I want you to know that I am a loyal American and I am also dedicated to my city of Los Angeles and I felt it was my duty to come before you today even though we at the present time have no agreement with the Los Angeles committee.[22]

Hammer said the $30 million guarantee by the Coin Group was generous: "We have already invested $2.5 million, $1 million of which was forfeited when we cancelled and $1 million or more which we lost in interest on the $5 million we gave the committee and on our expenses." Congressman Annunzio showed no sympathy, scolding the Coin Group for its intensive lobbying, which had cost $500,000. Annunzio referred to a meeting with Hammer at which "I asked you to fire the lobbyists." Hammer responded, "Well, unfortunately we cannot do without them in this era." Annunzio: "They are doing a good job for you now." Hammer: "Well, that is what they are paid for."[23]

When members of Annunzio's subcommittee attacked Hammer's patriotism, Hammer distributed testimonials from Representative Patricia Schroeder and Senators William Proxmire, Bill Bradley, and John Glenn. Robert Gray, a well-connected public relations executive from Washington, apparently had solicited the testimonials. Glenn's was typical: "Armand Hammer is certainly a remarkable example of our free enterprise system. His outstanding achievements are a credit to himself and the nation." After the acrimonious hearings ended, Hammer appeared to be victorious. Annunzio's "stop Hammer" movement lost in the full committee by a vote of 32 to 7. But he had no intention of quitting. The congressman took the debate to the full House of Representatives, saying his plan would allow the U.S. Mint to offer three coins, with all profits going to the Olympic Committee: "There is no middleman to siphon off profits under my bill. There are no lobbyists who have to be paid fat salaries to get my bill passed." He termed the opposition's bill "the Occidental relief act." Other members of the House brought up Hammer's less than exemplary conduct during Watergate, criticized Occidental's environmental record, and repeatedly questioned his loyalty to the United States.[24]

In a surprise, the House overturned its own committee's recommendation, supporting Annunzio 302 to 84. When the Senate Committee on Banking, Housing, and Urban Affairs called a hearing to debate the anti-Hammer House version, the Coin Group threw in the towel. Senator Alan Cranston tried to soften Hammer's defeat by telling the committee that

> I am sure Occidental Petroleum would like to have received the profits generated by the Senate-passed coin act, but profit is not Dr. Hammer's only motive in this or in many other matters. . . . I am confident that at this stage Dr. Hammer's real interest is to help the Olympic athletes and the Olympic committee stage the best summer Olympics possible. Dr. Hammer is one of California's finest citizens. His altruism is widely known.

Occidental executive Angelo Leparulo read a statement in which Hammer said Annunzio had won only because of misrepresentations: "More attention was given to vitriolic attacks upon Occidental and me personally than the merits."[25]

Of all Hammer's dizzying transactions with the Soviet Union, it was his $20 billion, twenty-year fertilizer deal that continued to cause the largest ripples in the world order. The commodities involved kept getting mixed up in the constant sparring between the two superpowers, assuring that Hammer would be in the position either of power broker or suppliant, depending on the situation. Because Hammer wanted the commodities to flow smoothly, he had an interest in America's granting most-favored-nation trading status to the Soviet Union, something Leonid Brezhnev also fervently desired. *Pravda* and *Izvestia* printed interviews with Hammer in which he called on Congress and the president to grant such status.[26]

One question about the deal that would not die was whether Occidental owned enough phosphate in Florida to supply the Soviets and the company's domestic markets without exhausting reserves, which would place the United States in a vulnerable position. George Brooks, who had convinced Hammer to mine northern Florida reserves in the first place, kept the controversy alive. The more he learned after leaving Occidental about Hammer's ties to Russia, the more upset the patriotic Brooks became. In July 1976, he surprised a House of Representatives hearing on phosphate leasing in Florida's Osceola National Forest by stating flatly that Occidental planned to mine the forest as part of its Soviet contract.

Maywood Chesson, Jr., Occidental's Florida vice president, denied Brooks's "allegations and insinuations." Although Chesson disagreed with the decision to ship superphosphoric acid to Russia, he continued to maintain that Occidental had no designs on the national forest. A lawyer representing Occidental wrote the subcommittee a seven-page letter intended to demonstrate that Occidental had never considered the possibility of mining the Osceola land. There the matter stood until the General Accounting Office, an arm of Congress, published its report *Phosphates: A Case Study of a Valuable, Depleting Mineral in America.* Noting that phosphate rock was crucial to fertilizer production, the report said that "over the next two decades the richest United States phosphate deposits are likely to be depleted. There is cause for concern as to how new sources may be developed to meet the nation's growing agricultural needs."[27]

Brooks, William Stowasser at the Bureau of Mines, and the GAO report reached a wider audience when Lee Smith of *Fortune* cited them in an article carrying the headline "Armand Hammer and the Phosphate Puzzle." Hammer told Smith that Occidental owned enough phosphate in Florida to last fifty years. Smith countered with the skepticism of his sources:

The fact that the sale to the Russians was approved by the federal government should not be taken as a guarantee that Hammer has the goods to deliver. The State Department evaluated the foreign policy implications, Commerce was responsible for seeing that none of the technology supplied to the Russians was classified, Treasury had to assess balance of trade and other economic ramifications, Agriculture sized up the effect on the American farmer, and the Export-Import Bank had to pro-

tect its loan. But no one questioned whether Occidental had the phosphate rock it claimed. William Casey, who was then chairman of the
Export-Import Bank . . . gives a reasonable explanation of his view at
the time — "As far as we were concerned, that was the Russians' problem."

Smith said the possible dependence on foreign supplies "might be more
acceptable if the exchange with the Russians guaranteed the United
States something equally valuable in return. It does not." In exchange
for the superphosphoric acid, the United States would receive three
commodities that its consumers had in abundance, Smith said.[28]

When two key Occidental executives involved in the phosphate negotiations looked back on the charges and countercharges from the
perspective of the late 1980s, they were unable to put to rest the controversy over whether Occidental actually had sufficient resources to fill
the Soviet contract without exploiting U.S. reserves. A. A. Guffey, one
of Occidental's phosphate pioneers, remembered being summoned from
Florida to Hammer's Los Angeles home on a Sunday morning sometime in 1972, right after "the doctor" returned from Moscow. "The
doctor asked us if we had sufficient reserves to deal with the Soviet
Union, then explained the details to us. He wanted to offer the Soviets
the latest, newest thing in fertilizer. We spent several million dollars
on drilling and computerizing to prove our gut feeling that we had
enough reserves. We proved more that one hundred million tons of
minable reserves. The twenty-year Occidental-Soviet deal required about
sixty million tons. The doctor wanted to feed the world. It might not
be highly profitable, but it could make money and do some good toward
meeting world hunger. . . . I had put together a white paper within
Occidental answering questions like what do we do if the Russians do
not take the SPA tonnage? It was well thought out, not just one of the
doctor's schemes. It had the approval of the board of directors."[29]

James Galvin, who chaired the Phosphate Rock Export Association
after leaving Occidental, said negotiating with the Soviets was tricky:
"What is the market for superphosphoric acid when there is only one
producer? Which shipping rate and destination do you use? We had
to make money on the superphosphoric acid to break even on the rest,
especially when you look at the huge capital outlay. I have to assume
that Occidental has been breaking even on the deal. Then you ask the
question, if it is only break even, could you not just put the money in
the bank and get interest?" But negotiating the deal of the century was
something Hammer was driven to do, and hang the opposition, Galvin
said.[30]

Avowed anti-Communists looked at the ammonia side of the equation, as well as the phosphate side, and became angered at what they saw. One of those anti-Communists, columnist Phyllis Schlafly, commented that the Soviet government was stealing the ammonia market from American producers. Russia was offering ten-year contracts with fixed prices for the first three years, coupled with a clause stating any increase after that would be no more than 3 percent. Schlafly said that because American ammonia companies were unable to match the Soviet government's current price or future guarantees, twenty-nine U.S. ammonia plants had closed in just two years. Schlafly carped that in no way was the "trade promoted by Occidental . . . mutual, reciprocal, the result of hard bargaining, or handled by Occidental on a philanthropic basis. It is highly profitable for those who promote it, but the United States taxpayer foots the bill and the United States worker lays his job on the line."[31]

Such criticism, in the end, did not stop Hammer. The construction proceeded on schedule. At one milestone, in August 1978, Hammer flew to the Ukraine to dedicate a $1 billion processing plant and port facility on the Black Sea coast. The site was less than an hour's drive from the ancestral home of his paternal grandparents. Hammer later called the ceremony "a very emotional experience." He arrived in a nineteen-car motorcade escorted by Soviet police. In the cars were officials from Occidental as well as the Soviet and American governments. Occidental chartered a plane to carry dozens of journalists to the site. A State Department diplomat cabled Washington that "the heavy and favorable Soviet press coverage was meant to demonstrate that he is a model of what United States–Soviet trade should be like. . . . Hammer was lavish in praise of Brezhnev and he ultimately . . . did give . . . Soviet reporters some of the critical words for which they were thirsting concerning United States trade restraints, et cetera."[32]

With the trade arrangement functioning, Hammer relied on the U.S. government to cut Occidental's costs whenever possible. The administration of Jimmy Carter was inclined to help. Hammer had been an early and important supporter of Carter's. Their first meeting had occurred during Carter's long-shot 1976 campaign, at the Los Angeles home of movie mogul Lew Wasserman, a Democratic power broker. Frances Hammer liked Carter and told Armand to take his candidacy seriously.

Hammer's presence at the Wasserman get-together had a negative impact on Carter's Mr. Clean image, mainly because of the recent Watergate taint. Nonetheless, when Hammer offered Carter advice on foreign affairs, Carter listened. In September 1976, during the height of the Carter-Ford race, Hammer reportedly carried a message to Plains, Georgia, from Soviet foreign minister Andrei Gromyko concerning the Kremlin's stance on arms control. Few people in Plains had seen anything like Hammer's jet; crowds gathered to view it land and take off. Hammer became a highly visible Carter supporter, wearing a gold peanut pin in his lapel.[33]

After Carter's election, Hammer pushed the president to arrange a summit with Brezhnev as soon as possible. Hammer's generosity with advice and gifts continued unabated during Carter's term. He had learned during the Johnson years that it was good public relations to cultivate the president's wife and children, so he did the same with the Carters. Hammer contributed to Rosalynn's favorite causes, including the Friendship Force, devoted to overseas exchanges involving ordinary citizens, and the Institutional Development Corporation, established to assist inner-city schools. The development corporation received $100,000 from Hammer, with the proviso that the money be split between his boyhood Bronx neighborhood and needy locales of Los Angeles. Collecting the first installment was Chip Carter, Rosalynn and Jimmy's son, who worked for the philanthropic group.[34]

One of Hammer's most appreciated acts was his donation of William Harnett's painting *Cincinnati Enquirer, 1888,* a favorite of the president's. Hammer bought it for $360,000 at the beginning of 1978 from J. William Middendorf, a Washington businessman, diplomat, and art collector. The painting had been on loan from Middendorf to the White House. Hammer changed the status from loan to gift, arranging a special White House ceremony for the presentation. He invited his grandson, Michael (Julian's son), his brother Victor, his sister-in-law Ireene, and assorted friends. One observer was *Washington Post* reporter Henry Allen, who noted that given the long tenure of the painting at the White House before Hammer's purchase, "the ceremony was largely an exercise in accounting and symbolism. But then symbolism is what Hammer is so good at." Rosalynn Carter wrote Hammer that the painting "will be a constant reminder of your warm generosity and friendship."[35]

In return, Rosalynn graced the opening of Hammer's art collection in Atlanta, guaranteeing Hammer even more publicity than usual. Armand and Frances arrived on their private jet, Rembrandt's *Juno* in tow under tight security. It was Hammer's favorite and most expensive painting, purchased from Middendorf in 1976 for more than $3 million. He refused to trust a commercial transporter with the picture, so he stowed it in the plane, where he could be certain of its safety as he and Frances drank wine and vodka, ate caviar and chicken. Hammer's employees and hangers-on arrived in Atlanta for the exhibition and the parties that accompanied it. At the museum, Hammer gave the First Lady a guided tour of his pictures. Afterward, she sent a photograph from the opening, inscribed to "my friend, Dr. Armand Hammer."[36]

Rosalynn agreed to serve as honorary chairwoman for a gala New York City dinner honoring Hammer as the year's "Man of Conscience." Jimmy Carter wrote a letter of congratulations to be read at the occasion. Senator Abraham Ribicoff of Connecticut gave the keynote speech, after New York governor Hugh Carey introduced Hammer as "one of the great figures on the world scene." Carey commented from the head table, "I have been sipping at [Hammer's] fount of wisdom, and if I sit there long enough, I will cure the energy crisis, the difficulty of the dollar, I will bring up the stock market." The program pictured Hammer on the cover; inside were pictures of him with the Carters, Lyndon Johnson, Brezhnev, Jonas Salk, and Prince Charles, among others.[37]

Jimmy Carter had frequent kind words for Hammer, writing on one occasion: "We know the dedication with which you have worked to make life better for our people, and your support for our efforts gives us strength and inspiration for the tasks that lie ahead." Hammer responded that he was deeply touched by those words.[38]

Hammer felt free to offer all manner of advice to the president, even suggesting Carter handle his televised fireside chats differently. During the controversy over whether the president should commute the sentence of kidnapped newspaper heiress Patty Hearst, who was serving time for terrorist activity, Hammer supported leniency. Patty's father, William Randolph Hearst, thanked Hammer "for your eloquent letter to President Carter about Patty. If your letter does not affect his thinking, nothing will. Frankly, our spirits are at a low ebb at the moment, because it appears that Carter is unwilling to take a stand." Shortly thereafter, Carter commuted the sentence, paving the way for Patty Hearst's release from prison.[39]

When Carter decided to sell the presidential yacht *Sequoia* as a sign that he was of the common people, Hammer saw an opportunity for publicity akin to Campobello. Working with Occidental executive Rear Admiral Tazewell Shepard, Hammer estimated how much it would take to buy the yacht at auction. They miscalculated, however. When the 174 sealed bids were opened, the high amount was $286,000. Hammer was third, at $251,000.[40]

Using his entrée to Carter, Hammer pushed his foreign agenda, especially with the Soviet Union; suggested a program for better relations between the United States and Mexico, a nation in which Occidental hoped to become deeply involved; and promoted Occidental's process for extracting oil from shale rock in Colorado. Despite the opposition of National Security Adviser Zbigniew Brzezinski, Hammer visited the White House more often than during any other presidency, flattering Carter by saying his inspiration had led to creation of the annual Armand Hammer Peace and Human Rights Conference.*

The Carter administration, despite an internal split over Hammer's motives, came through over and over again. During Nixon's presidency, Hammer had decided to have his staff design three special ships to carry Occidental's superphosphoric acid to the Soviet Union. The ships were expensive, but Carter's Maritime Administration promised to pick up 50 percent of the bill in return for Occidental's using a domestic shipyard instead of a substantially cheaper foreign yard. The agency issued an announcement in October 1978; it put the total cost of the three tug/barge units at about $156 million, making the government's share about $78 million. One vessel carried the name *Frances Hammer,* on Armand's orders. Another operated under the name *Julius Hammer.* Journalist Tom Gilroy, writing in the *Washington Monthly* under the headline "Tapping the Federal Till the Occidental Way," took issue with the deal, which he viewed as another memorial to Hammer's greed and vanity. Gilroy said "the only thing the subsidies will do is guarantee healthy profits to what otherwise would have been a shaky deal for Occidental." Hammer called the article "very biased and slanted" but in his letter to the editor failed to provide convincing evidence for that charge.[41]

With all the hubbub about the deal of the century, it seemed inevi-

---

* Hammer's access offended many White House staffers besides Brzezinski. At one point, aide Stuart Eizenstat drafted what was to be a personal reply to Hammer from the president. Carter's secretary, Susan Clough, objected: "As you can tell from attached files, Hammer is a frequent letter writer to the president. Because of this and the fact that it is not appropriate for him to have reason to . . . infer influence . . . each time he writes," Clough asked Eizenstat to sign the letter with his own name. (White House Central Files, General, box HE 5, Jimmy Carter Library, Atlanta.) Hammer had plenty of White House aides in his corner, though, having flattered them over the years with his gifts and his charm. Press secretary Jody Powell asked the president to see Hammer, commenting, "He has been extremely supportive, and I have the impression that his desire to meet with you privately and the various rebuffs he has received continue to bother him quite a bit." (Hammer to the president, April 18 and May 27, 1980; Powell to the president, May 13, 1980, Carter Library.) Carter's advisers at his reelection committee pushed for a meeting, too; they wanted Hammer to continue giving generously. Hammer got his meeting, although Carter aides scheduled it as off-the-record and omitted it from the White House schedule. (Robert Strauss and S. Lee Kling to Phil Wise, May 29, 1980, Carter Library.)

table that legal challenges would arise. They did. Domestic ammonia producers petitioned the U.S. International Trade Commission to halt Occidental's ammonia imports from the Soviets. The twelve producers, who accounted for about half of all domestic ammonia, raised the specter of dependency on Soviet supplies.[42]

Hammer responded that the opposition was based on avarice and inefficiency, that the domestic market was weak because of overexpansion and rising production costs. The case divided the five presidential appointees on the International Trade Commission, just as it split the industry and the nation. The agency voted 3 to 2 against Occidental, recommending that Jimmy Carter impose a three-year quota on ammonia from the Soviet Union. Hammer knew the president possessed the authority to disregard the commission, and he hoped the goodwill he had accumulated, combined with the president's substantial intellect applied to the facts, would lead to a reversal. Eventually Carter did decide that the nation was not under siege from the Soviet ammonia. Wasting no time, Hammer jetted to Moscow, where he signed a contract giving Occidental additional ammonia imports.[43]

But Hammer's victory was short-lived. When the Soviet Union invaded Afghanistan weeks later, Carter looked for ways to express his displeasure at what he believed to be a moral outrage. The president asked the International Trade Commission to reexamine ammonia imports, noting that "recent events have altered economic conditions." The commission reopened the case. Hammer, just back from a Moscow meeting with Brezhnev, testified at the hearing. Network television cameras recorded the proceedings for the evening news, an unusual occurrence at the obscure agency. Hammer hit away at the alleged greed of the domestic producers, wondering, "Should our American farmers be required to pay unreasonably high prices for their ammonia fertilizer?" One of the commissioners listening was Michael Calhoun, who had replaced Joseph Parker after the decision against Occidental. Calhoun found Hammer's case persuasive — this time, Occidental prevailed, in a 3-to-2 vote.[44]

Again, Hammer's joy was cut short. Although the ammonia imports seemed to be secure, the president lighted on Occidental's superphosphoric acid exports as a way to send a message to the Soviets. Carter already had curtailed grain exports to the Soviets; targeting phosphate was the next logical step because the Russians needed it to grow their own grain. Carter had no desire to get on the wrong side of Hammer, but the pressure to do something was intense. Longshoremen in Florida were refusing to load superphosphoric acid onto Occidental ships bound for Russia, as a protest against the Afghanistan invasion. Occidental, losing about $500,000 each day, obtained a court order requiring the laborers to load the ships. The two sides fought all the way to the United States Supreme Court, where Occidental prevailed.[45]

Carter kept Hammer informed about the administration's position. On January 29, 1980, the president promised that the special trade representative and secretary of commerce would be in touch with Hammer: "We cannot do business as usual with [Russia] if they continue their flagrant use of military force. . . . I express my appreciation for your . . . continued support as we take those decisions that we believe are best for our country and for the world." Hammer replied the next day, saying that he would support Carter publicly. Privately, however, he argued that the Soviets would replace Occidental's phosphate with Moroccan supplies, Florida would lose at least a thousand jobs, ports along the coast would be harmed, and the Soviet Union might retaliate against the Export-Import Bank and the American bank consortium financing the deal. Hammer reminded the president of all the services he had performed for the administration, including behind-the-scenes negotiations with the Iranians in an attempt to secure the release of American hostages.[46]

Hammer understood that his deal was the pawn in a political game. Syndicated journalists Rowland Evans and Robert Novak said in a column about Carter's "great new friend" Hammer that the phosphate cutoff had less to do with Soviet trade than with petty election-year politics. Vice President Walter Mondale, generally a supporter of Soviet-American trade, knew midwestern farmers would be furious if phosphate shipments continued while grain shipments were halted. Bob Bergland, the secretary of agriculture, was in Mondale's corner. Zbigniew Brzezinski, Carter's national security adviser, who despised Hammer, wanted a ban for global policy reasons. That trio was likely to win out, "despite the high cards held by the rich and mysterious" Hammer.[47]

Commerce Secretary Philip Klutznick and the State Department were rumored to favor allowing the phosphate shipments to continue but supposedly were outflanked. Actually, agreement was unanimous that something had to be done. The debate centered on whether to cancel or suspend Hammer's deal. Klutznick later related the decision-making process: "We spent a lot of time after the Soviet invasion of Afghanistan trying to figure out what to do. We set up an interagency committee of which I was chair, appointed by President Carter. I was new in the cabinet; it was tough to get agreement. One issue that came up was the Occidental contract with the Soviet Union. The National Security Council got into the act. We decided to suspend the contract. Then I asked who wanted to notify Armand Hammer. No one volunteered. I got the task, so I told my secretary to find Hammer, wherever he was. He was in his plane over Washington, D.C., when he called me. I told him the bad news. He said, 'That's wonderful.' I said, 'What do you mean?' He said, 'You didn't cancel it, you suspended it. Now I can tell the Russians there is hope, that you are reasonable people.' That is Armand Hammer; he never loses."[48]

Despite the cutoff, some people thought Hammer had been let off too easily. Senator James Exon, a Nebraska Democrat, asked Klutznick why the administration had waited until February 5, 1980, to signal a clampdown on the phosphate exports when cutoffs had been imposed on other commodities the previous month. Exon suggested that the delay "allowed three ships which were loading Florida phosphate to complete their loading and depart for the Soviet Union only shortly before the order became effective." Administration officials denied such favoritism.[49]

In his time of crisis, Hammer met with Brezhnev and other Soviet officials. He asked them to keep shipping ammonia to the United States; if the Soviet ammonia stopped in retaliation, he said, prices for farmers might double. When Brezhnev expressed puzzlement at the president's harsh reaction to the Soviets' Afghanistan adventure, Hammer replied that Carter felt betrayed and was worried Afghanistan would be a stepping-stone for an invasion of the Persian Gulf. According to Hammer, Brezhnev replied that such thinking was "sheer nonsense." Although Hammer might have agreed with Brezhnev's assessment, he supported Carter for reelection: "Ronald Reagan is a neighbor and a good friend, but I think the times are too perilous to make a change." Hammer's tolerance for Carter's world view was not infinite, however. Onetime Occidental executive James Galvin recalled Carter's picture disappearing for a while from the collection of leaders' photographs in Hammer's office.[50]

Ironically, it was the next president — the anti-Communist Reagan — who reinstated Occidental's shipments of phosphate to the Soviet Union. Hammer began lobbying as soon as it became clear who would be the key players in the new administration. He met with Secretary of State Alexander Haig in February 1981, reminding him of the Nixon administration's special commitment to the deal of the century; Haig had been an influential Nixon adviser. Hammer told Haig that resuming shipments would be a positive signal to the Soviets during a time of international tension over Afghanistan.[51]

Hammer was talking to Soviet officials in Moscow even as the

American public learned of the policy change. It appeared that Hammer had advance knowledge of the Reagan decision. Within six weeks of the announcement of the decision, the phosphate was moving overseas again. Not everybody was delighted. An editorial in the *Gainesville* (Florida) *Sun* said Hammer was taking unpatriotic advantage of American know-how "to improve the Communist diet, and is providing a rapidly depleted American resource to do just that. The Communists in turn provide marginally useful products and skim enough profit to repay the American loans with American money. With friends like Occidental around, Americans do not need enemies."[52]

20

The World Is
Made of Oil

A RMAND HAMMER'S WHEELING AND DEALING in the
Soviet Union overshadowed everything else he did in the public
mind. But during the 1970s and 1980s, Occidental was expanding into
dozens of other nations, influencing their economies and their governments. Hammer understood the importance, after the Libyan revolution, of never again becoming dependent on any one volatile nation. So
Occidental pushed harder to go global. Latin America was one of the
prime exploration areas. As Occidental began looking for oil there, accompanying the drilling rigs were Hammer's usual one-man diplomacy — and the usual controversy.

Nowhere was the controversy more intense than in Venezuela.
Hammer had visited there in 1966 and had apparently tried to sell the
government paintings by Venezuelan artists owned by Hammer Galleries. While there, he had talked to oil ministry officials about drilling
someday. About the same time, John Askew, a Fayetteville, Arkansas,
resident who had worked in the Venezuelan oil industry since 1945,
was conducting similar discussions independently of Hammer. Askew
heard that the government wanted to stimulate bidding for drilling
areas, so he sounded out U.S. oil companies. The reaction was unenthusiastic. Then he heard from the Wall Street firm of Loeb Rhoades
that Occidental might be interested. He arranged to meet Hammer.
The two men signed an agreement under which Askew would help
Occidental obtain exploration rights for one or more of five drilling
areas.

Occidental paid Askew $3 million for his services. (The money went
through a Swiss bank account to guard against competitors' learning

about it. Askew allegedly paid half his receipts to influential Venezuelans to work on Hammer's behalf.) In return Askew and his associates gathered intelligence about the plans of competing oil companies, hoping to place Occidental in an advantageous position when the government opened bids. Charles Hatfield, the head of Occidental's Venezuelan subsidiary, met almost daily with Askew. The strategy worked — in late 1970, Occidental won the bidding for three of the five blocks. Occidental began drilling.[1]

Prospects were bright. The American embassy cabled to the State Department that "Hammer has [the] type of charisma which will appeal to [Venezuela's president] and it is conceivable he could carve out for his company a much larger piece of the action in new oil arrangements." Meanwhile, Hammer opened a showing of his art collection and gave the Venezuelan president a statue of Simón Bolívar; the Venezuelan media loved it. The embassy reported that the art collection was "of truly outstanding quality, and the invitational opening maintained Dr. Hammer's flair for attracting public attention with well-conceived taste." Hammer sent an exhibition catalog to Secretary of State Henry Kissinger, who wrote back that the collection was making a "very real contribution" to cultural understanding.[2]

Controversy, however, was lurking beneath the surface calm, as it usually did when Hammer was involved. The fly in the ointment was John Ryan, who had joined Occidental in August 1973 from Texaco after hearing Hammer was looking for a Spanish-speaking lawyer. Ryan replaced Hatfield, reportedly fired because of unsatisfactory performance. The job would be a challenge, Ryan figured, because "Occidental's Venezuela operations had been marred by serious management problems. There had been internal rumors of fraud, corruption, and kickbacks, as well as indications of sloppy drilling work." By April 1974, Ryan was out. He alleged that he had been dismissed after he questioned possibly illegal payments by Askew and Occidental. His allegations sat like a time bomb in a Texas court.[3]

Five months after the lawsuit was filed, the *New York Times* published a story about it. Two days later, Hammer sent a denial of the allegations to the Venezuelan government. The charges snowballed, however, until Venezuela's president announced he was suspending talks with Occidental over compensation for a scheduled nationalization of its assets. Venezuela's judicial and legislative branches began investigations, calling Askew to testify. In a surprise move, the president appeared on national television to announce that his own investigation had turned up the names of the bribers and the bribe takers. The president displayed a copy of a $160,000 check signed by Askew, who was imprisoned.

Hammer believed the investigations were motivated by the Venezuelan government's desire to avoid paying Occidental tens of millions of dollars in compensation for its nationalized property. Occidental filed a compensation claim in 1977 against the government. Hammer hired a Caracas law firm with important ties to Venezuelan officials and asked the U.S. government to apply pressure. Hush-hush negotiations continued for more than a decade, with Hammer failing to recover anything. Then, surprisingly, the Venezuelan supreme court ruled in March 1989 that the government did indeed owe Occidental for the nationalization. The court recommended that a three-member panel decide the amount of compensation.[4]

Ryan's lawsuit had unpleasant repercussions for Occidental beyond Venezuelan borders. It inspired similar charges by another disgruntled former Occidental lawyer, John Shaver Nava, who had worked from 1972 to 1975 in Bolivia, Peru, and Guatemala. Shaver Nava alleged that he was forced to resign for refusing to ignore corruption by Occidental in Guatemala. Shaver Nava began a letter-writing campaign to newspapers and government officials in various South American nations. Hammer was furious at such tactics. Eventually, Shaver Nava and Occidental settled the case after seven years of legal jousting, without the oil company's admitting liability.[5]

At first, it appeared that Peru would be as nettlesome for Hammer as Venezuela. His chief antagonist was Texaco rather than a foreign government. The disagreement began with a letter from Texaco to Hammer, protesting about Occidental's hiring of geologist Jim Roth. Texaco alleged that Roth had carried away confidential information about the oil-rich Peruvian continental shelf. Roth had joined Occidental in late 1967, followed by fellow Texaco geologist James Taylor in mid-1968. Hammer said Texaco's charges were trumped up, intended to prevent Occidental from competing in an area it had been considering for exploration since 1959. Roth and Taylor had come to Occidental simply because they were unhappy at Texaco, Hammer said.

It was a dispute with a lot at stake. *Newsday* reported that "the case reeks with color and scandal potential. It pits Texaco, a member in good standing of the highly exclusive oil club, against fast-streaking upstart Occidental Petroleum, which has held a hot hand at the oil gaming tables for several years." Sources told the reporter the outcome could have "multi-million-dollar side effects" in the undercover world of industrial espionage. Other sources saw the main significance in the apparent effort by the major oil companies to punish Hammer's aggressiveness. Texaco's lawsuit and Occidental's countersuit dragged on for years; they eventually ended without any legal determination of guilt.[6]

Occidental, meanwhile, went on to considerable success in Peru. According to the conventional wisdom, Occidental was the only one of twenty oil companies to make a profit there. At one juncture, after a military takeover, Hammer decided to firm up Occidental's position with the new government. Tim Babcock, who accompanied Hammer to Lima, later recalled that the country's new president had been in power for a short time only. "I thought it was crazy to try to see him, but the doctor was insistent. We sat in a hotel room that was hotter than hell and within a few hours Dr. Hammer and I were talking to the new president. When the meeting was over, they hugged like old friends." Using his charm and his business acumen, Hammer convinced the military regime to waive a law forbidding foreign companies from drilling within fifty miles of Peru's borders, in this case the border with Ecuador. As a result, Occidental began looking for oil in the jungle.[7]

Hammer worked at cultivating Peru's rulers. On one occasion when he was visiting Lima, he decided impulsively to invite government officials for a lavish dinner the next evening. Occidental's Peruvian staff frantically began to make arrangements. Then Hammer received a call about a party that same night back in the States for President Nixon. Hammer decided to attend, ordering a halt to the planning for the dinner in Lima. Shortly thereafter he received another call from his staff in the United States, which let him know he would be just one of two thousand guests at the Nixon affair. He thereupon decided to stay in Peru and ordered the party planning to resume. The next call from stateside informed him that he would be at the head table with Nixon. Hammer wavered again. Finally, Occidental's local staff told him he must not continue the uncertainty; it was rude to Peruvian officials. His staff unilaterally canceled the party. Hammer left in a huff.[8]

Generally, though, his visits to Peru were happy ones as he viewed the black gold flowing from Occidental's wells. He brought his art collection to Lima and contributed to the restoration of a historic church. When the government was having trouble paying its foreign debt, thus endangering future loans, Occidental placed $25 million in a Peruvian bank to bolster the bottom line. It was a much-appreciated gesture. Hammer expressed pride:

We went into Peru several years ago and took a concession in the Amazon jungle where no oil had been found before. We have made some significant discoveries there. Seventeen other oil companies and governments followed us. Occidental is the only company that has been successful in finding commercial production in Peru. Right now, I believe we produce fifty percent of all oil that is produced in Peru. The government needs us.[9]

The biggest South American oil find for Occidental came in Colombia, after at least thirty dry holes that cost roughly $50 million. Because of those failures, Hammer was under pressure to pull out of Colombia, but he felt success was around the corner. As he had in Libya, he overruled the naysayers. Again he was right. The Cano Limon field turned out to be one of the largest in history. Hammer visited the Colombian wilderness in 1984 to see the billion-barrel strike for himself.[10]

When Hammer returned to Los Angeles from that visit, he heard rumors that the Colombian oil was making Occidental an especially attractive takeover target. One of the rumored predators was fabled corporate raider T. Boone Pickens. Hammer scoffed, replying that if Pickens was not careful, Occidental might buy *his* company. Whether Pickens was scared or not, he refrained from making a move. Meanwhile, Hammer continued business as usual — Occidental sold some of its Colombian holdings for $1 billion to reduce its debt, raked in the revenue from its remaining Colombian operation, and maintained a high philanthropic profile in the country with aid to volcano victims, among other activities.[11]

The Colombian government, putting greed before gratitude, announced that it was fining Occidental $800 million for the allegedly illegal sale of Colombian assets. Hammer called the proposed penalty an outrage. During two years of negotiating, Occidental whittled the amount down to $22 million. Hammer negotiated successfully not only with the government, but also with guerrilla fighters who threatened to terrorize Occidental's remote Colombian operations. He told a journalist that "we are giving jobs to the guerrillas. We give them the catering jobs, and we take care of the local population. It has worked out so far, and they in turn protect us from other guerrillas."[12]

Moral questions aside, the payoffs appeared to be money down a rat hole. Colombian guerrillas attacked Occidental's nearly five-hundred-mile-long pipeline repeatedly, threatened more destruction, and kidnapped two employees, one of them a North American expatriate executive. Some Occidental managers and Colombian government officials opposed Hammer's methods, contending that the guerrillas used the money to buy sophisticated weapons with which to accomplish further terrorism. James Sutton, a former FBI special agent who had been hired as Occidental's manager of security for the Western Hemisphere, was fired abruptly because of his opposition to the firm's negotiating with and making concessions to Colombian terrorists. In a lawsuit for damages stemming from his dismissal, Sutton criticized Occidental's "handling of a crucial hostage situation in Latin America, involving unethical, immoral, improper, ill-advised, and illegal actions."[13]

In other Latin American nations, the oil finds were smaller, but Hammer expended his usual energy on them anyway. He was especially popular in Ecuador, where the government moved a contract-signing ceremony from the capital, in Quito, to the governor's palace in Guayaquil out of deference to Hammer's health — doctors feared the high altitude of Quito might adversely affect his heart.

Mexican oil turned out to be elusive, despite repeated initiatives there. Hammer loved to be appreciated, and the Mexican hierarchy was most grateful for his attention. As he encouraged the Mexican and American governments to stop bickering about the particulars of oil exploration and start drilling, he built goodwill with his art collection.

Hammer was not content to stop there. He wanted improved U.S.-Mexican relations, the better to enhance Occidental's chances of oil exploration. When, accordingly, he talked with State Department experts, the diplomats were struck by his optimism. One noted in a memorandum, "Hammer observed that if he could do business with the Russians, he should certainly be able to work out something with the Mexicans." To that end he devised a detailed plan to remove obstacles to Mexican drilling, placing it in the context of America's desire for energy independence. Moreover, with more dollars from exploration, Hammer claimed, Mexico could purchase additional goods from the United States — everybody would win. The State, Treasury, and Energy departments and the National Security Council analyzed Hammer's plan and spent countless days preparing responses. Hammer disliked their slowness and their lack of enthusiasm; he warned Zbigniew Brzezinski that America was underestimating President José López Portillo's impatience.[14]

To build further bridges on his own, Hammer paid a reported $750,000 to transport precious stones and art objects from Mexico to Washington for a showing at the Smithsonian's Museum of Natural History. López Portillo and Hammer arranged to publish the color plates for the 205-

page exhibition catalog. *Washington Star* art critic Benjamin Forgey commented on the speed with which the show was put together, thanks to "a rich one-man band named Armand Hammer." Smithsonian Institution director S. Dillon Ripley called the show "the most impressive and important group of pre-Columbian objects ever to be taken out of Mexico for showing in the United States." Hammer sent the catalog to key aides in the Carter White House. Later, Rosalynn Carter viewed the exhibit with Hammer as her guide.[15] When the show left Washington, its next stops were the Hammer and Knoedler galleries, which thus increased Armand's visibility and cachet in New York.

Hammer held himself up as a good example of improved relations between the neighboring countries, philosophizing that the role of the multinational corporation was "to profit not at the expense of another country, but to profit with it." He related how Occidental had "Mexicanized" its chemical operations there by selling 51 percent of a subsidiary to local investors: "No Americans work for Quimica. The company has done better since Mexicanization, and Mexican law is such that we have a wider range of industrial opportunities than we would have if Quimica had remained foreign-owned." Hammer said everybody won with the change of ownership — Mexican investors profited, Mexican workers found some relief from unemployment, and Occidental gained revenues.[16]

The oil discoveries in Latin America helped turn Occidental Petroleum into one of the world's largest, most newsworthy companies. But not one of those successes matched in importance the discoveries in the British North Sea. For Hammer, Occidental's breakthrough there was a dream come true. North Sea oil provided Occidental with freedom from dependence on its Libyan operation at a crucial time. It also meant a foothold in a nation perceived as politically stable, giving investors confidence in Occidental's long-range outlook for the first time. Last but not least, the North Sea operation allowed Hammer to develop a relationship with the British royal family — the most glamorous world leaders of them all, in his book.

At the outset, Hammer himself had questioned the advisability of investing hundreds of millions of dollars searching for North Sea oil. It seemed the great discoveries were occurring in unbearably hot deserts or unbearably cold regions of less developed nations. That a highly developed, energy-dependent industrial nation might be the custodian of vast oil fields contradicted the conventional wisdom. When the Seven Sisters began to make sounds about exploring the North Sea, the Brit-

ish government harbored such doubts about the potential that it failed
to negotiate advantageous terms. By 1971, however, some successful
wells caused Britain to suspect the extent of its treasure. It opened
bidding for unexplored portions of the sea to all comers, on terms more
favorable to its treasury.[17]

Hammer focused his attention on what were to become known as
the Piper and Claymore fields, northeast of Scotland's coast. A winning
bid was more likely if the company formed a consortium with somebody who had Scottish connections. Hammer approached Roy Thomson, the media magnate whom he had met during the dispute over
Umm al Qaiwan (when, as Thomson recalled, "Dr. Hammer came to
see me, not being able to understand what the British government were
doing"). The two tycoons formed a bond, and Thomson, with his Scottish ties, was flattered to join the oil consortium. He was eager to diversify his empire in any case and perhaps move from multimillionaire
to billionaire in the process.[18]

Thomson sometimes despaired over working with what appeared to
be an obstinate British government, but Hammer, as usual, found ways
to surmount obstacles. One English policymaker, Lord Harold Lever,
provided British oilman-author Gerry Corti with an account of Hammer's approach. It was 1975, and Lever had invited Hammer and
Thomson to his home for a working lunch. The two tycoons had been
grousing about British exploration restrictions. According to Corti in
the book *The Nation's Oil*:

> When the two of them turned up, they started a tremendous tirade
> against the whole of the government's oil policy proposals. Harold Lever
> says he interrupted to say that they were enjoying a lunch with him
> under false pretenses. They understood the government's proposals per-
> fectly well, and they were raising arguments against them that he had
> heard thirty times already. He had expected them to come to seek clar-
> ification, and that was not what they were doing. Apparently this put
> something of a damper on the lunch, and Dr Hammer put some
> straightforward questions whilst . . . Lord Thomson looked flabber-
> gasted. After a reasonable interval, Harold Lever launched into a low-
> key explanation of the purposes and numbers. . . . The guests left with
> thanks. Lord Lever believes that after they left, Roy Thomson told Ar-
> mand Hammer that that was the end of it — the government was de-
> termined, and therefore would have their policy. Hammer is said to
> have replied . . . that Harold Lever was a man he could do business
> with.

Hammer regaled associates with stories of the North Sea negotiations, including one meeting when both men realized — as they rode in Thomson's Rolls-Royce to a restaurant — that they lacked enough pound notes to pay for lunch. The tycoons ended up dining at a club where Hammer's consultant John Tigrett had a charge account.

Another consortium member brought in by Hammer was J. Paul Getty, possibly the world's richest person at that time. Getty was so impressed by Hammer's risk taking that he purchased Occidental stock to demonstrate his confidence. Getty placed Hammer first on a list of entrepreneurs with "the innate capacity to think on a large scale"; he said that Hammer was "a man whose friendship I value most highly, and for whom I have the greatest respect both as a businessman and as a person."[19] Getty, Thomson, and Hammer signed a North Sea consortium contract giving Occidental operating authority and 36.5 percent of the investment. Getty would carry 23.5 percent, while Thomson and Allied Chemical each would carry 20 percent.

Combined with Thomson and Getty, Hammer had massive financial backing and an impressive English and Scottish presence. When the British government opened bids in March 1972, the Occidental consortium emerged with a 316,000-acre tract. Occidental told investors, "The North Sea has become one of the most sought-after petroleum exploration areas in the world, as multibillion-barrel discoveries by British Petroleum, Shell, and the Phillips group have confirmed. . . . Large reserves of low-sulphur oil, rapidly growing European markets, and political stability have attracted all of the world's important oil companies."[20]

Surprisingly, finding and marketing oil turned out to be almost as complicated in the United Kingdom as in nations hostile to capitalism. When the Labour government replaced the Conservatives, there were calls to nationalize the North Sea operations. Even without nationalization, it appeared that newly imposed taxes on oil would cut deeply into any revenues realized by Occidental. The Scots, concerned the English would siphon off revenue from any discoveries, developed their own brand of nationalism, which threatened the Occidental consortium. Difficult negotiations with British labor unions, opposition from environmentalists, and rough weather on the North Sea did nothing to ease Hammer's mind. Hammer was rewarded for his daring, however, when the consortium discovered retrievable oil in the Piper field.[21]

It was time to call the Bechtel Corporation again. Hammer needed an engineering feat equal in complexity to the one accomplished in Libya. The consortium ordered construction of a massive drilling plat-

form on rough waters far from land, an underwater pipeline for transporting the oil to land, and a terminal for processing, storing, and shipping the oil. Bechtel proposed laying a pipeline on the floor of the
North Sea that would stretch 135 miles from the Piper field to Flotta,
one of the Orkney Islands. Hammer realized there would be opposition
to any plan calling for an oil terminal in such an unspoiled setting. But
he also realized how badly the impoverished residents of the Orkneys
wanted employment. Accordingly, using Thomson's Scottish muscle and
giving resources to a public relations campaign run through Occidental's Tim Halford, Hammer put on a determined and masterful performance, taking environmental worries into account during the design
and construction stages and spreading money around in the name of
philanthropy. On one visit to the Orkneys, he received a request to
help raise $100,000 to purchase and remodel a building for an art col-
lection being offered the populace by a part-time resident. He announced he would donate the entire amount.[22]

Construction permits fell into place, and in January 1977 Hammer
attended the dedication of the facility. Also present was *New York Times*
reporter Peter Kilborn, who noted the presence of Anthony Wedgwood
Benn,

> Britain's best-known nemesis of private industry and leader of the Labor
> Party's left wing, which wants all Britain's North Sea oil nationalized
> outright. But Dr. Hammer and Mr. Benn, like most of the world oil
> industry and the British government, have worked out their differences,
> and the two men were enjoying the change. . . . In a huge assembly
> hall here, Dr. Hammer was greeted with even more appreciation than
> Mr. Benn. He had already agreed to pay the local government £500,000
> as a "disturbance" allowance for chewing up Orkney roads while the
> terminal was being built. Today, he gave the Orcadians . . . £25,000
> toward a new community center for Flotta. He gave another £50,000
> toward a museum. And he gave the local arts council a Steinway concert
> grand piano. The Orkney Islands County Council gave him an Orkney-
> built easy chair, and ninety-two-year-old Tom Rosie . . . presented a
> double-handled silver loving cup. . . . Then Occidental and its partners
> invited the three hundred to four hundred Orcadians and visiting dig-
> nitaries to a banquet that was easily up to the level of Dr. Hammer's
> London hotel, Claridge's. Clearly, much of the effort was part of Dr.
> Hammer's renowned knack for public relations, but no one here seemed
> to care.[23]

James Patten, later to be Occidental's chief lawyer in Scotland, recalled that Hammer "did things first-class in the Orkneys. They are a

sleepy bunch of islands, and people reacted violently against filthy terminals. But we built it out of sight with safeguards against spills." Looking back on the early years of the North Sea venture, Patten said, "Dr. Hammer always takes chances. He likes to operate on the ragged edge. He got the North Sea done even though he did not really have the financing to do it. . . . The North Sea was really expensive for the times. If Hammer had not been slapping people on the ass to keep them going, things would not have happened. If you have the bean counters sitting there looking at every little detail, things do not get done fast." [24]

Meanwhile Occidental was readying another money machine, at its other North Sea site, the Claymore field, about twenty miles west of Piper. Hammer ordered a drilling platform for Claymore from a French manufacturer, hoping to avoid further British labor problems — already, such complications had put the installation of the Piper platform a year behind Occidental's demanding schedule and cost it hundreds of millions of dollars. The French came through and installed the Claymore platform on time. Hammer was so pleased that he ordered a lavish dedication for February 1978. He would settle for no less a guest than Prince Charles, and he succeeded in getting him.

Hammer became a force in British public life partly because of his closeness with Margaret Thatcher. The Conservative prime minister of Great Britain was a staunch capitalist. Her administration reversed many policies of the previous Labour government, making Occidental's business more profitable. Hammer trusted Thatcher, and she liked him because of his enthusiasm for Britain, demonstrated by his huge commercial and philanthropic contributions there. Hammer liked to be identified with Thatcher. When William Scobie of the *London Observer* traveled to Los Angeles to interview Hammer for a profile, the tycoon insisted the photographer include an inscribed picture of Thatcher in the scene.[25]

Hammer and Thatcher were bound even closer together by Gordon Reece, her resourceful public relations adviser, whom Hammer hired to burnish his own image. *New York Times* reporter R. W. Apple described Reece as "a short, natty, jovial man who likes Havana cigars, and forty-dollar-a-bottle champagne." Even after Reece joined the Occidental payroll, Hammer gave him time off to help Thatcher with her campaigning.[26]

In the United Kingdom, responsibility for making Hammer a legend fell partly to John Smythe, who reported that "the increasingly frequent European visits by . . . Dr. Hammer proved to be ideal platforms to focus media and public attention. Inaugurations of the North

Sea facilities provided opportunities to invite large numbers of opinion-leader groups to distant Scottish locations to be entertained by show business–style ceremonies." By the time Thatcher was to visit Occidental's Orkneys terminal, in September 1980, Hammer was appearing in the English media regularly. He had rooms at Claridge's, a hotel described as one of the ten best in the world by *Travel and Leisure* magazine, with suites starting at $500 a night. Guests there "are greeted by liveried attendants. . . . The black and white marble floors gleam; the log fire crackles and scents the air. . . . State banquets and royal visits are a regular part of Claridge's social calendar."[27]

Journalist Daniel Yergin watched Hammer at Claridge's restaurant, making this observation about his retinue:

> There will be several empty chairs. But then, one after another, delegations of businessmen and trade officials — Russians, Italians, Frenchmen, Saudi Arabians — come to the chairs and make their cases. Hammer, with hooded eyes, attends like a tortoise, giving nothing away from under his impenetrable shell. Finally, the tortoise asks the question or two that the delegation did not want to hear. If the tortoise likes their answers, he keeps them for a few more minutes and plans the next step. Otherwise, he waves them away immediately, making room for the next group.[28]

Meanwhile, as Thatcher was on her way to the Orkneys, Hammer had surprised his staff by saying he planned to announce three big projects during her visit. None of the projects was ready to begin, but Hammer was in no mood to hear cautionary words. He immediately told Thatcher that Occidental would invest another $1.5 billion in Britain for a Claymore field floating rig, a gas-processing plant on Scotland's east coast, and a refinery at Canvey Island, less than an hour's drive from London. Thatcher was delighted. Turning to the assembled journalists, she said, "Get that down, it's news." She called Occidental's North Sea operation a "tremendous success story" and complimented Hammer by telling him, "The minute there is a hint of a smell you take it and build a successful enterprise faster than anybody else."[29]

British government agencies and Occidental's London staff privately expressed shock at the spontaneous commitment of such a huge sum by Hammer. Afterward, the staff spent months unruffling the hurt feelings of British bureaucrats, who could not understand why they had been kept in the dark. It was beyond the comprehension of the bureaucrats that Hammer's top executives truly had had no inkling either. One of Hammer's aides told a *Times* of London reporter that two of the three projects "were still at the internal planning stage." The reporter, John Huxley, commented that Hammer "always had a penchant for the dramatic."[30]

Hammer needed all the political clout and goodwill he could muster in the United Kingdom when Occidental's North Sea oil platform exploded in July 1988, killing 167 workers. Flying quickly to the disaster site, the shaken ninety-year-old millionaire reportedly was comforted by Thatcher herself after his arrival in Britain. He offered a substantial monetary settlement to every aggrieved family in an effort to stem litigation.* The accident cost Occidental tens of millions of dollars of production and set Britain back at least that much in lost revenue. Press reports appeared suggesting corporate negligence. An inquiry commenced in 1989. But somehow, as usual, Hammer seems to be emerging virtually untarnished. Editorialist Richard North noted in the *Independent,* a London daily newspaper, that "Dr. Hammer's response will combine with his famous history to see him through. . . . His image — in which Moses, Midas, Santa Claus, and imp are oddly combined — will survive intact."[31]

With its hugely successful operations in Colombia and the North Sea, Occidental Petroleum joined the ranks of the world's largest multinationals. And as Occidental grew, so did Hammer's plans for it. One route to growth was mergers and acquisitions, and he negotiated plenty of them. However, he liked acquisitions to be a one-way street. He had no intention of working for somebody else or of being forced out in a hostile takeover. Yet his successes made Occidental an increasingly attractive target. There were sharks out there even larger than Hammer, and they wanted to devour his company. The prospect of surrendering to the sharks and retiring would have tempted many other executives Hammer's age, who would have relished unimaginable wealth in their retirement. Hammer was not such a man. The thought of surrendering the helm at Occidental — giving up the base from which he conducted his citizen diplomacy, cultural exchanges, and relationships with princes, prime ministers, and presidents — was awful. So the eternally energetic Hammer set out to vanquish the sharks circling around him.

* As 1989 has progressed, it appears that many families will accept the settlement offer. Families of the thirty-one men whose bodies remained lost seem less than enthusiastic, however. They have asked for further undersea searches, but Hammer has responded that the risks were too great. Gavin Cleland, speaking for the families, said, "We expected so much more from Dr. Hammer, who has a reputation of being a very humane man." (*Daily Telegraph* [London], February 17 and 21, 1989.)

Teflon Tycoon

THE FIRST SERIOUS THREAT to Occidental Petroleum's independence came from Standard Oil of Indiana. It began in November 1974 with an innocent-sounding telephone call to Armand Hammer from John Swearingen, Standard's chairman, who asked for an appointment to talk.[1] Hammer, who says he assumed that Swearingen wanted to discuss a joint venture in Colorado, where Occidental was extracting oil from shale, agreed to the meeting. In fact, Swearingen was interested in entering the coal business by acquiring Occidental, which he believed might be an attractive target for a hostile buyer other than Standard Oil.

When he arrived, Swearingen was accompanied by a stranger. The stranger turned out to be Robert Greenhill, an executive of Morgan Stanley, the Wall Street brokerage firm, whose presence should have alerted Hammer that Swearingen wanted to discuss more than shale. But, as Hammer later said, he failed to ask Greenhill who he was and why he was there.

As Hammer talked about Occidental's shale operations, he said, he began to realize Swearingen had something else on his mind. Finally, Hammer said, Swearingen spoke up, saying he wanted to buy Occidental for $17 a share, above the current stock price. It added up to more than $1 billion; Hammer could walk away with $20 million for himself. He has said the thought of such riches made him angry, not happy. He probably would have rejected any offer for Occidental, no matter how it had been presented, but Swearingen appeared imperious, not solicitous. That attitude rankled Hammer, who later said he escorted his visitors out the door without indicating any interest in their offer, an important point.

Greenhill had a different recollection; he said Hammer indicated he felt a merger "seemed to be sufficiently feasible so it should be carefully studied. He would like to have Louis Nizer . . . discuss the matter with Standard Oil's general counsel." In Greenhill's version, Hammer bridled only when reminded that the two chief executives had a duty to disclose their discussions to the federal government.

> Dr. Hammer announced great reluctance to make any public disclosure. . . . He said he had had many discussions with companies. He did not report these discussions to his shareholders or often even his directors, and he alone made such decisions. . . . Dr. Hammer offered to simply return the financial material and act as though the meeting had not taken place, and we could then resume discussions after we were out of registration. John Swearingen and I demurred, and said counsel had advised we had disclosure duty. Dr. Hammer appeared quite excited, and he said any such disclosure would be "dynamite." He said it would foreclose the two companies getting together.[2]

On hearing Greenhill's and Swearingen's versions of events, Hammer acknowledged "a wide difference of opinion as to what happened" but insisted he was the one telling the truth. Recalling what had gone through his mind at the time, he said,

> I thought to myself I would try to draw them out and get as much information as I could because I knew then what the real purpose of their visit was, which had been hidden from me up until that time. When they, later on, said they wanted to put out an announcement that there had been talks and negotiations, I saw it was time to make it perfectly clear there was [sic] no talks or negotiations. . . . If I was really interested . . . do you think for one moment I would not have asked them what price they were offering for the stock? . . . What they wanted to do was trap me, was to get an announcement out to fool the public into thinking I was agreeable.[3]

There is no dispute that shortly after the meeting, Swearingen called Hammer to say Standard Oil was issuing a news release about the merger talks, in accordance with Securities and Exchange Commission rules. Nor is there any question that Hammer reacted in kind: He ordered his lawyers to deny that he had shown any interest in the offer, to sue Morgan Stanley for conflict of interest (because one of its subsidiaries represented Occidental in real estate transactions), to explore the possibilities of a lawsuit against Standard Oil, and to take the war to Congress and the Federal Trade Commission. Hammer believed his assiduous cultivation of policymakers in Washington would help him resist the takeover attempt.

The Senate subcommittee proved a receptive forum. Chairing the subcommittee was Floyd Haskell of Colorado, who launched the proceeding with a news release quite favorable to Occidental's side. Hammer's Washington staff drafted questions for Haskell to ask and supplied fifteen pages of answers as well. Although Hammer had a lot on his mind at the time, including the investigation of his Nixon contribution by the Watergate Special Prosecution Force, he focused intently on the phrasing of his testimony, telling the senators that the battle involved far more than his own selfish interests: "It is also of crucial relevance to the public interest, for if Occidental falls into the hands of one of the major oil companies, then the American people will have lost the nation's largest independent energy company, and with it a strong champion of competition in the world of oil, coal, chemicals, fertilizer, and international trade." William McSweeny, the head of Hammer's Washington office, considered the testimony so successful that he took photographs of the doctor in the hearing room, framed them, and presented them to key Occidental executives.[4]

Hammer's counteroffensive paid off at the FTC, too. Occidental somehow had obtained a report by a Standard Oil executive outlining how to drive gasoline retail competitors out of business. Because he was making monopolistic power the key issue, Hammer knew he had an explosive document. Unfortunately, he had obtained the document through a promise of confidentiality, so his lawyers told him he could not use it. But use it he did. When FTC examiners arrived in Los Angeles, preparatory to calling at Standard Oil's headquarters, Hammer suggested they look carefully at documents concerning independent retailers. After all, he said, such information was central to Occidental's case. Apparently, the FTC staffers understood the clue for they found the original copy of the damning report, which confirmed their doubts about antitrust violations. After that, Swearingen dropped his bid to acquire Occidental. Swearingen said later that Standard Oil changed course because of economic considerations, not because of Hammer's publicity offensive or antitrust allegations.

Daniel Yergin, who had access to Hammer while researching a magazine profile, was waiting in Occidental's New York office the day Standard Oil announced abandonment of its effort. Hammer's secretary was trying frantically to locate him when he burst in with Arthur

Groman, his Los Angeles lawyer. "They acted like two schoolboys who had pulled off a terrific prank and were barely able to control their mirth. Rosemary [the secretary] started to tell him the good news, but Hammer interrupted, 'I know, I know.'" Later, Yergin learned that Hammer had stopped at Blyth, Eastman, Dillon to discuss the stock market on his way to the office. It was there that a partner had scooped Rosemary. Yergin was fascinated to see that despite his elation over his victory, Hammer never stopped to relax. Instead, his faculties were focused on what move to make next.[5] One of those moves was to retain lawyer Joseph Flom, a legendary expert on corporate raids, to draft a protection plan for Occidental.

The next takeover threat came not from an oil company but from an oil government. The would-be acquirer was the shah of Iran; his offer came nearly eighteen months after Hammer vanquished Standard Oil. Hammer was in no mood for an overture from the shah, who he felt had betrayed Occidental during the battle of Umm al Qaiwan. But the shah was not to be deterred; he sent an emissary to Los Angeles with an offer to buy 10 percent of Occidental's stock and an option to buy 10 percent more. If Hammer agreed, Iran would become the largest Occidental stockholder by far.[6]

The U.S. Embassy in Teheran cabled to Washington that the announcement "came as [a] complete surprise." The Ford administration was puzzled and alarmed. Fear of foreign investment in the United States was high, and there was already consternation over Romania's role in Occidental's Virginia coal mine.[7]

Although the issue of sovereignty favored Occidental, Hammer had special reason to be wary of the Ford White House because he had played the wrong horse in the sweepstakes for vice president following Spiro Agnew's forced resignation. He had touted John Connally, the former Texas governor who had switched from the Democrats to the Republicans and now served as treasury secretary. The two men had done business together, had traveled together, and to all appearances liked each other. On October 11, 1973, Hammer had written to President Richard Nixon that Connally enjoyed the respect of Soviet leaders, negotiated skillfully with the Arabs, was well liked in Congress, and possessed an impeccable character. When the very next day Nixon announced Gerald Ford as his choice, Hammer, never lacking chutzpah, sent a congratulatory telegram to the White House.[8]

Ford's advisers had other reasons to be suspicious of Hammer, among them fear that the president would be perceived as giving special treatment to a corporate fat cat under investigation for campaign contributions to an embattled Nixon. But for the most part their concerns were those of state.

One specific administration worry about the proposed Iranian investment centered on Occidental's continuing involvement in strategic international bodies. The State Department commented that "we need to know whether Iranian participation on Occidental's board of directors would give Iran access to sensitive International Energy Agency and Industry Advisory Board material." The White House requested a cabinet-level review of the proposed transaction, a rare move stemming "from the unusually sensitive nature . . . in terms of possible public and Congressional reaction." The *Washington Post* noted that if the Iranian deal went through, it might be the last big deal of Hammer's unusual career: "Observers who have seen Hammer recently believe that Hammer's heart may indeed be giving him trouble. This, along with the litigation and investigations, may cause Hammer to spend more and more time with doctors and lawyers, and less with the foreign potentates whose company, and business, he so enjoys."[9]

The Office of Foreign Investment in the United States began asking questions. Gerald Parsky, an assistant secretary of the treasury, met with Iran's U.S. ambassador, who explained his nation's interest in Occidental by saying the company possessed expertise in agriculture, petrochemicals, fertilizers, and cattle raising. "With respect to the Caspian Sea," Parsky reported, "the ambassador noted the obvious benefits of having a partner with an established relationship with the Soviet Union. Occidental's participation . . . would take some of the pressure off any move towards a joint Iranian-Soviet venture to develop oil and gas." The next day, Parsky met with Hammer and McSweeny. Hammer said he liked the idea of exploring the Caspian's energy potential and the possibility of obtaining crude oil for Occidental's European refineries. He emphasized, however, that Iran had initiated the discussions.[10]

Although distrustful of the shah, Hammer decided to close the deal. After two months of negotiations involving about thirty lawyers, he flew to Paris, where he expected to sign a contract. He was confident that Occidental could block any later takeover attempts, but, just to be sure, he insisted on a provision that if the shah wanted to sell Iran's stock, Occidental would have first refusal. In the meantime, the corporate treasury would swell with cash, allowing Hammer to expand his empire anew.

In Paris, Hammer received a call from the Iranian negotiators ordering him to attend the signing session alone. Suspicious, he took along

Arthur Groman anyway. In the suite of the chief Iranian negotiator, they were told that the shah wanted one modification: elimination of the clause requiring Iran to offer its shares to Occidental first in the event of a divestment. Hammer knew right away that the modification demand meant trouble. Without the clause, Iran could throw out Occidental's management by initiating a takeover offer above the stock's market price. Or the shah could sell his stock to one of the Seven Sisters, which could mount its own takeover bid. Occidental's in-house lawyers had expressed doubt before Paris. This was the last straw. Hammer called off the negotiations on the spot, departing from Paris by the end of the day.[11]

After fending off Standard Oil and the shah, Hammer next found himself cast as the villain in yet another hostile takeover battle — this one perpetrated by Occidental itself. Hammer later denied responsibility for the initiative, saying he was misled by Occidental president Joseph Baird. It was Baird's idea, he said, to acquire the Mead Corporation, a diversified lumber and paper firm headquartered in Dayton. Baird, who had left the banking world to join Occidental, knew Mead's chairman and president professionally; everybody seemed to get along. Hammer liked the potential fit with Occidental and was under the impression from Baird that the Mead board of directors wanted to merge.

On August 10, 1978, Hammer flew directly from a White House lunch with President Jimmy Carter to Dayton, expecting a pleasant negotiating session. Instead, he found the top brass of Mead in high dudgeon. The already tense atmosphere worsened when, according to Mead president Warren Batts, Hammer declared "that he was not particularly interested in acquiring Mead, that this was Mr. Baird's project, that he [Hammer] preferred the petroleum business." Batts later commented, "If [Mead chairman] Mr. McSwiney and I were calling on a company to acquire them, one of us would not pipe up and say 'we are not interested.' So that was unusual."[12]

Mead officials told Hammer that Occidental would be hearing from attorney Joseph Flom. That alarmed Hammer because Flom was one of the few people he genuinely feared. During the ensuing controversy, a *Washington Post* article noted that Flom "is to mergers what Mickey Mantle was to baseball — a powerful switchhitter who is as adept in blocking an unfriendly takeover as he is in managing an unfriendly takeover."[13]

According to his own account, Hammer told Baird to insist that Flom withdraw, but Baird failed to do so. Flom then helped mount

one of the most aggressive defenses in corporate history, sending lawyers around the world to dig up information on Occidental. They gathered every piece of paper in sight; Mead's photocopying expenses alone
reportedly topped $300,000. Then Mead's lawyers petitioned the Ohio
Division of Securities to call hearings under a state law meant to protect Ohio companies from hostile takeovers. The state complied.

During questioning of Hammer and other Occidental executives,
Mead's lawyers sought to portray Occidental as corrupt. They introduced into evidence documents about Occidental's failure to write down
the costs of a proposed oil refinery in England, saying the papers established "conclusively that Mr. Baird . . . and Dr. Hammer . . . had
direct knowledge and direct intention of deliberately deceiving the pro-
spective purchasers . . . of stock . . . of Occidental . . . and that this
is another act in a long line of acts, commencing back in early 1975,
relative to . . . deceptive statements." [14]

After the hearings, Mead said the transcript "demonstrates that
Hammer's credibility and integrity have not improved. He was a key
participant in the [refinery] fraud, made intentional misrepresentations
to Occidental's accountants in that connection, and approved the sale
of hundreds of millions of dollars of Occidental securities pursuant to
prospectuses he knew were false. Moreover, any person who sat through
his testimony . . . involving as it did representations and predictions
concerning Occidental's financial condition and business prospects, observed the remarkable phenomenon of repeated reversals and virtually
complete abandonments of Hammer's grand claims about Occidental
when they were addressed in cross-examination, or in the testimony of
succeeding Occidental executives who recognized that Hammer's statements could not be supported." [15]

Hearing examiner Nodine Miller found fourteen instances of inade-
quate disclosure by Occidental. After complimenting Hammer on his
"entrepreneurial skills," she added, "The record is fraught with examples of senior management making plans and disregarding them;
recognizing risks but failing to plan for them; or spotlighting a project,
then abandoning it. Occidental's disclosures reflect its attempt to round
off the jagged edges of its capricious actions." [16]

The experience was a nightmare for Hammer, who told Baird to
drop the bid. According to Hammer, Baird refused, challenging him
in front of the Occidental board. Naturally, Hammer had the votes to
override him, although the decision against Baird was not unanimous.
Occidental general counsel Ronald Klein later commented that it was
the only time in his twelve years with the company that he saw any

directors oppose Hammer during a recorded vote.[17] But, despite their support, Baird's presidency was over.

The negative repercussions continued, however. *Forbes* noted the contrast between Hammer's testimonies in the Mead case and in the attempted Standard Oil takeover of Occidental, when he had "made sounds like the Statue of Liberty being raped. . . . This time, it is the raider who flies the free enterprise flag. That is the game." Mead also delivered its information to the SEC, which already possessed a fat Hammer file.[18]

The SEC — which until the Reagan administration possessed a reputation as the leanest, hardest-working, and most uncompromising of the regulatory agencies — treated Hammer one of two ways over the decades, depending on the viewpoint of the observer. Hammer partisans believed the commission persecuted him for imagined crimes, that the regulators failed to appreciate how a brilliant, global entrepreneur must operate in the real world. Hammer detractors believed the SEC was too lenient, that it uncovered serious wrongdoing only to cave in time after time by letting its target sign meaningless consent decrees. Hammer railed against the agency in private but in public dismissed its investigations as harmless inconveniences. In his 1987 autobiography, he failed to mention any of the four major investigations it conducted into his affairs.

Hammer had employed in his early business ventures many of the same practices he employed at Occidental. But it was only when he became an officer and director of Occidental, whose stock was traded on public exchanges, that he came under SEC jurisdiction. The commission's lawyers were amazed at what they saw; few if any chief executive officers at public companies were so bold, so omnipresent, so vain, so . . . well, self-promotional.

For a while, SEC lawyers just watched, collecting evidence. Their first move against Occidental came in 1966, after Hammer announced that his company had discovered an iron ore deposit at the Walker River Indian Reservation, about sixty miles southeast of Reno, Nevada. As the stock market opened the next day, Occidental jumped nearly five points. The SEC thought it detected promotional hype. Nevada mining experts said Hammer's announcement was overoptimistic, premature, or both. They wondered how and where Occidental would sell the iron ore, even if it existed in commercial quantities. The SEC called Occidental. Hammer, apparently under pressure, sent a clarifying letter to stockholders saying that further evaluation was needed to determine commercial feasibility. The mine never did become viable.[19]

The Walker River incident was child's play compared with what followed. As the federal agency began to examine Hammer more carefully, its lawyers became increasingly perplexed. In November 1970 the SEC privately authorized an investigation of numerous allegations dating back to 1966. It focused on creative accounting connected to land purchases and sales in the Southwest.[20] Arthur Groman accused the commission of falling for trumped-up charges from the recently departed Walter Davis, just four years earlier Hammer's heir apparent when he sold the Permian Corporation to Occidental.

Attempting to discredit Davis, Groman suggested that he was involved in unauthorized, possibly illegal land transactions of his own in his native North Carolina while supposedly acting on Occidental's behalf. Groman enlisted the help of Hammer's executive assistant, Thomas Wachtell, who had overheard that Davis possessed a criminal record. As Wachtell described it, "We were in court over a land deal in North Carolina, from which Davis might profit. When the day's deposition was over, the court reporter asked our lawyer if this was the same Walter Davis from so-and-so. Our lawyer said yes, and the court reporter said it is too bad that he did that time in prison."[21]

Occidental staffers began digging, turning up charges against Davis of attempted kidnapping, assaulting policemen, and gambling. They determined that Davis had served time in prison for his failure to file an income tax return. The alleged transgressions had occurred decades earlier; Davis certainly had rehabilitated himself. But Hammer showed no hesitation about impugning him now; after all, hadn't Davis tried to destroy Hammer's empire? Davis viewed it differently, saying it would have been dishonest to keep silent about Hammer's practices.

Occidental's witnesses and lawyers implored the SEC to drop the investigation before it became public. Dorman Commons, Occidental's chief financial officer, vigorously sought to deny that the company had been unfaithful to promises made about reforming its accounting practices during meetings in 1966 and 1967. Commons said it was "urgent" that the agency allow Occidental to release its 1970 financial statements, the veracity of which was in dispute. The delay was making it difficult to market a European bond issue and execute a domestic convertible debenture sale.

As evidence mounted against Occidental, the commission was in no mood to be sympathetic. It filed suit against both Occidental and Hammer in March 1971, alleging that they had issued "false and misleading earnings reports" for the last three quarters of 1969 and the first two quarters of 1970. More specifically, Occidental supposedly had "structured certain financing transactions to take on the appearance of land sales, and improperly recorded profits from these transactions." Occidental also was said to have failed to disclose that $14 million of its $49 million net income "resulted from extensive adjustments and changes in accounting in one of its consolidated subsidiaries, and that a major portion of the adjustments and changes related to prior years and to prior quarters of 1969." In addition, Hammer had issued a press release with "false and misleading statements concerning the volume of Occidental's crude oil production in Libya, the volume of coal production estimated to be mined by Occidental in 1970, and the estimated profitability of the company."[22]

Hammer reportedly wanted to fight all the way to the Supreme Court if necessary. What right, after all, did the SEC have to tell Arthur Andersen and Company, one of the nation's largest accounting firms, as well as Occidental's highly trained accountants that they were acting improperly? Some Occidental in-house lawyers encouraged Hammer to fight. But, instead, he accepted the advice of John McCloy, his outside counsel, to sign a consent decree.

Hammer's top in-house lawyer, Ronald Klein, agreed with the settlement strategy, fearing something more damaging in court. As he said later, "If there was an SEC vendetta against Dr. Hammer, it was not something that arose full-blown with no reason. The commission felt strongly about Hammer's noncompliance with public disclosure. It was not just a matter of numbers, of accounting. I left Occidental after twelve years because of my disagreements with Dr. Hammer over public disclosure. . . . The doctor was not evil or immoral. He was amoral, beyond morality."[23]

Many of Hammer's employees, stockholders, and acquaintances accepted at face value his explanation for failing to fight. Tim Babcock said Hammer "definitely felt that the SEC was out to get him, that the agency had a hidden motive. But you have to take his style into account. He was a plunger; he could not ever get the authorities to move fast enough for him." Still, it was very unlike Hammer to surrender. As his longtime, insightful lawyer Louis Nizer once wrote, if Hammer "feels he has been wronged, he is no respecter of powerful forces arrayed against him. He is unabashedly litigious. . . . When principle is involved, he rejects compromise. . . . It does not matter how great the gamble."[24]

Because many observers had seen Hammer fight back so often, they concluded that this time he was guilty and knew it. Afterward, Occidental faced at least twenty class-action lawsuits filed by stockholders angry about being misled. Rather than fighting them and winning, Hammer eventually settled out of court, with Occidental agreeing to pay about $11 million and its accounting firm of Arthur Andersen agreeing to pay almost $1 million. Nick Poulos, financial editor of the *Chicago Tribune,* put it succinctly: The public could draw one of two conclusions "from Hammer's statement — either Hammer is guilty of the SEC charges and does not dare fight them, or he is innocent but considers his integrity and that of his company of such small consequence [they are] not worth fighting for." [25]

The acrimony worsened when the agency reopened its investigation of Occidental in January 1972. John Carleton, representing the government, explained that the renewed inquiry went beyond possible noncompliance with the 1971 consent decree and would investigate possible perjury and obstruction of justice.

Again, the battle lines were starkly drawn. When SEC lawyers asked Hammer pointed questions, Groman told him not to answer. When Hammer did reply, he often was vague. When his vagueness became an issue, Groman complained that "some members of the commission seem to have the impression that Dr. Hammer is some universal computer genius who sits in Los Angeles when he is not traveling, and has instant knowledge and direction and control of the day-to-day activities of a two-billion-dollar corporation with . . . thirty-three thousand employees, and this impression, gentlemen, is just so unrealistic as to baffle the imagination." [26]

The questioning was so trying that Hammer uncharacteristically lost his composure during the inquiry: "I believe I never should have signed a consent decree, and if I had known that I was not getting my peace, I never would have signed the decree. I think we would have been better off to test this thing in the courts and put Arthur Andersen on the witness stand and take our chances. . . . I bit the bullet and on the advice of Mr. McCloy I was willing to accept the consent decree because he told me that was the only way we could get our . . . $125 million debenture through the SEC, which was so essential to us at that time. . . . I took the rap, and as a result of that I thought I was buying peace, and now I find that all I have invited was more aggravation . . . tying up the company and in effect jeopardizing our very existence, because it is hard to keep a secret, and news of another investigation of Occidental getting out could be very disastrous for this company." [27]

Occidental's outside law firm of Fried, Frank, Harris, Shriver and Jacobson sent the agency a forty-six-page memorandum about why the staff investigation should be dropped. That firm's Sam Harris, who had once toiled for the SEC himself, wrote enforcement chief Stanley Sporkin from London on Thanksgiving Day, 1973: "I would be eternally grateful to our good Lord if the Occidental matter was now put to final rest."[28]

The agency failed to grant his wish. Instead it issued a subpoena on December 6 for a new round of testimony by Hammer. But Hammer had no desire to undergo another grilling. He already had been damaged by testimony from other witnesses — for example, Robert Karlblom of the investment banking firm A. G. Becker had said there was concern in his company about Hammer's "basic integrity." Perhaps to avoid another session under oath, Hammer agreed to a second consent decree. In it, the SEC charged "that Occidental omitted or misrepresented material facts relating to its petroleum tanker fleet operations in its 1970 annual report to shareholders, in connection with its securities offerings in June and July 1971, and in certain subsequent press releases." Once more, Occidental told the public it was admitting no wrongdoing but was signing the document anyway "to avoid costly and protracted legal proceedings."[29]

Occidental stockholders filed at least sixteen class-action lawsuits. The company eventually paid another multimillion-dollar settlement, complaining bitterly that

> this case epitomizes the potentially disastrous financial penalty publicly held corporations face every time they attempt in good faith to describe in a prospectus the possible impact upon their operations of unpredictable, volatile market forces and events which, if they occur at all, will happen long after the document is read. Each time they do so, they must chart a very narrow course between the Scylla of pessimism and the Charybdis of optimism. When in hindsight they appear not to have been sufficiently optimistic, they are sued. They are also sued when hindsight suggests they were not sufficiently pessimistic. The only thing issuers can rely upon when they attempt to explain how future possibilities might affect their operations is that they will be sued by those who, having the benefit of twenty-twenty hindsight, claim the disclosures should have been phrased differently.[30]

If Hammer believed that signing the second consent decree, in December 1973, would put SEC investigations behind him, he was wrong again. In August 1975, the agency authorized a third inquiry, which focused on alleged bribes to foreign governments. Hammer, simultaneously fighting the Nixon campaign-contributions charge, pleaded illness when the commission requested his testimony. The agency responded by asking a federal judge to compel his cooperation, stating that he was "the only person to have knowledge of Occidental's operations, and since he took part in almost all of Occidental's negotiations with foreign governments, he and he alone has first-hand knowledge of what, if anything, was paid to government officials to obtain business for Occidental."[31]

Attorney Groman replied that Hammer was "a sick old man" who "lives four blocks from the office, goes in late, goes home for lunch, and takes a nap." Judge John Pratt was skeptical, noting an apparent "inconsistency between the diagnosis and the man's actual mode of living. He cannot be as sick as the doctors say he is and maintain this schedule. It is just contrary to fact." Pratt added, "We will assume Dr. Hammer has a serious heart problem. He is going to die someday like the rest of us, and every breath he takes is one breath less. But the commission is entitled to take Dr. Hammer's deposition." The deposition proceeded in January 1976, with Hammer hooked up to heart-monitoring equipment. Groman said he wanted to make sure the record reflected the government's responsibility if Hammer's health suffered further.[32]

After weighing the evidence, the SEC in May 1977 accused Occidental of various violations based on this third inquiry. The commission alleged that

> Occidental failed to disclose material facts relating to the existence of two related companies in foreign countries which generated income and profits of at least $220,000, which amounts were not reported on the books and records of Occidental. Funds from these companies and other sources were used to maintain secret funds of more than $200,000, part of which was distributed as illegal contributions.

The agency alleged further that Occidental "caused approximately $400,000 of its funds to be used for the making of illegal or questionable payments to or for the benefit of foreign officials." As part of the third settlement Hammer agreed to, he undertook to form a special committee of Occidental's board, to be assisted by outside counsel. The committee would file a report with the SEC after an intensive look at all the known domestic and overseas payments.[33]

The internal investigation turned out to be part competent detective work, part whitewash. Conducting the inquiry were three directors close to Hammer but not employed by Occidental, assisted by a prominent Los Angeles law firm, a former Columbia University law school dean, and two accounting firms. Significantly, the investigation was limited from the beginning, as the committee itself noted:

> The committee relied primarily upon Occidental personnel to identify relevant transactions and examined principally documents produced by Occidental personnel. . . . Although the committee is not aware of any omissions, it is possible that some questionable payments or practices were not identified. . . . The special committee did not attempt to conduct a complete audit of all of the company's books and records, or even to perform an audit of all transactions of a selected type. . . . The committee lacked power to issue subpoenas or to compel testimony under oath. It had no power to penalize any person not employed by Occidental for failing to cooperate with it. It was unable to compel testimony from persons who were known or believed to be officials of foreign governments or who were no longer employed by Occidental.[34]

At the committee's request, Hammer sent a questionnaire to 195 senior managers; a second questionnaire went later from Hammer to the same group, as well as to about 500 other persons with check-signing authority. When the answers were tabulated, the committee had information on "more than one hundred separate payments or related groups of payments." It determined that thirty-three of those were either definitely illegal or of questionable legal status. Those payments totaled about $1.5 million.[35]

One category of payments involved domestic political contributions; those illegal payments added up to slightly more than $21,000. Another category concerned "payments to persons possibly officially connected with foreign governments." Fifteen nations showed up on this list, with the case of Nigeria most flagrant. Payments there were intended to help Occidental win oil and gas drilling rights. Occidental had agreed to pay Nigerian official Joseph Tanko Yusuf for arranging introductions to other officials, providing information on political developments, and monitoring the activities of rival oil companies. With Hammer's authorization, Yusuf had received payments to educate his children in England and California. Some of the money entered a secret bank account in Liechtenstein. The sums paid to Yusuf totaled $300,000.[36]

The most damning section of the generally equivocal report was titled "off-balance sheet funds and accounts." One of these accounts carried the name Oil Trading A.G. About $70,000 of this $278,000 slush fund ended up in a Los Angeles safe-deposit box, conveniently located at a bank branch in Occidental's headquarters building. Dorothy Prellwitz, Hammer's personal secretary, said that two Occidental executives had asked her to rent the safe-deposit box sometime in 1968. As reported by the Occidental investigators, she said the executives

> told her that the safe deposit box had nothing to do with the business of Occidental or of Dr. Hammer, and she saw no reason to mention the matter to Dr. Hammer. To her knowledge, Dr. Hammer knew nothing about the box until January 1975 . . . [when] she gave a file regarding the safe deposit box to Dr. Hammer for the first time, in connection with the preparation by Dr. Hammer of a response to a subpoena from the Watergate special prosecutor. Prellwitz stated that Dr. Hammer appeared to be surprised and angered upon learning of the safe deposit box.

Her records showed twenty-seven trips to the safe-deposit box before it had been relinquished in September 1972.[37]

The Occidental special committee also noted that an unnamed former employee had charged

> that Dr. Hammer approved withdrawals from the box and that the money was sometimes delivered directly to Dr. Hammer. Dr. Hammer denied the allegations. . . . The committee considered and evaluated the evidence available to it. . . . The committee does not believe the hearsay statements reportedly made . . . concerning Dr. Hammer, and has concluded that Dr. Hammer did not have knowledge of the safe deposit box until January 1975.

The committee nevertheless roundly condemned the OTAG fund (and two similar funds), calling it

> in clear violation of the policy of Occidental. It could create distortions in the company's accounts, its financial reports to the SEC, and its reports to stockholders. Because it is outside of normal channels . . . disbursements made from such funds are unexplained and unaccounted for. This risks embezzlement of funds by unscrupulous employees as well as the making of unlawful or unethical payments.[38]

Three persons with direct knowledge of the safe-deposit box said later that they found the committee report difficult to believe on the question of Hammer's role. Others gave Hammer the benefit of the doubt. Dudley Miller recalled $5,000 bundles of cash moving from London and Basel, Switzerland, to Los Angeles, where they were handed over to one of Hammer's top aides. Ronald Klein said he himself was unaware of the safe-deposit box during its use, "so it is conceivable that the doctor did not know about it. Obviously, some people even within

Occidental thought he knew, and later told me so as general counsel. It had to go into the report. To this day, I do not know what he knew." Prellwitz politely refused to discuss the matter, even though she had been dismissed later on by Hammer after decades of loyal service.[39]

The board of directors' report, although ambiguous in spots, was still a remarkably damning document. Its mea culpas and promises of reform might have been expected to put an end to SEC investigations for a time. But in November 1978, the agency authorized its fourth inquiry in eight years. The impetus was information turned up by the Mead Corporation while defending itself against Occidental's unfriendly takeover attempt. The agency began to examine whether Occidental had "made untrue statements of material facts or omitted to state material facts" about undated resignation letters demanded by Hammer from executives and directors, and six other matters involving accounting, environmental pollution, and oil exploration.[40]

In July 1980, Occidental and Hammer signed a fourth settlement with the SEC. This last settlement was the broadest environmental pollution case ever filed by the commission. It found that Occidental was involved "in at least ninety legal proceedings with governmental units relating to the protection of the environment" but that stockholders were inadequately informed about such liabilities. One more time, angry stockholders sued their company. One more time, Hammer agreed to pay a multimillion-dollar sum.[41] Yet, despite the costly setbacks, his grip on the reins remained as sure as ever.

Through the Revolving Door

A T TIMES, it seemed as if Armand Hammer could do no wrong at the helm of Occidental Petroleum. Without his daring and his persistence, the oil finds in Libya, the North Sea, and Colombia might never have happened. Most people become more deliberate as they age. Not Hammer. As Occidental entered the 1980s and Hammer approached ninety, he played the entrepreneur more forcefully than ever while trying to guide the company's stock price to new heights. After the Mead Corporation takeover debacle, he paid closer attention to his targets. As a result of his renewed concentration, he completed a new run of multibillion-dollar acquisitions in the 1980s. The deals greatly expanded the already gigantic Occidental and also changed its character.

The most significant acquisition for Occidental's oil operations was Cities Service Company of Tulsa. Overnight, that deal turned Occidental from a large oil company with most of its resources outside the United States to a huge company with substantial resources inside America's borders. At first, the deal pursued Hammer rather than Hammer pursuing it. To be precise, takeover wizard T. Boone Pickens wanted Cities Service in his stable, and he wanted Hammer to help with the financing. The talks extended over many months, with plenty of ups and downs. At one point, Pickens met Hammer and Occidental president A. Robert Abboud late at night in Los Angeles. The abrasive Abboud was so negative about the deal that, according to Pickens, "all around the room, eyes were fixed on the ceiling or the floor. There was one set of eyes that was not directed at anything, however — the doctor's. His were closed; he had been asleep for twenty minutes." After some give-and-take with Abboud, Pickens commented tartly, " 'If the deal is that bad, why don't we just go to bed like Dr. Hammer.' I turned toward Hammer, who had started snoring."[1]

But Hammer was fully awake a few months later when Cities Service's investment bankers came calling. What appeared to be an imminent marriage with Gulf Oil Company had unraveled, leaving Cities Service executives demoralized and vulnerable to predators. They loathed the idea of being swallowed by Pickens. The investment bankers had spoken with David Murdock, an aggressive Los Angeles businessman who was Occidental's largest stockholder as well as a director. Murdock was interested. Was Hammer? He was.[2]

Negotiations were rocky at first. Hammer and Murdock disagreed; Hammer and Cities Service chairman Charles Waidelich disagreed; the Cities Service board seemed unenthusiastic. But all of them resolved their differences to complete the third-largest merger in American history to that time, valued at $4 billion. Waidelich said, "Negotiating is Dr. Hammer's fountain of youth. His eyes sparkle."[3]

Although most analysts were upbeat about Occidental's acquisition of domestic energy supplies, they worried about the huge debt load that resulted. But Hammer swiftly sold off Cities Service units that did not fit into Occidental's plans, and within several months of the merger those spin-offs allowed him to present a check for $1 billion to Occidental's bankers. It was done with his usual flair, in front of the media. An industry newspaper commented that "functions like Friday morning's are all but unheard of in the banking industry. Bankers generally shun such publicity unless demanded by a customer."[4]

Hammer slashed operations in Tulsa, which made him unpopular there. When the American Association of Petroleum Geologists invited him to speak at its annual convention, there were protests from members who had been laid off or whose colleagues had been. When they contemplated Hammer's annual compensation of nearly $2 million and his unlimited use of a customized, converted Boeing 727 with a reported value of $9 million, their anger increased. A Dallas member complained to the association's executives that Hammer had put four hundred geologists out of work: "He may have made millions on the deal and thereby be lauded as a successful entrepreneur, but by no stretch of our collective imagination can he be called a humanitarian when he so casually devastates so many in our profession." Hammer eventually canceled his appearance at the annual convention, citing unavoidable travel.[5]

The Cities Service work force dropped from about 20,000 to 4,000. An in-house joke made the rounds: "What is a Cities Service optimist?

An employee who brings his lunch to work." Congressman James Jones of Tulsa met with Hammer to discuss the reductions. Jones had served President Lyndon Johnson at the White House and knew Hammer from those years. "He understood my concerns, and told me his plan," Jones said. "He could not have been more cooperative. I think Dr. Hammer was better for Cities Service than Boone Pickens would have been."[6]

Another multibillion-dollar acquisition that expanded Occidental's energy capabilities was MidCon Corporation. Once again, it gave Hammer the opportunity to play the role of white knight. Hammer knew MidCon was perhaps the most desirable natural-gas pipeline company in the United States, but it had not been on the market. Then Hammer received a call from MidCon's investment banker, who was looking for an alternative to a hostile offer.

Hammer turned to Occidental president Ray Irani and suggested visiting MidCon right away, since its executives quite likely would be receiving many suitors. Hammer believed that Cliff Davis, who had built the company and was its chief executive, would decide on a buyer according to whom he liked the most. Davis, hearing of Occidental's interest, invited Hammer and Irani to fly to Chicago. As Hammer recalled later, Davis was waiting at O'Hare Airport in his car, which he was driving himself. They immediately launched into a discussion about a possible deal. Hammer and Irani had done their homework. They knew Davis had turned down an offer of $68 a share and had started buying his own stock at $75 a share. So when Davis asked Hammer how much he was willing to pay, Hammer quickly replied $75 a share. Davis extended his hand and said it was a deal. The three men were so absorbed discussing the details that they forgot to pay attention to the airport signs and drove around for half an hour looking for the correct exit.

The $3 billion transaction, consummated in a matter of minutes, surprised Wall Street analysts; oil companies generally disliked the pervasive regulation of the gas pipeline industry. But, as one analyst noted, "Occidental does things its own way." That was a euphemistic way of saying that Hammer was a deal junkie, and the bigger the better. Sometimes his impulsiveness made no sense in the context of Occidental's long-term plans. But he plunged ahead on his own, ignoring the memorandums from the cautious M.B.A.'s on his staff.[7]

When Hammer negotiated yet another billion-dollar deal, acquiring Cain Chemical, he was excited about expanding that segment of Occidental's business. Stagnant for years, it was beginning to turn around, partly because of Ray Irani's expertise. Irani had entered the Occidental presidency from the chemical side rather than from banking or oil. Analysts worried that the completion of another huge deal would increase Occidental's debt load beyond all reason. Hammer preferred to look at the positive side, emphasizing the $100 million addition to his company's net income. Besides, a highly leveraged, debt-heavy company made Occidental less vulnerable to would-be acquirers.[8]

But of all the billion-dollar deals, the one that most altered Occidental's character was the purchase of Iowa Beef Processors. Suddenly, a company earning virtually all its income from oil and gas became a company heavily dependent on meat packing. The Fortune 500 changed Occidental's category from oil to foods. Wags altered the company's long-established nickname from Oxy Pete to Oxy Meat.[9]

On his own, Hammer might never have considered expanding into meat packing. The idea came from David Murdock, whose office at the time was one floor above Hammer's in the building mostly occupied by Occidental. Murdock, chairman of Pacific Holding Corporation, owned 19 percent of Iowa Beef's stock and mentioned the possibility to Hammer of acquiring the largest company in the industry. Hammer, regularly attracted to the largest of anything in business, listened.

Hammer looked upon Iowa Beef as a challenge, to be sure, but also as an opportunity. When Occidental announced its bid, an Iowa Beef official said, "I understand that in the merger meetings . . . Mr. Hammer really talked about expansion and sales in the Soviet Union. He was talking millions, to which our response was that we cannot fill all our orders in this country. . . . Hammer is apparently after some other big food people besides us, and I believe that he truly believes that food is a negotiable world commodity." Murdock commented that Hammer "operates all over the world, and he has said more than once that food will be in the 1990s what oil has been in the 1980s. He thinks there will be a worldwide shortage of food." Once again, the federal government voiced no antitrust objections, and the merger went through. Within months, Hammer had treated the Soviets to a cookout and announced a meat-processing venture with them. The announcement was greeted with skepticism even within Occidental, where executives wondered how the Soviets, strapped for foreign exchange, would pay for meat imports.[10]

The Iowa Beef acquisition quickly confronted Hammer with new obstacles to surmount. Occidental generally had experienced little trouble with labor unions, but Iowa Beef was a company with a history of worker-management strife, especially at the main packing plant, in Dakota City, Nebraska. There were protracted, sometimes violent strikes over pay and working conditions. Hammer soon became the focus of the Iowa Beef unionists. After his article on the humanitarian lessons of Chernobyl appeared in the *Los Angeles Times,* the newspaper received a response from David Barry of the United Food and Commercial Workers Union. Barry said Hammer might be a global peacemaker, "but he has utterly failed in his responsibility to meet the challenge of correcting inhuman conditions in his own backyard." Hammer's ventures were "heavily financed by the savage exploitation of workers in a single labor-intensive . . . Occidental subsidiary." Barry tartly observed that "perhaps amid his global interests, the trivial matter of the broken bodies and damaged lives of his workers has simply escaped his attention."[11]

Ronald Asquith, Occidental's vice president for employee relations, responded that the company had few troubles with its forty labor contracts. Hammer "places great importance on positive, progressive employee relations. . . . We believe that the labor situation at this one IBP plant is an aberration, and it presents a picture of failed union leadership." That did nothing to placate the union. When Hammer spoke at the National Press Club, in Washington, union members picketed the building. They handed out brochures that were a takeoff on his art, titled "The Living Armand Hammer Collection at the IBP Plant in Dakota City, Nebraska." The type was superimposed on Rembrandt's *Study of a Beggar Man and Woman on the Street.* The last line said, "Enjoy Dr. Hammer's art. But remember, it was purchased with money stained by the blood of workers in Dakota City." The union received some satisfaction when the Occupational Safety and Health Administration levied a record fine against Iowa Beef — more than $2.5 million for at least 1,038 unreported or misreported violations.[12]

Another problem had its genesis within management, as Hammer and Iowa Beef chairman Robert Peterson clashed over who was in charge. To resolve that question, Hammer engineered the removal of Peterson from the Occidental board and sold 49 percent of Iowa Beef's stock in one of the largest public offerings ever. Hammer billed the sale as another step in Occidental's strategy of improving its balance sheet and concentrating on its main lines of oil and gas, chemicals, and coal. But because Iowa Beef was so lucrative in its way, Hammer made sure Occidental retained a controlling interest.[13]

Hammer could afford to undertake only so many billion-dollar acquisitions. But there were other ways to make money for Occidental and bring attention to himself in the process. On March 28, 1980, he called a news conference that left even veteran Hammer watchers openmouthed. He announced a $119 million profit for Occidental from his speculation in silver, at the expense of the Hunt brothers, who had tried but failed to corner the market and nearly caused international financial disaster. Occidental operated gold and silver mines in Nevada, so Hammer had a natural interest in the market and thus had sensed what Nelson Bunker Hunt was trying to do. Accordingly, he had invested heavily but prudently in silver futures and enjoyed a free ride. When the market collapsed, Hammer had already made his bundle and gotten out.[14]

Zoltan Merszei, Occidental's president at the time, remembered Hammer's calling with the plan one morning before sunrise. "He was sure the silver bubble was going to burst, that we must get in on it. It was entirely his idea. The company had never been in this business, and the rest of us were a little leery and nervous about it." *Los Angeles Times* reporter Linda Grant said Hammer "gave the order to buy and thereafter — with the intensity for which he is noted when a project captures his fancy — he tracked purchases hourly. Similarly, he orchestrated sales."[15]

Such a huge, quick profit was welcome to Hammer, whose critics charged him in lawsuits and in the media with using assets to satisfy his whims. It is unarguable that occasionally he used his absolute control within the company to favor ventures motivated by nostalgia or some other caprice. Examples were legion.

One venture harking back to Hammer's past was cattle breeding. After the death of his prize bull, Prince Eric, in 1953, and the dispersion of his herd, Hammer remained involved in the Aberdeen-Angus industry. His partner, Senator Albert Gore, had joined Occidental at a handsome salary after leaving Congress to manage the firm's coal subsidiary, Island Creek. Hammer also had a business arrangement with Mac Cropsey, the onetime veterinarian at Shadow Isle Farm, in New Jersey. For a while, though, Hammer pursued his cattle business completely apart from Occidental.

Then, in the mid-1970s, Hammer and Cropsey bought a herd for their twenty-three-thousand-acre spread near Loyalton, California, across the border from Reno, Nevada. Hammer involved Occidental in the sideline. The operation grew, opening an office in Colorado and running a state-of-the-art ranch in western Nebraska. Hammer again became visible in Aberdeen-Angus circles. He was the lunch speaker at the 1981 All-American Angus Futurity in Louisville, Kentucky, where a champion heifer of his had been the talk of the show thirty years before. Governor John Brown made the introduction. The advertising in cattle industry publications was shameless. One advertisement carried the headline "Dr. Armand Hammer: The Most Dedicated American to Mankind and His World." The text recited his accomplishments, ending, "Colleagues say Armand Hammer's genius is the ability to maintain an open mind. He is brutally honest with himself, while demanding the same from others. He searches for the truth, and makes his final decisions based on fairness and integrity."[16] What that had to do with cattle was anybody's guess.

Hammer, the frustrated doctor, had a penchant for investing in animals, which he could watch over. After David Murdock told Hammer about the value of Arabian horses, Hammer started acquiring them. As usual, he was unable to go halfway. Within a year, he was one of the nation's biggest enthusiasts, operating an oil-company subsidiary called Oxy Arabians.[17]

The big score, appropriately, came in the Soviet Union. Murdock wanted to buy a champion Soviet horse named Pesniar but needed an entrée. Hammer agreed to provide it in exchange for a share in the ownership. Along with Eugene LaCroix, probably the leading Arabian horse breeder in America, Hammer and Murdock paid $1 million for Pesniar. Within days, the new owners booked $3 million worth of stud fees.[18]

Hammer used his connections in other nations to buy the best, too. At a sale in Poland, he spent $373,000 for six lots of horses. Back home, Hammer jumped into the huge annual sale at Scottsdale, Arizona, paying more than $3 million in 1982.[19] Hammer looked forward to making a big splash at the annual Scottsdale event; so many other celebrities bought and sold Arabian horses, and Hammer loved being with them. One year, he compiled a scrapbook showing himself with country music star Tanya Tucker and television personality Merv Griffin, among others.

During an interview with *Arabian Horse World* magazine, Hammer recalled the stallion given to him in 1922 by Lenin and General Semen Budenny. He never thought his interest in horses would revive, but the trip to buy Pesniar

> whetted my appetite, and the more I learned about Arabians and the industry, the more I thought about getting involved, so I went to the sale in Poland. . . . I had seen some El Paso [a champion horse] daughters and was impressed, and I asked Dr. LaCroix what he thought of

El Paso, since Lasma [LaCroix's company] had had him on lease. He said he was the best stallion in Poland, but he was not for sale. I had already made up my mind to buy him, but Dr. LaCroix's opinion confirmed it.[20]

After making news in Poland and the United States because of the purchase, Hammer sold at least thirty shares in an El Paso syndicate, asking $65,000 a share. The purchasers met at a dinner, with California governor Jerry Brown as the speaker.

Hammer said profit was only part of his motive: "I think it would take a pretty insensitive person not to respond to an Arabian horse. There is a presence — a look, a bearing — that you do not find in other animals. I see that. I feel it." Hammer invoked his cattle background, from which he had learned "that to get the best you have to breed the best. Quality is the key to success." Hammer announced he would promote Arabian racing in the United States as an alternative to Thoroughbred racing. Two years later, the first annual Armand Hammer Arabian Classic race was run at Pompano Beach, Florida, with a purse of $50,000. Armand and Frances presented the winner's check. Hammer advertised that "Oxy Arabians is committed to the future of the breed — Arabian racing. In Europe, Arabians have starred on the race tracks; their beauty is matched by their speed and endurance. In the past few years, racing has grown phenomenally in the United States. We will continue to increase the racing pace with the bloodstock of El Paso."[21]

Tom Chauncey, a leading Arabian breeder, said Hammer "almost single-handedly got Arabian racing accepted in the United States. There had been no purses like that, not much movement. It is good for the whole industry, because it is another use for the horse." Eugene LaCroix said Hammer's quick study of the Arabian horse industry was amazing. "In 1981, I went with Dr. Hammer to Hungary to look at horses," LaCroix said. "On the flight back, he must have asked me questions for eight to ten hours. And they were good questions."[22]

Hammer donated six Russian-bred Arabian horses to Salem College in West Virginia, the favorite institution of Senator Jennings Randolph, who was a supporter of the tycoon's.[23] By 1986, Hammer was selling a good number of horses from his total stock of 142. Using his art collection as a come-on, the auction bill carried the headline "The Oxy Arabians Masterpiece Collection Sale." The text said Hammer "is proud to offer . . . a selection of mares that merit the consideration of serious breeders. They are all masterpieces, all collectibles." The sale grossed more than $5 million, with the average horse bringing $181,000 and the prize horse $575,000.

Despite Hammer's Johnny-come-lately status and his lack of humility, there was little resentment of him in the Arabian horse industry. He brought it so much positive publicity that prices stayed high several years longer than expected. Inevitably, though, whatever he touched meant controversy of some sort. For example, criticism arose when he lobbied in Washington for a waiver of duties on Arabian horses imported from the Soviet Union. The agency caught in the middle was the Animal and Plant Health Inspection Service of the Agriculture Department. Adoption of the rule change was expected to save Hammer and his partners about $200,000 on the importing of Pesniar. The only favorable comments on the rule change came from Arabian horse breeders. Nine members of Congress wrote in opposition. Summarizing their feelings, Representative Sam Hall, Jr., of Texas argued, "There is no valid reason to grant Mr. Hammer and the Soviet Union this preferential treatment. Let Mr. Hammer pay his import duties like everyone else, and send the Russian government a signal that before we grant trade concessions of any kind, they can abandon their aggression in Afghanistan and other areas of the world." The congressional objections went unheeded. Hammer obtained his duty waiver.[24]

Not all the lucrative sidelines in the world could erase Hammer's frustration at having to answer no when asked if he were the baking soda king. Off and on for decades, he thought about buying Church and Dwight, the New Jersey company that manufactured Arm & Hammer baking soda. There was little reason to do so except vanity. In 1986, Hammer succeeded in obtaining a piece of the business so he could answer yes more or less honestly. Occidental formed a partnership with Church and Dwight to produce and market potassium carbonate under the name of the Armand Products Company. Occidental became a 5 percent stockholder in Church and Dwight, and Hammer joined the board of directors. The *Wall Street Journal* headline joked, "ARMAND HAMMER AND ARM AND HAMMER FINALLY ARM IN ARM."[25] Church and Dwight over the decades had spread the word that its brand name was unrelated to Communism but instead represented Vulcan, the Roman god of fire and metalwork. The company had taken specific measures — especially after Hammer's guilty plea in the Watergate case — to disassociate itself from him. Now, after all the attempts at distancing, it was caught in his embrace.

Hammer sometimes failed in his attempts to acquire companies. Probably the most devastating failure involved Diamond Shamrock Corporation. The proposed $3 billion merger, announced in 1985, would have put Occidental much closer to the ranks of the Seven Sisters. Occidental president Ray Irani had served at Diamond Shamrock, so he was an obvious link. Several days after the merger announcement, the companies called a news conference. Journalists expecting details about the merged company instead received a news release stating that the agreement was off. Almost everybody attributed the surprise collapse to a clash of egos between Hammer and William Bricker, Diamond Shamrock's chairman. Bricker denied those reports, blaming instead a lack of enthusiasm from Wall Street, dissent on the Occidental board, and Diamond Shamrock's concern about the quality of Occidental's management. *Barron's,* the financial weekly, published a front-page column attacking Hammer in the wake of the deal's collapse. The headline said: "What Price Glory? For Armand Hammer's Fellow Shareholders — High."[26]

Another deal that fell through involved Zapata Corporation, founded by George Bush. David Murdock, a large stockholder in Zapata and Occidental, had introduced Hammer to B. John Mackin, his Zapata counterpart. Occidental made an offer, but it was so low even Murdock voted against it. Mackin said later that Hammer simply miscalculated how much he would have to spend to acquire Zapata.[27]

Hammer made miscalculations as well during his attempt to bring Husky Oil into Occidental. Although Husky had its headquarters in Wyoming, it was essentially a Canadian operation. Hammer had been holding laconic discussions with the Nielson family about acquiring Husky, but the negotiations unexpectedly took on urgency when PetroCanada made a hostile takeover bid, followed by a competing bid from the Alberta Gas Trunk Line Company. Hammer's attempt to play white knight was valiant, though futile, because of Canadian laws and nationalist sentiment that made it difficult for an American company to acquire anything over the border.[28]

As frustrating to Hammer as any of these failed acquisitions were the drawn-out controversies surrounding three matters on which he fervently wanted to get his way: marketing shale oil from Colorado's mountains, using Occidental's patented technology; cleaning up Love Canal, in Niagara Falls, New York; and drilling for oil in Southern California's Pacific Palisades. Each controversy, wrapped up in local and national politics, cost Occidental hundreds of millions of dollars and afforded new perspectives on Hammer's character.

Hammer's vision about the future for shale was tied to his belief that the United States desperately needed to attain energy independence through alternative sources of oil that would last hundreds of years. Hammer's study of shale oil's history should have given rise to pessimism — experiments with the technology in the 1920s and the 1950s had failed to excite government policymakers or consumers.[29] But Hammer rarely gave in to pessimism. He used Occidental's Garrett Research and Development subsidiary to develop in situ technology that extracted oil from the inside of the Rocky Mountains. The process meant tunneling into the mountains' interiors, blasting to produce broken-up rock, igniting it, then extracting the oil from the rubble without destroying the ecology of the mountain or the surrounding area. Hammer received reports during the height of the energy crisis, in the early 1970s, that Occidental's process could produce oil for three dollars a barrel during a time when the world price was many times higher. Experts outside Occidental were skeptical, wondering whether the technology would work on a commercial basis and questioning whether the federal government would offer substantial financial assistance.

Hammer and his executives began to lobby the government. Occidental's experiments were taking place on twenty-four hundred acres in Colorado, not enough land to accomplish all the tests. Hammer requested legislation allowing Occidental to acquire government-owned land in the vicinity at reasonable prices. In addition, Occidental used its unique technology to entice Ashland Oil Company to join a partnership on more desirable land. They envisioned a plant that would turn out 57,000 barrels a day at a cost of $440 million. Hammer said the total yield from the operation would top 1 billion barrels of oil. Occidental spent hundreds of millions of dollars of its own money, as well as millions more in Department of Energy funds.[30]

Despite substantial federal aid, Hammer thought the government was being stingy, and he criticized officials for their shortsightedness. He believed that with Occidental's help America could develop a vast new source of oil — admittedly, at great expense. In exasperation, he scolded Frank Zarb, the federal energy administrator, saying that his agency was placing greater emphasis on paper shuffling than on achieving energy independence. To Interior Department secretary Thomas Kleppe he complained about bureaucratic unresponsiveness.[31]

Hammer was relentless in his campaign to have the Occidental technology funded and adopted. He could be overbearing when discussing it, averring that all other companies were going about their research incorrectly. By mid-1983, he had engineered a multibillion-dollar assistance package from the federal Synthetic Fuels Corporation. But the agency appeared to be rife with inefficiency, causing Congress to waffle over whether to continue funding it. Congress eventually abolished the agency, despite Hammer's passionate plea for its retention. Occidental shut its shale oil project. Although Hammer expressed confidence that it would reopen, his was one of few such voices. The shale oil campaign further confirmed Hammer's reputation as the unusual kind of visionary who also was adept at playing hardball to get what he wanted. The shutdown of the Synthetic Fuels Corporation did nothing to damage his reputation; some Occidental stockholders were upset about the large expenditures that yielded no profit, but their dismay was moderated by Hammer's obvious good intentions on the issue.[32]

Hammer's reputation fared less well in the Love Canal matter. It was a thicket he had entered unwittingly as a result of Occidental's buying Hooker Chemical, in 1968. Unknown to Hammer, Hooker had deposited toxic waste at the Love Canal landfill site in Niagara Falls between 1942 and 1953, then deeded the land to the local board of education, which disposed of it to developers. They in turn built a residential area adjacent to the unrecognized poisonous dump. All manner of illnesses began to show up among area residents.

About a decade after Occidental's acquisition of Hooker, Hammer learned of the seriousness of the problem he had inherited. He was disturbed. After all, he had donated millions of dollars to the crusade against cancer, and here he was presiding over a carcinogenic dump. Hammer did not want to pay clean-up costs as the successor corporation of Hooker Chemical. Yet somebody clearly had to pay. Local residents, the state government, and the federal government became involved in litigation against Occidental as Hooker's parent company.

Hammer's case suffered from the public perception that Occidental was a major national polluter. Throughout the country, the firm was being charged with lackluster pollution control, often paying substantial penalties as a result. While Love Canal suits filed by governments and private citizens piled up, straining Occidental's legal budget, Hammer announced in October 1983 that the personal injury claims of 1,345 residents — about 95 percent of those outstanding — had been tentatively settled. Occidental's liability would be about $6 million; Hammer expected insurance to cover the rest. He emphasized that the proposed settlement was not an admission of negligence. In fact, he said, no link between the landfill and the claimed injuries had been proved.

The announcement did little to end the battles. The lawyer for the vast majority of the plaintiffs contested Occidental's characterization of the proposed terms. Environmentalists were enraged at Hammer's statement that no cause and effect had been established. Shortly thereafter, the federal government sued Occidental for another $45 million in clean-up and relocation costs. In 1988, Occidental suffered a further setback when a federal judge ruled that it had to pay hundreds of millions in costs assessed by the state. New York State attorney general Robert Abrams called the decision "a resounding defeat for Occidental's strenuous and expensive public relations campaign to shift the entire blame." The litigation continued into 1989. Throughout the controversy, Hammer — while conceding that Love Canal was causing him "considerable grief" — maintained that Occidental had done more than its share to guard the environment in general and to compensate Love Canal residents in particular.[33]

Occidental's operations in the Los Angeles area, meanwhile, had caused an even greater furor. Hammer's authorized biographer, Bob Considine, wrote in 1975 that the Pacific Palisades debate, as it was called, "makes Occidental's Libyan acquisition appear routine." Fourteen years later the controversy — over whether Occidental should be allowed to drill for oil next to a Los Angeles–area neighborhood a stone's throw from a beautiful residential area in one direction and an ocean beach in another — was still unresolved.

The controversy originated in the late 1960s, when the city and Occidental swapped pieces of land. The city received four and a half acres at the mouth of Portrero Canyon, near Palisades Park, and Occidental received two acres from the city, plus $175,000. The land Occidental gave up was not suitable for oil drilling; the land it received was. The transaction led to inconclusive grand jury and state legislative investigations, followed by years of litigation in California courts. Los Angeles city councilman Joel Wachs charged that municipal officials had "engaged in a highly irregular and improper series of actions whereby they in effect served as an agent for Occidental . . . in acquiring the two acres . . . in question at a fraction of its potential value, without public notice, without competitive bidding, and against the public interest." Council member Tom Bradley, later to play a major role in the controversy as Los Angeles mayor, testified against Occidental, disclosing that he had asked the Environmental Protection Agency and Governor Ronald Reagan to block oil drilling at the site on environmental grounds. Bradley termed the land swap "Watergate West."[34]

Hammer was so outraged at opposition from area residents, grouped under the name No Oil Incorporated, that he lobbied McGeorge Bundy, head of the Ford Foundation, to withdraw funding from the public-interest lawyers representing the homeowners. Bundy refused Hammer's unusual request, at which point Arthur Groman suggested that No Oil's lawyers were violating federal regulations for nonprofit groups, with the result that they might be endangering the tax-exempt status of the Ford Foundation. The lawyers' group, known as the Center for Law in the Public Interest, charged that Groman's veiled threat raised "serious ethical and professional questions." The No Oil lawyers filed a complaint with the Los Angeles County Bar Association ethics committee on the grounds that Hammer and Groman were employing "a calculated strategy of harassment designed to subvert the integrity of the judicial process." The bar association ruled that conduct of that kind was "ethically improper."[35]

Hammer, increasingly frustrated, became more involved himself, calling on city council members, targeting recipients of campaign contributions, and auditioning commercials that advocated drilling. Explaining why he had spent so much valuable time on a local rather than global matter, he said, "I don't care who it is — anyone who steps on my toes and tries to kick me in my lower regions and take advantage of me, and I think that is what is happening [sic]. I think this is the greatest injustice in my sixty years of business experience in the United States."[36]

Occidental had a majority of the Los Angeles City Council on its side, but Mayor Bradley kept exercising his veto to stymie Hammer, and the council majority was one vote shy of the number needed to overturn the veto. The *Los Angeles Times* commented that getting the additional vote has "been tougher [for Hammer] than negotiating with the Soviet Union." It was quite a different ball game from that in the preceeding administration, in which Mayor Sam Yorty had helped Hammer. Yorty traded in Occidental stock through his broker and accepted favors from Hammer; later investigations of his conduct turned up no actionable offense.[37]

One dramatic revelation came after Hammer hired private detective Herbert Itkin, a onetime informer for the FBI and the CIA, to conduct surveillance of the No Oil deliberations. (Hammer also was using Itkin to pry into the life of Tim Babcock in connection with the Watergate campaign-contributions case.) Itkin, living in Los Angeles under an assumed identity as a federally protected witness, reportedly received $120,000 for his efforts, part of which he paid to his friend Sandra Downs to infiltrate No Oil. Downs attended the group's meetings, purporting to be an interested neighborhood resident. The FBI interviewed Itkin at length after one of his associates reported the Hammer arrangement. But, again, nobody was charged with a criminal offense.[38]

Decisions by the city council, state agencies, and the courts kept switching the momentum from one side to the other. Hammer tried to influence the course of events by doing favors, including helping local leaders with the 1984 Olympics. Just as the U.S. government had boycotted the Moscow Olympics, the Soviets had decided to stay away from the Los Angeles competition. Mayor Bradley, hoping to change that decision, asked Hammer to intervene. Hammer failed to turn the Soviets around, but he made a determined effort, eventually receiving a personal reply from Ambassador Anatoly Dobrynin.[39]

Bradley went deeper into Hammer's debt when the tycoon helped dispel some of the gloom connected to the Soviet pullout by engineering the visit of Chinese pandas to Los Angeles during the Olympics. To accomplish that, Hammer had gone directly to Chinese leader Deng Xiaoping. Hammer even provided $150,000 toward the cost of transporting the pandas to and from Los Angeles.[40]

As usual, he wanted maximum recognition. Peter Ueberroth, director of the Los Angeles Olympic Organizing Committee, recalled Hammer's

> insistence that he be given an organizing committee title — special assistant to the president — and business cards and stationery to that effect. He scribbled a personal postscript on every note he sent me, wondering where his office supplies were. I did not think the title was necessary, so I finally told him "you fly in on your private jet wherever you go, and everybody knows who you are. I do not think . . . Olympic committee business cards can possibly enhance your international stature." But Hammer persisted, so we gave him the cards and stationery.[41]

Perhaps the accumulated good deeds and visibility helped. Occidental's drilling plans for the Pacific Palisades received an important boost in early 1985 when the mayor changed his position, saying the environmental safeguards promised by Hammer had been improved. The *Los Angeles Herald Examiner* commented that the mayor's flip-flop was tied to the mystique of Hammer, "who may be the most powerful non-government figure in the world today." Bradley called his shift of position "the toughest decision of my political career." Los Angeles resident Elizabeth Mortimer, complaining that Occidental's preliminary drilling was offensive, said she was writing a book tentatively titled *My Dinner with Oxy Smells*. Neighborhood residents James Garner and Ted Danson, both Hollywood stars, called the proposed drilling by Occidental "the most dangerous project to ever come before the city. . . . We all have things we hold dear. Mr. Armand Hammer . . . loves art. He would not appreciate our placing several thumbtacks into one of his

Monets or Picassos. We feel just as protective of the natural beauty of the Pacific Palisades and the Santa Monica Bay."[42]

Hammer and Groman saved some of their most vicious attacks for Marvin Braude, a city councilman since 1965. They charged that Braude knew at the time of the original land swap that Occidental planned to drill there but voiced no opposition. Then "he started to oppose us and make it impossible for us to do what he authorized us to do. . . . I do not like dishonesty and I do not like false statements," Groman said. Braude flatly denied the allegation and accused Hammer and Groman of "arrogance" for presuming they could drill without passing all necessary environmental reviews.[43]

When Occidental financed a pro-drilling group called the Los Angeles Public and Coastal Protection Committee, Braude and his followers were enraged. Heading the misleadingly named group was Edmund Brown, Sr., the former governor of California. During their public acerbic exchanges, Braude wrote Hammer a private letter, begging him to give up on Pacific Palisades because of the harm it was doing to political careers and because of the widespread opposition to drilling. "Armand, even a brilliant, successful, generous, charming man like you can have blind spots. But you are so exceptional, you are capable of changing your mind. I plead with you, please abandon the coast site in Los Angeles."[44] Hammer refused, continuing to marshal Occidental's resources for oil drilling that, if ever achieved, already would have cost tens of millions of dollars in staff time and legal fees.

Given Hammer's minuscule stockholdings in Occidental compared with the total, his whims underwritten at corporation expense, and his very advanced age, observers marveled that he continued to reign. The key was his control of the board of directors and the company's top executives, whom he kept in constant fear. With so many of Occidental's presidents and directors summarily dismissed, the perception arose of a revolving door in the boss's executive suite. James Pugash, Hammer's executive assistant in the early 1980s, remembered being told by Hammer's secretary as he reported for work: "Dr. Hammer has the highest estimation of you today that he will ever have. You had better accept that. It will be all downhill from here."[45]

The opprobrium of the revolving door was only partly deserved, however. Occidental's executive turnover was not unusual among Fortune 500 companies. Nor, considering that so many top executives came to Occidental through acquisitions, was it surprising that many failed to adjust. But, that said, Hammer's fickleness toward potential successors was rightly legend: He would meet a younger man who looked like a hotshot, woo him until the object of his affection could no longer resist, praise him to the skies, consult him on major decisions, perhaps even accept his advice from time to time, and then cashier him. In a twinkle the wunderkind was out the door with a generous settlement that included his agreement to keep quiet about what had happened. These people would then become nonpersons in Occidental literature; many rated not a single mention in Hammer's hefty 1987 autobiography.[46]*

After one such departure, that of Occidental president William Bellano, Hammer himself assumed the post of president, making the betting on a successor even more problematic.[47] Speculation centered mostly on the triumvirate of Marvin Watson, the Lyndon Johnson insider brought to Los Angeles after running Hammer's Washington office; Thomas Wachtell, a lawyer working as Hammer's executive assistant and said to be like a son to the old man; and Dorman Commons, Occidental's chief financial officer.

Commons said later that he knew he was doomed when his name started appearing in the media as a contender. He was right. Soon he was ushered out the door — only to become chief executive of another multinational. He was successful by any standard. But a full fifteen years after his departure from Occidental, he still dreamed of Hammer at night, he said. "I loved my father, and was influenced by him. When he died, I dreamed about him for a while. Eventually, those dreams stopped. My dreams about Dr. Hammer never did stop."[48]

Wachtell, after his departure, told an interviewer,

> You do not have any real idea how many people went in and came out. He is an acquisitor of people. Once you are in his camp he is continually looking for somebody else, because the grass is always greener, and because he figures if somebody else has a guy, then that guy must be alright. He would make promises that are impossible, or for one reason or another are not kept. A man comes aboard and Hammer says you are going to be number one man, you are after me, and you are going to know everything and do this, that, and the other thing. Then it does not turn out that way six months or two years later and the man leaves, and he bitterly blames the doctor for having misled him or having brought him aboard under false pretenses or taking his company away from him.[49]

* One of them, Thomas Willers, who lasted at the top for about two years, discussed his concerns about Hammer's business and personnel practices with Senate investigators. Willers had earned $200,000 a year and received $160,000 a year for three years after his departure. (Senate committee staff memorandum, November 20, 1973; and Willers, interview, November 11, 1987.)

When Hammer hired thirty-nine-year-old Joseph Baird from the London banking business in 1973, it looked like the real thing. By many accounts, Baird possessed a volcanic temper. But nobody questioned his business acumen, and for five years he and Hammer got along, at least on the surface. In 1978, Stephen Sansweet, the *Wall Street Journal*'s perceptive Hammer watcher, reported that the aging boss appeared to be relinquishing control voluntarily to Baird. Hammer thought the story was complimentary at first, until some members of his coterie told him that it was part of a Baird plot to depose him. He became suspicious, then began telling executives Baird was planting anti-Hammer stories with journalists.[50]

Hammer kept his doubts within Occidental for a time. During the Mead Corporation hearings, he described the Baird relationship as working well, saying that Baird operated the company "on a day to day basis." According to Hammer, Baird "discusses all important matters with me. . . . My office is right next to Mr. Baird's, so he just walks into my office at the close of each day when I am there and we discuss matters of importance, including planning, and then of course I sit at the board meetings." In the same forum, Baird said, "Dr. Hammer has a very active mind. He continuously thinks of ways to further the interest of Occidental, many of which involve very long-range planning."[51]

The failure of Occidental's Mead takeover attempt helped seal Baird's fate, however, along with his increasingly bold disagreement with Hammer in public. A *Wall Street Journal* reporter saw that disagreement firsthand during a joint interview when Baird scolded Hammer for predicting, in answer to a question, that Occidental expected to be "in the black for all of 1978. [']You know we do not make projections, Armand,['] Mr. Baird reminded his boss. The next day, Mr. Baird issued in the company's name a clarification of Dr. Hammer's remark, stating it is too early to make an estimate."[52]

After Baird's firing in July 1979, Zoltan Merszei took over that office, expecting to succeed Hammer in short order. Merszei had spent thirty years at Dow Chemical Company, where he rose to president, then chairman. Fifty-seven, Merszei was of Hungarian extraction, smart, handsome, and as outgoing as Baird was dour. The romance with Hammer was soon in full bloom. In a speech five months after becoming president, Merszei said that "on leaving Dow, Occidental Petroleum attracted me like a bee to flowers for a basic reason. Dr. Armand Hammer . . . and I think and work in much the same way." He called Hammer's success at Occidental "probably without equal in the history of business," citing the tycoon's "hard work, a highly unusual vision of the world," and a healthy reliance on individuals instead of on rigid organization.[53]

Not long afterward, as usual, the honeymoon seemed to be over. Within months, rumors of a rift were flying. Hammer denied them emphatically: "People cannot stand the idea that we are getting along. We have never had a quarrel or a fundamental disagreement. I think people would be disappointed if they did not hear such things."[54] It sounded like a vote of confidence, but it was the kiss of death. Three months later, Merszei was replaced as president by Robert Abboud, an intense, controversial, recently fired Chicago bank chief.*

Abboud brought to Occidental a reputation as one of the toughest chief executive officers in America. Subordinates feared him. But Hammer was not even slightly intimidated. Magazine writer Edward Jay Epstein, arriving at a hotel suite early for an interview, witnessed Hammer "glaring at Robert Abboud . . . with a focus that could wilt flowers. Abboud himself was on the telephone to Occidental's man in London, discussing a proposed British plan to increase the tax on Occidental's concession in the North Sea. Hammer instructed Abboud, sentence by sentence, as if he was dictating a letter, exactly how he should respond." Abboud lasted four years; under his contract he left with a minimum income from Occidental of $500,000 a year for four years. The news release announcing his departure was unusually revealing, acknowledging "honest differences" between him and Hammer. The candor ended there, however, as Abboud remained silent under the terms of his settlement.[55]

One thing was for sure: Abboud had found himself caught between Hammer and director David Murdock in their battle to control the company. Commenting on Abboud's firing, Murdock said,

> I believe Bob was the conservative member in the Hammer organization. His desire to pay down the debt, to stay out of new adventures, and bring more conservative operating methods to the company was in the best interests of all shareholders. But unfortunately this was in conflict with Dr. Hammer's more flamboyant method of operation. As in the past, no one has ever dared stand against . . . his singularly autocratic rule.[56]

Nobody challenged Hammer more seriously than Murdock, twenty-six years his junior. Until they became acquainted, in 1981, during

---

* Merszei stayed at Occidental nearly six more years but never regained the top spot. He left with a consulting contract worth $500,000 a year for two years, a guarantee given him when he joined Occidental. Publicly, he said he and Hammer were on good terms. Privately, he was disappointed by Hammer's refusal to relinquish the top spot. (Merszei, interview, February 22, 1989.)

negotiations to buy the Arabian horse Pesniar, they knew each other almost solely by reputation. They were attracted to each other, as many great salesmen are. Then Murdock gained a seat on the Occidental board by becoming the largest stockholder as a result of the Iowa Beef acquisition. It was no secret that he was ambitious — Hammer called him a "business barracuda" and "street fighter" — but few people foresaw his challenging Hammer for control of Occidental. Yet Murdock did just that. He quickly became a divisive force on a board that Hammer once had bragged voted unanimously every time. Murdock opposed Hammer's speculative shale oil project in Colorado and risky coal mine project in China. Eventually, he insisted Hammer amend their contract, which placed a cap on how much Occidental stock Murdock could acquire. Hammer said no but started looking over his shoulder, wondering if Murdock had found a loophole allowing him to mount a serious threat.

It is uncertain from currently available evidence whether Hammer or Murdock — or both — ever found usable dirt on the other. Hammer hired a private detective to look for skeletons in Murdock's closet, and Murdock scrutinized Occidental's ledgers for evidence of corporate assets being wasted on Hammer's personal crusades. In July 1984, Murdock sold back his common stock for a handsome premium, with the payout totaling $194 million. Some shareholders were so angry that they sued Hammer, Murdock, and their own company; nineteen separate suits were filed. To many small shareholders, Murdock's windfall looked like a classic case of greenmail. The next year, Murdock sold his preferred stock back to Occidental for about $86 million.[57]

One insider who observed the Murdock-Hammer wars was William McGill, the former president of Columbia University who had joined Occidental's board at Hammer's insistence. McGill, a psychologist, studied Hammer carefully, calling him "the most interesting, complex, capable individual I have ever known." McGill said that to comprehend Occidental in the 1980s, "it is important to understand David Murdock's attempt to drive out Dr. Hammer. One principle it illustrates is Dr. Hammer's failure to pay attention to details until disaster looms. He must have seen Murdock as benign, which shows a failure to correctly analyze his character." McGill said that Hammer's many projects outside Occidental sometimes caused him to lose sight of what was going on within the firm. "But just as disaster is about to strike, his head will clear and he will become the best manager I have ever seen by many orders of magnitude."[58]

Another insider who saw what was happening was Robert Teitsworth. Teitsworth joined the Occidental board in 1979 after twenty years of working his way up from staff geologist. "The only time it really got serious because of the revolving door at the top was when Bob Abboud came in," Teitsworth said. "You could not be sure whose side Abboud was on, and Murdock wanted to control the board. . . . Dr. Hammer was fighting for his life. He revered Murdock at first because of Murdock's wealth. Dr. Hammer is a romantic, falling in love with the man of the moment. Murdock and Abboud were out to get him. When I warned him, he said, 'Don't worry, Bob, I have eyes in the back of my head.' "[59]

Approaching ninety, Hammer clearly remained in command. Like many people at the top, though, he sometimes failed to receive the best possible information, and as he aged it became more difficult for him to cut through to the truth. James Pugash, his executive assistant, said that often Hammer failed to receive reliable information from his underlings because they were intimidated. "Before going in to see him, they would talk to me first about the bad news they were bringing," Pugash said. "Then we would enter his office. Dr. Hammer would start the session by saying what he expected to hear, which was usually good news. The messenger would then agree with Dr. Hammer, contradicting what he had told me just minutes earlier."[60]

A handful of top executives began the Occidental Mouseketeers Club, with various ranks such as chevalier. To learn if he qualified, an executive had to ask himself "Am I a man or a mouse?" when describing how he responded when Hammer called with an urgent request at an inopportune time. If the answer was "A mouse," membership was assured. The certificate of membership included a drawing of a mouse on a red carpet, looking over his shoulder in terror.

In such an atmosphere, a lot of responsibility fell on Ray Irani, the replacement for Abboud. Irani was a native of Lebanon, a forty-nine-year-old Ph.D. chemist who had joined Occidental's operations from the Olin Corporation. By the middle of 1989, he had served more than four years under Hammer in what appeared to be a comparatively placid atmosphere. Irani was popular, intelligent, blunt in private, and self-effacing in public. He let Hammer take the credit for Occidental's improved performance during the late 1980s, even though at times Hammer seemed to be failing mentally and physically.

Fortune writer Anthony Ramirez interviewed Hammer and Irani for hours during late 1988. Although he praised both men in his resulting article, Ramirez could not help noticing that the ninety-year-old tycoon's "voice is weak, his hearing weaker, his walk halting. When he sits, his clothes hang loosely on his bones, and he scarcely moves." But an examination of Occidental's 1989 notice of annual meeting to share-holders made it appear that Hammer was very much in control, what-ever the state of his health. He received nearly $2.5 million in cash compensation during 1988, in addition to dividends from his nearly 1.5 million shares of common stock. Hammer's employment agreement as he turned ninety-one provided him with minimum annual compensa-tion of about $1.5 million into 1998, the year in which he would turn one hundred. Furthermore, nobody was seeking to force him out. Ir-ani — earning well over $2 million annually — counseled patience. It appeared that he complemented Hammer, who called Irani "exactly the man I have been seeking."[61] But then, Hammer's praise had a familiar ring.

PART VI

CITIZEN-DIPLOMAT

23

Back-Channel
Ambassador

ALTHOUGH ARMAND HAMMER RECEIVED ACCLAIM
for his business acumen, at no time during the 1960s, 1970s, or
1980s was he merely a multinational tycoon. He was also an unparal-
leled citizen-diplomat, shuttling around the world as frequently as did
Henry Kissinger. Sometimes Hammer practiced his unique brand of
diplomacy in full view. At other times he kept a low profile, acting as
a back channel for the United States, the Soviet Union, or any other
nation that might be involved in superpower politics. Still other times,
he traveled incognito. Foreign governments almost always welcomed
his missions. His own government was more ambivalent, with presidents sometimes using his services against the advice of the State Department or the National Security Council, where Hammer tended to
be viewed as naive at best, traitorous at worst.

The mass media helped him spread his gospel of international cooperation. Hammer found his largest American forum yet in June 1974,
courtesy of NBC News, which aired a one-hour documentary about
him. The NBC crew shot much of the footage in the Soviet Union,
thanks to doors Hammer opened. He was at the service of host Edwin
Newman, producer Lucy Jarvis, and their television crew, arranging
for footage with Leonid Brezhnev inside the Kremlin wall.[1] As Joseph
Finder, a Harvard Sovietologist, found while researching his book *Red
Carpet:* "The rest of the Western news corps in Moscow, many of whom
had tried unsuccessfully for years to arrange a meeting with Brezhnev,
were flabbergasted. Edwin Newman, who had never been to Russia
before, had flown in one day, spoken with Brezhnev in the Kremlin

the next, and then left the country with Jarvis and the NBC team on Hammer's private jet."

Although a personal triumph for Hammer, the NBC documentary became a focal point of controversy. The anti-Communist magazine *Human Events* wondered before the broadcast whether NBC would show Hammer "as the Red sympathizer his every act proves he really is." Congressman Richard Ichord and his Internal Security Committee staff talked among themselves about whether to demand that Ichord be integrated into the show to provide balance. On the other hand, NBC ballyhooed the documentary in a news release, stressing its time-liness with President Richard Nixon's scheduled visit to the Soviet Union, and admirers of Hammer's encouraged rumors that he would be named U.S. ambassador to Moscow. The news media spread the rumors, which led the State Department to deny that an official offer had been tendered.[2]

Hammer, flattered but not interested, continued to act as unofficial ambassador. During a press conference in Moscow after a meeting with Brezhnev in 1975, he described his efforts to schedule a visit to the United States by the Soviet leader. He discounted rumors of Brezhnev's poor health, despite a much-discussed six-week disappearance from public view, and generally acted like a plenipotentiary without portfolio from Russia to the United States and vice versa.

Hammer decided the time was ripe to expand his recognition as a citizen-diplomat. The Soviets gave him remarkable access to the leadership and used those meetings to send messages — some private, some public — overseas. Hammer received special landing rights for his airplane, permission to show his art collection in international cultural exchanges, and the Soviet Union's Order of Friendship Between Peoples medal, the highest honor available to a non-Communist. Soviet print and television journalists attended the dedication of Occidental's superphosphoric acid terminal at Jacksonville, Florida. When Hammer traveled to Moscow for a session with 350 other American businessmen, Brezhnev singled him out during dinner remarks, assuring references to the tycoon in the next day's newspapers.[3]

Hammer was given living quarters in Moscow choicer than even the American ambassador's. In fact, nothing demonstrated his status in the Soviet Union quite so clearly as the suite given to him by Brezhnev — a living space previously occupied by five families. Hammer retained a Los Angeles architect and a West German contracting firm to renovate the space, transforming a rabbit warren into five spacious rooms, and he kept the gift secret from Frances until it was finished. He hung expensive art in the apartment, announcing that some of it would become the property of the Soviet government upon his death. When he subsequently opened his Moscow home to *Architectural Digest* magazine, the resulting article mentioned numerous Russian paintings on the walls, including *Children at the Piano,* by Nikolai Bogdanov-Belsky, *View from a Rocky Coast,* by Isaac Levitan, and *Peasant Girl,* by Isaac Brodsky.[4]

Mikhail Bruk, sometime Soviet journalist and Hammer's man about Moscow, described the dedication of the apartment in mid-1976:

> It was perhaps the most unusual housewarming in Moscow in recent years. To begin with, it was not in any of the new residential areas that keep cropping up on the outskirts of the Soviet capital. This party, given by Frances and Armand Hammer in their pleasant five-room apartment, took place in a nine-story house cater-cornered [sic] across the street from the Tretyakov Art Gallery and only a quarter of a mile from the Kremlin in Moscow's old Zamoskvorechye District.

One of the Soviet guests presented the Hammers with a kitten, "a traditional housewarming gift in this country. It is supposed, by legend, to bring happiness and luck to the new home." Attending the party were the American ambassador, the mayor of Moscow, top aides to Brezhnev, and various high-ranking trade, industry, and culture ministers.[5]

The momentum of Hammer's one-man diplomacy took off from there. After he met with Brezhnev in October 1976, *Pravda* placed the story on the front page, a clear signal to the United States that the Soviets wanted to increase the volume of trade. The ninety-minute discussion between Hammer and Brezhnev also covered the strategic arms limitations talks, war in the Middle East, U.S. presidential politics, and Soviet treatment of emigration requests from Jews. Not even the American embassy was fully informed about what was said. Hammer disclosed only what he chose to disclose, either on his initiative or at Brezhnev's request; he kept his own counsel about the rest of the goings-on at his private Kremlin sessions.[6]

Probably the most productive meeting with Brezhnev, at least for Hammer's image as citizen-diplomat, occurred during 1978 at Brezhnev's Yalta vacation home. The timing was propitious for all concerned because the United States and the Soviet Union were deadlocked over the fate of F. Jay Crawford, an American arrested on charges of black market currency dealings. The arrest of Crawford, the Moscow representative for International Harvester, quite likely was retaliation for the detention of two Soviet United Nations officials in New York. The Carter administration was getting nowhere trying to resolve the dispute, so Hammer wrote Brezhnev in July, then followed up in person during the August meeting. Before departing from the United States, Hammer was briefed by the State Department's Soviet expert, Marshall Shulman. Hamilton Jordan at the White House requested that Hammer report back after the session.[7]

At Yalta, Hammer asked Brezhnev to allow Crawford to leave the Soviet Union. Brezhnev replied that the evidence against Crawford was solid. What if it is? countered Hammer. Is the matter so important that you want to hurt Soviet-American relations irreparably and lose trade with American corporations in the process? Hammer predicted to U.S. ambassador Malcolm Toon at a post-midnight Moscow airport talk that Crawford would be expelled unharmed after a brief show trial. That is exactly what happened: The next week, a Soviet court convicted Crawford, gave him a five-year suspended sentence, and let him leave the country.[8]

A relieved Crawford later commented that he had begun to feel confident about obtaining his freedom when he heard Hammer's optimistic post-Yalta prediction about his fate. Like many other Americans, Crawford assumed that when Hammer spoke about Soviet intentions, he knew precisely what Kremlin rulers thought. Peter Maggs, a University of Illinois law professor on retainer to International Harvester, recalled meeting a Soviet KGB general in Moscow soon after Hammer's Yalta session. The officer told Maggs "he was authorized by the highest authority to comment on the press report about Armand Hammer, and that the information about Crawford was essentially accurate." To this day, the debate continues about Hammer's role in the Crawford release. Ambassador Toon said Hammer carried messages but was not influential in obtaining the release. Toon believed the Soviets trumpeted Hammer's virtues at every opportunity because of his value as an apologist for the Kremlin. Marshall Shulman was less skeptical, suggesting that Hammer's intervention combined with the Soviets' desire to improve relations worked in tandem to effect Crawford's release.[9]

Hammer used the Crawford affair as an opening to both superpowers, writing President Jimmy Carter that Brezhnev seemed eager to meet before the end of the year. As the leaders began to think seriously about such a summit, Hammer sent agenda items for consideration. Zbigniew Brzezinski, Carter's national security adviser, greeted the suggestions coldly. Brzezinski had never trusted Hammer. His special treatment at Yalta — including his transportation to the resort in a private Soviet airplane — ate away at the sternly anti-Communist adviser. When Hammer asked to see the president privately about a summit meeting, word passed from the National Security Council to the White House that "Brzezinski believes the president should not see Hammer. Hammer tends to abuse such meetings. Among other things, he misrepresented himself as a presidential emissary during his recent trip to Moscow."[10]

When Carter and Brezhnev finally met, Hammer took credit for planting the seed that had blossomed. He used the summit atmosphere to push for Senate ratification of the strategic arms limitation treaty, hoping it would ease tensions between the superpowers. Hammer believed the Russians were being falsely accused of violating SALT I. By early 1980, Hammer's lobbying of the Senate had taken on a plaintive note; the Soviet invasion of Afghanistan, at the end of 1979, had complicated superpower relations so profoundly that Hammer worried about war. Here was a chance to promote his deeply felt need for continuing dialogue and a chance to be a hero worthy of a Nobel Peace Prize. His first private report about Afghanistan came from Anatoly Dobrynin, the Soviet ambassador to Washington. After the briefing, Hammer told reporters the Soviet presence was certain to be short-term; that was what Dobrynin said, and he never lied to Hammer.[11]

Within weeks, Hammer was in Moscow discussing the Afghanistan impasse with Brezhnev. His account of the two-hour meeting caused a tremor in diplomatic circles and left insiders wondering more than ever about Hammer's loyalties. His version of Brezhnev's comments, if accurate, meant a softening of the Kremlin position, seeming to indicate interest in a negotiated settlement. But the official account, from the Soviet news agency, Tass, failed to signal a softening, which led experts to conclude either that Hammer had been set up or that his eternal optimism — perhaps combined with failing hearing and a misunderstanding of a key Russian colloquialism — affected his report of Brezhnev's meaning.[12]

Brzezinski decided that Hammer was consciously giving events a Soviet tilt. Hammer in turn likened Brzezinski to an aggressive little boy playing an international version of good guys / bad guys, poisoning the peaceful instincts of Carter in the process. The skepticism about Hammer's interpretation of the situation in Afghanistan failed to stop him from spreading it across the globe. During a speech in Chicago, he criticized the president for threatening to pull out of the summer Olympics and cutting back Soviet-American trade. He disclosed that he had suggested to the Russians that a pullout from Afghanistan might lead to a Pakistani withdrawal from the border, which was desired by the Kremlin. While in Chicago, he was treated like a head of state presenting a major foreign policy address. The chauffeur of his rented limousine said, "I have been driving people out to O'Hare for two and a half years, some real important people. But none of them was ever allowed to take the limousine out to the runway to meet the plane."[13]

Hammer worked both sides tirelessly. He spread the Soviet account in the United States, saying Brezhnev "explained to me that they believe Afghanistan, which since the revolution of 1978 had been a pro-Soviet government, was being threatened by forces unfriendly to the Soviet Union." According to Hammer, the Soviet leader said that as soon as he received guarantees from the American government and the countries neighboring Afghanistan that they would refrain from interfering, the Soviet Union would withdraw its troops. Brezhnev seemed truly bewildered at President Carter's anger, Hammer said, so he had explained that the president thought Brezhnev had tricked him by unexpectedly moving soldiers across the border. By Hammer's account, he and Brezhnev exchanged views on whether Carter was honest. Hammer said yes, but Brezhnev was of the opinion that Carter was acting politically.[14]

Newspapers attacked Hammer for serving as Brezhnev's mouthpiece. Some critics wondered why the federal government refused to invoke the Logan Act, a 1799 law meant to punish private citizens who tried to influence American foreign policy. The Justice Department responded that the law was antiquated, rarely used, and "never intended to prohibit attempts to convince foreign governments from doing something worthwhile." The unofficial explanation seemed patently clear — Hammer was serving a valuable function. Yet his background and perceived allegiances continued to cause concern among White House advisers.[15]

The suspicions troubled Hammer, so much so that he eventually sent a letter to Carter, in April 1980, inquiring why the president had not invited him for a tête-à-tête since August 1978, especially in light of his conversations with leaders of nine countries, as well as Pope John Paul II. National Security Council staff members, though wary as always, recommended a Hammer-Carter meeting. They knew Hammer possessed unmatched information pipelines in countless countries. They also knew they owed him something for swallowing a huge financial loss because of the administration's phosphate embargo, without making a public stink.[16]

When Hammer met with Carter on June 5, 1980, he suggested placing an international peacekeeping force in Afghanistan for five years, with elections scheduled at the end of that time. Carter was adamant that the Soviets should withdraw before negotiations could begin. Hammer responded that such thinking was unrealistic and unproductive, and he left the meeting saddened.[17]

As the year progressed, Hammer refined his suggestions for a peace plan, using Soviet ambassador Dobrynin as a sounding board, then writing Carter that with the help of Polish leaders there could be discussions about troop withdrawals from Afghanistan, after guarantees from the United States and Pakistan of noninterference and establishment of a peacekeeping force from neutral nations.

The U.S. government tried to keep up with Hammer, in order to use his connections constructively. Secretary of State Edmund Muskie cabled U.S. embassies for their reaction to a report that Hammer was planning to meet Pakistani president Zia al-Haq in August. Ambassador Arthur Hummel responded from Islamabad that the report appeared to be true; the Pakistanis "will undoubtedly speculate that there may be political overtones." Zia received Armand and Frances in his home, saying he would accept a Soviet government in Afghanistan in return for a troop withdrawal and safe passage for Afghan refugees in Pakistan to their homes without reprisals. Hammer, encouraged, flew to Moscow to present the proposal to Brezhnev, who accepted the terms — if China and India also agreed to noninterference pacts. Since the White House and State Department wanted to know what Hammer was saying to the Soviets, embassy personnel in Moscow pumped Occidental's representative there, Daniel Garine. The embassy cabled to Washington that "we have no way of knowing what . . . may be on Hammer's mind, and we doubt that Garine or anybody else in Occidental's shop here would know. That is not Hammer's style."[18]

Ambassador Thomas Watson, Jr., the longtime chairman of IBM, cultivated Hammer to learn Kremlin thinking firsthand. Watson kept the White House and State Department apprised of Hammer's initiatives, at one point cabling from Moscow that

Armand Hammer is back in town, and I think you should know about the idea he is pushing. He saw [French president] Giscard [d'Estaing] in Paris last week at a private dinner at Edgar Faure's apartment and thinks that he convinced Giscard to try to get something moving on the neutralization of Afghanistan by dealing through [Polish leader Edward] Gierek. Hammer is going to visit Poland and has undertaken to persuade Gierek to invite Giscard to Warsaw to discuss the matter. Hammer's idea seems to be that Gierek could invite Brezhnev at the same time, but it is not clear whether Giscard encouraged that aspect of the idea. . . . [Hammer] is an activist . . . and despite his recognition that the Soviets are probably not receptive to any scheme which would have them withdraw all or part of their troops from Afghanistan, he seems to feel that even a long shot is worth trying.

The next month, the embassy in Warsaw cabled: "In analyzing the developments leading up to Giscard-Brezhnev meeting at Gierek's invitation, I assume that the department has noticed that it coincides almost completely with the Armand Hammer idea." [19]

Watson was comfortable with Hammer as a fellow head of a multinational corporation and was unmoved by fears that Hammer was a traitor. In Watson's view, "he is a loyal American, one of the most brilliant men in business I have ever known, and . . . very misunderstood by a great portion of the population." While Watson served as ambassador, "Hammer was very helpful. I do not think there is anything odd in Hammer's relationship with the Soviet Union, though you might say he fails to accentuate the negative." Watson never ceased to be amazed at the reverence for Hammer in the Soviet Union: "I went to the ballet in Moscow with him. We had to check our coats; I was the last in line. The coat-check woman asked me if that had been Armand Hammer in front of me. When I said yes, she asked me to ask him to come back. He did. It turned out she wanted to shake the hand that shook the hand of Lenin." [20]

Senator Charles Percy, an Illinois Republican who served as chairman of the Foreign Relations Committee, was one of the most influential voices in the nation's diplomatic policy after Ronald Reagan's election. A former chief executive of Bell and Howell, Percy was a Hammer admirer. When Hammer asked Percy to set up a meeting with Secretary of State Alexander Haig about Afghanistan in early 1981, Percy was glad to help. "I have always found Dr. Hammer to be highly creative, deeply concerned about matters affecting the national interest of the United States, but also concerned about relationships between the United States and the Soviet Union," he said. Percy knew about the suspicions concerning Hammer's loyalties but dismissed such talk; Hammer's reputation with members of Congress "varied with the political persuasions of the politicians. The extreme right-wingers looked upon Dr. Hammer as soft on Communism, and other such clichés." [21]

Claiborne Pell of Rhode Island, Percy's successor as chairman of the

Foreign Relations Committee, watched Hammer intently. "When we get together, he does a lot of talking. I absorb and learn," Pell said. Because the Soviets at first perceived President Reagan as a Commie basher, Hammer's role as citizen-diplomat increased in importance. Through Hammer, Brezhnev spread the word about his interest in slowing the arms race. Hammer pushed Reagan and Brezhnev to meet, partly because of his faith in negotiations at the highest level, partly because of his desire to take credit for any summit that resulted.[22]

Sovietologist Joseph Finder said that Hammer "reveled in the art of private diplomacy, escalating it to a new level with his talents of self-promotion. If he was to be hounded by allegations of corporate impropriety, and even questionable connections to the Soviet leadership, at least he would make a concerted effort to create the image of a statesman."[23]

Hammer's detractors were fighting an uphill battle. He received the kind of attention most self-promoters only dream of, thanks in part to items like an Ann Landers column read by millions of people. Landers and her twin sister, fellow advice columnist Abigail Van Buren, were friends of Hammer's. In May 1982, Landers wrote about the horrors of nuclear war, suggesting that readers use the column as a basis for letters to Reagan. The president, though, proposed that readers send the column to Brezhnev. Landers told her audience she liked Reagan's suggestion so much that she had asked Hammer to deliver the column personally to the Kremlin. Hammer agreed to do so.[24]

By then, he was a Russian institution. When a Soviet actor portrayed a younger Hammer in the Moscow stage play *Thus We Shall Triumph*, about the last year of Lenin's life, Hammer went backstage to meet the cast. Finder, in Moscow doing research, heard a Hammer joke making the rounds. It seemed Hammer went to Red Square to visit Lenin's mausoleum but found it closed for repairs. The guards forbade Hammer's entry, infuriating him. "Don't you know who I am?" he asked. When the guards remained intransigent, Hammer drew a yellowed, wrinkled piece of paper from his pocket. "This is a personal letter to me from Vladimir Ilich himself. It says to come visit me anytime."[25]

After Brezhnev's death, in late 1982, Hammer read a eulogy at the grave, close to the Lenin mausoleum, as Senator Robert Dole and other dignitaries listened. *People* magazine published a photo essay about the Hammer-Brezhnev relationship, with Hammer providing the words. Hollywood film mogul Jerry Weintraub attended Brezhnev's funeral as Hammer's guest; Weintraub was flabbergasted at Hammer's access, at his treatment as a virtual head of state.[26]

Undiscouraged by the death of his "friend," Hammer, eighty-four, began over after the ascension of Yuri Andropov. Rather than perceiving his age as an impediment, Hammer believed it gave him the status of an elder statesman. Who understood the Soviet psyche better? Relying on his decades-long perspective, he pronounced contemporary Soviet-American relations the worst in sixty years but characteristically added that "sometimes, in foreign affairs, when relations are the worst, sudden breakthroughs can be made." Those who knew Hammer understood the implication — he alone could initiate that breakthrough. True to form, Hammer pushed for a Reagan-Andropov summit and worked relentlessly for his own meeting with Andropov. After obtaining an appointment for December 1983, he was disappointed when Andropov canceled. It was an early sign of the new Soviet leader's poor health. Hammer offered to send expert medical care, but because the Soviets were denying the seriousness of Andropov's problem they were loath to accept.[27] Andropov died in February 1984.

Hammer used his influence to help an acquaintance's television stations obtain exclusive, intimate coverage of the funeral. The acquaintance was John Kluge, a billionaire who served on the Occidental board of directors. Kluge wanted entry visas into Moscow for his journalists, but the Soviets reportedly were denying all requests. Hammer said he would make arrangements, so Kluge put New York journalists John Parsons and Christopher Jones on an airplane to London, where they met Hammer's luxury jet. During the flight, Hammer showed film footage about himself and gave Parsons a book and articles about his exploits. Upon landing in Moscow, the two journalists passed through Russian customs without any visas and with almost no delay. Before they knew it, Hammer had arranged for a Soviet film crew to help them. Parsons and Jones shot extraordinary footage of the funeral. Kluge had his scoop. Later, Parsons and Jones ate dinner in Hammer's Moscow apartment, where they interviewed him for a favorable profile that appeared on Kluge's stations.[28]

At the Andropov funeral, Hammer became acquainted with Konstantin Chernenko, the new Soviet leader, slipping him a piece of goodluck jade from his Wyoming mine. Before long, Hammer had achieved with Chernenko what shortness of time had denied him with Andropov — a highly publicized, face-to-face meeting. It took place at Chernenko's Communist party office, a more relaxed setting than the Kremlin. Hammer had built up to it, sending messages to the White House and the Kremlin and writing a commentary published in the *New York Times* that urged senators to ratify a strategic arms limitation treaty as a conciliatory sign. Since Andropov's funeral ten months earlier, no American other than a few journalists had succeeded in meeting with Chernenko to discuss issues.

That isolation worried Hammer, who pushed for a summit meeting. Hammer told Chernenko that if the Soviets were serious about signing a pledge to avoid first use of nuclear weapons, maybe the Reagan administration would do the same. Hammer also advocated a new cultural exchange agreement, one that would involve his own art collections. To make sure Chernenko remembered the meeting, Hammer had arrived bearing an 1871 letter written by Karl Marx, acquired earlier in the year at a London auction. Chernenko reciprocated with a replica of a huge czarist vase. The two men embraced at the end of the session. Immediately afterward, Hammer went to a Soviet news studio, where he gave successive live interviews to three American television networks.[29]

Hammer was also generous to American diplomats in the Soviet Union, helping to pay for a new piano in the ambassador's quarters, publishing a catalog of American artworks on display in Moscow, and donating Daumier lithographs to the consulate in Leningrad, where they were hung prominently in a public room. But, notwithstanding his gratitude, Ambassador Arthur Hartman cut through Hammer's public relations offensive to give an unbiased assessment of the Chernenko meeting to the State Department: "As described by Dr. Hammer, the meeting with Chernenko seems to have served primarily as a vehicle for him to publicize his views as to where the United States–Soviet relationship should be headed."[30]

Patrick Buchanan, reflecting the opinion of many Reagan administration officials, found Hammer's visit to be more insidious than that, saying Hammer "has hauled water" for every Soviet leader in return for riches and renown.[31]

Senator Alan Cranston disagreed, using the *Congressional Record* to disseminate the tycoon's views. According to Cranston, "Few analysts of United States–Soviet relations have more experience and greater understanding of the issues which divide us" than Hammer, whose firsthand knowledge "has provided important insights for American leaders."[32]

Hammer's political analysis may or may not have been keen, but his medical predictions left something to be desired. Throughout the early weeks of 1985, he told audiences that Chernenko was enjoying good health, despite rumors to the contrary. But just in case, he offered medical help for Chernenko, as he had done for Andropov. Only this time he brought lung specialist Daniel Simmons of Los Angeles with him on OXY-1.* The medical mission turned out to be fruitless. Simmons and Hammer did meet Chernenko's doctors, but they were defensive and refused to let Simmons examine their leader. Simmons understood: "It was probably as if a Russian doctor showed up at the White House to examine President Reagan."[33]

By March 1985, it was clear Chernenko was very sick. As rumors of his imminent death began to circulate, Hammer was packing for a business trip to Germany. He told Frances to include his Russian clothes, in case of a funeral on short notice. His foresight was accurate. With Chernenko's death confirmed, Hammer lacked time to obtain permission to fly OXY-1 into Moscow, so he took his first commercial flight in two decades. When he arrived at the Moscow airport, Mikhail Bruk had a visa waiting. No other private citizen would have been allowed entry under the circumstances. Hammer, age eighty-six, stood in bitter cold for three hours as he observed the pomp of another funeral for another departed Soviet head of state whom he had outlived. Afterward, he met Mikhail Gorbachev, soon to be named the new leader. Ambassador Arthur Hartman watched in awe as Hammer wended his way through the crowd at the reception: "He worked the line; he literally knew every head of state there." Warren Hoge, covering the event for the *New York Times,* said Hammer was the only guest willing to talk about the private reception publicly.[34] With Hammer, but keeping mum, were Vice President George Bush, Secretary of State George Shultz, and rulers from all over the globe.

The first substantive Hammer-Gorbachev meeting took place in June 1985, just three months after Gorbachev's succession. Shultz told Hammer before the meeting that "it would be particularly important that you underscore to Mr. Gorbachev . . . the president's determination to build a more constructive relationship. We have put forward a number of ideas for consideration in every area of our dialogue. We are frankly somewhat disappointed that they have refused to engage us in a serious discussion of many of these issues." Shultz asked Hammer to fill in Ambassador Hartman after the meeting, which Hammer did, leading Hartman to send Shultz a five-page cable with details.[35]

Hammer was pleased by Gorbachev's frankness, decisiveness, and charisma. As he often did with Soviet leaders, he conducted some of

---

* Simmons was impressed by the lavishness of Hammer's airplane and by Hammer's clout once they landed in Moscow. "When I had to take a taxi to Dr. Hammer's apartment during our stay, all I had to say to the driver was 'Hammer,' and he took me right there." (Simmons, interviews, January 8 and January 19, 1988.)

the conversation in Russian, speaking in an accented, largely correct manner. Hammer was distressed, however, at Gorbachev's poor understanding of American governance and his pessimism about being able to negotiate meaningfully with Reagan. The session produced at least two news items. First, Gorbachev revealed that he planned to skip the autumn opening session of the UN General Assembly. Second, a summit later in the year seemed certain if a site could be arranged. Hartman warned the State Department that Hammer "is clearly taken with his self-appointed role as midwife to a summit, and we expect he will argue vigorously upon his return to the United States that we should not stand on ceremony in insisting on a meeting outside the Union of Soviet Socialist Republics."[36]

After the talk with Gorbachev, Hammer met with Reagan at the White House to share his impressions. Reagan's advisers were adamant that the president should refuse to visit Moscow for the summit. It was the Soviet leader's turn to visit Washington, they said. Hammer urged Reagan to disregard such inflexible advice, telling him the need for a face-to-face meeting as soon as possible overrode concern over the site of such a summit.[37]

The *New York Times* printed Hammer's plan for the Reagan administration to share its Strategic Defense Initiative, or Star Wars, technology with the Soviets. He was derided by commentators who believed such an arrangement was impractical and possibly treasonous. Some critics wondered if Hammer was losing his grip on reality. Undaunted, Hammer replied that a negative reaction often greeted a good idea when first broached.[38] His supporters called him a visionary committed to peace on earth. Hammer distributed the plan to world leaders visiting the UN, members of Congress, and assorted other policymakers. He discussed its implementation during a ninety-minute meeting with Soviet foreign minister Eduard Shevardnadze.

At the end of the November 1985 Reagan-Gorbachev summit, in Geneva — which the Soviets credited Hammer with helping arrange, thus boosting his campaign for the Nobel Peace Prize — Hammer moved quickly to capitalize on the era of good feeling by using his art collection. He never divorced his paintings from his diplomacy. Earlier in the decade, his offer to transport five Soviet-owned pictures from Moscow to Harvard University's Fogg Museum — as part of a show of Jacob van Ruisdael's works — had become embroiled in the question of whether it would undermine Reagan's strictures following the invasion of Afghanistan. The Soviets would not release the paintings to Hammer unless the U.S. International Communication Agency determined that the pictures were protected from judicial seizure. To make such a promise, the agency had to state that the items were culturally significant and the exhibit was in the national interest. Gilbert Robinson, the agency's acting director, worried that such a ruling would cause the Soviets to believe it was business as usual. To complicate matters, the Soviets had rejected an earlier request by the Fogg Museum to ship the pictures, agreeing to do so only after Hammer's intervention. The State Department told Robinson to let Hammer have his way despite U.S. policy to the contrary.[39]

After that decision, the international situation improved, and Hammer wanted to use his pictures to continue the thaw. He termed an art exchange scheduled for 1986 "the first under the cultural exchange provisions" agreed to by Reagan and Gorbachev in Geneva. American art lovers would see forty Impressionists from the Hermitage and Pushkin museums; Soviet citizens would see Hammer's Old Masters collection plus additional paintings from the National Gallery of Art. Hammer, as usual, found significance that transcended art: "This is a first step in people-to-people exchanges, which, hopefully, will be followed by cooperation in other areas, such as arms reduction and the avoidance of nuclear war." Earl Powell, director of the Los Angeles County Art Museum, was delighted, saying of the exhibition when comparing it with the 1973 exchange arranged by Hammer: "This is the real show. The first was just hors d'oeuvres. This is a deeper and richer assembly of pictures."[40]

Hammer described the tough stance that got him his way: "I was in Moscow for five days, and then I refused to leave until I got the signed agreement. And every day I went to the ministry after the minister himself had agreed, and there was a lot of bureaucracy. At first they only said I could have it for two cities, because they did not want the paintings to be out of Russia for so long." Hammer told of refusing to depart from the Ministry of Culture until somebody assumed the authority to sign the agreement the way he had worded it. He sat for at least two hours while embarrassed Soviet functionaries wondered what to do with the living legend. Finally, a deputy minister signed.[41]

Hammer declined to rest there. When the Soviet First Lady, Raisa Gorbachev, joined the Soviet cultural fund board of directors to bring art to the masses, Hammer made the first donation — eighteen paintings from his collection. After he turned over one picture, by Russian artist Ivan Kulikov, accompanied by $100,000, the Soviet media hailed Hammer for days. Mrs. Gorbachev ordered the painting displayed in the Tretyakov Art Gallery, in the same neighborhood as Hammer's

Moscow apartment. The praise resumed three months later when Hammer donated a painting by Nikolai Bogdanov-Belsky. When he jetted to Siberia to open an exhibition of his art, on board were selected journalists and Neil Lyndon, the co-author of his autobiography in progress. Two stewards served drinks, fresh salmon, bagels, and brie. The guests settled into leather and velvet lounge chairs to watch movies. Two limousines met them at the remote airport. A Soviet woman who identified herself as a painter waited to meet Hammer. She told a journalist, "If one man can make a difference in relations between our countries, he is the man."[42]

Hammer tried to make that difference not only through art, but also by donating $200,000 and pledging many times that amount to the International Foundation for the Survival and Development of Humanity, which had offices in the United States, the Soviet Union, and Sweden. Hammer joined its international board, sitting alongside Robert McNamara and Andrei Sakharov, among other notables. The foundation promised to make grants to tackle "major global problems, with a special focus on the environment, international security, and social and economic development in areas such as health, education, and culture." As part of the start-up, Hammer journeyed to Moscow, where he attended the historic meeting between Gorbachev and Sakharov, the Nobel Prize–winning scientist who for years had been an outcast in his own land as the leader of Soviet dissidents. Hammer and Gorbachev talked privately for a half hour after Sakharov's departure.[43]

Through the vicissitudes of Soviet-American relations, Hammer continued his shuttle diplomacy on world problems, including the situation in Afghanistan. Using his art and his wealth were not enough; he was a man of action. He received unprecedented permission to enter the Soviet-occupied nation; at the Kabul airport, five Afghan officials and a Soviet diplomat met him. The official news agency called him "one of the outstanding personalities of the social, economic, and trade circles of the United States." After a round of meetings, he spoke to a news agency reporter, who wrote that Hammer "acclaimed the measures . . . taken under the leadership of . . . Najibullah to end the . . . bloodshed." Mike Hoover, an independent Los Angeles filmmaker hired by Hammer to document the Afghanistan trip, said, "I have not got a clue what makes him tick. He is phenomenal. He defies death, eats everything in sight, never gets jaded, has a little-boy attitude. On the way to Kabul, he exulted about going somewhere nobody else was going. He was not at all worried; he was enjoying it. . . . The Soviets were excited about Hammer going to Afghanistan, because they figured if they could convince him, it would help in the court of world opinion. You should have seen [Soviet foreign minister] Shevardnadze's face fall when Hammer told him if the Russians pull out, the current Afghan government will have to go also, because they are thought of as traitors. They may be nice people, Hammer said, but no one can govern in that atmosphere."[44]

Hammer wrote an article for the *New York Times* that touted his importance, perhaps because he believed he was failing to receive appropriate credit from the Western news media for his role in the Afghanistan negotiations. He expressed his pleasure at being a contributing factor in the signing of the April 1988 Geneva accords meant to solve the Afghanistan dispute. He said his citizen diplomacy on behalf of Afghanistan had been spurred by a February 1987 visit from Diego Cordovez, a high-ranking UN official. After that flattering visit, Hammer had begun new rounds of self-styled shuttle talks with government officials in Afghanistan, Pakistan, the United States, and the Soviet Union. Hammer said he had detected doubt within the Reagan administration about the sincerity of the Soviet leadership when Gorbachev talked about withdrawing his troops from foreign territory. Therefore, Hammer wrote, "I relayed this uncertainty to Mr. Gorbachev in the Kremlin. . . . I also told him that I felt sure the Pakistanis would not enter fully into the quickening peace process until and unless he dispatched [Deputy Foreign Minister Yuli] Vorontsov to negotiate personally with President Zia in Islamabad." Gorbachev asked Hammer to tell President Reagan that the Soviet Union would withdraw its troops by 1989 but wanted to avoid a bloodbath as a result of the withdrawal. Although the Soviet leader did not reply directly to Hammer's suggestion of a Vorontsov mission to Islamabad, when Hammer talked with Vorontsov the next day, the Soviet official reportedly said, "You did a job on the boss; Mikhail Sergeyevich ordered me last night to pack my bags and get to Pakistan." Hammer flew to Pakistan to be present when Vorontsov and Zia were meeting. Zia gave Hammer a letter to carry to Reagan. Hammer delivered it, telling Reagan to call Zia personally rather than respond with a staff-written letter. As Hammer noted proudly, Reagan did call Zia. Their conversation may have led to the Pakistanis' withdrawing their opposition to the Geneva agreement. After the Soviet departure from Afghanistan, in 1989, the government there asked Hammer to use his influence with President Bush. Afghan foreign minister Abdul Wakil hoped Hammer could persuade Bush to stop supplying weapons to the rebels trying to undermine the regime.[45]

Although Hammer normally aimed for maximum visibility when conducting his citizen diplomacy, on one matter he remained invisible for many years — his secret missions on behalf of Israel. Israel had many subjects to discuss with the Soviet Union but, after the Six-Day War of 1967 and the termination of relations with Arab nations and the U.S.S.R., lacked the diplomatic means to do so. At the request of Israeli leaders, starting with Golda Meir in 1972, Hammer served as a diplomatic back channel. That he remained undetected for so long in an age of pervasive communications media was amazing in itself, a testament to the sophisticated evasion he employed.

At first glance, Hammer seemed an unlikely emissary. He had demonstrated no discernible interest in Jewish affairs during the first seventy years of his life. In fact, he denied his Jewish heritage while conducting business in Libya and other anti-Semitic countries. When pushed to state his religion, he replied that he was Unitarian. So the 1972 contact from Golda Meir perhaps surprised him as much as it surprised others when they learned of it years later.

A primary concern of Meir's was the emigration of Soviet Jews. Hammer was uncomfortable with human rights issues, believing that one nation had no business trying to serve as a moral model for another. He knew the Soviets heatedly denied mistreating Jews, and thus he understood that discretion was vital if he were to serve Israel effectively.

Wolf Blitzer, apparently the first journalist to publish anything about the initial Hammer mission (more than a decade after it occurred), called it "one of the most spectacular but unpublicized incidents in Israel's history of diplomatic back channels." Blitzer's curiosity had been stimulated by a 1984 trip by Yitzhak Shamir to honor Hammer at a dinner in Los Angeles. It seemed like an unlikely journey for the Israeli foreign minister; when Blitzer asked questions, he was told the government was "deeply appreciative for Hammer's services over the years, and not just because he bought one million dollars or two million dollars in Israeli bonds."[46]

The background turned out to be this, Hammer has said: Meir wrote him on September 5, 1972, then asked Zvi Dinstein, her deputy finance minister, to make personal contact. (Dinstein has said he was unaware of any letter from Meir to Hammer.) Hammer and Dinstein eventually met in Houston. Reportedly commenting that he had been a bad Jew, Hammer said he would think over the request to meet with Meir. He and Dinstein met again later at Hammer's Greenwich Village home, the location of which Hammer asked Dinstein to keep secret. Hammer agreed to see Meir in Israel but only if certain conditions were met.

First, he would fly his own plane to Rome, where an Israeli plane —
with nobody on board but Dinstein and the crew — would pick him
up. Second, Hammer would land in Israel after dark, without a visa,
so nobody could trace his movements later. Third, he would stay, unannounced, in the government's guesthouse, then leave twenty-four hours
later, again after dark. The Israelis agreed to the plan.[47]

All went smoothly until Hammer's arrival at the guesthouse, where
he became convinced that the dark-skinned guards were Arabs, despite
Dinstein's assurances that they were trustworthy Israelis. Hammer insisted that Dinstein stay with him. Together they drove to Dinstein's
home, where Dinstein picked up pajamas and accompanied Hammer
back to his government sleeping quarters. During meetings the next
day, Hammer agreed to carry messages to Moscow. Hammer then re-
joined his own airplane in Rome and returned to his point of departure, without even Frances's knowing where he had been.[48] In his own
account, which differs from Dinstein's in many particulars, Hammer
emphasized Meir's desire to have the Soviets lift the onerous education
tax on Jews wishing to emigrate, a tax few could afford. Hammer has
said he raised that issue with Brezhnev in their meeting of February
1973. His autobiography suggested cause and effect between his plea
and the removal of the tax by the Soviets in April, something that may
or may not be true.

The Israelis gave Hammer the code name Patishi, which translates
literally as "my hammer." They continued to deal with the Soviets
through him, although after a time Hammer decided there was too
great a risk of being detected. He began sending emissaries to Israel in
his place — first Paris lawyer Samuel Pisar, then international lawyer
Harry Simon Levi, whom Israeli diplomat Eli Mizrachi described as
an unlikely courier for Hammer: "They were a strange combination:
an old Jewish revisionist working for a friend of Lenin." Levi became
an especially valuable contact after the surprise election of Menachem
Begin in 1977 as Israel's head of government. The two men went way
back in the Israeli resistance movement.[49]

Hammer had retained Levi as a counsel in the early 1970s, when he
also hired two top Occidental executives from Yardney Electric Corporation, whose owner Hammer apparently knew through art collecting. Levi was ending a career at Yardney. Until his death, in 1979, he
remained Hammer's confidant and link to the Jewish world. Levi's
widow, Mara, recalled flying secretly to Israel with her husband and
Hammer, where General Ariel Sharon escorted them on a helicopter
tour of the troubled nation. She also remembered early morning tele-

phone calls from Hammer when the Jewish Defense League was pick-
eting his home or office to protest his ties to anti-Semitic governments.
Hammer would yell to Levi, "Get them to stop this demonstrating."
With a few well-placed telephone calls, Levi would do just that.[50]

After Levi made the introductions, Begin developed a genuine fondness for Hammer, addressing him as "my friend." The feeling was
mutual. Hammer admired Begin's intellect and his drive to change the
world. With Begin's blessing, Hammer worked to develop the economies of Israel and Egypt, sometimes through joint ventures based on
his immutable belief that business partners are less likely to make war.
On a personal level, Hammer provided medical experts for Begin's
dying wife, Aliza.[51]

In return, Begin defended the tycoon at the White House, telling
Reagan to disregard intelligence reports questioning Hammer's loyalty.
Begin asked his ambassador in Washington, Ephraim Evron, to write
Secretary of State Alexander Haig on Hammer's behalf; Evron did so.
Even after Begin resigned from office and cut himself off from almost
all outsiders, his special relationship with Hammer continued. When
Begin took ill in retirement, Hammer flew California urologist Willard
Goodwin to Jerusalem.[52] Hammer probably extended Begin's life by
convincing him that surgery would be necessary. It was the frustrated
doctor in Hammer coming to the fore.

Despite his disdain for organized religion, Hammer proved his good
faith to Israel over and over, as when Israeli leaders approached him
about asking the Soviets to intervene in Ethiopia on behalf of Falasha
Jews trying to escape the Marxist regime there. Israeli military aide
Ephraim Poran said Hammer's inability to prevail in "the Ethiopian
business is not so important as the fact that he was willing to try hard.
It was his willing attitude which we highly appreciated." In the matter
of emigration for Soviet Jews, Hammer presented Brezhnev with a
secret document that suggested flying refuseniks from Moscow to Tel
Aviv on KLM, or from Moscow to Bucharest, Romania, on Aeroflot,
to be picked up for the final leg to Israel by El Al. He pointed out to
Brezhnev that it would be a gesture toward American Jewry that might
help obtain congressional approval of SALT II. Later, as world tensions eased, Israeli prime minister Shimon Peres asked Hammer to
approach Konstantin Chernenko about reestablishing diplomatic relations between Israel and the Soviet Union.[53]

While Hammer carried on his behind-the-scenes diplomacy, he also
began to contribute to Israeli philanthropic causes, especially as Occidental's dependence on Middle East oil waned. But even his philan-

thropy stirred controversy. Hammer's name had been anathema to Jews
for so long that a decision by the Jewish Federation–Council of Greater
Los Angeles granting him its Maimonides Award caused unusual debate in the normally congratulatory philanthropic world. Writing in
the newspaper *Israel Today,* journalist Yehuda Lev commented that if
any Jew in America were "less deserving of recognition and honor
from the Jewish community, I am not aware of his existence." Lev laid
responsibility for the award on Arthur Groman, Hammer's lawyer and
a power in the Los Angeles Jewish community. An explanation and
apology were in order, Lev said: "I do not think that either will be
forthcoming. But when someone sells you like a common whore, you
have at least the right to know for how much you were peddled."[54]

Responding to the criticism, the Jewish Federation convened to reconsider the award but let it stand. That opened the floodgates. Afterward, Hammer received honors from Jewish organizations virtually
every month; Jewish newspapers were filled with articles and advertisements about the latest dinner in his behalf. One of the biggest galas
was sponsored by Bar-Ilan University in Israel, which awarded Hammer an honorary doctorate. Novelist Elie Wiesel, the 1986 Nobel Peace
Prize–winner, attended the $1,000-a-couple dinner in Los Angeles, where
Frank Sinatra serenaded Hammer with the song "Mr. Wonderful, That
Is You." The program said Hammer had been "a confidant of every
American president since Herbert Hoover."[55]

One of Hammer's most visible philanthropies in Israel was the Armand Hammer Fund for Economic Cooperation in the Middle East,
conceived by Haim Ben-Shahar while he was president of Tel Aviv
University. Its purpose was "to foster economic cooperation between
Israel and her neighbors." The fund churned out reports on topics such
as water supplies, fertilizer production, and gas pipelines. One board
member was Guilford Glazer, a Los Angeles real estate developer generally credited with bringing Hammer into Judaism's fold. As Occidental increasingly withdrew from Middle Eastern ventures, and as Hammer increasingly campaigned for the Nobel Peace Prize, Glazer became
more vocal on his behalf.[56]

For example, after a favorable profile of Hammer in the *Los Angeles
Times,* one Joseph Ribakoff wrote to the editor and criticized Hammer's apparent failure to help with individual dissident Soviet Jews.
The letter carried extra significance because of Ribakoff's position as
executive director of the Southern California Council for Soviet Jews.
Springing to the defense, Glazer replied that Hammer gave priority
"to the countless requests we make of him to aid us in securing exit

visas for Jews who wish to leave the Soviet Union. Dr. Hammer is highly respected in the Soviet Union, and he does not hesitate to go right to the top in matters concerning Soviet Jews." After a separate controversy spawned by a *Jerusalem Post* article, Glazer wrote that Hammer had visited Israel many times incognito (where he stayed at the homes of Golda Meir and Moshe Dayan), had contributed to the United Jewish Appeal, had given $600,000 to Tel Aviv University and raised another $1 million for it.[57] This was news to most observers of Hammer.

Neal Sandler, reporting from the Middle East for *Business Week,* picked up on the rumors of Hammer's investment in oil exploration, noting that

> the Israelis believe that major oil companies and oil equipment suppliers have shied away from Israeli prospecting . . . because of pressure from Arab oil-producing countries. . . . Negotiations between Hammer and the Israelis had been hush hush until he mentioned them in Los Angeles. After Hammer visited Israel in mid-September to open his art collection, General Ariel Sharon, former defense minister and now industry and trade minister, took time out from his libel suit against *Time* magazine to fly to Los Angeles to talk with him about Israeli development projects. Longtime Hammer watchers are puzzled by the apparent switch in his allegiances.[58]

Israelis were pleased to have Hammer's name and money behind one of their first serious efforts to achieve energy independence. Hammer's investment vehicle was not Occidental Petroleum, because of the problems that could have caused for the company in Arab nations. Instead, he invested privately, acting on encouraging assessments from Occidental geologists. Hammer claimed credit for raising $12 million from friends, supplemented by $2 million from private Israeli sources and $4 million from the Israeli government. The resulting partnership used the name Isramco; it announced a $20 million oil and gas exploration program covering three million acres. Hammer told *Los Angeles Times* correspondent Dan Fisher in Jerusalem that "I am determined to find oil for Israel. I think when the Lord put oil in the world, he did not mean to keep it from Israel and give it all to the Arabs."[59]

Despite Hammer's investments, philanthropy, and diplomacy on behalf of Israel, his identification with Judaism was known to only a limited audience until a dramatic event in 1986 — the release of David Goldfarb by the Soviet Union. Goldfarb, a war hero and eminent scientist, had been denied permission to emigrate for years. He was diabetic, blind, and an amputee. The Soviets put forth their reasons for the denial, but human rights activists rejected the explanations, believing it was another case of Soviet discrimination against Jews.

In 1983, Joseph Ribakoff had criticized Hammer for his inaction on emigration cases, including Goldfarb's. Guilford Glazer's assurances seemed hollow. If Hammer was doing so much behind the scenes, why was he uncharacteristically refusing credit? Whatever the answer, in the Goldfarb case Hammer was spurred to effective action by Alex Goldfarb, David's son, who had left Russia in 1975. In one of life's ironies, Alex became a microbiology professor at Columbia University, Hammer's alma mater, where his office building had been underwritten by a $5 million donation from Hammer and named for Armand and his father, Julius.[60]

Alex's mother, Cecilia, who had remained in the Soviet Union, had suggested contacting Hammer as a desperation measure; unless somebody helped, David Goldfarb appeared quite likely to die in a Moscow hospital. Accordingly, Alex tried to reach Hammer by letter and telephone but was unable to get through. So he tried his court of last resort — the media. The *Wall Street Journal* published an editorial-page plea to Hammer in July 1986.[61]

The strategy worked. Whether Hammer truly was moved, feared public embarrassment, or saw a chance to bolster his campaign for the Nobel Peace Prize, he acted. Alex received a call that same day. Hammer promised to help but provided no details about how he planned to proceed. The next day, Richard Jacobs, Hammer's executive assistant, told Alex that Occidental would handle all media inquiries. Alex was to say nothing except to confirm that he and Hammer had talked.[62]

For weeks Alex heard nothing else. He decided that Hammer had never intended to provide assistance and gave up on him. Hammer has said he had no chance to argue the case until a meeting in Moscow with Anatoly Dobrynin, one month after publication of Goldfarb's plea in the *Wall Street Journal*. In any case, Hammer called Alex again, saying there was reason for hope; just be patient. Soon thereafter, Secretary of State Shultz announced the upcoming emigration of several Soviet Jews. Alex's hopes rose, only to be dashed when David Goldfarb's name was not on the list. Again, Alex gave up on Hammer. Instead, he traveled to the Reagan-Gorbachev summit in Iceland himself to plead his father's case to anybody who would listen — vainly, it turned out. He returned to New York on October 14, 1986, empty-handed.[63]

On October 16, Hammer called Alex from OXY-1, high over Russia. Incredulous, Alex heard that David and Cecilia were on board, sipping champagne and watching the movie *My Fair Lady*. Next, Alex received a call from William McSweeny, the head of Hammer's Washington office, saying a limousine would pick him up to take him to Newark Airport to meet his parents. Alex was speechless with disbelief and elation. So were the Goldfarbs, riding in luxury on OXY-1. To be on the flight himself, Hammer had canceled an appearance in Kiev, where he was supposed to open his art collection at a local museum.[64]

That same night in Kiev, American singer John Denver was performing in a benefit arranged by Hammer for victims of the nuclear power plant disaster at Chernobyl earlier in the year. But the Goldfarb mission took precedence, for humanitarian and publicity reasons. So Hammer had called Robert Gale, a Los Angeles physician who had traveled to Moscow with him to study Chernobyl's aftermath, and told him to fly with Denver to Kiev on an Occidental backup plane. The Goldfarb mission was so secret that Hammer said nothing about the reason for the change in plans. It was only when Gale flew out of the Soviet Union several days later that he read about Goldfarb.[65]

As David Goldfarb told it later, he had started receiving improved hospital care in September 1986 because of unspecified orders from the highest levels of the Kremlin. A pleased but puzzled Goldfarb said the pieces began to fit only when he read in the Soviet press about a meeting between Hammer and Dobrynin:

> After the president and the secretary of state, Armand Hammer is the best-known American in Russia, the mysterious foreigner who mingles with the top members of the Soviet hierarchy. . . . After a lifetime's experience with proper political evaluations, I still would be at a loss if asked to give a Marxist assessment of Armand Hammer. Is he the friendliest of our adversaries or the most independent of our friends? Whichever is true, his status in Moscow is unique. In the subculture of Moscow refuseniks, Dr. Hammer's visits were watched with special attention. Each time he appeared in the news together with Soviet leaders, we wondered whether somebody's release had been negotiated behind the scenes.[66]

This time it was Goldfarb's turn. He received two hours' notice that Hammer would be arriving at the hospital. Hammer's first words were "Dr. Goldfarb, I want to take you to New York tomorrow." When Goldfarb replied he would not leave without his wife, Hammer went to see Mrs. Goldfarb at her apartment, persuading her to leave her native land on the very next day. The publicity was immense. Alex Goldfarb had not been the only recipient of a telephone call from OXY-1. Journalists, including the editor of the *Wall Street Journal,* received midair calls as well. Quickly, Hammer was awash in praise.[67]

When David Goldfarb landed at Newark, one of the people who greeted him was his friend Nicholas Daniloff, who earlier in the year had been arrested in the Soviet Union by the KGB, jailed, questioned, and finally released — but not before the case became an international cause célèbre that involved Hammer. Daniloff, a Moscow correspondent for *U.S. News & World Report,* barely knew Hammer, although he had written articles about Occidental's Soviet ventures and knew members of Hammer's Washington staff. Daniloff knew David Goldfarb well; they had developed a professional relationship, then become friends. Soviet intelligence agents had approached Goldfarb about framing Daniloff as a spy, with the implicit promise that cooperation could mean approval of his emigration request. Goldfarb had refused to participate in the plan. Five days after Alex Goldfarb's open letter to Hammer appeared in the *Wall Street Journal,* Daniloff also had written Hammer, asking him to intervene on David Goldfarb's behalf.[68]

Unbeknown to Daniloff, at the same time the KGB was plotting to frame him, without Goldfarb's help. The KGB carried out its plan, using a different decoy, and arrested Daniloff. Hammer did nothing but observe at first: He happened to be in Moscow when the arrest became public knowledge but failed to realize its overarching significance right away. It seemed like yet another trumped-up charge by the Soviets in retaliation for the U.S. government's arrest of an alleged Soviet spy in New York the week before. The Soviet media gave little attention to the Daniloff case, so Hammer simply was not focusing on it during his previously scheduled discussions with Soviet leaders.

He decided to become involved in the Daniloff affair only after it was obvious the incident indeed was important, that in fact it was imperiling the Reagan-Gorbachev summit scheduled for Iceland. Since Hammer had political, diplomatic, and emotional capital invested in that summit's taking place, he inserted himself into the Daniloff negotiations. After all, the Daniloff case had parallels to the F. Jay Crawford case of eight years earlier, and Hammer had helped reach a resolution there.

Hammer began by keeping a low profile, figuring if his intervention failed to help free Daniloff, almost nobody would be the wiser. Hammer wrote a compromise plan, then called Anatoly Dobrynin at his country home outside Moscow. Dobrynin promised to present the plan to Gorbachev. Simultaneously, Hammer proposed to his own government that he and Deputy Secretary of State John Whitehead travel to Moscow to negotiate personally with Gorbachev. The White House opposed the plan, however, preferring to stick to its original position on Daniloff's release: no deals, just release him. Hammer was told to stop interfering. He did that quietly for two weeks. Then word leaked.[69]

When the Soviets released Daniloff after a month of detention, Hammer received scant mention for his role. To rectify that, he supplied his own account to a national audience. *Life* correspondent Marie-Claude Wrenn recorded and then edited interviews with Hammer, wrote the article in the form of his own journal, and cleared it with him. According to Hammer's retrospective account, he told President Reagan at a White House reception three weeks after Daniloff's arrest, "I am going to Moscow to see if I can help," and the president replied: "I wish you well." Whitehead has said Reagan simply was being courteous, although Hammer apparently interpreted the remark as permission to get involved. The next day, Hammer met with the Soviet ambassador and the Soviet representative to the UN in New York, entering through the back door of the mission to avoid being noticed by journalists. Then Hammer jetted to Moscow to see Dobrynin, who set the table in his office with cookies because he knew how much Hammer loved sweets.[70]

After talking with Dobrynin, Hammer drafted a letter to Gorbachev in Occidental's Moscow office, staying up almost all night despite the rigorous demands of the past two days on his eighty-eight-year-old body. Hammer told Gorbachev that if he released Daniloff, the Reagan administration probably would release Gennadi Zakharov, the accused Soviet spy. Hammer also suggested that the U.S. government might delay its order to expel twenty-five Soviet UN employees suspected of spying. Dobrynin delivered the letter to Gorbachev, calling Hammer the next day to express the Soviet leader's appreciation. "Where does Hammer get his energy?" Gorbachev reportedly had inquired of Dobrynin. In his account of the Daniloff affair, Hammer stopped short of claiming full credit, but his words shouted for the interpretation that he was vital to the happy ending. Daniloff himself was uncertain, saying Hammer might have exaggerated his role, but he added, "I am grateful to Armand Hammer, don't get me wrong."[71]

Hammer soon strengthened his image as the savior of Soviet prisoners and refuseniks with the release of Ida Nudel. She had been trying to leave Russia for seventeen years. Politicians, movie stars, and human rights activists had worked hard for her release. During that time, Hammer's name never appeared on the list of crusaders, although he later said he had started working on the case years earlier. One thing was certain: When Nudel arrived in Israel during October 1987, it was on OXY-1, accompanied by Hammer. He told reporters he had raised the issue of her release successfully after Gorbachev requested his help with the Afghanistan quagmire. On Nudel's first day in Israel, she and Hammer visited the reclusive Menachem Begin at his home. Whatever the circumstances of Hammer's involvement, Nudel was grateful to him. She later appeared at a Los Angeles dinner in his honor. Myrna Shinbaum, at the National Conference on Soviet Jewry, was unsure why the Soviets gave Hammer credit by placing Nudel on his plane. Maybe Hammer had been the deciding factor, maybe not: "We know who brought her out, but we do not know who got her out."[72]

Hammer inserted himself into other emigration tangles that had defied resolution by others for years. One such case was that of Abe Stolar, an elderly Soviet resident with American citizenship. He had moved with his parents from Chicago to Russia in 1931; when he requested permission to leave in 1974, the Soviets refused to allow his Russian wife to go with him. Stolar called on Senator Paul Simon, an Illinois Democrat, who in turn requested Hammer's help. Hammer wrote to Soviet ambassador Yuri Dubinin, who responded positively (although Stolar would not be released until 1989). Hammer also helped Inessa Weintraub obtain freedom from the Soviet Union for her brother Naum Kogan and his family. Representative Bill Lowery of California said Hammer served as "a back channel" to the Kremlin during negotiations.[73]

Hammer gained further acclaim from world Jewry by intervening in the case of John Demjanjuk, who had been extradited by the United States to Israel to stand trial on charges of Nazi war crimes. To aid its prosecution, the Israeli government needed the World War II identification card of Demjanjuk, who had served as a Ukrainian soldier before his capture by the Nazis — for whom he allegedly put Jews to death. The Soviet Union had refused to deliver the identification card to Israel because the nations did not have diplomatic relations with each other. But the Soviets agreed to lend the card to Hammer for use in the case, telling him to return it when the Israeli government no longer needed it. Demjanjuk's lawyers were furious; they claimed the card was a forgery, noting that "Hammer has for seventy years been a known collaborator with the notorious KGB." Demjanjuk asked the Israeli court to hear testimony from Count Nikolai Tolstoy, a descendant of the famous novelist, who as a devoted anti-Communist had developed a visceral hatred of Hammer. The Israeli court refused to allow Hammer's character to be put on trial. Demjanjuk was found guilty.[74]

Ray Errol Fox, a Manhattan-based writer, watched Hammer enhance a reputation as a demigod in Israel. Hammer played host to Fox's acquaintance Tel Aviv mayor Shlomo Lahat in Occidental's Los Angeles dining room. Present were twenty guests, a veritable who's who of Los Angeles. Lahat described the need for a spot in his city where Arabs and Jews could meet and perhaps get to know each other better. Fox reported that Hammer, between dessert and coffee, "bemusedly supervised the raising of a prerequisite $1.6 million in seed money toward the construction of the Armand Hammer–Guilford Glazer Arab-Jewish Community Center" in a Tel Aviv neighborhood. Later, Fox traveled with Hammer in Israel, where there were ninetieth-birthday celebrations planned for the citizen-diplomat. Within hours after his arrival, Hammer attended a four-hour performance of an opera. At each intermission, younger members of his retinue left to get some sleep. Not Hammer — he stayed until the end, chatting with Israeli president Chaim Herzog and other admirers during the breaks.[75]

Such diplomatic coups by Hammer, as a bridge between hostile nations, were enough to make the mind reel. But the greatest goodwill gesture of all was still to run its course.

24

Hero of the Soviet People

NOTHING ELSE that Armand Hammer had attempted in the diplomatic realm was as dramatic, and as meaningful to so many people so quickly, as his role in the nuclear disaster at Chernobyl. Hammer saw it as his life coming full circle, from his medical aid to Russia as a young doctor in 1921 to another mission of mercy there sixty-five years later.

After hearing about the disaster at Chernobyl, about fifty miles northwest of Kiev, Hammer almost certainly would have taken the initiative to try to help. But before he could act on his own, he received a call from Dr. Robert Gale, a University of California–Los Angeles bone marrow transplant specialist.

Gale had met Hammer by chance eight years earlier in Russia, where he was vacationing after a Moscow medical conference. The hotel where he had planned to stay in Odessa was in turmoil when he arrived. Dozens of guests had been thrown out of their rooms because an American dignitary and his entourage had shown up unexpectedly. The dignitary turned out to be Hammer. Gale saw him in the hotel restaurant and introduced himself as a fellow Angeleno and fellow physician. They became better acquainted in 1984, when Hammer asked Gale to fly with him to Israel to inspect a hospital seeking money from Hammer's foundation. Gale replied that his passport was tied up at the Chinese consulate in San Francisco, which was studying a visa request. Hammer said not to worry. A day later, Gale received an emergency passport.[1]

When Gale called Hammer on April 29, 1986, his intention was to help the Chernobyl victims through the International Bone Marrow

Transplant Registry. For this he needed permission from Soviet authorities, since their country had not joined the registry. "I tried to think who in the world could help me get a message to Mr. Gorbachev of our offer to help. Because no matter how good our intentions might be, we really had to deliver it to the right person. And it became immediately clear to me that we could not really achieve anything without the help of Armand Hammer." Gale reached Hammer at the plush Madison Hotel in Washington, where he was staying while attending an opening of paintings from the Soviet Union at the National Gallery of Art. Gale's idea struck a chord in Hammer, who reportedly discussed it with four senators and the State Department, then cabled Gorbachev.[2]

The answer was quick — permission granted for Gale to enter the Soviet Union. The Kremlin had rejected a U.S. government offer of assistance, but Soviet authorities knew they could count on Hammer to refrain from using the disaster for propaganda purposes in the international court of public opinion. Hammer arranged for Gale and his team of specialists to enter Russia and to bring in sophisticated equipment gathered from all over the world on short notice, at Hammer's expense.[3] It was a near-miraculous airlift. As usual, Hammer's subordinates never asked how to get it done. They knew better. When he gave an order, the proper response was to work day and night making seemingly outrageous demands until everything fell into place.

After arriving in Russia, Gale was on the telephone regularly to Hammer's executive assistant Richard Jacobs. They discussed needs ranging from fresh bagels (so the doctors could eat quick, palatable lunches in the Russian hospital between surgeries) to technologically advanced equipment costing hundreds of thousands of dollars. Jacobs arranged for all of it to reach Gale. Another facilitator was Mikhail Bruk, Hammer's mysterious Moscow representative. As Gale noted, Bruk "was variously identified as a KGB official, a high-ranking member of the Soviet Army, a higher-ranking member of the Communist Party, and just about anything else good or bad people could think of. Ask Bruk what his job was, and he would say he was an editor for Novosti Press. What he edited, I do not know. But he was very well connected. . . . Whether he was paid by Occidental Petroleum or the Soviet government, I do not know and doubt I could find out."[4]

Two weeks after Gale's arrival in Moscow, Hammer was on his way to see the rescue effort for himself. Coincidentally, he had scheduled the trip before the Chernobyl tragedy in order to open his art collection in Moscow; the timing could not have been better to reap maximum

publicity. OXY-1 left Los Angeles filled with medical supplies as journalists swarmed around Hammer at the airport. On arrival, Hammer
insisted on visiting Hospital Number Six right away. The Soviet authorities said no. They preferred to avoid the publicity about the disaster that such a visit would mean. They also worried about the strain
on the elderly Hammer, not to mention the health hazards.[5]

The resulting negotiations between a stubborn government and an
even more stubborn Hammer were almost comical. Hammer finally
told Soviet officials he would camp outside the hospital until admitted
inside. "And he would have," Gale commented.[6] Characteristically,
Hammer went to the top when he failed to achieve what he wanted
from midlevel bureaucrats. After appealing to Anatoly Dobrynin, he
received permission to enter. The tour lasted thirty minutes. Hammer,
saying he was moved beyond words by the sight of the dying Chernobyl victims, decided to make a gift of the doctors' efforts and the massive imported supplies. That meant the Soviets would not have to spend
their scarce Western currency. It was a goodwill gesture meant to
counteract attempts by Western governments to capitalize on the accident for propaganda purposes. Hammer used his announcement as a
platform from which to spread his views on the importance of world
peace. If governments were unable to cope with treating several hundred
victims of a reactor malfunction, how could they hope to handle the
casualties from a neutron bomb? he asked.

As Gale and Hammer were holding a joint news conference, a call
came from the foreign ministry. Would Hammer meet later that day
with Mikhail Gorbachev? Gale could come, too. Hammer was thrilled.
Dobrynin escorted them to the Kremlin.

Despite all Hammer's previous meetings with world leaders, each
new opportunity validated his hard-won image as a man deserving
respect. As always, he was impressed with the leader of the Soviet
people. The phrases he used on this occasion could have been substituted for his evaluations of Leonid Brezhnev or Konstantin Chernenko; Gorbachev was "tough but frank and candid and very outgoing." Also in typical fashion, Hammer discussed his agenda for peace,
suggesting that Gorbachev cite Chernobyl as a reason for a second summit with Reagan. To the delight of the human rights advocates, his
onetime critics, Hammer brought up the matter of Jewish emigration.
Later, he suggested that his persuasiveness at the meeting had led to
exit visas for 117 members of divided families, about one third of them
Jewish. As Gale remarked, "I realized that this was not simply a congratulatory meeting where someone gives you a tie clip and an autograph. This was a diplomatic exchange at a fairly high level."[7]

Hammer left Moscow soon after the Gorbachev meeting, returning to Los Angeles for his gala eighty-eighth birthday party. Gale accompanied him, taking a rest from nearly three weeks of exhausting surgery. As the American heroes departed, Soviets showered them with gratitude. The Soviet doctors who had worked alongside Gale embraced him as their eyes welled with tears. *Pravda* praised Hammer, contrasting him with his fellow countrymen who cruelly used Chernobyl as a vehicle for anti-Soviet statements.[8]

In his own country, Hammer received accolades just as lavish. Charlotte Curtis of the *New York Times* wrote a column praising his humanitarianism. Hammer encouraged the praise by announcing he had spent $600,000 on the Chernobyl effort.[9] A few detractors asked prickly questions, like whether that money had come from Occidental's treasury, but they were very few and Hammer ignored them. The Occidental board of directors supported such uses of company funds with the theory that Hammer represented the corporation in the minds of the public, so anything reflecting positively on him helped Occidental's image.

After a heroes' welcome in Los Angeles, Hammer and Gale boarded OXY-1 for Washington, where an Occidental limousine met them at the airport and whisked them to the Madison Hotel. The next day, Gale accompanied Hammer to a meeting with Secretary of State George Shultz. After some three-way talk, Gale was ushered outside while Hammer and Shultz met privately for thirty minutes. President Ronald Reagan, on the other hand, did not receive Hammer and Gale, despite an apparent recommendation from Shultz that he do so. Hammer attributed the snub to a feud between Shultz and National Security Adviser John Poindexter. What Hammer perhaps failed to realize was that he himself was the issue, that many presidential advisers considered him a Soviet agent and a shameless self-promoter.

Hammer bounced back quickly from his disappointment at the Reagan rejection; he found ways to keep his name in the headlines because of Chernobyl. Occidental issued a news release that he and Gale were winging back to the Soviet Union to implement a long-term study of Chernobyl's effects. The formal mechanism would be called the Armand Hammer Center for Advanced Studies in Nuclear Energy and Health. The Gales' three children traveled with their father, mother, and Hammer. Elan, the two-year-old, "developed the habit of kicking Hammer in the shins when he wanted attention," according to Gale. "Hammer was gracious about the whole thing, and said Elan would do very well in life because he knew how to make his desires known."[10]

Upon arriving in Moscow, Hammer made sure there would be op-

portunities for journalists to write about the visit. He announced another tour to the hospital where Gale had performed his operations, as
well as a visit to Kiev, where some bone marrow transplant recipients
were convalescing. Since Kiev was so close to Chernobyl, Hammer obtained permission for himself, Gale, and photographer John Bryson —
chronicling the tycoon's every publicity offensive — to view the disaster
site from a helicopter. Afterward, Hammer reflected, "I thought to
myself, we have about twelve thousand nuclear warheads and the Russians have ten thousand. If one explosion could do this amount of damage, what would happen if these missiles got out of control?" Hammer
combined the medical mission with the opening of his art collection in
Novosibirsk. All the gestures solidified his relationship with Gorbachev, who knew a useful conduit to the West when he saw one.[11]

Aided by his help at Chernobyl, Hammer maintained his amazing
access to Soviet officialdom. At the December 1987 Reagan-Gorbachev
summit, in Washington, he seemed to be omnipresent, the only person
without official status on the published guest lists for both the White
House and the Soviet state dinners. The National Gallery of Art staff,
working overtime to plan for a visit by Raisa Gorbachev, wondered
when the inevitable call from Hammer would come. He was a large
contributor, demanding recognition on his terms. Sure enough, the day
before Mrs. Gorbachev's arrival, Hammer's office phoned to say he
would give the Soviet First Lady a tour of his art in the gallery. That
meant rearranging the minute-by-minute plans. To complicate matters
the next day, Mrs. Gorbachev was running behind schedule. It was a
hurried tour, but as Mrs. Gorbachev was about to leave the museum,
Hammer rushed in — with television personality Barbara Walters in
tow. Hammer took Mrs. Gorbachev by the arm and guided her around
his collection as reporters and photographers followed.[12]

During the May 1988 summit, in Moscow, Hammer was in the news
again, as the only Western "special guest" of the Soviets. The official
magazine *Soviet Life* pictured him chatting and laughing with Reagan
and Gorbachev. When Gorbachev visited New York several months
afterward, he found time to discuss diplomacy with Hammer despite a
demanding official schedule. A few days later, Hammer was on his
way to earthquake-ravaged Armenia with a reported $1 million in
medical supplies. Hammer and Gorbachev seemed to be so close that
Walter Scott's "Personality Parade" column, from *Parade* magazine,
received a letter from a reader in California asking whether the Soviet
leader was the tycoon's illegitimate son.[13]

Perhaps one reason Hammer kept working so hard at his relationship with the Soviet Union as he passed ninety was the whispering that he might be losing his preferred position among the Soviet leadership to Dwayne Andreas, chief executive of Archer-Daniels-Midland, an agribusiness conglomerate. Journalists seemed to be promoting a competition between the two men. It made for good copy. The *Wall Street Journal,* in a widely read front-page story, emphasized Andreas's ability to discuss agriculture with Gorbachev in depth, unlike Hammer. Reporter Mark D'Anastasio wrote that at a December 1985 Kremlin reception for U.S. business leaders, "the moment Mr. Gorbachev spied Mr. Andreas, he sped across the polished agate jasper floor, past Dr. Hammer and others, and asked the grain and oil seed magnate to sit with him at dinner."[14]

The *New Yorker* heightened the perception of rivalry with a profile of Andreas, which noted that a recent Gorbachev biography had contained more references to Andreas than to Hammer. Andreas tried to discourage the comparisons, saying Hammer had been "criticized a lot for getting involved in so many things with the Russians, but I think he does great work. I try to stick to my knitting. My role is strictly one of trade and business, and that is enough for me." John Chrystal, a Des Moines banker and citizen-diplomat in American-Soviet affairs, questioned the validity of the comparison. He said Hammer's "main motive seems to be headlines, while Andreas's seems to be more profit-oriented."[15]

Without question, Andreas's influence was narrower. Americans of all sorts approached Hammer when they hoped for hard-to-win favors from the Soviet Union. Louisiana State University basketball coach Dale Brown wanted to recruit seven-foot-three Soviet star Arvidas Sabonis but knew the Kremlin would oppose losing a sports hero. A Baton Rouge friend suggested that Brown contact Hammer. Brown, flamboyant and well connected, nonetheless hesitated about approaching so august a figure. He called Senator Russell Long and religious leaders Robert Schuller and Norman Vincent Peale, all known to have ties to Hammer. Hammer received Brown's message, contacted him, and agreed to cable Gorbachev about the situation. Then Hammer offered Brown the use of Occidental's Moscow office when the coach made his recruiting trip. Once in Russia, Brown was "amazed at doors that opened because of Armand Hammer. Everybody knows him, even the cab drivers. I'll bet he's more popular there than any U.S. president."[16]

When Los Angeles ear surgeon Howard House wanted to visit Soviet hospitals in 1987, he asked Hammer for help in arranging the trip.

Hammer was glad to do it for his physician friend. The trip was going nicely until House reached Leningrad, where he suffered a heart attack. His traveling companion, worried about care for House in a foreign land, roused Hammer at 1:00 A.M. in Los Angeles. Without hesitating, Hammer made calls that resulted in an examination of House by top Soviet cardiologist Andrei Pulatov. The Soviet physician noticed House was carrying a copy of Hammer's recently published autobiography and looked at it longingly. House presented it to Pulatov as a gift: "You would have thought I had given him the hospital, he was so pleased." When a vastly improved House returned to Los Angeles, he received a fresh, autographed copy of the book from Hammer.[17]

Often Hammer did not wait to be asked for help. His commitment to peace combined with his incessant need for recognition led to such trips as the one to Bonn and East Berlin during September 1987. He had been fretting that delayed destruction of U.S.-controlled warheads on West German missiles might sabotage Soviet-American arms-reduction talks. West German chancellor Helmut Kohl received Hammer for a private meeting, after which Hammer crossed the Iron Curtain to meet East German leader Erich Honecker. Then Hammer talked by telephone with Dobrynin in Moscow about the discussions.[18] Such unfettered access to all those capitals would have been unthinkable for any other private citizen.

The consensus was overwhelming, among Hammer's admirers and detractors alike, about the unprecedented nature of his seventy-year involvement with the Soviet Union. Authors Gale Warner and Michael Shuman chose Hammer as one of nine citizen-diplomats profiled in their book. He was the only one of the nine to decline an interview, apparently because of recent unhappy experiences with writers. They pressed ahead anyway. Their profile concluded that

> Hammer's what is good for Occidental is good for the world philosophy sets him apart from other citizen diplomats whose primary motivation is creating peace. Yet his accomplishments — his steadfast advocacy of East-West trade, his art exchanges, his aid to Chernobyl victims, and his role as a personal liaison between world leaders — have merit independent of his motivations. Historians may someday conclude that Hammer has done the right things in Soviet-American relations for the wrong reasons. But his legacy of right things may remain long after the reasons have faded.[19]

Retired senator J. William Fulbright, formerly chairman of the Foreign Relations Committee, said Hammer is "one of the very few people in this country who keep doors open to the Soviet Union when our blind, inept government considers that nation beyond the pale. Armand Hammer might make the Soviets feel that what our government says in its blindness is not the last word. The psychological element of international relations is extremely important; it colors everything else."[20]

Gorbachev has stated that "it is always a pleasure to meet Dr. Armand Hammer. He does much to promote understanding and friendly contacts between our two countries."[21]

For Hammer's ninetieth birthday, Soviet television aired a one-hour documentary about his life, the ultimate gift for somebody so image-conscious.

Hammer in China

ARMAND HAMMER had unmatchable ties to the Soviet Union.
He eventually could make the same claim about his connections
with the People's Republic of China, even though he did not start cultivating the leaders of the world's most populous country until he was
past eighty. Hammer began his rapid climb to the top of citizen diplomacy with China on February 2, 1979, as Deng Xiaoping visited Houston for a barbecue during a tour of the United States.

Before Deng's visit, Occidental Petroleum's only link with China
had been forged through sales there by its subsidiary International Ore
and Fertilizer Company. But Hammer had grander designs. China was
rich in coal; another Occidental subsidiary, Island Creek, possessed advanced technology that the Chinese might find attractive. Albert Gore,
whom Hammer had hired to run the coal subsidiary after his departure
from the Senate, helped plan a major incursion into the Chinese market. The time was right. The United States and China had just up-
graded their diplomatic relations; an era of good feeling had begun.[1]

The immediate problem was getting Deng's attention, because Hammer had not been invited to meet him. As he explained later, "This
was a much celebrated visit of which the Carter administration was
justifiably quite proud. Because of my long history of relations with the
Soviet Union, the State Department did not want me to meet Mr.
Deng."[2] But Hammer's prominence, connections, and gifts to President
Jimmy Carter led Robert Strauss, a Democratic power broker serving
as Carter's special trade representative, to promise Hammer tickets.

However, when Armand and Frances arrived at the Houston arena,
their names were nowhere to be found on the Secret Service list. Ham-

mer has said that he suspected a plot by Zbigniew Brzezinski, Carter's Hammer-hating national security adviser, and asked to see the list. Scanning it, he noticed the name Robert McGee. A person by that name was an executive in Hammer's Washington office, the son of a senator. Hammer has said he told the list's custodian that McGee had arranged for the tickets; his name must have been included by mistake in place of Hammer's.

The Secret Service let Armand and Frances through. According to Hammer, they proceeded to "their" table, where they introduced themselves to a couple already there — Mr. and Mrs. Robert McGee, no relation to the Occidental executive. Undaunted, by his own account, Hammer excused himself from the table to enter the receiving line for Deng. He related what happened next: "When I was introduced to him [Deng], he said, 'I know about you. You were a friend of Lenin. We want you to come to China to help us the way you have helped Russia.' I replied, 'I will be glad to come if you let me land in my own plane.' He said, 'It can be arranged.'" Robert Strauss has said it happened differently from Hammer's oft-repeated version. Hammer's name was omitted from the Secret Service list through a simple snafu. Strauss said he took care of the misunderstanding on the spot, then escorted Hammer to sit with Deng. "Dr. Hammer clearly captivated Deng," Strauss said. "I turned to somebody and said 'in a few minutes they'll be friends.'" Strauss said he has scolded Hammer for telling the embellished tale, but Hammer keeps relating it his own way.[3]

Within weeks, Hammer received unprecedented permission to arrive in China in his private jet. With him were Occidental energy and agriculture experts ready to negotiate deals. The most ambitious involved a coal mine. Hammer knew the China Coal Society had sent a nineteen-person delegation to America. Its hope was to double Chinese coal production within a decade. In exchange, James Schlesinger, Carter's energy secretary, had visited China and had heard of the government's interest in working with American coal companies. It was no secret that the Chinese wanted to develop a mine in the coal-rich Pingshuo region of Shanxi Province, approximately three hundred miles west of Beijing.[4]

Other coal companies believed they had nothing to fear from Occidental. But they were wrong, then and later, when they failed to realize how much progress Hammer made.[5] He signed agreements to participate in South China Sea and South Yellow Sea oil explorations, to work with China on developing hybrid cotton and hybrid rice, and to export coal. As was so often the case in Hammer's dealing with the

Soviet Union, the signings with the Chinese were only agreements to agree. But they were an important beginning. It was a diverse, imaginative package that probably only Hammer would have devised.

Richard Chen, an interpreter at Hammer's early meetings with Chinese officials, later became a top Occidental executive. He recalled how during Hammer's first visit to China, an energy minister commented, "In the past three days, Dr. Hammer met with the leaderships of our eight ministries. He has broken all records of foreign friends doing business with China. We are impressed by his energy, efficiency, enthusiasm, and dedication."[6]

A banquet for the Occidental delegation on its first night in Beijing began with nine appetizers, which Chen recognized as a good omen — in China, the number nine signifies supremacy. At such an early stage of the negotiations, Hammer chose to keep quiet, although he could not contain himself when he returned to Los Angeles for Occidental's annual meeting. He waxed enthusiastic about Deng Xiaoping. He told stockholders in general terms about the promise of China trade. In a tone that some observers interpreted as braggartly, he said he had engineered the sale of fifty thousand tons of Russian urea to China, the Soviet Union's arch rival.[7]

Hammer's next sleight of hand came two weeks after the annual meeting, when Chinese vice premier Kang Shien visited the United States. Waiting for Kang was a detailed schedule of his trip, covering fourteen cities. Kang and his delegation would be guests at numerous receptions paid for by U.S. Steel, Amoco, Exxon, Pennzoil, Texaco, Amax, and Arco. Occidental had not been included, and Hammer was angry about it. The schedule, which had been carefully arranged over several months, showed the evening of June 3 to be one of the few unplanned segments of the trip. On that day Kang's delegation would fly from New Orleans to Houston after touring an offshore oil platform, proceeding to the Whitehall Hotel for an informal, unsponsored dinner.

So federal officials and those of the National Council for United States–China Trade accompanying Kang were surprised, on arriving in Houston, to receive an engraved invitation. It read: "Dr. Armand Hammer . . . requests the pleasure of your company at a reception and dinner in honor of his excellency Kang Shien . . . the third of June at half after six o'clock, the Concourse Rooms, Whitehall Hotel." At the elaborate meal, Hammer gave an interminable speech from the head table, stressing his decades of accomplishments and how much he could do for the Chinese. But what members of the audience recalled years later was their wonderment at how he had worked the dinner into the schedule. To this day they remain unsure, but they have an idea — Richard Chen, listed as the State Department's interpreter for Kang's delegation, quietly arranged the dinner at Hammer's behest.[8]

Throughout the remainder of 1979 and into 1980, almost nothing appeared in print about Hammer's China dealings. If competitors had been worried at all, they relaxed. As always when dealing with Hammer, that was a mistake. He was building bridges. One clue came in mid-1980, when the *China Business Review* reported that China was on the verge of helping feed the world's starving hordes, with assistance from Ring Around Products, Occidental's seed division. The company's researchers in conjunction with Chinese scientists were developing ways to mass-produce and distribute

> Chinese hybrid rice seeds, with a per hectare yield reportedly twenty percent higher than that currently achieved by any other seed varieties. Ring Around's seventeen-year licensing agreement grants it exclusive rights to market Chinese hybrid rice in five countries — the United States, Brazil, Italy, Spain, and Portugal. . . . Ring Around has not disclosed the potential worth of the agreement, but has compared the Chinese invention to the effect of corn hybrid technology on its output and commercial value over the last twenty-five years. . . . The conclusion of a second agreement to introduce Ring Around's recently developed hybrid corn to textile-conscious China is just around the corner, as well as a third one covering seed genetics.

It was all part of Hammer's mosaic for even bigger contracts, involving coal and oil.[9]

By mid-1981, Occidental was one of twenty-four American companies with a registered representative's office in China. Oil diplomacy seemed to be more on Hammer's mind than coal. When Hammer met Deng in Beijing, they discussed promises by the U.S. government that an Internal Revenue Service team would visit China to clear up tax questions before China opened bidding for offshore oil leases. Hammer also called on Arthur Hummel, the new American ambassador to China, whom Hammer already knew from Hummel's tour in Pakistan, where Occidental had business interests and where Hammer had practiced shuttle diplomacy after the Soviet invasion of Afghanistan. Hammer's patience paid off on the oil front. In August 1983, Occidental announced that China had awarded the company "two contract areas in the South China Sea, each area covering approximately 312,000 acres.

Our contract was the first awarded to a United States company under China's competitive bidding procedure."[10]

It soon turned out that Occidental was in the running for the Ping-shuo coal mine, too. Hammer viewed the project as the equivalent of his fertilizer deal with the Soviet Union. Nearing ninety, he figured he did not have forever to make a big impact in China. If he could become the number-one trading partner — and the coal mine would be the biggest Sino-American joint venture ever — perhaps he could influence Sino-American diplomacy as well. So, in March 1982, he surprised the coal industry and diplomats by winning permission to conduct a feasibility study on developing the world's largest open-pit mine. The Chinese government agreed to build railroads and highways to transport the coal. That commitment was important because the lack of an infrastructure had scared away larger American coal firms. The government also promised to construct a city to house seventeen thousand mine workers and their families. Occidental said it would contribute $250 million initially, with profits to be split fifty-fifty until the company recovered its investment, after which China would receive 60 percent of any profits.[11]

All of a sudden, Occidental Petroleum had the advantage, but Hammer had no intention of relaxing. To cement his special standing, he shipped his art collection to Beijing. The Armand Hammer Foundation and Occidental shared the costs.[12]

Hammer meanwhile began to build other cultural bridges. He and Hollywood producer Jerry Weintraub announced a partnership to promote entertainment exchanges with China and the Soviet Union. Entertainment-industry analysts immediately expressed doubt about the venture — the market seemed weak, and neither Hammer nor Weintraub was likely to be comfortable in a secondary role. The analysts were right about the soft market. The venture never realized a profit as far as anybody knows. They were wrong, however, about the personality clash. Hammer and Weintraub got along; in fact, Weintraub became one of the few business associates who could tell Hammer off without severing the relationship.[13]

Hammer demonstrated the same diplomatic prowess with China that he had achieved with Russia. On one occasion he sat for ninety minutes with Deng Xiaoping, afterward conveying to Washington Deng's message that China, upset about American arms sales to Taiwan, had no intention of moderating its opposition to the sales. He followed up that meeting with a letter to the Reagan White House, in which he offered to help negotiate with China on issues dividing the superpowers. When the State Department listed people who might accompany Secretary of State George Shultz to China, Hammer's name was at the top. Hammer sent Shultz a letter accompanied by sixteen news clippings about his special status with the Chinese.[14]

In the meantime, Occidental executives, contractors, subcontractors, and government trade experts were wondering how Hammer would raise the money to develop the proposed coal mine. Hammer had the answers. Although he was a government unto himself, he never hesitated to enlist the U.S. government when he thought he could benefit. So Occidental applied to the U.S. Export-Import Bank for financing help. The bank eventually approved a $28 million credit that would support $43 million of exports. The interest rate was a favorable 7.4 percent. A decade earlier, a credit to assist Occidental's Soviet fertilizer deal had unleashed a firestorm of criticism. The China credit passed nearly unnoticed.[15]

Despite Hammer's well-thought-out plan, there were delays. By summer 1983, press reports started sounding skeptical, even in the face of Hammer's reassurances. Perhaps the most pessimistic was the most widely read, appearing as it did in the *Wall Street Journal*. Datelined Beijing and written by Amanda Bennett, it said, "Four years of negotiations brought Occidental Petroleum Corporation and China close to building a major open-pit coal mine in this country. But plummeting coal prices have sent them back to the drawing board." Hammer was quoted as saying that "all costs have to be reduced" if the venture was to succeed. So, Bennett reported, "in the past several days dozens of bankers, lawyers, Coal Ministry officials and finance specialists have been huddling here, trying to save the giant project. They are poring over everything from wage rates to railway tariffs, looking for places to prune costs." Bennett paid homage to the Hammer factor:

> One big advantage this project has going for it is the fierce desire both parties have to make it work. They both have staked an enormous amount of time and prestige on it. "Occidental's top officials spend eighty percent of their time on China," marvels one observer close to the company. Dr. Hammer fancies himself a pioneer and an entrepreneur, having successfully completed many business deals in the Soviet Union and other Communist countries. The China venture could be the last hurrah for the octogenarian industrialist. China, for its part, needs a successful conclusion to the project . . . to persuade those waiting in the wings. Since Dr. Hammer is such a China booster, the reasoning goes, if China can-

not successfully conclude a deal with him, there is not much hope for others.[16]

The reports continued into 1984 that the project was in trouble. Hammer was having none of it. In March 1984, he reassured Deng that Occidental had no intention of pulling out. Hammer's contacts with Deng impressed everybody involved; the relationship helped Occidental's negotiators overcome obstacles in the Chinese bureaucracy. In a speech at the National Press Club, in Washington, Hammer said, "We are very, very close to closing our deal with China."[17]

On April 5, 1984, Occidental executive John Dorgan and Chinese officials signed an agreement that included Bank of China loan guarantees, which caused skeptics to rethink their concern about the financing. The Chinese made concessions over pay scales for miners and purchases of excess coal if Occidental failed to sell it all in export markets. Peter Kiewit Sons, a construction company based in Omaha, joined Occidental as a fifty-fifty partner. Bankers took heart at Kiewit's participation and inquired about joining a consortium of lenders.[18]

But just when the financing seemed assured, the deal went sour again. Near the end of 1984, Peter Kiewit Sons withdrew as Occidental's partner. Its reasons were vague. Ken Stinson, Kiewit's manager of business development, said, "We just could not get arrangements to our satisfaction with the [Chinese] coal ministry. . . . Occidental's financing was on a parallel track . . . the financing and the [coal ministry] negotiations were dependent on each other." With the pullout of Kiewit, a seven-bank consortium thinking of helping with the financing backed off from its $120 million letter of credit and its $40 million bridge loan. At least one bank identified with the consortium pulled out.[19]

Hammer and Deng refused to let the project fail — it had come so far despite so many obstacles. The Bank of China announced it would pick up the slack, something insiders attributed to Hammer's clout at the top. *China Daily,* a government newspaper, praised Hammer extravagantly, saying the mention of his name in the world's most populous land "is likely to trigger a train of associations in the minds of well-informed Chinese. . . . The 1982 Armand Hammer Collection exhibition remains a fresh memory; Bob Considine's *Larger Than Life* [Hammer's authorized biography, translated into Chinese] is still a reader favorite. . . . Hammer has become a living legend in Chinese business and intellectual circles."[20]

The legend prevailed. In May 1985, Hammer released the text of a communiqué signed in Beijing "securing basic agreement on the terms of a final joint-venture contract." Despite the breakthrough, there had been so many false starts that, the *International Coal Report* noted, the communiqué "was greeted with almost universal skepticism from the coal community." But much of that skepticism dissolved in June 1985, when Occidental issued a three-page news release and a three-page background sheet tied to the signing of what Hammer termed "the final joint-venture contract."[21]

George Keyworth, Reagan's science adviser, and Arthur Hummel, the U.S. ambassador, attended the ceremony at which the final contract was signed, in Beijing. Anticipating the doubters, Hammer remarked: "I guess you are wondering whether this is just another signing and there will be another. There will be no other signing. This is it." Hummel wondered, though, if there were more to the deal than met the eye. He cabled the State Department: "Both Occidental and the Chinese are keeping this very close. Few details have been allowed to leak. . . . Aside from a vague tidbit or two concerning financing and the relative position of the several participants, the Occidental representative has either given a no-comment or referred all questions to the United States office."[22]

Wall Street analysts and Occidental stockholders expressed skepticism, too, noting how many of Hammer's Communist bloc megadeals had brought attention for the doctor but seemingly little profit to the company. The United Mine Workers and congressional representatives complained about the depressing effect the mine could have on world markets for U.S. coal when Occidental began sending its Chinese output to Japan and Korea.[23]

Hammer rebutted the criticisms while he willed the mine to happen. At the end of 1986 — in a full-length mink coat and beaver hat to ward off the cold — he watched as one hundred tons of explosives detonated 240 feet below the ground at the mine site, in Shanxi Province. A trial production period followed. The Chinese government, proud of the progress under difficult conditions, devoted a large chunk of *China Pictorial* magazine to the venture, showing off the new roads to the mining site, the new railroad to haul out the coal, high-voltage electric transmission lines strung across the countryside, a river-diversion project, three apartment buildings of fourteen stories each to house workers and their families, an office building, movie theater, department store, and airport.[24]

The big dedication party took place in September 1987. Hammer flew his entourage to the mine site in the Chinese countryside — among those in that group was Abigail Van Buren, the advice columnist. At the ceremony were Winston Lord, the new U.S. ambassador, and thousands of Chinese. Hammer maintained a hectic schedule during the trip, meeting with Deng Xiaoping and other Chinese leaders not only about the coal mine, but also about how to end the Soviet occupation of Afghanistan. *Newsweek* crowned him as one of America's "twenty-five top Asia hands," a remarkable honor considering his late start in that part of the world.[25]

Problems at the coal mine continued into 1989, but the Chinese showered Hammer with honors nonetheless. When construction began on the nation's first golf course, the government named seven honorary members: five Chinese, one Japanese, and Hammer. The government magazine *China Reconstructs* devoted a full-length feature to Hammer's life, the only feature that entire year on an American industrialist. One of China's leading painters, Yao Youxin, completed portraits of Armand and Frances, which showed up in the catalog of Yao's work when Hammer Galleries mounted his exhibition. When Hammer reached ninety, Chinese president Yang Shangkun gave him a porcelain likeness of the god of longevity. Armand and Frances planted trees for peace in a hallowed Beijing garden, then used a photograph of the ceremony on their Christmas card.[26]

PART VII

THE QUEST FOR
IMMORTALITY

26

The New Medici

ARMAND HAMMER'S REPUTATION suffered virtually no
harm after four serious run-ins with the Securities and Exchange
Commission, a guilty plea in a campaign-contributions cover-up, and
diplomacy with Communist nations during various anti-Communist eras.
Part of the reason was his pervasive, highly publicized philanthropy,
including the sharing of his art collections.

Not until the second half of the 1960s did Hammer begin building
what were to become his most famous collections, far surpassing those
that he began during the 1920s in Moscow. When he did start anew,
he was a man in a hurry. Some of his newly acquired art was on
display at Hammer Galleries during the fortieth-anniversary celebration of the family business, in November 1968. Victor Hammer, who
did much of the purchasing, told a visiting reporter that Armand did
not trust him completely with money: "I would buy up every painting
I see. . . . There are so many millions [of dollars], that Armand and
Harry now have to concentrate on giving it away. Me? I am buying —
Renoirs, Monets, Utrillos, Russells, and Western art."[1]

Recognizing Armand's stature as a collector and gallery owner, the
Los Angeles County Museum of Art invited him onto its board of
trustees at about the same time that he donated a Modigliani, a Renoir,
and $1 million in cash to the institution in his adopted home city. Part
of the museum, known as the special exhibitions gallery, became the
Frances and Armand Hammer Wing. His purchases of artworks for
high prices at national and international auctions began to make headlines. His improved collection had a showing at the Brooks Memorial

Art Gallery, in Memphis, thanks to the influence of Hammer Galleries client and Occidental director Morrie Moss.[2]

By 1970, Hammer had spent millions and felt he had accomplished what the experts thought impossible — building a quality assemblage of Old Master paintings despite their scarcity on the market. Hammer was ready to take the pictures to Washington to impress the policy-makers. The occasion started off well, with a gala dinner in the Gem Hall of the Smithsonian Museum of Natural History, where the collection would be displayed. In attendance were ambassadors, senators, a Supreme Court justice, and leaders from the art world. Hammer gave each guest a chunk of his polished good-luck jade. The *Washington Post* published a flattering profile under the headline "ARMAND HAMMER: MORE PLEASURE IN GIVING."[3]

But four days later, Paul Richard, the *Post*'s new art critic, savaged the show, hinting at fakes among the paintings. The rumors refused to die, Richard said, because "never have so many major masters been represented in this city by canvasses so poor." Richard called Hammer's Goya trivial, the van Gogh ugly, and the Cézanne landscape botched up. There were first-rate paintings in the exhibition, Richard said, but they were overwhelmed by the second-rate ones. Even the greatest of artists, like other people, suffered off days on which they produced dreadful work, Richard commented, and by the time Hammer began building his collection, "masterpieces by the blue-chip painters he prefers were already hard to come by. . . . He has . . . bought sweepings, as many museum directors seem to be aware." For nearly forty paragraphs Richard continued, attacking the quality of the collection and Hammer's motives for displaying it in Washington.[4]

Devastated and furious, Hammer called *Washington Post* publisher Katharine Graham. She offered him a "Point of View" article in the news pages under his own name, an unusual practice by a major metropolitan daily. Hammer put his rebuttal on paper picture by picture. His defense was longer than Richard's article, and it was displayed just as prominently. He accused Richard of incompetence and misrepresentation. A knowledgeable art critic would have understood "that the uniqueness of the collection lies largely in the fact . . . that it shows the first thoughts of many of the great masters." Richard was astonished at the length and heat of Hammer's reply. "I am embarrassed at my lead [beginning paragraphs] today," Richard said in retrospect. "I was new at being a critic. But the story was based on solid research."[5]

Despite his angry rebuttal, Hammer took Richard's criticism to heart.

Swallowing his pride, he approached John Walker, the recently retired director of the National Gallery of Art. They knew each other slightly from their common trustee position at the Los Angeles County Museum. Walker was reluctant to help Hammer. As he strolled through the Smithsonian exhibition, he realized "that half the pictures were mediocre, a few unauthentic, but a number [were] of acceptable quality, with a scattering of masterpieces." He warned Hammer that he might recommend discarding up to half the paintings and in fact did so. As Walker commented later, Hammer "did accept my judgments, not one hundred percent as he is fond of saying, but about ninety percent. . . . I have known very few collectors as willing to recognize mistakes. With his brilliant mind, he quickly grasped why he had erred. . . . He had been a colossal bargain hunter! There is no better way to be an unsuccessful collector."[6]

Pride played a role in Hammer's drive to revamp his collection, but he had other reasons as well for his refusal to be discouraged. Walker observed that Hammer was "not like other collectors. His delight is in the quest, not the possession. None of his great paintings or drawings hang in his house. He is satisfied to live with a fine copy by Mrs. Hammer of the Modigliani portrait . . . and with a few Impressionist paintings of slight importance." After getting to know Hammer, Walker called him "the most astounding" collector in his experience, a statement that encompassed Bernard Berenson, Kenneth Clark, Andrew Mellon, and Paul Mellon, among others.[7]

The metamorphosis of the collection was amazing, as well as expensive. Hammer went on a buying spree probably unmatched in modern times. Within eighteen months, Kenneth Donahue, director of the Los Angeles County Museum, could write that

> the development of his collection from the time of its first public exhibition only two years ago is still astonishing. At that time, the collection numbered seventy-nine works, most of them European paintings and drawings from Corot to Chagall. Today the collection is almost double that number. In 1969, there were no drawings earlier than the Boudin of 1869. Today the old master drawings in the collection, including works of the rarest masters Raphael and Dürer, would do honor to a veteran connoisseur of drawings. Two years ago the collection included only one American painting, the Sargent portrait of Mrs. Edward Livingston Davis and her son; today there is a distinguished group of Americans from Gilbert Stuart to Andrew Wyeth. In the field of concentration of the collection, the nineteenth and early twentieth century, master works of

Moreau, Pissarro, Monet, Degas, Renoir, van Gogh, and Cézanne have been added.[8]

The Los Angeles County Museum showed the revamped collection at the end of 1971, to positive reviews. The show traveled to London and Dublin, then to Leningrad and Moscow. It did not stop touring until the end of 1987. Commentators looked for clues to Hammer's character in his collecting. Bernard Denvir, writing in the magazine *Art and Artists,* said,

> Here we have an enigma. . . . Unlike his predecessors, he collects paintings not for private pleasure but for public consumption. . . . They are basically peripatetic pictures charged with some mission which eludes the comprehension even of those to whom they give so much pleasure. . . . This indeed gives us a clue to one of the dominant characteristics of the collection. It has none of those quirky eccentricities of taste, none of those inexplicable lapses which so often throw an unexpected light on the personality of the owner. There is an impeccable quality about the Hammer collection which seems to transpose it from the private into the public domain. There are of course certain accents perceptible. Of the one hundred and nine paintings and drawings, some ninety are of human figures.[9]

When the lithographs of Honoré Daumier first attracted Hammer's fancy, he bought six thousand at once from George Longstreet, who had spent fifty years assembling them. Immediately, Hammer vaulted to the top of Daumier collectors. He said he wanted the public "to share in the timeless quality of Daumier's work and the universal genius of his vision. Daumier's comments on the social and political situation in nineteenth-century France are as humorous and perceptive today as they were when they were created. . . . It is his deep compassion for the human condition that has made Daumier's works the preoccupation of my collecting." When Hammer donated some of his Daumier collection to the Corcoran Gallery of Art, he noted that "it is particularly fitting that this collection should be a permanent fixture here in Washington, D.C., since the leading lights of our capital city are often the target of the political cartoonist's sometimes acerbic pen."[10]

Two particular works brought Hammer the most publicity. The first was his 1976 purchase of Rembrandt's *Juno,* for $3.25 million, nearly $1 million more than a Rembrandt ever had brought before. After its creation in about 1665, the picture had disappeared for more than two hundred years. When it emerged, it was incorrectly cataloged by a

German museum, which then sold it for about $200. When someone finally realized its provenance, the price increased dramatically. The painting changed owners four times in four decades before entering Hammer's collection. Each time, the price shot up. But Hammer did not hesitate before buying it, feeling that it was a bargain.[11]

The other attention-getting purchase came at the end of 1980, when Hammer bid at a London auction for a Leonardo da Vinci manuscript composed in mirror writing and illustrated with 360 sketches concerning water and cosmology. Lord Coke was selling it because of a tax dispute with the British government. Hammer tried to negotiate privately with the family but failed to reach an agreement. The bidding was expected to be intense; some predicted that the price might reach $14 million.

At the last minute, the Italian government pulled out of the bidding because it needed all available funds for relief in the wake of a destructive earthquake. Jack Tanzer, one of Hammer's art gallery executives, accompanied the tycoon to the auction. He recalled how relaxed Hammer seemed: "There was a long wait in a hot room. He dozed off, telling me first to wake him when the bidding started. When I did, he was as alert as could be." The opening bid was $1.4 million; eighty-five seconds later it was over, with Hammer the winner at $5.28 million, plus a 10 percent commission to the auctioneer. Part of the reason for Hammer's success was the element of surprise; he kept his interest quiet until the auction began. Apparently not even Frances knew his intentions. It was only when he bid successfully for an Old Master painting earlier in the auction that "a knowing buzz spread among the several hundred people packed into the sales room," according to *Washington Post* correspondent Leonard Downie. They realized then that Hammer would be a bidder for the da Vinci.[12]

The British government tried to persuade Hammer to keep the treasure in the country and even considered denying him an export license when he refused. Hugh Legatt, secretary of the group Heritage in Danger, protested that the government had a weak case, since it had bungled the opportunity to buy the manuscript for the entire nation. Legatt also pointed out that Hammer was "a generous benefactor" to England. Hammer finally compromised with the government, promising to display the manuscript in England every year during his life and for ten years after his death. To solidify his place in da Vinci lore and attach his name in perpetuity to yet another institution, Hammer donated $1 million to the University of California at Los Angeles to establish the Armand Hammer Center for Leonardo Studies and Research. The money funded the salary of da Vinci expert Carlo Pedretti, an annual award for the best da Vinci studies, and a scholarly journal.[13]

Citing research that the da Vinci manuscript never was intended to be bound, Hammer ordered the eighteen double-sided sheets (with four pages a sheet) split into thirty-six pages for display purposes. He renamed it the Codex Hammer. Despite the revision, when he took the renamed manuscript to Italy for its return after a 265-year absence, he was treated like a national hero. In fact, Hammer was treated like a hero everywhere he took any part of his collection. The critics had changed their tune since the 1970 debacle at the Smithsonian. When the collection returned to Washington in 1980, this time at the Corcoran Gallery, Paul Richard wrote, "In its present incarnation, Dr. Hammer's art collection is a trove of treasures." In *Smithsonian* magazine, Frank Getlein compared the two exhibitions, admitting that in 1970 "I myself was then art critic on the *Washington Star* and led the hoots. . . . [Today], all in all, the collection is museum-worthy and may well be the last substantial private collection to be amassed in the classical area."[14]

Museum-worthy indeed. Across the United States, museums were fighting for any or all of Hammer's holdings. The first big gifts came during 1971, when Hammer promised sixty paintings with a total value of $10 million or more to the Los Angeles County Museum. "In monetary terms, Hammer's gift is the most significant the . . . museum . . . has ever received," said *Los Angeles Times* art critic Henry Seldis. Museum director Kenneth Donahue commented that Hammer "has matched if not surpassed the generosities of such early supporters . . . as William Randolph Hearst, Alan Balch, and George DeSilva." The collection began its display in the Frances and Armand Hammer Wing.[15]

The euphoria was nearly as great in Washington, where the National Gallery of Art received a promise from Hammer of Gauguin drawings that he valued at more than $2 million. Director J. Carter Brown said the gift bolstered the museum's weakest area. Brown had approached Hammer initially during the Smithsonian fiasco, complimenting him on the collection's Gauguin sketchbook. The timing was right; Hammer needed praise just then. After reflecting on Brown's praise, Hammer impulsively sprang into action, flying from Los Angeles to the East Coast, pulling Brown from a dinner party, and taking him to his Greenwich Village carriage house to strike a bargain for the sketchbook.[16]

At Harvard University, Hammer gave so liberally to the Fogg Art Museum that his name became attached to galleries four through eight.[17]

But no other major American museum would rely so heavily on Hammer's generosity as the Corcoran Gallery of Art, in Washington. It was a wise choice for somebody who wanted recognition from policymakers. The National Gallery already claimed so many wealthy, prominent donors that Hammer never could have stood alone at the top there. The Corcoran, by contrast, boasted few extremely large contributors, but it still offered visibility among the power set in Washington. Hammer and the Corcoran were no strangers. He had featured the museum in the March 1943 issue of his magazine *Compleat Collector.*

Hammer's involvement as the museum's leading light began in 1979, when David Kreeger — a Washington insurance mogul and art collector — invited him to join the board of directors. Hammer's first suggestion was that the museum stop charging its $1.50 admission fee. To compensate for the loss of income free entry would mean, Hammer pledged more than $1 million. The museum's old guard was dubious about ending the admission charge, since even Hammer's generous contribution apparently would fail to cover the lost income.[18]

But Hammer was right, said Peter Marzio, the museum's director at the time. "He is a visionary," Marzio said. "Ending the admission increased attendance a lot, and the money from the contributions box just about equaled the fees. . . . He is amazing. . . . Some people try to act like big givers, but you look behind the scenes and there is not much there. . . . Not him. You read about his enthusiasm, and it sounds corny, but it is true. I have seen it. He gave the board three extra levels of energy. It is like having Mickey Mantle on your baseball team. 'Before you do anything, you have to dream.' Dr. Hammer told me that once when I wanted to move fast. I have never forgotten that — dream first, then move. And that from a man often said to move without thinking."[19]

Michael Botwinick, who succeeded Marzio as Corcoran director and then left to work for Hammer, said perhaps more important than the patron's dollars was his presence: "His participation has helped the trustees validate their own efforts. He has helped them see the Corcoran is big league. . . . It is what he is, and who he is. When the doctor blows in from the Hermitage or from buying the Codex and says 'I like what you are doing,' it helps."[20]

Marzio and Botwinick acknowledged Hammer's controversiality; they heard endless speculation about his motives. Botwinick tuned it out: "In the end, a collection is its own justification. We do not collect collectors, we collect art. . . . The transience of human considerations means little or nothing in the long run. I think Dr. Hammer is drawn to the beauty or the force of the individual objects. He collects things that he responds to." Nearly every year, the Corcoran staged a party in Hammer's honor, which the cream of Washington society attended. He always made a splash, announcing a new gift, revealing a previously secret discussion with a Soviet ruler.[21]

To be sure he was appreciated in the New York museum world as well as in Los Angeles and Washington, Hammer gave $1 million to renovate the Arms and Armor Gallery at the Metropolitan Museum of Art. Considering Hammer's horror of war, observers were puzzled by his decision to help display the very stuff of war. He had an answer, saying of the objects: "While we shall never praise their use, they are valuable to us in historical terms . . . as we seek to preserve the world from the war and the battle they represent." Once again, his name went up on a structure; the museum christened the gallery the Armand Hammer Equestrian Court. When in New York, Hammer occasionally used it as a stage for lavish parties.[22]

To Hammer's lasting credit, he took his collection to the hinterlands as well as major metropolitan centers. Often his choice was dictated by a political or a business connection. But whatever the motive, residents of towns across the country saw great art free because of him. Almost everywhere the collection went, Hammer showed up to be showered with adulation. In return, he used the occasion as a forum for talking about superpower relations and often left behind a large contribution for the local museum.

During 1981, the collection made a trip to the Norton Gallery of Art, in West Palm Beach. The state of Florida, already grateful to Hammer for his phosphate-mining employment in an underdeveloped region, honored him at a ceremony in which he was presented with a medal as "ambassador of the arts." The secretary of state called Hammer "an American legend." The governor called him "a Renaissance man." Because of the ceremony, Hammer arrived at the Norton Gallery ninety minutes late for a news conference, but nobody had left. A newspaper reporter captured the mood: "As though God himself had made an appearance, a hush came over the crowd. There was none of the usual pushing and shoving to get microphones up front. . . . A long line formed as Hammer led his followers into the gallery, pausing from time to time to admire a special painting." Hammer pledged $50,000 for a new wing in addition to picking up the $100,000 tab to transport and display the collection.[23]

Norton director Richard Madigan said the display "was the biggest undertaking in this museum's history, going back to 1941. We had one hundred and ten thousand visitors in six weeks, higher than the attendance in any previous entire year. It attracted people who never had been here. They are curious about Armand Hammer; he is so identified with his collection and so controversial. They came because of him, but they also saw the greatest traveling art collection. It raised awareness of this museum, and has meant long-term increased attendance."[24]

Madigan enjoyed watching Hammer enjoy his art. On one occasion, he observed Hammer being met at the door of the Norton Gallery by Occidental president Ray Irani. "Doctor, the first thing we have to do is take a picture [for some report]," Irani said. Hammer replied, "No, the first thing we're going to do is look at my collection." Generally, though, Hammer was available for the camera. Madigan later displayed to the author a photograph album of a Hammer visit, presented to the museum by the tycoon. The caption under one picture read that Madigan was "requesting" Hammer's autograph on a coffee-table book about his life. Madigan laughed. "I requested nothing. The book was thrust into my hands for the picture."[25]

The smallest town to warrant an exhibition was Moultrie, Georgia, the home of Jimmy Carter's aide Tom Beard. Hammer sent fifteen of his paintings to the southwestern Georgia community of 20,000 people. When Hammer showed up in person, he was swamped by autograph seekers. Melody Jenkins, director of the Moultrie–Colquitt County Library, where the pictures were being displayed, said attendance was 15,000 over thirteen days. Hammer's staff trained locals to be school group guides. Rural residents traveled 150 miles to see the show, some signing the registration book with an *X*. Jenkins found Hammer to be "kind, warm, and down to earth." The city and county paid for security; Hammer's money was donated to the arts center for improvements.[26]

When Hammer sent his art collection overseas, it was usually connected to his citizen diplomacy or his business initiatives. That was especially true in the Soviet Union. In 1972, Soviet culture minister Yekaterina Furtseva had admired Goya's portrait of Dona Antonia Zarate while touring the Los Angeles County Museum. Hammer had bought the portrait not long before, placing a value on it of $1 million, more than six times what he had paid. He decided to donate it to the Soviet state. The donation coincided with the opening of Hammer's Old Masters collection at the Hermitage, in Leningrad, apparently the first time the Soviets had invited an American citizen to exhibit a private collection. The crowds thronged to see it. One viewer, a Leningrad architect,

sentimentally presented Hammer with an old pencil from the Allied
American factory of the 1920s.[27]

The Goya was the first of many gifts from Hammer to the Soviets.
In 1973 he donated the painting *Triumph of Amphitrite,* by French artist
Raoul Dufy, to Moscow's Pushkin Museum. Soviet officials had mentioned their dismay at owning just one small Dufy. Hammer has said
he decided that a museum as prestigious as the Pushkin deserved to
have one of Dufy's best paintings. The Soviets, touched by the generosity, reciprocated by giving Hammer a twentieth-century abstract
painting by Kasimir Malevich. It was the type of art little appreciated
by Furtseva; Anthony Astrachan noted in the *New York Times* that a
strategy of showing avant-garde art abroad but suppressing it at home
"would fit the pattern of détente with the West while continuing to
restrict cultural and political dissension in the Soviet Union."[28]

Later, there were allegations by David Karr that Hammer had paid
Furtseva $100,000 to allow the art exchanges. Karr apparently had no
hard proof, although Hammer's detractors saw circumstantial evidence
in the reprimand Furtseva received from the Communist party for lavish living. Reports circulating in Moscow said she had been ordered to
repay $80,000 for materials used in her country cottage. She possessed
enough money to make restitution, a surprising development considering her monthly salary of $500.[29]

Karr's allegations had been made privately, but they entered the
Hammer lore after publication in the *New York Times* as part of a
lengthy article by reporter Judith Miller. Joseph Baird, Occidental's
president at that juncture, complained to the newspaper that its story
referred three times to Hammer's alleged $100,000 payment but failed
to mention Hammer's emphatic denial. Baird scolded that "this scan-
dalous rumor is based on the alleged statement of an unidentified business associate that Victor Hammer told him so, which Victor Hammer
vehemently denies. This is hearsay triply compounded and . . . did not
merit publication by any responsible test of journalism."[30] Lacking concrete evidence, neither Soviet nor American governmental authorities
took action against Hammer.

The truth of the rumor is uncertain judging from currently available
records; Furtseva could have obtained her wealth any number of ways.
It seems likely that the Soviet government welcomed Hammer's art not
because of payoffs, but rather as an easy way to satisfy the culture-
hungry intelligentsia in Leningrad and Moscow, as well as other cities
to which the paintings traveled — Kiev, Minsk, Riga, and Odessa. As
for the Soviet decision to show masterpieces in the United States, it was

a logical step by which to promote détente while also putting a gloss on Hammer's reputation at a time when the Soviets needed him as a bridge to the West. Prominent American officials praised Hammer lavishly for the exchange. Senate Majority Leader Mike Mansfield said he regretted he was unable to join Hammer in Moscow for the opening there, adding, "I am delighted that you are undertaking this initiative, and I feel confident that this showing, coupled with the one at Leningrad earlier this year, will do much to bring about a better understanding and a better relationship between the Union of Soviet Socialist Republics and our own country."[31]

Without Hammer's influence, the exchange never would have occurred. He began with a wish list of thirty-seven Impressionist and post-Impressionist paintings in the collections of the Hermitage and Pushkin museums. None had been exhibited in the United States. J. Carter Brown, the director of the National Gallery of Art, asked Hammer to add four paintings to the list. The Soviets granted permission for all forty-one paintings on the list to be part of the tour. Hammer made certain the National Gallery was the first stop; he put other museums in his debt by lobbying with Furtseva on their behalf, too. At the National Gallery reception to celebrate the show, Hammer and Furtseva were the center of attention, despite the presence of such other luminaries as the chief justice of the Supreme Court, the secretary of state, and three senators.[32]

Joy Hakanson of the *Detroit News* wrote a typically laudatory column when the paintings reached her city: "How he convinced the Soviets to loan their paintings after top museum men tried and failed is the latest episode in an incredible career." She talked about the "charmed influence of Dr. Hammer, who has experienced just about everything but failure." In the exhibition catalog, Leonid Brezhnev and Richard Nixon thanked Hammer for his initiative in bringing the two superpowers closer during a treacherous age.[33]

It was the first of numerous large-scale art exchanges involving the two nations, with Hammer the key figure in many of them. Each time, the praise was widespread and effusive. In 1975, Hammer announced from Moscow that the Hermitage would send thirty of its most valuable paintings for a six-month tour of museums in Washington, Chicago, Los Angeles, and — of course — his gallery in New York. The American museums would send some of their treasures to the Soviet Union. Paul Richard, the *Washington Post* art critic, called the exhibition "unprecedented," noting that some of its Old Masters "have not been seen outside Russia since the days of Peter the Great."[34]

Hammer experienced two minor frustrations — he missed the preview dinner in Washington because of illness, and President Gerald Ford refused to write a glowing statement for the exhibition catalog, even though Nixon had written one two years earlier for a similar catalog. Hammer discussed the matter personally with Ford. J. Carter Brown composed a follow-up request. When the National Security Council advised against a Ford letter, despite Brezhnev's agreement to contribute an introduction, Hammer asked Senate Minority Leader Hugh Scott, a Pennsylvania Republican, to plead the case. Scott did, but the National Security Council stood firm, charging that Brezhnev's words carried political overtones and recommending that Ford avoid being drawn into a propaganda exercise.[35]

Later in the decade, Hammer persuaded Soviet authorities to send their only painting by Leonardo da Vinci, the priceless *Madonna with a Flower,* to the United States. As Hammer related the story of his coup,

> I was talking to Mr. Brezhnev . . . and he asked me "What can I do for you now?" I asked him "Let us have the Leonardo." Some of his assistants shook their heads and said nyet. But Mr. Brezhnev said da. I asked for the Leonardo and a small group of paintings from the period — we got a list from Carter Brown — and they gave us everything we asked for except a few pieces whose condition would not allow them to be moved.

Hammer was the guest of honor at the Soviet embassy in Washington, where the ambassador read a letter from Brezhnev congratulating him on the exhibition of the da Vinci as well as his long-standing friendship with the Soviet Union and presented him with a sculpture of himself by a Soviet artist.[36]

Outside the Soviet Union, he sometimes took a shine to a particular foreign museum, sustaining it over the long term. The primary example was the Musée Jacquemart Andre in Paris. Edouard Andre had been a nineteenth-century French art collector; his widow, Nelie Jacquemart, willed their mansion to L'Institut de France (she died in 1912), which converted it to a museum. Hammer fell in love with the gallery on a trip to Paris, likening it to the Frick, in New York — if it could be repaired. Martha Kaufman, curator of his collection at the time, said Hammer "was determined that this gem of a museum would shine again. He endowed it with a concern that would return it to its former glory." He arranged for his paintings to hang there at the same time some of his drawings were being exhibited at the Louvre. The show was a huge success. French experts credited Hammer with saving the Musée Jacquemart Andre from obscurity or even ruin. Before long, the name of the Armand Hammer Foundation was emblazoned on a gold plaque at the entrance.[37]

It was through Hammer's foundation, established in 1968, that museums, universities, charities, religious groups, and municipalities received his largess. There were no independent trustees — the captive board consisted of Victor, Harry, and Frances; Frances's sister, Helen Andrews; and Hammer's lawyer Arthur Groman. As a result, the giving reflected Hammer's broad, idiosyncratic interests. Early nonart donations included $1,000 for the Monmouth Museum in Hammer's former home of Red Bank, New Jersey, and $850,000 for the Salk Institute for Biological Studies in La Jolla, California.[38]

As the years passed, Hammer channeled his gifts — large and small — to the Soviet government, presidential libraries, Prince Charles's favorite English causes, a financially strapped Los Angeles municipal golf course near his home that later was renamed for him, Norman Vincent Peale's church-affiliated Center for Positive Christianity, other religious groups ranging from evangelist Robert Schuller's Crystal Cathedral to the Wilshire Boulevard Jewish Temple, and an American College of Surgeons scholarship honoring Nancy Reagan's father.[39]

By 1988, the foundation's assets totaled $24 million. Nearly $10 million was in the form of interest-free, unsecured loans from Hammer. When Hammer became a heavy investor in Financial General Bancshares of Washington, he donated his stock to the foundation, which eventually sold it for a gain of nearly $8 million. In any given month, the foundation might sell substantial amounts of Occidental Petroleum stock, sometimes registering a gain, sometimes a loss.[40]

The Internal Revenue Service occasionally expressed doubts about the valuations of Hammer's gifts, especially artworks. In 1974, he received unwanted attention as the tax agency's charges against him became public. The dispute centered on whether Hammer had overvalued paintings donated to the University of Southern California and Western sculpture given to the Johnson White House. If the IRS valuations were correct, Hammer had failed to meet the standard qualifying him for unlimited tax deductions: Such unlimited deductions were available only to persons who gave away at least 90 percent of their income in eight of ten previous years. The IRS wanted a substantial sum from Hammer as a result of the allegedly incorrect values on the donations, plus an even larger amount as a result of his failing to qualify for the unlimited deductions.[41]

When *Newsweek* suggested Hammer might be a tax cheat, Louis Nizer sprang into action, notifying the magazine that there were wide disagreements on just two of many donations and that, anyway, the government was wrong. Hammer had valued a Rubens painting, *Venus Wounded by a Thorn,* at $75,000 when donating it to USC, but the government believed the value to be just $2,000. "When Dr. Hammer protested the absurdity of this ruling, a government art expert appointed by the Internal Revenue Service, Professor Seymour Slive of Harvard University, after spending a week studying the painting, joined with the two greatest living authorities on paintings by Rubens in agreeing that the painting" was genuine, Nizer said. As for the Frederic Remington bronze sculpture, *The Bronco Buster,* Nizer said the two sides were $45,000 apart.

> The amounts in dispute . . . are relatively small compared to the $6.5 million which Dr. Hammer donated to charities during the years in question, and which the Internal Revenue Service has not disputed. If a citizen's right to test in an appropriate court the evident arbitrariness of a disallowance is to be characterized as fudging . . . then every disagreement with a government department would automatically subject the citizen to condemnation.[42]

In 1976, Hammer and the IRS quietly settled the case. For the allegedly overvalued donations, Hammer paid slightly more than $77,000 in back taxes, which split the difference between him and the agency. He paid another $190,000 in a related settlement. Seven years later, when the *New York Times* published an article about an IRS crackdown against overvalued art donations, the agency used the "celebrated" Hammer case as an example.[43]

Hammer was controversial not only for his aggressive collecting and his donations, but also for his ownership of M. Knoedler and Company Galleries. Owning a New York gallery was nothing new to Hammer; he and his brothers had run the establishment named after them since 1928. But the purchase of Knoedler's in 1971 was truly news. At the time of the acquisition, Hammer was viewed in the art world much as he was in the realms of the Seven Sisters and by the foreign policy establishment — as a brash, unwelcome outsider. Knoedler's represented everything Hammer did not. It was one of the oldest (founded in 1846), most prestigious galleries in the nation, with old-fashioned ways of doing business that usually excluded hype.

When rumors circulated in October 1971 that the venerable gallery was in financial trouble and that Hammer planned to buy it, Grace Glueck of the *New York Times* reported them. Roland Balay, Knoedler president, denied the report. Years later, Balay said Hammer actually had approached him about buying the gallery at least two years before Glueck's story appeared in print. In December, Glueck's tip panned out. The purchasers were Armand and Victor Hammer; Maury Leibovitz, the accountant turned psychologist; and Bernard Danenberg, whiz kid New York gallery owner. Danenberg told Glueck he and Victor had been in Omaha attending the fortieth anniversary of the Joslyn Art Museum when they found themselves defending Knoedler's to museum officials, who felt they had been treated poorly by the gallery during the purchase of a painting. Danenberg impishly told Victor since they had defended the gallery so vigorously, maybe they should buy it; they had heard the sale rumors. When they presented the idea to Armand, Danenberg said, he liked it so much that he and Leibovitz flew to Omaha, picked up the other two men, and structured a deal in the air. The purchase price turned out to be $2.5 million, with Danenberg to pay 30 percent.[44]

Balay eventually accepted the offer, telling Glueck he would stay on. In fact, Balay was unhappy from the start and finally retired after numerous spats with the Hammers and Leibovitz. Danenberg failed to get along with his partners, too. He was upset by what he felt was Leibovitz's crass marketing, selling works of art as if they were shoes. Leibovitz, of course, disagreed with that criticism. At a meeting with Hammer in Los Angeles, Danenberg issued a warning that it was he or Leibovitz. Within three months of the purchase, Danenberg was gone, bought out for a reported $180,000. The turmoil took its toll as some of the top Knoedler salespeople departed, taking artists along.[45]

Hammer gave Leibovitz authority to move quickly to rebuild the gallery's reputation, improve its bottom line, and lure back the departed artists. He hired John Richardson, a respected art historian and author, as well as Jack Tanzer, a knowledgeable art dealer — who represented Hammer — with a reputation as a publicist. To direct Knoedler's, Leibovitz and Hammer eventually brought in Lawrence Rubin. Although he was happy running his own gallery, Rubin said,

> When I met Dr. Hammer . . . I was bowled over in many ways. . . . The notion of working with Knoedler's intrigued me, I liked Dr. Hammer, and I felt I would lose none of my freedom by getting involved. Also, a lot of money would be available to do things that I had not been able to do on my own, such as dealing with the work of earlier twen-

tieth-century painters like Léger, Miró, Picasso. I wanted to show those
artists simultaneously with American post–World War Two painting.
In 1973, we formed a joint venture, a fifty-fifty partnership, called Knoedler
Contemporary Art, which went on for a few years. The older business of Knoedler and Company had not been going too well, so Dr.
Hammer asked if I would take over the whole thing and give it a new
direction. After dealing in American art for fifteen years, I had come
to feel a little stale; Knoedler's gave me the opportunity to get a much
broader mix.

Hammer expanded the gallery, spending more than $1 million on an
adjoining building and renovation of the existing quarters. The gallery
acquired significant works, such as the eighty-eight-piece collection of
movie actor Edward G. Robinson for more than $5 million.[46]
The biggest step came in 1977, when Knoedler's merged with Modarco, an art investment fund based in Switzerland. Modarco was managed by two banks that invested in paintings, selling them at a profit
when the timing seemed right. Its worth was estimated at $20 million.
Hammer, crowing that the merger was the most substantive ever accomplished in the commercial art world, told of his plan: "The Arabs
are already into stocks and real estate, and given particularly the de-
preciation in the stock market, we think they might be attracted by
solider investments in the art market. We have sold a lot already to
the Iranians, and we are hopeful about the Arabs." Hammer requested
an IRS ruling adjudging the merger to be tax-free and obtained it.
Tanzer, reviewing the transaction more than a decade later, remained
impressed: "The merger brought us lots of inventory, which we sold
off and got a ten-million-dollar cash infusion, which was a lot of money
in those days."[47]
At Hammer Galleries, Leibovitz and director Richard Lynch played
increasingly major roles, since Victor's health was failing. The family
gallery became known for its marketing of contemporary artist LeRoy
Neiman; its occasional shows for worthy causes in conjunction with
celebrities such as actor Paul Newman; and its role in the art-buying
spree of Imelda Marcos, wife of the Philippine dictator. Hammer knew
Ferdinand and Imelda through an Occidental Petroleum venture and
through his citizen diplomacy. When Mrs. Marcos went shopping during 1983, she patronized Hammer Galleries, buying at least seventy-
seven paintings for more than $4 million. One itemized bill from Ham-
mer Galleries to Mrs. Marcos listed seven paintings by Grandma Moses,
a Gauguin, an Andrew Wyeth, a Pissarro, a Lippi, and a Monet. The

total came to $3,069,000. Attached was a note from Lynch that knocked off the $69,000 to make the price an even $3 million. It appeared that Mrs. Marcos spent at least as much at Knoedler's. One receipt that turned up during an investigation contained the notation "Above prices are special prices authorized by Dr. Armand Hammer for Mr. and Mrs. Marcos."[48]

Hammer did nothing illegal by mixing his art collecting, museum directorships, and gallery ownerships. But there was cause for concern on an ethical plane. Some eyebrows went up when Hammer openly used his gallery ownership to obtain Rembrandt's *Juno,* in 1976. J. William Middendorf had approached Knoedler's about selling the masterpiece, with $5 million reportedly the minimum acceptable offer. When nobody came forward at that price, Middendorf decided to sell lower and called Hammer to tell him so. Hammer reminded Middendorf that when Knoedler's had agreed to handle the sale, he had insisted on a right of first refusal. He was exercising that right, Hammer said; Middendorf was obligated to sell *Juno* to him.[49]

John Walker, Hammer's art adviser and frequent defender, explained in his memoirs why he planned to loosen his ties to the tycoon:

> I decided he no longer needed my advice, for his collection had begun to rank with the most important in the country. Moreover, he had started to curtail his own private collecting, and had further complicated his position as an amateur by purchasing the oldest firm dealing in art in the United States, Knoedler and Company. I thought it was time for me to bow out in the friendliest manner. His ownership of the Hammer Galleries was from my point of view questionable enough, but his deeper involvement in dealing made my position as a former museum director even less tenable.[50]

Walker continued to respect Hammer. But elsewhere in the museum world, Hammer's reputation was muddied by testy negotiations and broken promises concerning the resting place for his various collections. The doubts struck first at the National Gallery of Art. Hammer's relationship with the leading museum in the nation's capital never had been contractually well defined. His promises of gifts were viewed skeptically. Hammer's relationship with the Corcoran made his loyalties suspect anyway, although nobody at the National Gallery wanted to discourage his largess.

His insistent demands kept him on the minds of the museum's administration. When Larry Van Dyne profiled National Gallery director J. Carter Brown in the *Washingtonian,* he began the article with a tell-

ing scene involving Hammer. Brown was returning from an exhausting
day in Detroit when he learned Hammer was waiting to meet him in
a VIP lounge at National Airport. Brown would have preferred to
avoid a meeting until he could prepare but knew Hammer waited for
nobody. Brown had used Hammer's services to help arrange otherwise
impossible exchanges with the Soviet Union. In return, Brown had
made available to Hammer the expertise of the museum's curators in
assembling his drawings collection. As Van Dyne noted:

> Hammer had allowed these drawings to be exhibited at the gallery as
> "promised gifts" on two occasions in the 1970s. Even so, nearly fifteen
> years after the first show, there was no written agreement on the exact
> terms of the gift, a situation that had caused some nervousness inside
> the gallery as Hammer aged into his late eighties. Lawyers for Hammer
> and the gallery had been working on an agreement for months, sending
> versions of the proposed terms back and forth. But Hammer's sudden
> and surprising demand for an airport rendezvous left Brown without
> the latest paperwork in his briefcase. So the gallery's car was dispatched
> to National with the appropriate documents. . . . To Brown, the biggest
> issue still hanging is the disposition of a rare fifteenth-century drawing
> by Leonardo da Vinci, which Hammer acquired in 1972 and exhibited
> in those earlier National Gallery shows of his promised gifts. From the
> latest list of Hammer's proposed gifts, it now appears that he wants to
> renege on his precious Leonardo, perhaps intending to reserve it for an
> institution on the West Coast.
>
> Normally, the bargaining power would rest with the donor. After all,
> he owns the art. But Brown has some cards of his own to play. He
> knows that Hammer, whose ego and desire for publicity are legendary,
> is deeply interested in having his name associated with the National
> Gallery, figuratively chiseled up there on the marble with the Mellons
> and other donors to certify him as a man of respectability, generosity,
> and taste. Time also is on Brown's side. The gallery already has told
> Hammer that it must have the matter settled soon if it is to permanently
> install the collection within a few months and celebrate the event to
> coincide with the appearance of his autobiography. . . . The argument
> is heated, and swings back and forth between the two skillful negotia-
> tors. . . . Negotiation, Brown understands, is a game that Hammer en-
> joys, and as always the old man blusters and postures to the hilt. Ham-
> mer is holding out on the Leonardo, and Brown is being just as insistent,
> giving the impression that he might take a walk. In that case, there
> would be no deal, no special installation, no opening-night party, and

no publicity; the whole thing would go back to the lawyers. Finally Hammer relents.[51]

The news release announcing the gift was just in time for a major exhibition of Hammer's art at the museum — and for the publication of his autobiography. In the lush 134-page exhibition catalog, Brown recounted his adventures with Hammer. During an interview, he stressed the intoxicating unpredictability of working with Hammer but admitted to occasional exasperation.[52]

It was Brown's counterpart at the Los Angeles County Museum of Art, Earl Powell, who ended up more exasperated. In 1988, Hammer decided to withdraw his artworks from the major museum in his adopted hometown and to place them in his own museum, which he would build a stone's throw from Occidental's headquarters — just a few miles from the county museum. In so doing he broke a previous pledge to the museum; eight months earlier, he had reacted angrily to a newspaper report that he wanted an entire museum with his name on it, responding, "I have repeatedly stated that on my death . . . the paintings in my collection will be given to the Los Angeles County Museum of Art . . . I have never considered establishing a private museum of my own."[53]

Hammer understandably did not refer to that letter when he announced a $30 million art museum and cultural center that would house his collections, estimated to be worth at least $250 million and maybe $400 million. Without even a mention of the county museum, the news release quoted Hammer's rationale: "I have always said that I planned to leave these collections for the enjoyment of the people of Los Angeles, and with construction of this new art museum and cultural center, that will be assured. Not only will the works be on display to the public, but this museum will provide for continued scholarly study of the artists and their works." Hammer noted that his museum would "be located only a few blocks from the University of California at Los Angeles, where the Armand Hammer Foundation, with the support of Occidental, has endowed the Armand Hammer Center for Leonardo Studies."[54]

Nobody disputed Hammer's right to change his mind. What troubled the museum trustees — most of them respected civic, state, and national leaders — was his disregard for promises made. The *Los Angeles Times* called for the community to unite behind the county museum's leadership, which would be forced into an expensive rethinking of overall collection strategy in the wake of Hammer's withdrawal. For two decades, the editorial said, "the museum has, correctly, based its acquisition strategy on the understanding that the Hammer collection would be part of the museum's treasures. There may be no way to compensate for lost purchase opportunities now that hyperinflation has seized the world's art auctions."[55]

The true story slowly unfolded. A turning point had occurred at a lunch the previous July between Hammer and Daniel Belin, a Los Angeles attorney who chaired the museum board, on which Hammer served. Hammer had presented Belin with a thirty-nine-page proposal to nail down the promises of the past. When other trustees saw the proposal, they were upset — Hammer, who presumably knew the museum's policies, apparently was suggesting violating them. To aggravate matters, the proposal seemed outrageously vain. It called for his collection to be displayed intact on a floor of its own named after him; it requested that names of other major donors be removed from that floor, so as not to detract from his glory; it ordered the museum never to sell any of the pieces; it mandated a full-length portrait of Hammer at the floor's entrance. Furthermore, Hammer would hire and fire the curators, effectively creating a museum within a museum.[56]

Some trustees were especially angry about the loss of the Daumier lithographs. Hammer had bid for them against the museum while he was a trustee. That seemed to be a breach of museum policy, but the board went ahead and accepted it. Now he was withdrawing his collection and keeping the Daumiers, too. The trustees decided to play hardball over the proposal, apparently believing Hammer would respect forceful business negotiators, being one himself. The trustees were wrong. As Robert Jones explained in the *Los Angeles Times Magazine,* the trustees' response

> missed something. To Hammer, giving his art collection away was not business. It was everything that business was not. It was the thing that won him love in Beijing, and Moultrie, Georgia. Chinese boys sold their bicycles to buy tickets, and they were grateful for the chance. Hammer might bargain over the details of his gift, just as he had bargained with the National Gallery [of Art], but the bargainers could damn well be grateful for the chance. This letter was not grateful. As Hammer read it through, he was hurt and outraged.[57]

Hammer got the last word. After announcing the plans for his own museum, he showed up at the county museum with a high-ranking Soviet minister in tow. Museum director Powell accompanied them on the tour. Hammer was friendly. As it ended, according to Jones's account, "Hammer turned to Powell and asked if the museum owned any Daumiers. Powell, wondering if this was a joke, said no, not since the new museum was announced, anyway. Hammer patted him on the shoulder. 'I will send you some,' he said, climbed into his limousine and sped away." He added insult to injury by hiring a county museum staff member, Alla Hall, to direct his center.[58]

As work on the museum began, it became clear that Occidental stockholders would be the ones to pay the price. Stockholders filed three separate lawsuits aimed at the costs of the museum and additional Hammer causes. Hammer justified the expense — which by early 1989 had jumped to an estimated $50 million — on the grounds that Occidental benefited substantially from the name recognition the art collections brought. It seemed ironic, therefore, as Hammer made clear frequently, that "Occidental does not own in whole or in part one single object in my collection of over ten thousand items. All of the paintings, drawings, sculptures, manuscripts, and books in my collection are either owned by myself, were purchased by the Armand Hammer Foundation with funds that I made available to it for that purpose, or were first purchased by me and subsequently donated to the foundation."[59]

27

Philanthropist with a Vengeance

A RMAND HAMMER attributed his dedication to finding a cure
for cancer to the influence of his father, the devoted doctor.
Hammer has said he made the decision to spend a substantial portion
of his wealth on cancer research sometime in the late 1960s, as he
watched Walter Cronkite interview Jonas Salk on television. Salk, who
had helped conquer another dread disease, polio, spoke about cancer
research at the institute he founded in La Jolla, California. Hammer
recalled spontaneously getting in touch with Salk and pledging $5 mil-
lion for cancer research. A plaque of acknowledgment containing the
name Armand Hammer Center for Cancer Biology has been appropriately placed at the institute.[1]

Apparently, Hammer liked the ring of $5 million donations — in
1977, he gave a like amount to his alma mater, Columbia University,
to help pay for a twenty-story tower on the medical school campus. Its
name became the Julius and Armand Hammer Health Sciences Center.
University president William McGill called it "one of the largest private donations in Columbia's two hundred and twenty-three years."
Hammer found time in his hectic life to write the medical school dean
about the size, placement, and composition of the building plaque bearing his name. The next year, the university presented Hammer with
an honorary degree in a ceremony at the site. When Hammer gave the
commencement speech two years after that, *New York Times* reporter
Lawrence Altman, a doctor himself, wrote, "When asked if medical
schools should name buildings for individuals who have broken the law
and make them role models for future physicians, Dr. Hammer re-

plied, 'That is for the Columbia trustees to decide. I did not solicit them, they solicited me.' "[2]

That was true. McGill recalled the solicitation. He recently had become president of Columbia. In an early action, he sent out birthday letters to potential donors. The letter carried no mention of money but was meant as a subtle reminder that the alma mater needed contributions. According to McGill, Hammer wrote back, saying "thank you for the letter. I am not in a position to give." McGill added, "I was fascinated by his perceptiveness. I learned about him. . . . I was stunned at his life, could not wait to meet him. . . . He burst into tears when we handed him the medical school transcripts of himself and his father. He was generous and calculating with his gifts. Our only problem was that the name of the new building had already been given to Augustus Long, the chairman of Texaco. . . . I called on Gus Long and told him that the library would be named for him, but the building would be named for the Hammers. . . . we worked it out." Long had done prodigious volunteer work for Columbia University's Presbyterian Hospital. "I felt it was a somewhat unkind and harsh way to do business," Long said. "I was upset and embarrassed." Long said he felt no resentment toward Hammer, who after all helped pay for a much-needed building.[3]

Having his name on buildings meant a kind of immortality, but it was not enough for Hammer. He was looking for a more active role in cancer research, and he found it. One of the positions Ronald Reagan needed to fill after entering the White House was the chairmanship of the President's Cancer Panel. It had been a backwater volunteer position attracting almost no attention. Word reached the White House that Hammer would love to be nominated. It seemed like a good fit — Reagan would make a campaign contributor happy, and Hammer's medical degree would make the appointment easier to justify.

No matter how logical, the appointment caused raised eyebrows, partly because of Hammer's Watergate guilty plea, partly because of Occidental's reputation as a carcinogenic polluter. *Time*'s Laurence Barrett wrote that the appointment "was hardly a major matter, and Hammer is an esteemed United States business leader. But if the president wanted a successful corporate executive to chair this panel, surely there was someone available who had not openly confessed to illegal political activities." *Mother Jones* magazine editorialized that "at first glance it seemed like a wildly inappropriate appointment, something on the order of asking the late Sid Vicious to head a program for battered women, or making Colonel Qaddafi director of the Jewish Relief Fund." But, the magazine added, maybe Hammer would be inspired to clean up Occidental's carcinogens.[4] Hammer brushed off the attacks, bragging to acquaintances that his loyalty to America had been validated — the FBI background check had cleared his appointment to the volunteer position.

Probably nobody realized just how bully a pulpit the cancer panel would prove to be. Hammer used the first meeting to announce that his foundation would give $1 million to any scientist finding a cancer cure. In the interim, the foundation would award $100,000 annually for the discovery advancing research the most. With his usual optimism, Hammer said, "A scientific breakthrough in the cure of some cancers is closer than we know." The *New York Times* responded that "many scientists, however, suspect that cures have been so elusive because cancer represents complex biological processes that are not yet understood." *Science* magazine commented,

> The cancer panel appears to be taking on a more active role than it has in the past. The new chairman is off to a flashy start. . . . But the money is unlikely to speed up the discovery of an ultimate weapon against cancer, given the billions of federal dollars that have been pumped into the cancer program so far, and given the complexity of the disease. What remains are tougher issues. . . . They are questions that a million-dollar cash prize cannot answer.[5]

Hammer, along with two cancer researchers serving on the panel, began considering those questions. He was vain and opinionated, but he worked hard at the volunteer position. Elliott Stonehill, a physician whose National Cancer Institute position included serving as the panel's executive secretary, said that during meetings Hammer would have his Occidental executive assistant manning the telephone. "Dr. Hammer might be working on Occidental business during the meetings, but he still paid attention," Stonehill said. "When it looked like he was dozing, he was writing in his lap. A minute later, he asked a sharp medical question." Ann Landers, the nationally syndicated advice columnist, watched Hammer during her six years on NCI's advisory board. Hammer attended board meetings, even though nobody expected him to do so. "I was amazed at how well prepared he was," Landers said. "It was so impressive; he was up-to-date."[6]

Hammer began trying to influence cancer research at centers across the nation, hoping scientists would focus on monoclonal antibodies as a solution. He organized an international symposium at the Salk Institute on the topic. *Los Angeles Times* science reporter Harry Nelson commented that medical researchers believed monoclonal antibodies had potential for diagnosing and treating cancer, but "some stiffen at the thought of a nonscientist, especially a businessman, setting their priorities. Also, they are fearful that too much premature publicity about such antibodies might raise public expectations too high, resulting in a backlash that could adversely affect funding." To nobody's surprise, the first recipients of Hammer's annual $100,000 prize won for their work on monoclonal antibodies.[7]

When Hammer issued the cancer panel's first report to the White House, his cover letter stressed his own agenda almost to the exclusion of the body's work. It was a marked contrast to the self-effacing reports from past chairmen. Hammer took the panel on the road, for the first time holding meetings away from Washington. They generated controversy. At a 1983 session in Houston, cancer researchers took issue with Hammer's projection of a cure by 1990, but he was not fazed. When Hammer heard about especially promising research, he visited the laboratory within days rather than waiting for an invitation. For example, Hammer read in a medical journal about the work of Ronald Levy, at Stanford University. He went to see Levy and was shocked by his cramped quarters. Hammer gave the university $500,000 to triple the size of his laboratory. Stanford University held a dedication ceremony to unveil a plaque by the door of the refurbished area; it read: "The Armand Hammer Cancer Research Laboratory."[8]

Levy recalled his first exposure to Hammer, several years earlier at a Salk Institute cancer seminar. At that time, Levy had never heard of the tycoon: "He came to lunch and talked about how great he is, passed out autographed copies of a book about him." Levy thought it was bizarre behavior for a scientific conference. It wasn't long before Levy came to know Hammer better: "I won his cancer prize, and later served as a judge. It is not that well known, but it has the potential to stimulate cancer research because it's designed to recognize very recent advances." Due to their association, Hammer would call Levy in the middle of the night and say, "Ron, I have been reading your article, and do not understand one of the words." Levy was amazed and pleased at Hammer's interest and comprehension. When Levy observed Hammer at a subsequent conference, the researcher was fascinated as people "would come up one by one to ask for his favor in getting an audience in the Soviet Union, getting his political campaign support, or whatever."[9]

Sherry Lansing, a Hollywood movie producer deeply affected by her mother's death from cancer, helped Hammer seek out researchers deserving of money. Steven Rosenberg at the NCI became one of the favored recipients. Hammer heard Rosenberg's name during a discus-

sion with Vincent DeVita, the head of the institute, about the researcher's work with a colon cancer patient. "When I got the news I immediately left for Bethesda [Maryland] to see Dr. Rosenberg and to see
for myself what he was doing in his laboratory. . . . I then immediately
asked him, what do you need to repeat this work, to do more in this
regard?" Hammer thought the answer would be millions of dollars.
Rosenberg said $100,000; Hammer pledged it on the spot.[10]

Outspoken as ever, Hammer criticized the White House and Congress for failing to see how far such relatively small sums would go.
"They have no trouble in spending billions of dollars on another dread-
nought or an aircraft carrier, but to get extra money for our program
is a very difficult task." A few minutes later, Hammer switched to his
more typical upbeat message: "I am promoting hope rather than de-
spair, optimism rather than pessimism, and extra efforts and renewed
dedication by all of us. This is the formula I have always found produces success in my own business, and I feel sure it will produce success here."[11]

When the *Wall Street Journal* published an article citing pessimistic
cancer mortality statistics, Hammer replied that America was not losing the war on cancer. Just the opposite, he said: "The innovative and
imaginative work being done by many researchers makes this the most
exciting and promising time ever to be involved in the battle, a battle
from which I firmly believe we will emerge victorious in the relatively
near future."[12] Despite the controversy surrounding his views, Hammer received a vote of confidence from the medical establishment when
the American Cancer Society presented him with its service award,
placing him in the company of Edward Kennedy, Frank Borman,
Laurance Rockefeller, and Betty Ford. The Reagan White House gave
him a vote of confidence, too, appointing him to new terms as panel
chairman.

Demonstrating the synergy of his interests, Hammer helped organize
a cancer summit during which American and Soviet researchers discussed advances by means of teleconferencing satellite. More than twelve
hundred American hospitals reportedly received the broadcast, as did
sites in forty-three foreign cities. Steven Rosenberg, Vincent DeVita,
and Robert Gale spoke. Ronald Reagan offered videotaped greetings,
while Mikhail Gorbachev had a spokesman read a message. Actor Bill
Cosby and Hammer provided commentary. Hammer had convinced
Cosby to take a special interest in cancer research. Two months earlier,
Hammer made a guest appearance on the popular Cosby situation comedy aired by NBC. He played a generous donor to a hospital where his

fictional high school–age grandson was a cancer patient. Cosby, a doctor on the show, was lobbied by Hammer, as part of the plot, to write members of Congress for more research money. When "Dr." Cosby told Hammer, "You're pushy," Hammer replied with a grin, "Thank you." The guest spot demonstrated that he liked to have fun, to try new experiences. Many chief executives would have been too stodgy to appear in a situation comedy. It was great public relations.[13]

Hammer used the visibility from the television appearance to launch a $1 billion campaign for cancer research. He addressed a star-studded lunch in New York. Attending were Cosby, *New York Times* publisher Arthur Sulzberger, prominent medical researchers, Wall Street leaders, and members of Congress. Hammer made a personal pledge of $100,000 and announced he had persuaded nine other people to pledge an equal amount. Later in the year he raised about $2 million in one evening at a dinner concert to which tickets cost $2,500; featured were Mstislav Rostropovich conducting the National Symphony Orchestra and violinist Isaac Stern. New York governor Mario Cuomo said that if anybody could raise $1 billion for cancer, it was Hammer.[14]

Hammer's support of an experimental school in the wilds of New Mexico was a different sort of crusade, something that had its genesis in his desire to help Prince Charles. The tycoon's relationship with Charles surprised even the most seasoned Hammer watchers. The two met in 1977, when the London branch of Knoedler's presented an exhibition of Winston Churchill's art to celebrate Queen Elizabeth II's silver jubilee. Charles, an amateur painter, attended. Hammer was so taken with the prince's enthusiasm for Churchill's work that he offered a picture as a gift. It was the beginning of something special; Hammer, old enough to be Charles's grandfather, talked about the joy of being "close enough to observe this remarkable young man as he has grown to full manhood. More than that, I have seen him emerge completely from the chrysalis of his late youth as a man who stands ready to impress the stamp of his character upon the world."[15]

When the prince gave a controversial speech decrying the decline of entrepreneurial spirit in Britain, Hammer defended Charles against criticism by calling him a wise man with vision and a conscience. Hammer showered him with personal gifts, contributed heavily to his philanthropies, and advised him on business and world diplomacy. Charles had to do nothing in return but grace Hammer's life with his presence from time to time. Many people who viewed the relationship from close up concluded that Prince Charles could tap the doctor for his causes; here was this little man from Los Angeles who came over and gave the prince lots of money to play with. But when they were together, there seemed to be genuine affection between them.[16]

Not long after they met, Hammer invited Charles to visit Occidental's North Sea drilling operation. In early 1978, Buckingham Palace informed Hammer that Charles would make the journey on February 24. Occidental's staff worked around the clock to plan the affair. Public relations counselor John Smythe recalled that "in military style, final schedules were exchanged in sealed boxes a week before the visit, and traveling instructions were mailed under confidential cover to our guests." The visit meant publicity for the special relationship between Hammer and Charles. It was hard to ignore Hammer in England because of his relationships with Prince Charles and Margaret Thatcher. His ties appeared to influence the civil servants who had to make decisions about North Sea contracts.[17]

Shortly after Charles's North Sea visit, Hammer exhibited his art collection at the Edinburgh Festival, in Scotland. Armand and Frances carried Rembrandt's *Juno* on their jet, unwrapping it "for the inspection of reporters at the foot of the airport steps, standing proudly by and waving as cameras rolled," according to an account in the *Daily Telegraph* of London. At a gala meal with Charles present, Hammer announced three gifts of more than $50,000 each to causes held dear by the prince. Charles commented, "Doctor, that was an expensive lunch." [18]

Hammer settled his largess on other favorite causes of Prince Charles. One was the Mary Rose Trust, dedicated to raising the British ship sunk in 1545 during a battle with the French armada. Charles made numerous dives as part of the salvage effort. The trust lifted the remains of the ship during 1982. Another was rebuilding the Old Globe Theatre, famous because of its affiliation with William Shakespeare, on the site where it had been torn down in 1644. During a reception in Los Angeles, Hammer announced his donation of $250,000, along with like amounts from four of his wealthy acquaintances. Attending were Prince Philip, Cary Grant, Elizabeth Taylor, and Richard Burton, who did a reading. Additional recipients of Hammer's Charles-inspired gifts were the decaying Wells Cathedral, in Somerset, for restoration; Salisbury Cathedral, in Wiltshire, also for restoration; and such London institutions as the Royal Opera House and the Royal Academy. After Hammer won a libel case from *Private Eye,* an English magazine, he donated the $41,000 settlement to Business in the Community, a philanthropy of the prince's.[19]

When Charles married Diana Spencer, Hammer gave them a creation by the California sculptor Pascal. There was a story behind the gift. Hammer had introduced Charles to Pascal at a gala for the Royal Ballet in New York. That night, the sculptor was wearing a jewel openly admired by the prince. As a result, Hammer commissioned Pascal to fashion a glass horse's head, two and one half inches high, with topaz eyes and a mane of gold chains. It could be worn as a jewel on a gold collar or could hang from a gold stand. Hammer's generosity seemed to be limitless: Princess Diana happened to mention to him that Neil Diamond was her favorite singer, so he arranged for Diamond to give a birthday concert for her in England, with proceeds going to charity.[20]

Hammer, taken with Charles's paintings and seeing a way to publicize his art galleries, asked the prince to exhibit his watercolors at Knoedler's. Charles refused, saying he was too much of an amateur. Not missing a beat, Hammer offered to bring watercolorist Bob Timberlake to Buckingham Palace to give him private lessons. Timberlake, from a tiny North Carolina town, had seen little of the world. He had begun painting professionally late; after a year of filling canvases, he carried them by train to New York, loaded them in a taxicab, and got out at Hammer Galleries because he knew somebody who once exhibited there. Timberlake arrived without an appointment, but, luckily, Victor Hammer was free. Victor liked Timberlake's work and, on the spot, agreed to exhibit it. That was the beginning of a long-term artist-patron relationship.[21]

Armand's call to Timberlake to visit England came on a Saturday during 1979; the artist was vacationing away from home, but Occidental's switchboard operators tracked him down. "I don't even know how he found me." Timberlake said. "He wanted me to meet him in London the next Tuesday. I went on a commercial flight because he was already there. I had just got to Claridge's when he phoned my room. He wanted to see the prince right away. I was tired, but he didn't even give me time to wash up." Within hours, Timberlake was touring Buckingham Palace with the prince and Hammer. He observed the "truly warm relationship" between the old man and the royal youth. Timberlake gave the prince some tips on watercolors, then was on his way back to North Carolina. "Dr. Hammer is amazing," Timberlake said. "I'm not sure we will see this kind of man pass by us again. . . . I thank my lucky stars he passed my way. I cannot be around him without feeling the electricity, that positive attitude."[22]

Profiling Hammer for the *London Telegraph Sunday Magazine,* Andrew Duncan said the tycoon's "admiration for the royal family is boundless, and he has given about fourteen million pounds to charities associated with Prince Charles. . . . Yet he is not, it must be said, a parvenu royal groupie on the make." When a *Los Angeles Times* columnist asked Frances and Armand what royal personage they would like to be, Frances answered Queen Elizabeth, because of her wealth. Armand replied, "I would be a grand duke, an advisor to kings."[23]

Tim Halford, hired in 1975 to handle public relations for Occidental in Europe, became the pathway between Hammer and the prince. He performed his job so well that Hammer's increasingly close identification with Charles started to cause consternation in some quarters. A *Chicago Tribune* gossip column reported that as Hammer had approached Princess Diana at a lunch, she had muttered, "Oh no, please, no," just before he seated himself next to her. Other gossip columns claimed that Prince Philip was upset about the possibility of Charles's naming Hammer godfather to Prince Henry, his second son. At Henry's birth, Hammer sent Charles a baby stroller designed especially to be pushed by joggers. When the prince wrote a thank-you, Hammer sent a copy to Phil Baechler, the Yakima, Washington, manufacturer of the stroller.[24]

But nothing Hammer did for the prince matched the significance of their work together for United World Colleges, a group of colleges in different locations around the world that promoted cultural exchange. After Prince Charles encouraged Hammer, the octogenarian threw himself into the effort to establish the first U.S. campus. By that time, Hammer was wary of taking on new philanthropic projects. He received so many requests that his secretary prepared a master list for him to skim from time to time. This project was different, however. It was a perfect match — Hammer could promote internationalism and gain gratitude from the man who would be king of England.

Campuses already existed in Canada, Singapore, Swaziland, Italy, and Wales. They were the brainchild of Kurt Hahn, an educator who had fled Nazi Germany and founded the Gordonstoun School, in Scotland, which Prince Charles had attended. Hahn's concepts excited Lord Mountbatten, Charles's uncle, who had worked hard to spread the idea. Students attended for two years, taking courses roughly equivalent to those covered during the senior year of an American high school and the freshman year of an American college. When Hammer agreed to underwrite a campus, he planned to accept fifty young men and fifty young women from forty countries, including twenty-five students from the United States. In that way, Hammer hoped to create a cadre of internationalists devoted to world peace. He raised money from various circles of associates. The board of trustees consisted almost entirely of Occidental directors, business partners, and social acquaintances who attended Hammer's parties and basked in his glow.

Hammer hired as the first headmaster Theodore Lockwood, recently president of Trinity College in Hartford. Acting impulsively, as he often did, Hammer had offered the position to someone else first, even though it was clear to others that the person was ill suited for the post. Hammer's staff breathed easier when that person declined. After Lockwood's hiring, the big questions were whether Hammer could find the right site and then build on it quickly enough to open classes by his self-imposed deadline of September 1982.

The site needed to be spacious, attractive, conducive to outdoor activities, affordable, and available right away. The burden of locating it fell on James Pugash, Hammer's executive assistant fresh from the staff of a U.S. Senate committee. When Pugash had decided to leave public service and seek a job in the corporate world, he sent inquiries to chief executives of Fortune 500 companies. His boss, Senator Bennett Johnston, wrote a cover letter — "That is the kind of mail Dr. Hammer reads," Pugash said. Hammer invited Pugash to Los Angeles for a Sunday interview at his home. He was in his bathrobe, surly and distant, when Pugash arrived. Then a call came from Washington, apparently a positive report on the potential aide. "Dr. Hammer was all smiles after that," Pugash recalled. "I still was not sure that I liked him, so I named a high price. He gulped and said okay. At first he gave me a week to decide, but when he found out there was competition for me, he wanted an answer by the end of the day." Pugash enjoyed the work and developed a strong affection for Hammer. But after a year, he wanted to strike out on his own, so told Hammer he planned to look for a new job. Hammer made Pugash a vice president of Occidental and doubled his salary. Pugash stayed. The development of the United World Colleges campus turned out to be his most satisfying accomplishment at Occidental.[25]

Pugash looked at dozens of sites, including a hard-to-reach one in Montezuma, New Mexico, along the Gallinas River at the edge of the Pecos Wilderness in the Sangre de Cristo Mountains. The Atchison, Topeka & Santa Fe Railroad had developed the site, which had a pleasant climate and natural hot springs, as a resort during the late nineteenth century. The centerpiece, a lodge known as the castle, was completed in 1895 but closed less than a decade later because it couldn't compete with other resorts. The Baptist church acquired the building in 1921, operating it for ten years as a college. In 1937, the Catholic church bought it as a site for training seminarians. By 1972, it was vacant again, and falling into disrepair.[26]

Hammer pronounced himself "enchanted" by the site's possibilities but worried about the time and money needed to make the property usable. At first, he thought the site could be readied for no more than $1 million. An abandoned Catholic school seemed as if it might be a bargain, since so many were in trouble at that time. The church was paying $80,000 a year for insurance alone. But the $1 million estimate turned out to be much too low. The land alone cost that much, and Hammer had to do some skillful negotiating to win the competition at that price. Businessman Wid Slick had made a similar offer before Hammer entered the picture, but the church was hesitating over whether to sell to a commercial developer. Hammer came out on top at least in part because church officials felt more comfortable selling to a philanthropic venture.[27]

Owning the property was just the beginning. As one college publication noted later, "To accomplish these renovations in only one year seemed impossible. Yet because of the vision and determination of Dr. Hammer, the renovations were completed in time." William McGill, the former Columbia University president who chaired the school's board, agreed with that immodest phrasing: "Dr. Hammer drove us unmercifully. With someone else in charge it would have been much less painful, but less effective." McGill said the elderly Hammer pushed to open the college quickly because "he wants to direct the way he is remembered, and he will work indefatigably to construct the edifice."[28]

Early construction focused on five buildings, to be used as classrooms, a library, residence halls, and a dining room. The school encountered difficulty receiving accreditation by its deadline. So Senator Harrison Schmitt reportedly intervened with the Immigration and Naturalization Service, persuading the agency to admit international students to a worthy, but unaccredited, institution.[29] When the school opened in the fall of 1982, Hammer was there to greet each student. At the end of October, Prince Charles arrived in Montezuma after a journey on Hammer's airplane, setting not only the town but also the entire nation abuzz.

By the first graduation, in May 1984, Hammer had spent $5.5 million for facilities and raised millions more for operations and scholarships. The graduations were gala affairs, with celebrity speakers such as Abigail Van Buren, Malcolm Forbes, and Senator Pete Domenici. Parents of graduates included King Constantine and Queen Anne-Marie of Greece. Hammer's delight with his college struck just about everybody as sincere.

The climax of his efforts came in 1985. Prince Charles and Lady Diana visited the United States, and on their agenda was a Hammer-sponsored ball in Palm Beach, Florida, to raise money for United World Colleges. Invitations to the ball could be had for a donation of $10,000, which provided one scholarship for an international student. A donation of $50,000 brought the opportunity to be photographed with the prince and princess. What Hammer left out of his account of the ball in his 1987 autobiography were details of perhaps the ugliest debate ever to rip through the elite Florida city of Palm Beach. Many year-round members of local high society expressed outrage that Hammer was milking the community for charity dollars to be sent out of state. Town council member Nancy Douthit led the opposition, voting against issuance of a charitable solicitation permit. The majority of the council members voted yes, after Hammer gave $75,000 to the community chest. The council president explained cryptically that Hammer's gift "may have looked like moral blackmail, but there is a very thin line between legality and morality."[30]

Failing to understand the deep-seated resentment, Hammer blithely sent the media promotional packets with letters of praise from Prince Charles and President Reagan. Florida governor Bob Graham proclaimed Armand Hammer Day to coincide with the ball. The unpleasantness only worsened. Some of the anger centered on Hammer's appointment of Patricia Kluge, an out-of-towner, as chairwoman of the charity event. The statuesque Patricia was married to John Kluge, thirty-four years her senior, a media baron reputed to be the second-wealthiest person in America. John Kluge served on Occidental's board of directors. Publications appeared stating that Patricia Kluge had posed in the nude for a magazine. When the reports turned out to be accurate, the Kluges decided that European travels would prevent their attendance at the Palm Beach festivities.

Joseph Kamp, a Palm Beach–area resident known as the dean of American anti-Communists, circulated leaflets exposing Hammer's supposedly subversive activities. Kamp commented that the British Foreign Office "should have warned Prince Charles about the dangerous implications . . . in accepting the help of anyone with the weird and sinister background of Dr. Hammer. . . . It is a bit odd that England's royal family should be honoring Soviet agent Hammer, who has probably done more damage to England than all of these KGB agents put together."[31]

In the end, the ball was a success on one level — it raised millions of dollars for United World Colleges. But that institution was almost completely overshadowed by the heaping of praise on Hammer. A trib-

ute book produced by Hammer's staff and given to every guest contained a full-page color photograph of the tycoon, accompanied by this
quotation from him: "During my lifetime, I have been a man of many
dreams, and have been fortunate that so many of them have come true.
But my greatest dream, for which I have been working throughout my
life, is to help to secure a lasting peace in the world." A letter on
Charles's Buckingham Palace stationery thanked Hammer for his support. Then came sugary letters from President Reagan, Governor Graham, Senators Lawton Chiles and Paula Hawkins, California governor
George Deukmejian, Los Angeles mayor Tom Bradley, and many other
notables. The booklet included a twelve-page synopsis of Hammer's life
and ended with a purportedly inspirational poem by Edgar Guest on
accomplishing the impossible.[32] The evening of self-promotion was a
reminder of Hammer's penchant for riding roughshod over even important people, of his gaucheness when headlines were at stake.

Marylouise Oates, a columnist for the *Los Angeles Times,* captured
Hammer's excitement when she accompanied him to the New Mexico
campus in 1986: "The last time we saw Dr. Armand Hammer, he was
in the middle of an African folk dance line, winding its way conga-
like through a former Jesuit seminary secluded in the New Mexico
highlands. None of this should surprise anyone." Oates told of "the
ubiquitous industrialist" and his wife that morning boarding their private jet in Los Angeles. On the flight, Hammer waxed enthusiastic
about his college, spinning stories about the son of a former Greek king
volunteering as a fireman with the school's brigade, about an Israeli
student saving an Arab classmate who had fallen into a stream. A
television film crew traveled with Hammer, Oates said, to produce a
fund-raiser for the college. The cameras rolled as cheering students
greeted Hammer entering the castle. After lunch, the audience interrupted Hammer's speech with cheers that appeared to surprise even
him. He announced that two students and a teacher from the Soviet
Union planned to participate during the next term. After Oates returned to Los Angeles, she received from Hammer a scrapbook com-
memorating her visit to the campus; it contained fifteen color pictures,
including one of herself.[33]

Despite the glamorous fund-raisers, the school's income failed to cover
its expenses. During the early years, Pugash recalled, he used to enter
Hammer's inner sanctum every month to ask for a $200,000 check to
pay its bills. "You can be cynical about Dr. Hammer's philanthropy
because of all the self-interest involved, but when it is just you and he
in the room and he writes those checks, you have to be impressed. He
loves to go to the campus. Being with the kids rejuvenates him. He has

a sincere interest in them."[34] Hammer made sure Prince Charles knew about his generosity, sending him bound reports of construction progress with an engraved gold plate on the cover.

Another international forum devised by Hammer was the annual Armand Hammer Conference on Peace and Human Rights. It was the activity most transparently tied to his desire for the Nobel Peace Prize. Yet, like his other philanthropic ventures, it sprang from more than self-interest; Hammer's decades-long commitment to peace on earth was sincere. The first conference took place during 1978 in Norway, home of the Nobel Peace Prize. It was uncharacteristically low-key; before Hammer publicized a conference named for himself, he wanted to make sure the concept worked. By 1979, when the conference was held at Campobello, the publicity was in full bloom as Hammer took advantage of the site's natural news value and his past connection with it. Once again, Hammer's dizzying life had become a seamless whole.

President Jimmy Carter sent a warm message and a representative from the White House. Samuil Zivs, one of the Soviet Union's three representatives present, noted that Hammer "has done much to make United States–Soviet relations stable and positive. All his long and tireless life, Dr. Hammer has actively promoted economic and cultural cooperation between the United States and the Soviet Union." Twenty other nations were represented by the twenty-nine delegates, whose ranks included two Nobel Peace Prize–winners. Their conclusions were mostly platitudinous, their key theme being that "the right to peace should be recognized as a human right." For the most part, the purpose seemed to be the glorification of Armand Hammer. Over and over, he recalled his ties to Franklin and Eleanor Roosevelt, his proud decade of owning Campobello.[35]

The 1980 conference, in Poland, was spicier, for delegates became embroiled in debate over the Soviet invasion of Afghanistan and the Polish government's suppression of unionists and intellectuals. During the conference, Hammer met Polish leader Edward Gierek and praised him for demonstrating the independence that allowed the conference to be held behind the Iron Curtain. Polish dissidents were aghast at Hammer's remarks, criticizing him for supporting a government that refused to respect human rights. To them, Hammer was mistaken in believing that the conferences helped hold Communist nations accountable on human rights. The State Department disapprovingly commented that the message emanating from Hammer's Warsaw session "complements the current Soviet peace campaign in Europe."[36]

Hammer held the 1981 conference at Aix-en-Provence, France. In

1982, he again evoked the memories of Eleanor and Franklin Roosevelt by choosing Hyde Park, New York, as the locale. There was a hiatus in 1983. In 1984, Hammer chose Spain, coordinating the meeting with a display of the Codex Hammer at Madrid's Prado museum. The size of the conference had ballooned, with 132 delegates representing thirty-six countries.[37]

Despite their varied locations and elegant trappings, the conferences had begun to take on a sameness in their messages to world leaders. Hammer loved the adulation bestowed upon him at the meetings, but he halted them after Madrid, channeling his money to other international peace ventures. He must have been pleased with one outcome, though. Attending the conferences convinced U.S. Senator Jennings Randolph of Hammer's commitment to peace. As a result, the West Virginian nominated Hammer for the Nobel Prize.[38] Having a senior senator in his corner was a coup, especially because Randolph represented one of just seven categories of people who could make nominations to the Nobel committee. To supplement Randolph's push, Hammer's Washington office supplied an eighteen-page summary of his accomplishments to potential nominators. The package included the address of the Nobel committee, the deadline, and a reminder to recipients: "Please do not attach a copy of the Armand Hammer biography to your nomination," perhaps a safeguard against discovery of the orchestrated campaign.

This kind of campaigning for the Nobel had a long tradition; the effort was sometimes mounted by the hopeful's adherents, sometimes directly by the hopeful. About half the members of Congress reportedly backed someone or other each year. Hammer's desire for the prize became known beyond his associates, who long had talked about it among themselves. In a *Fortune* profile of Hammer, reporter Brian O'Reilly noted that critics considered his Nobel Peace Prize campaign unbecoming. Zbigniew Brzezinski said, "If it can be bought, his chances of winning are quite high." Hammer told O'Reilly he was not campaigning, adding, "But if it happens, I will be very happy." After Donald Woutat of the *Los Angeles Times* spent months researching Hammer for a cover piece in the Sunday magazine, the tycoon's quest for the prize stood out so strongly he opened the article with it. Woutat said Hammer's executive assistant Richard Jacobs was keeper of the nomination letters: "The staff at Occidental answers questions about a Nobel for Hammer about as readily as an apprehensive pitcher talking about a no-hitter in the seventh inning. Hammer's aides only reluctantly acknowledge the existence of any letters of nomination, and they reject as inappropriate a request to read them."[39]

Sometimes it seemed the Nobel Peace Prize was the only honor to elude Hammer. Despite the publicity that came with each award, Hammer wanted more. He took matters in his own hands — to publicize his doings, he oversaw the creation of the *Occidental Report,* a newsletter whose first issue appeared in July 1972, and *Oxy Today,* a slick, full-color magazine published several times a year beginning in 1973. To nobody's surprise, the first issue of *Oxy Today* contained a five-page profile of Hammer. The author was Bob Considine, sportswriter, syndicated columnist, and prolific book author. The editor's note said nothing about Considine's being retained to write a full-scale biography of Hammer, although that is what happened. The *Oxy Today* article previewed the adulation that infused the 1975 biography, saying of Hammer that Occidental's thirty thousand employees "look to him and him alone to supply all their answers and give substance to their aspirations."[40]

The founding editor of *Oxy Today* was Joe Maranto, whom Hammer hired from ITT specifically to create the magazine. It was a tough job. Hammer wanted an award-winning, credible magazine. Maranto recalled that Hammer, despite his daunting responsibilities and worldwide travel, "got involved in everything — the photograph selection, the paper stock, everything. I didn't mind; he knew what he was doing. When it was time to go to press, I would sit outside his office waiting for him to get off the phone or conclude his meetings with an endless stream of business associates. But he would always find time to see what I had to show him. For instance, he would knock out references to a particular executive, telling me he would not be there much longer."[41]

The intensity of Maranto's working relationship with Hammer left vivid memories. "Part of my job was to set up lunches and dinners for foreign dignitaries," Maranto said. "Dr. Hammer would get involved with the typeface to be used on the menus, the wine selection, everything." At the sumptuous meals, it was difficult to enjoy the food: "By the time I would have three sips of soup, he would be done and the butler would bring in the second course. That happened with each course, and Dr. Hammer would excuse himself to make telephone calls. The next day I consciously tried to keep up with him at the table, and was unable to do it. He obviously has the digestive system of a mountain goat. I rode with him once in his white convertible Rolls-Royce down Wilshire Boulevard, and he drives like he eats. Quick. He shifted lanes with impunity, driving like a twenty-one-year-old." Maranto never ceased to be amazed at Hammer's accessibility. "I later worked for twelve years at Mobil Oil, and I only dealt directly with the chairman on a few occasions. . . . You simply didn't get in to see him. Not so

with Hammer. You heard from him directly, especially if he was unhappy about something. And then he could bruise your eardrums. You
generally deserved it."[42]

Hammer certainly was accessible to his in-house filmmakers. Of all
his Occidental vanity ventures, the film company probably was the most
egregiously self-promoting. The subsidiary's original name was Fireline
Productions, later changed to Armand Hammer Productions. It suffered from a split personality, reflecting Hammer's two minds on the
matter: He wanted the subsidiary to be a profit center, making feature
films for television and movie theaters, but he also wanted it to serve
as a cinematic scrapbook that would document his every meeting with
world leaders. One of the company's earliest efforts carried the title
Occidental: Visions for the Future. It contained footage of Hammer with
the leaders of Egypt, England, Hungary, Poland, Peru, Pakistan, Abu
Dhabi, and the United States. The credits thanked Armand and Frances
Hammer in large letters; the lettering for the remainder of the credits
was so small as to be virtually unreadable.[43]

Establishing a film company apparently had been on Hammer's mind
for some time. What finally spurred him to action was a call in 1979
from Prince Charles, asking for help in finding donated fuel supplies
for the daring Transglobe Expedition of explorer Ranulph Fiennes.
After Hammer lined up the fuel, he wrote Fiennes and offered to help
in other ways. In response, Fiennes asked if Hammer could find an
American television company to film the years-long voyage, which would
circle the earth from pole to pole. The English crews Fiennes wanted
were on strike. Hammer had no success lining up an independent crew,
so, as Fiennes said, "the doctor formed his own film company, and
started hiring a team to join us." One filmmaker Hammer wanted was
Mike Hoover, but he was on the Red Sea shooting footage for the
National Geographic Society. Hammer sent a messenger to the location
and had him row out every day to wherever Hoover was shooting to
repeat the job offer; finally Hoover agreed.[44]

The record of the Fiennes expedition eventually became the subsidiary's earliest feature, *To the Ends of the Earth,* with Richard Burton
narrating. Hammer made two cameo appearances with Prince Charles,
at different stages of the expedition. Fiennes later cut back on his exploring to become Hammer's spokesman in London. As one British
journalist noted, "For a super-fit adventurer and comic-strip hero like
Ranulph Fiennes to act as Dr. Hammer's clerk says a lot about the
man's power." Fiennes said Hammer was "perhaps the only man alive

for whom I would willingly have subjected myself to office life." Another feature, *Backstage at the Kirov*, was an inside look at a Soviet ballet company, filmed in Russia thanks to Hammer's entrée. Although it and some other Armand Hammer Productions films were of high quality, the venture reportedly lost money for Occidental. That failed to stop Hammer. During 1988, the subsidiary launched work on a miniseries for Home Box Office that was based on the saga of a Russian family. Derek Hart, president of the film company, said the project demonstrated Hammer's continuing commitment to better Soviet-American relations.[45]

Periodically, Hammer concluded that his publicity machine was not doing enough to achieve lasting recognition for him. One solution — produce a book. His 1932 memoir had been intended to sell his czarist art and bring his name before the American public after his decade in the Soviet Union. That was just a warm-up. In 1975, Harper & Row published *The Remarkable Life of Dr. Armand Hammer,* by Bob Considine, one of the best-known journalists of the era between World War II and Watergate. Hammer hired Considine for a reported $75,000, exercised editorial control, and pledged to buy a large number of copies from Harper & Row. Amy Bonoff, the editor who worked with Considine, recalled how Hammer "read the manuscript before publication and made lots of suggestions. He would call daily to check sales."[46]

As serious biography, it was an embarrassment, characterized by careless research, one-sided arguments, glaring omissions, and a lack of documentation. In Considine's defense, the book was done near his death and to some extent beyond his control.

The reception from readers and reviewers was mixed. Those who already worshipped Hammer thought it a classic; those who despised him considered it a whitewash. Abigail Van Buren promoted it in her "Dear Abby" column: "If you enjoy biographies, beg, borrow, or buy [the book]. . . . It is a fascinating book about one of the world's most successful, creative, talented, yet warmly human men of our time. I loved it!" In the *New York Times Book Review,* Robert Alberts called it "a biography of a character so versatile and unbelievable that most writers of topical-events fiction would be embarrassed to put him in a novel." Although Hammer's exploits were inherently fascinating, Alberts said, he was bothered by the work's lack of balance; he suggested it be subtitled "The Case for the Defense." Hammer gave it as a gift to colleagues, journalists, and policymakers.[47]

At the end of the book, Considine wondered when Hammer would take the time to write his autobiography. Hammer began to consider that enterprise in the early 1980s. First, he retained John Bryson, a former *Life* magazine photographer, to follow him for three years, camera at the ready. The result was a 256-page coffee-table book, *The World of Armand Hammer,* published by Abrams in 1985. The photographs were superb. Bryson was proud of his effort, saying he had wanted to avoid "a fawning piece of work" like Considine's.[48] But the consensus was that a fawning piece of work was exactly what he had produced. Bryson developed a deep admiration for Hammer during their traveling. Furthermore, he operated under Hammer's approval and took money from him.

Michael Kinsley, writing in the *Washington Post* and the *New Republic,* savaged the book as "executive porn," described Walter Cronkite's introduction as "sycophantic," and noted that "the vanity of this enterprise almost defies description. . . . Apart from one obvious customer, is there a market for this preposterous book?" Kinsley feared there might be:

> In this age of the glamorized businessman, even serious business magazines feed their readers' gray-flannel fantasies with salacious photographs of high-powered executives posed with suggestive self-importance against a background of corporate luxury. . . . On the one hand, the important executive has overwhelming duties and works all the time. On the other hand, he socializes incessantly with famous people. . . . [Hammer] is a sad man, measuring his self-worth by the size of his airplane, attracted to people solely because they are rich or powerful or famous, and unaware or indifferent that his so-called friends are attracted to him for the same shallow reasons.

Hammer's concept of heaven, Kinsley said, would be a party attended by dictators and duchesses, magnates and movie stars, who journeyed from all over the world specifically to drink a champagne toast on his one hundred and fiftieth birthday. "Not incredible," Kinsley said. "Just pathetic." Bryson led the counterattack on Kinsley, replying that *The World of Armand Hammer* was an honest recording of what had taken place before his eyes.[49]

During the controversy over the Bryson book, it became known that Hammer was working on a full-scale autobiography, also partially financed by Occidental Petroleum. Ray Irani, then the company's president, seemed perplexed about the uproar over Occidental's underwriting the books: "[Hammer's] first priority always has been the shareholders. It is fitting, then, that the company's directors chose to make the story of Armand Hammer, which is in many ways the story of Occidental, available to the shareholders and the general public in the form of photographic and historical books." Irani noted that public relations budgets of other companies exceeded what Occidental was spending on the volumes and that any profits from book sales would replenish the treasury.[50] *

Both books rewrote the histories of Hammer and Occidental, mostly by omission. Key men and women received no mention in the text, no place in the hundreds of photographs. James Pugash, by then departed as Hammer's executive assistant, was shown once; Bryson told him he had been included only because Bryson insisted, thus saving him from the status of nonperson. Key clerical staff, completely loyal to Hammer despite his seemingly unreasonable demands, appeared nowhere in the photographs.

For the autobiography, titled simply *Hammer,* the tycoon had sought an eminent collaborator. He approached Robert Kaiser, a former Moscow correspondent for the *Washington Post.* Surprised at the feeler, Kaiser suggested Hammer read his Russian dispatches before proceeding, since he realized some would be perceived as negative. Soon thereafter, Kaiser received a note telling him he would receive a copy of the book upon publication.[51]

Negotiations went further with Clay Blair, a prolific, respected author of books and magazine articles. Blair flew to Los Angeles, where Hammer's limousine met him at the airport. He and Hammer liked each other, and they signed a tentative agreement to produce the book. Hammer wanted to pay Blair with Occidental funds or personal funds, but Blair suggested drafting a proposal and selling it to a publisher; that would give the book more credibility. Hammer, who apparently never had thought of such an approach, agreed. As Blair began his research, Hammer started calling in the very early morning hours, inviting him to travel to exotic places on short notice. But worries arose in Blair's mind as Hammer continued to be vague about access to his files. Rather than granting access, Hammer sent Blair a videocassette recorder and tapes from Armand Hammer Productions. They were nearly useless to a serious biographer. It looked more and more as if Hammer wanted a book of self-promotion, not a candid biography or autobiography. When Hammer objected to Blair's outline, the two men amicably ended the relationship.[52] Eventually, Hammer settled on Neil Lyndon, a talented British journalist. Lyndon, on his own, had tried to

---

* In early 1989, Occidental reported that royalties from the autobiography topped $600,000. Those royalties went into the corporate treasury as reimbursement for book expenses. (Occidental proxy statement, 1989.)

interest English publishers in a Hammer biography in years past but found no takers. It was only when London's *Sunday Times* needed an article to go with Bryson's photographs that Lyndon received a call to write a profile. Hammer liked the published result, so he approached Lyndon about collaborating. Lyndon reportedly was offered $200,000 plus royalties.

He began traveling the world with Hammer, writing as he went. With the massive manuscript in draft form, Hammer hired high-powered literary brokers from the William Morris agency to find a publisher. Putnam ended up acquiring the manuscript for a reported $1 million. When the book appeared, in May 1987, sales soared. Hammer bought copies to distribute. Stockholders at Occidental's annual meeting received coupons to buy the book at a discount; the *Wall Street Journal* mentioned the coupons under the sarcastic headline "WHAT A PERK!" Hammer appeared on television to promote the autobiography; the "Today" show put him on two days in a row. The *Los Angeles Times* syndicate sold excerpts to newspapers. Portions appeared all over the world. *Newsweek* won the bidding for a preview and accompanied it with a glowing review. The book was translated into at least thirteen languages. In England, a reporter noted that Hammer launched the book "with his usual flair — a come-and-be-seen champagne party in the Hellenic and Egyptian jewel room at the Royal Academy."[53] It reached number two on the national best-seller lists, number one on local newspaper lists in selected cities.

The reviews were divided about evenly between praise and disgust. Some commentators concentrated on the dust jacket rather than the book, an unsurprising reaction to the large number of effusive blurbs that appeared on it. There were so many celebrities willing to comment favorably on *Hammer* that Putnam sent reviewers a separate pamphlet containing those paeans failing to fit on the jacket. The *New Republic* offered a prize to any celebrity willing to prove he or she had read the 544-page book before sending in the blurb.[54]

Reviews that brought heated reactions from the Hammer camp appeared in the *St. Louis Post-Dispatch* and *Manhattan, inc.* magazine. The newspaper's review was sarcastic and negative, ending, "This is not the profoundest autobiography of our time, but it wins the boasting awards hands down." The book editor received an unexpected rebuttal from best-selling novelist Irving Stone, a member of Hammer's social circle. Stone slammed the newspaper's "prejudiced review" and called the autobiography "a testimonial to a life lived on a grand scale, most of it contributing to the economic, political, and cultural well-being of our one world." Stone argued with the criticism of Hammer's vanity: "Armand Hammer is a man filled with delight in himself and his seventy years of astonishing accomplishment. . . . He has no time for humility. He would find it a waste of energy in his indomitable concept that one person can help."[55]

The *Manhattan, inc.* review was longer and nastier. Joseph Nocera called the book "a consumer fraud." Nocera homed in on the omissions, listing some in a lengthy paragraph. To him, Hammer seemed to be saying to the reader, "You have to trust me. I was there." But, Nocera said, "you do not trust him. . . . By the end of the book, you just cannot. The omissions, the distortions, the convenient oversights and lapses of memory, piling up as they do for page after page after page . . . finally, it is just too much." Even a reader accepting the book at face value, he wrote, would find Hammer to be "a fairly unpleasant character," somebody "lacking any kind of moral compass."[56]

Bruce Kauffman, a Philadelphia lawyer working on the Watergate pardon for Hammer, expressed his outrage at Nocera's review. He wrote a letter to *Manhattan, inc.* but the magazine refused to publish it unless Hammer signed it. Otherwise, said editor Clay Felker, it would be akin to giving public relations practitioners free space for their clients. Shut out of the letters column, Kauffman bought a full-page advertisement in the magazine, attacking Nocera as vituperatively as Nocera had attacked Hammer.[57] As usual, the truth was somewhere in the middle. Both Nocera and Kauffman appear to have overstated parts of their cases. It seems plausible that Neil Lyndon either did not know about the omissions or that he mentioned certain episodes but had them excised by Hammer. As for the errors of commission, it appears that Lyndon had little access to primary documents, relying instead on Hammer's memory, which turned out to be faulty on numerous occasions.*

The primary evidence certainly existed for Hammer's hired writers to study, if given the opportunity. Several months after the publication of Hammer's autobiography, the Library of Congress, in Washington, announced it had been promised Hammer's personal papers. Daniel Boorstin, in his final week as librarian of Congress before retirement,

---

* The controversy over the autobiography failed to dull Hammer's desire for another book. In early 1989, Occidental disclosed that it had spent $255,000 and planned to spend at least $120,000 more for a sequel to the 1987 book. The newest volume would "describe Dr. Hammer's worldwide endeavors since [1987] in international affairs, art, and other philanthropic concerns, as well as significant domestic and international business activities of Occidental." (Occidental proxy statement, 1989.)

was delighted. The library had first approached Hammer twelve years earlier about the donation. The competition with other depositories had been spirited; after all, few individuals had recorded so broad a span of twentieth-century events.

Early in January 1989 Hammer finally signed the necessary documents. A large reception was held in his honor in the Great Hall of the Library of Congress on January 18, during George Bush's inaugural week. The present librarian of Congress, James Billington; Boorstin, librarian of Congress emeritus; and Hammer all spoke. The long-promised gift had finally been made.[58]

28

Family Feuds

A S ARMAND HAMMER CARVED OUT HIS PLACE in his-
tory, his family often took a backseat. By the time he reached his
ninetieth birthday, his brothers were dead, as were most of his other
relatives. Those who were alive usually saw him only at one of his gala
parties with hundreds of other guests present, if they saw him at all.
The only family members who were part of his supporting cast were
his third wife, Frances; his son, Julian; his grandchildren, Michael and
Casey; and his great-grandchildren.

Frances was Hammer's constant companion. By all accounts, she was
patient with her sometimes trying husband and with everybody else
around her. Acquaintances agreed that she remained unspoiled by her
vast wealth. She and Armand lived in the same house she had owned
before they married. She redecorated frugally and continued to cook
and clean. Daniel Yergin, who observed her while preparing a profile
of Hammer, noted that although she termed gardening and painting
her hobbies, her full-time preoccupation was Armand. She accompanied him on almost every flight, leaving the plane if necessary during
stopovers to purchase a tie or a coat for him.[1]

During his younger days, Hammer, handsome and dashing, had a
roving eye. In his 1987 autobiography, he commented on the sexual
appetites of many other wealthy men but provided little information
about his own. By the time he married Frances and launched his career
as an oilman, he was nearly sixty. Despite the gossip, sexual conquests
probably played a small role in his life by then. Thomas Wachtell, his
executive assistant during the 1960s, recalled one chaste but amusing
incident: "We were working at night when he got an unexpected call

from a high school sweetheart whose husband had died, and who knew about Armand through the newspapers. He was touched and excited, and arranged to see her in Newark or thereabouts. He got dressed snappily, with a flower in his lapel, and drove with his chauffeur to a modest neighborhood. He rang the bell. What he described as 'an old lady' answered. He left as quickly as he could." Wachtell commented that Hammer was about seventy at the time but did not think of himself as "an old man."[2]

Armand and Frances had no children together, and she had none from her previous marriage. Thus Julian had no competition. He was a disappointment all the same. After his acquittal on the 1955 murder charge, Julian continued to get into scrapes involving guns. He ended up in a mental hospital, diagnosed as a chronic paranoid schizophrenic. When he went through a divorce as a middle-aged man, his lawyer said he had been unemployed for five years, "living on funds loaned him by his father." Occasionally Hammer tried to enhance his son's self-esteem, as well as his image, by making him sound successful. In a 1980 magazine interview, he was quoted as saying that Julian "works with me. He is an electronics engineer and a scientific writer."[3] Julian distributed a business card that read: "Consultant — audio, graphics, video, the Armand Hammer Foundation."

Occidental and Hammer Foundation employees recalled Julian's copying television shows that mentioned his father and keeping the tapes in a storage room that held shelves of footage documenting Armand's life. They said that in later years Julian exhibited fewer symptoms of the mental illness that had led to violent episodes and hospitalization during the 1960s. Armand occasionally allowed photographers to capture him with Julian; in the glitzy commemorative booklet published by Hammer for his ninetieth-birthday bash, sandwiched between the dozens of congratulatory letters from world leaders, was a picture showing four generations of Hammer men: Armand, Julian, Armand's grandson, Michael, and great-grandson Armand. But it was revealing that in Armand's hefty 1987 autobiography, there are no more mentions of Julian after the story of his acquittal for murder in 1955 is told.

Michael filled a gap in Armand's life that Julian never could. Occidental staff lawyer James Patten remembered being in a meeting when the doctor took a telephone call. As he hung up, he was chuckling. The caller had been Michael, who wanted to borrow $300 to enter the lawn-mowing business. Armand commented later that he made the loan but should have structured the deal differently, because Michael had earned far more than Grandpa had thought possible. Armand saw that his grandson made it through college, retaining John Boles — a former Occidental executive and university economics professor — to help the youth navigate the undergraduate curriculum at the University of San Diego. "Dr. Hammer told me once that the only thing he had left in life was his two grandchildren," Boles said.[4] Michael completed a master's degree in business administration at Columbia University and, at age twenty-six, joined Occidental.

Armand could not resist pushing his grandson's career. Robert Teitsworth was pressured to find Michael a good job in the oil and gas division. Teitsworth objected, telling Hammer it was unfair to place Michael where he would be resented. He suggested instead that Michael learn the business at another oil company, where the pressure would be less intense. Hammer rejected the advice, and eventually Boles received a call from Paul Hebner, the veteran Occidental corporate secretary about to be displaced in that role by Michael. Hebner told Boles he liked Michael but was having trouble adjusting to the arrangement whereby Michael was supposed to know everything Hebner knew. After inviting Michael to lunch, Boles advised him to resist Grandpa's pressure to climb the ladder so fast. "Paul Hebner is very popular," Boles told Michael. "Wait until he tells everyone that you are qualified. Then you will have everyone's support." Michael apparently stalled his grandfather, but only temporarily — at Occidental's 1988 stockholder meeting, he was onstage at his grandfather's elbow as the corporate secretary, leading the Pledge of Allegiance, taking notes, prompting Armand by whispering in his ear. When Armand introduced everybody on the stage, he commented, "Here's another Hammer." The crowd applauded enthusiastically.[5]

In 1985, Michael had married Dru Ann Mobley at a Methodist church wedding with 950 guests. The bride came from a prominent Tulsa family involved in banking and real estate. Dru was a personal-fitness instructor. The couple had met on an airplane and married within five months. When they moved to Los Angeles, Armand helped them buy a home with a reported sales price of $337,000. Shortly thereafter, in June 1987, Armand's granddaughter, Casey, who had graduated from Pepperdine University and taken a job with a women's clothing manufacturer in Los Angeles, was married. Her husband, Victor Swab, worked as a filmmaker. The couple settled in Beverly Hills, not far from Hammer.[6]

One of the rare family stories about Hammer's interaction with other relatives made the rounds in Massachusetts. Cousin Robert Springer, a Boston-area lawyer, read that Hammer would be in the area to accept an award from Brandeis University and to open an exhibition of his art collection in Holyoke. Springer's maternal grandmother and Hammer's maternal grandmother had been sisters. When Springer invited Hammer to visit his home, everybody said Hammer would ignore the letter. They were wrong. Hammer replied that he would be delighted to come for lunch. After accepting his Brandeis award on a Thursday evening, he jetted back to New York so he could sleep in his converted carriage house. But the next day, he returned to Boston and took a limousine to Springer's home. Accompanying him was his executive assistant Richard Jacobs.

"Dr. Hammer was delightful," Springer recalled. "He was a gentleman, complimenting me on my garden, and my wife on the lunch. One of the group tried to argue politics. I was embarrassed. But Dr. Hammer stopped him in the nicest way." Springer has a photograph of himself and thirteen others assembled around Hammer, who autographed the picture. When asked why he had accepted Springer's invitation, Hammer replied, "Because you are family."[7]

Any perception of Hammer as a loving family man was battered by the storm over his handling of his brothers' estates. Harry Hammer died on November 11, 1970, at the age of seventy-seven, two years after his wife, Bette. Harry succumbed at Methodist Hospital in Houston, where Armand had insisted he go to see the best heart specialists in America. But no amount of money could save Harry, who died a millionaire thanks to his Occidental stock. Part of his estate consisted of property he had inherited from Bette — a family homestead in Vicksburg, Mississippi, her hometown. Armand, as executor of the estate, planned to sell the property.[8]

Frances Colmery, Bette's sister, recalled Armand's offering to sell her the family property for $40,000. She was shocked and angry, especially because she possessed a letter from Bette pledging that the family home would one day belong to her. Mrs. Colmery could not and would not pay Armand's price for a home she felt was rightly hers. So Armand put the house on the market and sold it to an outsider for a reported $22,000. Nearly twenty years later, Mrs. Colmery said his decision "is a very painful thing for me to write about or talk about, and, in fact, to think about."[9]

The bitterness over Harry's estate was little known. But the claim that Armand filed in 1985 against the estate of his brother Victor became exceedingly public. That claim was one of the most inexplicable acts of Hammer's career, something that caused even his closest associates to shake their heads. Here was a wealthy, self-proclaimed humanitarian — who professed to love his brother — making a claim that not only threatened to leave Victor's seriously ill widow and adopted daughter penurious, but also sullied his hard-won image.

Throughout his life, Victor had been content to serve his older brother however he could. Armand sometimes treated him coldly, but there were moments of warmth. For example, after Victor wrote Armand about the Soviets' changing the flowers daily in front of the Goya painting that was Armand's gift to the Soviet Union, his big brother replied that he had never dreamed he would be paired with Lenin in the minds of the Russian people. He then commented that their parents would have been proud. Armand signed the letter "Lots of love."[10] However, such demonstrativeness was rare.

As Victor and Ireene began to fail mentally and physically, their care became the burden of Nancy Wicker Hammer Eilan, the biological daughter of Ireene and adopted daughter of Victor. The last decade of Victor's life was filled with hospitalizations, but by most accounts Armand rarely if ever visited him. (Some family members believed that Armand feared confronting impending death, being so concerned about his own mortality.) Nancy accordingly corresponded with Armand and Frances and telephoned them to consult about living arrangements for Victor and Ireene, asking questions about payment of certain bills.[11]

Nancy lived in Stamford, Connecticut, in a home bought by Victor and Ireene. She maintained the house and entertained there often for Victor's Hammer Galleries clients. Victor had said he would place the home in Nancy's name, but he never got around to it. When he died, in July 1985, Armand was hospitalized himself, reportedly for prostate surgery.[12] Ireene, confined to a nursing home, was unable to do anything for herself. So Nancy handled some of the arrangements for Victor's funeral, after Armand decided to hold the service in Los Angeles. Conducted by a rabbi related to the family on Rose Hammer's side, it sometimes seemed more a hymn of praise to Armand than a eulogy for Victor. Nancy was upset.

Nancy knew Armand probably cared little for her, but she saw no reason to worry about his role as executor of Victor's estate. After all, the will was straightforward enough: Victor had left everything to Ireene in trust, with Nancy and her Moscow stepbrother, Armasha, to split the estate after Ireene's death. The liquid assets totaled about $700,000. The biggest nonliquid asset was the Stamford house, appraised at $400,000.[13]

After the funeral, Nancy and Armand found themselves together at a memorial service for Victor in New York. By then, Nancy had received the news that Armand was making a claim against his brother's estate for approximately $667,000, the sum he alleged Victor owed him for certain notes at 12 percent interest signed in 1983, 1984, and 1985. Before requiring Victor to sign the notes, Armand had questioned him about repaying certain expenses to Hammer Galleries. The terminally ill Victor replied, "I was amazed getting such a letter from you. Pay these bills from what funds? You know my financial position better than anyone."[14]

The notes Victor signed were authentic enough, but some friends were certain he had never expected Armand to demand repayment. Nancy's lawyer raised the possibility that Victor was unable to understand the four-page, legalistically phrased documents; even if competent, the lawyer said, he would have signed anything Armand asked him to. Armand's response was that this was a matter in which he had lent money to his brother over a period of years, and for which his brother gave him promissory notes. Armand said it was a simple claim against his late brother's estate, to be determined by the probate court.[15]

The situation went from bad to worse during a meeting in Hammer's New York office the day after the memorial service. Nancy asked for an explanation of the claim; Armand apparently interpreted her words as a threat to expose him to ridicule if he pressed on. Declaring that he would never give in to moral blackmail, he steeled himself for whatever bad publicity might result. After the media learned about the claim, the publicity came in waves; much of it was of a soap opera variety. As *People* magazine commented, "Who says the television show 'Dynasty' is improbable and unbelievable?"[16]

Armand demonstrated no intention of capitulating. He employed his resources against Nancy's estimated annual income of $11,000 and savings of $8,000. Nancy, who received occasional commissions as a sculptor, sold a dozen precious chairs Victor had given her for the Stamford house. The chairs, which had graced Armand's opulent United Distillers office in the Empire State Building, were Nancy's source of income to meet her daily living expenses. Armasha eventually sided with his uncle against his half sister; he needed Armand's goodwill in the Soviet Union. In an affidavit from Moscow, he told the probate court he objected to Nancy's contesting Armand's claims.

As Victor's executor, Armand refused to pay Ireene Hammer's nursing home bills from the estate, thus escalating the pressure on Nancy. Nancy sold her mother's stocks and put Ireene's Florida condominium on the market to make ends meet. She sued to have Armand and family lawyer James Nemec removed as executors for allegedly mismanaging Victor's estate. The judge allowed Hammer and Nemec to retain their positions, giving great weight to the fact that Victor had appointed them: "This court is hard-pressed to countermand his desires. . . . To find otherwise would require the court to be carried away by street-corner gossip and gut feelings . . . which advocate the philosophy that rich people who have plenty of money ought not pursue claims against those who have less."[17]

Although Armand had defeated Nancy in round one, his 185-page deposition contained damaging insights into his own character. He made clear that he intended to sell the Stamford house, despite her moral and legal rights to it. "I felt that she was ungrateful, and wanted to go her own way, and as far as I was concerned I had no responsibility toward her," Armand said. "She is not a blood relation of mine. She was adopted when she was forty-eight . . . by my brother. I never could understand why, except she wanted the prestige of being known as a Hammer." His version ignored the facts that Nancy had been a devoted stepdaughter for decades before the adoption, had entertained Hammer Galleries clients in the Stamford house, and was the diligent keeper of the Hammer family's history, as well as a member of the prominent Wicker family. When questioned by Nancy's lawyers about details that might damage his case, Hammer sometimes could not remember matters, even some occurring during the week of his deposition.[18]

As the case dragged on, Ireene died. Nancy buried her, wondering how she would continue the court battle. Then, all of a sudden, the case ended as unexpectedly as it began. The lawyer appointed to defend the estate against Armand's claim discovered a conflict of interest in his firm's simultaneous work for Occidental Petroleum. The firm withdrew, and Armand offered to settle out of court. Nancy kept the Stamford house and all rights to her mother's "artistic and intellectual property," in case she wanted to tell the story of Ireene's stardom and downfall. She received no cash. Her stepbrother in Moscow inherited $200,000 and concluded a related private agreement with Armand. According to an unusual provision, Nancy in effect surrendered her First Amendment rights, agreeing "that in any book which she may write about Ireene she will not mention Dr. Hammer's claim against Victor's estate or make derogatory comments about Dr. Hammer. Further, she agrees not to make any derogatory remarks against Dr. Hammer in any book or in any other media."[19]

In his 1987 autobiography, Armand Hammer wrote that the acrimony with Nancy Eilan was an unhappy send-off for his beloved brother. Victor was buried in Westwood Memorial Park, within walking distance of Occidental's Los Angeles headquarters and Armand's home. In 1981, Armand had removed the remains of his parents and his half brother from their resting place in Middletown, New Jersey, so they could be together in death at Westwood. It was a decidedly unpeaceful spot, filled with tourists gawking at the graves of the celebrities buried there, especially that of Marilyn Monroe. Dwarfing the graves of all the stars was the mausoleum near the cemetery's entrance engraved with the words "The Armand Hammer Family." Tombstones were already in place: Frances Hammer, 1902–, and Armand Hammer, 1898–. Hammer wanted to live for many more years, though. The seemingly immortal Armand continued to jet around the world, practicing his commerce, philanthropy, and citizen diplomacy, collecting the headlines that meant so much to him. A Los Angeles columnist for the *New Republic* commented, "When Armand is out of the papers for more than a few days, I look for signs of activity around the mausoleum."[20]

Epilogue

"An Impossible Recovery"

A S ARMAND HAMMER APPROACHED his ninetieth birthday, he had other personal concerns besides his family. Among
other things, he was determined to undo his guilty plea in the Watergate contributions case twelve years earlier.[1] It was an indisputable blotch
on a life of extraordinary achievement. He was convinced that his criminal record was denying him the two honors he desired most: a knighthood from the queen of England and the Nobel Peace Prize. Moreover,
he was sure he had been set up by his former executive Tim Babcock,
abetted by overzealous federal prosecutors. His campaign for exonera-
tion — perhaps more than any other episode of his astonishing life —
demonstrated his capacity for self-deception.

In a sense, the campaign was as old as the plea itself. When FBI
agents and Watergate special prosecutors began asking him questions
in the summer of 1973, Hammer had expressed incredulity that he was
under suspicion. He had promised $100,000 to the reelection campaign
of President Richard Nixon by the cutoff of April 7, 1972, so why
would he stall on the donation of the final $54,000? Such a sum was
peanuts to him. Their scenario made no sense, Hammer told the investigators. He swore that he had handed Babcock $54,000 on April 5
during a meeting in Reno, Nevada, and assumed that Babcock had
turned over the money to chief Nixon fund-raiser Maurice Stans by
the cutoff date for anonymous contributions.

Babcock told prosecutors that Hammer was lying, that he had waited
until September 6, 1972, before providing the balance and then had
participated in an elaborate cover-up to hide his identity as the donor.

Among other things, the cover-up involved recruitment by Babcock of prominent Montana Republicans willing to be listed falsely as the donors and a sham loan to Babcock from John Tigrett, Hammer's consultant in London. The prosecutors granted immunity to an uncooperative Tigrett in return for his version of events. Despite conflicting testimony on various points, there was no controversy about whether a cover-up had taken place. The only uncertainty revolved around Hammer's exact role in it.

The FBI interviewed Hammer intensively on August 23, 1973. He continued to claim that he had given money to Babcock before the deadline. But the normally thorough tycoon could provide no proof of the money transfer — no receipt, no witnesses. It was Hammer's word against Babcock's. Fortunately for Hammer, Babcock's credibility was suspect; he had, after all, lied in early interviews with federal agents. But as the months passed and the prosecutors labored to piece together the puzzle, Babcock seemed to have more convincing documentation.

The turning point came in June 1974, when Babcock received a subpoena to testify before a federal grand jury. He resolved to come clean, filling in the evidentiary gaps. He told prosecutors he had lied orginally to protect himself, Hammer, and other Occidental participants in the cover-up, including Marvin Watson. Babcock theorized that Hammer had waited until September 6, 1972, to turn over the remaining $54,000 because he wanted to be as sure as possible that Nixon would win reelection. Babcock said one reason he remembered the September 6 meeting so well was that Hammer had slipped an extra $50 bill into the pile of cash, then asked him to count the pile — apparently as a test of his integrity. "He could have done what he did without leaving me hanging out to dry," Babcock said later. "I don't think he tried to hurt me intentionally, and I sure as hell didn't want to hurt him. I worked for him, and I was loyal. But you can only go so far. I would have been a felon if I had lied to the prosecutor, to the grand jury."[2]

The Watergate Special Prosecution Force lawyers finally decided the evidence compelled them to move against Hammer. Word had leaked out. By the time the *Washington Star* and *Business Week* published details of the previously secret investigation in September 1974, the government was negotiating with Hammer's lawyers in the case, Edward Bennett Williams and Louis Nizer. Yet when *Business Week* questioned Hammer for its story, the reporter quoted him as saying, "There is no truth to it. You have really got me floored."[3]

Behind the scenes, Hammer approved an internal Occidental investigation to turn up evidence that Babcock had lied, but it was inconclusive. Herbert Itkin, a private investigator who later admitted he was working for Hammer, posed as a businessman interested in buying Babcock's properties in Helena, Montana. Itkin had been living in Los Angeles under a new identity as a federally protected witness after testifying for the government in New York City–area criminal cases. He obtained access to Babcock's financial records, learning details of his money troubles. When Watergate lawyers found out about the ruse, they asked the FBI to determine whether Hammer or his subordinates were trying to obstruct justice.

As Babcock, Marvin Watson, Stans, and other witnesses began cooperating with the prosecution, the walls closed in on Hammer. In December 1974, Babcock pleaded guilty to making an illegal campaign contribution in the name of another. Watson, in September 1976, pleaded guilty to being an accessory after the fact to the same offense. Watson's closed-door sessions with the prosecutors suggested strongly that Hammer had possessed knowledge about the cover-up from the early stages. But, to the prosecutors, Watson's statements seemed roundabout. As one Watergate Special Prosecution Force memorandum noted:

> Generally . . . Watson couches all references to discussions with Hammer with phrases such as "I believe," "I assume," "As best as I can recall," while in referring to discussions with other persons involved in the transactions he appears to be much more certain. There is no explanation for Watson's clear recollection with respect to discussions with lesser staff members of Occidental than with discussions with Dr. Hammer, other than the fact that Watson is still in fear of Hammer and refuses to directly implicate him.

(Watson later said he had been straightforward and certainly never was in fear of Hammer.)[4]

Uncharacteristically discouraged, Hammer agreed to a plea bargain in September 1975. But he never accepted the veracity of his participation in the cover-up. In a remarkable twenty-page letter to his probation officer three weeks after the apparent settlement, he blamed only his memory, "which might have played a trick on me. Did my intention to make the payment before April 7 become confused with the actual deed? In the hectic life I lead, with problems of global scope often engaging me day and night, this matter could conceivably have been overlooked, although I had it checked off in my mind as done." He told James Walker, the probation officer, that the prosecution's case contained legal and factual flaws throughout. But fighting the charges, which would put a strain on his heart, might finish him. He did not want to die; he also did not want to go on living under a legal cloud. He felt he was Babcock's victim, not the perpetrator of a crime.[5]

"I cannot describe the anguish I am suffering by being placed in this humiliating position," he wrote.

> It is as if a whole life of usefulness is being wiped out by the making of an anonymous political contribution of my own money, an act which concededly was perfectly legal prior to April 7, 1972. This event threatens to terminate my hopes to be of continued service in the final years of my life. The situation I find myself in is a nightmare. I trust the court will be compassionate, and mindful of my efforts through my entire life to contribute to society in a positive and helpful way and to make use of my wealth for worthy charitable purposes.[6]

Attorney Edward Bennett Williams warned Hammer that sending the letter would intensify his nightmare rather than end it. Williams was right. The chief federal judge in Washington, presiding in the case before it was moved to Los Angeles because of Hammer's poor health, withdrew the guilty plea on the basis of the letter. Williams resigned as Hammer's lawyer. The Watergate Special Prosecution Force began preparing for a full-scale trial.

Hammer responded by pulling out the stops; he did not want to go on trial or to serve a prison sentence. The sight of his father going to prison fifty-five years earlier still burned in his memory. He hired eminent physicians to certify his failing health, solicited famous friends to testify to his sterling character. Nizer tried a novel argument, telling prosecutor Thomas McBride that Hammer should not go to jail because he was "a national resource." McBride said later, "I will never forget that phrase. Nizer had a lot of chutzpah to say that, when we had been thinking of prosecuting the president of the United States."[7]

Legal fees in the case approached $1 million. On the one hand, Hammer was stressing the private nature of his contribution to Nixon, made from his own funds. On the other, he was emphasizing the propriety of Occidental's paying the legal bills because he had contributed the money to help the corporation. The executive committee of Occidental's board approved payment of the legal expenses on March 3, 1975. The full board agreed in May. Later, while defending that decision against a lawsuit by stockholders, Occidental's lawyers explained that Hammer was responsible for the company's "phenomenal growth. . . . His prosecution presented the real danger that Occidental might lose Dr. Hammer's services should he be sentenced to prison. Occidental was entitled to defend against such a possibility as it would have been entitled to defend against a legal challenge to any of its other assets." Nicholas von Hoffman commented in his syndicated column that "such obtuse and comic indifference to the moral sentiments of others has seldom been seen outside the brutal, upper-class cynics of Molière's theater."[8]

As the prosecutors considered whether to charge Hammer with a felony rather than a misdemeanor, Hammer apparently decided it was prudent to reinstitute his guilty plea. That is what occurred on March 4, 1976, in Judge Lawrence Lydick's courtroom. Ironically, Lydick had been associated in law practice with Richard Nixon. Nineteen days later, Hammer again was wheeled into the courtroom, where the judge decided against prison — on humanitarian grounds. He sentenced Hammer to one year of probation and a $3,000 fine.

So, Hammer would be allowed to die outside of a prison cell. Death seemed certain in the near future. The previous month, Arthur Groman — Hammer's friend, personal attorney, and an Occidental director — wrote, "Since his disease is irreversible, Dr. Hammer is not going to get better. It may be possible that temporary relief could result from critical heart surgery, a coronary bypass, but such an operation itself is hazardous to the life of a seventy-seven-year-old man."[9]

Groman, it turned out, was wrong. By April 2, 1976, the week after sentencing, Frances Hammer could write to Armand's brother and sister-in-law that Armand was feeling fine and working hard. At Occidental's annual meeting on May 21, his seventy-eighth birthday, reporters in attendance commented on Hammer's vigorous health. Nizer, in his memoirs, called it "an impossible recovery" that "astounded" the doctors. Nizer conceded he could understand skepticism about the truth of such dire medical reports during a criminal proceeding.[10]

Because Hammer was ever the Teflon tycoon, his guilty plea had little adverse impact on his reputation. It did contribute to his failure to receive a minor but coveted appointment from Jimmy Carter, whose administration generally was marked by a high moral tone. In the Reagan administration, where morality appeared to be less important, Hammer had been named chairman of the President's Cancer Panel. Hammer liked to tell interviewers the campaign-contributions guilty plea involved a technical violation no more serious than a speeding ticket.[11]

But the guilty plea still rankled Hammer, despite the passage of time; despite the dozens of honors he later received from the federal government, foreign nations, museums, and universities; and despite the media coverage that made him a household name. Hammer began to spread the theory that his prosecution had occurred not because of a solid case, but because of the Watergate atmosphere. He accused Tim Babcock of lying and mounted a renewed investigation of him.

One day in early 1987, a Houghton, Michigan, banker named Alex Sample received a telephone call at his home from Hammer. Sample never had spoken to Hammer in his life, so naturally he was surprised to hear the world-famous tycoon asking about the condition of his throat cancer. Hammer obviously had done his homework on Sample before placing the call. Finally, he came to the point. He was writing his autobiography and needed information about Babcock. Sample, previously a banker in Nevada, had done business with Babcock many years earlier. Would the loan records still be available? Sample told Hammer where he might find such records in Nevada. Hammer made the follow-up calls, Sample verified from his old Nevada sources, but the old records had been discarded. It was only later that Sample realized Hammer's purpose in making the calls might have been to dig up new evidence for a pardon.[12]

In addition to focusing on Babcock, Hammer accused Watergate Special Prosecution Force lawyers of misconduct. At least two members of the prosecution team received requests from Hammer to support — or refrain from opposing — a pardon application. Those two, Thomas McBride and Henry Ruth, Jr., refused to help.[13] Part of Hammer's argument for a pardon was based on a seemingly similar case, one in which the prosecutors had failed to press charges. Ironically, that case involved Dwayne Andreas, the agribusiness tycoon being portrayed in the media as Hammer's arch rival for the attention of Soviet leader Mikhail Gorbachev.

Hammer asked the Justice Department to recommend a pardon by President Ronald Reagan and hired top-flight lawyers to pave the way. Until he had a pardon in hand — even if obtained through a technicality, using the best attorneys money could buy — he would not rest. Perhaps the knighthood, the Nobel Peace Prize, maybe even his place in history, depended on the outcome.[14]

As a result, he worked to win friends at the Reagan White House. It was a formidable task. There was no reason Reagan should have granted Hammer favors. Hammer had supported a second term for Carter in 1980. Even after Carter's defeat, Hammer had stayed in touch with the Georgian, contributing heavily, for example, to the former president's library in Atlanta.[15]

With the advent of the Reagan presidency, Hammer definitely had

lost his insider status at the White House. Although he and Reagan
were more or less of the same generation and were fellow transplanted
Californians, they never had been close. During Reagan's governorship
of California, Hammer had made campaign contributions, but that was
about all. He had supported Reagan's Democratic predecessor as governor, Edmund Brown, Sr., and Reagan's successor, Edmund Brown,
Jr.[16] Finally, Reagan had too much staked on his reputation as a hard-
line anti-Communist to be identified with Hammer.

Just as Zbigniew Brzezinski was suspicious of Hammer, so was Richard
Allen, Reagan's first national security adviser. Allen's attitude was summarized by an unidentified Reagan administration official who talked
to Robert Lenzner of the *Boston Globe*: "Where do his loyalties lie?
When he goes to the great beyond, will he be buried inside or outside
the Kremlin walls?" Hammer bitterly blamed Allen for stifling his
access to President Reagan, something Allen acknowledged in an interview with Edward Jay Epstein, author of a widely read profile of
Hammer that appeared in a November 1981 *New York Times Magazine*.[17]

That profile reinforced the feeling of many Reagan administration
officials that Hammer was untrustworthy and maybe treasonous. Free-
lancer Epstein had approached Hammer at the suggestion of the magazine's editors. "He was enthusiastic," Epstein said. "He could envision
seeing himself on the cover. He was friends with [*New York Times*
publisher] Punch Sulzberger, so expected the article would turn out
well." Hammer instructed his key aides to talk with Epstein. But Epstein's in-depth research began to irritate Hammer, who tended to rely
on memory while repeating his own well-crafted life story. Hammer
suggested he write the article himself, with Epstein simply adding color
from his extensive travels on OXY-1.[18]

"Hammer took everything away from his aides, started calling me
from all over the world," Epstein said. "He said 'Hey, I thought we
had a continuing relationship.' He said that I could write a book about
him under my name and make millions of dollars. He was trying to
control the piece. He took me to the Royal Ballet to meet Prince Charles,
and sat me next to Punch Sulzberger. It was his way of showing me
he thought he had Sulzberger in his hip pocket. . . . When I asked
Hammer questions he did not expect, he just did not hear me. He had
programmed what he would tell me on the plane, like a prerecorded
cassette. He seemed perplexed and upset when I would change the
subject." After Epstein's article appeared, Hammer responded by writing a complaint of more than twenty-five pages to the *Times,* demand-

ing the magazine print it in full. The editors found nothing requiring a correction. They finally ran a long excerpt of Hammer's rebuttal, devoting the entire letters page to it.[19] On a normal Sunday that page contained about a dozen short letters.

Hammer was determined that the damage from the Epstein article would be temporary. Philip Klutznick, Carter's commerce secretary and an insider in seven administrations, said he never was surprised at Hammer's being shut out or at his finding a way in. "I would assume that every president would be hesitant about seeing Armand Hammer," Klutznick said, "not so much because of his ties to the Soviet Union or China, but because of his reputation as a wheeler-dealer. Any president would isolate himself from people like Dr. Hammer, partly because presidents have to limit access. They have only so much time. I never was concerned about dealing with him. He is an impressive character."[20]

Malcolm Forbes — magazine publisher, confidant of heads of state, and a Hammer admirer — suggested that Hammer's access problems originated with the State Department, where his personal diplomacy "ruffles feathers. . . . I have been at White House dinners where Armand presented ideas directly to the president, and the president listened. But his entrée in Washington is probably less than in Moscow or Beijing. The State Department could make better use of his contacts. . . . His information is almost always good. His sources are indisputably valuable. . . . There is no doubt that he is a patriot, despite what some have tried to prove."[21]

Realizing the opposition he faced, Hammer worked to buy his way into the administration, beginning with the first Reagan inaugural. He campaigned in England to export temporarily the Leonardo da Vinci manuscript for which he had just paid more than $5 million and renamed the Codex Hammer. The British government was studying the propriety of granting Hammer an export license. Hammer promised to abide by the decision, but in the meantime he wanted to show off the treasure in Washington. The British agreed to his plan. Nancy Reagan cut the ribbon at the unveiling. Hammer followed that grand gesture by pledging $20,000 to her White House redecoration fund. Hammer was tailoring his strategy to a socialite Reagan administration, so different from the ascetic Carter atmosphere. *New York Times* reporter Barbara Gamarekian saw Hammer at a benefit for Ford's Theatre the night after Occidental Petroleum had sponsored a postrehearsal party at the Corcoran Gallery. Hammer told her, "This is where the action is. If the government cuts back on the arts budget, it means corporations are going to have to pick up the slack."[22]

Ford's Theatre, where Abraham Lincoln was assassinated, had re-opened as a performing center under the National Park Service. Ham-mer, with his brilliance for picking attention-getting causes not yet staked out by others, pledged $100,000 to the theater and found four addi-tional donors to pledge the same amount. He captivated Frankie Hew-itt, the theater's executive producer. She told how he took the initiative to make a retrospective film about Ford's Theatre at a cost of several hundred thousand dollars, then presented it as a gift. "At difficult times, when he probably should be doing other things, Dr. Hammer comes to our meetings, or, if he can't be here, he gives me a personal expla-nation instead of leaving it to somebody else. When I get a letter from him, I know he wrote it. . . . There is always a personal touch. . . . He follows up when he solicits contributions; he does not leave it for me to collect. All this is a part of life to him," Hewitt said.[23]

Hammer's generosity to the National Symphony Orchestra was even more headline-grabbing, making him hard to ignore in Washington society. Hammer pledged $250,000 to the orchestra. In response, con-ductor Mstislav Rostropovich scheduled a concert to honor Hammer on his eighty-fourth birthday. The audience of twenty-five hundred dig-nitaries sang "Happy Birthday"; the symphony boomed out the *1812 Overture*. Hammer was so moved he increased his pledge to $500,000 and threw in another $250,000 for the renovation of New York's Car-negie Hall, a special interest of Isaac Stern's, the featured violinist at the birthday concert. Hammer adopted additional Washington institu-tions as objects of his charity, including Meridian House.[24]

As always with Hammer, it was difficult to separate philanthropy from politics or diplomacy. Elisabeth Bumiller reported in the *Washing-ton Post* that "the crowd was generally Democratic, a group less apt to growl about Hammer's longtime business ties to the Soviets than does the current administration. Hammer, although he is chairman of the President's Cancer Panel, has generally been kept at a healthy distance by a mistrusting White House." When Bumiller asked Hammer how he was getting along with the Reagan administration, Hammer replied, "Oh, fine." Bumiller countered that the White House seemed to be nervous about his Soviet links; he responded that he expected Leonid Brezhnev and Reagan to meet within months, at which time they would find common ground on an arms limitation treaty.[25]

All the goodwill masked political considerations. In January 1984, Hammer tried to convince Reagan to attend a Ford's Theatre showing of the film *Backstage at the Kirov,* produced by Hammer's own crew thanks to his special status in the Soviet Union. Hammer suggested that Reagan's attendance would be a positive follow-up to a recent presidential speech on U.S.-Soviet relations. Soviet ambassador Anatoly Dobrynin would be attending with his family. Richard Burt at the State Department wrote to Secretary of State George Shultz that Hammer's

> interest in promoting this film is . . . clear. The film will show a positive element in Soviet society, its dedication to fostering classical ballet. We are receiving no reciprocity in the Union of Soviet Socialist Republics by the commercial showing of any comparable production there portraying a positive element in American society. We believe that for the president or you to attend this premiere would convey a message of better atmospherics than the bilateral situation warrants, and one which Andropov, in his apparent state of health, could not reciprocate.[26]

By the time of Reagan's second inaugural, Hammer had made himself impossible to ignore. To celebrate Reagan's reelection, he decided on an exhibition of his American paintings, at the National Gallery of Art. The black-tie reception brought together Supreme Court justices, cabinet members, ambassadors, and other dignitaries, with Hammer at center stage. Paul Richard, the *Washington Post* art critic, observed that the exhibition was "perplexing. It mixes splendors and embarrassments. It suggests the man himself . . . at ease with contradictions. . . . He is a generous philanthropist and a ceaseless self-promoter." Richard said the National Gallery and the Corcoran were hosting Hammer's inaugural celebrations largely because of his financial largess. The showing would appear to be "an embarrassing payoff to a donor were it not subtitled 'an inaugural celebration.' Indeed, frivolity is permissible at parties."[27]

With Reagan entrenched in the White House for a second term, he worried less about any criticism he might receive for consorting with an apparent pro-Communist like Hammer. The president wrote Hammer, "I value your insights on our policy toward the Soviet Union." Hammer framed copies of a separate praiseworthy letter from Reagan and displayed them in Occidental offices around the country. At the president's request, National Security Adviser Robert McFarlane met with Hammer to hear his views on world peace. Reagan awarded Hammer a coveted National Medal for the Arts at a White House ceremony. When the president spoke to the World Affairs Council in Los Angeles, Hammer was on the dais with him. When Reagan's supporters held a lunch at which each attendee was asked to pledge $100,000 for a Reagan Library, Hammer was there; his pledges topped $1 million. When White House curator Clement Conger decided to place western art in the West Wing and settled on a Charles Russell scene titled *Fording the Horse Herd,* on loan from Hammer Galleries, he called William McSweeny, Hammer's main man in Washington, to suggest how wonderful it would be if Hammer contributed the painting to the White House. It was no small request; the painting carried an estimated value of $750,000. Hammer said yes, in return for a White House presentation ceremony. The deal was done.[28]

Washington Post reporter Sarah Booth Conroy summarized the Hammer phenomenon in the Reagan-Bush years: "Washington partygoers have become blasé with getting those glossy receiving line photographs of themselves being greeted by someone richer, thinner, and/or better-known. So billionaire Dr. Armand Hammer has found a way to impress them — and make other hosts look like Instamatic pikers." Hammer's innovation, Conroy wrote, was sending personalized photograph albums to guests at a National Gallery reception for an opening of his art. Each album contained about seventy color photographs with printed captions.[29]

In the end, even Hammer critic Edward Jay Epstein was impressed. Writing in *Manhattan, inc.* magazine, Epstein related all the strikes against Hammer at the beginning of the Reagan regime. Not only had the president heard negative reports from his advisers, but he also had become spooked by Hammer's regularly appearing in the next chair at a Beverly Hills barbershop when Reagan showed up for a haircut. At a 1981 diplomatic reception in Ottawa, Reagan had given Hammer the cold shoulder as Epstein watched. Epstein could see the hurt, yet he saw, too, the determination. After Hammer obtained his appointment to the President's Cancer Panel, Epstein said, the rest of the scenario was predictable. "Once he got his proverbial camel's nose into the tent . . . Hammer proceeded to ingratiate himself further through his usual mixture of art, charity, and charm." By 1988, the determination had paid off. Hammer again was a force at the White House. Epstein concluded that Hammer "can take considerable pride in this achievement. He has against all odds charmed the Reagan administration."[30]

But all of Hammer's inroads failed to produce the presidential pardon he so desperately wanted from Reagan — in the end, the Teflon president would not absolve the Teflon tycoon. At the tail end of his second term, Reagan issued thirty-two pardons, including one to New York Yankees owner George Steinbrenner, who had also pleaded guilty to an illegal contribution during the 1972 Nixon campaign.[31] Reagan said nothing about why he chose to ignore Hammer's entreaties.

As George Bush took the oath of office, Hammer was anything but ready to give up. At ninety-one, with so many accomplishments behind him and so much fame enveloping him, he kept up his campaign for respect and respectability. He contributed generously to the Bush inaugural festivities. The exhibition of his papers at the Library of Congress coincided with inaugural week, when the high and mighty would be in the nation's capital. United States senators, the Soviet ambassador, and other dignitaries attended the opening of the collection and applauded when Hammer announced a surprise $100,000 gift to the library. They gawked at samples of Hammer's private correspondence — from Lenin, Brezhnev, Mikhail Gorbachev; from Franklin Roosevelt, Nixon, Gerald Ford, Carter, Reagan; from Margaret Thatcher, Menachem Begin, Prince Charles.[32]

There was a letter from George Bush, too. That was no surprise. After all, Bush had provided a blurb for the dust jacket of Hammer's autobiography. Many who knew Hammer understood that the old man would be currying favor, would be pushing for the presidential pardon that Reagan refused to grant. But those same Hammerologists also understood that Hammer was no Bush insider.

So even they were surprised as they watched George and Barbara Bush walk into the Capitol immediately after the new president took his oath of office. There, at the top of the Capitol steps, with the Reagans, Quayles, and congressional leaders, was Hammer. The president and the First Lady shook hands with him and chatted. Hammer had done it again.[33] Not long afterward, on August 14, 1989, Hammer received a pardon from President Bush.

Notes

I talked with more than seven hundred people for this biography, either face-to-face, by telephone, or by letter. The conversations and correspondence that I have used in the text are cited in the Notes. To those persons whose names fail to appear in the text or Notes, my thanks as well.

Books, dissertations, and certain other stand-alone works are cited in the Notes using a short form, with fuller citations found in the Bibliography. Articles from general circulation or specialized newspapers, magazines, and newsletters are cited in the Notes only, not in the Bibliography. Uncited anywhere in this book are thousands of additional articles that I read but relied on little or not at all.

As for primary documents, I located hundreds of thousands of pages within government agencies, some of which required me to use the federal Freedom of Information Act or similar state access laws; and within library special collections, private archives, and personal papers. The primary documents on which I relied heavily are cited in the Notes.

To keep the notes manageable, I sometimes cited selected sources when I could have cited many more. In such instances, I chose the most authoritative or the most accessible information. In the interest of readability, I sometimes omitted detailed document location numbers from archival references. I have tried to provide enough detail so that other researchers can locate the information on their own. More specific location information is available from me on request when it exists.

When I cite secondary sources, such as newspaper or magazine articles, I usually do so for one of three reasons: to convey a useful opinion stated by the writer, to share an eyewitness account, or to provide a citation when no other verifiable information is available.

AUTHOR'S NOTE

  1. Ronald Kessler, *Washington Post,* May 29, 1987.
  2. After a dozen telephone calls brought no response, I sent five letters to Dr. Hammer telling him about what I had learned so far and asking him to comment in general or specifically. The first letter was dated January 12, 1986; the last was dated September 29, 1987. By then, he had made it clear he would not cooperate. Nonetheless, I sent one more letter, in November 1988, as I neared completion of the manuscript.
  3. During my research and writing, I read extensively about the craft of biography. Some of the most thought-provoking books were by Milton Lomask, *The Biographer's Craft* (Harper & Row, 1986); Stephen B. Oates, ed., *Biography as High Adventure* (University of Massachusetts Press, 1986); Marc Pachter, ed., *Telling Lives: The Biographer's Art* (New Republic Books, 1979); Eric Homberger and John Charmley, eds., *The Troubled Face of Biography* (St. Martin's Press, 1988); and William Zinsser, ed., *Extraordinary Lives: The Art and Craft of American Biography* (Houghton Mifflin, 1986). I also read dozens of biographies specifically to ponder technique.

Prologue: A RECKONING IN COURT

This introductory chapter is a synthesis of research spanning five years. Almost everything mentioned in this chapter is treated in greater detail later in the book, with accompanying notes to identify sources. Throughout this biography, I have taken into account Hammer's own versions of events as told in his 1932 memoir, *The Quest of the Romanoff Treasure,* among other places. I read and reread that memoir and each of his three later books — Bob Considine's *Remarkable Life of Dr. Armand Hammer,* 1975; John Bryson's *World of Armand Hammer,* 1985; and the autobiography with Neil Lyndon, *Hammer,* 1987 — comparing them line by line for internal consistency, checking the accuracy of every verifiable sentence, and trying to determine what Hammer had omitted. In the early stages of research, I consulted hundreds of additional books that mentioned Hammer, read thousands of articles by or about him, and located radio and television tapes and transcripts. Most contained little insight into the how or why of his life. Many were inaccurate. I am, however, indebted to a small number of groundbreaking shorter accounts: the books *Red Carpet,* by Joseph Finder, John Walker's *Self-Portrait with Donors,* and Robert Williams's *Russian Art and American Money;* profiles by Spencer Klaw, *Saturday Evening Post,* March 12, 1966; Daniel Yergin, *Atlantic,* June and July 1975; James Cook, *Forbes,* April 28, 1980; Edward Jay Epstein, *New York Times Magazine,* November 29, 1981; Donald Woutat, *Los Angeles Times Magazine,* June 7, 1987; and the NBC-TV documentary narrated by Edwin Newman and produced by Lucy Jarvis that aired June 18, 1974.

  1. Physicians' reports filed with U.S. District Court, Washington, D.C., case 75-668, and U.S. District Court, Los Angeles, case 76-164-LTL.
  2. Watergate Special Prosecution Force files, National Archives of the United States, Washington, D.C., Record Group 460, Occidental Petroleum file. Steven Tilley at the National Archives went to great lengths to process the prosecution files pursuant to my federal Freedom of Information Act request. Information from the court cases and the Watergate Special Prosecution Force files undergirds almost all of the specifics in this chapter about the campaign contribution and cover-up.
  3. I obtained information from every presidential library in the National Archives system, either through personal visits or correspondence. Those repositories cover the administrations of Herbert Hoover, Franklin Roosevelt, Harry Truman, Dwight

Eisenhower, John Kennedy, Lyndon Johnson, Richard Nixon, Gerald Ford, and Jimmy Carter.
4. FBI documents released pursuant to FOIA request. Joe Iazzetta handled the request, reviewing and releasing documents over a three-year span.
5. *Business Week,* June 8, 1987.
6. Nizer, *Reflections Without Mirrors.*

Chapter 1: A BANKRUPT FAMILY

1. Zipperstein, *The Jews of Odessa;* Sanders, *Shores of Refuge;* Howe, *World of Our Fathers.*
2. The State Department supplied passport applications for Julius, Rose, Victor, and Harry Hammer under the author's FOIA request. The applications range from 1911 to 1973. Much of the information from Armand Hammer's four books about his ancestors and formative years is unverifiable. Unless evidence was found that cast doubt on Hammer's version, his account was accepted.
3. Jacob Hammer's citizenship application, handled by the Superior Court, New York State, bundle 282, record 87.
4. New Haven city directories from the 1890s (researcher Betty Linsley located the directories and supporting information); and Socialist Labor party archives, State Historical Society of Wisconsin, Madison (Harold Miller guided the author through the voluminous materials there).
5. Sandy Robinson Vorspan, interview, November 9, 1987. She is Rose Hammer's niece.
6. Julius Hammer bankruptcy records, U.S. District Court, Southern District of New York, case 8748, stored at Federal Records Center, Bayonne, N.J. New York City researcher Ben Bedell located the previously unreported case.
7. Julius and Rose Hammer passport applications, State Department FOIA release; and Wolfe, *A Life in Two Centuries.*
8. Julius Hammer bankruptcy records; land records in Manhattan and Bronx courthouses; city directories at the New York Public Library and the New York State Library, Albany; letter to the author from Leanore Bona, associate registrar, Columbia University, December 3, 1986; and Howe, *World of Our Fathers.*
9. All surviving federal censuses from 1870 on that are open to the public at the National Archives; Julius Hammer bankruptcy records; city directories, New York Public Library; land records, Manhattan and Bronx courthouses; and New York State Education Department, Division of Professional Licensing Services, medical license 5552, issued October 14, 1902 (verified in a letter to the author from Elaine Alston, September 22, 1986).
10. Julius Hammer bankruptcy records.
11. Ibid.
12. Ibid.
13. Ibid.
14. Irwin Hymes's recollections appeared in the *New York Times,* August 6, 1982; and Hammer's in his 1987 autobiography, *Hammer.*
15. Meriden city directories, viewed at Library of Congress, Washington, D.C.; *Meriden Record-Journal,* January 25, 1933; Harry Wellington, interview, October 7, 1988; passport applications, released by State Department under FOIA; *Daily People* (a Socialist newspaper), August 20, 1907; and annual reports and incorporation documents, New York Secretary of State, Division of Corporations, Albany.
16. Hammer's records from the school's archives, covering his entrance, on September 10, 1913, through his graduation, on June 25, 1915.

17. Syrkin, *New Republic,* November 7, 1983, based in part on her high school year-books; and Syrkin, interview, June 6, 1987.

Chapter 2: RADICAL POLITICS

1. *New York Times,* August 20, 1907; Socialist Labor party archives, State Historical Society of Wisconsin, Madison; and Wolfe, *A Life in Two Centuries.*
2. Socialist Labor party archives, State Historical Society of Wisconsin.
3. Ibid.
4. Documents released by State Department and FBI under FOIA; various documents at National Archives, especially from Record Groups 59, 84, and 261.
5. *Columbian,* Columbia University yearbook, 1915–1920, read at the university's library; back issues of the fraternity's publications, supplied by James Greer at national headquarters, July 1986.
6. Résumé of Armand Hammer; and draft registration card, signed September 12, 1918, National Archives, Atlanta branch, East Point, Georgia.
7. New York State census, 1915; Isabel Crystal Sacher, interview, September 15, 1987 (Sacher is a longtime Hammer family acquaintance); photographs from the collection of Ireene Wicker Hammer and Victor J. Hammer; testimony by Julius Hammer during his 1920 manslaughter trial, New York State Archives, Albany; and collection of Ireene Wicker Hammer and Victor J. Hammer.
8. Tax and land records, including book 5202, p. 449, Office of City Register, New York County; testimony of Armand Hammer and Angela Zevely Hammer from their divorce, Chancery Division, New Jersey Superior Court, Monmouth County, file M-1075-54; *Architectural Digest,* August 1985; and interviews with neighborhood residents conducted by the author and New York City researcher Anne Fullam.
9. Socialist Labor party archives, State Historical Society of Wisconsin; Draper, *The Roots of American Communism;* and Wolfe, *A Life in Two Centuries.*
10. New York State Legislature Joint Committee to Investigate Seditious Activities, also known as the Lusk Committee, numerous documents from its files at New York State Archives, Albany; U.S. House of Representatives, *The Communist Party of the United States as an Agent of a Foreign Power,* April 1, 1947, report 209; and U.S. House of Representatives Committee on Un-American Activities, *Organized Communism in the United States,* August 19, 1953, report 1694.
11. Incorporation papers and periodic reports filed with secretaries of state in New York, New Jersey, and Delaware; Wilson, *American Business and Foreign Policy, 1920–33,* and *Ideology and Economics;* Reitzer, "United States–Russian Economic Relations, 1917–20"; and Norbert Gaworek, *Jahrbücher für Geschichte Osteuropas,* no. 23, 1975.
12. Lusk Committee files, New York State Archives, Albany; and National Archives, Record Group 59, April 15, 1919.
13. Powers, *Secrecy and Power;* and various documents from National Archives and FBI.
14. Bronx County Courthouse, indictment 473-19, microfilm reel 118; and *New York Times* and *New York World,* August 16, 1919.

Chapter 3: CONVICT FATHER, MILLIONAIRE SON

1. Fingerhood filed two suits in New York Supreme Court, New York County, cases 10575-1919 and 2684-1920. Armand Hammer referred to Fingerhood in his writings as Henry. That apparently was Fingerhood's commonly used middle name.
2. Steuer obituary, *New York Times,* August 22, 1940.
3. Various advertisements, including one in *American Perfumer and Essential Oil Review,* December 1921.

4. Annual proceedings of Flavoring Extract Manufacturers' Association, 1918–1921; articles in *American Perfumer and Essential Oil Review,* especially April 1919, July 1920, and December 1920.

5. U.S. House of Representatives, Judiciary Committee, *Prohibition Legislation 1921,* May 16, 1921; Kobler, *Ardent Spirits;* Charles Kiely et al., "An Epidemic of Motor Neuritis in Cincinnati, Ohio, Due to Drinking Adulterated Jamaica Ginger," *Public Health Reports,* vol. 47, no. 42, October 14, 1932; and *Prohibition — the Eighteenth Amendment, the Volstead Act, the Twenty-first Amendment,* National Archives and Record Administration series "Milestone Documents in the National Archives," text by David E. Kyvig.

6. National Archives, Bureau of Investigation file 61, subject 2272; and *New York Times,* January 13, 1914, January 24–25, 1914, and February 4, 1917. In his writings, Armand Hammer incorrectly rendered the name as Kunz.

7. Trial transcript, New York State Archives, Albany.

8. *New York Tribune* and *New York World,* June 24, 1920.

9. *Journal of the American Medical Association,* July 17 and July 31, 1920.

10. Trial transcript, New York State Archives, Albany.

11. *New York Times,* September 19, 1920 (Sing Sing Prison blotter with Julius's entry viewed at New York State Archives, Albany); *New York Times,* September 21, 1920; and information compiled by Roberta Arminio, Ossining Historical Society.

12. Bronx County Courthouse, indictment 711-20, microfilm reel 118.

13. Reported at 194 A.D. 712, and 232 N.Y. 564.

14. Hammer talk in Cleveland, September 14, 1979, reprinted in *Vital Speeches,* November 1, 1979; land records in Bronx County, New York; Hammer family passport applications; and State Department FOIA releases.

Chapter 4: YOUNG DOCTOR

1. "A Biographical History of the College of Physicians and Surgeons, 1767–1976," pamphlet from Columbia University.

2. The honorary society's national headquarters verified Hammer's admission; the framed picture is hanging in the public relations office of the College of Physicians and Surgeons; Ruth Rosenzweig, interview, September 22, 1987 (she is Maxwell's widow); Mishell's wife, Helen, to the author, June 6, 1987 (Daniel's poor health prevented an interview); letters to the author from Jacqueline Frost Knapp, August 30, 1987, and Wilbur Moore, June 15, 1987; and Maurice Richter, interview, June 6, 1987.

3. Unidentified newspaper clipping, March 19, 1921, in files of *New York Post;* and files at New York Division of Professional Licensing Services, Albany.

4. Records of State Department, National Archives.

5. National Archives, Record Group 59, location 800.11-332, June 11, 1921.

6. Turack, *The Passport in International Law;* and State Department records, National Archives.

7. National Archives, Record Group 59.

8. MacKenzie, *Russia Before Dawn,* and Bassow, *The Moscow Correspondents.*

9. Robert Mishell, interview, June 9, 1987; Joseph Mishell, interview, October 13, 1987; and Boris Mishell papers, courtesy of Joseph Mishell. Robert and Joseph are the sons of Boris.

Chapter 5: MEETING LENIN

1. A. A. Heller, *The Industrial Revival in Soviet Russia;* and Morray, *Project Kuzbas.*

2. Heller, *Industrial Revival.*

3. Senator William Borah papers, Library of Congress, manuscript division, box 218;

and archives of Women's Committee for the Recognition of Russia, Swarthmore College Peace Collection.

4. Heller, *Industrial Revival.*
5. *Istoricheskii Archiv,* 1958, no. 5. James Curtis, a Russian-language professor at the University of Missouri–Columbia, provided translations of Martens's article and many others.
6. Levine, *Eyewitness to History;* and Socialist Labor party archives, State Historical Society of Wisconsin, Madison.
7. The author is indebted to Philip Gillette for his interpretation of the Hammer-Lenin relationship, and for his interview, January 25, 1987. See *Slavic Review,* Fall 1981, for Gillette's article, plus his dissertation, "The Political Origins of American-Soviet Trade."
8. Most of Lenin's letters referring to the Hammers are translated and printed in *V. I. Lenin: Collected Works,* vol. 45 (Progress Publishers, 1970).
9. Ibid.
10. Liberman, *Building Lenin's Russia.*
11. *New York Times,* November 6, 1921; and *Chicago Tribune,* November 10, 1921.
12. National Archives, Justice Department memorandum, November 29, 1921.
13. Mishell letter of October 16, 1923, Boris Mishell papers, courtesy of Joseph Mishell.
14. Sheridan, *Naked Truth.*
15. State Department notice, July 7, 1920, in *Foreign Relations of the United States 1920,* vol. 3, p. 717; Kennan, *Russia and the West Under Lenin and Stalin;* Strong, *The First Time in History;* Wilson, *Ideology and Economics;* Ball, *Russia's Last Capitalists;* and *Foreign Relations of the United States 1921,* vol. 2, p. 775.
16. *Dokumenty Vneshney Politiki SSSR,* vol. 4, March 19–December 31, 1921.
17. New York and Delaware state corporation records.

Chapter 6: BARON OF THE BROWN HOUSE

1. London telephone directory, 1922; and Kunetskaya, *Lenin: Great and Human.*
2. *Soviet Life,* April 1965 and May 1973.
3. Again, the main source for the Lenin letters is *V. I. Lenin: Collected Works,* vol. 45 (Progress Publishers, 1970). These translations were compared with two other Soviet versions — *V. I. Lenin: On the United States of America,* a 1967 publication; and *Vladimir Ilyich Lenin, Biograficheskaya Khronika,* vol. 11, a 1980 publication.
4. Boris Mishell papers.
5. Newspaper accounts indicate that Boris Mishell rather than Armand Hammer visited Henry Ford. See *New York American,* September 27, 1922; *New York Tribune* and *Detroit Times,* September 29, 1922. For scholarly interpretations that seem to contradict Hammer, see Filene, *Americans and the Soviet Experiment, 1917–33,* and Nevins and Hill, *Ford: Expansion and Challenge, 1915–33.* Researchers seeming to validate Hammer's version are Fithian in his dissertation, "Soviet-American Economic Relations, 1918–33"; Wilkins and Hill, *American Business Abroad;* Wilson, *Ideology and Economics;* and Christina White, "Ford in Russia: In Pursuit of the Chimeral Market," *Business History,* October 1986. Evidence was gleaned from the Ford Archives and Library, Henry Ford Museum, Dearborn, Mich., with the help there of David Crippen.
6. *Ekonomicheskaya Zhizn,* December 10, 1922; State Department, National Archives, Record Group 59; and Mikoyan, *V Nachale Dvadtsatykh.*
7. The University of Illinois Slavic and East European Library has Moscow directories from the 1920s. The author received help there from Helen Sullivan.
8. National Archives, Record Group 59, September 6, 1922; and *New York Times,* February 28, 1924. The State Department reaction was on March 5, 1924, National Archives, Record Group 59.

9. *New York Times,* November 30, 1922.
10. IRS case 31704, decided at 25 BTA 1276; *New York Times,* July 9, 1923; incorporation papers, New York Secretary of State, Division of Corporations, Albany; Lyons, *The Red Decade;* and Salisbury, *Without Fear or Favor.*
11. *Pravda,* August 24, 1923; Finder, *Red Carpet;* and U.S. Tax Court, reported at 25 BTA 1276.
12. "Asbestos: Sources and Trade," U.S. Commerce Department, Bureau of Foreign and Domestic Commerce, Mineral Section, Trade Information Bulletin 442, October 1926.
13. *New York Times,* June 14, 1922; and *New York World,* undated but probably the same week.
14. *Ekonomicheskaya Zhizn,* December 10, 1922; and *New York Times,* February 20, 1923.
15. *Ekonomicheskaya Zhizn,* June 1, 1926.
16. *Pravda,* March 9, 1924.
17. National Archives, Record Group 59, March 29, 1924; and *Pravda,* May 6, 1924.
18. Passport applications, State Department, FOIA release.
19. New York State Archives, Albany, Sing Sing Prison blotter; *New York Times,* January 24, 1923; and State Department, FOIA release.
20. State Department, FOIA release.
21. Ibid.; and *Chicago Tribune,* April 28, 1923.
22. Julius Hammer to Ford Motor Company, June 1, 1923, box 38:47, Ford Archives.
23. Ibid., June 3, 1923; and Julius Hammer's affidavit attached to a 1927 passport renewal application, State Department FOIA release.
24. Boris Mishell papers.
25. New York State Archives, *Executive Restorations of Citizenship Rights,* series B0046-79, vol. 8, p. 54; and American Relief Administration archives, Hoover Institution, Stanford University.
26. Lyons, *Assignment in Utopia.*
27. Lucita Williams, unpublished memoir written in 1973, courtesy of Rhys Williams II.
28. Papers of Alexander Gumberg and James Frear, State Historical Society of Wisconsin, Madison; Frear's report, *Congressional Record,* December 13, 1923, and King's report, April 24, 1924; King's diary of the trip, Special Collections, Brigham Young University, Provo, Utah; and Levine, *Eyewitness to History.*
29. Conway, *Art Treasures in Soviet Russia;* and Joseph L. Wieczynski, ed., *The Modern Encyclopedia of Russian and Soviet History,* vol. 5.
30. Joseph Mishell, interview, October 13, 1987; and Robert Mishell, interview, June 9, 1987.
31. *Chicago Daily News,* January 16, 1924; Mishell obituary, *New York Times,* July 20, 1943; and Boris Mishell papers.
32. Zinsser, *As I Remember Him;* Zinsser obituary, *New York Times,* September 5, 1940; and New York Division of Professional Licensing Services to the author, September 22, 1986.

Chapter 7: PENCIL KING

1. DeJonge, *Stalin and the Shaping of the Soviet Union;* and Taubman, *Stalin's American Policy.*
2. Corson and Crowley, *The New KGB;* Fithian, "Soviet-American Economic Relations, 1918–33"; Robert Williams, *Russian Art and American Money;* Wilson, *Ideology and Economics;* and State Department, National Archives, Record Group 59.
3. National Archives, Record Group 59.
4. National Archives, file 61, subject 5431.

5. J. Jaakson, "Estonian Financial System: Its Development and Present Position," *The Banker,* March 1938.

6. Background reading included documents from the National Archives, U.S. Commerce Department, Bureau of Foreign and Domestic Commerce, Record Group 40, group 151, file 448; back issues of *Pencil Collector,* supplied by Jack Batterson; and Eric Voice's speech, "The History of the Manufacture of Pencils," November 15, 1950, reprinted by Newcomen Society, *Transactions,* vol. 27.

7. *New York Times,* October 4, 1925.

8. Moscow telephone directory listings from the late 1920s, University of Illinois Slavic and East European Library.

9. Diary, collection of Ireene Wicker Hammer and Victor J. Hammer.

10. *Economic Review of the Soviet Union* (an Amtorg publication), January 1, 1928, and July 1, 1929.

11. Barmine, *One Who Survived.*

12. Ashmead-Bartlett, *The Riddle of Russia.*

13. State Department passport documents, FOIA release.

14. *Pravda,* June 10, 1928.

15. *Pravda,* July 8, 1928.

16. *Economic Review of the Soviet Union,* January 1, 1928.

17. Letter from Sherwood Eddy, August 15, 1929, Senator William Borah papers, Library of Congress, manuscript division, box 284; Charles Muchnic, *Harper's,* September 1929; Chase et al., *Soviet Russia in the Second Decade;* John Brophy diary, Brophy papers, Catholic University of America, located by archivist Anthony Zito; and report 16, American-Russian Chamber of Commerce, box 21, Alexander Gumberg papers, State Historical Society of Wisconsin, Madison.

18. *Chicago Daily News,* March 6, 1929; and *New York Times,* December 22, 1929.

19. Passport applications of Victor Hammer, State Department FOIA release.

20. Lucita Williams, unpublished memoir, courtesy of Rhys Williams II; and various documents filed by Julian Hammer, such as his voter registration, Los Angeles County. The 1928 birth date in the authorized Considine biography is almost surely wrong.

21. Lyons, *Assignment in Utopia; Chicago Daily News,* July 18, 1929; cummings, *Eimi;* and Francis Ferguson, *Kenyon Review,* Autumn 1950.

22. Sutton, *Western Technology and Soviet Economic Development,* vol. 2.

23. *Izvestia,* March 2, 1930.

24. *Soviet Life,* September 1985.

Chapter 8: SELLING ART LIKE SHOES

1. In addition to Armand Hammer's four books, see *Palm Beach Times,* March 13, 1978, and *Palm Beach Daily News,* January 26, 1982.

2. Tolstoy, *Stalin's Secret War.*

3. Sakho's business listing, New York City directories, 1925. A reconstituted Peasant Art Importing Company filed a certificate of incorporation on May 25, 1927, New York State Secretary of State, Division of Corporations, Albany; and Agnes Sakho, interview, March 2, 1988.

4. L'Ermitage Galleries filing at Division of Corporations, Albany; and Hammer's deposition before Palm Beach County Circuit Court, case 85-2705-CP, January 8, 1986.

5. U.S. District Court, Southern District of New York, case 48588, stored at Federal Records Center, Bayonne, N.J.; *New York Times,* March 6, March 28, April 11, and August 21, 1930; and Gest obituary, May 17, 1942.

6. Paris researcher Donna Evleth investigated Hammer's activities during his short stay there, but documentation was virtually nonexistent.

7. Knickerbocker, *Fighting the Red Trade Menace.*

8. Passport documents of the Hammer family, State Department, National Archives, Record Group 59; and State Department FOIA request.

9. National Archives, Record Group 59.

10. Ibid.

11. Ibid.

12. State Department FOIA request; and documents in Styles Bridges papers, New England College, Henniker, N.H. Curator James Kiepper and his assistant David Carle guided the author through the Bridges collection.

13. New York Supreme Court, New York County, case 3248-1931; *New York Times,* February 8 and February 28, 1931; and Luba Elianoff, interview, August 4, 1988.

14. *New York Times,* May 1, 1935.

15. St. Louis newspapers gave the Hammers attention throughout 1932. See, for example, *St. Louis Post-Dispatch,* November 18, 1932; and *St. Louis Globe-Democrat,* November 20, 1932.

16. *Buffalo Evening News,* March 29 and March 30, 1932.

17. *Detroit News,* April 11, 1932.

18. *San Francisco Call,* May 18, 1932.

19. *Chicago Tribune,* October 3, 1932.

20. *New York Times,* November 20, 1932.

21. New York Supreme Court, New York County, case 49358-1932.

22. Lord & Taylor promotional brochure, New York Public Library; *New York Times,* February 18 and February 20, 1933; and correspondence between Post and the Hammers, located by Anne Odom, a curator at the Hillwood estate, Washington, D.C.

23. *New Yorker,* December 23, 1933.

24. *Art News,* June 1, 1935; *New York Times,* May 25, 1935; Bridges papers; Palm Beach city directories, 1935–1940; and *Palm Beach Daily News,* January 14, January 15, and January 17, 1938.

25. *Time,* August 16, 1937; and *Art News,* August 1, 1937.

Chapter 9: BEER BY THE BARREL

1. Correspondence between Hollis and Roosevelt, Franklin D. Roosevelt Library, Hyde Park, N.Y.

2. "Prohibition," National Archives and Record Administration series "Milestone Documents in the National Archives," text by David E. Kyvig.

3. *Foreign Markets for Cooperage,* U.S. Commerce Department, Bureau of Foreign and Domestic Commerce, Trade Promotion Series 144, April 1933; and New York Secretary of State, Division of Corporations, Albany.

4. *Coopers International Journal,* June and September 1933; *Wooden Barrel,* September 1933, February, May, June, and July 1934, and September 1937; and *National Coopers' Journal,* May 1935 and April 1937.

5. *Time,* August 21 and September 25, 1933.

6. *New Yorker,* December 23, 1933; and *New York Post,* September 14, 1933.

7. Summary by William Shaw, September 22, 1972, based on FBI files, Richard Ichord papers, University of Missouri manuscript collection, Columbia; and memorandum, December 7, 1939, FBI FOIA release.

8. New York Supreme Court, New York County, case 37436-1934; filings before New York Court of Appeals, bound vols. 51 and 52, New York State Library, Albany; and opinions reported at 242 A.D. 803, 245 A.D. 829, and 272 N.Y. 479.

9. Ibid.; *Wooden Barrel,* May 1935; and *New York Times,* March 28, 1935.

10. Property records, Orange County, New York, located by researcher Ben Bedell.

11. Hayes, interview, April 11, 1988.

12. 8th Judicial Circuit of Nevada, Clark County, case 19039; and Hammer, *Hammer*.
13. Sandy Robinson Vorspan, interview, November 2, 1987; and Nancy Hammer Eilan, interview, August 21, 1987.
14. Marriage license, New York Department of Health, no. 31948.

Chapter 10: SELLING SPIRITS, TOO

1. Tebbel, *The Life and Good Times of William Randolph Hearst;* and Swanberg, *Citizen Hearst*.
2. McCabe to James Wilson, November 1, 1945, Styles Bridges papers, New England College, Henniker, N.H.
3. Gimbel to James Wilson, June 21, 1945, Bridges papers.
4. *New York Times,* December 29, 1940.
5. Ibid.
6. Every issue of *Compleat Collector* was examined by the author at the Library of Congress.
7. Hammer to Eleanor Roosevelt, January 16 and January 24, 1941, and Eleanor Roosevelt to Hammer, January 25, 1941, Franklin D. Roosevelt Library, Hyde Park, N.Y.
8. *New York Sun,* January 29, 1941; *New York News,* February 16, 1941; and *New York Times,* June 28, June 30, September 20, and September 22, 1942.
9. Russell Brown speech to the Newcomen Society, February 18, 1965; and Associated Press, dispatches of November 15 and December 22, 1943, and April 10, 1944.
10. "Memorandum on Loan to Nahum Chapin Distilling Company," no date, Bridges papers; and land records, book M, town clerk, Newmarket, N.H., located by researcher David Carle.
11. *New York Post* advertisement, July 19, 1944.
12. Getz, *Whiskey; Progress Report on Industrial Alcohol,* War Production Board, document 271, January 3, 1944, Harry Hopkins papers, Roosevelt Library; *Business Week,* March 25, 1944; Harold Szacik, interview, December 30, 1986 (Szacik worked at the plant); and Royce Carpenter, interview, December 30, 1986 (Carpenter is a longtime local resident).
13. *New York Times,* May 18 and May 20, 1944; and *Wooden Barrel,* June 1944.
14. *Alcohol Policies of the War Production Board and Predecessor Agencies, May 1940 to January 1945,* Virginia Turrell, War Production Board, study 16, Library of Congress.
15. U.S. Tax Court, docket nos. 60897 and 60907, reported at 18 CCH Tax Court memo 207; and U.S. District Court, Western District of Kentucky, reported at 189 F. Supp. 821.
16. *Spirits,* November 1944 and October 1946; *New York Times,* October 30, 1944; and *Business Week,* July 20, 1946.
17. *Ye Olde Treaty House,* published by Hammer Galleries, 1946, collection of Ireene Wicker Hammer and Victor J. Hammer; Carolynne Hearmon, *Uxbridge: A Concise History,* Hillingdon Borough Libraries, 1982; *Middlesex Advertiser and Gazette,* September 13, 1929; *Daily Mirror* (London), February 1, 1961; and Bridges papers. London researcher Dominic Higgins discovered much of the material located in England.
18. *Spirits,* October 1946; and *Congressional Record,* May 23, 1949.
19. FBI memorandum, September 14, 1951, FOIA release; and U.S. House of Representatives, *The Communist Party of the United States as an Agent of a Foreign Power,* report 209, April 1, 1947; House Committee on Un-American Activities, *Organized Communism in the United States,* August 19, 1953.
20. Pamphlet, June 11, 1940, Bridges papers; Hammer to Marion Dickerman, July 5

and July 17, 1940, and to Franklin Roosevelt, September 21, 1940, Roosevelt Library.

21. Letters and telegrams exchanged by Hammer and the Roosevelts, August 19, October 3, October 23, November 1, and November 7, 1940, Roosevelt Library; and Ben Gross column, *New York News,* November 1, 1940.

22. White House staff memorandum, Roosevelt Library; *New York Times,* November 29, 1940; and transcript of press briefing, Roosevelt Library.

23. Bridges papers.

24. Hammer telegram to Truman, April 13, 1945, Harry S. Truman Library, Independence, Mo. Also there are Hammer's April 27, 1946, letter concerning wheat flour; the reference to the Pearson broadcast; and the material on Hammer's White House meeting.

25. *New York Times,* April 29, 1946; and Herbert Hoover Presidential Library, West Branch, Ia.

26. Comments on Truman's appointments for July 19, 1946, Truman Library; and *New York Times,* July 20, 1946.

27. Luckman, *Twice in a Lifetime;* and *Spirits,* November 1947.

Chapter 11: DOMESTIC DIFFICULTIES

1. New York Division of Professional Licensing Services, Albany; and letters on Julius Hammer's behalf to the New York State Board of Medical Examiners from Bernard Barron, July 15, 1940, James Gerard, March 12, 1943, and Alfred Smith, April 30, 1943, all from Styles Bridges papers, New England College, Henniker, N.H.

2. The engraved invitation, guest book, and photographs are all in the collection of Ireene Wicker Hammer and Victor J. Hammer.

3. *New York Times* and *New York Sun,* October 20, 1948; records of Fairview Cemetery, Middletown, N.J.; Surrogate's Court, New York City, p. 11469; and edited transcript of remarks, *Los Angeles Times,* May 21, 1986.

4. Correspondence between Victor Hammer and Armasha, collection of Ireene Wicker Hammer and Victor J. Hammer; private papers of Nancy Hammer Eilan; *New York Daily News,* January 13, 1941; *The Singing Lady's Favorite Songs,* W. K. Kellogg Company, 1934, Library of Congress; and Harry Hopkins papers, Franklin D. Roosevelt Library, Hyde Park, N.Y.

5. Ireene Wicker Hammer to Armand Hammer, November 11, 1949, collection of Ireene Wicker Hammer and Victor J. Hammer; Nancy Hammer Eilan, interview, August 21, 1987; *Counterattack* news release, October 27, 1950; *New York World Telegram* and *New York Daily News,* October 27, 1950; Cogley, *Report on Blacklisting, Volume II, Radio-Television;* and testimony of Vincent Hartnett, July 1956, U.S. House of Representatives Committee on Un-American Activities, *Investigation of So-Called Blacklisting in Entertainment Industry — Report of the Fund for the Republic — Part I.*

6. *Workplan for Ordnance Works Disposal Areas, Morgantown, West Virginia, Remedial Investigation Feasibility Study, Volume I,* U.S. Environmental Protection Agency, December 20, 1985.

7. U.S. House of Representatives, Armed Services Committee, *Investigation of Proposed Lease of Morgantown Ordnance Works by Department of the Army,* 1951; presidential appointments calendar, Harry S. Truman Library, Independence, Mo.; Kilgore papers, West Virginia University, Morgantown, including a Hammer telegram of August 7, 1951; *New York Times,* August 18 and August 31, 1951; *Morgantown Post,* August 18, 1951; Frank McGrath, Manufacturers Trust Company, to Army Corps of Engineers, July 25, 1951; William DuBois, Chase Na-

tional Bank, to Army Corps of Engineers, July 25, 1951; and letter from James C. Wilson, Perth Amboy First Bank and Trust Company, to the undersecretary of the army, August 30, 1951, Bridges papers.

8. U.S. Defense Department news release, September 5, 1951; and *Baltimore Sun,* December 11, 1951.

9. Hammer to Vinson, December 1, 1951, and Vinson to members of U.S. House, Armed Services Committee, November 27, 1951, Bridges papers.

10. Hammer's testimony before U.S. House, Armed Services Committee, October 24, 1951.

11. Alexander's testimony before U.S. House, Armed Services Committee, October 20, 1951.

12. Galusha to Bridges, November 27, 1951, Bridges papers. Galusha later rose to the rank of brigadier general. I spoke to his widow.

13. Teletype, November 14, 1951, FOIA release (also see Jack Anderson's October 15, 1951, memo to Drew Pearson in Pearson papers, box G284, Lyndon Baines Johnson Library, Austin, Tex.); and Bridges papers.

14. *The Reporter,* July 20, 1954 (underlying research for the exposé of Bridges is in Max Ascoli papers, Special Collections, Boston University; Charlie Niles guided the author through the documents); and *Congressional Record,* August 19, 1954.

15. Bridges papers, including Hammer to Bridges, December 23, 1949.

16. State Department memorandum, May 6, 1952, FOIA release.

17. New York State Liquor Authority minutes, December 13 and December 14, 1949, New York City (Richard Chernela at the Liquor Authority helped locate the documents); and Edward Beenstock, interview, September 25, 1987 (Beenstock worked for Hammer at United Distillers).

18. Hammer's testimony before U.S. House of Representatives, Special Subcommittee to Investigate the Department of Justice, June 27, 1952.

19. Real estate records, Rockingham County, N.H., including book 1160, p. 319; Hoyt telegram, June 21, 1952, and Mason telegram, July 1, 1952, Bridges papers; Marquis Childs column, *Washington Post,* June 24, 1952; and Rowe, *Newington, New Hampshire.*

20. *Journal of Commerce,* March 26, 1952; *Dallas Times Herald* and *San Antonio Express,* June 27, 1952; *New York Herald-Tribune,* May 7, 1952; *Editor & Publisher,* April 11, 1953; *Business Week,* February 7, 1953; and *Spirits,* May 1952 and March 1953.

21. Hammer telegram to U.S. ambassador in London, June 2, 1953, Bridges papers; documentation at Victoria and Albert Museum, London; *Middlesex Advertiser and County Gazette,* August 15, 1958; Schenley Industries annual report, 1953; *Business Week,* February 21, 1953; and *New York Times,* March 4 and March 18, 1953.

22. 18 CCH Tax Court Memo 207, docket nos. 60897 and 60907; files at the IRS and U.S. Tax Court have been destroyed, so secondary sources have been relied upon for the most part. No living member of Eleanor Roosevelt's family interviewed recalled her testifying to Hammer's good character.

23. Towne and Wentworth, *Cattle and Men;* Alvin Howard Sanders, *A History of Aberdeen-Angus Cattle* (New Breeder's Gazette, 1928); and *New Yorker,* December 1, 1963.

24. Armand Hammer–Angela Hammer divorce proceedings, New Jersey Superior Court, Monmouth County, Chancery Division, C-1712-53. Other documents from the divorce are in related cases, New Jersey Superior Court, Appellate Division, docket A-312-54, decision reported at 36 N.J. Super. 265 and 115 A.2d 614; New York Supreme Court, New York County, index number 31954-54; and scattered documents in Bridges papers, including a letter from Angela's attorney Samuel

Nashel to Bridges, March 2, 1955. The author interviewed Nashel on January 19, 1988.

25. Mary Kotick Feinstein, interview, September 16, 1987.

26. Sales reports in *Aberdeen-Angus Journal* (every monthly issue from 1944 to the present was examined); and *Aberdeen-Angus Review,* Summer 1951.

27. Martha Walker Sturtevant, interview, June 29, 1988.

28. Allen, interview, September 24, 1987; *Aberdeen-Angus Journal,* August 1954; New York Supreme Court, New York County, case 17170-54; New Jersey Superior Court, Monmouth County, docket nos. L-8167-53 and L-4059-55.

29. *Times* (London), May 12, 1954; and *New York Times,* May 13, 1954.

30. New Jersey Superior Court, Monmouth County Chancery Division, C-1712-53.

31. Ibid.

32. Ibid.

33. Ibid.

34. Ibid.

35. Ibid.

36. *New York Daily News,* December 8, 1954.

37. *New York Daily News,* January 18 and October 7, 1955; and January 20, 1956.

38. Deed, October 4, 1971, Monmouth County, New Jersey, book 3753, p. 836; and *National Register of Lost or Stolen Archival Materials,* list B, July 1980, published by Society of American Archivists.

Chapter 12: GOING WEST

1. Chell, interview, March 8, 1988; Galina Perry, interview, February 26, 1988; Armand Hammer–Olga Vadina divorce file, 8th Judicial District Court, Clark County, Nev., file 19039; and Olga Vadina's death certificate, Orange County, Calif., Health Department, no. 3000-03237. Los Angeles researchers Don Ray, Victor Cook, and David Ritchie helped locate information throughout California.

2. Mary Kotick Feinstein, interview, September 22, 1987; and Nancy Hammer Eilan, interview, August 21, 1987.

3. Registrar's office, Marshall College, Huntington, W. Va.; marriage license, Los Angeles County, book 3890, p. 314; and divorce file, Superior Court, Los Angeles County, case WE-D-20136-1972.

4. Superior Court, Los Angeles County, criminal case 173163; and various newspaper articles, including *Los Angeles Times,* May 9, 1955, and *Huntington Herald-Dispatch,* May 9–11, 1955.

5. Ibid.

6. Land records for 10431 Wyton Drive, Los Angeles County; *Architectural Digest,* August 1985; and probate in Lake County, Illinois, book 176, p. 58. Armand and Frances Hammer both have said the tabloid detailing the divorce was *Police Gazette.* Numerous publications have carried that name or a similar one, but research failed to uncover any reference to Julian's case in any such publication at the Library of Congress. The case received such heavy coverage, however, that Frances undoubtedly read about it in some broadsheet or tabloid.

7. Marriage license, Los Angeles County, book 3878, p. 294.

8. Gore papers, Middle Tennessee State University, Murfreesboro. James Neal, custodian of the papers, searched for the Hammer references.

9. *San Jose Mercury,* September 23, 1957; *New York Times,* December 15, 1957; New-York Historical Society museum news release about the exhibition there; and "The Private Collection of the Hammer Brothers," fifty-three-page catalog prepared by W. R. Valentiner and Paul Wescher, author's collection.

10. *Los Angeles Times,* January 15, 1958; documentation at Fisher Gallery, University

of Southern California; publications of Armand Hammer Foundation; *New York Times,* January 14, 1965; *Los Angeles Times,* January 15, 1965; and John Walker's foreword, 1977 catalog of Armand Hammer Collection, prepared for a showing in Paris.

11. Eleanor Roosevelt letter, October 25, 1951, and Hammer Galleries news release, November 10, 1951, both from Franklin D. Roosevelt Library, Hyde Park, N.Y.; Muskie, *Campobello;* Joseph Lash, *Eleanor Roosevelt on Campobello,* Roosevelt Campobello International Park Commission, 1984; Minnewa Roosevelt Bell, oral history, Roosevelt Library; Armand Hammer to Victor Hammer, April 14, 1967, collection of Ireene Wicker Hammer and Victor J. Hammer; Franklin Roosevelt, Jr., interview, August 27, 1987; and Roosevelt and Brough, *Mother R.*

12. *New York Times* and *New York Herald-Tribune,* July 10, 1952.

13. Victor Hammer to Eleanor Roosevelt, box 3990, general correspondence, Ha-Har, 1952, Eleanor Roosevelt papers, Roosevelt Library.

14. Bette Barber Hammer, *A Guide Book to FDR's Beloved Island,* Hammer Library for Regional Research, Vicksburg, Miss.; *Jackson Clarion-Ledger and Daily News,* October 16, 1955; and *New Bedford Standard-Times,* September 7, 1958.

15. Ireene Hammer to Armand Hammer, August 5, 1956, and Victor Hammer to Ireene Hammer, August 14, 1956, both from collection of Ireene Wicker Hammer and Victor J. Hammer.

16. *Montreal Gazette,* October 24, 1959; *New York Times,* October 25, 1959; and Victor Hammer to real estate brokers, June 10, 1960, collection of Ireene Wicker Hammer and Victor J. Hammer.

17. Galina Perry, interview, February 26, 1988; annual reports, Delaware Corporation Office, Dover; Delaware Chancery Court, case 1298-1960; District Court, 7th Judicial Circuit of Wyoming, case 11277-1962; and correspondence between Gore's Senate office and Hammer's office, including June 4, 1956, Gore papers.

18. Contract between Imperial Jade and Donald Brann, October 2, 1956; and Brann's resignation letter, November 8, 1957.

19. "Washington Scene" newspaper column by George Dixon, King Features, June 17, 1958; and Dwight D. Eisenhower Library, Abilene, Kan., location PPF 1-L, H.

20. Gore to Hammer, July 29, 1957, Gore papers.

21. *Broadcasting/Telecasting,* July 22, August 5, August 12, August 19, October 14, October 21, December 9, and December 30, 1957; and *Television Digest,* July 27, 1957.

22. Fitzpatrick obituary, *New York Times,* July 2, 1977; *Current Biography,* 1948; *New York Times,* May 25, 1948; annual reports of FCC, 1948–1955; Hennock obituary, *New York Times,* June 21, 1960; and Stevens to the author, March 30, 1988.

23. Occidental Petroleum proxy statement, April 23, 1958.

24. H. Roy Roberts, interview, March 13, 1988; Blair Walliser, interview, September 13, 1987; *Television Digest,* March 1, 1958; *New York Times,* March 3, 1958; and New York Supreme Court, New York County, index number 4001-1958.

25. Blume, interview, February 11, 1988.

26. Walliser, interview, September 13, 1987.

27. *Television Digest,* September 13, 1958; and Walliser, interview, September 13, 1987.

28. Mutual Broadcasting System history, *Broadcasting,* September 10, 1984.

29. Walliser, interview, September 13, 1987; and Blume, interview, February 11, 1988.

Chapter 13: ACCIDENTAL OCCIDENTAL

1. Annual Reports of Occidental Petroleum from 1955 on at SEC (John Heine there helped obtain older reports from storage); and H. Roy Roberts, interview, March 13, 1988.

2. Harris's answers to interrogatories, U.S. District Court, Southern District of California, Central Division, case 61-636-K, stored at Federal Records Center, Laguna Niguel.

3. Hammer speech to Petroleum Club of Los Angeles, November 27, 1973; Occidental form 8-K, November 1956; and Abrons obituary, *New York Times,* May 26, 1977.

4. Coggin, *J. K. Wadley;* and land records, Los Angeles County, book 52930, p. 431.

5. Hammer to Bridges, November 6, 1959, and Bridges to Hammer, November 14, 1959, location LF 3, Hammer, 102, Bridges papers, New England College, Henniker, N.H.

6. Occidental filings at SEC; *Oil and Gas Journal,* December 19, 1960, and March 26, 1962; and *New York Times,* July 25, 1957.

7. Occidental filings at SEC; Gimbel obituary, *New York Times,* June 11, 1966; and decision concerning Gimbel's contested probate, Connecticut Supreme Court, reported at 166 Conn. 21.

8. *Los Angeles Times,* June 5, 1969; Leibovitz deposition before SEC, January 12, 1971, obtained under FOIA; Robert Rose, interview, November 5, 1987; Dorman Commons, interview, April 10, 1987; and Sheldon Eisner, interview, November 18, 1987.

9. Registrar's office, University of Southern California; *Dissertation Abstracts,* 1968, vol. 29; Jack Tanzer, interview, September 10, 1987; and *New York Times,* November 8, 1980.

10. American Stock Exchange listing application, no. 3278; and Occidental filings at SEC.

11. Eugene (Bud) Reid, Jr., interview, November 16, 1987.

12. Louis Rezzonico, Jr., interview, January 29, 1988; and Louis Rezzonico, Sr., obituary, *New York Times,* September 4, 1969.

13. Teitsworth, interview, November 19, 1987; U.S. District Court, Western District of Oklahoma, case 10807, stored at Federal Records Center, Fort Worth, Tex.; Occidental news release, March 10, 1961; Occidental form 8-K, August 1960; and numerous articles from the files of *Tulsa Tribune,* including Orville Parker obituary, April 8, 1963.

14. Ibid.

15. Robert Davis article in *Stanford Law Review,* January 1967; Goulden, *The Benchwarmers;* and 10th Circuit Court of Appeals, reported at 303 F.2d 55.

16. U.S. District Court, Central District of California, 68-611-JVC, stored at Federal Records Center, Laguna Niguel; and *Los Angeles Times,* April 18, 1968.

17. This refers to current and former employees, current and former directors of Hammer's businesses, federal investigators, journalists and authors, politicians, and relatives. The speculation referred to appeared in hundreds of articles and books and cropped up in dozens of interviews.

18. Leonard Lyons column, *New York Post,* September 20, 1959.

19. General correspondence, box 4464, Ha-Har, Eleanor Roosevelt papers, Franklin D. Roosevelt Library, Hyde Park, N.Y.

20. Hammer to Gore, January 23, 1961, Lyndon Baines Johnson Library, Austin, Tex.; and Gore to Anastas Mikoyan, January 27, 1961, Gore papers, Middle Tennessee State University, Murfreesboro.

21. Hodges, *A Governor Sees the Soviet.*

22. Tumarkin, *Lenin Lives!*

23. Hammer to Gore and Hodges, February 5, 1961, U.S. Commerce Department FOIA release; and Gore papers.

24. Hammer to Hodges, February 19, 1961, Johnson Library.

25. Whitman Bassow, interview, March 2, 1988; Bassow, *The Moscow Correspondents;*

Seymour Topping, interview, March 22, 1988; R. G. Ensz, interview, August 13, 1987; and State Department memorandum, February 19, 1961, FOIA release.

26. Packet of reports submitted by Hammer to various officials after the meetings; copies were located at the Johnson Library and in the Gore papers.

27. Mikoyan obituary, *New York Times,* October 22, 1978.

28. Frances Hammer's letter is in the private papers of Victor and Ireene Hammer.

29. Hammer-Strauss correspondence, Strauss papers, Herbert Hoover Presidential Library, West Branch, Ia.; and Strauss obituary, *New York Times,* January 22, 1974.

30. Reports submitted by Hammer, Johnson Library and Gore papers.

31. *Pravda* account of Khrushchev speech, June 30, 1962.

32. Ibid.

33. Hammer to Gore and Hodges, February 19, 1961, Gore papers.

34. Hodges memorandum to Rusk, March 3, 1961, U.S. Commerce Department FOIA release.

35. Evelyn Lincoln to Kennedy, February 25, 1961, president's office files, countries, box 125, folder 12, and Rusk to Kennedy, February 26, 1961, both from John Fitzgerald Kennedy Library, Boston; *New York Times,* March 10 and March 21, 1961; and Gore to Hammer, March 17, 1961, Johnson Library.

36. Eleanor Roosevelt to Victor Hammer, March 9, 1961, collection of Ireene Wicker Hammer and Victor J. Hammer.

37. Hammer to Gore, August 10, 1961, and Gore to State Department, August 16, 1961, both from Gore papers.

38. *Daily Kennebec Journal* (Augusta, Me.), August 11, 1962.

39. Muskie, interview, January 8, 1986.

40. Transcript of conversation, Armand Hammer oral history for Hollywood Museum, conducted by Norman Corwin, October 22, 1963; Corwin to the author, March 16, 1988; and Hammer's handwritten apology to the president for keeping him on the line, May 12, 1963, Kennedy Library.

41. May 12, 1963, stories in *Los Angeles Times, Washington Post, Boston Globe,* and *Detroit News,* among others.

42. Hammer to Kennedy, May 23, 1963, Kennedy Library; White House announcement, August 19, 1963; and *Los Angeles Times,* August 19, 1963.

43. State Department documents, FOIA release; Senate report 1097, 88th Cong., 2d session; *The Public Papers of the President,* 1964, items 137 and 138; and correspondence in Johnson Library.

44. Lady Bird Johnson to Hammer, September 22, 1964, Johnson Library.

Chapter 14: SHAKING UP THE SEVEN SISTERS

1. Financial figures are from Occidental Petroleum's reports to SEC.

2. Eugene (Bud) Reid, Jr., interview, November 16, 1987; Teitsworth, interview, November 19, 1987; various *Oil and Gas Journal* articles; and *Wall Street Journal,* February 13, 1962.

3. Reports to SEC; *Wall Street Journal,* December 4, 1961; and Jim Clark newspaper column, September 10, 1961, in *Los Angeles Times* files.

4. *Business Week,* March 23, 1963.

5. Information about Occidental's directors and top executives comes from many sources, including a 1973 company booklet, "A Profile of Occidental and the Men Who Manage It."

6. Ten Eyck, interview, October 19, 1987.

7. Rose, interview, November 5, 1987; and SEC release 16950, July 2, 1980, administrative proceeding 3-5936.

8. Rose, interviews, November 5, 1987, and December 16, 1988.

9. Alioto, interview, April 5, 1988.
10. Leir to the author, April 20, 1988.
11. Occidental letter of intent, September 1, 1963; American Stock Exchange listing application 4735; *Wall Street Journal*, September 12, 1963; and Hammer telegram to White House, September 21, 1963, John Fitzgerald Kennedy Library, Boston.
12. Occidental-Best agreements, May 23, 1963, and June 14, 1963; American Stock Exchange listing application 4619; Barbara Berry Corneille, interview, August 31, 1987; William Quinlan, interview, August 31, 1987; and Superior Court, Los Angeles County, WE-C-6272.
13. Gore to Hammer, March 8, 1965, Gore papers, Middle Tennessee State University, Murfreesboro.
14. SEC release 16950, July 2, 1980; Trost, *Elements of Risk;* and *Wall Street Journal*, June 20, 1979.
15. Occidental proxy statement, February 3, 1964; *Wall Street Journal*, October 17, 1963; and *New Orleans Times-Picayune*, October 30, 1963.
16. New York Stock Exchange listing application A-21482, January 23, 1964; *Staff Report on Organization, Management, and Regulation of the American Stock Exchange*, SEC document, January 3, 1962; and *Wall Street Journal*, February 17 and April 1, 1964.
17. Occidental proxy, December 29, 1967.
18. Brooks, interview, October 10, 1987; and his employment contract, September 8, 1963.
19. Guffey, interview, October 28, 1987; *Who's Who in America;* Continental Can annual reports; *Wall Street Journal*, October 14 and November 2, 1964; and Lehman obituary, *New York Times*, August 10, 1969.
20. *Florida Times-Union*, November 1, 1964, and October 30, 1965; and Occidental prospectus, January 19, 1965.
21. Brooks's testimony before U.S. District Court, Central District of California, 64-1219-FW, March 13, 1967.
22. Ibid.
23. Occidental reports to SEC; Thomas Wachtell to George Abell, May 31, 1966, Lyndon Baines Johnson Library, Austin, Tex.; Shwadran, *The Middle East, Oil and the Great Powers;* and *Wall Street Journal*, December 16, 1964, and August 10, 1966.
24. Gore to Hammer, January 3, and January 17, 1967, Gore papers; Lotos Club invitation to Hassan dinner, February 11, 1967, Victor Hammer papers; and *Wall Street Journal*, March 10, 1964, and February 25 and March 8, 1966.
25. Land records in Manhattan; Maclay obituary, *New York Times*, May 28, 1944; Louise Maclay obituary, *New York Times*, September 9, 1973; and interviews at Pâtisserie Claude, May 20, 1987.
26. Real estate and partnership records in Manhattan.
27. Surrogate's Court, New York State, Richmond County, file P-84/87; and Bureau of Vital Records, Health Department, New York City, death certificate A-233958.
28. Occidental reports to SEC, especially prospectus of July 19, 1967.
29. SEC investigation HO-494, leading to litigation release 4922, March 4, 1971, and a consent decree the same day in U.S. District Court, Southern District of New York. The underlying investigatory files were obtained under the FOIA. Those testifying included William and Lawrence Weinberg, Maury Leibovitz, Lawrence Kagan, and Dorman Commons.
30. Ibid.; Wansell, *Tycoon;* and *Jackson Sun* and *Memphis Commercial Appeal* files.
31. No-action letter request, April 27, 1967, and SEC approval, May 3, 1967; and Feldman to Hammer, October 15, 1963, Kennedy Library.

32. Occidental SEC filings; and *Los Angeles Times,* December 27, 1974.
33. Hammer telegram to Johnson, November 29, 1963, Johnson Library; John Mecom, Jr., interview, April 15, 1987; *New York Times,* February 15, 1971; *Wall Street Journal,* July 9, 1971; and Feldman, interview, December 8, 1988.
34. O'Brien to Hammer, March 10, 1964, and Valenti to Bundy, July 20, 1964, both from Johnson Library.
35. Lynda Johnson to Hammer, April 23, 1965, Luci Johnson to Hammer, April 25, 1965, and Lady Bird Johnson to Hammer, May 24, 1965, all from Johnson Library.
36. Watson memorandum, June 17, 1966; and Aziz cable, June 18, 1966, Johnson Library.
37. *New York Times,* June 24, 1966.
38. Watson to Johnson, June 21, 1966, White House Central Files, executive, FG 1, PL/ST5, Johnson Library; and list compiled by Arthur Krim, December 1966, Johnson Library.
39. *Saturday Evening Post,* March 12, 1966.
40. Hammer to Johnson, Johnson Library.
41. Invitation list, January 27, 1967, for the dinner February 9, 1967, Johnson Library.
42. White House news release, May 23, 1967; Hammer to Johnson, October 7, 1966, Johnson Library; and Lady Bird Johnson to the Hammers, July 26, 1968, Johnson Library.
43. *Congressional Record,* October 23, 1967; *Washington Star,* August 25, 1967; *New York Times,* October 22, 1967; and Mike Mansfield papers, University of Montana, Missoula.
44. Ketchum to Hammer, September 20, 1967, Johnson Library; and Lady Bird Johnson, *A White House Diary.*
45. Backup material on White House lunch, June 20, 1968, Johnson Library; and presidential announcement, August 23, 1968, Johnson Library.
46. Johnson to Rostow, May 7, 1967, and Rostow to Watson, May 9, 1967, Johnson Library.

Chapter 15: FAME

1. Unsell, interview, August 18, 1987.
2. *Los Angeles Times,* January 8, 1962; *New York Times,* October 19, 1962; and *New Yorker,* December 1, 1963.
3. Spencer Klaw, "Man with the Golden Touch," *Saturday Evening Post,* March 12, 1966.
4. Braudy, *The Frenzy of Renown.*
5. Richard Vaughan's deposition beginning August 30, 1968, U.S. District Court, Southern District of New York, case 67-4011, stored at the Federal Records Center, Bayonne, N.J.
6. Hammer to John Connor, October 11, 1965, U.S. Commerce Department FOIA release.
7. Gore to Hammer, August 15, 1963, Gore papers, Middle Tennessee State University, Murfreesboro; and Lightner, interview, September 29, 1987.
8. Akins's testimony before U.S. Senate Foreign Relations Committee, *Multinational Corporations and United States Foreign Policy,* pt. 5, October 11, 1973; and Schuler, interview, August 7, 1987.
9. U.S. District Court, Southern District of New York, case 67-4011, especially Hammer's deposition beginning February 7, 1968, and his testimony of September 13, 1973. Also, Hammer's testimony of April 18, 1978, U.S. District Court, Southern District of New York, case 75-1160, stored at the Federal Records Center, Bayonne.

10. Ibid.
11. Ibid.
12. Galic letter, March 15, 1966, exhibit 164, ibid. The waiver is dated August 27, 1966.
13. Kabazi's deposition to U.S. District Court of New York, case 67-4011, April 24, 1969; opinion of Judge Edward Weinfeld, reported at 382 F. Supp. 1052; and appeals court opinion upholding Weinfeld, reported at 519 F.2d 788.
14. Phillips's own books, including *Qataban and Sheba;* Merilyn Phillips Hodgson, interview, September 23, 1987; numerous conversations with Gordon Hodgson; Phillips obituary, *New York Times,* December 5, 1975; U.S. District Court, Central District of California, 87-1461-ER, including Hammer's deposition, September 18, 1987.
15. Orser, interview, November 13, 1987; and U.S. District Court, District of Columbia, case CIV-88-1169.
17. Occidental Petroleum filings at SEC, including prospectus of July 19, 1967; and *Wall Street Journal,* April 1, 1966.
18. Orser, interview, November 13, 1987.
19. *Wall Street Journal,* May 10, 1967; and untitled pamphlet published by Occidental in 1967, author's collection.
20. State Department FOIA release, declassified at author's request; and Wall, *Growth in a Changing Environment.*
21. July 17, 1967, State Department FOIA release.
22. Staff notes from interviews with McGuire on June 27 and July 9, 1973. I talked to John Henry, one of the subcommittee investigators, April 9, 1988. Another subcommittee investigator, Jack Blum, wrote to me on April 18, 1988, cautioning that McGuire might have been unreliable in his testimony. I talked to John Sitzler, the lawyer for the late McGuire, on April 11, 1988.
23. State Department FOIA release.
24. Rostow, memorandum, April 22, 1968, White House Central File, Executive ME 4-3/0, Lyndon Baines Johnson Library, Austin, Tex.
25. Occidental news release, March 12, 1968.
26. *New York Times,* October 22, 1967; and *West,* November 9, 1969.
27. *Fortune,* July 1968.
28. SEC filings by Occidental and by Kern County Land; and court decisions in the resulting litigation, including those reported at 284 F. Supp. 843, 323 F. Supp. 284 and 570, 450 F.2d 157, and 411 U.S. 582. I examined underlying documents in some of the cases, receiving some directly from Cecil Munn, who represented Kern. Some of the most useful early articles about Occidental-Kern appeared in the *Wall Street Journal,* May 9, 1967; *Los Angeles Times,* May 10, May 14, May 23, and June 5, 1967; and *Newsweek,* May 29, 1967; also Mrs. Dwight Cochran, interview, April 6, 1988.
29. Ibid.
30. Ibid.
31. Ibid.
32. U.S. District Court, Northern District of Texas, Fort Worth Division, case CA 4-902, reported at 284 F. Supp. 843.
33. Ibid.
34. U.S. District Court, Southern District of New York, case 67-CIV-2858, reported at 323 F. Supp. 570.
35. U.S. Supreme Court decision is reported at 411 U.S. 582.
36. Superior Court, Los Angeles County, case C-37601; and *Los Angeles Times,* May 13, 1975. I talked to Rogers's widow on November 4, 1988.
37. Davis, interview, March 14, 1988; transcript of Hammer talk to New York Society of Security Analysts, November 18, 1968; Thomas Wachtell, interview, November

5, 1987; Robert Teitsworth, interview, November 19, 1987; *Wall Street Journal,* October 28, 1966; *Los Angeles Times,* May 14, 1967; Associated Press story in *Charlotte Observer,* December 24, 1968; and *Raleigh News and Observer,* February 21, 1982.

38. Occidental filings at SEC; U.S. District Court, Central District of California, case 68-1671-JWC; Forrest Shumway to the author, March 6, 1989; and *New York Times,* February 4, 1968.

39. *Fortune,* May 15, 1969.

40. Docket C-1450-1968; and Boggs to SEC, October 10 and October 16, 1968, part of investigatory file HO-494, SEC FOIA release.

41. Gore to Hammer, May 24, 1968, Gore papers; Getty to Hammer, April 19, 1968, in Considine, *The Remarkable Life of Dr. Armand Hammer;* Getty, *As I See It;* and Lenzner, *The Great Getty.*

42. Transcript of Hammer talk to New York Society of Security Analysts, November 18, 1968.

43. *Los Angeles Times,* May 22, 1969; and Hammer's testimony before the U.S. Senate Subcommittee on Antitrust and Monopoly, *Government Intervention in the Market Mechanism: The Petroleum Industry,* July 31, 1969.

44. Miller, interview, November 17, 1987.

Chapter 16: HOT SPOTS

1. State Department documents, FOIA release; *New York Times,* September 2, 1969; Reuters article in *New York Times,* September 9, 1969; and Terzian, *OPEC.*

2. Arra, interview, January 26, 1988.

3. *Wall Street Journal,* September 5, 1969; and Terzian, *OPEC.*

4. American embassy in Tripoli to State Department, October 1969, FOIA release.

5. Bradford, *Fragile Structures;* and *Bangor Daily News,* July 25, 1968.

6. Buckley, interview, May 18, 1988.

7. U.S. Senate Subcommittee on Antitrust and Monopoly, *Government Intervention in the Market Mechanism: The Petroleum Industry,* July 31, 1969.

8. Ibid.

9. Ibid.

10. Continental Oil executives to secretaries of interior and commerce, September 9, 1968, Lyndon Baines Johnson Library, Austin, Tex.; *Oil and Gas Journal,* November 25, 1968; and Frank Ikard, interview, October 5, 1987.

11. *Independent Petroleum Monthly,* May 1969.

12. *New Orleans Times-Picayune,* September 29, 1968; and Unsell, interview, August 18, 1987.

13. Bradford, *Fragile Structures.*

14. Ibid.; and Nixon, interview, May 13, 1988.

15. Vahlsing, Sr., obituary, *Bangor Daily News,* September 3, 1969; *New York Times,* March 1, 1970; Vahlsing, Jr., interview, January 26, 1988; Muskie, interview, January 8, 1986; and Bradford, *Fragile Structures.*

16. Bradford, *Fragile Structures.*

17. *Congressional Record,* October 14, 1968.

18. Pierson to Johnson, October 17, 1968, and Aspinall to Johnson, October 31, 1968, Johnson Library; and *Oil Daily,* October 30, 1968.

19. Hammer to Johnson, November 8, 1968, Johnson Library.

20. *Washington Post,* October 28, 1968; *Fortune,* December 1968; and Associated Press, December 14, 1968.

21. Senate Banking and Currency Committee, *Foreign Trade Zone Application of the State of Maine,* December 19, 1968; and "Let Us Keep the Record Straight on Machiasport," Occidental Petroleum, 1968, author's collection.

22. Hammer speech to Maine Sugar Beet Growers Association, September 13, 1969, printed in *Congressional Record,* September 16, 1969.
23. Bradford, *Fragile Structures.*
24. Hammer to Nixon through Ehrlichman, February 1970, Nixon Presidential Materials Project, National Archives, Alexandria, Va.
25. Flanigan to Lincoln, August 19, 1970, Nixon Presidential Materials Project.
26. *Wall Street Journal,* November 20, 1969; report of special committee of Occidental board of directors on overseas payments, filed at SEC; and *Los Angeles Times* and *Wall Street Journal,* April 21, 1978.
27. U.S. District Court, Central District of California, 70-1397-HP; and 9th Circuit Appeals Court, case 71-1984.
28. British Court of Appeal, Civil Division, reported at 3 All ER 1025; House of Lords ruling, October 29, 1981; and *Times* (London), October 30, 1981.
29. Northcutt Ely, interview, November 11, 1987; and *Times* (London) coverage by Clive Callow, starting June 1, 1970.
30. Hammer to J. William Fulbright, December 4, 1971, and January 5, 1972, and Fulbright to Hammer, December 18, 1971, all from Fulbright papers, Special Collections, University of Arkansas, Fayetteville; Fulbright, interview, August 18, 1987; and Hammer to Mike Mansfield, December 3, 1971, Mansfield papers, University of Montana, Missoula, especially series 10, box 336.
31. Ely, interview, November 11, 1987.
32. Ibid.; and MacArthur, interview, December 8, 1987.
33. Shwadran, *The Middle East, Oil and the Great Powers;* and *International and Comparative Law Quarterly,* January 1983.

Chapter 17: HAMMER AND QADDAFI

1. U.S. Senate Foreign Relations Committee, *Chronology of the Libyan Oil Negotiations, 1970–1971,* print of January 25, 1974.
2. Williamson, interview, October 24, 1987; and Miller, interview, November 17, 1987.
3. Hammer to stockholders at Occidental Petroleum's 1970 annual meeting, as rendered in a fifteen-page account of the meeting published by Occidental.
4. State Department memorandum, October 15, 1970, FOIA release.
5. Occidental public reports to SEC, plus my examination of tens of thousands of pages of previously private files compiled by SEC investigators, obtained through FOIA release. Occidental sued the SEC to stop the release of documents to me; see U.S. District Court, District of Columbia, case 86-3428; and Court of Appeals, District of Columbia Circuit, case 87-5279. I also found dozens of useful documents concerning Hammer in Libya as part of the hearing "In the Matter of Occidental Petroleum Corporation Exchange Offer for the Mead Corporation," conducted in September 1978 by the Ohio Division of Securities. The entire hearing record (23 volumes) and all the underlying documents were made available to me in Columbus.
6. State Department FOIA release of January 1971 cables; and Jamieson letter to the author, February 27, 1989.
7. *Lloyd's Law Reports,* Q.B. Commercial Court, 1976, vol. 1, p. 293; and SEC FOIA release.
8. Boles, interview, May 11, 1988.
9. State Department cables between Tripoli and Washington, September 1970, FOIA release; and Boles, interview, May 11, 1988.
10. Williamson, interview, October 24, 1987.
11. *Times* (London), October 6, 1970; and Schuler, interview, August 7, 1987.
12. *Forbes,* April 28, 1980.

13. Adrian Hamilton, *Oil.* For a Libyan view, see Ghanem, *The Pricing of Libyan Crude Oil.*

14. Barran to U.S. Senate Foreign Relations Committee, August 16, 1974, *Multinational Corporations and United States Foreign Policy,* pt. 8; and Hammer's testimony before U.S. District Court, Southern District of New York, case 75-1160, April 18, 1978.

15. Brown, interview, November 26, 1986.

16. Occidental's annual report for 1971, SEC.

17. Vicker, *The Kingdom of Oil.*

18. Patten, interview, June 2, 1987.

19. Considine, *The Remarkable Life of Dr. Armand Hammer;* and Orser, interview, November 13, 1987.

20. Hammer to Ford, and Koch to Brent Scowcroft, October 2, 1975, both from Gerald R. Ford Library, Ann Arbor, Mich.; and *Sunday Times* (London), October 26, 1975.

21. *Los Angeles Times,* February 18, 1984; *Business Week,* January 20, 1986; *Wall Street Journal,* February 10, 1986; *New York Times,* June 30, 1986; State Department FOIA release; *Federal Register,* February 7, 1986; GAO Fact Sheet, "Terrorism — Laws Cited Imposing Sanctions on Nations Supporting Terrorism," NSIAD-87-133FS, April 1987; *New York Times,* March 27, 1986; Hammer to the editor, *New York Times,* April 7, 1986; *Wall Street Journal,* January 17, 1989; and Hammer's presentation to New York Society of Security Analysts, January 24, 1989.

Chapter 18: DÉTENTE THROUGH TRADE

1. Hammer speech at Salem College, reprinted in the *Congressional Record,* May 14, 1979.

2. James Roosevelt to Llewellyn Thompson, June 11, 1962, attached to Hammer memorandum for Marvin Watson, April 28, 1967, Lyndon Baines Johnson Library, Austin, Tex.; Gore to Hammer, May 12, 1964, and Gore to Dobrynin, May 19, 1964, both from Gore papers, Middle Tennessee State University, Murfreesboro.

3. Ten Eyck, interview, October 19, 1987.

4. Hammer's accounts of meeting with M. N. Gribkov, June 8, 1964, and with Furtseva, June 10, 1964.

5. Hammer account of meeting with Khrushchev, June 12, 1964, State Department FOIA release.

6. Kohler, interview, October 20, 1987.

7. *Wall Street Journal,* July 21, 1964; and *Oil, Paint and Drug Reporter,* July 27, 1964.

8. *Izvestia,* September 27, 1964, translated in *Current Digest of the Soviet Press,* October 21, 1964; and *New York Times,* September 27, 1964.

9. *Soviet Life,* April 1965.

10. *New York Times,* April 14, 1965.

11. Finder, *Red Carpet;* and Greg Stricharchuk, *Cleveland* magazine, September 1981.

12. Eaton, Jr., interviews, September 30 and October 26, 1987.

13. Ibid.

14. Ibid.

15. *Dun's Review,* October 1975; and *Chicago Tribune,* June 24, 1973.

16. Armasha Hammer letters, collection of Ireene Wicker Hammer and Victor J. Hammer; and George Krimsky, interview, October 27, 1987.

17. Charles Maynes, interview, August 14, 1987; Kennan letter to the author, September 19, 1986; and Kennan, *The Nuclear Delusion.*

18. Beam cable, April 21, 1970, State Department FOIA release; and Beam, interview, January 2, 1986.
19. *Soviet Life,* May 1973; *New York Times,* July 19, 1972; and State Department FOIA release.
20. *Times* (London) and *New York Times,* July 19, 1972.
21. Frank Vogl, *Times* (London), July 14, 1975.
22. *New York Times,* July 19, 1972.
23. *Barron's,* July 24, 1972.
24. SEC investigation HO-494, box 453, FOIA release.
25. *Los Angeles Times,* July 20, 1972.
26. Peterson to the author, January 6, 1988; *New York Times,* July 21, 1972; and *U.S. News & World Report,* September 4, 1972.
27. Peterson to the author, January 6, 1988.
28. H. R. Haldeman papers, Nixon Presidential Materials Project, National Archives, Alexandria, Va.; W. Marvin Watson comments to the author, March 18, 1989; and *Washington Post,* July 21, 1972.
29. Reuters dispatch, July 20, 1972; and editorial, *Washington Post,* July 25, 1972.
30. White House fact sheet, October 18, 1972; and Clausen to Hammer, July 20, 1972, Hammer to Haldeman, July 27, 1972, and Hammer-Stans exchange mentioned in July 26, 1972, memo to Haldeman from Lawrence M. Higby, of Nixon's staff, all from H. R. Haldeman papers.
31. *Washington Post,* August 30, 1972; Associated Press, September 15, 1972; *L'Express,* September 25, 1972; Occidental Petroleum filings at SEC; and CIA, *Appearances of Soviet Leaders,* an annual publication.
32. *Washington Post,* January 14, 1973.
33. Armand Hammer Foundation annual report, 1972.
34. Bachert, interview, September 25, 1987.
35. *Pravda,* November 9, 1972; and *Soviet Life,* May 1973.
36. Hammer speech to Petroleum Club of Los Angeles, November 27, 1973, inserted in *Congressional Record,* December 21, 1973.
37. *Pravda,* February 16, 1973.
38. U.S. Embassy cable from Moscow, February 1973, State Department FOIA release.
39. Eight-page agreement, April 12, 1973, author's collection; *Sunday Times* (London), April 15, 1973; and *New York Times,* April 13, 1973.
40. *Izvestia,* May 8, 1973, translated in *Current Digest of the Soviet Press,* June 6, 1973; and James Giffen, interview, May 18, 1987.
41. Dent to V. S. Alkhimov, June 1, 1973, and Alkhimov to Dent, June 1, 1973, author's collection (see *Washington Post,* June 2, 1973); and Hammer to Nixon, May 10, 1973, Nixon Presidential Materials Project.
42. Holles, *New York Times,* May 20, 1973; and Holles obituary, *New York Times,* June 10, 1978.
43. Stowasser memo, June 5, 1974, author's collection; and Stowasser, interview, December 8, 1987.
44. Shaw to Ichord, June 1, 1973, Ichord papers, University of Missouri–Columbia; and Ichord to the author, May 27, 1986. .
45. *Congressional Record,* July 10, 1973.
46. Hammer speech to Petroleum Club of Los Angeles, November 27, 1973.
47. Hammer to Flanigan, April 11, 1974, and Flanigan to Hammer, April 16, 1974, both from Nixon Presidential Materials Project.
48. Hammer to Sauer, February 5, 1974, and Sauer to Hammer, February 15, 1974, Export-Import Bank, FOIA release.
49. Stevenson to Casey, March 28, 1974, U.S. Senate Banking, Housing, and Urban

Affairs Committee, *The Role of the Export-Import Bank and Export Controls in United States International Economic Policy,* 1974 hearings on bills 1890 and 3282.

50. Ibid., as well as Stone, interview, December 16, 1985; and Glick, interview, October 5, 1987.

51. Hammer's testimony before U.S. Senate Banking, Housing, and Urban Affairs Committee, *The Role of the Export-Import Bank and Export Controls in United States International Economic Policy,* 1974 hearings on bills 1890 and 3282.

52. Ibid.

53. Ibid.

54. *Washington Post,* May 19, 1974.

55. Occidental International Corporation annual report to the District of Columbia; McSweeny, profile in "A Profile of Occidental and the Men Who Manage It," Occidental Petroleum, 1973; *Boston Globe,* April 10, 1969, and December 17, 1979; and Occidental news release, February 6, 1984.

56. Babcock, interviews, November 20, 1985, and June 2, 1987; Shepard, interviews, January 27, 1986, and August 31, 1987; *Des Moines Register,* February 7, 1973; *Oxy Today,* no. 5 (1975); Gore, interview, January 31, 1986; filings with the clerk of the U.S. House of Representatives (Washington, D.C., researcher Richard Pretorius helped gather the reports); and Tunney, interview, November 4, 1987.

57. NBC-TV "Today," September 10, 1973; Nixon to Casey, May 20, 1974; and Export-Import Bank announcement, May 21, 1974, FOIA release.

58. One of many letters from members of Congress to the bank, FOIA release.

59. Morris Amitay, interview, August 11, 1987; Stern, *Water's Edge;* and Shevchenko, *Breaking with Moscow.*

60. Amitay, interview, August 11, 1987; Stern, *Water's Edge;* and Daniel Yergin, *Atlantic,* July 1975.

Chapter 19: DOLLARS AND RUBLES

1. Associated Press, June 9, 1973.

2. *New York Times,* June 9, 1973; *Fortune,* July 1973; and *American Review of East-West Trade,* September-October 1973.

3. U.S. Senate Foreign Relations Committee, multinational corporations subcommittee, *Multinational Corporations and United States Foreign Policy,* hearings, June 17, 1974, and report, December 18, 1974; United Press International in *Washington Post,* February 22, 1974; and Bill Hall, interview, March 1, 1988 (Hall worked for Senator Church).

4. *Chicago Daily News* and *Los Angeles Times,* July 26, 1973.

5. McCartney, *Friends in High Places;* Dorman obituary, *San Francisco Chronicle,* May 15, 1974; U.S. Commerce Department memorandum, July 9, 1980, FOIA release; and Howard Boyd, interview, December 8, 1987. In a February 14, 1989, letter, Boyd said some of the information is "inaccurate and misleading," but would not specify.

6. *Washington Post,* September 19, 1973; and *Izvestia,* September 21, 1973.

7. File on credit 5178, examined by the author; Associated Press in *Washington Post,* April 20, 1974; *New York Times,* September 2, 1975; copy of Hammer dedication speech from the files of Joyce Barnathan, Moscow correspondent for *Newsweek,* author's collection.

8. *Information Moscow* (Western edition), 1985–1986; *New York Times Magazine,* September 21, 1986; and Michael Parks, Moscow correspondent, *Los Angeles Times,* March 1, 1989.

9. Hammer speech to Petroleum Club of Los Angeles, November 27, 1973; Dwyer interview in *Portland Oregonian,* July 1, 1975; and Jones to Scowcroft, December 23, 1975, Gerald R. Ford Library, Ann Arbor, Mich.

10. *New York Times,* May 5, 1978; *New Republic,* June 27, 1988; *Los Angeles Times,* August 3, 1988; *New York Times Magazine,* November 13, 1988; *Golf Digest,* January 1989; and *Regardie's,* February 1989.
11. Numinter B.V. literature from the files of Charles Simonelli; Simonelli, interview, June 27, 1988; *Numismatist,* November 1979; *New York Times,* March 4, 1979; and Mikhail Bruk, *Oxy Today,* no. 13 (1979).
12. *New York Post,* December 3, 1979; and Hammer's testimony before U.S. House of Representatives Banking, Finance, and Housing Committee, consumer affairs and coinage subcommittee, *Olympic Coin Legislation,* May 12, 1982.
13. New York Supreme Court, New York County, index numbers 03536-1979 and 18735-1979, reported at 123 Misc. 2d 574, and NYS 2d 372; Henzel, interviewed by Anne Fullam, July 11, 1988; and *New York Post,* December 20, 1979.
14. Cates, interview, October 19, 1988.
15. New York Supreme Court, New York County, index numbers 15105-1982 and 19493-1982; and *New York Jewish Week,* September 3, 1978.
16. *Fortune,* June 1961; *Business Week,* May 19, 1975; *New York Times,* October 5, 1979; *Fortune,* December 3, 1979; Jeff Gerth, interview, March 31, 1987; Andrew Karr, interview, January 28, 1988; Karr to Ford, June 23, 1975, Ford Library; and Evans, *Ari.*
17. Simonelli, interview, June 27, 1988.
18. Gerth, interview, March 31, 1987; Karr obituary, Associated Press, July 14, 1979; and Andrew Karr, interview, January 28, 1988.
19. Tunney, interview, November 4, 1987; and *Spotlight,* September 30, 1985.
20. Annunzio, interview, November 25, 1985; and Jack Anderson column, April 2, 1982.
21. Hammer's testimony before U.S. House of Representatives Banking, Finance, and Housing Committee, consumer affairs and coinage subcommittee, *Olympic Coin Legislation,* May 12, 1982.
22. Ibid.
23. Ibid.
24. Ibid.; and *Congressional Record,* May 20, 1982.
25. *Congressional Record,* May 20, 1982; and U.S. Senate Banking, Housing, and Urban Affairs Committee hearing on bill 1230, June 10, 1982, document 97-65.
26. *Pravda* and *Izvestia,* January 16 and January 22, 1975.
27. U.S. House of Representatives Interior and Insular Affairs committee, mines and mining subcommittee, July 23, 1976, serial 94-67; Brooks, interview, October 10, 1987; Chesson, interview, October 12, 1987; John Galvin, interview, October 12, 1987; A. A. Guffey, interview, October 28, 1987; and *Phosphates: A Case Study of a Valuable, Depleting Mineral in America,* GAO, November 30, 1979, EMD-80-21.
28. *Fortune,* April 7, 1980.
29. Guffey, interview, October 28, 1987.
30. Galvin, interview, October 12, 1987.
31. Phyllis Schlafly, *St. Louis Globe-Democrat,* November 14, 1979.
32. Hammer's testimony before the hearing "In the Matter of Occidental Petroleum Corporation Exchange Offer for the Mead Corporation," Ohio Division of Securities, September 11, 1978, 23 vols., stored at division archives in Columbus; Dan Fisher, *Los Angeles Times,* August 23, 1978; and State Department FOIA release.
33. Witcover, *Marathon;* Stroud, *How Jimmy Won;* Hammer to Carter, December 1976, Jimmy Carter Library, Atlanta; and *Palm Beach Daily News,* December 27, 1976.
34. *Washington Post,* January 31, 1978; *Women's Wear Daily,* April 3, 1978; and Armand Hammer Foundation annual report, 1978.
35. Clement Conger, interview, September 14, 1987, and Conger to the author, Sep-

tember 22, 1987; *Washington Post,* September 20, 1978; Rosalynn Carter to Hammer, October 2, 1978, Carter Library; and Armand Hammer Foundation annual report, 1978.

36. Jody Jacobs, *Los Angeles Times,* November 23, 1977.
37. Program book, dated October 31, 1978, author's collection.
38. Hammer to Carter, February 14, 1977, Carter to Hammer, February 22, 1977, and Hammer to Carter, March 4, 1977, all from Carter Library.
39. Hammer to Carter, January 15, 1979, Carter to Hammer, January 23, 1979, William Hearst to Hammer, January 26, 1979, and Hammer to Carter, January 29, 1979, all from Carter Library.
40. Shepard, interview, January 28, 1986; and *Washington Post,* May 19, 1977.
41. News release, October 19, 1978; U.S. District Court, Eastern District of Louisiana, case 82-4034; U.S. District Court, Southern District of New York, case 84-CIV-9174, reported at 681 F. Supp. 169; U.S. Claims Court, Washington, case 652-83C, reported at 7 Claims Court 556; Occidental news release, June 5, 1981; Shepard, interview, January 27, 1986; Leigh Bundick, interview, August 27, 1987; and *Washington Monthly,* June 1978, and Hammer to the editor, July-August 1978.
42. *Anhydrous Ammonia from the USSR,* publication 1006, October 11, 1979; and *Chemical Week,* July 18, 1979.
43. *Federal Register,* vol. 44, p. 71809; and Associated Press, December 15, 1979.
44. *Federal Register,* vol. 45, p. 3875; International Trade Commission hearing transcript, March 3, 1980; and Calhoun, interview, December 4, 1986.
45. *Florida Times-Union,* January 29 and February 2, 1980; and U.S. Supreme Court decision, reported at 457 U.S. 702, June 24, 1982.
46. Hammer correspondence, January 29 and January 30, 1980, Carter Library.
47. Evans and Novak, *Washington Post,* February 20, 1980.
48. Klutznick, interview, April 28, 1987, and letter to the author, February 20, 1989; and *Chemical Week,* February 13, 1980.
49. U.S. Senate Committee on Commerce, Science, and Transportation, *Embargo of Phosphate Exports to the Soviet Union,* February 19, 1980, serial 96-81.
50. *Los Angeles Times,* February 28, 1980; *Time,* March 10, 1980; Hammer speech to United Nations Association of San Francisco, reported in *San Francisco Examiner,* October 27, 1980; and Galvin, interview, October 12, 1987.
51. Charles Percy to the author, November 20, 1987.
52. *Florida Times-Union,* April 24, 1981; *New York Times,* April 25 and June 26, 1981; *Chemical Week,* May 6, 1981; and editorial, *Gainesville Sun,* August 20, 1981.

Chapter 20: THE WORLD IS MADE OF OIL

1. U.S. Tax Court, docket 15898-80, with a reported decision of March 6, 1985; and related litigation, U.S. District Court, Western District of Arkansas.
2. State Department FOIA release; and Nixon Presidential Materials Project, National Archives, Alexandria, Va.
3. U.S. District Court, Southern District of Texas, Laredo Division, CIV-76-L-51; U.S. Court of Appeals, 5th Circuit, 577 F.2d 298; Ryan, interview, October 2, 1986; *New York Times,* October 9, 1975; and *Mother Jones,* July 1977.
4. SEC investigatory file HO-846, FOIA release, including Hammer's depositions of January 15 and August 5, 1976; *Wall Street Journal,* December 17, 1975, and February 20, March 31, June 4, June 11, and July 15, 1976; Venezuelan legislative report, June 9, 1976; Occidental Petroleum news release, June 10, 1976; Oxy's reply brief of December 22, 1988, to Trade Policy Staff Committee; *Wall Street Journal,* December 27, 1988; and *New York Times,* March 31, 1989.
5. U.S. District Court, Central District of California, case 79-2089-MRP; Shaver Nava, interview, September 24, 1986; and SEC FOIA release.
6. U.S. District Court, Central District of California, case 68-1393-JWC; *Newsday,*

August 5, 1968; Sigmund, *Multinationals in Latin America;* and Richard Palmer, interview, May 8, 1988.

7. Babcock, interview, June 2, 1987.
8. J. D. Ratcliffe, interview, March 4, 1988.
9. *Oxy Today,* no. 16 (1981); John Dorgan's testimony before the hearing "In the Matter of Occidental Petroleum Corporation Exchange Offer for the Mead Corporation," Ohio Division of Securities, September 1978, 23 vols., stored at division archives, Columbus; Superior Court, Los Angeles County, case C-631015; and *Wall Street Journal,* August 30, 1985, and January 5, 1987.
10. *Oxy Profiles* newsletter, October 1987.
11. Hammer speech to Los Angeles Stockbroker Society, reported in *Los Angeles Times,* October 3, 1984; Occidental annual report, 1985; *Wall Street Journal,* June 6, 1985; and Occidental news release, November 15, 1985.
12. *El Tiempo* (Bogotá, Columbia), November 1, 1986, translated by Zy Weinberg; *Wall Street Journal,* November 4, 1986, and October 14, 1987; Hammer quoted by Youssef Ibrahim, *Wall Street Journal,* May 13, 1985; *New York Times,* March 31, 1988; and *Journal of Commerce,* October 6, 1988.
13. Sutton's lawsuit, Superior Court of California, Kern County, case 202003-1988; and ELN to Hammer, April 15, 1987, concerning hostage Albert Ricky Paulson.
14. Hammer and McSweeny correspondence with White House, Central Files, ST 10, Jimmy Carter Library, Atlanta; State Department FOIA release; and Hammer to White House, December 16, 1977, Brzezinski to Hammer, January 12, 1978, Hammer to Brzezinski, June 13, 1978, Brzezinski to Hammer, August 1, 1978, and Hammer to Brzezinski, August 4, 1978, all from Carter Library.
15. *Washington Post* and *Washington Star,* March 30, 1978; and Ripley to Brzezinski, March 8, 1978, Carter Library.
16. Hammer's article, *American Banker,* July 29, 1981.
17. Guy Arnold, *Britain's Oil.*
18. Thomson, *After I Was Sixty;* and Goldenberg, *The Thomson Empire.*
19. Getty, *As I See It.*
20. Occidental news release, April 5, 1972; Occidental reports to SEC.
21. Annual reports to Occidental United Kingdom subsidiaries located by London researcher Bill Britt.
22. *Times* (London), January 14, 1977; and Armand Hammer Foundation annual report, 1977.
23. Peter Kilborn, *New York Times,* January 12, 1977.
24. Patten, interview, June 2, 1987.
25. Coleman, *Thatcher's Britain;* and *London Observer,* October 9, 1980.
26. *New York Times,* June 8, 1983; Junor, *Margaret Thatcher;* and *Evening Standard,* October 9, 1980.
27. *Travel and Leisure,* April 1987.
28. Yergin, *Atlantic,* July 1975.
29. J. D. Ratcliffe, interview, March 4, 1988; *Oxy Today,* no. 16 (1981); and *Sunday Times* (London), September 7, 1980.
30. *Times* (London), September 6, 1980.
31. *New York Times,* July 8, 1988; Occidental quarterly reports to stockholders and SEC; *Independent,* July 25, 1988; *Wall Street Journal,* August 30 and November 25, 1988; *Business Insurance,* November 14, 1988; and Bernard Ingham (Margaret Thatcher's press secretary) to the author, March 6, 1989.

Chapter 21: TEFLON TYCOON

1. Swearingen, interview, December 16, 1987.
2. U.S. Senate Interior and Insular Affairs Committee, special subcommittee on in-

tegrated oil operations, *Standard Oil Company of Indiana–Occidental Petroleum Corporation Merger,* December 3, 1974.

3. Ibid.

4. Steve Stern, interview, November 10, 1987; Haskell news release, November 20, 1974; and U.S. District Court, Central District of California, case 74-3527.

5. Yergin, *Atlantic,* June and July 1975.

6. Occidental news release, June 21, 1976.

7. State Department FOIA release.

8. Hammer to Nixon, White House Central Files, Executive, FG38/A, Nixon Presidential Materials Project, National Archives, Alexandria, Va.

9. State Department memorandum, FOIA release; and *Washington Post,* June 27, 1976.

10. Analyses and reports, White House Central Files, FO 4-3, Gerald R. Ford Library, Ann Arbor, Mich.

11. Ronald Klein, interview, November 15, 1988; *Times* (London), August 28, 1976; and *Wall Street Journal,* August 30, 1976.

12. "In the Matter of Occidental Petroleum Corporation Exchange Offer for the Mead Corporation," Ohio Division of Securities, September 1978, 23 vols., stored at division archives, Columbus; filings by both companies at SEC; and Warren Batts to the author, March 9, 1989.

13. *Washington Post,* October 22, 1978.

14. "In the Matter of Occidental Petroleum Corporation Exchange Offer for the Mead Corporation."

15. Ibid.

16. Ibid.

17. Klein, interview, May 24, 1988.

18. *Forbes,* December 11, 1978; *New York Times,* February 13, 1979; and *Wall Street Journal,* April 3, 1979.

19. *Wall Street Journal,* August 22 and August 24, 1966; *New York Times,* August 24, 1966; Joe Tingley, interview, June 24, 1987; and Bureau of Indian Affairs report 21, II, 1985.

20. SEC investigations HO-494 and HO-557, FOIA release.

21. Davis, interview, March 14, 1988; and Wachtell, interview, November 5, 1987.

22. U.S. District Court, Southern District of New York, detailed in SEC litigation release 4922.

23. Klein, interview, May 24, 1988.

24. Babcock, interview, June 2, 1987; and Nizer, *Reflections Without Mirrors.*

25. U.S. District Court, Central District of California, case 74-2895; and Poulos, *Chicago Tribune,* January 2, 1974.

26. SEC FOIA release.

27. Ibid.

28. Ibid.

29. U.S. District Court, Southern District of New York, case 73-5505, accompanied by SEC litigation release 6186.

30. U.S. District Court, Southern District of New York, case 74-1.

31. SEC investigative file HO-846; *Washington Post,* December 12 and December 18, 1975; *New York Times,* December 18, 1975; and U.S. District Court, Central District of California, case 76-2097-ALS.

32. Ibid.

33. U.S. District Court, District of Columbia, case 77-0751, accompanied by SEC litigation release 8121.

34. "Investigated Payments and Accounting Practices of Occidental Petroleum Corporation, 1969–1975," filed with SEC.

35. Ibid.

36. Ibid.
37. Ibid.
38. Ibid.
39. Miller, interview, November 17, 1987; and Klein, interview, November 15, 1988.
40. SEC administrative proceeding 3-5936, with release 16950; and U.S. District Court, Central District of California, case 80-3018-WPG.
41. Ibid.

Chapter 22: THROUGH THE REVOLVING DOOR

1. Pickens, *Boone.*
2. Ibid.; Lampert, *Behind Closed Doors;* Mary Hargrove and Dale Ingram analysis, *Tulsa Tribune,* October 18, 1982; and *Washington Post,* August 14, 1982.
3. Waidelich, interview, November 12, 1987.
4. *American Banker,* January 24, 1983.
5. *Explorer,* American Association of Petroleum Geologists, April 1987; and Larry Nation, interview, December 21, 1987.
6. *Tulsa Business Chronicle,* September 9, 1985; Jones, interview, August 31, 1987; and David Hentschel to the editor, *Wall Street Journal,* January 9, 1985.
7. *Wall Street Journal,* January 2, January 13, and November 21, 1986; Barbara Rehm's coverage in *Natural Gas Week;* Irani to the editor, *Barron's,* February 3, 1986; U.S. District Court, Southern District of New York, case 88-0179; and James Pugash, interview, December 13, 1988.
8. Occidental Petroleum filings at SEC; and *Wall Street Journal,* April 15 and April 22, 1988.
9. Occidental news release, June 1, 1981; *Des Moines Register,* July 22, 1979, June 2, 1981, August 13, 1981, and September 18, 1988; and Kwitny, *Vicious Circles.*
10. Occidental filings at SEC; *Wall Street Journal,* March 2, 1983; Occidental reports to stockholders; Merszei, interview, February 22, 1989; and *New York Times,* January 18, 1981.
11. Barry to the editor, *Los Angeles Times,* May 2, 1987.
12. Asquith reply, *Los Angeles Times,* May 9, 1987; copy of brochure from Washington, D.C., researcher Reagan Walker, author's collection; notices of the Occupational Safety and Health Administration, July 1987; and *Wall Street Journal,* November 25, 1988.
13. Sales prospectus; and Occidental news releases, October 1 and October 9, 1987.
14. Occidental release, March 28, 1980; *Wall Street Journal,* March 31, 1980; Jefferson County District Court, Denver, case 80-1332, researched by Sarah Fisher; and U.S. District Court for Nevada, case CIV-R-81-229-BRT, reported at 662 F. Supp. 1002.
15. Merszei, interview, November 8, 1988; Fay, *Beyond Greed;* and *Los Angeles Times,* May 21, 1980.
16. *Aberdeen-Angus Journal,* March 1976 and June 1979; *Chicago Tribune,* March 21, 1981; *Louisville Courier-Journal,* August 4, 1981; *Angus Journal,* October and November 1985; and Cropsey, interview, October 9, 1987.
17. *Arabian Horse World,* 1981–1988, especially June 1982.
18. LaCroix, interview, June 18, 1987.
19. Occidental news release, February 4, 1986.
20. *Arabian Horse World,* June 1982.
21. Ibid.
22. Chauncey, interview, June 16, 1987; Lasma Arabians East booklet, "The Alluring Arabian"; Pereira, *The Majestic World of Arabian Horses;* and *Los Angeles Times,* November 28, 1982.
23. Randolph, interview, June 8, 1987.

24. *Federal Register,* April 21 and August 23, 1982; FOIA release of comment letters; *Washington Post,* April 28, 1982; and Lambro, *Washington.*

25. News release, September 1986; Ray Shaffery, interview, September 30, 1986; Dwight Minton to the editor, *Barron's,* February 23, 1987; and *Wall Street Journal,* September 23, 1987.

26. Occidental filings at SEC; *Los Angeles Times,* January 5, 1985; and *Barron's,* January 14, 1985.

27. Mackin letter to the author, October 25, 1987; and *Wall Street Journal,* September 22, 1981.

28. J. D. Ratcliffe, interview, March 4, 1988; Foster, *The Blue-Eyed Sheiks; Toronto Globe and Mail,* June 17, 1978; and research by Jock Ferguson in Toronto.

29. Yanarella and Green, *The Unfulfilled Promise of Synthetic Fuels.*

30. U.S. House of Representatives Science and Technology Committee, *Loan Guarantees for Commercial-Size Synthetic Fuel Demonstration Plants,* September 29, 1975; U.S. Senate Energy and Natural Resources Committee, *Oil Shale Technologies,* especially Hammer's testimony, March-April 1977, publication 95-45; and Hammer's testimony before same committee, *Energy Supply Act,* June 28, 1979.

31. Hammer to Zarb, June 24, 1975, and Hammer to Kleppe, September 23, 1976, both from Gerald R. Ford Library, Ann Arbor, Mich.

32. Hammer to Carter, October 14, 1977, Jimmy Carter Library, Atlanta; Hammer article in *New York Times,* February 19, 1977; Occidental synthetic fuels booklet, July 1979; Synthetic Fuels Corporation's July 1983 letter of intent to Occidental; *Newsday* series, November 28–December 5, 1983, especially December 1; Hammer to the editor, *New York Times,* July 26, 1985; U.S. Bureau of Land Management to the author, August 19, 1987; and John Rigg, Sr., interview, October 31, 1987.

33. SEC enforcement proceedings; court decisions reported at 430 NYS 2d 982; 477 NYS 2d 242; 749 F.2d 968; 607 F. Supp. 1057; Occidental booklet, "Love Canal: The Facts"; Brown, *Laying Waste; Business Insurance,* October 17, 1983; *Wall Street Journal,* February 24, 1988; and Stanley Grossman, interview, September 17, 1987.

34. California General Assembly Committee on Planning and Land Use, *1969 Land Exchange Between the City of Los Angeles and Occidental Petroleum Corporation,* December 4, 1972, and March 26, 1973, hearings.

35. Los Angeles County Bar Association ethic committee opinion 339, September 27, 1973; and California Supreme Court decision reported at 13 Cal. 3d 68, along with underlying documents.

36. Hammer's quote in Bill Boyarsky's story, *Los Angeles Times,* September 9, 1978.

37. Yorty, interview, November 2, 1987.

38. FBI tapes of Itkin; *Wall Street Journal,* January 11, 1980; KNBC-TV, Los Angeles, December 12, 1984; *LA Weekly,* February 22, 1985, and August 7, 1987; Mark Ryavec, interview, November 13, 1987; Marvin Braude, interview, November 20, 1987; *Los Angeles Times Magazine,* September 25, 1988; *Los Angeles Times,* October 13, 1988; and *Wall Street Journal,* November 10, 1988.

39. Dobrynin to Hammer, May 21, 1984, copy in author's collection.

40. Payne and Ratzan, *Tom Bradley.*

41. Ueberroth, *Made in America.*

42. *Los Angeles Herald Examiner,* January 23, 1985; *Los Angeles Times,* May 12, 1987; and Garner and Danson letter to the editor, *Los Angeles Times,* May 12, 1987.

43. Author's notes from Occidental annual meeting, May 23, 1988; and Braude, interview, November 20, 1987.

44. Braude to Hammer, May 20, 1987, author's collection.

45. Pugash, interview, November 20, 1987.

46. Ibid.; *Business Week,* December 18, 1971; *Forbes,* November 15, 1971; and Neil Jacoby to the editor, *Forbes,* December 1, 1971.

47. Occidental news release, January 28, 1972.
48. Commons, interview, April 10, 1987; and Commons, *Tender Offer.*
49. Wachtell, interview, November 1987; *Atlantic,* June and July 1975.
50. Occidental news release, November 1973; *Wall Street Journal,* May 12, 1978; *Esquire,* January 30, 1979; Baird letter, January 25, 1979; and Bruce McWilliams, interview, February 9, 1988.
51. "In the Matter of Occidental Petroleum Corporation Exchange Offer for the Mead Corporation," Ohio Division of Securities, September 1978, 23 vols., stored at division archives, Columbus.
52. *Wall Street Journal,* July 25, 1979.
53. Transcript of Merszei speech at Purdue University, December 7, 1979; *Los Angeles Times,* May 21, 1980; and *New York City Tribune,* August 7–8, 1986.
54. *Los Angeles Times,* May 12, 1980.
55. Edward Jay Epstein, *New York Times Magazine,* November 29, 1981; Occidental news release, August 23, 1984; and *Los Angeles Times,* August 25, 1984.
56. *Los Angeles Times,* August 25, 1984.
57. Superior Court, Los Angeles County, case 1984-0864; *New York Times,* March 31, 1984; and *Los Angeles Times,* April 5–6, 1984.
58. McGill, interview, November 6, 1987.
59. Teitsworth, interview, November 19, 1987.
60. Pugash, interview, December 13, 1988; Lamb, *Running American Business;* Vancil, *Passing the Baton;* Meyers, *When It Hits the Fan;* and Hammer, interviewed by Frederick Rose, *Wall Street Journal,* July 13, 1987.
61. *Fortune,* November 7, 1988; and Anthony Ramirez, interview, November 2, 1988.

Chapter 23: BACK-CHANNEL AMBASSADOR

1. Copy of the transcript, courtesy of James Polk at NBC-TV News, author's collection (program aired June 18, 1974); Jarvis, interview, January 7, 1987; and *New Times,* May 31, 1974.
2. *Human Events,* March 30, 1974; Bill Stapleton to Ichord, March 28, 1974, Ichord papers, University of Missouri–Columbia; NBC-TV news release, May 23, 1974; *Newsweek* and *Le Point* (French newsmagazine), July 30, 1973; and *New York Times,* August 28, 1973.
3. United Press International, February 9, 1975; State Department documents, FOIA release; *Los Angeles Times,* May 26, 1978; Tass, May 11, 1979; *Jacksonville Journal,* May 30, 1979; and *World Affairs Report,* December 5, 1979.
4. Charlotte Curtis column, *New York Times,* November 22, 1976; Edward Jay Epstein, *New York Times Magazine,* November 29, 1981; and *Architectural Digest,* August 1985.
5. Mikhail Bruk, *Soviet Life,* October 1976.
6. *Pravda,* October 21, 1976; State Department cables, FOIA release; and *Los Angeles Times,* October 27, 1976.
7. Hammer to Brezhnev, July 6, 1978, and Hammer to Carter, July 20, 1978, both from Jimmy Carter Library, Atlanta; *Chicago Tribune,* July 14, 1978; *Washington Post,* September 5, 1978; and Marshall Shulman, interview, October 22, 1987.
8. Toon, interview, January 4, 1986; and Toon cables, August 1978, State Department FOIA release.
9. Peter Maggs, interview, March 2, 1987; and Robert Booth, interview, April 28, 1987.
10. Hammer to Carter, September 5, 1978, Carter Library; and Reginald Bartholomew at the National Security Council to Rick Hutcheson at the White House, September 23, 1978, Carter Library.

11. Hammer speech at his human rights conference, Campobello Island, August 1979; and *Los Angeles Times,* January 31, 1980.
12. *Pravda, Washington Post,* and *Christian Science Monitor,* February 28, 1980.
13. Quoted by Mark Potts, *Chicago Tribune,* February 23 and February 25, 1980.
14. Hammer, interview in *San Diego Union,* May 18, 1980.
15. *New York Post,* March 1, 1980; *Detroit News,* November 10, 1980; Logan Act, 18 USC 953; State Department FOIA release of constituent letters to Senators Jake Garn and Orrin Hatch; and interview with Justice Department spokesman John Martin, September 30, 1987.
16. Hammer to Carter, April and May 1980, Carter Library; and Marshall Brement and Steve Larrabee, National Security Council memorandum, June 2, 1980, Carter Library.
17. Hammer to Carter, June 30, 1980, c-track 74526, Carter Library.
18. State Department cables, FOIA release.
19. Watson letter to the author, February 2, 1988; Watson, interview, March 7, 1988; and State Department FOIA release.
20. Ibid.
21. Percy to the author, February 2, 1988; and chapter by Hammer in Newsom, *Private Diplomacy with the Soviet Union.*
22. Pell, interview, October 2, 1987; and *Pravda,* December 17, 1981.
23. Finder, *Red Carpet.*
24. Ann Landers column, June 14, 1982.
25. *Pravda,* January 12, 1982; *Moscow News,* no. 13 (1982); Finder, interview, June 19, 1986; and Finder, *Red Carpet.*
26. *People,* November 29, 1982; and Weintraub to the editor, *Los Angeles Times,* November 27, 1982.
27. Hammer speech to Overseas Press Club, May 5, 1983, excerpted in *Christian Science Monitor,* June 10, 1983; *New York Times,* December 21, 1983; and State Department FOIA release.
28. Parsons, interview, September 23, 1987; and *New York Post,* February 16, 1984.
29. Hammer, interview in *USA Today,* March 28, 1984; Hammer to the editor, *Atlantic,* November 1986; Armand Hammer Foundation annual report, 1984, California Registry of Charitable Trusts, Sacramento; and live interviews given to CBS-TV, NBC-TV, and CNN-TV.
30. Hartman, interview, October 9, 1987; and State Department FOIA release.
31. Buchanan, *Washington Times,* December 5, 1984.
32. *Congressional Record,* January 24, 1985.
33. *Washington Post,* February 23, 1985; "CBS Morning News," February 8, 1985; and Simmons, interviews, January 8 and January 19, 1988.
34. Hoge, *New York Times,* March 14, 1985.
35. Shultz to Hammer, June 15, 1985, and Hartman to Shultz, both from State Department FOIA release.
36. Tass, June 18, 1985; *Soviet Life,* April 1985; John Bryson on "The Tonight Show" with Hammer, NBC-TV, October 3, 1985; and State Department FOIA release.
37. *New York Times,* June 25, 1985; and *Congressional Record* insert by Pell, June 26, 1985.
38. *New York Times,* July 7 and September 22, 1985.
39. Associated Press, June 18, June 21, and July 5, 1985; and International Communication Agency–State Department exchanges, March 9 and March 10, 1982, FOIA release.
40. Occidental Petroleum news release, December 13, 1985; *New York Times* and *Los Angeles Times,* December 14, 1985; and Hammer on "MacNeil-Lehrer Newshour," PBS-TV, May 2, 1986.

41. *New Yorker,* July 14, 1986; and Gregory Guroff, interview, May 7, 1987.
42. Armand Hammer Foundation annual report, 1986; *Pravda,* February 15, 1987; and Anna Christensen article for United Press International in *Newsday,* August 2, 1986.
43. Foundation news release, January 15, 1988; publicist Amanda Bowman, interview, March 4, 1988; and *New York Times,* January 16, 1988.
44. Foreign Broadcast Information Service, NES-87-198, October 14, 1987; and Hoover, interview, December 6, 1987.
45. *New York Times,* June 4, 1988; and Reuters, February 24, 1989.
46. Blitzer, *Between Washington and Jerusalem;* Blitzer, interview, December 11, 1985; *Jerusalem Post,* November 16, 1984; *Los Angeles Times,* November 19, 1984; and *B'nai B'rith Messenger,* Los Angeles, November 23, 1984.
47. Dinstein, interviewed by researcher Macabee Dean, December 1987 and April 18, 1988.
48. Ibid.
49. Ephraim Poran, interviewed by Dean, April 28, 1988; and Mizrachi, interview, May 17, 1988.
50. Mara Levi, interviews, April 30 and August 11, 1988.
51. Samuel Lewis, interview, August 10, 1987; and Yehiel Kadishai, interviewed by Dean, March 27, 1988. Lewis was American ambassador to Israel; Kadishai was one of Begin's closest aides.
52. Evron, interviewed by Dean, June 1988.
53. Poran, interview, April 28, 1988; Rapoport, *Redemption Song;* Hammer to Carter, Carter Library; and *Jerusalem Post,* January 29, 1985.
54. *Israel Today,* Los Angeles, October 23, 1980; Lev, interview, June 1, 1987; *Heritage,* Los Angeles, November 5, 1980; and Tom Tugend, interview, February 23, 1987.
55. *Heritage,* 1985–1989; Herb Brin, interview, February 16, 1987; copy of program, author's collection; and *Heritage,* December 11, 1987.
56. Ben-Shahar, interviewed by Dean, May 21, 1987; and reports and studies from the Armand Hammer Fund for Economic Cooperation in the Middle East.
57. *Los Angeles Times,* May 1, 1983; Ribakoff to the editor, *Los Angeles Times,* May 22, 1983; Glazer to the editor, *Los Angeles Times,* May 29, 1983; *Jerusalem Post,* September 19, 1984; and Glazer to the editor, *Jerusalem Post,* October 17, 1984.
58. *Business Week,* December 10, 1984; and Dan, *Blood Libel.*
59. Reports at SEC; news release, February 11, 1987; *Jerusalem Post,* March 1, March 5, April 28, and April 29, 1985; Isramco news release, January 13, 1989; and *Los Angeles Times,* July 13, 1988.
60. *California,* April 1983; and Goldfarb, interview, May 18, 1987.
61. *Wall Street Journal,* July 31, 1986.
62. Alex Goldfarb, interview, May 18, 1987.
63. Ibid.
64. United Press International, October 17, 1986.
65. Gale and Hauser, *Final Warning.*
66. David Goldfarb, *New York Times Magazine,* December 28, 1986.
67. Hammer speech to California Institute of Technology, October 20, 1986; and *Heritage,* February 20, 1987.
68. Daniloff, interview, March 9, 1987; Daniloff to the author, February 15, 1989; and Daniloff, *Two Lives, One Russia.*
69. *New York Times,* September 27, 1986; "This Week with David Brinkley," ABC-TV, September 27, 1986; and *Washington Times,* September 29, 1986.
70. *Life,* January 1987; Wrenn, interview, March 9, 1987; and Whitehead to the author, March 10, 1989.
71. Daniloff, *Two Lives, One Russia.*

72. *Los Angeles Times,* October 15, 1987; *Jerusalem Post,* October 18, 1987; *Heritage,* November 13, 1987; and Shinbaum, interview, October 30, 1987.

73. Stolar to Simon, January 7, 1987; Simon to Hammer, March 12, 1987, with help from Pam Huey in Simon's office; *Los Angeles Times,* May 17, 1987; Lowery, interview, November 25, 1987; *Los Angeles Times,* June 6, 1987; Susan Graham, interview, November 2, 1987; *Los Angeles Times,* July 21, 1988; and Alfred Bloom, interview, November 2, 1988.

74. Copies of the Soviet transmittal letter to Israel, December 3, 1986, and of Hammer to Shimon Peres, December 11, 1986, author's collection; Glazer to the editor, *New York Times,* April 7, 1987; and *Los Angeles Times,* November 4, 1987.

75. *Arete,* October-November 1988; and Fox, interview, November 1, 1988.

Chapter 24: HERO OF THE SOVIET PEOPLE

1. Gale and Hauser, *Final Warning;* and Gale's remarks at Hammer's birthday party, reported in the *Los Angeles Times,* May 21, 1986.

2. Ibid.

3. Interviews with State Department spokesmen Tom Switzer, June 11, 1986, and Scott Thayer, June 21, 1986; and Occidental news release, May 5, 1986.

4. Gale and Hauser, *Final Warning.*

5. Hammer article distributed by United Press International, May 20, 1986.

6. Gale and Hauser, *Final Warning.*

7. *Soviet Life,* August 1986; *Life,* January 1987; State Department FOIA release; and Gale and Hauser, *Final Warning.*

8. Harry Nelson's account in *Los Angeles Times,* May 18, 1986; and *Pravda,* May 25, 1986.

9. Charlotte Curtis, *New York Times,* May 27, 1986; and *Science,* July 4, 1986.

10. Occidental news release, July 17, 1986; and Gale and Hauser, *Final Warning.*

11. *Life,* January 1987; and Hammer and Gale column in *New York Times,* April 26, 1987.

12. *Washington Post,* December 8, 1987; *New York Times,* December 10, 1987; *Wall Street Journal,* December 11, 1987; *Washington Times,* December 14, 1987; Milton Esterow, interview, May 10, 1988; and material from National Gallery's press officers, especially Ruth Kaplan and Randall Kremer.

13. *Soviet Life,* August 1988; *Wall Street Journal,* December 9, 1988; *Los Angeles Times,* December 11, 1988; White House and State Department briefings, December 12, 1988; and *Parade,* January 17, 1988.

14. *Wall Street Journal,* December 26, 1986.

15. *New Yorker,* February 16, 1987; and Chrystal, interview, April 17, 1987.

16. Brown, interviews, June 24 and August 27, 1987, and February 13, 1989; his correspondence with Hammer; and Associated Press in *Portland Oregonian,* June 18, 1986.

17. House, interview, November 16, 1987; and *Los Angeles Times,* November 12, 1987.

18. Hammer speech, September 20, 1987, covered by Erin Kelly, *Orange County Register,* September 21, 1987; and news dispatches from the East German news agency ADN, September 1987, translated for the author by Birgit Wassmuth.

19. Warner and Shuman, *Citizen Diplomats.*

20. Fulbright, interview, August 18, 1987.

21. Gorbachev, *Perestroika.*

Chapter 25: HAMMER IN CHINA

Some of the material in this chapter first appeared in my article for *Regardie's* magazine, May 1986.

1. Gore, interview, January 31, 1986.
2. Hammer's article, *Journal of International Affairs,* Winter 1986.
3. Hammer speech in Cleveland, September 14, 1979; *China Reconstructs,* October 1985; and Strauss, interview, February 21, 1989.
4. Hammer to Carter, May 7, 1979, Jimmy Carter Library, Atlanta; and U.S. Energy Department news release, May 25, 1979.
5. Ronald Greenfield, interview, November 13, 1985; Joe Cerenzia, interview, November 12, 1985; and Joseph Yancik, interview, January 6, 1986.
6. Richard Chen's article in *Oxy Today,* no. 14 (1980).
7. *Wall Street Journal* and *Los Angeles Herald Examiner,* May 22, 1979.
8. Chen, interview, January 8, 1986; Daniel Stein, interview, January 8, 1986; Stephanie Green Lawson, interview, January 9, 1986, Priscilla Bynum, interview, February 4, 1986; and author's copy of itinerary.
9. *China Business Review,* July 1980; Occidental news release, May 7, 1980; *Oxy Today,* no. 16 (1981); *Scientific American,* March 1983; and Wilbur Johnson, interviews, January 21, 1986, and October 7, 1987.
10. *China Business Review,* July-August 1981; Hummel, interview, January 3, 1986; and Occidental Petroleum report to SEC.
11. Don Forest, interview, January 3, 1986; Melvin Searls, interview, January 6, 1986; Daniel Stein, interview, January 8, 1986; *International Coal Report,* October 1981; and *Los Angeles Times,* March 26, 1982.
12. Armand Hammer Foundation annual report, 1982; and Associated Press, March 28, 1982.
13. Gordon Crawford, interview, February 3, 1986; James Pugash, interview, November 21, 1987; and Kenneth Locker, interview, November 30, 1987.
14. *Los Angeles Times,* April 5, 1982; and State Department FOIA release.
15. Ann Frey, interview, December 7, 1987; and FOIA releases.
16. Amanda Bennett, *Wall Street Journal,* August 10, 1983.
17. Stonie Barker, interview, December 23, 1985; Associated Press, March 20, 1984; James Patten, interview, June 2, 1987; and Hammer speech to National Press Club, Washington, D.C., March 19, 1984.
18. United Press International, April 5, 1984; and *Omaha World-Herald,* April 24, 1984.
19. Stinson, interview, November 6, 1985.
20. *China Daily,* January 29, 1985.
21. Su Guang, interview, November 26, 1985; Jim Mann, interview, October 2, 1987; Ken Bailes, interview, December 16, 1985; *International Coal Report,* May 24, 1985; and Occidental news release, June 29, 1985.
22. Keyworth to the author, December 2, 1985; and State Department FOIA release.
23. Gregory Mounts, interview, January 2, 1986; Joe Corcoran, interview, December 6, 1985; and Jim Zoia, interview, November 5, 1985.
24. Steve Liu, interview, November 27, 1985; John Murphy, interview, December 9, 1985; Jack Milliken to the author, November 7, 1985; *Wall Street Journal,* December 4, 1986; *Beijing Review,* April 13, 1987; and *China Pictorial,* no. 3 (1987).
25. Marylouise Oates, *Los Angeles Times,* August 14, 1987; Associated Press in *New York Post,* September 11, 1987; *Beijing Review,* September 21, 1987; Xinhua (news agency), September 11–13, 1987; and *Newsweek,* February 22, 1988.
26. *Journal of Commerce,* October 4 and December 20, 1988; *Beijing Review,* December 12–18, 1988; Xinhua, July 12, 1985; *China Reconstructs,* October 1985; Xinhua, April 25, 1988; and Armand and Frances Hammer Christmas card, author's collection.

Chapter 26: THE NEW MEDICI

1. *New York Daily News,* November 20, 1968.
2. Annual reports from 1967 on; news releases supplied by the museum's public relations office; *Los Angeles Times,* June 2 and September 6, 1968, and August 20, 1969; United Press International story in *Los Angeles Times,* October 16, 1969; *Chicago Tribune,* November 7, 1969, for example; catalog for the show opening October 2, 1969, author's collection; and *Memphis Commercial Appeal,* September 28, 1969.
3. Copy of the engraved invitation, author's collection; and *Washington Post,* March 24, 1970.
4. *Washington Post,* March 28, 1970.
5. Graham confirmed the offer through Evelyn Small, February 21, 1986; *Washington Post,* April 30, 1970; and Richard, interview, February 21, 1986.
6. Walker, *Self-Portrait with Donors.*
7. Ibid.
8. Catalog of the Armand Hammer collection, 1971.
9. Armand Hammer Foundation annual reports; and Denvir, *Art and Artists,* October 1978.
10. Corcoran Gallery of Art news releases, April 22 and October 14, 1983.
11. Armand Hammer collection catalogs; and *ARTnews,* November 1976.
12. Tanzer, interview, September 10, 1987; Occidental Petroleum news release, December 18, 1980; *Washington Post,* December 13, 1980; and *Times* (London), December 13, 1980.
13. Legatt to the editor, *Times* (London), December 17, 1980; *ARTnewsletter,* March 3, 1981; Department of Trade (London), export license no. B131180; and University of California–Los Angeles news release, March 25, 1985.
14. Occidental news release, June 12, 1985; *New York Times,* April 18, 1982; Richard, *Washington Post,* October 2, 1980; and *Smithsonian,* October 1980.
15. *Los Angeles Times,* December 20, 1971; and news releases from Los Angeles County Museum of Art, with help from Pam Jenkinson.
16. Brown, interview, September 14, 1987; and *Washington Post,* December 21, 1971.
17. Fogg Museum newsletters, especially December 1976; and author's visit there.
18. Kreeger, interview, January 3, 1986.
19. Marzio, interview, November 14, 1985.
20. Botwinick, interview, January 3, 1986; and Corcoran Gallery news releases and reports, with help from Roberta Faul.
21. Botwinick, interview, January 3, 1986; and *Washington Post,* September 20, 1979.
22. Metropolitan Museum news release, May 1985; *New York Times,* May 15 and October 11, 1985; and *USA Today,* November 1, 1985.
23. *Palm Beach Times,* January 16 and January 19, 1981.
24. Madigan, interview, October 14, 1987.
25. Ibid.
26. Jenkins, interview, May 18, 1988.
27. Hammer, interviewed by Fred Ferretti, *ARTnews,* April 1973; Armand Hammer Foundation annual report, 1973; United Press International interview of Hammer, August 2, 1973; and *United States of America: Economics, Politics, Ideology* (Soviet magazine), May 1973, translated by Philip Gillette.
28. *New York Times,* May 4, 1973; and *Washington Post,* February 22, 1973.
29. *New York Times,* May 13, 1974; and *Newsweek,* July 1, 1974.
30. *New York Times,* February 13, 1979; and eight-paragraph letter from Baird to the editor, *New York Times,* March 12, 1979. The full letter, written February 14, 1979, contained twenty-two paragraphs.

31. Mansfield to Hammer, December 4, 1972, series 15, box 215, Mike Mansfield papers, University of Montana, Missoula.

32. National Gallery of Art news release, February 16, 1973; John Richardson, *Apollo,* September 1975; Brown, interview, September 14, 1987; and *Washington Post,* March 31, 1973.

33. *Detroit News,* September 2, 1973; and exhibition catalog, *Impressionist and Post-Impressionist Paintings from the USSR,* Ellis Library, University of Missouri–Columbia.

34. *Pravda,* April 4, 1975; and *Washington Post,* April 2, 1975.

35. *Los Angeles Times,* July 30, 1975; and Hammer to Hugh Scott and to Ford, June 26, 1975, Scott to Hammer, June 27, 1975, Brown to Paul Theis, May 16, 1975, and National Security Council internal memorandum, all from Gerald R. Ford Library, Ann Arbor, Mich.

36. Hammer, interviewed by Joseph McLellan, *Washington Post,* May 11, 1979; and Tass, May 11, 1979.

37. *Oxy Today,* no. 11 (1978); catalog of 1977 exhibition, *Apollo,* June 1977; *Le Point,* April 4, 1977; and author's visit there, October 1986.

38. Armand Hammer Foundation annual reports, starting in 1968; and Dennis Gould letter to the author, June 7, 1985. The annual reports are available at the California Registry of Charitable Trusts in Sacramento.

39. Armand Hammer Foundation annual reports, starting in 1968.

40. Ibid.

41. All pertinent files at the U.S. Tax Court in Washington, D.C., were examined with help from researcher Deborah Simon; and *Wall Street Journal,* March 14, 1974.

42. *Newsweek,* March 25, 1974; and Nizer letter to the editor, *Newsweek,* April 29, 1974.

43. Geoffrey Taylor, interview, September 3, 1987; and *New York Times,* May 2, 1983.

44. *New York Times,* October 29, 1971; Balay, interview, September 15, 1987; and *New York Times,* December 9, 1971.

45. Leo Biga, interview, October 5, 1987; *New York Times,* February 17 and May 28, 1972; *Newsday,* May 6, 1973; and Leibovitz to the author, March 1, 1989.

46. Richardson, interview, September 23, 1987; Rubin, in de Coppet and Jones, *The Art Dealers;* Rubin to the author, March 1, 1989; New York City property records; Armand Hammer Foundation annual report, 1973; *Variety,* March 21, 1973; and *Los Angeles Times,* March 15, 1973.

47. *New York Times* and *Washington Post,* July 1, 1977; IRS ruling, September 1977; and Tanzer, interview, September 10, 1987.

48. Hole in the Wall Gang Camp Fund news release, May 4, 1987; *USA Today,* May 5, 1987; New York Supreme Court, New York County, case 9842-86; Michael Ratner, interview, September 16, 1987; Jane Perlez, *New York Times,* April 27, 1986; and *Arts and Antiques,* Summer 1986.

49. *New York Times,* September 30, 1976.

50. Walker, *Self-Portrait with Donors.*

51. Van Dyne, "J. Carter Brown," *Washingtonian,* April 1988.

52. National Gallery of Art, April 23, 1987; and Brown, interview, September 14, 1987.

53. Occidental news release, January 21, 1988; *New York Times, Washington Post,* and *Wall Street Journal,* January 22, 1988; and Hammer to the editor, *Wall Street Journal,* May 15, 1987.

54. Occidental news release, January 21, 1988.

55. Editorial, *Los Angeles Times,* January 24, 1988.

56. Documents, including August 30, 1968, agreement between Hammer and the museum; and board of trustee meeting minutes.
57. George Longstreet affidavit, January 19, 1988; Daniel Belin to Hammer, February 2, 1988; and draft of thirty-nine-page agreement.
58. *Los Angeles Times Magazine,* May 22, 1988; Occidental news release, September 21, 1988; *Los Angeles Times,* September 23, 1988, and March 13, 1989; Alla T. Hall to Hammer, March 2, 1989, author's collection; and Occidental's 1988 annual report.
59. Hammer to the editor, *Arts and Antiques,* May 1987; Occidental's proxy statement of April 25 and May 12, 1989, supplement; Delaware Chancery Court, New Castle County, civil actions 10808 and 10823-1989; and California Superior Court, Central District, *Levitan* v. *Occidental,* Hammer et al., May 1989.

Chapter 27: PHILANTHROPIST WITH A VENGEANCE

1. Patterson, *The Dread Disease;* Rettig, *Cancer Crusade;* news releases, Salk Institute, including April 21, 1970, with help from Dianne Carter and researcher Linda Puig; and Salk to Hammer, December 23, 1969, transcribed by researcher Liz Ruskin.
2. News releases, including July 18, 1977; Hammer to Paul Marks, October 28, 1977, author's collection; *New York Times,* May 27, 1980; and McGill, interview, November 17, 1987.
3. McGill, interview, November 17, 1987; and Long, interview, January 23, 1988.
4. *Time,* January 4, 1982; and *Mother Jones,* January 1982.
5. *New York Times,* December 4, 1981; *Science,* December 18, 1981; and Harold Amos, interview, September 15, 1986.
6. Stonehill, interview, August 19, 1987; and Ann Landers, interview, December 10, 1987.
7. *Los Angeles Times,* February 11, 1982; Hammer Prize Foundation annual reports, California Registry of Charitable Trusts, Sacramento; and Raymond Erikson, interview, September 24, 1986.
8. National Institutes of Health publication 83-2609; transcript of 1983 meeting; *Houston Post,* March 5, 1983; Levy, interview, April 13, 1987; and *San Jose Mercury,* August 19, 1983.
9. Levy, interview, April 13, 1987.
10. Transcript of Hammer's remarks, President's Cancer Panel, June 3, 1985; *COPE: Living with Cancer,* August 1986; Lansing, interview, October 20, 1987; *Discover,* March 1986; *Business Week,* December 23, 1985; and President's Cancer Panel transcripts.
11. Hammer remarks, President's Cancer Panel transcript, February 25, 1985.
12. *Wall Street Journal,* May 8, 1986; and Hammer to the editor, *Wall Street Journal,* July 18, 1986.
13. Armand Hammer Productions news release, March 14, 1988; *Los Angeles Times,* March 30, 1988; and "The Cosby Show," January 21, 1988, supplemented by NBC-TV publicity packets from Mary Neagoy.
14. Guest list, author's collection; *New York Times,* March 2 and October 14, 1988; *Los Angeles Times,* October 14, 1988; *New York Times,* December 13, 1988; and Ted Stevens, *Congressional Record,* February 2, 1989.
15. *Sunday Times* (London), December 1, 1985.
16. Patten, interview, June 2, 1987.
17. *Oxy Today,* no. 11 (1978); *IPRA Review,* April 1982; and Patten, interview, June 2, 1987.
18. *Daily Telegraph,* August 17, 1978; and *Oxy Today,* no. 13 (1979).

19. Armand Hammer Foundation reports; research in England by Dominic Higgins; and High Court of Justice, Queen's Bench Division, case 1985-H-6820.
20. Betty Beale column, August 2, 1981; Beale, interview, September 8, 1987; and *St. Louis Post-Dispatch,* June 5, 1984.
21. Timberlake, interview, February 9, 1988.
22. Ibid.
23. *London Telegraph Sunday Magazine,* July 24, 1983; and Marylouise Oates, *Los Angeles Times,* February 29, 1988.
24. Halford to the author, February 15, 1988; "Inc." column, *Chicago Tribune,* November 17, 1985; Hall, *Philip; Newsday,* November 7, 1984; *Ladies' Home Journal,* March 1985; *Los Angeles Times,* November 5, 1987; and author's correspondence with Baechler.
25. Lord Mountbatten's article, *Times* (London), February 3, 1977; and Pugash, interview, November 21, 1987.
26. Nomination form, National Register of Historic Places, December 28, 1971.
27. United World Colleges literature, including "Fact Book" and the newsletter *Kaleidoscope;* William ("Wid") Slick, interviewed by New Mexico researchers Kingsley and Jerilou Hammett, December 3, 1987; Emiliano Saiz, interviewed by the Hammetts, November 25, 1987; and San Miguel County, N.M., land records, including book 229, p. 2437.
28. McGill, interview, November 17, 1987.
29. *Albuquerque Journal,* July 10, 1982.
30. Douthit, interview, October 14, 1987; minutes of Town Council meeting, September 18, 1985; *Washington Post,* November 5, 1985; permit application; final solicitation report, February 28, 1986; and Occidental Petroleum news release, October 28, 1985.
31. Copies of Kamp's pamphlets; and *Spotlight,* September 30, 1985.
32. Tribute book, author's collection.
33. Oates, *Los Angeles Times,* October 4, 1986.
34. Pugash, interview, November 21, 1987.
35. Zivs, *Human Rights;* Hammer booklets on each conference; and Richard Bilder, interview, May 13, 1987.
36. State Department memorandum, July 11, 1980, FOIA release; and *New York Times,* July 5, 1980.
37. Occidental news release, December 3, 1984.
38. Randolph, interview, June 8, 1987.
39. Irwin Abrams, interview, March 31, 1987; discussions with Jakob Sverdrup at the Nobel Committee for the author by Manny Paraschos, and by Torbjorn von Krogh, April and May 1987; *Fortune,* August 3, 1987; and *Los Angeles Times Magazine,* June 7, 1987.
40. *Oxy Today,* no. 1 (1973).
41. Maranto, interview, November 18, 1987; and all back issues of *Oxy Today* and *Occidental Report.*
42. Maranto, interview, November 18, 1987.
43. Kenneth Locker, interview, November 14, 1987; Marty Nicholson, interview, March 15, 1987; Laja Holland, interview, November 14, 1987; Robert Wise, interview, November 18, 1987; Mike Hoover, interview, December 6, 1987; and author's viewing of twenty-two films produced by the unit.
44. Fiennes, *To the Ends of the Earth;* Hoover, interview, December 6, 1987; and *Variety,* February 9, 1983.
45. Rupert Morris, *Today,* June 5, 1987; Fiennes, *Living Dangerously; Variety,* January 13, 1984; *San Diego Union,* February 17, 1984; Armand Hammer Productions promotional literature; and Hart to *Los Angeles Times Magazine,* July 10, 1988.

46. Bonoff, interview, January 24, 1986; Finder, *Red Carpet;* and *Wall Street Journal,* May 2, 1985.

47. Van Buren, column, September 8, 1985, and interview, October 17, 1987; *New York Times Book Review,* July 13, 1975; and inscribed copy of the biography in Stuart Symington papers, University of Missouri–Columbia.

48. Bryson, *Washington Post,* January 4, 1986.

49. Kinsley column, *Washington Post,* January 1, 1986; Bryson, *Washington Post,* January 4, 1986; and Bryson, interview, November 18, 1985.

50. Occidental proxy statement for 1985 annual meeting; and *Wall Street Journal,* May 2, 1985, and June 10, 1987.

51. Kaiser, interview, March 2, 1988.

52. Blair, interview, May 17, 1988, and his letter to the author, May 24, 1988.

53. News release, July 17, 1986; *New York,* August 4, 1986; *Wall Street Journal,* June 10, 1987; NBC-TV "Today," April 30 and May 1, 1987; and Andrew Nibley dispatch for Reuters, June 16, 1987.

54. *New Republic,* May 4, 1987.

55. *St. Louis Post-Dispatch,* July 11, 1987; copy of Stone's response, author's collection.

56. *Manhattan, inc.,* June 1987.

57. Kauffman's reply, *Manhattan, inc.,* September 1987.

58. News release, September 11, 1987; *Washington Post* and *New York Times,* September 12, 1987; John Broderick, interview, October 16, 1987; John Haynes, interviews, May 19, 1988, and January 10, 1989; and Boorstin to the author, March 28, 1989.

Chapter 28: FAMILY FEUDS

1. *Atlantic,* June and July 1975.

2. Wachtell, interview, November 19, 1987.

3. Julian Hammer divorce records, Superior Court, Los Angeles County, case WE-D-20136; cases in Superior Court, Los Angeles County, WE-P-6138, WE-C-37822, WE-C-49676, and D-978945; and *Modern Maturity,* October-November 1980.

4. Patten, interview, June 2, 1987; and Boles, interview, May 23, 1988.

5. Teitsworth, interview, November 19, 1987; Boles, interview, May 23, 1988; and Occidental Petroleum news release, February 12, 1988.

6. *Tulsa World,* January 9, 1985; *New York Times,* January 13, 1985; *Women's Wear Daily,* January 17, 1985; land records, Los Angeles County, at 86-972176; and *New York Times,* June 15, 1987.

7. Springer, interview, May 25, 1987; his letter to the author, September 23, 1987; and Eileen Springer Katz, interview, October 7, 1988.

8. Surrogate's Court, New York County, case 6903-1970; Harry Hammer obituary, *New York Times,* November 12, 1970; Galina Perry, interview, February 26, 1988; Eilan, interview, August 21, 1987; Surrogate's Court, Westchester County, N.Y., case 3945-1968; and Bette Barber obituary, *New Orleans Times-Picayune,* October 24, 1968.

9. Colmery to the author, September 30, 1987; and Bette Barber Hammer to Colmery, December 2, 1956, author's collection.

10. Victor Hammer to Armand, March 7, 1976, and Armand to Victor, March 15, 1976, collection of Ireene Wicker Hammer and Victor J. Hammer.

11. Eilan to Armand Hammer, April 5, 1981, January 6, 1984, and April 3, 1985, Eilan papers.

12. Victor Hammer obituary, *New York Times,* July 23, 1985; and *San Diego Tribune,* July 24, 1985.

13. Palm Beach County Circuit Court, cases 85-2705-CP, 85-9811-CA-L, 87-4298, with

help from Jean Dubail; Stamford Probate Court, file 135; and Stamford town records, vol. 1045, p. 432.

14. *Wall Street Journal,* November 13, 1985; Eilan news release, November 12, 1985; and Victor Hammer to Armand, February 1983, collection of Ireene Wicker Hammer and Victor J. Hammer.
15. Occidental news release, November 12, 1985.
16. *People,* December 9, 1985.
17. Palm Beach County Circuit Court, case 85-2705-CP; and Florida Court of Appeals decision, reported at 499 South 2d 853.
18. Ibid.
19. Ireene Wicker Hammer obituary, *Los Angeles Times,* November 19, 1987; settlement papers, Palm Beach County Circuit Court, April 1988; *Wall Street Journal,* July 25, 1988; and James Nemec to the editor, *Wall Street Journal,* August 5, 1988.
20. Author's visit to Westwood Memorial, November 8, 1987; Fairview Cemetery records check, September 14, 1987 (the removal occurred on November 4, 1981); and *New Republic,* April 18, 1988.

Epilogue: "AN IMPOSSIBLE RECOVERY"

1. U.S. District Court, Washington, D.C., case 75-668; and Lydick, interview, February 13, 1989.
2. Babcock, interview, June 2, 1987.
3. *Business Week,* September 21, 1974.
4. U.S. District Court, Washington, D.C., cases 74-727, 75-163, 75-668, and 76-618; GAO report, April 8, 1974; Stans, interview, February 27, 1989; and Watson to the author, March 18, 1989.
5. Hammer to Walker, October 27, 1975.
6. Ibid.
7. McBride, interview, April 13, 1987.
8. U.S. District Court, Central District of California, case 76-2097-ALS; and von Hoffman, *Washington Post,* June 24, 1976.
9. U.S. District Court, Washington, D.C., case 75-668.
10. Postcard, April 2, 1976, collection of Ireene Wicker Hammer and Victor J. Hammer; *New York Times,* May 22, 1976; and Nizer, *Reflections Without Mirrors.*
11. *Times* (London), August 25, 1976; WTTW-TV, Chicago, "The John Callaway Show," October 8, 1981; Howard Rosenberg column, *Los Angeles Times,* October 19, 1981; and *London Telegraph Sunday Magazine,* July 24, 1983.
12. Sample, interview, June 25, 1988.
13. McBride, interview, April 13, 1987; Ruth, interview, April 16, 1987; and *Los Angeles Times,* December 29, 1988.
14. Periodic conversations during 1987 and 1988 with pardon attorney David Stephenson and his staff; and Myer Feldman, interview, December 8, 1988.
15. Hammer's name is on a plaque there.
16. California Secretary of State, Political Reform Division filings; Occidental Petroleum reports to SEC on questionable contributions; Edmund Brown, Jr., interview, October 27, 1987; Edmund Brown, Sr., interview, November 10, 1987.
17. *Boston Globe,* April 13, 1982; *New York Times Magazine,* November 29, 1981; and Epstein, interview, October 17, 1987.
18. Epstein, interview, October 17, 1987.
19. Ibid.; Clifford May, interview, June 29, 1988 (May edited the Epstein article); and *New York Times Magazine,* December 20, 1981.
20. Klutznick, interview, April 28, 1987.
21. Forbes, interview, May 20, 1987.

22. *Oxy Report,* January-February 1981; Armand Hammer Foundation annual report, 1981; and *New York Times,* March 20 and March 23, 1981.
23. Hewitt, interview, December 13, 1985.
24. *Washington Post,* May 25, 1982; and annual reports of Armand Hammer Foundation.
25. *Washington Post,* May 25, 1982.
26. Burt memorandum, January 27, 1984, State Department FOIA release.
27. News release, November 27, 1984; *Los Angeles Times,* January 11, 1985; and *Washington Post,* January 12, 1985.
28. Copy of letter seen by the author at Island Creek Coal Company headquarters, Lexington, Ky., during a visit there in June 1986; Reagan to Hammer, March 4, 1988; McFarlane, interview, February 12, 1986; White House news release and Associated Press dispatch, June 10, 1987; Armand Hammer Foundation annual report to IRS for 1987, on form 990-PF; William Allman to the author, September 14, 1987; and Conger to the author, September 22, 1987.
29. *Washington Post,* September 6, 1987.
30. *Manhattan, inc.,* May 1988.
31. White House press briefings by Marlin Fitzwater, January 9 and January 18, 1989; David Stephenson, interview, January 19, 1989; *USA Today,* January 19, 1989; and *Wall Street Journal,* February 3, 1989.
32. Washington, D.C., researcher Liz Ruskin studied every item in the Hammer papers and transcribed many; Library of Congress news release and brochure, author's collection; and *Washington Post,* January 20, 1989.
33. Communications to the author about Hammer's place among dignitaries from numerous Washington sources who attended the inauguration or saw it on television.

Select Bibliography

I consulted the works that follow to learn about Armand Hammer himself or about the environments in which he was born, grew, and conducted his affairs. The chapter reference notes make clear where I relied on specific sources from this select list. The Bibliography covers only books, dissertations, and pamphlets; newspaper articles, magazine pieces, and other periodical secondary sources are cited only in the Notes, as are primary documents that I used.

Abdrabboh, Bob, ed. *Libya in the 1980s: Challenges and Changes.* International Economics and Research, 1985.

Abrams, Irwin. *The Nobel Peace Prize and the Laureates: An Illustrated Biographical History, 1901–1987.* G. K. Hall, 1988.

Ahrari, Mohammed E. *OPEC: The Failing Giant.* University Press of Kentucky, 1986.

Allan, John Anthony. *Libya: The Experience of Oil.* Westview, 1981.

Allen, Everett S. *The Black Ships: Rumrunners of Prohibition.* Little, Brown, 1979.

Allen, Loring. *OPEC Oil.* Oelgeschlager, Gunn and Hain, 1979.

Allen, Michael Patrick. *The Founding Fortunes: A New Anatomy of the Super-Rich Families in America.* Talley/Dutton, 1987.

Allison, Eric W. *The Raiders of Wall Street.* Stein & Day, 1986.

Al-Otaiba, Mana Saeed. *The Petroleum Concession Agreements of the United Arab Emirates.* 2 vols. Croom Helm, 1982.

American Jewish Biographies. Lakeville Press, 1982.

American-Russian Chamber of Commerce. *Economic Handbook of the Soviet Union.* 1931.

Amtorg Trading Corporation. *Soviet-American Trade Outlook.* 1928.

An, Taeg-Won. "Soviet Perceptions of Soviet-American Trade." Ph.D. diss., University of Georgia, 1984.

Anderson, Charles A., and Robert N. Anthony. *The New Corporate Directors: Insights for Board Members and Executives.* John Wiley, 1986.

Anderson, Jack, with James Boyd. *Fiasco.* Times Books, 1983.

Angier, Natalie. *Natural Obsessions: The Search for the Oncogene.* Houghton Mifflin, 1988.

Apostol, P., et al. *Soviet Russia: Legal and Economic Conditions of Industrial and Commercial Activity in Soviet Russia.* P. S. King and Son, 1924.

Arbatov, Georgi A., and Willem Oltmans. *The Soviet Viewpoint.* Dodd, Mead, 1983.

Arnold, Arthur Z. *Banks, Credit and Money in Soviet Russia*. Columbia University Press, 1937.

Arnold, Guy. *Britain's Oil*. Hamish Hamilton, 1978.

Ashmead-Bartlett, Ellis. *The Riddle of Russia*. Cassell, 1929.

Axelbank, Albert. *Soviet Dissent: Intellectuals, Jews and Détente*. Franklin Watts, 1975.

Baer, George W., ed. *A Question of Trust: The Origins of U.S.-Diplomatic Relations; The Memoirs of Loy W. Henderson*. Hoover Institution Press, 1986.

Baer, Jean. *The Self-Chosen: "Our Crowd" Is Dead, Long Live Our Crowd*. Arbor House, 1982.

Bainbridge, Henry C. *Peter Carl Fabergé, Goldsmith and Jeweller to the Russian Imperial Court: His Life and Work*. 1949. Reprint. Spring Books, 1966.

Ball, Alan M. *Russia's Last Capitalists: The NEPmen*. University of California Press, 1987.

Barmine, Alexandre. *One Who Survived: The Life Story of a Russian Under the Soviets*. Putnam, 1945.

Barnaby, Frank, ed. *The GAIA Peace Atlas*. Doubleday, 1988.

Barnet, Richard J. *The Giants: Russia and America*. Simon & Schuster, 1977.

Baron, Samuel H., and Carl Pletsch, eds. *Introspection in Biography: The Biographer's Quest for Self-Awareness*. Analytic Press, 1985.

Bassow, Whitman. *The Moscow Correspondents: Reporting on Russia From the Revolution to Glasnost*. William Morrow, 1988.

Baykov, Alexander. *Soviet Foreign Trade*. Princeton University Press, 1946.

Beam, Jacob D. *Multiple Exposure: An American Ambassador's Unique Perspective on East-West Issues*. W. W. Norton, 1978.

Bearman, Jonathan. *Qadhafi's Libya*. Zed Books, 1986.

Bennett, Edward M. *Recognition of Russia: An American Foreign Policy Dilemma*. Blaisdell, 1970.

Bennett, Steven J., and Michael Snell. *Executive Chess*. NAL, 1987.

Berger, John J. *Restoring the Earth: How Americans Are Working to Renew Our Damaged Environment*. Alfred A. Knopf, 1985.

Bessedovsky, Grigory. *Revelations of a Soviet Diplomat*. Williams & Norgate, 1931.

Bezveselny, S. F., and D. Y. Grinberg, compilers. *They Knew Lenin: Reminiscences of Foreign Contemporaries*. Progress Publishers, 1968.

Blackwell, Earl. *Earl Blackwell's Celebrity Register*. Times Publishing, 1986.

Blair, John M. *The Control of Oil*. Pantheon Books, 1976.

Blitzer, Wolf. *Between Washington and Jerusalem: A Reporter's Notebook*. Oxford University Press, 1985.

Blundy, David, and Andrew Lycett. *Qadafi: A Biography*. Little, Brown, 1987.

Boehm, Helen F. *With a Little Luck: An American Odyssey*. Rawson, 1985.

Bohlen, Charles E. *Witness to History, 1929–69*. W. W. Norton, 1973.

Boss, Barbara D., et al., eds. *Monoclonal Antibodies and Cancer*. Academic Press, 1983.

Botein, Bernard. *Trial Judge: The Candid, Behind-the-Bench Story of Justice Bernard Botein*. Simon & Schuster, 1952.

Boyer, Richard O. *Max Steuer: Magician of the Law*. Greenberg, 1932.

Bradford, Peter Amory. *Fragile Structures: A Story of Oil Refineries, National Security, and the Coast of Maine*. Harper's Magazine Press, 1975.

Braudy, Leo. *The Frenzy of Renown: Fame and Its History*. Oxford University Press, 1986.

Brenner, Lenni. *Jews in America Today*. Lyle Stuart, 1986.

Brezhnev, L. I. *Following Lenin's Course: Speeches and Articles 1972–75*. Progress Publishers, 1975.

———. *Leonid I. Brezhnev: His Life and Work*. Sphinx Press, 1982.

————. *Peace, Détente and Soviet-American Relations.* Harcourt Brace Jovanovich, 1979.

Bron, Saul G. *Soviet Economic Development and American Business.* Liveright, 1930.

Brookstone, Jeffrey M. *The Multinational Businessman and Foreign Policy.* Praeger, 1976.

Brough, James. *Auction!* Bobbs-Merrill, 1963.

Brown, Michael H. *Laying Waste: The Poisoning of America by Toxic Chemicals.* Pantheon Books, 1980.

————. *The Toxic Cloud.* Harper & Row, 1987.

Brownstein, Ronald, and Nina Easton. *Reagan's Ruling Class: Portraits of the President's Top 100 Officials.* Pantheon Books, 1983.

Brozen, Yale. *Concentration, Mergers, and Public Policy.* Macmillan, 1982.

Bruck, Connie. *The Predators' Ball: The Junk-Bond Raiders and the Man Who Staked Them.* American Lawyer/Simon & Schuster, 1988.

Bryant, Louise. *Mirrors of Moscow.* Thomas Seltzer, 1923.

Bryson, John. *The World of Armand Hammer.* Abrams, 1985.

Brzezinski, Zbigniew. *Power and Principle: Memoirs of the National Security Adviser, 1977–81.* Farrar, Straus & Giroux, 1983.

Burger, Chester. *The Chief Executive: Realities of Corporate Leadership.* CBI, 1978.

Burnet, Alastair. *In Private/In Public: The Prince and Princess of Wales.* Summit, 1986.

Bush, George H.W. *Looking Forward.* Doubleday, 1987.

Butler, J.R.M. *Lord Lothian (Philip Kerr), 1882–1940.* St. Martin's, 1960.

Butson, Thomas G. *Gorbachev: A Biography.* Stein & Day, 1985.

Byrne, John A. *The Headhunters.* Macmillan, 1986.

Carlson, Don, and Craig Comstock, eds. *Citizen Summitry: Keeping the Peace When It Matters Too Much to Be Left to Politicians.* Tarcher, 1986.

Carr, Edward Hallett. *Socialism in One Country, 1924–26,* vol. 3. Macmillan, 1964.

Carter, Jimmy. *Keeping Faith: Memoirs of a President.* Bantam, 1982.

Cassini, Oleg. *In My Own Fashion: An Autobiography.* Simon & Schuster, 1987.

Catalog of the Library of the Museum of Modern Art, vol. 6. G. K. Hall, 1976.

Caudill, Harry M. *Theirs Be the Power: The Moguls of Eastern Kentucky.* University of Illinois Press, 1983.

The Celebrity Who's Who. By the editors of *Who's Who in America.* World Almanac/Pharos, 1986.

Celler, Emanuel. *You Never Leave Brooklyn: The Autobiography of Emanuel Celler.* John Day, 1953.

Central Intelligence Agency. *The Soviet Economy in 1973: Performance, Plans and Implications,* A(ER) 74-62, 1974.

Chagy, Gideon. *The New Patrons of the Arts.* Abrams, 1973.

Chamberlain, William Henry. *Soviet Russia: A Living Record and a History.* Little, Brown, 1930.

Chase, Stuart, Robert Dunn, and Rexford Guy Tugwell, eds. *Soviet Russia in the Second Decade: A Joint Survey by the Technical Staff of the First American Trade Union Delegation.* Day, 1928.

Chester, Edward W. *U.S. Oil Policy and Diplomacy: A Twentieth Century Overview.* Greenwood Press, 1983.

Clark, Kenneth, rev. by Martin Kemp. *Leonardo da Vinci.* Viking, 1988.

Clarke, A. *Flavouring Materials: Natural and Synthetic.* Frowde & Hodder & Stoughton, 1922.

Clemens, John K., and Douglas F. Mayer. *The Classic Touch: Lessons in Leadership from Homer to Hemingway.* Dow Jones–Irwin, 1987.

Clinard, Marshall B., and Peter C. Yeager. *Corporate Crime.* Free Press, 1980.

Coates, James. *Armed and Dangerous: The Rise of the Survivalist Right.* Hill & Wang, 1987.

Cockerell, Michael, Peter Hennessy, and David Walker. *Sources Close to the Prime Minister*. Macmillan, 1984.

Coggin, James E. *J. K. Wadley: A Tree God Planted*. Southwest Printers, 1971.

Cogley, John. *Report on Blacklisting, Volume II, Radio-Television*. The Fund for the Republic, 1956.

Coleman, Terry. *Thatcher's Britain*. Bantam, 1987.

Commission on Russian Relief of the National Information Bureau Inc. *The Russian Famines, 1921–22, 1922–23*. 1923.

Commons, Dorman L. *Tender Offer: The Sneak Attack in Corporate Takeovers*. University of California Press, 1985.

Conlin, Joseph R. *The American Radical Press, 1880–1960*, vol. 1. Greenwood Press, 1974.

Considine, Bob. *The Remarkable Life of Dr. Armand Hammer*. Harper & Row, 1975.

Conway, Martin. *Art Treasures in Soviet Russia*. Edward Arnold, 1925.

Cooley, John K. *Libyan Sandstorm*. Holt, Rinehart & Winston, 1982.

Coronel, Gustavo. *The Nationalization of the Venezuelan Oil Industry: From Technocratic Success to Political Failure*. Lexington Books, 1983.

Corson, William R., and Robert T. Crowley. *The New KGB: Engine of Soviet Power*. William Morrow, 1985.

Corti, Gerry, and Frank Frazer. *The Nation's Oil: A Story of Control*. Graham & Trotman, 1983.

Costello, John. *Mask of Treachery*. William Morrow, 1988.

Cowhey, Peter F. *The Problems of Plenty: Energy Policy and International Politics*. University of California Press, 1985.

Cowles, Fleur. *Friends*. William Morrow, 1978.

Coyne, Franklin E. *The Development of the Cooperage Industry in the United States, 1620–1940*. Lumber Buyers Publishing, 1940.

Crawford, Ann Fears, and Jack Keever. *John B. Connally: Portrait in Power*. Jenkins, 1973.

Crowe, Kenneth C. *America for Sale*. Doubleday, 1978.

Crozier, Brian. *Strategy of Survival*. Arlington House, 1978.

———, Drew Middleton, and Jeremy Murray-Brown. *This War Called Peace*. Universe Books, 1985.

cummings, e. e. *Eimi*. Covici, Friede, 1933.

Dallek, Robert. *Franklin D. Roosevelt and American Foreign Policy 1932–45*. Oxford University Press, 1979.

Dan, Uri. *Blood Libel: The Inside Story of General Ariel Sharon's History-Making Suit Against* Time *Magazine*. Simon & Schuster, 1987.

Daniloff, Nicholas. *Two Lives, One Russia*. Houghton Mifflin, 1988.

Davidson, Kenneth M. *Megamergers*. Ballinger, 1985.

Davis, William. *The Innovators: The Essential Guide to Business Thinkers, Achievers and Entrepreneurs*. Amacom, 1987.

Day, Donald. *Will Rogers: A Biography*. David McKay, 1962.

Dayan, Moshe. *Moshe Dayan: Story of My Life*. William Morrow, 1976.

de Coppet, Laura, and Alan Jones, eds. *The Art Dealers: The Powers Behind the Scene Tell How the Art World Really Works*. Clarkson N. Potter, 1985.

Dedmon, Emmett. *Challenge and Response: A Modern History of the Standard Oil Company (Indiana)*. Mobium Press, 1984.

De Gaury, Gerald. *Faisal: King of Saudi Arabia*. Arthur Barker, 1966.

De Jonge, Alex. *Stalin and the Shaping of the Soviet Union*. William Morrow, 1986.

Delano, Daniel W., Jr. *Franklin Roosevelt and the Delano Influence*. Nudi Publications, 1946.

De Pauw, John W. *Soviet-American Trade Negotiations*. Praeger Books, 1979.

Dewey, John. *Impressions of Soviet Russia and the Revolutionary World: Mexico, China, Turkey.* New Republic, 1929.

Doder, Dusko. *Shadows and Whispers: Power Politics Inside the Kremlin from Brezhnev to Gorbachev.* Random House, 1986.

Doyle, Jack. *Altered Harvest: Agriculture, Genetics, and the Fate of the World's Food Supply.* Viking, 1985.

Draper, Theodore. *The Roots of American Communism.* Viking, 1957.

Druks, Herbert. *Harry S. Truman and the Russians, 1945–53.* Robert Speller, 1966.

Dull, James. *The Politics of American Foreign Policy.* Prentice Hall, 1985.

Duncan, Ronald, and Colin Wilson, eds. *Marx Refuted.* Ashgrove Press, 1987.

Dunne, Dominick. *Fatal Charms and Other Tales of Today.* Crown, 1987.

Dunning, John. *Tune In Yesterday: The Ultimate Encyclopedia of Old-Time Radio.* Prentice Hall, 1976.

Eastman, Max. *Love and Revolution: My Journey Through an Epoch.* Random House, 1964.

Eban, Abba. *The New Diplomacy: International Affairs in the Modern Age.* Random House, 1983.

Eisenhower, Dwight D. *The White House Years.* 2 vols. Doubleday, 1963, 1965.

Elderkin, Kenton W., and Warren E. Norquist. *Creative Countertrade: A Guide to Doing Business Worldwide.* Ballinger, 1987.

Ellison, Katherine. *Imelda: Steel Butterfly of the Philippines.* McGraw-Hill, 1988.

Engler, Robert. *The Brotherhood of Oil: Energy Policy and the Public Interest.* University of Chicago Press, 1977.

Epstein, Edward Jay. *Deception: The Invisible War Between the KGB and the CIA.* Simon & Schuster, 1989.

Epstein, Samuel S. *The Politics of Cancer.* Sierra Club Books, 1978.

Evans, Peter. *Ari: The Life and Times of Aristotle Onassis.* Summit, 1986.

Fahy, Everett Philip. *The Legacy of Leonardo: Italian Renaissance Paintings from Leningrad.* M. Knoedler, 1979.

Fay, Stephen. *Beyond Greed.* Viking, 1982.

Feinberg, Richard E. *Subsidizing Success: The Export-Import Bank in the U.S. Economy.* Cambridge University Press, 1982.

Ferguson, Thomas, and Joel Rogers. *Right Turn: The Decline of the Democrats and the Future of American Politics.* Hill & Wang, 1986.

Fiennes, Ranulph. *Living Dangerously: The Autobiography of Ranulph Fiennes.* Macmillan, 1987.

———. *To the Ends of the Earth.* Hodder & Stoughton, 1983.

Fike, Claude Edwin, Jr. "A Study of Russian-American Relations During the Ominous Years 1917–21." Ph.D. diss., University of Illinois, 1950.

Filene, Peter G. *Americans and the Soviet Experiment, 1917–33.* Harvard University Press, 1967.

Finder, Joseph. *Red Carpet.* New Republic/Holt, Rinehart & Winston, 1983.

First, Ruth. *Libya: The Elusive Revolution.* Penguin, 1974.

Fischer, Louis. *The Life of Lenin.* Harper & Row, 1964.

Fisher, Harold H. *The Famine in Soviet Russia, 1919–23: The Operations of the American Relief Administration.* Macmillan, 1927.

Fithian, Floyd James. "Soviet-American Economic Relations, 1918–33: American Business in Russia During the Period of Nonrecognition." Ph.D. diss., University of Nebraska, 1964.

Forbes, Christopher. *Fabergé Eggs: Imperial Russian Fantasies.* Abrams, 1980.

Forbes, Malcolm. *Around the World on Hot Air and Two Wheels.* Simon & Schuster, 1985.

Ford, Gerald R. *A Time to Heal: The Autobiography of Gerald R. Ford.* Harper & Row, 1979.

Ford, Henry. *My Life and Work.* Garden City Publishing, 1927.

Foster, Peter. *The Blue-Eyed Sheiks: The Canadian Oil Establishment.* Collins, 1979.

———. *Other People's Money: The Banks, the Government and Dome.* Collins, 1983.

Frankland, Mark. *The Sixth Continent: Russia and the Making of Mikhail Gorbachev.* Harper & Row, 1987.

Frear, James A. *Forty Years of Progressive Public Service.* Associated Writers, 1937.

Freedom House. *Glasnost: How Open?* 1987.

Funigiello, Philip J. *American-Soviet Trade in the Cold War.* University of North Carolina Press, 1988.

Gaddis, John Lewis. *Russia, the Soviet Union and the United States: An Interpretive History.* John Wiley, 1978.

Gale, Robert Peter, and Thomas Hauser. *Final Warning: The Legacy of Chernobyl.* Warner Books, 1988.

Gerard, James W. *My First Eighty-three Years in America: The Memoirs of James W. Gerard.* Doubleday, 1951.

Getty, J. Paul. *As I See It: The Autobiography of J. Paul Getty.* Prentice Hall, 1976.

Getz, Oscar. *Whiskey: An American Pictorial History.* David McKay, 1978.

Ghanem, Shukri Mohammed. *The Pricing of Libyan Crude Oil.* Adams, 1975.

Gillette, Philip Spencer. "The Political Origins of American-Soviet Trade." Ph.D. diss., Harvard University, 1969.

Gitlow, Benjamin. *I Confess: The Truth About American Communism.* E. P. Dutton, 1940.

Godson, Roy, ed. *Intelligence Requirements for the 1980s: Domestic Intelligence.* Lexington Books, 1986.

Goette, John. *Jade Lore.* Ars Ceramica, 1976.

Goldberg, Paul. *The Final Act: The Dramatic, Revealing Story of the Moscow Helsinki Watch Group.* William Morrow, 1988.

Goldenberg, Susan. *Hands Across the Ocean: Managing Joint Ventures with a Spotlight on China and Japan.* Harvard Business School Press, 1988.

———. *The Thomson Empire.* Beaufort Books, 1984.

Golder, Frank A., and Lincoln Hutchinson. *On the Trail of the Russian Famine.* Stanford University Press, 1927.

Goldman, Marshall I. *Détente and Dollars: Doing Business with the Soviets.* Basic Books, 1975.

———. *Gorbachev's Challenge: Economic Reform in the Age of High Technology.* W. W. Norton, 1987.

Goodman, Melvin Allan. "The Diplomacy of Nonrecognition: Soviet-American Relations 1917–33." Ph.D. diss., Indiana University, 1972.

Gorbachev, Mikhail. *Perestroika: New Thinking for Our Country and the World.* Harper & Row, 1987.

———. *Toward a Better World.* Richardson & Steirman, 1987.

Gottlieb, Robert, and Irene Wolt. *Thinking Big: The Story of the Los Angeles Times, Its Publishers, and Their Influence on Southern California.* Putnam, 1977.

Gould, Milton S. *The Witness Who Spoke with God and Other Tales From the Courthouse.* Viking, 1979.

Goulden, Joseph C. *The Benchwarmers: The Private World of the Powerful Federal Judges.* Weybright and Talley, 1974.

Grant, Steven A., and John H. Brown. *The Russian Empire and Soviet Union: A Guide to Manuscripts and Archival Materials in the United States.* Kennan Institute and Wilson Center/G. K. Hall, 1981.

Grayson, George W. *Oil and Mexican Foreign Policy.* University of Pittsburgh Press, 1988.

Green, Mark, and John F. Berry. *The Challenge of Hidden Profits: Reducing Corporate Bureaucracy and Waste.* William Morrow, 1985.

Greenberg, Martin. *The Jewish Lists: Physicists and Generals, Actors and Writers, and Hundreds of Other Lists of Accomplished Jews.* Schocken Books, 1979.

Gromyko, Andrei A. *Only for Peace: Selected Speeches and Writings.* Pergamon Press, 1979.

Haensel, Paul. *The Economic Policy of Soviet Russia.* P. S. King, 1930.

Haines, Gerald K. *A Reference Guide to United States Department of State Special Files.* Greenwood Press, 1985.

Halberstam, David. *The Reckoning.* William Morrow, 1986.

Hall, Unity. *Philip.* O'Mara, 1988.

Halliwell, Leslie. *Halliwell's Film Guide,* 4th ed. Scribner, 1983.

Hamilton, Adrian, ed. *Oil: The Price of Power.* Michael Joseph/Rainbird, 1986.

Hamilton, Charles. *Auction Madness: An Uncensored Look Behind the Velvet Drapes of the Great Auction Houses.* Everest, 1981.

Hammer, Armand. *The Quest of the Romanoff Treasure.* Payson, 1932.

———, with Neil Lyndon. *Hammer.* Putnam, 1987.

Hammer, Olga, and Jeanne D'Andrea, eds. *Treasures of Mexico from the Mexican National Museums, an Exhibition Presented by the Armand Hammer Foundation.* Los Angeles County Museum of Art, 1978.

Hammond, Thomas T. *Red Flag Over Afghanistan: The Communist Coup, the Soviet Invasion, and the Consequences.* Westview, 1984.

Hannaford, Peter. *The Reagans: A Political Portrait.* Coward, McCann & Geoghegan, 1983.

Hanson, Philip. *Trade and Technology in Soviet-Western Relations.* Columbia University Press, 1981.

Harriman, W. Averell. *America and Russia in a Changing World.* Doubleday, 1971.

Hawkes, Nigel, et al. *Chernobyl: The End of the Nuclear Dream.* Vintage Books, 1987.

Hayes, Helen. *On Reflection: An Autobiography.* M. Evans, 1968.

Heard-Bey, Frauke. *From Trucial States to United Arab Emirates: A Society in Transition.* Longman, 1982.

Heller, A. A. *The Industrial Revival in Soviet Russia.* Thomas Seltzer, 1922.

Heller, Mikhail, and Aleksandr Nekrich. *Utopia in Power: The History of the Soviet Union from 1917 to the Present.* Summit, 1986.

Heller, Robert. *The Age of the Common Millionaire.* E. P. Dutton, 1988.

Herlihy, Patricia. *Odessa: A History 1794–1914.* Harvard University Press, 1986.

Herman, Edward S. *Corporate Control, Corporate Power.* Cambridge University Press, 1981.

Herrmann, Frank. *Sotheby's: Portrait of an Auction House.* W. W. Norton, 1981.

Hewitt, Ed A. *Energy, Economics and Foreign Policy in the Soviet Union.* Brookings Institution, 1984.

Hillquit, Morris. *Loose Leaves from a Busy Life.* Macmillan, 1934.

Hills, Stuart L., ed. *Corporate Violence: Injury and Death for Profit.* Rowman & Littlefield, 1987.

Hines, Lawrence Gregory. *The Market, Energy and the Environment.* Allyn & Bacon, 1988.

Hird, John Wynne. *Under Czar and Soviet: My Thirty Years in Soviet Russia.* Hurst & Blackett, 1932.

Hobbs, James B. *Corporate Staying Power: How America's Most Consistently Successful Corporations Maintain Exceptional Performance.* Lexington Books, 1986.

Hodges, Luther H. *A Governor Sees the Soviet: Letters From Governor Luther H. Hodges of North Carolina.* Privately printed, 1959.

Hoffman, Paul. *The Dealmakers: Inside the World of Investment Banking.* Doubleday, 1984.

———. *Lions of the Eighties: The Inside Story of Powerhouse Law Firms.* Doubleday, 1982.

Holden, Anthony. *King Charles III.* Weidenfeld & Nicolson, 1988.

Hook, Sidney, et al., eds. *Soviet Hypocrisy and Western Gullibility.* Ethics & Public Policy Center/University Press of America, 1987.

Howe, Irving. *World of Our Fathers.* Harcourt Brace Jovanovich, 1976.

Howe, Russell Warren, and Sarah Hays Trott. *The Power Peddlers: How Lobbyists Mold America's Foreign Policy.* Doubleday, 1977.

Hullinger, Edwin Ware. *The Reforging of Russia.* E. P. Dutton, 1925.

Ichord, Richard H., with Boyd Upchurch. *Behind Every Bush.* Seville, 1979.

Impressionist and Post-Impressionist Paintings from the USSR, Lent by the Hermitage Museum, Leningrad; and the Pushkin Museum, Moscow. National Gallery of Art and M. Knoedler, 1973.

Ingham, John N. *Biographical Dictionary of American Business Leaders* (H-M). Greenwood Press, 1983.

Jacoby, Neil H., Peter Nehemkis, and Richard Eells. *Bribery and Extortion in World Business: A Study of Corporate Political Payments Abroad.* Macmillan, 1977.

———. *Multinational Oil: A Study in Industrial Dynamics.* Macmillan, 1974.

Jagoe, A. L. *The Winning Corporation: Management Practices That Work.* Acropolis Books, 1987.

Jentleson, Bruce W. *Pipeline Politics: The Complex Political Economy of East-West Trade.* Cornell University Press, 1986.

Johnson, Lady Bird. *A White House Diary.* Holt, Rinehart & Winston, 1970.

Johnson, Lyndon Baines. *The Vantage Point: Perspectives of the Presidency 1963–69.* Holt, Rinehart & Winston, 1971.

Johnston, Moira. *Takeover: The New Wall Street Warriors.* Arbor House, 1986.

Jones, Jesse H., with Edward Angly. *Fifty Billion Dollars: My Thirteen Years with the RFC.* Macmillan, 1951.

Jones, Proctor. *Classic Russian Idylls.* Proctor Jones, 1985.

Jones, Robert Huhn. *The Roads to Russia: United States Lend-Lease to the Soviet Union.* University of Oklahoma Press, 1969.

Junor, Penny. *Charles.* Sidgwick & Jackson, 1988.

———. *Margaret Thatcher.* Sidgwick & Jackson, 1983.

Kallir, Otto. *Grandma Moses.* Abrams, 1973.

Karlsson, Svante. *Oil and the World Order: American Foreign Oil Policy.* Berg, 1986.

Kashlev, Y. *Cultural Contacts Promote Peaceful Coexistence.* Novosti Press Agency, 1974.

Kazmer, Daniel R., and Vera Kazmer. *Russian Economic History: A Guide to Information Sources.* Gale Research, 1977.

Kehrer, Daniel. *Doing Business Boldly: The Art of Taking Intelligent Risks.* Times Books, 1989.

Kennan, George F. *The Nuclear Delusion: Soviet-American Relations in the Atomic Age.* Pantheon Books, 1982.

———. *Russia and the West Under Lenin and Stalin.* Atlantic Monthly/Little, Brown, 1961.

Kent, Robert W., ed. *Money Talks: The 2500 Greatest Business Quotes from Aristotle to Iacocca.* Pocket Books, 1986.

Kessler, Ronald. *The Richest Man in the World: The Story of Adnan Khashoggi.* Warner Books, 1986.

Kets de Vries, Manfred F.R., and Danny Miller. *Unstable at the Top: Inside the Troubled Organization.* NAL, 1988.

Khrushchev, Nikita. *Khrushchev Remembers.* Little, Brown, 1970.

Kiernan, Thomas. *Citizen Murdoch.* Dodd, Mead, 1986.

Kipnis, Ira. *The American Socialist Movement, 1897–1912.* Columbia University Press, 1952.

Kissinger, Henry. *White House Years.* Little, Brown, 1979.
———. *Years of Upheaval.* Little, Brown, 1982.
Klass, Rosanne, ed. *Afghanistan, the Great Game Revisited.* Freedom House, 1987.
Kleinfield, Sonny. *Staying at the Top: The Life of a CEO.* NAL, 1986.
Klinghoffer, Arthur Jay, with Judith Apter. *Israel and the Soviet Union: Alienation or Reconciliation?* Westview, 1985.
———. *The Soviet Union and International Oil Politics.* Columbia University Press, 1977.
Klitz, J. Kenneth. *North Sea Oil: Resource Requirements for Development of the U.K. Sector.* Pergamon Press, 1980.
Klurfeld, Herman. *Winchell: His Life and Times.* Praeger, 1976.
Knickerbocker, H. R. *Fighting the Red Trade Menace.* Dodd, Mead, 1931.
Knight, Misha G. *How to Do Business with the Russians: A Handbook and Guide for Western World Business People.* Quorum Books, 1987.
Kobler, John. *Ardent Spirits: The Rise and Fall of Prohibition.* Putnam, 1973.
Kohler, Foy D. *Understanding the Russians: A Citizen's Primer.* Harper & Row, 1970.
Korman, Abraham K. *The Outsiders: Jews and Corporate America.* Lexington Books, 1988.
Kosnik, Joseph T. *Natural Gas Imports from the Soviet Union: Financing the North Star Joint Venture Project.* Praeger, 1975.
Kotkin, Joel, and Paul Grabowicz. *California, Inc.* Rawson, Wade, 1982.
Krantz, Les. *American Art Galleries: The Illustrated Guide to Their Art and Artists.* Facts on File, 1985.
Krassin, Lubov. *Leonid Krassin: His Life and Work.* Skeffington, 1929.
Krefetz, Gerald. *Jews and Money: The Myths and the Reality.* Ticknor & Fields, 1982.
Krueger, Robert B. *The United States and International Oil: A Report for the Federal Energy Administration on U.S. Firms and Government Policy.* Praeger, 1975.
Kunetskaya, L. *Lenin: Great and Human.* Progress Publishers, 1970.
———. *Lenin in the Kremlin.* Novosti Press Agency, 1969.
Kwitny, Jonathan. *Vicious Circles: The Mafia in the Marketplace.* W. W. Norton, 1979.
Lacey, Robert. *Ford: The Men and the Machine.* Little, Brown, 1986.
Lamb, Robert Boyden. *Running American Business: Top CEOs Rethink Their Major Decisions.* Basic Books, 1987.
Lambro, Donald. *Washington: City of Scandals; Investigating Congress and Other Big Spenders.* Little, Brown, 1984.
Lampert, Hope. *Behind Closed Doors: Wheeling and Dealing in the Banking World.* Atheneum, 1986.
Laqueur, Walter. *America, Europe and the Soviet Union: Selected Essays.* Transaction Books, 1983.
———. *Confrontation: The Middle East and World Politics.* Quadrangle, 1974.
Larkin, Emmet. *James Larkin: Irish Labor Leader, 1876–1947.* MIT Press, 1965.
Lash, Joseph P. *A World of Love: Eleanor Roosevelt and Her Friends, 1943–62.* Doubleday, 1984.
Laurent, Eric. *La Corde pour les pendre.* Fayard, 1985.
Lawson, Eugene K., ed. *U.S.-China Trade: Problems and Prospects.* Praeger, 1988.
Lee, Ivy Ledbetter. *Present-Day Russia.* Macmillan, 1928.
Lehman, John F., Jr. *Command of the Seas.* Scribner, 1988.
Leighton, Frances Spatz. *The Search for the Real Nancy Reagan.* Macmillan, 1987.
Leiteizen, C., compiler. *V. I. Lenin on the United States of America.* Progress Publishers, 1967.
Lenzner, Robert. *The Great Getty: The Lives and Loves of J. Paul Getty, Richest Man in the World.* Crown, 1985.
Leontiades, Milton. *Managing the Unmanageable: Strategies for Success Within the Conglomerate.* Addison-Wesley, 1986.

Lesley, Parker. *Fabergé: A Catalog of the Lillian Thomas Pratt Collection of Russian Imperial Jewels.* Virginia Museum, 1976.

Let Us Live in Peace and Friendship: The Visit of N. S. Khrushchev to the USA, September 15–27, 1959. Foreign Languages Publishing House, 1959.

Levchenko, Stanislav. *On the Wrong Side: My Life in the KGB.* Pergamon-Brassey's, 1988.

Levin, Hillel. *Grand Delusions: The Cosmic Career of John DeLorean.* Viking, 1983.

Levine, Isaac Don. *Eyewitness to History.* Hawthorn, 1973.

Levinson, Charles. *Vodka Cola.* Gordon and Cremonesi, 1978.

Levinson, Harry, and Stuart Rosenthal. *CEO: Corporate Leadership in Action.* Basic Books, 1984.

Lewery, Leonard J. *Foreign Capital Investments in Russian Industries and Commerce.* U.S. Department of Commerce, Bureau of Foreign and Domestic Commerce, Government Printing Office, 1923.

Libbey, James K. *Alexander Gumberg and Soviet-American Relations 1917–33.* University Press of Kentucky, 1977.

Liberman, Simon. *Building Lenin's Russia.* University of Chicago Press, 1945.

Lieberthal, Kenneth, and Michel Oksenberg. *Policy Making in China: Leaders, Structures and Processes.* Princeton University Press, 1988.

Linkletter, Art. *Old Age Is Not for Sissies: Choices for Senior Americans.* Viking, 1988.

Luckman, Charles. *Twice in a Lifetime: From Soup to Skyscrapers.* W. W. Norton, 1988.

Lydenberg, Steven D., et al. *Rating America's Corporate Conscience: A Provocative Guide to the Companies Behind the Products You Buy Every Day.* Addison-Wesley, 1986.

Lynes, Russell. *The Lively Audience: A Social History of the Visual and Performing Arts in America.* Harper & Row, 1985.

———. *The Tastemakers: The Shaping of American Popular Taste.* Harper & Brothers, 1955.

Lyons, Eugene. *Assignment in Utopia.* Harcourt, Brace, 1937.

———. *The Red Decade: The Stalinist Penetration of America.* Bobbs-Merrill, 1941.

MacKenzie, Frederick Arthur. *Russia Before Dawn.* T. Fisher, Unwin, 1923.

Macleod, Roderick. *China Inc.: How to Do Business with the Chinese.* Bantam, 1988.

Madrick, Jeff. *Taking America: How We Got from the First Hostile Takeover to Mega-mergers, Corporate Raiding and Scandal.* Bantam, 1987.

Marer, Paul, ed. *U.S. Financing of East-West Trade: The Political Economy of Government Credits and the National Interest.* Indiana University, International Development Research Center, 1975.

Marples, David R. *Chernobyl and Nuclear Power in the USSR.* St. Martin's, 1986.

Martz, John D. *Politics and Petroleum in Ecuador.* Transaction Books, 1987.

Mathur, Ike, and Chen Jai-Sheng. *Strategies for Joint Ventures in the PRC.* Greenwood Press, 1987.

McCartney, Laton. *Friends in High Places: The Bechtel Story.* Simon & Schuster, 1988.

McCoy, Doris Lee. *Megatraits: Twelve Traits of Successful People.* Wordware, 1988.

McElwain, M. Scott. "Challenge and Response: An Analysis of Soviet-American Relations 1961–62." Ph.D. diss., Claremont McKenna College, 1974.

McGill, Michael E. *American Business and the Quick Fix.* Holt, 1988.

McGovern, James. *The Oil Game.* Viking, 1981.

McJimsey, George. *Harry Hopkins: Ally of the Poor and Defender of Democracy.* Harvard University Press, 1987.

McKenna, Marian C. *Borah.* University of Michigan Press, 1961.

Meiburger, Anne Vincent. "Efforts of Raymond Robins Toward the Recognition of Soviet Russia and the Outlawry of War, 1917–33." Ph.D. diss., Catholic University of America, 1958.

Melanson, Richard A., ed. *Neither Cold War Nor Détente?: Soviet-American Relations in the 1980s.* University Press of Virginia, 1982.

Metcalfe, Robyn Shotwell. *The New Wizard War: How the Soviets Steal U.S. High Technology and How We Give It Away.* Tempus, 1988.

Meyers, Gerald C., with John Holusha. *When It Hits the Fan: Managing the Nine Crises of Business.* Houghton Mifflin, 1986.

Mikoyan, A. I. *V Nachale Dvadtsatykh.* Moscow, 1975.

Miller, Sally M. *Victor Berger and the Promise of Constructive Socialism, 1910–20.* Greenwood Press, 1973.

Milton, Joyce, and Ann Louise Bardach. *Vicki.* St. Martin's, 1986.

Mokhiber, Russell. *Corporate Crime and Violence: Big Business Power and the Abuse of the Public Trust.* Sierra Club Books, 1988.

Mongan, Elizabeth. *Daumier in Retrospect.* Los Angeles County Museum of Art, 1979.

Morray, J. P. *Project Kuzbas: American Workers in Siberia 1921–26.* International Publishers, 1983.

Morris, Joe Alex. *Deadline Every Minute: The Story of the United Press.* Doubleday, 1957.

Morrison, Donald, ed. *Mikhail S. Gorbachev: An Intimate Biography.* Time, 1988.

Mosley, Leonard. *Power Play: Oil in the Middle East.* Random House, 1973.

Muskie, Stephen O. *Campobello: Roosevelt's Beloved Island.* Roosevelt Campobello International Park Commission/Down East Books, 1982.

Nader, Ralph, and William Taylor. *The Big Boys: Power and Position in American Business.* Pantheon Books, 1986.

Nansen, Fridtjof. *Russia and Peace.* George Allen & Unwin, 1923.

Nash, Bruce, and Allan Zullo. *The Misfortune 500.* Pocket Books, 1988.

Naylor, Thomas H. *The Gorbachev Strategy: Opening the Closed Society.* Lexington Books, 1988.

Nelson, Donald M. *Arsenal of Democracy: The Story of American War Production.* Harcourt, Brace, 1946.

Nevins, Allan, and Frank Ernest Hill. *Ford: Expansion and Challenge, 1915–33.* Scribner, 1957.

Newsom, David D., ed. *Private Diplomacy with the Soviet Union.* University Press of America, 1987.

Nixon, Richard. *The Memoirs of Richard Nixon.* 2 vols. Warner Books, 1979.

Nizer, Louis. *Reflections Without Mirrors: An Autobiography of the Mind.* Doubleday, 1978.

Norton, Howard. *Rosalynn: A Portrait.* Logos International, 1977.

Norton, Thomas E. *One Hundred Years of Collecting in America: The Story of Sotheby Parke Bernet.* Abrams, 1984.

O'Brien, Gregory. *Lenin Lives!* Stein & Day, 1984.

O'Connor, Richard. *The Oil Barons: Men of Greed and Grandeur.* Little, Brown, 1971.

O'Connor, Timothy Edward. *Diplomacy and Revolution: G. V. Chicherin and Soviet Foreign Affairs, 1918–30.* Iowa State University Press, 1988.

O'Toole, Patricia. *Corporate Messiah: The Hiring and Firing of Million-Dollar Managers.* William Morrow, 1984.

Pack, Robert. *Edward Bennett Williams for the Defense.* Harper & Row, 1983.

Parks, J. D. *Culture, Conflict and Coexistence: American-Soviet Cultural Relations 1917–58.* McFarland, 1983.

Patterson, James T. *The Dread Disease: Cancer and Modern American Culture.* Harvard University Press, 1987.

Payne, J. Gregory, and Scott C. Ratzan. *Tom Bradley: The Impossible Dream.* Roundtable, 1986.

Peale, Norman Vincent. *The True Joy of Positive Living: An Autobiography.* William Morrow, 1984.

Pereira, William L., Jr. *The Majestic World of Arabian Horses.* Abrams, 1986.

Perlmutter, Amos. *The Life and Times of Menachem Begin.* Doubleday, 1987.

Petzinger, Thomas. *Oil and Honor: The Texaco-Pennzoil Wars.* Putnam, 1987.

Phalon, Richard. *The Takeover Barons of Wall Street.* Putnam, 1981.

Philip, George. *Oil and Politics in Latin America: Nationalist Movements and State Companies.* Cambridge University Press, 1982.

Phillips, Wendell. *Qataban and Sheba: Exploring Ancient Kingdoms on the Biblical Spice Routes of Arabia.* Gollancz, 1955.

Pickens, T. Boone, Jr. *Boone.* Houghton Mifflin, 1987.

Pinkus, Benjamin. *The Jews of the Soviet Union: The History of a National Minority.* Cambridge University Press, 1988.

Pisar, Samuel. *Of Blood and Hope.* Macmillan, 1980.

Pottker, Jan, and Bob Speziale. *Dear Ann, Dear Abby: The Unauthorized Biography of Ann Landers and Abigail Van Buren.* Dodd, Mead, 1987.

Powell, S. Steven. *Covert Cadre: Inside the Institute for Policy Studies.* Green Hill, 1987.

Powers, Richard Gid. *Secrecy and Power: The Life of J. Edgar Hoover.* Free Press, 1987.

Pratt, Norma Fain. *Morris Hillquit: A Political History of an American Jewish Socialist.* Greenwood Press, 1979.

Press, Jacques Cattell, ed. *Who's Who in American Art,* 16th edition. R. R. Bowker, 1984.

Pullerits, Albert, ed. *The Estonian Year-Book 1927.* Government Printing Office, Tallinn, 1927.

Pyadyshev, B. *USSR-USA: Confrontation or Normalization of Relations?* Novosti Press Agency, 1977.

Rand, Christopher T. *Making Democracy Safe for Oil: Oilmen and the Islamic East.* Atlantic Monthly/Little, Brown, 1975.

Rapoport, Louis. *Redemption Song: The Story of Operation Moses.* Harcourt Brace Jovanovich, 1986.

Reagan, Maureen. *First Father, First Daughter: A Memoir.* Little, Brown, 1989.

Reeve, Carl. *The Life and Times of Daniel DeLeon.* American Institute for Marxist Studies/Humanities Press, 1972.

Regenstein, Lewis. *America the Poisoned: How Deadly Chemicals Are Destroying Our Environment, Our Wildlife, Ourselves — And How We Can Survive.* Acropolis Books, 1982.

Rein, Irving J., et al. *High Visibility.* Dodd, Mead, 1987.

Reitzer, Ladislas F. "United States–Russian Economic Relations, 1917–20." Ph.D. diss., University of Chicago, 1950.

Renner, Frederic G. *Charles M. Russell.* Abrams, 1974.

Reswick, William. *I Dreamt Revolution.* Henry Regnery, 1952.

Rettig, Richard A. *Cancer Crusade: The Story of the National Cancer Act of 1971.* Princeton University Press, 1977.

Rheims, Maurice. *The Glorious Obsession.* St. Martin's, 1980.

Richmond, Yale. *U.S.-Soviet Cultural Exchanges, 1958–86: Who Wins?* Westview, 1987.

Rigby, Douglas, and Elizabeth Rigby. *Lock, Stock and Barrel: The Story of Collecting.* J. B. Lippincott, 1944.

Roberts, Charles. *LBJ's Inner Circle.* Delacorte, 1965.

Robinson, Edward G. *All My Yesterdays: An Autobiography.* Hawthorn, 1973.

Robock, Stefan H., and Kenneth Simmonds. *International Business and Multinational Enterprises.* Richard D. Irwin, 1973.

Rocca, Raymond G., and John J. Dziak. *Bibliography on Soviet Intelligence and Security Services.* Westview, 1985.

Rogers, David J. *Waging Business Warfare: Lessons from the Military Masters in Achieving Corporate Superiority.* Scribner, 1987.

Rogers, Will. *There's Not a Bathing Suit in Russia and Other Bare Facts.* Boni, 1927.

Roosevelt, Elliott, and James Brough. *Mother R.* Putnam, 1977.

Roosevelt, James, with Bill Libby. *My Parents: A Differing View.* Playboy, 1976.

Roquet, Louis L. "The Process of Top Management Succession in Large Public Companies." Ph.D. diss., Harvard University, 1978.

Rowe, John Frink. *Newington, New Hampshire*. Phoenix, 1987.

Rubenstein, Joshua. *Soviet Dissidents: Their Struggle for Human Rights*. Beacon Press, 1985.

Ruddy, T. Michael. *The Cautious Diplomat: Charles E. Bohlen and the Soviet Union 1929–1969*. Kent State University Press, 1986.

Russell, Paul L. *History of Western Shale Oil*. Center for Professional Advancement, 1980.

Russian Information Bureau. *Commercial Handbook of the USSR*. 1926.

Rustow, Dankwart A. *Oil and Turmoil: America Faces OPEC and the Middle East*. W. W. Norton, 1982.

Sale, Kirkpatrick. *Power Shift: The Rise of the Southern Rim and Its Challenge to the Eastern Establishment*. Random House, 1975.

Salisbury, Harrison E. *A Journey for Our Times: A Memoir*. Harper & Row, 1983.

————. *Without Fear or Favor: The New York Times and Its Times*. Times Books, 1980.

Sampson, Anthony. *The Seven Sisters: The Great Oil Companies and the World They Shaped*. Viking, 1975.

Sandberg, Neil C. *Jewish Life in Los Angeles: A Window to Tomorrow*. University Press of America, 1986.

Sanders, Ronald. *Shores of Refuge: A Hundred Years of Jewish Emigration*. Holt, 1988.

Scheer, Robert. *Thinking Tuna Fish, Talking Death: Essays on the Pornography of Power*. Hill & Wang, 1988.

Scheffer, Paul. *Seven Years in Soviet Russia*. Putnam, 1931.

Schlesinger, Arthur M., Jr. *The Cycles of American History*. Houghton Mifflin, 1986.

————. *A Thousand Days: John F. Kennedy in the White House*. Houghton Mifflin, 1965.

Schneider, Steven A. *The Oil Price Revolution*. Johns Hopkins University Press, 1983.

Schoenebaum, Eleanora W., ed. *Political Profiles: The Nixon/Ford Years*. Facts on File, 1979.

Schuller, Robert H. *Success Is Never Ending, Failure Is Never Final*. Nelson, 1988.

Schuman, Frederick Lewis. *American Policy Toward Russia Since 1917: A Study of Diplomatic History, International Law and Public Opinion*. International Publishers, 1928.

Schwartz, Morton. *Soviet Perceptions of the United States*. University of California Press, 1978.

Seagrave, Sterling. *The Marcos Dynasty*. Harper & Row, 1988.

Seligman, Joel. *The Transformation of Wall Street: A History of the Securities and Exchange Commission and Modern Corporate Finance*. Houghton Mifflin, 1982.

Seretan, L. Glen. *Daniel DeLeon: The Odyssey of an American Marxist*. Harvard University Press, 1979.

Seward, Ingrid. *Diana*. Weidenfeld & Nicolson, 1988.

Shapiro, Susan P. *Wayward Capitalists: Target of the Securities and Exchange Commission*. Yale University Press, 1984.

Sharnik, John. *Inside the Cold War: An Oral History*. Arbor House, 1987.

Sheridan, Clare. *Naked Truth*. Harper & Brothers, 1928.

Sherrill, Robert. *The Oil Follies of 1970–1980: How the Petroleum Industry Stole the Show (and Much More Besides)*. Anchor/Doubleday, 1983.

Shevchenko, Arkady N. *Breaking With Moscow*. Grafton, 1986.

Shoumatoff, Alex. *Russian Blood: A Family Chronicle*. Coward, McCann & Geoghegan, 1982.

Shultz, Richard H., and Roy Godson. *Dezinformatsia: The Strategy of Soviet Disinformation*. Berkley, 1986.

Shwadran, Benjamin. *The Middle East, Oil and the Great Powers*. John Wiley, 1973.

————. *Middle East Oil Crises Since 1973.* Westview, 1986.

Sigmund, Paul E. *Multinationals in Latin America: The Politics of Nationalization.* University of Wisconsin Press, 1980.

Silver, Eric. *Begin: The Haunted Prophet.* Random House, 1984.

Simon, Paul. *Winners and Losers: The 1988 Race for the Presidency — One Candidate's Perspective.* Continuum, 1989.

Simpson, Colin. *Artful Partners: Bernard Berenson and Joseph Duveen.* Macmillan, 1986.

Singer, David G. "The U.S. Confronts the Soviet Union, 1919–33: The Rise and Fall of the Policy of Non-Recognition." Ph.D. diss., Loyola University of Chicago, 1972.

Sivachev, Nikolai V., and Nikolai N. Yakovlev. *Russia and the United States.* University of Chicago Press, 1979.

Skaggs, Jimmy M. *Prime Cut: Livestock Raising and Meatpacking in the United States, 1607–1983.* Texas A & M University Press, 1986.

Smith, Glen Alden. *Soviet Foreign Trade: Organization, Operations and Policy, 1918–71.* Praeger, 1973.

Smith, Gordon B., ed. *The Politics of East-West Trade.* Westview, 1984.

————. *Soviet Politics: Continuity and Contradiction.* St. Martin's, 1988.

Sobel, Lester A., ed. *Corruption in Business.* Facts on File, 1977.

Sonnenfeld, Jeffrey. *The Hero's Farewell: What Happens When CEOs Retire.* Oxford University Press, 1988.

Sono, Themba, ed. *Libya: The Vilified Revolution.* Progress Press, 1984.

Sorensen, Charles E. *My Forty Years with Ford.* W. W. Norton, 1956.

Sorin, Gerald. *The Prophetic Minority: American Jewish Immigrant Radicals, 1880–1920.* Indiana University Press, 1985.

Soviet–American Relations Yesterday and Today. Novosti Press Agency, 1973.

Spitz, Peter H. *Petrochemicals: The Rise of an Industry.* John Wiley, 1988.

Staar, Richard F. *USSR Foreign Policies After Détente.* Hoover Institution Press, 1987.

Stannard, David E. *Shrinking History: On Freud and the Failure of Psychohistory.* Oxford University Press, 1980.

Stans, Maurice H. *The Terrors of Justice: The Untold Side of Watergate.* Everest House, 1978.

Starr, Martin K., ed. *Global Competitiveness: Getting the United States Back on Track.* W. W. Norton, 1988.

Steibel, Gerald L. *Détente: Promises and Pitfalls.* National Strategy Information Center/ Crane Russak, 1975.

Stephan, John J., and V. P. Chichkanov, eds. *Soviet-American Horizons on the Pacific.* University of Hawaii Press, 1986.

Stern, Paula. *Water's Edge: Domestic Politics and the Making of American Foreign Policy.* Greenwood Press, 1979.

Sterne, Margaret. *The Passionate Eye: The Life of William R. Valentiner.* Wayne State University Press, 1980.

Stettinius, Edward R., Jr. *Lend-Lease, Weapon for Victory.* Macmillan, 1944.

Steuer, Aron. *Max D. Steuer: Trial Lawyer.* Random House, 1950.

Stevens, Edmund. *Russia Is No Riddle.* Greenberg, 1945.

Stobaugh, Robert, and Daniel Yergin, eds. *Energy Future.* Ballantine Books, 1980.

Strong, Anna Louise. *The First Time in History: Two Years of Russia's New Life.* Boni and Liveright, 1924.

Stroud, Kandy. *How Jimmy Won: The Victory Campaign from Plains to the White House.* William Morrow, 1977.

Sullivan, Gerald, and Michael Kenney. *The Race for the Eighth: The Making of a Congressional Campaign.* Harper & Row, 1987.

Sutton, Antony C. *Wall Street and the Bolshevik Revolution.* Arlington House, 1974.

————. *Western Technology and Soviet Economic Development.* 2 vols. Hoover Institution Press, 1968, 1971.

Swanberg, W. A. *Citizen Hearst: A Biography of William Randolph Hearst.* Scribner, 1961.

Szajkowski, Zosa. *Jews, Wars and Communism: The Impact of the 1919–1920 Red Scare on American Jewish Life.* KTAV Publishing, 1974.

Szulc, Tad. *The Illusion of Peace: Foreign Policy in the Nixon Years.* Viking, 1978.

Taubman, William. *Stalin's American Policy: From Entente to Cold War.* W. W. Norton, 1982.

Tebbel, John. *The Life and Good Times of William Randolph Hearst.* E. P. Dutton, 1952.

Temko, Ned. *To Win or to Die: A Personal Portrait of Menachem Begin.* William Morrow, 1987.

Terzian, Pierre. *OPEC: The Inside Story.* Zed Books, 1985.

Tetreault, Mary Ann. *Revolution in the World Petroleum Market.* Quorum Books, 1985.

Thayer, Charles W. *Diplomat.* Harper, 1959.

Thompson, Jacqueline. *The Very Rich Book.* William Morrow, 1981.

Thomson, Lord. *After I Was Sixty: A Chapter of Autobiography.* Hamish Hamilton, 1975.

Tolstoy, Nikolai. *Stalin's Secret War.* Jonathan Cape, 1981.

Towne, Charles Wayland, and Edward Norris Wentworth. *Cattle and Men.* University of Oklahoma Press, 1955.

Trost, Cathy. *Elements of Risk: The Chemical Industry and Its Threat to America.* Times Books, 1984.

Tuccille, Jerome. *Kingdom: The Story of the Hunt Family of Texas.* PaperJacks, 1987.

Tugwell, Franklin. *The Politics of Oil in Venezuela.* Stanford University Press, 1975.

Tumarkin, Nina. *Lenin Lives!: The Lenin Cult in Soviet Russia.* Harvard University Press, 1983.

Turack, Daniel C. *The Passport in International Law.* Lexington Books, 1972.

Turner, Louis. *Invisible Empires: Multinational Companies and the Modern World.* Harcourt Brace Jovanovich, 1971.

Turrell, Virginia. "Alcohol Policies of the War Production Board and Predecessor Agencies, May 1940 to January 1945." War Production Board Special Study 16, 1945.

Ueberroth, Peter. *Made in America: His Own Story.* William Morrow, 1985.

Ulam, Adam B. *Expansion and Coexistence: The History of Soviet Foreign Policy, 1917–1967.* Praeger, 1968.

Vance, Cyrus. *Hard Choices: Critical Years in America's Foreign Policy.* Simon & Schuster, 1983.

Vancil, Richard F. *Passing the Baton: Managing the Process of CEO Succession.* Harvard Business School Press, 1987.

Vanderlip, Frank A. *From Farm Boy to Financier.* Appleton-Century, 1935.

Vernon, Raymond, ed. *The Oil Crisis.* W. W. Norton, 1976.

Vestal, Bud. *Jerry Ford, Up Close: An Investigative Biography.* Coward, McCann & Geoghegan, 1974.

Vicker, Ray. *The Kingdom of Oil: The Middle East, Its People and Its Power.* Scribner, 1974.

Wachtel, Andrew, and Eugene Zykov. *At the Dawn of Glasnost.* Proctor Jones, 1988.

Waddams, Frank C. *The Libyan Oil Industry.* Johns Hopkins University Press, 1980.

Waldmann, Raymond J. *Managed Trade: The New Competition Between Nations.* Ballinger, 1986.

Walker, John, ed. *The Armand Hammer Collection: Five Centuries of Masterpieces.* Abrams, 1980.

————. *Self-Portrait with Donors: Confessions of an Art Collector.* Atlantic Monthly/Little, Brown, 1974.

Wall, Bennett H. *Growth in a Changing Environment: A History of Standard Oil Company (New Jersey), Exxon Corporation, 1950–1975.* McGraw-Hill, 1988.

Wansell, Geoffrey. *Tycoon: The Life of James Goldsmith.* Atheneum, 1987.

Warner, Gale, and Michael Shuman. *Citizen Diplomats: Pathfinders in Soviet-American Relations, and How You Can Join Them.* Continuum, 1987.

Weihmiller, Gordon R., and Dusko Doder. *U.S.-Soviet Summits: An Account of East-West Diplomacy at the Top, 1955–85.* Georgetown University Institute for the Study of Diplomacy/University Press of America, 1986.

Weisberg, Richard C. *The Politics of Crude Oil Pricing in the Middle East, 1970–75: A Study in International Bargaining.* University of California, Institute of International Studies, 1977.

Weisberger, Bernard A. *Cold War, Cold Peace: The United States and Russia Since 1945.* American Heritage, 1984.

West, R. L., and J. Stoyle, eds. *The Better Blacks.* Better Blacks Inc., 1956.

White, Theodore H. *The Making of the President, 1972.* Atheneum, 1973.

Whiteside, Henry Overton. "Kennedy and the Kremlin: Soviet-American Relations 1961–63." Ph.D. diss., Stanford University, 1968.

Wieczynski, Joseph L., ed. *The Modern Encyclopedia of Russian and Soviet History.* Academic International Press, 1976.

Wiley, Peter, and Robert Gottlieb. *Empires in the Sun: The Rise of the New American West.* Putnam, 1982.

Wilkins, Mira, and Frank Ernest Hill. *American Business Abroad: Ford on Six Continents.* Wayne State University Press, 1964.

Williams, Robert C. *Russian Art and American Money.* Harvard University Press, 1980.

Williams, William Appleman. *American-Russian Relations, 1781–1947.* Rinehart, 1952.

Wilmerding, John. *Andrew Wyeth: The Helga Pictures.* Abrams, 1987.

Wilson, Joan Hoff. *American Business and Foreign Policy, 1920–33.* University Press of Kentucky, 1971.

———. *Ideology and Economics: U.S. Relations with the Soviet Union, 1918–33.* University of Missouri Press, 1974.

Winchell, Walter. *Winchell Exclusive.* Prentice Hall, 1975.

Wirth, John D., ed. *Latin American Oil Companies and the Politics of Energy.* University of Nebraska Press, 1985.

Witcover, Jules. *Marathon: The Pursuit of the Presidency, 1972–76.* Viking, 1977.

Wolfe, Bertram D. *A Life in Two Centuries: An Autobiography.* Stein & Day, 1981.

Woodward, Bob. *Veil: The Secret Wars of the CIA, 1981–1987.* Simon & Schuster, 1987.

Wright, John. *Libya: A Modern History.* Johns Hopkins University Press, 1982.

Wright, Peter. *Spycatcher: The Candid Autobiography of a Senior Intelligence Official.* Viking, 1987.

Wulff, Kurt. *How to Profit from the Coming Oil Crisis.* Bantam, 1988.

Wyden, Peter. *The Unknown Iacocca.* William Morrow, 1987.

Yanarella, Ernest J., and William C. Green, eds. *The Unfulfilled Promise of Synthetic Fuels.* Greenwood Press, 1987.

Yurovsky, L. N. *Currency Problems and Policy of the Soviet Union.* Parsons, 1925.

Zimand, Savel. *State Capitalism in Russia: The Soviet Economic System in Operation, 1917–26.* Foreign Policy Association, 1926.

Zinsser, Hans. *As I Remember Him: The Biography of R.S.* Little, Brown, 1940.

Zinsser, William, ed. *Inventing the Truth: The Art and Craft of Memoir.* Houghton Mifflin, 1987.

Zipperstein, Steven J. *The Jews of Odessa: A Cultural History, 1794–1881.* Stanford University Press, 1985.

Zivs, Samuil. *Human Rights: Continuing the Discussion.* Progress Publishers, 1980.

Zobel, Myron. *The Fourteen-Karat Trailer.* Frederick Fell, 1955.

Index